COVENANT OF PEACE

COVENANT OF PEACE

The Missing Peace in New Testament Theology and Ethics

Willard M. Swartley

WILLIAM B. EERDMANS PUBLISHING COMPANY
GRAND RAPIDS, MICHIGAN / CAMBRIDGE, U.K.

Wm. B. Eerdmans Publishing Co.
255 Jefferson Ave. S.E., Grand Rapids, Michigan 49503 /
P.O. Box 163, Cambridge CB3 9PU U.K.

Printed in the United States of America

10 09 08 07 06   7 6 5 4 3 2 1

Library of Congress Cataloging-in-Publication Data

Swartley, Willard M., 1936-
    Covenant of peace: the missing peace in New Testament theology and ethics /
    Willard M. Swartley.
        p.   cm.
    Includes bibliographical references.
    ISBN-10: 0-8028-2937-6 / ISBN-13: 978-0-8028-2937-5 (pbk.: alk. paper)
    1. Bible. N.T. — Theology.   2. Peace — Biblical teaching.
    3. Christian ethics — Biblical teaching.   I. Title.

    BS2397.S93 2006
    261.8′73 — dc22

                                2005034317

www.eerdmans.com

Contents

Studies in Peace and Scripture

Visions of peace abound in the Bible, and so do the language and tales of battle. In this respect, the Bible is thoroughly at home in the modern world: a history filled with visions of peace accompanying the reality of war bridges the distance between the Bible's world and our own. That alone would justify study of peace and war in the Bible. However, for those communities reading the Bible as Scripture, the matter is more urgent. For them it becomes crucial to understand what the Bible says about peace — and about war. These matters have often divided Christians from each other, and the way Christians have understood them has had terrible consequences for Jews and, indeed, for the world. A series of scholarly investigations cannot hope to resolve these issues, but it can hope, as this one does, to aid our understanding of them.

Over the past century a substantial body of literature has grown up around the topic of the Bible and war. Studies in great abundance have been devoted to historical questions about ancient Israel's conception and conduct of war and about the position of the early church on participation in the Roman Empire and its military. Motivating many of these studies have been theological and ethical concerns, which may themselves be attributed to the Bible's own seemingly disjunctive preoccupation with peace and, at the same time, with war. If not within the Bible itself, then at least since Aqiba and Tertullian, the question has been raised whether — and if so on what basis — those who worship God may legitimately participate in war. With the Reformation, the churches divided on this question. The division was unequal, with the majority of Christendom agreeing that, however regrettable war may be, Christians have biblical warrant for participating in it. A minority countered that, however necessary war may appear, Christians have a biblical mandate to avoid it. Modern historical studies have served to bolster one side of this division or the other.

Meanwhile, it has become clear that a narrow focus on participation in war is not the only way, and likely not the best way, to approach the Bible on the topic of peace. War and peace are not simply two sides of the same coin; each is broader than its contrast with the other. In spite of agreement on this point, the number of studies devoted to the Bible and peace remains quite small, especially in English. Consequently, the most basic questions persist. For example, What does the Bible mean in speaking of *shalom* or *eirēnē*, the Hebrew and Greek terms most often translated as "peace"? Questions also persist about the relation of peace, in the Bible, to considerations of justice, integrity, and — in the broadest sense — salvation. And of course there still remains the question of the relation between peace and war. In fact, what the Bible says about peace it often frames in the language of war. The Bible very often uses martial imagery to portray God's own actions, whether in creation, in judgment against or in defense of Israel, or in the cross and resurrection of Jesus Christ — actions aimed at achieving peace.

This close association of peace and war presents serious problems for the contemporary appropriation of the Bible. Are human freedom, justice, and liberation — and the liberation of creation — furthered or hindered by the martial, frequently royal, and pervasively masculine terms in which the Bible speaks of peace? These questions cannot be answered by the rigorous and critical exegesis of the biblical texts alone; they demand serious moral and theological reflection as well. But that reflection will be substantially aided by exegetical studies of the kind included in this series, even as these studies will be illumined by including just that kind of reflection within them.

"Studies in Peace and Scripture" is sponsored by the Institute of Mennonite Studies, the research agency of the Associated Mennonite Biblical Seminary, and the series' volumes have been published by different publishers. The seminary and the tradition it represents have a particular interest in peace and, even more so, an abiding interest in the Bible. We hope that this ecumenical series will contribute to a deeper understanding of both.

BEN C. OLLENBURGER
Series Editor

Foreword

I remember clearly when I received the vision. I was sitting near the front on the left side of the church, looking up at my pastor, a teacher-preacher, as he was telling of his recent visit to Moscow Baptist Church. It was the period dominated by the rabid anticommunist, Senator Joseph McCarthy, during the height of the Cold War, and I was only a young teenager, but my pastor's words about Jesus and peacemaking were demonstrated by his visit to Russian Baptists — a somewhat courageous and symbolic prophetic action at that time. I received a vision of the church as spreading a meaningful witness to Jesus' peacemaking at a time — like now — when the world deeply needed that witness. My pastor was V. Carney Hargroves, president of both the American Baptist Churches and the Baptist World Alliance. As part of his witness, he had also welcomed the pastor of Moscow Baptist Church to preach in our church. He showed us pictures of Russian Baptists. We prayed for peace with the Russians.

That Sunday, the vision came as I was looking at my fellow church members, at the vaulted ceiling of the church, and at my pastor. I got the vision of the church as truly following Jesus, truly making a difference for peacemaking — not only Second Baptist Church of Germantown, but churches throughout the nation — witnesses for following Jesus and Jesus' teachings on peacemaking.

The world needs that witness from the churches now, and the churches need to recover that vision if they are not to be blown about by every shifty wind of ideology (Eph. 4:14).

It was Dr. Hargroves who called me to the ministry. In seminary some outstanding New Testament scholars fascinated and influenced me and deepened my understanding of the way of Jesus. I almost decided to study for a

Ph.D. in New Testament. But I *knew* the New Testament was already clear about the call to peacemaking, so I decided to study Christian ethics and think through some of the practical implications of Jesus' teachings. Now Willard Swartley has deepened my understanding enormously.

The faithfulness of the churches depends on what New Testament scholars teach and write. They have to make the connections, write the interpretations, and teach the implications that we depend on if we are to fulfill Jesus' vision of the good news of peace and salvation (Isa. 52:7) and Paul's vision of a church that embodies "grace and peace." Churches will not make the connection Dr. Hargroves modeled or fulfill that vision if New Testament scholars and the pastors they train and the Sunday School teachers who read their studies do not make the connections.

Willard Swartley points out that the word *peace* appears one hundred times in the New Testament, and *reconciliation* four times. But New Testament theologians write more about reconciliation than peace, and often limit it to individual reconciliation with God — without significant attention to God's work to reconcile us with others or with enemies — and sometimes move it off the stage of history into a purely future eschatology waiting in the wings invisible in our actions and invisible to observers' eyes. They often reduce it to inner peace, or peace with God, without attention to God's will for peace among God's creatures.

In his appendix, Swartley measures twenty-five major studies of New Testament theology or ethics by three criteria. Not one of the studies pursues the significance of the theme of peace (and righteousness/justice) in Luke and Acts — one-fourth of the New Testament. Only one of them has significant discussion of Paul's distinctive term "God of peace" — an important indicator of whether New Testament theologies do justice to Paul's peacemaking theology. Only four authors use Isa. 52:7 on the good news of peace and salvation for their explication of New Testament peace theology or ethics.

The Christian ethicist in me wants to ask whether this remarkably extensive systematic omission is caused by unconscious or uncritical introjection of our society's faulty ethical assumptions or of church traditions shaped by medieval and nationalist traditions of deference to governmental authority. Have New Testament scholars consciously or unconsciously avoided speaking of peace and its central role in the good news of salvation because they do not want to tread on the toes of some supporters of secular authorities? Gerd Theissen's studies of the history of German New Testament scholarship have sharpened this question.

Willard Swartley fills the hole, the missing peace, in New Testament studies. He does it with careful attention to the ways that peace is integrated into the New Testament's wider theological vision and emphasis. He shows how peace and other key terms occur not merely as isolated words, but in their semantic field relations and conceptual associations. Peace is crucial in the New Testament understanding of Jesus, of salvation, of the mission of the church, and of eschatology. Swartley's lifelong attention to the Old Testament roots of New Testament teaching, as shown in his *Israel's Scripture Traditions and the Synoptic Gospels,* gives him special expertise.

He shows that the world of the New Testament was characterized by "imperial occupation, war, and brutality against subjected peoples," persecution, suffering, and martyrdom. We cannot understand the New Testament without noticing this, and the same is true of our world. Jesus' message of *the kingdom of God* is centrally tied to the *gospel* and *peace,* as in Isa. 52:7. "Lacking attention to any of these three themes, . . . the historical Jesus, as well as the proclaimed Jesus, would be altogether different from what the Gospel portrait boldly and joyfully presents." A recurring emphasis in historical Jesus studies is that Jesus is the initiator of a peace movement. New Testament theology and New Testament interpretation need to pay attention to that, for accuracy of interpretation as well as for our world's desperate need.

Swartley's findings "demonstrate that the New Testament consistently not only supports nonviolence but also advocates proactive peacemaking, consisting of positive initiatives to overcome evil, employing *peaceable means* to make *peace.*" This is true in Matthew as well as in the other Gospels and in Paul. In Mark, two opposing views of messiahship lock horns: Peter's Maccabean view and Jesus' Suffering Servant view. "Willing solidarity in suffering and death" rather than defense with the sword is required for identification with this Messiah. In Luke, the theme is glad tidings — great joy — of salvation as peace. Luke presents the theme of peace in twelve different texts. Luke's use of justice receives an analysis by Swartley that I have not been able to find in other treatments.

This is a careful and insightful inductive study. The case builds as it goes, and it adds up to a detailed and powerful *tour de force.* The payoff comes especially clearly in the chapters on the Johannine literature and the concluding chapters that follow. Some impatient or hurried readers, or Christian ethics-concerned readers like me, might read the first two or three chapters and then skip to those concluding chapters. That way they will see the implications before they have worked carefully through all the data on which the conclusions are based. But I encourage them eventually to come back and see the case build as it proceeds. Swartley says he thought of writing a popular book but decided on a scholarly book instead. I hope he helps many scholars see what they have been missing. But I also hope upper-level college, university, and seminary courses on New Testament theology or ethics can benefit from it, especially if read in the order I have suggested.

GLEN H. STASSEN

Preface

This book has been brewing for over twenty years. Only in the last four years, however, with a sabbatical and leave in 2001-2002 did the book as such begin to take shape. During that year I submitted a prospectus of my work along with a draft of Chapter 3 to the AMBS Teaching and Research Seminar for critique and direction. I thank my colleagues for their helpful suggestions and for their encouragement in the task. I am also grateful to the AMBS administration in their encouragement and support, who in approving my sabbatical put this book proposal at the top of the list of four proposed projects.

The title, *Covenant of Peace,* came to me one morning serendipitously as I was reading in Ezekiel 34. Having considered other titles, I intuitively knew this was the right one. We speak of Old and New *Testaments,* but "Covenants" is a viable synonym. Ezekiel prophesied that God would make a new covenant, a covenant of *peace.* My thesis is that the New Testament is to be viewed as precisely such. My hope is that this contribution will aid our vision, help us to see God's covenant made through Jesus Christ in that perspective, a point that too often has been neglected or marginalized in New Testament theology and ethics.

In the beginning stages of my work, I considered pitching the book at a semi-popular level, though from the start I wanted it to serve as a companion volume to textbooks in New Testament Theology and New Testament Ethics. In light of my publications on peace in the New Testament between 1992 and 1996 (see Bibliography) it was inevitable that this volume developed more in the scholarly direction, to adequately serve its purpose in the seminary classroom and among peers in the scholarly guild. Dialogue with scholarship became thus an important part of the book's substance. The many footnotes, some quite long, may be a "put-off" to some, but to others an important resource. I recognize the need for a more popular version of this book, and perhaps that will appear in due time.

I am especially grateful for the 2002 summer of research and writing in England and Scotland. I thank Justin Meggitt and Melanie Wright for providing wonderful hospitality in their home for five days and a few days as residence guest at Corpus Christi College (Cambridge University's central area) for my (and Mary's) first week in Cambridge. In the providence of God, Wesley House on Jesus Lane provided a flat for three weeks, the home also of the Centre for Jewish-Christian Relation (CJCR), where Edward Kessler and Melanie Wright, Director and Academic Dean respectively, welcomed me, guided me in use of their library's rich resources, and gave counsel to me on my project. I thank Justin Meggitt for his counsel on my Pauline chapters. For the three weeks at St. Andrews in Scotland I thank Paul and Chiharu Yokota for assisting us to find a comfortable flat in New Hall. But even more important, I thank them both for their friendship and fellowship during this time and their hospitality in their home, where on one occasion we shared a meal with them and Professor Richard Bauckham, Paul's faculty advisor. I thank Paul also for his helpful suggestions on Chapter 3, and granting me access to his doctoral dissertation in process. The summer experience was most delightful and enriching, contributing considerably to progress on my project.

I thank all those who read portions of my manuscript and gave helpful responses: AMBS Professors Jacob Elias, Dean Loren Johns, Alan Kreider, Ben Ollenburger, Mary Schertz, and Perry Yoder and others who gave helpful comments in the Teaching and Research Seminar. From the wider community of scholars I thank Professors Richard Hays and Glen Stassen for their responses to parts I sent to them and their encouragement in the project. I thank William Klassen for several stimulating phone calls, for mentioning sources I might otherwise have overlooked. I express appreciation to AMBS for a Faculty Research Grant that enabled me to hire Reuben Glick Shank for work represented in Appendix 1, for which I am most grateful. I am also grateful to both AMBS and Canadian Mennonite University students (summer 2003 in Winnipeg) who read chapters and gave helpful critique and counsel. I am also grateful for papers by students Alastair McKay, Darrin Belousek and Wanda Stopher that enriched my work in Chapters 4 and 10 respectively, and to Douglas Yoder for a stimulating conversation at the 2004 SBL meeting that resulted in the addition of the Addendum to Chapter 1.

I acknowledge also the support staff of AMBS, especially Rosalie Grove's assistance in preparing a draft of the Bibliography from the footnotes and in catching mistakes and for her readiness to assist in managing some of the technology connected with producing a manuscript. I thank also Brent

Graber, Director of Technology, who helped me out when I was at my wit's end with an uncooperative computer. To others who helped me with details here and there I am grateful. For all who helped me in other ways, including my pastors Duane Beck and Nina Lanctot caring about my health and spiritual well-being, I am grateful.

Most of all, I am grateful to Mary, my spouse, who gave generously of her time, doing much valuable work for me, not only in editing but also in her wise discernment and counsel at numerous points in my writing, for her preparation of the indexes, and for encouraging me lest I get bogged down from the tedium of such a project. Without her aid I may have given up on this project at particular stressful times. I thank her for her assistance in this project and in my publications over the years.

I express gratitude also to Eerdmans for accepting the manuscript, and for the warm collegial relationship with the editors who brought this work to publication: New Testament Editor John Simpson, Managing Editor Linda Bieze, and Editor-in-Chief Jon Pott.

While this book was in progress of publication much of it was also being translated into Japanese. I express much gratitude to Robert Lee, International Director of the Tokyo Mission Research Institute, an arm of Tokyo Biblical Seminary, for negotiating this vision and task with a team of translators headed by Takio Tanase of the Tokyo Honancho Christian Church (Mennonite), Saturo Kanemoto of the Tokyo Biblical Seminary, and Billy Nishioka, Director of the Tokyo Mission Research Institute. I am grateful to those who translated specific chapters: Takio Tanase, Kaz Enomoto, Katsuya Kawano, Mitsuru Matsuki, Hideo Okayama, and Paul Yokota. Their careful work and email queries saved me from numerous small errors, refined my expression on occasion, and contributed to a stronger manuscript.

Above all, I thank God, Jesus Christ, and the Holy Spirit for sustaining me in this project. I receive the health I have as a gift. I am glad that in God's providence I have been able to contribute in this way to Christ's kingdom gift and task of making peace. Hence the acclaim:

Solo Dei Gloria!

WILLARD M. SWARTLEY

Abbreviations

AnBib	Analecta Biblica (Rome)
ANRW	*Aufstieg und Niedergang der römischen Welt. Geschichte und Kultur Roms im Spiegel der neueren Forschung*
ASMS	American Society of Missiology Studies
BBB	Bonner biblische Beiträge
BCBC	Believers Church Bible Commentary
BibInt	*Biblical Interpretation*
BibLeb	*Bibel und Leben*
BJRL	*Bulletin of the John Rylands Library*
BR	*Biblical Research*
BT	Babylonian Talmud
BTB	*Biblical Theology Bulletin*
BZAW	Beihefte zur *Zeitschrift für die alttestamentliche Wissenschaft*
CBQ	*Catholic Biblical Quarterly*
CBQMS	*Catholic Biblical Quarterly* Monograph Series
CGR	*Conrad Grebel Review*
ChrCent	*Christian Century*
COV & R	Colloquium on Violence and Religion
CurrTheolMiss	*Currents in Theology and Mission*
ETL	*Ephemerides theologicae lovanienses*
EvQ	*Evangelical Quarterly*
ExpT	*Expository Times*
FOR	*Fellowship of Reconciliation*
FS	Festschrift
GNB	Good News Bible
HBT	*Horizons in Biblical Theology*

HeyJ	*Heythrop Journal*
HNT	Handbuch zum Neuen Testament
HSM	Harvard Semitic Monographs
HTR	*Harvard Theological Review*
ICC	International Critical Commentary
IDBSupp	*The Interpreter's Dictionary of the Bible, Supplementary Volume*
IMS	Institute of Mennonite Studies
Int	*Interpretation*
JAAR	*Journal of the American Academy of Religion*
JBL	*Journal of Biblical Literature*
JEH	*Journal of Ecclesiastical History*
JR	*Journal of Religion*
JRE	*Journal of Religious Ethics*
JRS	*Journal of Roman Studies*
JRT	*Journal of Religious Thought*
JSNT	*Journal for the Study of the New Testament*
JSNTS(S)	*Journal for the Study of the New Testament* Supplement Series
JSOT	*Journal for the Study of the Old Testament*
JT	Jerusalem Talmud
KJV	King James Version
m.	Mishnah
MQR	*Mennonite Quarterly Review*
MWR	*Mennonite Weekly Review*
NASB	New American Standard Bible
NEB	New English Bible
NIB	*The New Interpreter's Bible*
NICNT	New International Commentary on the New Testament
NIGTC	New International Greek Testament Commentary
NIV	New International Version
NovT	*Novum Testamentum*
NovTSup	*Novum Testamentum* Supplements
NRSV	New Revised Standard Version
NT	New Testament
NTS	*New Testament Studies*
OBO	Orbis biblicus et orientalis
OP	Occasional Papers
OT	Old Testament
OTP	*Old Testament Pseudepigrapha*

par.	parallel(s)
QD	*Quaestiones disputatae*
RelStudRev	*Religious Studies Review*
RSV	Revised Standard Version
SBL	Society of Biblical Literature
SBLDS	Society of Biblical Literature Dissertation Series
SBLMS	Society of Biblical Literature Monograph Series
SBLSP	*Society of Biblical Literature Seminar Papers*
SBM	Stuttgarter biblische Monographien
SBS	Stuttgarter Bibelstudien
SBT	Studies in Biblical Theology
SNTSMS	Society for New Testament Studies Monograph Series
SPS	Studies in Peace and Scripture
ST	*Studia theologica*
SWJTh	*Southwestern Journal of Theology*
TDNT	*Theological Dictionary of the New Testament*
THAT	*Theological Handwörterbuch zum Alten Testament*
TR	Text Reader series (Institute of Mennonite Studies)
TRE	*Theologische Realenzyklopädie*
TRINJ	*Trinity Journal* NS: New Series
WBC	Word Biblical Commentary
WUNT	Wissenschaftliche Untersuchungen zum Neuen Testament
ZAW	*Zeitschrift für die alttestamentliche Wissenschaft*
ZTK	*Zeitschrift für Theologie und Kirche*

Introduction

This book is a study of peace in the New Testament, a topic often marginalized in texts on NT Theology and Ethics. Most people want *peace.* Jesus promised blessing to *peacemakers:* "for they shall be called sons (children) of God" (Matt. 5:9). Some first-century Roman emperors claimed for themselves the title *peacemaker (eirēnopoios),* but those living under their occupation experienced life otherwise. Humans during the centuries, and certainly we today, continue to long for peace. In this decade, designated "The Decade to Overcome Violence" by the World Council of Churches, we do well to consider anew the NT witness on peace.

Peace, however, is often "used in vain," in that what we really mean by the word is getting good things for oneself, even if it means that others suffer so we can achieve our peace goal. In the social and political realm, peace most always assumes also "peace with security" — that is, *my* or *our* security. A tacit assumption in most public thinking about achieving this goal is that *peace* is to be won through superior power and violence; "just war" criteria would add "when necessary." *Necessary* usually means by the standards of self-protection of some sort, often "protection of national expansionist interests" of one type or another, usually economic advantage and/or political gain. Yet the goal hoped for often becomes more and more illusory the harder one works to secure it.

If one examines the Israeli-Palestinian conflict over the last decades, for example, the point is graphic. More power and violence from Israel only brings more violent subversive tactics from Palestinians, followed by more violence from Israel. The grinding, devastating war in southern Sudan for two decades is especially heart-rending, since so many have died as a result — some counts are two million. Now with a new front in the western Darfur province, some 1.2 million have been displaced as refugees (mostly in Chad). Until recently the larger world and especially the U.S. paid scant attention. The ethnic wars in the Balkans and in sub-Saharan Africa only compound the dismal picture of God's shalom project for humans gone terribly awry. Lamentably, these wars are often between Christian groups. How can such things be?!

The persisting challenge of the Mideast conflict exemplifies in microcosm the more macrocosmic situation in which the U.S. extends its enormous power to crush opposing interests, whether in Afghanistan or Iraq. A similar pattern of domination appears in the ever-increasing global expansion of multinational corporations. Though corrective analyses and protests to these strategies abound, few put forward concrete alternatives that carry persuasive hope for achieving peace.

So why another book on peace, especially when written by one trained in biblical studies, not in political analysis and strategic planning for national or international security? Indeed, this book makes no direct contribution to enhancing the national security of the United States, Iraq, Sudan, Israel, or the Palestinians, to name specific cases. Nor does it prescribe self-help formulas that promise to help people find peace personally in the sense of prosperity and personal accomplishment. But this book is important for those who wish to know how Christian faith bears on the formation of personal and corporate societal values, which in turn shape our personal and corporate ambitions and the means we use to achieve them. It contributes also to thinking about political issues, for example, how nations might win peace with security by addressing underlying enmity-creating factors. Put another way, this book seeks to shape human character formation so that different foundational questions are asked. Rather than thinking first and foremost about peace with security, the exposition leads one to think about peace through repentance, personal and corporate, and then transforming enmity into valued friendship.

This book raises vexing questions that challenge and at times irritate: Why are certain specific people our enemies? Why do they want what we also want? What does it mean to overcome evil with good? Is peace something *we* can achieve, or does it have a gift and grace dimension, both in personal and sociopolitical dimensions? How does Christian Scripture contribute to our thinking about peace? Do the many self-identified Christians today seek peace by the *means* prescribed in Christian Scripture, in the New Testament? What could happen to current conflicts if all Christians would refuse the use of violence? Would evil overwhelm good, or would good prevail? Do we have the capacity to live by faith, or are we hopeless victims consigning the future to fate? Do we think of justice and prosperity as a good for all people, or just for those who share in our identity, be it familial, social, economic, or political? Do we think only in national terms or international as well when we speak of justice, the common good, and shalom?

In one respect, this book addresses these broad questions. In another respect it is focused on a more modest and clearly defined task, namely, to show that the major writings in the NT canon speak to the topic of peace and peacemaking. Further, it intends to show *how* we are to seek peace, the *motivations* that guide such actions, and what "habits of the heart" or *practices* lead to peacemaking. Surprisingly, this task has been largely neglected in the textbooks on NT theology that have been in the staple diet of seminary and graduate students in biblical studies of the past several generations. Texts devoted to NT ethics have done little better, with some exceptions. How is it that a massive volume on NT theology or Pauline theology would have only one or two references to peace, even though that word and associated motifs permeate NT literature? Put simply, why have *peace* and *peacemaking* been topically marginalized in the NT academic guild?[1]

During the last twenty-five years I have taught a course on Theology and Ethics of the New Testament every other year, more recently focusing on the Gospels. What I have noticed is how sparse, if at all, the treatment of peace is in numerous NT theologies especially, and also in NT ethics texts as well. Richard B. Hays's *The Moral Vision of the New Testament* does more than most, but while *nonviolence* appears in his Topic Index with three citations, *peace* does not appear (there is one reference to "peace churches"). Even N. T. Wright's magisterial *Jesus and the Victory of God* has no *peace* listing in his "Index of Selected Topics," though he speaks more than most about peace as an integral part of messianic hope and Jesus' mission. Thus while both authors speak about peace at numerous places, the topic as such is elusive, buried within other topical discussions. Major Pauline theologies are even more deficient, as a long footnote in Chapter 7 below will point out.[2]

For this reason it is urgent to bring together in an accessible volume an understanding of peace in the NT as a companion volume to texts in NT theology and ethics. No other book in English makes this contribution. Some of the volumes I edited in the series "Studies in Peace and Scripture" provide important resources for this project, but they are mostly more narrowly topi-

---

1. There are exceptions, as we note. An area of study that has spoken more about peace and peacemaking is "historical Jesus" studies, despite the many hazards that accompany its methodology and the diversity in results. Recent postcolonial studies have also attended to peacemaking issues.

2. See note 1 in Chapter 7 (p. 190).

cal contributions. They do not pursue the topic through the full NT canonical witness. The exception (though it does not treat the entire NT or each Gospel separately) is volume 1 in the series, *The Gospel of Peace,* by Ulrich Mauser. I am indebted to him for some key emphases in this volume. Another exception, as a model for Paul only, is Virginia Wiles's *Making Sense of Paul,* which I include in my analysis of NT theologies and ethics in Appendix 1, even though it is not a NT theology or ethics study as such. Much work on peace has been done in German, and my writing will incorporate some of the good exegesis available there.[3] William Klassen's numerous essays contribute significantly, as does his book *Love of Enemy.*[4]

This marginalizing of peace in standard NT theologies and ethics is dismaying when many of the authors carry also keen concern for peace in our world. The disparity may arise from the limitations of the discipline.[5] To hold a scholarly discipline accountable to moral values may seem to smack of doctrinal sectarianism and thus not reflect objective research. Recent developments in NT studies, however, have exposed that illusion.[6] Matters of social location, economic and political allegiances, and religious convictions are valued as part of the academic enterprise. Hence scholarship seeks to honor diversity and discerning dialogue with one another, even when disagreements exist.

3. See the extensive bibliography in *The Meaning of Peace,* ed. Perry B. Yoder and Willard M. Swartley. See our introductory articles to both the OT and NT sections and my introduction to the Bibliography in the same volume.

4. Klassen's contribution is extensive: "Peace," in *A Dictionary of Jewish-Christian Relations,* p. 338; "Ascetic Way"; "Authenticity of the Command: 'Love Your Enemies'"; "Jesus and the Zealot Option"; "Pursue Peace"; Review of *The Meaning of Peace: Biblical Studies;* "'Love Your Enemies': Some Reflections on the Current Status of Research"; "Peace," in *Anchor Dictionary of the Bible* (see also "War [NT]" 6:867-75); "The God of Peace"; "Jesus and the Messianic War"; "Peace," in *Illustrated Dictionary and Concordance of the Bible; The Realism of Peace; Love of Enemies: The Way to Peace;* Summary of "Frieden, Altes Testament"; "Religion and the Gift of Peace"; "Child of Peace"; "Love Your Enemy: A Study of New Testament Teaching on Coping with an Enemy."

5. Klassen identifies two unfortunate tendencies: the neglect of the NT "pursue peace" commands due to fear of too easily equating the NT teaching with current "peace movements" (which may have little to do with the biblical teaching) and dissociation of peace from historical reality. He cites Schrage's *The Ethics of the New Testament,* which he generally applauds, to illustrate the first (see also my analysis of Schrage in Appendix 1), and Brown's commentary on John for the second (Klassen, "Pursue Peace," pp. 199-201).

6. See, among others, the critique against "neutrality" in scholarship by Elisabeth Schüssler Fiorenza in her 1987 SBL Presidential address, "The Ethics of Biblical Interpretation: Decentering Biblical Scholarship."

Documenting the Neglect

With the research help of a graduate student,[7] I discovered that fifteen of twenty-five NT "Theology" or "Ethics" textbooks included *peace* in their subject indexes.[8] Of the remaining ten, four have no subject index and the other six fail to list the word *peace*. Indexes, of course, do not tell the whole story. One needs to read the text to determine whether the neglect is in the Index or in the theology or ethics textbook itself. Further, the idea or notion of peace/reconciliation may be present though the words are not used.

One would think that the term *peace,* however, which occurs one hundred times in the NT and in every canonical book except 1 John would get some showing in theological or ethical treatments. To assess the extent of this deficiency we summarize what has and has not been done in numerous textbooks (see Appendix 1 for data and analysis).

In analyzing major texts on New Testament theology or ethics, research student Shank looked also for associated terms and emphases, such as love of enemy, reconciliation, and verbal or adjectival forms of *peace*. On the basis of the number of occurrences of *peace,* Rudolf Bultmann, I. Howard Marshall, Ben Wiebe, and, most outstanding, Virginia Wiles receive high marks. But in these works, perceptions and emphases differ significantly. Bultmann speaks of peace mostly in personal relational terms, in keeping perhaps with his existential mode of "translating" kerygmatic meaning into (then!) contemporary relevance. Marshall mentions *peace* often, but never as a subject of discussion. Wiebe understands peace to be at the core of the messianic movement inaugurated by Jesus, which expresses itself in NT ecclesiology. But Wiebe's work is limited to the Jesus section of the NT canon. Wiles is a basic introduction to Pauline theology (200 pages), and does not develop Pauline theology at the level of the other volumes analyzed. While *peace/shalom* literally laces her treatment and provides a thematic unity to the various facets of Pauline theology, her book does not exploit the full range of *peace* emphases in Paul. Nonetheless, it is a remarkable and outstanding contribution demonstrating how *shalom/peace* might function to provide coherence to Pauline theology

7. I am indebted to Reuben Glick Shank for his insightful analysis of twenty volumes in New Testament theology or ethics.

8. I did not include Historical Jesus studies. Many of these present a quite different emphasis. When we examine N. T. Wright, Marcus Borg, John Dominic Crossan, William Herzog, and others, we find a prominent emphasis on Jesus as bringer of peace or inaugurating an alternative peace party to that of nationalist self-interest parties and politics. This is striking and leads one to query the reason for the gap between Historical Jesus studies and "theologies" and "ethics."

(and to NT theology and ethics more broadly). See Appendix 1 for the detailed analysis of these twenty-five contributions.

When these limiting factors are taken into account, Bultmann is seriously deficient in lacking any clear trajectory between the personal and the corporate, even for the corporate life of believers (the ecclesial dimension), let alone the church's peace witness socioeconomically and politically. Wiebe's and Wiles's constraints are also significant, though the two together might function well to provide an elementary *shalom/peace* theology and ethics of Jesus and Paul.

If one examines the theological understanding of *peace* and related terms — as surely one should — at least eight of the twenty-five sources give significant attention to the topic. Overall, *reconciliation* receives more attention than *peace,* however, even though *peace* in nominal, verbal, adjectival, and compound forms occurs one hundred times in the NT, while reconciliation in its noun and verb forms occurs only seven or eight times! Richard Hays's *Moral Vision of the New Testament,* while lacking a Topic Index entry on *peace,* nevertheless gives considerable attention to peace and related topics. Even more, he devotes a complete chapter to "Violence" and uses the term *nonviolence* numerous times.

This dominant attention to *nonviolence* occurs also in Walter Wink's influential contribution in his "*Powers*" trilogy as well. This raises the question whether *nonviolence* is the contemporary word replacing *peace* and *peace-making.* If so, why? This term, like *nonresistance* (Matt. 5:39 KJV has "resist not" for *mē antistēnai*[9]), connotes what one does *not* do. Stanley Hauerwas makes a similar point:

> . . . pacifists cannot let their understanding of Christian nonviolence be determined by what we are against. . . . The very phrase "Christian nonviolence" cannot help but suggest that peace is "not violence." Yet a peace that is no more than "not violence" surely cannot be the peace that is ours in Christ.[10]

If the term is coupled with *resistance* (i.e., nonviolent resistance), that objection is only partially overcome, since the witness of the church still appears to be mostly reactive rather than proactively initiating peacemaking. Here Glen Stassen's work is salutary, since he accentuates transforming initiatives.[11] An

---

9. In Mennonite discussion over the past century *nonresistance* has been a prominent emphasis, but it occurs rarely in the NT. The key text is Matt. 5:39.

10. Hauerwas, "Explaining Christian Nonviolence," 173.

11. Stassen, *Just Peacemaking: Transforming Initiatives for Justice and Peace;* "Fourteen

injunction oft-repeated in the NT, "do not return evil for evil" (in the Synoptic Gospels, Paul, and 1 Peter) would valorize *nonretaliation*. Though the term as such is not used, it expresses the meaning of the imperative. This also emphasizes what not to do, but it is also often accompanied with positive action: *love enemies,* more frequently *overcome evil with good,* and occasionally *bless those who curse you.* Jesus' blessing on the *peacemakers* also connotes positive action. For it speaks not of merely *thinking* peace or *avoiding* evil, but a proactive *making of peace. Nonviolence* might be taken as denoting the work of peacemakers, but *nonretaliation, peacemaking, reconciliation* (noun and verb form for the latter two), *loving the enemy,* and *overcoming evil with good* are biblical terms.

This serious *peace* deficiency is not limited to NT studies in theology and ethics. It shows also in some of the best contributions on mission in the NT, for example, in David Bosch's magnum opus *Transforming Mission.*[12] It illustrates the anomaly of how an excellent scholar in missiology, much concerned about peace and justice in South Africa and the wider world, could exposit mission in the NT in its distinctive theological character and yet miss completely its relationship to peace emphases, also prominent in the same texts that authorize mission. The same omission on peace emphases occurs, most lamentably, in Joseph A. Grassi's valuable treatment of social justice in the NT.[13]

May this volume, as a companion to other works in NT theology and NT ethics, begin a corrective and spur other scholars to continue the task. One of the weaknesses of the contemporary church's peace witness is that so often its rationale is grounded not in Scripture but in general cultural notions of justice and fairness. Equally lamentable, Christians who stress biblical authority and preach "biblical" sermons react by criticizing peace and justice proponents and then put peace and peacemaking on discount, regarding it secondary, perhaps even unimportant, to the evangelistic mission of the church. In his insightful study of Eph. 2:11-22, Thomas Yoder Neufeld puts the point provocatively,

> This text reminds us that there is no evangelical and missional way of speaking of Christ that is worthy of him that does not come to terms with the radical spiritual, social, and even cosmic dimensions of peace. Were it not for the fact that we see it all around us in churches great and small, we

---

Triads"; with David P. Gushee, *Kingdom Ethics,* especially 19-145; Stassen, ed., *Just Peacemaking: Ten Practices for Abolishing War.*

12. Bosch, *Transforming Mission.* See my "Bosch and Beyond: Biblical Issues in Mission."

13. Grassi, *Informing the Future: Social Justice in the New Testament.*

would find it inconceivable that one could come to know the peace of God without being drawn into the costly making of peace in our world.

. . . if remembering Christ, but forgetting peace is a terrible truncation of the gospel, so also is remembering peace while forgetting the Christ who is our peace. Such forgetfulness results in losing touch with the core of peace, its roots, and its pedigree. Peace thus becomes divorced from the mission of reconciling people not only with each other but with God. Worse, the proclamation of Christ as peace is viewed as exclusivistic and arrogant, as maintaining or erecting new walls when they should be coming down.[14]

Any dichotomy between evangelistic mission and peace/peacemaking is inconceivable when the foundational NT texts for both emphases are examined, as Chapter 1 and this entire contribution shows. Let us then as Christian leaders and the communities we lead, shepherd, and nurture seek a holistic gospel of Jesus Christ, with peacemaking, reconciliation, and associated NT emphases guiding our theology and moral praxis.

The Method and Shape of This Project

In this investigation of peace and peace-related teaching in the New Testament I chose to put at the center texts that speak directly of peace-*eirēnē* and to consider also *nonretaliation, love of enemies, overcoming evil with good, blessing those who* curse, and *reconciliation* texts as close seconds in importance. *Nonviolence,* technically not a NT term, is discussed at numerous points. The double love command in its various NT uses also has foundational bearing upon the discussion and is considered as it relates to love of enemies or peace.[15] The texts on warfare, both where believers are involved and where the believers' relation to government is addressed, are also considered.

But no ethical emphasis in the NT can be understood adequately as a theme discrete to itself. Ethics is closely intertwined with christology throughout the NT; in Luke and Paul especially salvation is linked with peace. Further, because instruction on the moral life appears in life contexts in which people either respond in faith or refuse Jesus' teachings or Paul's gospel-proclamation, judgment enters the picture as well. Hence, this study

14. Yoder Neufeld, "For He Is Our Peace: Ephesians 2:11-22," 229-30.

15. The love of enemy command functions also as a critique of the love of neighbor command when the latter limits scope of application to one's own kind, racially or nationally.

frequently treats aspects of christology, soteriology, judgment, and other themes pertinent to peacemaking in particular literary contexts.

The aim of this study is to focus and honor the contribution that the various NT books and authors make to an understanding of peace, while noting on the one side the theological and christological matrix of this thought and, on the other side, observing features that alert us to issues of war or violence within the narrative as well.

Chapter 1 shows how fundamental the *peace-gospel* emphasis is to core NT teachings, especially Jesus' announcement and inauguration of the reign of God. It bridges the Testaments on basic themes of Jesus' gospel proclamation: gospel, kingdom/reign of God, and God's inauguration of peace in and through Jesus Christ. This sets the stage for the entire endeavor. For even amid diversity of moral emphases, the strength and coherence of this vision permeate the whole NT canon.

The second chapter takes up a study of OT understandings of *shalom* and *eirēnē* in Greco-Roman usage and addresses as well what may appear to be contrary emphases, texts that are often used to defend use of violence for self-defense or Christian participation in war. With Chapter 1 functioning as foundational to the project as a whole, Chapter 2 presents a necessary definitional component.

While Chapter 1 may suggest that my method for this investigation into NT theology and ethics falls into the type known as *salvation*-history,[16] my method of treatment is largely canonical, as becomes clear in the order of Chapters 3-12, with the exception of treating the Gospel of John as part of the larger Johannine corpus and thus contiguous to Revelation. Beyond the matter of order, the method is also canonical in the sense defined by Brevard Childs.[17] I focus on the final form of the document, not on the history of the development of the tradition.

The three concluding chapters (13-15) are more *thematic*. Chapter 13 is a cross-sectional NT study of "discipleship and *imitatio Christi*" together since both are related to modeling Jesus' way of peace. Chapter 14 then loops back to issues raised in Chapters 2 and 3 but latent throughout as well: To what extent does the peacemaking imperative reflect God's moral character? What does one make of the warrior-God so prominent in OT thought? As this study shows, some texts portray Jesus coming to battle against evil, thus ex-

---

16. See Hasel, *New Testament Theology: Basic Issues in the Current Debate.*

17. With Childs I recognize the value of knowing the history of texts prior to the canonical form, but such cannot serve as the basis for the text's authority. I focus on the text's final form for its theological and moral significance.

tending the OT warrior motif. Hence Chapter 14 wrestles with this issue and makes a distinctive, though modest, contribution to recent discussion. Finally, Chapter 15 takes up the hermeneutical and "performance" challenge prompted by this study. It also summarizes in schematic format key elements discussed in Chapters 3-12 directed toward moral formation of character.

In the Summary and Conclusion I identify leading emphases of this study, including test-criteria for the NT Theologies and Ethics volumes analyzed in Appendix 1. I also identify important issues to be considered as we take up the challenge of this study: to be people of peace who seek to promote peace in our world. I raise the life-commitment question: what does it mean to live in light of this teaching, personally and corporately as God's people?

Appendix 1 is a close analysis of twenty-five books on either NT theology or NT ethics, in order to assess the degree *peace* and cognate emphases are present in these treatments. This matter is crucial, since these books — often seminary texts — construct the "settings," to use computer language, that determine what is essential in NT theology and ethics. Except for Wiebe and Wiles, none of the twenty-five attend to *peace* and *peacemaking* in such a way that the emphasis shapes the presentation. Since the two exceptions are not complete treatments of the NT, *peace* and *peacemaking* are *neglected* — in *central* emphases even *missing* — in texts on NT theology and ethics. Hence the need for this contribution, to restore *peace* in the study of NT theology and ethics. To the extent that peacemaking, reconciliation, and related themes are *neglected,* to that same extent the student's grasp of the gospel's content is abortive. What is grasped is thus a distorted version of the gospel of Jesus Christ. As Paul would say, may it never happen (*mē genoito*)! God forbid that such occur in the formation of those who live and preach the gospel as leaders in the churches of Jesus Christ.

1   Jesus and Peace:
The Gospel of the Reign of God

How beautiful upon the mountains
are the feet of the messenger
who announces peace,
who brings good news,
who announces salvation,
who says to Zion, "Your God reigns."   ISA. 52:7

Your kingdom come,
Your will be done,
As in heaven,
So upon earth.   MATT. 6:10

This chapter focuses on three interrelated themes of Jesus' proclamation: the reign (kingdom) of God, gospel, and peace.

In the Lord's Prayer, which is modeled after the Jewish Kaddish prayer, Jesus instructs us to pray boldly, simply, and with adoration, sanctifying the divine name and entreating God's will in heaven to be done on earth. In light of the angel's announcement to the shepherds, "peace on earth," what does it mean to pray God's "will be done on earth," and thus claim the angel's promise? With the long-term conflict in the Middle East (which, thank God, shows signs in early 2005 for some peace gains) and a prolonged (peacekeeping?) war in Iraq, what does peace on earth really mean? The gap between prayer and reality is so great; we are tempted to mistrust the peace vision of Scripture. The dissonance between reality and vision is poignant. And yet we pray, hope, plead, and sometimes trust. Will the admonition to "overcome evil with good" ever root itself in this world and its culture? Or are true believers destined to find fulfillment of this vision only in some "other world" reality yet to come, where enemies no longer exist?

The Lord's Prayer does not speak of such delay. It speaks of God's will being done on earth, presumably in the here and now. But promised peace is so illusive. Can it ever become reality? The AIDS crisis of this coming decade will reach unimaginable proportions, so that we are unable to comprehend the number of deaths, in scores of millions. What does it mean to long for a better world when the triumph of love appears to dwindle, and retaliation, revenge, and death press in on us to have the last word?

Clearly, focusing on peace theology and ethics in the New Testament cannot be done in some sanitized ideal environment. Such is not our world, and such also was not the world of NT times. Imperial occupation, war, and brutality against subjected peoples were much at home in the first century, including the persecution, suffering, and martyrdom of many, both Christians and Jews.[1] In light of this historical realism as the context of the NT literature, I take up the awesome task of seeking to understand the NT call to peacemaking as the core component of proclaiming the gospel of Jesus Christ.

I examine the meaning and relationship of three major related themes of the first three Gospels: kingdom of God, gospel, and peace. Jesus means all three together. Lacking any one of these, the historical Jesus, as well as the proclaimed Christ, would be altogether different from what the Gospel portrait boldly and joyfully presents. In order not to confess and preach an abortive gospel, it is essential to see what these three motifs mean and how they relate to each other in the earliest Gospel narratives.

I translate literally from the Greek the above quotation from the Lord's Prayer in order to capture the sense that God's will done in heaven serves as the pattern for God's will to be done on earth. Heaven as the prototype is not a small point, but it is lost in English translations. It reminds us that God's will done in heaven precedes and infuses all human effort to seek peace and to replicate God's kingdom pattern. In recent theological literature the doctrine of the trinity provides a model of the community of love that inspires and empowers the community of believers on earth. The

---

1. Here the work of Daniel Boyarin on martyrdom is most insightful and instructive, even to the point of showing empathic relationship between Jews and Christians well into the sixth century in their common experience of martyrdom. See his *Dying for God: Martyrdom and the Making of Christianity and Judaism,* especially chapter 1.

book of Revelation follows the same logic: a scene in heaven is followed by a scene on earth. Heaven becomes the exemplar for the earthly experience. And ultimately it becomes the end-pattern and "home" for human life, in that we have both come from and return to God. Jesus in his mission and message fleshes out in human life the heaven–earth connection. This is essential for grasping his role as peacemaker and understanding his call for his followers to be peacemakers. Thus the OT meaning of shalom is necessary background for understanding the peace emphasis of the NT. Furthermore, the meaning and role of peace *(eirēnē)* in the Greco-Roman world are relevant (see Chapter 2).

Though historical Jesus studies come these days in many brands and flavors, one recurring emphasis is that Jesus is the initiator of a peace movement (Borg, Crossan, Wright, Powell, and others). The earlier work of S. G. F. Brandon from the 1960s argued for Jesus' sympathies with the Zealots, if indeed Jesus was not a Zealot himself. Martin Hengel, Oscar Cullmann, Ron Sider, John Howard Yoder, and others dissented from this view and exposed its tendentious thinking. In reviewing Brandon's book,[2] I pointed out that his evidence is at most inferential and flies in the face of the Gospels' evidence, which marks Jesus as a Leader for peace and not a proponent of violence. By now that era of construing Jesus as a violent revolutionary figure is pretty well ended.[3] Further, most scholars hold that the proclamation of the reign (kingdom) of God was central to Jesus' teaching and actions. Indeed, many gospel sub-themes are interwoven with Jesus' proclamation of the kingdom. At the heart of these is the core declaration that this kingdom comes through the

2. I prepared the extensive review (unpublished) for a doctoral class in Social Ethics taught by Charles West at Princeton Theological Seminary in the 1968-69 school year.

3. Horsley's argument that Jesus' conscientization for justice sets up a cycle that may lead to violence is essentially different from Brandon's views, since Horsley holds that Jesus seeks to break the cycle of violence (Horsley, *Jesus and the Spiral of Violence*). Horsley also holds that Zealots as such did not exist in the time of Jesus, though many resistance and rebellion groups did (see Horsley's *Jesus and Empire: The Kingdom of God and the New World Disorder,* pp. 35-53, for a good overview of his earlier work). He holds that "the Zealots" in the work of Hengel, Klassen, Yoder, Sider, and others is a "scholarly construct," a "foil" to portray Jesus' stance as *nonviolent,* to which Horsley objects. William Klassen has examined Horsley's claims, and Morton Smith's, which Horsley follows, and has found them wanting. That "a Zealot party" did not exist until 66 CE (based on Josephus), the Horsley-Smith argument, does not mean that the early disparate bands of *lēstai* are not "zealot" in aims, use of violence, and ideology of revolt. Evidence is not adequate to deny "connection" between these earlier groups and the Zealot party. Nor is it impossible for more than one group to call itself "Zealot" (Klassen, "Jesus and the Zealot Option"). Klassen's review of the scholarly debate is superb and is crucial to further discussion. Comparison to current numerous terrorist groups connected loosely to or acting independently of al-Qaida may illumine the first-century reality.

word and work of the gospel of peace. Few contributions wed these three themes of kingdom, gospel, and peace together.[4]

To grasp the meaning of the motif of the reign or *kingdom of God* in its close relation to *gospel* and *peace,* we must trace these three interwoven strands that form a strong cord uniting the OT and NT. In fact, these dominant motifs form the center of a biblical theology oriented to the concrete historical expression of the reign of the One God (Deut. 6:4). It is essential, therefore, to locate the OT roots of the relationship between peace, gospel, and the kingdom of God.

As part of the full scope of the kingdom's gospel of peace, Jesus' victory over the powers of evil is an important dimension of the peacemaking gospel of Jesus' kingdom mission. Different portions of the NT use different sets of terms and develop different emphases. But within this diversity arising from contextual demands, opportunities, and challenges, a common horizon of vision emerges: the establishment on earth of God's will for peace, the reconciliation of former enemies, and the bringing together of many peoples in one new creation that fulfills the ancient vision of making sacred the name of God in the world. To provide a larger overview of the topic, I use the following diagram of tripartite clustering of complementary NT emphases with *peace* as a focal motif in each distinctive language cluster:

Jesus in the Synoptics   Jubilee, social justice (Luke 4:18-19)
Kingdom of God   Paul's justice-fication and
Love of enemies   reconciliation and nonretaliation
Nonretaliation and peacemaking   suffering for the faith
              (Hebrews, James, and 1 Peter)

PEACE

Victory over Satan, evil, sin, and death
no condemnation
in the Synoptics, Paul, and Peter

Abiding in love/Receiving the peace of Jesus (John)

Each of these fields of thought is connected to peace in NT thought, and each contributes a significant part to the full meaning of peace. Further, each clus-

---

4. See Appendix 1, the first section of my book analyses for authors of NT theology or ethics who approximate this achievement. Ben Wiebe, in *Messianic Ethics,* does this most adequately.

ter of emphases contains foundational missional meaning. Each aspect of peacemaking moves toward inclusion of the outsider, the overcoming of enmity, and the extension of the kingdom of God to all people. Jesus' proclamation of the kingdom of God permeates the Synoptic Gospels. Thus we must understand the OT roots of Jesus' kingship and seek to discern why and how the metaphor "kingdom of God" was so central to Jesus' mission.

The key OT texts that NT writers use to authorize this interpretation of Jesus' mission are Isa. 52:7-10 and 61:1-3. Key NT texts are Mark 1:14-15; Matt. 4:23 (and 9:35; 24:14); and Luke 4:16-19 and 10:1-20. The larger Lukan emphasis on the *gospel* as a gospel of *peace* is very important (see Chapter 5 below). In Chapter 7 we examine Paul's declaration that Christ is our peace (Eph. 2:14-17), and Paul, too, draws on OT texts and traditions to enunciate his claim. Throughout this study we pay special attention to Israel's royal traditions, since these are the tenor of the metaphor "reign of God."

The Roots of the Gospel of the Kingdom of Peace in Isaiah

The specific term "kingdom of God" is virtually absent from the OT.[5] For this reason it is surprising to see how central it is in the earliest Gospel, Mark, and in Matthew and Luke as well. Indeed, the *idea* is present throughout the OT in the repeated assertion that "the Lord reigns." The Lord's kingship is a dominant theme throughout the Hebrew Scriptures (Exod. 15:18; 1 Sam. 8:7; Pss. 24:7-10; 47; 48:1-2; 74:12-13; 84:3; 93; 95–99; 145:1, 12-13; Isa. 43:15; 44:6). In Exod. 19:3-6 God's covenant with Israel gives to Israel their kingdom identity: "You shall be to me a kingdom of priests." Hence the basic components of the metaphor "kingdom of God" are indeed present in the OT.

But because of the virtual absence of the phrase "kingdom of God" from the OT, it has been a puzzle for NT scholars to determine where Jesus got the metaphor and why it is so central to his mission. Jesus comes preaching "the kingdom of God has come; repent and believe in the gospel" (Mark 1:14-15). His many parables are either explicitly or implicitly presented as parables of the kingdom of God. Certainly he could say something new, and indeed he did — more than the people could receive. But this phrase is presented in the Gospel accounts in such a way that it appears that both Jesus

---

5. One exception occurs in 1 Chron. 28:5, which speaks of the Lord choosing "Solomon to sit upon the throne of *the kingdom of the Lord* over Israel." See also Wis. 10:10, where "kingdom of God" appears. But these two uses are not adequate to explain the dominant role of the motif in the Synoptic Gospels. Some other factors must have influenced this, which I take up in the ensuing discussion.

and the hearers had it already in their thoughts and hopes. In other words, when Jesus announces that God's kingdom has come, it sounds as though he is saying: "what we have been praying for and longing for has now come to pass. Believe me, it's here, and you all must repent."

Recent contributions by Bruce Chilton have provided the key to the link between the OT emphasis on God as king and the NT phrase "kingdom of God." From Chilton's extensive study of the Isaiah Targum,[6] that is, the Aramaic translation-paraphrase of Isaiah, Chilton discovered that in several key Isaiah texts the Targum actually uses the precise phrase "kingdom of God." Four of these (24:23; 31:4; 40:9; 52:7) are in Zion theology texts. Zion theology is royal theology, related to the Davidic kingship tradition, but consisting essentially of the proclamation of God's own kingship and sovereign rule in Israel. Ben Ollenburger shows convincingly that Zion must be distinguished from Davidic kingship. Zion denotes God's rule, and Davidic kingship and its policies may indeed come under Zion's judgment. Even after Jerusalem falls and there is no Davidic heir on the throne, Zion continues.[7] It is a foundational metaphor for the reign of God in justice and steadfast love.

Of these four Zion texts, we shall focus on the one most significant for this topic, 52:7-10 (RSV modified for word consistency):

> How beautiful upon the mountains
>   are the feet of him who announces gospel *(mebasser)*,
> who proclaims *(mashemia)* peace *(shalom)*,
>   who announces the good gospel *(mebasser tob)*,
> who proclaims *(mashemia)* salvation *(yeshuah)*,
>   saying to Zion, "Your God reigns *(malak elohayikh)*." (v. 7)

Vv. 8-10 continue with celebrative responses, singing for joy on seeing the Lord return to Zion, breaking forth into jubilant song because the Lord is redeeming Israel, and all the ends of the earth seeing "the salvation of our God."

This text contains the key themes gospel, peace, and reign of God. But the phrase "kingdom of God" *per se* does not occur. However, the Aramaic Targum renders the last clause of v. 7 as "the kingdom of your God is revealed." In all four Isaiah texts both the phrase "the kingdom of God" and the passive form of the verb *reveal* in either the present or future tense occur. *What* or *who* here does the revealing? In 52:7 it is *the one announcing gospel (mebasser)* that reveals the kingdom of God. This gives us a significant perspective for under-

6. This information is accessible in Part II of Chilton's *A Galilean Rabbi and His Bible* and "Regnum Dei Deus Est."

7. Ollenburger, *Zion, City of the Great King.*

standing Jesus and his mission. In the Greek translation (LXX), this subject is represented by the participle *euangelizomenos*, which includes both the subject, *the one announcing*, and the object, *gospel*. Since *gospel* is already present in the participle, we might view *peace, good, salvation*, and "*Your God reigns*" as the objects or outcomes of the verbal action. Thus, the *gospel* declares *peace*, and it is *good*, echoing perhaps the refrain in Genesis 1. It is important to note that Isa. 52:7 forms the backdrop to the famous Isaiah 53 text (the unit actually begins with 52:13), which influenced Jesus' own perception of his ministry. But it is less well known that 52:7 also played a crucial role in shaping Jesus' ministry, as well as the early church's understanding of Jesus and his mission.[8]

A crucial text complementing the impact of Isa. 52:7 on Jesus' self-understanding of his mission is Isa. 61:1-2a:

> The spirit of the Lord GOD is upon me,
>   because the LORD has anointed me;
> he has sent me to bring good news to the oppressed,
>   to bind up the brokenhearted,
>   to proclaim liberty to the captives,
>   and release to the prisoners;
> to proclaim the year of the LORD's favor.

The connection between the two texts hinges on two points. The "me" of 61:1-2a appears to be the *servant/ebed* of chs. 40-55. V. 1 uses the word *anointed (mashiach)* to describe the vocational call and empowerment of the servant. Since anointing was used primarily for the installation of kings, we have here already the blending of the traditions of kingship and servant, similar to what occurs at Jesus' baptism. Significantly, the verb *basar* is used to describe the servant's mission. The Lord has anointed the servant to "announce the gospel to the poor."

The positive OT view of kingship, which contrasts to the negative view in 1 Samuel 8, merits fuller description here, since this political conception lies at the heart of the "kingdom of God" metaphor. While the kingship theme in the OT is rich and vast,[9] Bernhard W. Anderson's study of the king-

---

8. Peter Stuhlmacher paved the way in showing these connections. See his "The Theme: The Gospel and the Gospels." See also William Horbury's excellent study "'Gospel' in Herodian Judaea." The definitive work showing the influence of this text on early Christian writings is Frankemölle, "Jesus als deuterojesajanische Freudenbote?"

9. Key studies are Ringgren, *Messiah in the Old Testament*; Eaton, *Kingship and the Psalms*; Cook, "The Israelite King as Son of God"; Gerbrandt, *Kingship according to the Deuteronomic History*; and Ollenburger, *Zion*. David M. Hay's study of Psalm 110 and its influence on the NT is also crucial: *Glory at the Right Hand: Psalm 110 in Early Christianity*.

ship traditions as background for understanding Peter's confession "You are the Christ"[10] summarizes well the crucial data.[11] The Davidic king as son of God is also the anointed one *(mashiach)* from whence the messianic hope and the title Messiah arose. The anointed king functions as the anointed of Yahweh who is the cosmic King enthroned in the heavens; Yahweh as King reigns in Zion. The metaphor "son of God," which was applied in the Mosaic tradition to Israel as God's people (Exod. 4:22-24; Hos. 11:1-11; Jer. 31:9; Isa. 1:2-3b), is applied to the king in the royal Davidic and Zion traditions (Ps. 2:7; Isa. 9:2-7; 2 Sam. 7:11-17). Through Israel's exile and chastened hopes on the return to Jerusalem the David/Zion tradition "survived intact and provided a major resource, if not hermeneutical guide, for understanding the messianic identity of Jesus." Anderson then sums up three basic components of the tradition: "(a) God's cosmic kingship in heaven and on earth; (b) the elected king (the Anointed One) as the Son of God and therefore God's viceroy on earth; and (c) the exaltation of the 'messiah' on Zion, the 'holy hill,' against which the assaulting hosts of chaos and evil cannot prevail."[12]

Indeed, this tradition provides a major resource for the early church's understanding of Jesus. But the NT also shows significant transformation of the tradition, so much so that the OT *per se* cannot be said to provide an unambivalent understanding. This ambivalence is indeed present already in the OT. A major stream of OT tradition viewed human kingship negatively. 1 Samuel 8 clearly depicts Israel's desire to have a king, like the nations, as a departure from God's pattern for Israel — a direct threat to Yahweh's kingship. Some of the prophets echo this tradition: "I have given you kings in my anger, and I have taken them away in my wrath" (Hos. 13:11). Indeed, Israel's entire experience of human kingship may be viewed negatively as the usurping of Yahweh's role as King, as willful disobedience of God.[13]

But whether viewed positively or negatively, the strong influence of the kingship tradition on the entire canon of Scripture cannot be disputed. Jesus' use of "the kingdom of God" to describe his mission and message — even using "king" to denote God in some parables — shows how central this metaphor was to Israel, even in the first century, when Israel had no human king. In fact, during times like those, it was safer to speak of kingship. For then it

10. Bernhard W. Anderson, "The Messiah as Son of God: Peter's Confession in Traditio-Historical Perspective."

11. A more complete summary is to be found in my *Israel's Scripture Traditions and the Synoptic Gospels: Story Shaping Story,* pp. 199-200.

12. Anderson, "Messiah as Son of God," p. 169.

13. This view is textually explicated at many levels of the Pentateuchal narrative and in the Primary History by Millard C. Lind in *Yahweh Is a Warrior,* pp. 50-170.

was clear that one spoke of the true king, the Lord God who called Israel into being and promised to continue to work through the covenant people.

Jesus and the Gospels

Mark, likely the earliest Gospel, portrays Jesus via the combined motifs of kingship, servant, and gospel. At Jesus' baptism (1:9-11) the voice from heaven uses two OT texts. "You are my son" is from Ps. 2:7, a Psalm used for the coronation of the king in Israel. Hence, anointed by the Spirit in his baptism, Jesus is identified as God's royal Son. He is declared to be also the Beloved One, which connects the citation to Genesis 22, to Isaac, Abraham's only beloved son. Jesus is so designated in John 3:16.

Further, Jesus is identified as God's *servant,* for the second part of the Voice's statement speaks of "one in whom I am well pleased," from Isa. 42:1, which describes the servant of the Lord and his mission to bring justice to the nations. Here again is an echo of Isa. 61:1-2, for its subject is the same servant as in Isaiah 42.

Mark uses the word *gospel* already in the title of his book: "The beginning of the *gospel* of Jesus Christ, the Son of God." He is thus the only Gospel writer to call his Gospel explicitly a Gospel. His keynote description of Jesus' ministry in 1:14-15 accentuates the word by using it two times: "Jesus came into Galilee, preaching the *gospel* of God, and saying, 'The time is fulfilled, and the *kingdom* of God is at hand; repent, and believe in the *gospel*'" (RSV). Mark's three-point summary thus uses the word *gospel* to sum up Jesus' mission. As in Isa. 52:7, *gospel* and *the reign of God* are linked together. In the LXX *euangelion,* "gospel," is used to translate the Hebrew word *šemuʿah* in Isa. 53:1 ("Who has believed our *report*"), the noun form of the participle *mebasser.* This is the same word used in Isa. 52:7 in the participle form ("him who announces gospel") and in Isa. 61:1 in the infinitive ("to bring good news").

In what language did Jesus hear and read the Scripture? Quite certainly, he heard the synagogue readings in Aramaic and scholars agree that he spoke and taught in Aramaic. Since the Targum already rendered "Your God reigns" with "the kingdom of God is revealed," and both Isa. 52:7 and Mark 1:14-15 use the word *gospel* twice, it is quite probable that Mark and indeed Jesus himself understood his mission in light of and as fulfillment of Isa. 52:7.[14]

---

14. It is striking that C. H. Dodd, a pacifist, did not include this text in his dozen-plus key texts shaping NT theology in his seminal *According to the Scripture: The Sub-Structure of New Testament Theology.* Some of the NT Theology or NT Ethics authors analyzed in Appendix 1 did

Further, it is striking to see the correlation between Jesus' parables of the kingdom of God in Mark and Targum Isaiah's emphasis on *reveal*. The Targum says, "the kingdom of God is revealed." In Mark the "to be *revealed*" aspect of the kingdom is so strong that we read, "To you is given the secret of the kingdom of God" and "there is nothing hid, except to be made manifest," that is, *revealed*. Each of the four parables in Mark 4 is oriented to the *revealing* of the kingdom of God: the sower (see especially vv. 14-20), the lamp and bushel (vv. 21-25), the seed growing secretly (vv. 26-29), and the mustard seed (vv. 30-32). All develop different aspects of the *revealing* of the kingdom.[15]

When Jesus later in Mark speaks to his disciples about entering the kingdom of God (9:41-50), he concludes the section by calling them to be at peace with one another, a point also carrying forward a central emphasis of Isa. 52:7 (see Chapter 4 for further treatment of this section in Mark).

Matthew also shows similar connections. He regularly describes the mission of Jesus with the phrase "preaching the gospel of the kingdom" (4:23; 9:35; 24:14). All three components of our title — gospel, kingdom, and peace — are found also in Matthew. For the Sermon on the Mount links the theme of the kingdom of God to that of peace by identifying peacemakers as the sons (children) of God, using here an image from Israel's royalty tradition.

With Luke the point intensifies in significance. Luke strongly emphasizes all three components: *announcing the gospel, the kingdom,* and *peace.* While Mark uses *gospel* only as a noun, Luke frequently uses forms of *euangelizomai,* "announce the gospel," and thus provides even a stronger witness to the point that Jesus' mission unfolded and was understood in the light of the gospel-kingdom proclamation of Isa. 52:7. The verb "announce gospel" is a favorite for Luke, occurring twenty-five times. In several texts it occurs in combination with "kingdom of God" (Luke 4:43; 8:1; 16:16; Acts 8:12) and in several others with Luke's emphasis on peace (Luke 2:10, 14; Acts 10:36). Luke 10:1-12, an important text, links *peace* and *kingdom.* Though the word for *gospel is* not found there (but see *euangelizomenoi* in 9:6, where Jesus sends out

---

see the Isa. 52:7 text's importance to Jesus' gospel announcing the kingdom. I will comment on this in my "Summary and Conclusion." Nonetheless, Dodd recognized that Jesus' gospel of the kingdom stands opposed to war and violence. He held that war, by its very nature, contradicts the gospel and is "fundamentally antagonistic" to the kingdom Jesus proclaimed. See Dodd's "The Theology of Pacifism," pp. 11-12. See also William Klassen's discussion of Dodd in "The Eschatology of Jesus: Is Apocalyptic Really the Mother of Christian Theology?" pp. 86-87. Significant also is Jewish NT scholar David Flusser's similar view of Jesus' proclamation and embodiment of the kingdom message as standing for peace and opposed to war. See Flusser's *Jesus,* pp. 37-55.

15. For further treatment see my *Mark: The Way for All Nations,* pp. 62-74.

the twelve), Jesus' *sending (apesteilen)* of the seventy in 10:1 echoes his own *having been sent* by the Spirit of the Lord to *announce gospel* to the poor in 4:18, which draws on Isa. 61:1. Luke has introduced Jesus' public ministry there with Jesus reading the Isaiah text in the synagogue. Jesus himself is the anointed one, who as God's servant of justice has come "to announce gospel" to the poor *(euangelisasthai* translates *lebasser):*

a   To *preach good news* to the poor,
  b   To proclaim *release* to the captives,
    c   And recovering of *sight* to the blind,
  b′   To send forth the *oppressed in release,*
a′   To proclaim the *acceptable year* of the Lord.

This great text of liberation outlines the mission of Jesus around five powerful declarations, with Luke's great word for *gospelize (euangelizomai)* at the head of the list.

Another important Lukan text is Luke 2:10, 14, one of fourteen uses of "peace" *(eirēnē)* in the Gospel. This text links "gospel" and "peace," and v. 11 connects both to the royal tradition, for the baby born is of "the house of David." Peace *(eirēnē)* is one of Luke's narrative emphases, especially in the Gospel's central section (this will be taken up in detail in Chapter 5 below).

The above analysis of word uses shows that Luke strongly accentuates three interrelated themes: announcing the gospel, the kingdom, and peace. Another important Lukan contribution to these themes occurs in Acts in Peter's summary of Jesus' mission and message (Acts 10:36-37), which combines *gospel, peace,* and Jesus' Lordship. In this sermon on the occasion of Cornelius' admission into the new "Way" covenant community, Peter sums up the message of Jesus as that of "preaching the gospel of peace." V. 38 then describes how Jesus "went about doing good [recall this adjective in Isa. 52:7] and healing all that were oppressed by the devil, for God was with him." Just as v. 36 echoes Isa. 52:7, so v. 38 echoes Isa. 61:1-3. Clearly, Luke understands Jesus as the fulfillment of these Isaiah texts. The gospel of Jesus inaugurates the year of the Lord's favor, that is, Jubilee (Luke 4:19). All this is set within the overarching accent on the kingdom of God which Jesus inaugurates and which the early church proclaims, so that Acts ends with Paul teaching and preaching the kingdom of God in Rome, the capital of the empire (see Chapter 6 for more on this point).

The Synoptic Gospels' presentation of Jesus thus draws on OT texts and traditions to mark Jesus as the gospel-herald of *peace.* Jesus is the long expected Messiah, but one of a different sort than most Israel-covenant folk anticipated. Matthew, Mark, and Luke deepen this understanding of Jesus in specific ways, as Chapters 3-5 will show.

The *gospel*, the *reign of God*, and *peace* permeate Paul's letters (see Chapters 7-8). The good news of God's salvation is the heart of his proclamation, foundational to his understanding of the manifestation/revelation of God's righteousness and justification. Further, Paul speaks often of God's defeat of the principalities and powers through the cross of Jesus Christ, an important precondition of God's establishment of the messianic peace. As a term, *peace* occurs in almost all Paul's letters. It lies at the heart of Paul's eschatological hope, for "The God of peace will soon crush Satan under your feet" (Rom. 16:20).

Hebrews, James, and 1 Peter continue the proclamation of God's reign of peace, under conditions of severe testing, even persecution. The moral imperative of non-retaliation and seeking to overcome evil with good intensifies, given the limitations of the socio-political situations in which these books were written.

John's Gospel contributes different but not contradictory emphases on peace. Peace is Jesus' bequest to his disciples in the midst of a hostile world (14:27; 16:33). In his post-resurrection appearance to his disciples, Jesus' *peace*-greeting occurs twice (20:19d, 21a), marking Jesus' character and the empowerment he imparts in the distinctive Johannine form of Jesus' commission: "As the Father has sent me, so I send you" (v. 21b; the *peace*-greeting recurs in his appearance a week later as well, with Thomas present, v. 26d). Empowered by Jesus' gift of peace, love for one another is the key mark of Jesus' followers (13:35). Both peace and love stand in opposition to the world's character. In both the Gospel and Epistles Jesus by doing fully the works of him who sent him gains victory over the evil ruler of the world. Further, believers are protected from the evil one (John 17:15; 1 John 5:18). While "world" is negative here in connotation, it is not always so, for God loves the world and seeks its salvation (see Chapter 10).

The book of Revelation adds yet another depth perspective, for it celebrates God's triumph amid the worldly idolatrous kingdoms arrayed against God's kingdom. God's people are called to be faithful witnesses to the gospel, even at the cost of martyrdom. Worship God, not the beastly empire, is the central imperative of the book (Chapter 12).

To be sure, the term *reign of God* does not occur often in John, Paul, Hebrews, James, 1 Peter, or Revelation, but the notion is not absent either. Paul's *righteousness of God* and John's *eternal life* are close approximations, as is 1 Peter's *chosen people/holy nation/royal priesthood* and Hebrews' *kingdom that cannot be shaken.* In Revelation "the *kingdom of our Lord and of his Christ*" triumphs over Satan's and the beast's kingdoms; it culminates in the majestic vision and promise of the *new heavens and new earth.*

This chapter has set forth the foundational thesis of this study: *peace* is integral to the *gospel* of the *kingdom* that Jesus proclaimed and brought in his own person. Chapters 3-6 will explicate expressions of this in the Synoptic Gospels and Acts. Chapters on Paul and later NT writings will extend the same point, but with different terms. Paul speaks of *kingdom of God* quite infrequently, but his *righteousness of God* manifest in Jesus Christ conveys a similar notion to *kingdom of God.* Paul's peace emphases occur in his explication of the meaning of Christ's death on the cross. In a recently published article by the late Robert Guelich the problem of the relation between the Gospels and Paul in these differing emphases is posed and resolved. As Guelich put it: the Synoptic Gospels emphasize the *kingdom of God* and Paul emphasizes *Christ crucified.* This has given rise to two different gospels, the first more social and the second more personal. But Guelich rightly notes that both are formulations of the same good news of salvation. The *gospel of the cross* and the *gospel of the kingdom* are both derived from God's promised *gospel of peace,* announced by the prophet Isaiah.

> The answer to our dilemma of how the gospel of the Kingdom and the gospel of the cross relate is that the gospel of the cross is integral to the gospel of the Kingdom in Jesus' ministry. But the gospel of the cross is only integral to the gospel of the Kingdom if we understand both to be an expression of the same "gospel," namely, Isaiah's promised "gospel" of God. The "gospel," then, is the message that God acted in and through Jesus Messiah, God's anointed one, to effect God's promise of *shalom* — God's reign.[16]

As Guelich perceives, Isa. 52:7 is important both to the Gospels' presentation of Jesus and to Paul. Both affirm that in Jesus the long-awaited messenger of peace has come, bringing salvation and a new creation. God's saving gospel of peace encompasses the personal, social, and cosmic dimensions of a new creation through Jesus Christ. Subsequent chapters will exposit the pluriform dimensions of this pillar of salvation-truth.

To build further the foundations for this study, the next chapter takes up an intensive study of the meaning of *peace* (both *shalom* and *eirēnē*).

16. Guelich, "What Is the Gospel?" 7.

Addendum: Aramaic Daniel as Another Source

Another likely influential OT source for Jesus' use of *kingdom of God* is the Aramaic portion of Daniel, 2:4–7:28.[17] Both Daniel 2 and Daniel 7 conclude with emphasis on the kingdom from above that subverts earthly empires. God's establishment of an everlasting kingdom forms the inclusio-theme of this Aramaic portion. Since Aramaic was the dominant Palestinian language of Jesus' time, this OT portion of Scripture may have carried special import, indeed messianic significance, for Jewish people from 200 BCE into the time of Jesus.

The *mystery* of the *kingdom* that God establishes is revealed through dreams in both Daniel 2 and 7. King Nebuchadnezzar of Babylon in the second year of his reign "dreamed such dreams that his spirit was troubled and his sleep left him." He called for the recognized wise people, the magicians, enchanters, sorcerers, and Chaldeans, to make known to him *his dream and its interpretation.* His was a high demand and the Chaldeans replied, "There is no one on earth who can reveal what the king demands" (2:10). Further, they said no king had ever asked for such a thing before "of any magician or enchanter or Chaldean."

The "king flew into a rage and issued a decree that all the wise men of Babylon be destroyed" (2:12). The decree was averted when Daniel heard of it and responded with "prudence and discretion to Arioch," the executioner. Daniel entreated his three companions to pray for him that God would hear his prayer and reveal the mystery so that they and all the wise men of Babylon would not perish. "Then the mystery was revealed to Daniel in a vision of the night, and Daniel blessed the God of heaven" (v. 19).

When Daniel goes to the king to give the answer to the mysteries of the dream, he repeats what the wise men earlier said, that no one on earth is able *to make known* to the king his request. But "there is a God in heaven who reveals mysteries" (v. 28). Then Daniel *makes known* to the king both the dream — what the king has seen — and its interpretation. A statue composed of four metals (gold, silver, bronze, and iron mixed with clay) represents the kingdom that now is (gold = Babylon) and those to come. In the days of the kings of the last kingdom "the God of heaven will set up a kingdom that shall never be destroyed, nor shall this kingdom be left to another people. It shall

17. For this analysis of Daniel 2 and 7 my observations arise from a conversation with Douglas Yoder who is currently doing his doctoral dissertation, "Tanakh Epistemology: A Philosophical Reading of an Ancient Semitic *Text,*" at Claremont Graduate University on the epistemic significance of *yadha* in the Tanakh.

crush all these kingdoms and bring them to an end, and it shall stand forever" (2:44). Further, the stone cut from the mountain represents this kingdom that stands forever and crushes all the parts of the statue. "The dream is certain and its interpretation trustworthy" (v. 45).

The story is told with great effect, repeating seventeen times Aramaic *yadha*, "tell, reveal, understand, inform, know, make known." Another key term used seven times is *mystery(ies)* (*raz*: 2:18, 19, 27, 28, 29, 30, 47). This term had great significance to the Qumran Covenanters, for whom it denoted the manifestation of God's end-time victory over evil (including Roman oppressors).[18] Daniel 2, therefore, with its use of these two key words along with the *kingdom* that "the God of heaven will set up" provides perspective to understand the puzzling text of Mark 4:11-12, "To you is *revealed* the *mystery* of the *kingdom of God.*" Strikingly, in Daniel's prayer (2:20-23) "he reveals deep and hidden things" (v. 22a) sounds like a precursor to Mark 4:22, "For there is nothing hidden except to be disclosed."

Daniel 7 is analogous to ch. 2 in that here *Daniel* has a dream during the time of King Belshazzar. He sees four beasts, one like a lion, one like a bear, one like a leopard, and a terrifying fourth beast with iron teeth. As he watches this astounding scene, he sees thrones set in place and an Ancient One taking his throne, with dazzling visuals, and thousand thousands serve the Ancient One and ten thousand times ten thousand stand attending him, and he takes the seat of judgment over humans. Then the dominion of the beasts is ended, and there appears in the night visions "one like a human being [Son of Man], who receives dominion and glory and kingship" (v. 13). "To him was given dominion and glory and kingship, that all peoples, nations, and languages should serve him. His dominion is an everlasting dominion that shall not pass away, and his kingship is one that shall never be destroyed" (v. 14). Concerning the end of the fourth beast, judgment is certain (vv. 23-27). The last verse proclaims: "The kingship and dominion and the greatness of the kingdoms under the whole heaven shall be given to the people of the holy ones of the Most High; their kingdom shall be an everlasting kingdom, and all dominions shall serve and obey them."

Against this background it is hardly accidental that Jesus identifies himself as the Son of Man with authority to forgive sins (Mark 2:10). Not only is the book of Daniel laden with kingdom/dominion motifs, but the texts together explain two of the Gospels' key emphases, "to you is revealed

---

18. Among the Qumran scrolls have been found seven manuscript fragments of the Aramaic portion of Daniel, indicating its importance to the community. The term *pesher*, important at Qumran, occurs numerous times in Daniel 2.

the mystery of the kingdom of God" and Jesus' self-identification as "Son of Humanity."

Hence, this Danielic Aramaic portion blends with the Isaian Aramaic "the kingdom of God shall be revealed" to provide a substantial theological context for both Jesus' self-understanding and his proclamation of the kingdom of God come and coming. Daniel's contribution adds to that of the Isaiah Targum by marking God's kingdom as one that subverts earthly empires. It will counter imperial pretenses to lordship, savior-claims, and certainly all emperor-divinization, recurring emphases in this study. God's kingdom, contra the Pax Romana, will be the locus of authentic *peace.*

2 *Shalom* and *Eirēnē* in Hebrew Scripture, the Greco-Roman World, and the New Testament

Steadfast love and faithfulness will meet;
righteousness and peace will kiss each other.   PS. 85:10

Righteousness and justice are the foundation of your throne;
steadfast love and faithfulness go before you.   PS. 89:14

Glory to God in the highest heaven,
and on earth peace among those whom he favors!   LUKE 2:14

For he [Christ] is our peace . . . that he might create in himself one new
humanity in place of the two, thus making peace.

EPH. 2:14-15

Shalom in the Old Testament and Rabbinic Writings

Shalom is an iridescent word, with many levels of meaning in Hebrew
Scripture. The base denominator of its many meanings is *well-being, wholeness, completeness.* "It ranges over several spheres and can refer in different
contexts to bounteous physical conditions, to a moral value, and, ultimately, to a cosmic principle and divine attribute."[1] Understanding its

1. Ravitsky, "Peace," p. 685.

meaning in the Hebrew Bible is an essential prerequisite for the study of peace in the NT.

Shalom occurs well over 200 times in the Hebrew Bible[2] and has many dimensions of meaning: wholeness, completeness, well-being, peace, justice, salvation, and even prosperity. It occurs often in inquiries about one's *welfare* (Gen. 29:6; 37:14; 43:27; Exod. 18:7; 1 Sam. 10:4; 17:18, 22; 25:5; 30:21; Jer. 15:5 on the *shalom* of Jerusalem; 38:4). It thus "includes everything necessary to healthful living: good health, a sense of well-being, good fortune, the cohesiveness of the community, relationship to relatives and their state of being, and anything else deemed necessary for everything to be in order."[3] English versions may translate it as "prosperity" (Ps. 30:6; Isa. 54:13). It can also have moral connotations. For example, deceit destroys *shalom* (Ps. 34:13-14; Jer. 8:22–9:8). The notion of *well-being* shades over into *shalom's* cognate, *shalem* (used 33 times), meaning wholeness and health, spiritually and physically.[4]

In an introductory article to seven essays on *shalom* in the OT, Perry Yoder identifies three main dimensions of meaning.[5] For von Rad *shalom* denotes material, physical well-being within a social context.[6] Thus it has relational dimensions also. Eisenbeis concurs that *shalom* designates "wholeness" and "intactness" of life but notes that the primary meaning describes some aspect of relationship with God. It is theological and closely associated with *salvation*.[7] Westermann concurs that *shalom* denotes wholeness and well-being, but argues that it designates a *state* or *condition*, rather

2. Claus Westermann, "Peace [*Shalom*] in the Old Testament," in *The Meaning of Peace*, p. 44 (1992 edition, p. 20), specifies 210 for the number of occurrences and notes that it occurs in virtually all the OT books. But J. Douglas Harris, in *Shalom! The Biblical Concept of Peace* (Grand Rapids: Baker, 1970), lists over 350 occurrences, including cognates (pp. 75-78). The number 250 is cited most frequently, however. See, e.g., H. Beck and C. Brown, "Peace," in *The New International Dictionary of New Testament Theology*, ed. Colin Brown, vol. 2 (Grand Rapids: Zondervan, 1976, 1986), p. 777. The variation in count depends on inclusion of verbal forms *(shalam)* and cognates.

3. Westermann, "Peace [*Shalom*] in the Old Testament," p. 49.

4. Healing may be used to denote restoration of *shalom*. See Joseph M. Savage, "Shalom and Its Relationship to Health/Healing in the Hebrew Scriptures: A Contextual and Semantic Study of the Books of Psalms and Jeremiah" (Ph.D. dissertation, Florida State University, 2001).

5. I have adapted portions of this chapter from my article, "War and Peace in the New Testament," in *ANRW* 2.26.3, ed. W. Haase and H. Temporini (New York: de Gruyter, 1996), pp. 2305-14.

6. G. von Rad, "Shalom in the Old Testament," in *TDNT* 2, pp. 402-6.

7. Walter Eisenbeis, "A Study of the Root Shalom in the Old Testament" (Ph.D. dissertation, University of Chicago, 1966, published as *Die Würzel shlm im Alten Testament* [BZAW 113; Berlin: Töpelmanns, 1969]).

than a relationship.[8] Gerleman holds that *shalom* refers to both a state and a relationship.[9]

A second scholarly perspective argues that *shalom* refers to the concept of a correct order of life and that the notion of creation order binds together the various uses of *shalom* into a unified whole. War is not an antithesis to *shalom* (David asks Uriah about the *shalom* of a war in 2 Sam. 11:7), and may in Israel's later literature be understood as an act of divine judgment in order to restore the *shalom* of the creation order.[10] Whatever blocks Yahweh's order for the world, materially or relationally, is the foe and antithesis of *shalom*. In Jerusalem's cult the king was authorized to execute and defend the *shalom* of God's order against injustice and oppression.

Extending this emphasis and in keeping with the thrust of Hans Walter Wolff's work on Isa. 2:1-5,[11] Yoder proposes that *shalom* also contains a moral quality. It stands against oppression, deceit, fraud, and all actions that violate the divine order for human life.[12] Klaus Wengst says *violence* is the opposite of *shalom*.[13] Violence and *evil (raʿ)* are certainly close antonyms of *shalom*. *Shalom* also designates innocence of moral wrong-doing (Gen. 44:17; 2 Kgs. 5:19) and is paired with *mishpat* (Isa. 59:8) and *tsedaqah* (Ps. 72:7; Isa. 54:13-14; 48:18; 60:17). *Shalom* is indeed a gift,[14] but its maintenance in human life depends on human response to God's order that values and acts in accord with the divine moral order for human society.

In order to grasp the wide range of meaning *shalom* connotes in the OT,

8. C. Westermann, "Der Frieden *(shalom)* im Alten Testament," in *Studien zur Friedenforschung* 1, ed. G. Picht and H. E. Tödt (Stuttgart: Klett, 1969), pp. 144-77.

9. G. Gerleman, "*shlm,*" *Theological Handwörterbuch zum Alten Testament* 2, pp. 919-35.

10. H. H. Schmid, *Shalom: Frieden im Alten Orient und im Alten Testament* (Stuttgart: KBW, 1971), and "Frieden II: Altes Testament," in *Theologische Realenzyklopädie*, vol. 11, pp. 605-10; Odil Hannes Steck, "Jerusalem Concepts of Peace and Their Development in Ancient Israelite Prophecy," in *The Meaning of Peace*, ed. P. Yoder and W. Swartley, pp. 129-48 (1992, pp. 49-69). This is taken from Steck's larger study, *Friedensvorstellungen im alten Jerusalem. Psalmen, Jesaja, Deuterojesaja* (Zurich: Theologischer Verlag, 1972).

11. Hans Walter Wolff, "Swords into Plowshares — Misuses of a Word of Prophecy?" *Currents in Theology and Mission* 12 (1985): 133-47, also in *The Meaning of Peace*, ed. P. Yoder and W. Swartley, pp. 211-28 (1992, pp. 110-26).

12. Perry Yoder made this point in an article titled "Shalom Revisited" (unpublished, 1984), p. 18.

13. Klaus K. Wengst, *Humility: Solidarity of the Humiliated: The Transformation of an Attitude and Its Social Relevance in Graeco-Roman, Old Testament-Jewish and Early Christian Tradition* (Philadelphia: Fortress, 1988), p. 21.

14. Jacob Kremer, "Peace — God's Gift: Biblical Theological Considerations," in *The Meaning of Peace*, ed. P. Yoder and W. Swartley, pp. 21-36 (1992, pp. 133-47), translated from "Der Frieden — eine Gabe Gottes: Bibeltheologische Erwägungen," *Stimmen der Zeit* 200 (1982): 161-73.

it is helpful to see it in relationship to other major themes in OT thought. I propose the following semantic and conceptual context for *shalom:*

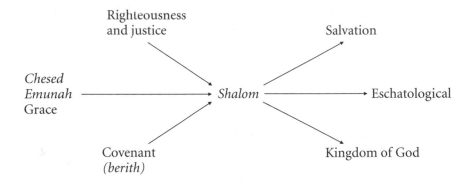

Conceptual diagram with terms carrying corporate and relational significance

To the left of *shalom* in this diagram are covenantal moral attributes that make *shalom* possible and are rooted in God's character and initiative. Indeed, *shalom* is a gift of God, but the people must actualize that reality by living in accord with the righteous and just statutes that God gives and prescribes in the covenant (Ps. 119; Exodus 20; Deut. 18:16-18). The two Psalm texts cited at the beginning of the chapter identify the key moral qualities of steadfast love *(chesed)*, faithfulness *(emunah)*, righteousness *(tsedaqah)*, and justice *(mishpat)*. These are *sine qua non* for *shalom* to flourish (Ps. 89:14; 97:2b; 85:10). The covenant is the relational framework that states what God expects from the people and what the people are to expect from God. OT scholars have compared the covenant to political treaties, and there is indeed a structural similarity. But the content is specific to Israel's God and God's people in holy relationship. The Ten Commandments may indeed be viewed as Israel's covenant response to God's redemptive action in delivering them from slavery in Egypt. Hence, they begin with "Since I am the Lord your God who redeemed you from bondage. . . ."

The terms to the right of *shalom* in the diagram show that the God-people relationship is on the march toward realization of the salvation God has begun and toward the fuller establishment of God's kingdom. Thus the eschatological dimension cannot be minimized. Against this background one can appreciate the futuristic visions of *shalom* permeating the prophetic corpus. Further, the NT proclamation continues and brings to greater fulfillment this *shalom* vision, as in Paul's declaration "Christ is our peace" (Eph. 2:14).

Paul Hanson proposes that the understanding of *shalom* underwent significant shifts throughout Israel's history. In early Yahwism it was understood "as something other than a human achievement. It was a condition of life, received by those allowing themselves to be drawn into a pattern of community manifested by the God who delivered Hebrew slaves from their bondage."[15] During the monarchy, the wars of the kings, waged mostly not "in the name of God's order of righteousness and peace but rather in the name of an imperialistic ideology,"[16] competed against *shalom*, which the prophet Isaiah identified with quiet trust in God (30:15). Israel's royal ideology threatened the early Yahwistic and Isaianic view of *shalom*. With the close identification of the Davidic king's reign with Yahweh's reign and the growth of the temple and kingship in power and popularity, "shalom came increasingly to be identified as the achievement not of the deliverer God of the exodus but of the king as the chosen son of God."[17]

The prophets unrelentingly criticize this trend, but only the exile delivers Israel from royalist perversions. Out of the crisis of the exile Second Isaiah forged new visions and understandings of *shalom*. Not only is God's order of *shalom* now seen in cosmic proportion, but Israel's vocation is defined as one of agent and witness through which *shalom* extends to the whole world. Further, Second Isaiah sees that the chaos of the exile itself is an act of divine judgment subservient to God's purpose of salvation for Israel; exile enables a prophetic, universal vision for God's *shalom*. Building on Second Isaiah, Trito-Isaiah extends this cosmic vision, specifically to "a renewal of creation to its divinely intended wholeness."[18] But in postexilic Israel internal community strife and exclusivism toward neighbors subvert this vision of *shalom*. Hence in much of Israel's subsequent apocalyptic writings the realization of Yahweh's order of *shalom* "ceases to be taken up as the community's earthly vocation, but is awaited as a divine act which inflicts stinging defeat on outsiders even as it imbues the insiders with paradisaical blessing."[19] The apocalyptic turn also sends out shockwaves of cosmic destruction resulting from the collapse of God's *shalom* order for the world.[20]

The approaches of Yoder and Hanson to the understanding of *shalom* in Hebrew Scripture differ markedly from each other. Yoder's is focused more on linguistic textual analysis while Hanson's reflects the dynamics of Israel's

15. Paul D. Hanson, "War and Peace in Hebrew Scripture," *Int* 38 (1984): 347.
16. Hanson, "War and Peace," p. 351.
17. Hanson, "War and Peace," p. 353.
18. Hanson, "War and Peace," pp. 356-59 (quoting p. 359).
19. Hanson, "War and Peace," p. 361.
20. Hanson, "War and Peace," p. 361.

changing history and echoes many aspects of Brueggemann's *Biblical Reflections on Shalom*.[21] The two approaches may be viewed as complementary. Yoder, taking account of the history of scholarship, calls for more careful semantic field analysis of all text occurrences to enable clearer definition of *shalom*.[22] Hanson, on the other hand, shows how the understanding of *shalom* is affected by changing historical circumstances. Both approaches, taken together, contribute to a fuller understanding of *shalom*.

A pertinent consideration is the impact that war in the OT had on *shalom*. While war is not an antonym to *shalom*, Hanson rightly regards it as interrupting *shalom*, introducing chaos, which is the antithesis of *shalom*. As he puts it, "War in the Bible can be understood only in relation to shalom and chaos, and can best be described as that which transforms the realm of shalom into the condition of chaos."[23]

Shemaryahu Talmon, in his thorough study of *shalom*, affirms the wide range of meaning — personal well-being, greetings, inter-group relations — and observes several levels of meaning in reference to the political sphere. *Shalom* may denote an offer of peace prior to war or a peace that is forced on to people by war. Further future utopian visions of peace are based on a type of *Pax Solomonica*. Talmon understands Isa. 2:1-5 in that context.[24] In response to Talmon's paper presented at the 1999 meeting of the Society of Biblical Literature, Hanson emphasized that remembering that the primary meaning of *shalom* as relational, even covenantal, is important when considering the nature of the eschatological visions of *shalom*, whether or not *Pax Solomonica* promises a utopian future. Indeed, this is important when considering the relation of *shalom* to the use of *eirēnē* in the NT.

Reflection on the meaning of *shalom* continued in Judaism among the Rabbis from the second century to the medieval period and later. Hillel defined the heart of Judaism as "love peace and pursue it" (m. *Abot* 1.12).

> Aaron is regarded as the prototype of those who "love peace and pursue peace and love all creatures," and every Jew is enjoined to follow this example (*Avot* 1.12). R. Shim'on ben Ḥalafta' said, "God could find no better

---

21. Walter Brueggemann, *Peace* (St. Louis: Chalice, 2001). This edition slightly revises *Living toward a Vision: Biblical Reflections on Shalom* (Philadelphia: United Church, 1976), with an excellent new preface.

22. P. Yoder, "Shalom Revisited," pp. 14-17.

23. Hanson, "War and Peace," p. 347.

24. Shemaryahu Talmon, "The Signification of שׁלם in the Hebrew Bible," in *The Quest for Context and Meaning: Studies in Biblical Intertextuality in Honor of James A. Sanders*, ed. Craig A. Evans and Shemaryahu Talmon (Leiden: Brill, 1997).

vessel of blessing for Israel than peace" (*'Uqts.* 3.12). Indeed, peace is the ultimate purpose of the Torah (*Tanhuma' Shofetim* 18) according to the sages. Every single prayer of importance (e.g., Birkat ha-Kohanim, the Qaddish, the 'Amidah, the Birkat ha-Mazon) ends with a prayer for peace and the hope that the same peace that exists among the heavenly spheres shall also reign on earth.[25]

Two emphases emerge in rabbinic texts: peace, especially in later mystical texts, is more and more associated with the notion of *shelemut,* perfection. Thus it is descriptive not only of well-being in various historical spheres, but also becomes ultimately "a cosmic principle and divine attribute."[26] In rabbinic texts as a whole, however,

> *shalom* primarily signifies a value, an *ethical category* — it denotes the overcoming of strife, quarrel, and social tension, the prevention of enmity and war. It is still, to be sure, depicted as a blessing, a manifestation of divine grace, but in a great many sayings it appears in a normative context: The pursuit of peace is the obligation of the individual and the goal of various social regulations and structures. The majority of passages on the subject of peace are concerned with family or communal life, that is, with internal peace among the people, and only a minority are concerned with external relations between Israel and other peoples, between nations and states. . . . The series of regulations ordained by the Sages "in the interest of peace" . . . were also meant to affect relations both among the Jews themselves and between the Jews and the Gentiles.[27]

A favorite saying of Rabbi Abbaye illustrates powerfully the emphasis on making peace within the community:

25. *The Oxford Dictionary of Jewish Religion,* ed. R. J. Zwi Werblowsky and Geoffrey Wigoder (Oxford: Oxford University Press, 1997), p. 523. The Sages comment several times on "the unhewn stones" (stones of perfection, *shelemot*) prescribed for building in Deut. 27:6 as "stones that bring peace" *(shalom).* See Ephraim E. Urbach, *The Sages: The World and Wisdom of the Rabbis of the Talmud,* trans. Israel Abrahams (Cambridge: Harvard University Press, 1975), pp. 370-71, 597. Urbach also specifies an important link between peace in heaven and peace on earth, consisting of study of the Torah. He cites numerous rabbis on this (pp. 179-80), e.g., "Whoever occupies himself with the Torah for its own sake makes peace in the Heavenly Court and in the Earthly Court" (R. Joshua b. Levi).

26. Ravitsky, "Peace," p. 685.

27. Ravitsky, "Peace," p. 686. Hillel, praised for his "humility, patience, love of one's fellows, and the pursuit of peace," also stressed each person's responsibility to make peace in the community — "What is hateful to you do not do to your fellow" (Urbach, *The Sages,* pp. 588-89).

There were two men whom Satan incited against each other. Every Friday evening they wrangled with one another. It happened that Rabbi Me'ir came thither, and he restrained them three Friday evenings running, till he made peace between them. Then he heard Satan cry, "Woe is me; R. Me'ir has driven me away from my house."[28]

The Rabbis reflected on the relationship of peace to justice, truth, and mercy. Rabbi Eleazar ben Simeon said that "one may deviate from the truth for the sake of peace" (BT *Yevamoth* 65b). Rabbi Joshua ben Korha taught that "where there is strict justice there is no peace, and where there is peace there is no strict justice," so he mediated the two by calling for a compromise, justice tempered with peace (JT *Sanhedrin* 1.5; BT *Sanhedrin* 6b), while an opposing view held to justice at all costs: "let justice pierce the mountain." Still another approach seeks harmonization of all three: "By three things the world is preserved, by justice, by truth, and by peace, and these three are one: if justice has been accomplished, so has truth, and so has peace" (JT *Ta'anith* 4.2).[29]

This rabbinic tradition provides a rich resource that complements Christian understandings of peace,[30] both in the NT and even more in the appropriation of NT teaching into the doctrinal and ethical conceptions of church teaching. Ravitsky notes a dual development that arrests Christian theological reflection. In the early medieval period Jewish reflection spiritualized biblical war imagery, while Christian theologians, notably Augustine, spiritualized or internalized the pacifist teachings of the NT. Christian thought began to take OT war imagery literally to develop "just war" doctrine and justify imperial extension, leading in subsequent stages to theological justification of the Crusades.[31] It is thus urgent for Christian believers to recover what the NT actually teaches about peace.

---

28. Entry 1504 in *A Rabbinic Anthology,* ed. C. G. Montefiore and H. Loewe (New York: Schocken, 1974), p. 535.

29. Ravitsky, "Peace," pp. 686-87. Later, Ravitsky cites Rabbi Judah Loew of Prague who, in linking *shalom* to perfection *(shelemut),* holds that God's essence is peace and that, because of *shalom's* comprehensiveness, it is supreme over all other attributes, such as truth (p. 689).

30. For helpful analysis of Judaism's contribution to peacemaking, see Marc Gopin, "Judaism and Peacebuilding," in *Religion and Peacebuilding,* ed. Harold Coward and Gordon S. Smith (Albany: SUNY Press, 2004), pp. 111-27.

31. Ravitsky, "Peace," pp. 692-93.

Eirēnē in the New Testament

In assessing the meaning of war and peace language in NT writings some analysis of the understanding and role of war and peace in the Greco-Roman world is essential. On the one hand, there is the question of what *eirēnē* meant in classical and Greek usage. On the other hand, what did the Pax Romana mean to the various peoples living in such a vast empire, extolled for its peace and prosperity?

Dinkler rightly points out that we cannot know the precise degree of influence that the classical Greek use of *eirēnē* had upon the Koine, and certainly not upon the NT writers.[32] Further, though the NT, especially Acts, cites several Greek writings (Aratus's *Phaenomena* in Acts 17:28b; Euripides' *Bacchae* quite possibly in Acts 26:14, and others), none of these citations are linked with NT peace sayings or texts. When *eirēnē* is used in classical Greek literature it is not always clear whether the term refers to a socio-political condition or to the Greek goddess *Eirēnē*.

The Greek artist Cephisodotus, born at Athens, is credited with the celebrated statue of *Eirēnē* holding the young child Plutus, the god of wealth, on her arm.[33] Scheibler points out that the poet of the *Iliad* condemned war because it brought suffering and death, and the *Odyssey* associates peace with riches.

Historians Herodotus (1.87) and Thucydides (2.61.1) present peace as desirable on humanitarian considerations and for political reasons. For the "spear-raging" Hellas may destroy herself; thus one should turn to Eirene and accept her blessings.[34] The goddess Eirene gained significantly in popularity so that the peace treaty between Sparta and Athens in 375-74 BCE[35] was celebrated by the inauguration of an annual offering to Eirene. In 375 a statue of Eirene was erected on the Agora in Athens.[36] Several decades later silver coins

32. Erich Dinkler, "*Eirēnē* — The Early Christian Concept of Peace," in *The Meaning of Peace*, ed. Yoder and Swartley, pp. 89-90 (1992, pp. 177-78). For what follows I have drawn from Dinkler's article and my previous formulation in "War and Peace in the New Testament," pp. 2309-14.

33. See Ingeborg Scheibler, "Götter des Friedens in Hellas und Rom," *Antike Welt* 15.1 (1984): 39-40, fig. 1. Two other portraits of Eirene appear in Scheibler, pp. 45-46, figs. 12-13. See also the *Tellus-Italia-Reliefs* from the east side of the Ara Pacis in Ludwig Budde, *Ara Pacis Augustae: Der Friedensaltar des Augustus* (Hannover: Tauros, 1957), plates 2-3.

34. Here Dinkler cites Euripides' *Cresphonte's Song of Peace;* "*Eirēnē* — The Early Christian Concept," p. 84 (1992, p. 174).

35. Dinkler, "*Eirēnē* — The Early Christian Concept," p. 85 and n. 50 (1992, p. 174, n. 49 on pp. 196-97), where Dinkler cites Isocrates' *Antidosis, Oratio* 15.109-10 and gives further documentation of research.

36. Literary evidence of this comes from Cephisodotus who portrays Eirene holding the

The goddess *Eirēnē* holding Plutus (in the Glyptothek at Munich)

originating from Locri picture "Eirene, sitting on an altar embellished with bukranion, in her right hand holding a staff with a snake coiled around it, the caduceus *(kerykeion)*."[37] Even with this degree of visibility, Eirene never emerged beyond minor goddess status in Greco-Roman culture. Dinkler cites H. Fuchs: "Although she is peace, she is not the one that brings peace."[38]

Complementing this emergence of Eirene as a significant minor deity in the Greek-speaking East, Augustus in the Latin West introduced the Pax cult into Roman imperial politics not many years before the birth of Jesus. The older Roman *Concordia* cult was now nicely balanced with a Pax cult. The former was directed to internal policy, the latter toward imperial policy. Through this relationship, *eirēnē* as Pax Romana became a power of pacification of foreign nations in order to enable concord and harmony to continue at home. The erection of the *Ara Pacis Augustae* (Altar of Peace to Augustus)[39] on the field of Mars in Rome in 9 BCE is telling. The location discloses the means of Pax Romana: subjugation of the nations of the empire.[40] The classic example is Vespasian's building of a Peace Temple (the *Templum Pacis*) in 75 CE celebrating Rome's victory over the Jews, with the famous arch depicting both Rome's victory and the Jews' defeat.[41]

The Pax Romana was celebrated as an ideal state of affairs, a time of one worldwide Greco-Roman language and culture, a time of prosperity and order. These latter features accord with the Hebrew notion of *shalom*. But the

---

boy Plutus on her arm, in Dinkler, "*Eirēnē* — The Early Christian Concept," pp. 85-86, documentation in n. 53 (1992, p. 174, n. 52 on p. 197).

37. Dinkler, "*Eirēnē* — The Early Christian Concept," p. 86 (1992, p. 174). Dinkler cites P. R. Franke and M. Hirmer, *Die griechische Münze* (Munich: Hirmer, 1964), plate 101, and Stefan Weinstock, "Pax and the 'Ara Pacis,'" *JRS* 50 (1960): 44. Dinkler cites evidence in his note 53, p. 85 (1992, n. 52, p. 197). For pictorial reproduction of the coin see also Scheibler, "Götter des Friedens," p. 45, fig. 11.

38. Fuchs, *Augustin,* p. 171, 1.

39. Dinkler, "*Eirēnē* — The Early Christian Concept," p. 87 (1992, p. 175), and Klaus Wengst, *Pax Romana and the Peace of Jesus Christ,* trans. John Bowden (Philadelphia: Fortress, 1987), p. 11. On the *Ara Pacis* see Ludwig Budde, *Ara Pacis,* pp. 5-13, and the excellent reproduction in plate 1; plates 2-18 contain details from all sides of the altar; S. Weinstock, "Pax and the Ara Pacis," *JRS* 50 (1960): 44-58; I. Scheibler, "Götter des Friedens," p. 52, and figs. 17 (p. 48) and 19 (p. 49).

40. Evidence for this dual war/peace thinking abounds on Roman coins, a form of Pax Romana propaganda. See Wengst, *Pax Romana,* pp. 11-12; Scheibler, "Götter des Friedens," pp. 54-56.

41. I. Scheibler, "Götter des Friedens," p. 54 and fig. 21 on p. 51. Here also Titus's minting the *IVDAE CAPTAE* coin ca. 80 CE can be cited. See Franke and Hirmer, *Die griechische Münze,* p. 31, #240 on plate 62, and B. Overbeck's description in Part II, p. 107, for #240 (cf. also #228 on p. 106 and see plate 225 for a similar coin under Vespasian).

Pax Romana was also a situation in which many subjugated peoples suffered oppression from Rome's "golden age" of prosperity — features that oppose and mock *shalom.*

When early Christian readers of the NT saw and heard the word *eirēnē,* to what extent did they connect it positively or negatively with the Pax of the Roman imperial order? And to what extent did they connect it to *shalom* in the Hebrew Scriptures, since *shalom* is translated in the LXX by *eirēnē* in the majority of its uses? *Eirēnē* occurs 199 times in the LXX; only fourteen times does it translate words other than *shalom* and its cognates.[42] Dinkler cautions us not to overestimate the impact that the Pax Romana had in the eastern provinces, nor the concept it carried with it. But he also demurs when considering whether "early Christian terminology remained uninfluenced by the history of the peace cult."[43] His thesis, however, stated at the beginning and end of his essay contends that the NT use of *eirēnē* is best understood by the OT use of *shalom.*[44]

Klaus Wengst describes the Pax Romana under seven categories of analysis:

> "A Golden Age"?
> "A peace established through victories" — the military aspect of the Pax Romana
> "Being able to enjoy one's possessions in peace" — the political aspect of the Pax Romana
> "The common market for the produce of the earth" — the economic aspect of the Pax Romana
> "Imposing Roman law on the vanquished" — the legal aspect of the Pax Romana
> "When there are so many cities . . ." — culture and civilization under the Pax Romana
> "Serving on earth as the vicar of the gods" — the religious aspect of the Pax Romana.[45]

Wengst's incisive analysis echoes the prophetic critique of the OT prophets against those who enjoy peace and prosperity at the cost and sacrifice of subjugated peoples. Revolts and wars at the peripheries of the empire were

---

42. Harris, *Shalom,* p. 36.
43. Dinkler, "*Eirēnē* — The Early Christian Concept," pp. 88-89 (1992, p. 176).
44. Dinkler, "*Eirēnē* — The Early Christian Concept," p. 89 (1992, p. 176).
45. Wengst, *Pax Romana,* pp. 7-51.

largely disregarded, even assigned mythical status, by those at the power center, whose prosperity and security were assured by Rome's vast armies and a tax system odious to the vanquished. As Wengst says, "Despite all the assertions to the contrary, the Pax Romana was not really a world of peace. This peace, gained by military force, had its limits at the limits of the Roman empire. In the Annals of Tacitus the description of this war occupies page after page."[46]

Three vignettes represent the underside of this "Age of Peace": (1) The Roman general Germanicus in the battle against the Germani calls on his soldiers "to go with the carnage. Prisoners were needless; nothing but the extermination of the race would end the war."[47] (2) Tacitus puts on the lips of the Britain Calgacus a caustic description of the dangerous Romans: "To plunder, butcher, steal, these things they misname empire; they make a desolation and call it peace."[48] (3) 4 Ezra 11:39-46 pronounces doom on the arrogant eagle Rome:

> You, the fourth has come, have conquered all the beasts that have gone before you: and you have held sway over all the world with much terror, and over all the earth with grievous oppression; and for so long you have dwelt on the earth with deceit. And you have judged the earth, but not with truth; for you have afflicted the meek and injured the peaceable; . . . your insolence has come up before the Most High, and your pride to the Mighty One. . . . Therefore you will surely disappear, you eagle . . . so that the whole earth, freed from your violence, may be refreshed and relieved, and may hope for the judgment and mercy of him who made it.[49]

Connected to Rome's unrivaled power and its "glorious peace" was the emergence of the emperor cult demanding devotion, worship, and sacrifice.[50]

---

46. Wengst, *Pax Romana,* p. 17.

47. Wengst, *Pax Romana,* p. 18; Tacitus, *Annals* 2.21.2.

48. Wengst, *Pax Romana,* p. 52 (see his fuller citation of the speech), from Tacitus, *Agricola* 30.3-31.

49. Wengst, *Pax Romana,* p. 53; 4 Ezra 11:39-46, from Charlesworth *OTP* I, p. 549. The seer of Revelation fits this perspective also.

50. On the nature and pervasive influence of the emperor cult see the extensive bibliography by P. Herz, "Bibliographie zum römischen Kaiserkult," *ANRW* 2.16.2, ed. W. Haase (Berlin/New York: de Gruyter, 1978), pp. 834-910, and related articles in the same volume. See also the treatments by C. Habicht, "Die Augusteische Zeit und das erste Jahrhundert nach Christi Geburt," in *Le culte des souverains dans L'Empire Romain,* ed. E. J. Bickermann, et al. (Vandœuvres-Genève: Fondation Hardt, 1973), pp. 41-69, and Stefan Weinstock, *Divus Iulius* (Oxford: Clarendon, 1971).

Pliny's statement describing his testing of his subjects for Christian identity is well known for its evidence of this point.[51] John Helgeland has also shown that "religion" itself was an essential aspect of the Roman army, and that extending the Roman reign meant extending the Roman religion. He cites Tacitus's account of Germanicus's ritual celebration of newly acquired territory: "First eulogizing the victors in an address, the Caesar raised a pile of weapons, with a legend boasting that the army of Tiberius Caesar, after subduing the nations between the Rhine and the Elbe, had consecrated that memorial to Mars, Jupiter, and to Augustus."[52]

As Hubert Frankemölle sums it up,

> Sword and cross as symbols of political power were not limited to Paul (as Roman citizen) or Jesus (as Jewish criminal and seditionist). They were symbols much more for the fact that the politically proclaimed "pacification" by Rome, the *Pax Romana*, rested on countless dead bodies. For Roman power policy, crucifixion was an instrument of war and securing the peace in order to wear down rebellious cities under siege, to humiliate defeated powers, to bring to reason mutinous troops or restive provinces. That it was employed in excess in order to "pacify" rebellious provinces is evident from Josephus's many examples from Judea (on mass crucifixions, cf. *War* 2.75; 2.241; 5.449-451; *Ant.* 17.295; etc.).[53]

"Peace" and Related Words

This brief survey of Hebrew and Greek backgrounds indicates that *war* and *peace* are not exact antonyms, but they are interrelated. War creates non-shalom for many people. The dominant Hebrew word for evil *(ra')* is a more exact antonym to *shalom*. Certainly, in its effects upon humans, war is more evil than it is good. The NT, we will see, regularly calls believers to overcome evil with good. War is never mentioned, directly or indirectly, as a possible means of accomplishing this. The vast literature on warfare in the OT often

---

51. Pliny, *Epistles* 10.96.5; cited in Wengst, *Pax Romana*, p. 50.

52. John Helgeland, "Roman Army Religion," *ANRW* 2.16.2, ed. W. Haase (Berlin/New York: de Gruyter, 1978), p. 1503. Helgeland cites in n. 128 the Latin text of *Annals* 2.22. That Christianity threatened this religious, spiritual foundation of Roman power is argued well by Torben Christensen in *Christus oder Jupiter. Der Kampf um die geistigen Grundlegen des römischen Reiches* (Göttingen: Vandenhoeck und Ruprecht, 1981).

53. Hubert Frankemölle, "Peace and the Sword in the New Testament," in *The Meaning of Peace*, ed. Perry B. Yoder and Willard M. Swartley, pp. 197-98 (1992, p. 217).

fails to study *eirēnē*. Further, studies of *shalom* in the OT have not systematically investigated how *war* functions in the narrative. Similarly, the studies of *eirēnē* in the NT have perhaps, as Desjardins points out (see below), given only little attention to war or warfare traditions or images in the NT.

At the same time the semantic field of war and peace, in both Testaments, relates *shalom* and *eirēnē* to other terms. We noted above the semantic field of *shalom*. For peace *(eirēnē)* the semantic field includes:

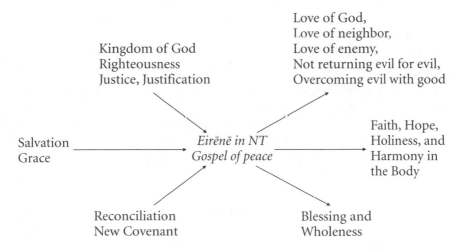

Conceptual diagram with terms carrying corporate and relational significance

This diagram puts to the left of *eirēnē* God's gifts through Jesus Christ which are the fruit of the gospel of peace in relation to restored relationship with God and with fellow humans. The terms on the right represent the fruit of peace expressed in the new creation that salvation brings. These are both personal and corporate. See especially Chapters 3 and 7 for further exposition of peace in Jesus (Matthew) and Paul, especially Klassen's diagram and the many uses of the distinctive appellation "the God of peace."

For war, in the OT, the semantic field includes victory, salvation, judgment, faith and trust, death and martyrdom, and sacrifice; and in the NT, resurrection and exaltation, principalities *(exousiai)* and powers *(archai)* and God's armor to resist the powers. Again, these terms and the conceptual fields they represent are not in opposition to each other, but are integrally interrelated. Much NT language utilizes war and peace language in an inter-explicatory relationship. For this reason Egon Brandenburger rightly contends, contra Erich Dinkler's and Werner Foerster's studies, that the larger messianic royal traditions, which in apocalyptic writings include a messianic war to defeat evil, are part of the NT scope of study of *eirēnē*. Thus the gospel story involving conflict between Jesus and the political powers and Paul's theology of atonement must be considered specifically for their linkage of peace with conflict, battle, and victory at a fundamental level. Specific texts like Luke 10:1-20; Rom. 16:20; and Eph. 6:10-18 are paradigmatic and foundational. It is important, therefore, to treat *eirēnē* from the broader conceptual perspective, via semantic field relations and conceptual associations, rather than simply from word-occurrences, though these, to be sure, are most important and serve as a control to limit the scope. Related emphases on nonretaliation against evil and love of the enemy occur in the Synoptics, Paul, and 1 Peter.

Although the uses of *eirēnē* vary in their emphases, its recurring use in the majority of NT books, a total of 100 in its variant forms,[54] indicates the extent of its significance.[55] While encyclopedia articles identify numerous dimensions of meaning for *eirēnē*,[56] Peter Stuhlmacher argues for a certain development in meaning within the NT tradition, contra Beck and Brown who say, "It is not possible to trace any development of the idea of *eirēnē* within the NT."[57] Stuhlmacher, in his important article on the concept and meaning of *eirēnē* in the NT,[58] develops his contribution structured by twelve theses (see Appendix 2). He holds that the NT use of *eirēnē* in salutations (Paul's letters) and formulas such as "Go in peace" (Mark 5:34 par.; Luke 7:50) extend the OT and Jewish usages of *shalom*. Other uses of *eirēnē* by Jesus and the Gospel writers, such as Matt. 10:13, 34; Luke 10:5-6; 12:51, reflect in addition the significance of Jesus' proclamation of the kingdom of God. Jesus' blessing on

---

54. J. B. Smith, *Greek-English Concordance to the New Testament* (Scottdale: Herald, 1955), p. 104; W. F. Moulton and A. S. Geden, *A Concordance to the Greek Testament,* 3rd ed. (Edinburgh: Clark, 1926), pp. 297-98. The noun *eirēnē* occurs 92 times (Matthew has 4, Mark 1, Luke 14, Acts 7, the Pauline epistles 44, John 6, Hebrews 4, James 3, 1 Peter 3, 2 Peter 1, 2 John 1, 3 John 1, Jude 1, and Revelation 2). The verb *eirēneuō* occurs four times (Mark 9:50; Rom. 12:18; 2 Cor. 13:11; 1 Thess. 5:13), the adjective *eirēnikos* two times (Heb. 12:11; Jas. 3:17), and compound forms of the noun and the verb two times (Matt. 5:9; Col. 1:20). This count includes Luke 24:36, for which I argue (see Chapter 5), but not Rom. 10:15, which has weak textual support.

55. For summary treatment of the terms "peace" (*shalom* and *eirēnē*), "violence," and "war," see my articles in *The Westminster Theological Wordbook of the Bible,* ed. Donald E. Gowan (Louisville: Westminster John Knox, 2003), pp. 354-60, 520-22, and 524-28 respectively.

56. Beck and Brown, "Peace," pp. 780-82; W. Foerster in *TDNT* II, pp. 412-17.

57. Beck and Brown, "Peace," p. 780.

58. Peter Stuhlmacher, "Der Begriff des Friedens im Neuen Testament und seine Konsequenzen," *Historische Beiträge zur Friedensforschung,* ed. Wolfgang Huber, Studien zur Friedensforschung 4 (Stuttgart: Klett/Munich: Kösel, 1970), pp. 21-69. See Appendix 2 below.

the peacemakers in the Beatitudes belongs in its present form to Matthew's composition.

But none of these uses contains the degree of theological reflection that appears in Paul, the later Pauline writings, the Lukan redaction, and the Johannine tradition. These later uses developed from Paul's theological reflection on the meaning of Jesus Christ's death for salvation, atonement, and ecclesial experience.

The majority of Stuhlmacher's theses explicate this Pauline theological contribution (peace between humans and God and among humans through the work of Christ on the cross), and its bearing upon the post-Pauline, Lukan, and Johannine writings. Stuhlmacher notes also that the Passion narratives are theologically congruous with this theology, in that Jesus' words and conduct that culminate in his death are presented with atoning significance. In Paul *peace* is christological, in that atonement and reconciliation are the gifts of Jesus Christ's work on the cross. Post-Pauline writings reflect in differing ways this central Pauline perception that *peace* is christologically oriented. Experience of this *peace* marks the community (church/*Gemeinde*), in contrast to the world (John's uses especially). The eschatology of the community, arising from atonement and Easter-resurrection, anticipates the end-time appearing and lordship of Jesus. From this perspective, those whose lives are shaped by this christology and eschatology of Jesus' rule, begun in his proclamation of the kingdom and to be consummated in the end time, regard war as denial of the peace of Jesus Christ.

Stuhlmacher's systematic explication of *peace* in the NT is helpful indeed. It lacks, however, several aspects that could more fully unfold its meaning. First, in focusing sharply on *peace*, related moral teachings such as love of enemies, nonretaliation, overcoming evil with good are neglected, not only in his treatment of the Gospels, but also in his discussion of the deutero-Pauline and Petrine traditions (the latter he largely overlooks). Second, by placing Paul at the center of the NT *theological* reflection on *peace*, the insights arising from Guelich's reflection, for example (see Chapter 1), are neglected. To see Jesus' proclamation of the kingdom of God and Paul's theology of the cross as both fulfilling Isa. 52:7, the "messenger of the gospel of peace" text, is lacking in Stuhlmacher's treatment. This has the effect of putting the contribution of Jesus' life and teaching to *peace* on discount. Nor does Stuhlmacher take up the *peace* perceptions of Hebrews, James, and 1 Peter. Finally, Stuhlmacher's treatment, helpful as it is, does not connect adequately *peace-theology* to *peace-ethics*.

The following chapters seek to show this intrinsic connection and also attend to the pluriform testimony of the NT to peace and peacemaking.

Peace, Yes, but What about Violence in the New Testament?

This important question will be addressed in multiple ways and levels throughout this study. I address the issue of Jesus' violence in "cleansing" the temple when I discuss Mark (Chapter 4, where I also refer to John's account). For Jesus' language regarding Jewish religious leaders, I address this in Matthew (for the Pharisees, Chapter 3) and in John (for "the Jews," Chapter 10).

A deeper strand of warfare theology permeates the Gospels, as an extension of "divine warfare" in the OT. I summarize below the OT divine warfare perspective as it expresses itself in the Gospels, especially Mark and Luke. Martial imagery throughout the NT is addressed in Chapter 8 in the context of the believers' stance of "wrestling against the principalities and powers." The matter is taken up also in the treatment of Revelation (see Chapter 12).

While NT scholars generally agree that Jesus repudiates violence and that peace is an essential aspect of the gospel of the kingdom, some dissent, seeing considerable violence in the NT, thus presenting fundamental dissonance on this issue. Michel Desjardins contends that the NT underwrites both peace and violence.[59] Among texts that condone violence he cites Jesus' cleansing of the temple in John 2:13-15 and Jesus' harsh language in his "Woes" on the Pharisees (Matthew 23) and saying to "the Jews," "You are from your father the devil" (John 8:44). Desjardins contends,

> The tension in the New Testament Scriptures themselves between advocating peace and condoning violence presents the interpretive challenge out of which my study emerges. I am unable to reduce the evidence either to one option, "the New Testament is fundamentally peace-promoting," or to the other, "the New Testament encourages people to be violent." The strong presence of both is striking and intriguing.[60]

After treating the NT's numerous texts that advocate peacemaking and those that reflect violence in either word or deed, Desjardins concludes, "The New Testament strongly promotes peace and it strongly promotes violence."[61] He then considers efforts of scholars to live with this bifurcation. He describes two views that hold this phenomenon to be consistent: "*Opposites Are Needed to Make the Whole*" and "*Mythic and Ritual Violence Is Needed for People to Live in Peace*" (Yarbro Collins and Thompson on Revelation; see my Chapter 12 below, and René Girard for sacral/ritual violence to make peace).

59. Michel Desjardins, *Peace and Violence in the New Testament.*
60. Desjardins, *Peace and Violence*, p. 11.
61. Desjardins, *Peace and Violence*, p. 111.

He also assesses the opposing view that these moral opposites in the NT are inconsistent, and lists numerous contributing factors for that to be the case: the many people and communities involved in making the NT, the stretch of time over which the books were written, the differing social and political situations reflected in the literature, and our perceptions of this question constrained by our culture (e.g., we cringe at the notion of a wrathful God, but biblical writers seem not to have been offended). Desjardins rejects interpretations that argue for a NT literary pacifist cover over a revolutionary Jesus and finds unsatisfying the argument that the core of Jesus' and Paul's teaching promoted peace, not violence.[62] He concludes, saying that the "violence-promoting side . . . disturbs me, all the more because I rarely find it discussed in academic and non-academic circles. . . . The New Testament, I am now convinced, advocates both peace and violence."[63]

In my review of Desjardins's work I note several strategic methodological decisions that, I believe, preclude a satisfying resolution. His definition of violence is broad, anything that "violates the personhood of another in ways that are psychologically destructive," and he does not intend to provide a historical-critical reading of the texts.[64] His first decision opens the door to both a subjective element as to what counts for violence and the hegemony of modern psychological perceptions in his work. By passing up historical-critical analysis (for the most part, at least) he fails to do what Klaus Wengst does well, comparing the Pax Christi with the Pax Romana, setting the NT in its socio-political context of imperial violence (see above), and what Hubert Frankemölle's theological assessment of the data against a historical-critical

---

62. Desjardins, *Peace and Violence*, pp. 112-19.

63. Desjardins, *Peace and Violence*, p. 121. Earlier Desjardins says, "Violence abounds in the New Testament" (p. 108). Desjardins failed to note a study published four years earlier than his that focuses precisely on the ambiguity of both the OT and NT on war/violence and peace: Albert Curry Winn, *Ain't Gonna Study War No More: Biblical Ambiguity and the Abolition of War*. This study provides helpful perspectives toward resolving the ambiguity. A former student of Desjardins, Philip L. Tite, has expanded Desjardins's theses into the ideological nature of the definitions of violence and peace, the ambiguity of the biblical text, and the practical dimensions of the use of Scripture and violence in gender issues, anti-Semitism, and gay culture. See Tite, *Conceiving Peace and Violence*. My critique of Desjardins applies to Tite as well, though he acknowledges his subjective bias on what constitutes violence. Violence in NT texts spirals in Hector Avalos's *Fighting Words* (also for Judaism and Islam). The essays in *Violence in the New Testament* (ed. Matthews and Gibson) represent a wider grid of analysis for the NT and a more exegetically viable approach, though Horsley's well-argued case for Jesus' exorcisms as divine violence against imperial Rome (pp. 51-80) is problematic.

64. Desjardins, *Peace and Violence*, pp. 12, 14. For my review, see "Review of *Peace, Violence and the New Testament*," *CGR* 17 (1999): 122-24.

grid does in producing a rigorous grappling with this dilemma.[65] Further, Desjardins's comment that this issue is glossed over in academic work is not sustainable, as the vast literature cited in several bibliographies indicates.[66]

In sharp contrast to Desjardins's view, Richard Hays takes an opposing stance in *The Moral Vision of the New Testament*, which I treat in both Appendix 1 and my Conclusion. Hays contends there is nothing in Pauline literature that supports use of violence. Hays claims the NT nowhere supports use of violence: "With regard to the issue of *violence*, the New Testament bears a powerful witness that is both univocal and pervasive, for it is integrally related to the heart of the kerygma and to God's fundamental elective purpose."[67] My following study of the NT literature examines these issues, for the alleged violence in the NT needs to be dealt with in its literary and historical context. My findings complement Hays's remarks in that they demonstrate that the NT consistently not only supports nonviolence, but also advocates proactive *peacemaking*, consisting of positive initiatives to overcome evil by employing *peaceable means* to make *peace*.

Jesus' teaching on nonretaliation and love of enemies and his refusal to fight because his kingdom is not of this world, that is, does not exist by worldly power (John 18:36),[68] have functioned as pillars in the pacifist interpretation.[69] Those holding either that the NT supports Christians participating in war or does not clearly disallow it have cited various specific texts as well. In my study of this topic[70] I have listed twenty-four such texts; fifteen occur in the Synoptics. They are:

Luke 22:36-38	sell mantle . . . buy a sword
Mark 12:13-17 par.	pay taxes to Caesar (cf. Matt. 17:24-27)
Matt. 10:34-35 par. Luke 12:51	I bring not peace, but a sword

65. Hubert Frankemölle, "Peace and the Sword in the New Testament," in *The Meaning of Peace*, ed. P. Yoder and W. Swartley, pp. 191-210 (1992, pp. 213-33).

66. See, for example, the Bibliography in Swartley, "War and Peace in the New Testament," pp. 2389-2408.

67. Hays, *Moral Vision of the New Testament*, pp. 331, 314.

68. As N. T. Wright says, this text does not mean that Jesus' kingdom is otherworldly: "Kingdoms of the world fight; physical power, strategic, revolutionary, or military power is the rule of the game. Jesus' kingdom has a different *modus operandi*" (*Jesus and the Victory of God*, p. 13).

69. Swartley, *Slavery, Sabbath, War, and Women*, pp. 118-22. Richard McSorley's *New Testament Basis for Peacemaking*, pp. 20-45, also considers some of these texts as well as similar texts in Paul and 1 Peter and shows why they do not provide support for war.

70. Swartley, *Slavery, Sabbath*, pp. 99-101, 250-55.

Luke 7:2-10 par. Matt. 8:5-10	Jesus commends a soldier's faith
Luke 11:21-22 par.	a strong man fully armed
Mark 12:1-9 par., etc.	Jesus' parables speak of force and violence
Mark 13:7-13 par.	Jesus predicts wars
Luke 3:14	John the Baptist does not ask soldiers to quit
Luke 14:31-32	a king goes to war fully armed
Mark 9:42	should be cast into the sea with a millstone around his neck
Matthew 23 par.	woes against Pharisees
Matt. 26:52	take sword, perish by sword — assumes defense
Matt. 11:12 par. Luke 16:16	violent people seize the kingdom
Mark 8:34-35	willing to sacrifice in death
Luke 12:39-40 par. Matt. 24:43-44	guard house against thief

In the other NT books the cited texts are:

John 2:13-17	Jesus' cleansing the temple
John 15:13	love sacrifices life for a friend
John 18:36	the world's kingdoms fight
Acts 10-11	the church admits Cornelius, a Roman general
Rom. 13:1-7 (1 Pet. 2:13-17)	be subject to the powers that bear the sword
Eph. 6:10-17	martial imagery supports war
Rev. 19:15	God uses the sword and treads the winepress of wrath
Rev. 12:7-9	war in heaven (if so, why not on earth?)
Rom. 1:19-21; 2:14-15	the basis for just war

The last seven in the Synoptic Gospels have played only minor roles in the literature, but the first eight have been more significant.[71] Scholarly com-

---

71. For a good analysis of these arguments see Macgregor, "Does the New Testament Sanction War?" For the first three and the problematic John 2:13-17 see the summary of pacifist exposition as well as my citation of pagination from eight different writers for treatment of twenty-four texts (Swartley, *Slavery, Sabbath*, pp. 250-55). Note also how these texts are used to argue for NT support for war (pp. 99-101). The eight pacifist writers represent the range of

mentary on most of these texts, however, does not consider them as portraying Jesus' condoning the use of violence or providing support for believers' participation in war.[72] But as I. H. Marshall observes, "the question of war is not addressed directly in the NT."[73] Marshall points to five "indirect indications" that bear on the subject: 1) numerous references to war and strife, 2) the central role of the kingdom of God and Jesus' kingship in the Gospels' narratives (see above and Chapters 2-4), 3) Jesus' commands of nonretaliation and love of enemies (see Chapter 3), 4) the relevance of Jesus' personal behavior (Is it unique because of his messianic mission, or is it a pattern for his followers in all times and places?), and 5) the significance of texts that discuss or reflect the state's role, the use of force, and the roles of military officials.[74]

In respect to 1) above, Jewish revolts and Rome's retaliation were indeed part of the first-century world, and this reality punctuates the biblical narratives (Luke 13:1-3; Acts 5:36-37; Mark 13:7 par.).[75] Since the Gospels were likely all written after 65-70 CE, both Nero's blaming of the Christians for the fire of Rome and the awful sufferings of the Jews in the 66-70 revolt[76] inform the narratives also. Jesus' statement that there will be wars and rumors of wars does not justify war, nor does it mean that his followers should not work to prevent war, just as his saying that the poor will always be with us should not be used to counter efforts to alleviate poverty.[77]

Christian traditions: Herbert Booth, Salvation Army; John Ferguson, Anglican; Henry Fast, Mennonite; Guy Hershberger, Mennonite; G. H. C. Macgregor, Anglican; Richard McSorley, Roman Catholic; Jean Lasserre, Reformed; Culbert G. Rutenber, Baptist.

72. See Victor P. Furnish, "War and Peace in the New Testament," *Int* 38 (1984): 369-71; I. H. Marshall, "New Testament Perspectives on War," *EvQ* 57 (1985): 115-32; Joseph Blank, *Im Dienst der Versöhnung: Friedenspraxis aus christlicher Sicht* (Munich: Kösel, 1984), pp. 14-18, 26-28 (also his "Gewaltlosigkeit — Krieg — Militärdienst," in *Orientierung* 46 [1982]: 158-59, 161-62).

73. I. H. Marshall, "NT Perspectives," p. 115.

74. Adapted from I. H. Marshall's list in "NT Perspectives," pp. 115-16.

75. The revolt headed by Judas the Galilean in 6 CE in Sepphoris (Josephus, *Antiquities* 17.271-72; *War* 2.56), a few miles from Nazareth and when Jesus was around ten years old, was crushed by Roman retaliation; two thousand Jews were crucified (*Antiquities* 17.295; *War* 2.75). Martin Hengel has described Palestine in the time of Jesus as "a politico-religious tinderbox," in *Victory over Violence: Jesus and the Revolutionists*, trans. David E. Green (Philadelphia: Fortress, 1973), p. 30. For a good study of Josephus's sources and the volatile political history consummating in the Jewish revolt, see David M. Rhoads, *Israel in Revolution, 6-74 C.E.: A Political History Based on the Writings of Josephus* (Philadelphia: Fortress, 1976). See also the masterful study by Martin Hengel, *The Zealots: Investigations into the Jewish Freedom Movement in the Period from Herod I until 70 A.D.*, trans. D. Smith (Edinburgh: Clark, 1989).

76. Josephus, *War* 5.11-38.424-45, 512-18 and all of Book 6.

77. Cf. Marshall, "NT Perspectives," p. 118. To use the texts in this way is tantamount to condoning burglary since Jesus also speaks of the Son of Man coming as a thief in the night.

These texts witness to the fact that Jesus' gospel of peace entered a world that knew much war and violence. That war and violence are reflected in Jesus' language and predictions of the future cannot be used to legitimize war or provide warrant for Christian participation in war. The fact that military officials are not told to leave their service (Luke 3:14; Matt. 8:5-10; Acts 10-11) has been cited as evidence that Jesus did not regard it as "inherently wrong to be a soldier." But we do not know whether leaving the military was an option open to these soldiers, as Marshall acknowledges.[78]

The texts outside the Synoptic Gospels are of the same nature. They do not speak directly to whether believers ought morally to participate in war. The most direct logic occurs with Romans 13, where, since war was approved for Israel (that too is debatable in light of 1 Samuel 8), the command to be subject strongly implies that every citizen, especially believers who desire to obey Scripture's commands, should assist the authorities as servants of God in bearing the sword when asked to do so.[79]

To base a positional argument on evidence of indirect reasoning or inference is hermeneutically dubious. As will be argued later (in Chapter 14) human moral obligation is not always symmetrical to God's moral freedom and action. Nor does the reasoning on Romans 13 take into account the separation of the church from the state, in the sense that the state functions outside the "perfection of Christ," a view held by the Anabaptists,[80] who sought to recover what they understood the NT to teach and what was practiced by the early church in its members' refusal to participate in the military during most of the first two centuries. A constructive moral proposal must rest rather on the explicit teachings of Jesus and the NT as a whole regarding human moral obligation. Further, our contemporary theological and ethical reflection must seek to discern the impact of Jesus' call to be peacemakers — transforming enmity into friendship — upon our moral decisions and posi-

78. Marshall, "NT Perspectives," p. 118. Frankemölle, "Peace and the Sword," makes the point that the early Christian believers had no access to political power and thus "had no reason to offer a general theological reflection on power." But he also says that Jesus' "peace concepts can have social-political relevance even if not in the sense of political power" (p. 200; 1992, p. 219). Jesus' contrast of his way of servant obedience to the powers who lord it over people makes it clear that Jesus intends his followers to constitute a contrast community to the powers (see Chapter 4 on Mark 10:42-45).

79. For exegesis of this text see my "How to Interpret the Bible: A Case Study of Romans 13:1-7 and the Payment of Taxes Used for War," *Seeds* 3 (June 1984): 28-31. The literature on this text abounds: see Chapter 8 below and more in my article, "War and Peace in the New Testament," pp. 2357-65, esp. n. 234.

80. This was articulated in 1527 in the Schleitheim Confession, in which Michael Sattler was influential in bringing together emerging Anabaptist beliefs on church-state relations.

tions. Ulrich Mauser has pointed the way by asserting that "the starting point" must be "the New Testament's attitude to hatred, oppression, war, and all forms of violence."[81]

While warfare imagery is used to describe the Christian life, occurrences of the word "war" are relatively infrequent — twenty-five, with the majority in Revelation.[82] Numerous NT texts use language of violence and warfare metaphorically to refer to *spiritual* warfare, in which the opponent is Satan (see Chapter 8 below).[83] On the saying, "I have come to bring a sword," Mauser persuasively explicates this in tandem with Luke 10:17-20; 11:21-22, and Matt. 11:12.[84] In all these texts images of violence are associated with the kingdom of God. Mauser rightly maintains that they describe the warfare between the kingdom of God inaugurated by Jesus and the stronghold of Satan. This warfare language

> expresses the dialectic between the arrival of a complete rule of God and, with it, the inauguration of the ultimate peace in the world, and the continued, and even intensified, determined resistance to this dawn of a new age. But it must be noted that both sides of the dialectic are expressed in terms of violent, warlike encounters that are set in motion by Jesus' coming: He has indeed come to bring a sword![85]

Jesus' battle against evil is thus a strategic aspect of his peacemaking mission. As shown below, Jesus comes to render evil powerless over human life. The warfare metaphor is an essential part of Paul's proclamation of God's defeat of the powers of Satan in Jesus' death and resurrection. As Mauser deftly puts it,

> The whole struggle is not against but, without abridgment and reservation, for the benefit of and on behalf of all human life, including the human adversary. The battle against Satan does include the command, "Love your enemies and pray for those who persecute you" (Matt. 5:44);

---

81. Mauser, *The Gospel of Peace*, pp. 166-89. Mauser further states that if the NT has pronounced "a blanket condemnation of persons in military service, or on the institution of slavery, or on the practice of economic exploitation, . . . it would have reintroduced the notion of enemies whose form of life renders them immune to the power of faith" (p. 184).

82. Smith, *Greek-English Concordance*, p. 298; Moulton and Geden, *Concordance*, p. 832.

83. Marshall, "NT Perspectives," p. 118.

84. Mauser, *Gospel of Peace*, pp. 41-45. I. H. Marshall, however, takes the more common interpretation that the "sword" simply refers to "division" within households, as Luke 12:51 explicitly says ("NT Perspectives," p. 128).

85. Mauser, *Gospel of Peace*, p. 45.

in fact, love to the human enemy is the very battle line at which the victory over God's adversary is decided.[86]

The following chapters return to these issues as they arise in their literary context.

The Interrelation of War and Peace in the New Testament

To adequately understand the *peace* teaching of the NT it is essential to set it within the longer biblical theology perspective on war and peace throughout canonical Scripture. Arising from my study and teaching of war and peace in the Bible over twenty-five years, seven strands of biblical-theological emphasis are crucial as the larger backdrop of this more focused study of New Testament texts. These emphases inform my study of Jesus and the gospel, with the goal to seek peace through peaceful means in the face of evil.

1. The over-arching emphasis of Scripture presents God as Peacemaker who is also the Divine Warrior fighting against evil to establish and maintain peace and justice. God's people are called to trust in God for the divine victory, and are not to take vengeance and judgment into their own hands. "Holy War," as presented in the OT's Deuteronomic history, is motivated by God's judgment on idolatry and God's jealousy for Israel. God commands that they not worship other gods or engage in pagan practices of divination and sorcery or trust in wealth and military power (see Deut. 18:9-14; Isa. 2:6-22), but depend upon the power of God's prophetic word (Deut. 18:15-20; Isa. 2:1-5).

2. Jesus comes as divine warrior to overcome and defeat the powers of evil (see below on Mark). Exorcisms and healings play a major role in his ministry, to announce the breaking in of God's reign.

3. In Jesus' combat against and victory over evil, his disciples are called not to fear, but to believe, have faith. The NT "believe" *(pisteuō)* matches the OT "have faith" *(batach)*.

4. Jesus refuses easy identification with Jewish expectations of the Messiah (Mark 8:29-33) because those hopes violated God's way for the victory to be won. Jesus denounces the domination system with its redeemer myth that lives by violence.[87] Instead, Jesus identifies himself with the Danielic "Son of

---

86. Mauser, *Gospel of Peace*, p. 174.
87. Walter Wink, *Engaging the Powers: Discernment and Resistance in a World of Domination,* Part 1, pp. 13-104.

humanity"[88] and indirectly with the Isaiah "servant" traditions, in which victory comes through suffering. Jesus' entry into Jerusalem on a donkey shows him as king of peace, based on humility and trust in God.

5. Jesus includes "the enemy" in his circle of ministry: the marginalized Jews, the Samaritans, and the Gentiles. This incarnates his teaching: "Blessed are the peacemakers, for they shall be called the children of God." Love of the enemy and nonretaliation are cardinal teachings of the gospel. So also is confrontation of and expulsion of demonic spirits — God's kingdom against Satan's kingdom. See Chapter 3 for discussion of the "kingdom coming with violence" in Matthew.

6. Luke provides us with twin themes in his travel narrative in which peace and justice are Jesus' gifts through his ministry, on the one hand, and presuppose, on the other, this onslaught against and victory over Satan and the demonic powers. See Chapter 5. Further, each major section of Acts shows confrontation with evil spirit-powers as the first stage of ministry in the evangelistic spread of the gospel (Acts 8 in Samaria, ch. 13 in Asia Minor, ch. 16 in Macedonia, and ch. 19 at the culmination of Paul's journeys).[89]

7. The Pauline teaching on the powers is a gospel proclamation of the theological meaning of Jesus' ministry (see especially Col. 2:12-15). Wink is correct that the method of Christ's defeat of the powers is the nonviolence of the cross. But he is less correct when he views the powers as spirit-personality manifestations in structures and institutions. See Chapter 8 for discussion of this point.

In this context, the aim of this study is to exposit the contribution that the various NT books and/or authors make to an understanding of peace, while noting on the one side the theological and christological matrix of this thought and, on the other side, observing elements of conflict, combat, and violence within the narratives as well.

88. Scholarly views abound regarding the origin and meaning of "Son of Humanity," as used by Jesus (which some scholars deny, assigning its origin to the early church — a most implausible view in my judgment). For a recent survey of the issues and a distinctive view that it was not a title, but a name that Jesus chose, see Hurtado, *Lord Jesus Christ*, pp. 290-306.

89. See Garrett, *The Demise of the Devil*, for detailed study of the gospel's encounter with magic and the demonic in Luke-Acts.

3 Matthew: Emmanuel, Power for Peacemaking

"Look, the virgin shall conceive and bear a son,
and they shall name him Emmanuel,"
which means, "God is with us."   MATT. 1:23

"[R]emember, I am with you always, to the end of the age."

MATT. 28:20

"Blessed are the peacemakers, for they will be called children of God."

MATT. 5:9

The Gospel of Matthew is unique among the Gospels in that its bookends promise the presence of God ("Emmanuel") and the Risen Christ (Jesus said, "I am with you always") with the people of God.[1] Further, peacemakers are marked in their identity as "children of God."[2] This promise is not an idyllic

---

1. The bookends contain also a royal portrait of Jesus. In ch. 1 Jesus is of the lineage of David. In the final paragraph of the Gospel, Jesus is on a mountain, echoing royal Mt. Zion traditions. He declares, "All authority *(exousia)* in heaven and on earth has been given to me." This statement contrasts to Satan's offer in 4:9, "All these [the kingdoms of this world] I will give you." See my treatment of this "mountain" scene in *Israel's Scripture Traditions*, pp. 228-32.

2. The Greek here is "sons" *(huioi)* in accord with OT royal traditions. Similar to modern inclusive Bible versions that render "sons" as "children," Paul expands the 2 Sam. 7:13-14 promise of "royal sonship" to include "daughters" in 2 Cor. 6:18. No textual precedent exists to explain this bold move. Paul subverts the male royal tradition by making women also heirs to the royal

53

vision, but is intertwined with the life-reality of suffering and persecution. In Matthew, Jesus' birth includes the political repercussion of Herod's massacre of babies in Bethlehem. Jesus encounters unbelief from and conflict with the religious leaders.

The Beatitudes name persecution as an expected experience of those who seek to be God's people in the world (5:10-12). The Olivet discourse (ch. 24) also designates persecution of Jesus' followers as a result of living the gospel in this world. In his final promise, "I am with you always," Jesus commissions his disciples to worldwide mission, to proclaim the gospel to all nations. The proclamation of the gospel of the kingdom throughout the whole world (24:14) is woven into the predicted persecution that believers will endure before the end comes (24:9-14 and ff.).

The Beatitudes, in all their beauty, are really about God's sustaining presence for lowly people as they experience difficulties and encounter obstacles. They mark out the fundamental nature of life in the kingdom of God:

> Blessed are the poor in spirit, for theirs is the kingdom of heaven.
> Blessed are those who mourn, for they will be comforted.
> Blessed are the meek, for they will inherit the earth.
> Blessed are those who hunger and thirst for righteousness,
>   for they will be filled.
> Blessed are the merciful, for they will receive mercy.
> Blessed are the pure in heart, for they will see God.
> Blessed are the peacemakers, for they will be called children of God.
> Blessed are those who are persecuted for righteousness' sake,
>   for theirs is the kingdom of heaven.
> Blessed are you when people revile you and persecute you and utter
>   all kinds of evil against you falsely on my account.
>   Rejoice and be glad, for your reward is great in heaven,
>   for in the same way they persecuted the prophets who
>   were before you.

This is not a list of virtues of human achievement. Rather, they reflect life-conditions and describe virtues that reflect character.[3] The life-conditions in and of themselves do not by any means *produce* happiness. Rather, *blessing* is

---

Davidic promise fulfilled in Christ. This adds to other texts like Rom. 16 where Paul clearly affirms women in ministry. For more on this topic, see my *Slavery, Sabbath, War, and Women*, pp. 150-91.

3. See Glen Stassen's excellent discussion of the Beatitudes as virtues that characterize God's kingdom people in Stassen and Gushee, *Kingdom Ethics*, pp. 32-54.

God's word of grace and hope for precisely such people. Further, the entire Sermon is to be understood within an ecclesial-eschatological context.[4] It is *gospel*, a present and future gift from the heart of God for the people of the *ekklēsia* (16:16-19) whose lives are marked by: *poverty in spirit, mourning, meekness, hungering and thirsting for righteousness, mercy, purity in heart, peacemaking*, and *persecution for righteousness' sake*.

To promise *blessing* means a miracle occurs by God's grace through the messianic kingdom herald, Jesus. Jesus in his coming, proclaiming and inaugurating the kingdom, actualizes the *blessing*. Sanction for this incredible vision appeals to God's own nature (5:48; cf. 5:16). But such emphasis is not totally *de novo*, for the righteous piety of those who trusted in the Lord in the OT was marked by these same attributes. They, often described as those who "fear the Lord," were the *blessed* of God,[5] those on whom God's favor rests (Pss. 18:27; 25:9; 34:17-19; 37:11; 73:1; 149:4).

Jewish scholar David Flusser has developed this at some length for the first Beatitude.[6] The Hebrew scriptural home of this beatitude is Isa. 57:15; 66:2 and Ps. 51:17, specifically in the Hebrew text, with English translation, "contrite and humble":

> For thus says the high and lofty one who inhabits eternity, whose name is Holy: I dwell in the high and holy place, and also with those who are contrite and humble in spirit, to revive the spirit of the humble, and to revive the heart of the contrite (Isa. 57:15).

> All these things my hand has made, and so all these things are mine, says the LORD. But this is the one to whom I will look, to the humble and contrite in spirit, who trembles at my word (Isa. 66:2).

> The sacrifice acceptable to God is a broken spirit; a broken and contrite heart, O God, you will not despise (Ps. 51:17).

Flusser cites the Tannaitic Midrash *Mekilta*, which in its commentary on Exod. 20:21 discusses the meekness of Moses (Num. 12:3). It cites all these

---

4. Lischer, "The Sermon on the Mount as Radical Pastoral Care."

5. In the LXX *makarios* (blessed) translates either *bārûk* or *'ašrê*. Whether *'ašrê*, as occurring in Pss. 1:1; 84:4, 5, 12 (MT, v. 13), or *bārûk*, used widely in the OT, lies behind the Beatitudes is debatable. In his study of comparative usage Waldemar Janzen concludes that *'ašrê* is used consistently by humans blessing humans whereas *bārûk* has wider usage, including God blessing humans. See Janzen, "*'Ašrê* in the Old Testament," especially p. 224. In light of this distinction, it would seem to me that *bārûk* lies behind the Beatitudes, since Jesus speaks God's blessing.

6. Flusser, "Blessed are the Poor in Spirit."

texts plus Isa. 61:1, "The spirit of the Lord hath anointed me to preach good tidings unto the *meek*."[7] This catena of texts combines Beatitudes one and three (Matt. 5:3, 5).

Qumran's Thanksgiving Scroll 18.14-15 also confirms the Jewish home of these gospel proclamations, and includes also the second Beatitude. The sectarian author thanks God:

> To [have appointed] me in Thy truth a messenger [of the peace]
>   of Thy goodness,
> To proclaim to *the meek* the multitude of Thy mercies,
> And to let them *that are of contrite spirit* he[ar salvation]
>   from [everlasting] source.
> And to *them that mourn* everlasting joy.[8]

Clearly, these beatitudes promise divine blessing to those who are poor in spirit, mourning, meek, and humble. In first-century Palestine, as in many places in our world today, such blessing comes amid suffering, deprivation, poverty, mourning, and yearning for peace and justice.

Blessed are the peacemakers is no less such a promised blessing. Doing the work of peacemaking in a violent world is not itself a task that produces happiness. John Paul Lederach's recounting of his experiences in peacemaking in Nicaragua, Somalia, and in other settings of dangerous and violent conflicts often generated threats of violence and death, hardly a recipe for happiness. Yet he writes about reconciliation, the fruit of this *meek, broken in spirit* approach to horrendous evil and violence through painstaking, patient mediation.[9] This is the peacemaking that disarms violence and effects reconciliation. The Beatitude promises *blessedness* precisely where it does not exist in this world, for people who are meek, lowly of heart, humbly trusting in God. These are those who fear the Lord and are friends of God (Ps. 25:14).

Add to these *peacemaking* beatitudes the seventh beatitude promise: "for they shall be called children of God." As in Matt. 5:45-48, peacemaking is rooted in God's moral character. Children bear the image of the parent. Being

---

7. Flusser, "Blessed," p. 2. The citation in the Exodus *Mekilta* of Isa. 61:1 uses the word *meek,* instead of *poor,* as in the NRSV and Luke's citation (4:18) of the text. In Qumran the poor are the *anawim,* who are meek and humble. This reality makes the Matthean and Lukan versions agree, though Luke, as we shall see, emphasizes the economic dimension.

8. Flusser, "Blessed," p. 3. The reconstruction of missing words, based on J. Licht's editing (Jerusalem, 1957), has been done in the belief that the text alludes to Isa. 52:7 in its use of the Hebrew *mebasser* for messenger (see ch. 1 above for the importance of this text in Jesus' proclamation of the kingdom of God).

9. John Paul Lederach, *Journey toward Reconciliation,* pp. 25-44.

children of peace is the gospel's mark of identity for those who follow Jesus. Here is the charter for Christian vocation, to reflect the character of being God's children. Jesus called disciples to be trained in this new radical thought and action. The Gospel narratives are Jesus' catechism of the disciples.

To do this peacemaking, Jesus taught his disciples to do the unthinkable: to love enemies. This is beyond human capacity, for the natural human response to enemy actions against us is to retaliate, to wipe out the enemy if possible. Rarely does one think of responding in such a way that might convert the enemy into a friend! But this is the gospel with which Jesus inaugurates his ministry.[10] Flusser says that while Rabbi Hanina taught to love the righteous and not to hate the sinner, Jesus' "commandment to love one's enemies is so much his definitive characteristic that his are the only lips from which we hear the commandment in the whole of the New Testament."[11] Elsewhere, mutual love is commanded, building on the double love commandment to love God and neighbor. Indeed, the double love command, especially the second part, is pervasive in the NT (Gospels, Paul, and James).[12] While Flusser is correct, Paul's moral commands in Rom. 12:14-21, especially v. 20, demonstrate action consistent with love of enemies.

The analogous emphasis between Beatitudes seven and eight and the command to love enemies even when persecuted is noted by Ulrich Mauser:

> The seventh and eighth blessing in Matthew's form of the Beatitudes show strong verbal and thematic affinities to his wording of Jesus' command to love enemies. "Blessed are the peacemakers, for they will be called *children of God*. Blessed are those who are *persecuted* for righteousness' sake, for theirs is the kingdom of heaven" (5:9-10) is analogous to "love your enemies and pray for those who *persecute* you, so that you may be *children of your Father* in heaven" (5:44-45a).[13]

As Mauser further observes, Luke has no parallel to these Beatitudes, which attests Matthean composition, and this deliberate arrangement in Matthew 5 to highlight these interrelated emphases of peacemaking and love of enemies even when persecuted; both mark one's identity as God's child. The reality of persecution is indicated not only in Matt. 24, but also in ch. 10, where perse-

---

10. The Sermon is likely a condensation, perhaps an *epitomē*, of Jesus' teaching. As such, it stands as the frontispiece of Jesus' proclamation of the kingdom in Matthew.

11. Flusser, *Jesus*, p. 88.

12. The literature is vast on the love commands generally. For a good study see Furnish, *Love Command*.

13. Mauser, *Gospel of Peace*, p. 36.

cution originates with governmental and political forces (10:17ff., 23) as a result of announcing the gospel of peace (10:12-13).[14]

Is this command to love enemies unique to Jesus? Since the Torah calls for kindness and help to the enemy in need (Exod. 23:4-5; Deut. 22:1-4), Jesus' love command is not altogether novel, William Klassen contends.[15] But Marius Reiser's close study of both the Greek and Jewish ethical traditions argues the opposite. While in both traditions one can find injunctions not to retaliate in kind (Plutarch, Musonius Rufus, several other Stoics, Prov. 25:21; Exod. 23:4-5), the explicit positive initiative to love *enemies* is unique to Jesus. Reiser proposes that Jesus was the first to interpret the sequence of three terse commands in Lev. 19:17-18 as extending neighbor love to include enemy love.[16] Gordon Zerbe's study concurs with Reiser in respect to Judaism. After examining numerous Jewish writings of 200 BCE–100 CE, he concludes, "there is no evidence in early Judaism of an explicit exhortation to love one's enemies," though there are many "exhortations to good will or kind actions in response to adversaries or abuse. The theme of 'love' toward injurers, however, applies only to local, personal conflict *(Testaments of the Twelve Patriarchs)*, not to situations of socio-political oppression by outsiders."[17] In Jesus' and Matthew's social worlds, enmity between Jews and Gentiles was not only socio-racial, but also political (see below on Wink) and religious (see below on Weaver). Thus, the mixed Jewish and Gentile crowds depicted in Matthew's Galilean narrative as well as Jesus' response to the centurion (4:25; 8:5-13) exemplify Matthew's own appropriation of Jesus' love of enemy command (see also 15:21ff.).[18]

14. Mauser, *Gospel,* p. 37. Mauser develops at length the opposition to the gospel/persecution theme in Matthew, noting parallel emphases in Luke. I comment on this briefly in this chapter; more extensive discussion will come in Chapter 5 on Luke.

15. Klassen, *Love of Enemies,* pp. 12-66. Klassen's cited texts refer more to nonretaliation (which as in Greek thought is motivated often by calculated prudent outcomes) than to proactive love of enemies. The cited texts from T. of Gad 6:1, 3 speak of loving response when wronged by a *brother,* not an enemy (p. 59). See also his essay, "The Novel Element in the Love Commandment of Jesus," which holds that the novel element is calling into being a community that seeks to model the love command. See p. 112, note 5, in "Novel Element" for sources that discuss the degree of newness in Jesus' love command.

16. Reiser, "Love of Enemies in the Context of Antiquity."

17. Zerbe, *Non-retaliation in Early Jewish and New Testament Texts,* pp. 171-72. For fuller reporting and analysis of this helpful work, see my review. Flusser's position above concurs with Reiser and Zerbe.

18. I hold that the Sermon on the Mount is an integral part of Matthew's narrative and theology, contra Hans D. Betz's proposal that the Sermon is an earlier literary document (an *epitomē*) composed in a Palestinian Jewish Christianity milieu around A.D. 45 with different theological features than the Gospel; Betz, "The Sermon on the Mount: In Defense of a Hypoth-

Illustrating the radical challenge this approach to evil calls for, Walter Wink cites a marvelous testimony from Sheila Cassidy in *When the Powers Fall*. On the basis of her healing ministries, she observes that "Hatred is a devil to be cast out, and we must pray for the power to forgive, for it is in forgiving our enemies that we are healed."[19] Of all the strategies that we may advocate for response to the powers, this command to love our enemies must ever be kept in view, since it is easy to absorb the very evil we seek to resist.[20] The goal of all nonresistance or nonviolent resistance is to overcome evil with good — this is pervasive in NT parenesis — and to transform hostile relationships into friendship through reconciliation, truth-telling, and forgiveness. This is love for the enemy: to convert from hostility by extending to the enemy the indiscriminate love of God. This does not mean annulling the judgment of God on violence and evil. Understanding the fifth super-thesis,[21] Matt. 5:38-42, requires us to see this in deeper profound perspective.

To understand these radically creative responses to evil I address five areas for investigation. First, I examine how several scholars have understood Jesus' teachings "love enemies" and "do not resist." Second, I take up a most difficult question, the consistency between Jesus' teaching and how he is portrayed in his own ministry, especially in his mounting conflict with the Pharisees. Third, I look at the Sermon on the Mount to identify the spirituality which underlies this teaching and what this means for our current commitment to peacemaking. Fourth, I ask "What then is the greater righteousness" that Jesus, according to Matthew, asks of us. Fifth, I conclude by presenting a distinctive portrait of Matthew's royal christology, which deepens the peaceable portrait of King Jesus as Messiah and Son of God.

---

esis." But the Sermon in its love of enemy command matches perfectly the Gospel's positive depiction of Gentiles. Granted, however, the Sermon does not develop a Christological portrait of Jesus beyond the prophetic, as does the Gospel as a whole. However, the Antitheses/Supertheses imply that Jesus is greater than Moses. The Lord's Prayer in its "Our Father" address (in Luke 11:2 the vocative *Pater*, which was likely the Aramaic *Abba* on Jesus' lips), as well as the recurring "my Father in heaven," also discloses Jesus' unique intimate relationship with God.

19. See Wink's *When the Powers Fall*, p. 24.

20. Wink, *The Powers That Be*, pp. 122-27.

21. I concur with Pinchas Lapide that "But I say to you" *(egō de legō hymin)* should be translated, "*And* I say to you," so that the so-called *Antitheses* are understood as *Supertheses;* Lapide, *The Sermon on the Mount*, pp. 42-46. Similarly, W. D. Davies understands the Sermon within the context of New Exodus and New Moses themes and extensive OT backgrounds and Jewish literature more broadly, with such taking 90% of the space in his over 500-page study, *The Setting of the Sermon on the Mount.*

Interpretations of Jesus' Teaching

In *The Love of Enemy and Nonretaliation in the New Testament,* I included three essays that present differing interpretations of this "nonresistance" text, Matt. 5:38-48.

Examining Jesus' words in Matthew's narrative context, Dorothy Jean Weaver understands Jesus' commands *not to resist the evil one* and *to love the enemy* as referring to those who revile (5:11), persecute (5:11, 44), say evil things (5:11), and tell lies about the disciples (5:11). The referents include the adversary (5:25), the "council" (5:22), the judge (5:25), and the court assistant (5:25). These "are the 'evil one' (*tǭ ponerǭ:* 5:39a) and 'the enemies' (*tous echthrous;* 5:44)."[22] In Matthew's setting, these people were likely part of the Gentile world, though Jewish persecution cannot be ruled out. Weaver sees a marked contrast between Jesus' response to one doing evil and that prescribed in the Torah, where the evil one is to be removed from the community (Deut. 19:15-21). Verbal resemblance between the two texts is striking.[23] Weaver proposes that Jesus' word fulfills the law. Rather than cutting off the evildoer from the community or simply responding in kind, which sparks a cycle of violence, Jesus prescribes a redemptive response that shows forth God's love manifested in sending rain on the just and unjust (5:45-46). The sanction for such response is being children of God the Father in heaven.[24]

Richard A. Horsley argues that "'love your enemies' pertains neither to external, political enemies nor to the question of nonviolence or non-resistance."[25] Following Tannehill,[26] Horsley considers 5:39-42 as referring to "focal instances." He identifies the life-setting, however, as local social-economic relationships within village life. The instruction was addressed thus to "people caught in . . . severe economic circumstances." "Love your enemy," therefore, hardly has the wealthy ruling elite in mind,[27] but "apparently referred to persecutors outside the religious community, but still in the local residential community — and certainly not the national or politi-

---

22. Dorothy Jean Weaver, "Transforming Nonresistance," p. 49.

23. Weaver, "Transforming Nonresistance." Compare the texts printed on pages 40-41 and 50-51.

24. Weaver, "Transforming Nonresistance," pp. 55-58.

25. Horsley, "Ethics and Exegesis: 'Love Your Enemies' and the Doctrine of Non-Violence," p. 3 (= *The Love of Enemy,* p. 72).

26. Robert C. Tannehill. "The 'Focal Instance' as a Form of New Testament Speech"; *The Sword of His Mount.*

27. Horsley, *Jesus and the Spiral of Violence,* pp. 262-69.

cal enemies (Romans)."[28] Horsley argues against using the Zealots as a foil for understanding Jesus' love of enemy command. In this identification of the "enemies," no correlation can be made with Matthew's portrayal of Gentiles elsewhere in the Gospel, since the enemies are local compatriots who compete for economic survival.

Walter Wink regards Horsley's reconstruction of the socioeconomic setting for Jesus' teaching as correct, but also rightly holds that such peasant life included the reality of the Roman occupation. Indebtedness was the most serious socioeconomic problem of Jesus' Galilean life-context. Jesus addressed the poor who "share a rankling hatred for a system that subjects them to humiliation by stripping them of their lands, their goods, finally even their outer garment."[29] Addressed to people under Roman occupation, all five "instances" point Jesus' hearers to an unexpected response that disarms the enmity. Jesus commands a nonviolent shock-tactic that exposes the indignity of the oppression.

On the basis of his extensive study of contemporary usage, especially Josephus, Wink holds that "do not resist" *(mē antistēnai)* means not to resist violently. The examples show a form of nonviolent resistance whereby the poor or oppressed claim their dignity and open the door to a new relationship between the oppressor and oppressed. The enemy is disarmed by a "surprise" response: turn the *other (left)* cheek to one who insultingly hits you with a backhanded *right-fist* slap on your *right* cheek; when sued for your coat in court give your *undergarment* also, and thus stand there naked; and offer to go a *second* mile when required to carry a Roman soldier's load *one* mile *(angareia)*. Such response throws the opponent off-balance, introducing a third way, an alternative to flight or fight; the situation is radically redefined.[30] This approach of nonviolent resistance does not guarantee that the other side will refrain from violence or that there will be no casualties. It rather creates a new paradigm by using "moral jujitsu" to disarm the enemy.

Thus Jesus sets forth a "way of fighting evil with all one's power without being transformed into the very evil we fight."[31] Although Wink does not explicitly link his exegesis of 5:38-42 to the love of enemy command in 5:44, his later response to Horsley affirms "that Jesus taught love of enemies in refer-

---

28. Horsley, "Ethics and Exegesis," p. 24 (= *The Love of Enemy,* p. 93). Following Morton Smith, "Zealots and Sicarii," p. 9, Horsley argues that a Zealot party did not exist until 66 CE.

29. Walter Wink, "Neither Passivity nor Violence," p. 24 (revised in *The Love of Enemy,* p. 107).

30. Wink, "Neither Passivity," in *The Love of Enemy,* pp. 104-11.

31. Wink, "Neither Passivity," p. 223 (*The Love of Enemy,* p. 117).

ence to Romans and their puppets."[32] Jesus' radical "third way" expresses love for the enemy by seeking to transform the relationship so that dehumanization of both the oppressor and oppressed, aggressor and victim, comes to an end. Horsley excludes the national enemy (the Romans) from the "enemy," but his application of the teaching to conflict situations among village factions is not to be excluded. In contrast, Wink leaves the scope of application open to wherever enemy relations exist — socioeconomic, racial, political, or personal. In Wink's analysis, the enemies to be loved certainly include Gentiles of the Roman occupation. Since Wink contends that Jesus prescribes a tactic intended to disarm the enmity and put the human relationship on a new basis, such response toward Gentile oppressors readily harmonizes with Matthew's favorable portrait of the Gentiles' response to Jesus.

Love of enemy matches Matthew's depiction of the Gentiles in some key texts. At the beginning and near the end of the Galilean ministry, Matthew depicts the strong faith of Gentiles in receiving the gospel: 8:5-13, the centurion's great faith; 15:21-28, the Canaanite woman's extraordinary faith.[33] This book-end feature of the Galilean narrative in Matthew depicts Jesus overcoming boundaries of enmity. The Canaanite woman is a hero in faith, persuading Jesus to overcome the boundary. Further, his encounter with her stands in tension with 10:5, where he commands his disciples in their gospel-proclamation mission to "go nowhere among the Gentiles." But positive depiction of Gentiles in 12:15-21, citing Isa. 42:1-4, points to another reality by which the trajectory of the narrative moves beyond the limitation of 10:5 and several negative references to Gentiles in the narrative (6:7, 31; 18:17; 20:25). The positive depiction emerges also from Gentile choirs singing the praises of Israel's God in 9:33b and 15:31c: "And they praised the God of Israel." Weaver proposes that this tension is finally and fully resolved in Matthew's ending, in Jesus commissioning his disciples to go to all nations (Gentiles) to preach the gospel.[34]

Interpretations of the "nonresistance" command that connect it meaningfully to love for the enemy are more persuasive. Likewise, those interpretations are stronger that also relate love of enemy to Matthew's depiction of Jesus'

---

32. Wink, "Counterresponse to Richard Horsley," p. 134.

33. For an insightful exposition of this text, see Schipani, "Transformation in the Borderlands." See also my discussion in *Israel's Scripture Traditions*, pp. 66, 70; Bauckham, *Gospel Women*, pp. 41-46; Love, "Jesus, Healer of the Canaanite Woman's Daughter." For exposition of the Markan account of this encounter, see my "The Role of Women in Mark's Gospel." For still wider perspective, see Dewey, "Women in the Synoptic Gospels," who too easily dismisses the cultural conventions in assessing the silence of women, though she acknowledges this story to be an exception.

34. Dorothy Jean Weaver, *Matthew's Missionary Discourse*, pp. 124-53.

own actions. Peter Ellis persuasively argues that the Sermon on the Mount "is funneled through 28.16-20 to become the standard of Christian existence for the ongoing community — both Jewish and Gentile — of Matthew's day."[35]

Does love of enemy, nonresistance, or nonretaliation ever express itself in stern judgment? On this crucial matter I find Luise Schottroff's interpretation of these commands of Jesus profound and helpful.[36]

> Matthew 5:38-41 . . . commands the refusal to retaliate as well as prophetic judgment of violent persons. . . . As imitators of God, Christians are supposed to confront the enemies of God with his mercies. . . . Loving one's enemy is the attempt to change the violent person into a child of God through a confrontation with the love of God. That is, love of one's enemy can be concretely presented as the prophetic proclamation of the approaching sovereignty of God.[37]

Schottroff contends that this behavior breaks the spiral of violence and grows out of "the assurance that God's judgment is just." She summarizes her threefold emphases:

> This behavioral ensemble consisting of refusal to pay retribution, expecting prophetic judgment, and loving the enemy has its reason or its goal in the justice of God or in the sovereignty of God.[38]

Further, Rom. 12:2 and 13:2 present a normative pattern similar to that in Matthew. In 12:2 the believer is called to "resist" with the command "do not be conformed to this age/world," but in 13:2 "not to resist." The word (*anthistēmi*) used in Matt. 5:39 occurs in Rom. 13:2 and Eph. 6:13. The resistance, Schottroff says, is against Satan and the world. In principle the believer does not resist the powers that God ordained. But living out the command to resist the evil of the world often puts Christians in collision with the state powers, because in them the very Satan that Christians must resist is at work. Christians did not desire conflict with the empire and even at times sought to avoid it, but their faithfulness to the command to "resist" brought them into

35. Ellis, *Matthew: His Mind and His Message,* p. 42.

36. Schottroff, "Give to Caesar."

37. Schottroff, "Give to Caesar," p. 232. She correlates this teaching with Paul's in Romans under the topic "Make Room for God's Wrath: Romans 12:14-21" and takes up a study of Romans 13:1-7 (see Chapter 8 below). She presents a persuasive case that Matthew 5:38-48 and Romans 12-13 are entirely compatible and represent a consistent pattern of early Christian response to evil (found also in 1 Peter; see Chapter 9 below).

38. Schottroff, "Give to Caesar," p. 236.

conflict. "The root of the problem was their resistance against Satan and sin as the true rulers of this world." The "resistance of Christians against Satan is not the resistance of the powerless. God's power is on their side."[39] Living through this paradox gave early Christians freedom to live for God, even in hostile environments.

Both nonresistance and resistance, of whatever type, must witness to Jesus' lordship over all, a way to overcome evil with good.[40] It is a sign of both our subjection to and freedom from the powers, because we know our citizenship is in heaven (Phil. 3:20-21). It is motivated not by disrespect for the powers or refusal to recognize their authority. Rather, it has the surprising dimension of the folly of the cross — the defeat of evil by extending genuine unlimited love that stands for truth, justice, and shalom precisely where evil seeks to reign. In this way of loving we seek to extend God's justice in human relationships, reflecting God's love and divine justice for all humanity.

Schottroff's treatment closely correlates the command not to resist with the command to love the enemy, as does Luke's account (6:17-30) — which lacks the "instance" of going the second mile. The command to love one's enemies, bless those who curse, and pray for those who abuse *precedes* the four "focal instances." Wink speaks of achieving a new relationship that restores dignity to both parties. In the court suit "instance," however, the publicly humiliated "adversary" would likely be angered more. Nor does the "shock"-logic Wink uses for the first three "instances" apply to the last two: give to one who begs and do not refuse one who asks to borrow.

Elements of Wink's proposals are persuasive, but these weaknesses are significant. That the "victim" takes initiative to turn humiliation into restoring dignity, fundamental to his position, is good, but I am not persuaded that the offender would thereby be shocked into a new respectful relationship. Rather, such a tactical response may aggravate more aggression, which means that the "surprise tactic" violates love of enemy. For these reasons, Schottroff's explanations are more cogent. Further, her work is correlated with the wider canonical teachings on nonretaliation and love of enemy.

John Piper's thorough study does the same. Piper's approach is to "isolate the elements of the paraenetic tradition which possibly represent the reception and application of Jesus' command of enemy love."[41] He regards Rom. 12:14, 17-20; 1 Thess. 5:15; and 1 Pet. 3:9 as expressive of the parenetic tra-

39. Schottroff, "Give to Caesar," pp. 242-44.

40. See here the helpful article by Thomas Yoder Neufeld, "Resistance and Nonresistance: The Two Legs of a Biblical Peace Stance."

41. John Piper, *Love Your Enemies*, p. 4.

dition that developed from Jesus' command to love enemies. These texts have at their core the nonretaliation command, "Do not return evil for evil." Piper proposes that this command, *mē apodidontes kakon anti kakou*, "became a fixed rule early in the Christian paraenetic tradition. As the community reflected on this rule and endeavored to apply it to life-situations a process of specification occurred."[42] He examines the contextual situations to which it was applied.

In his insightful study of the Sermon on the Mount, Glen Stassen focuses on the *positive initiatives* that are part of each of the Sermon's fourteen triads, which are made up of (1) a statement of traditional teaching, (2) the vicious cycle that perpetuates the wrong, and (3) the action-initiative that *transforms* the person and/or relationship. His structural analysis is impressive and persuasive, in that the repeated use of the same grammatical features for the three elements (negative command, descriptive indicative, and imperative verbs) is hardly coincidental.

The Fourteen Triads of the Sermon on the Mount[43]

Traditional Teaching	Vicious Cycle	Transforming Initiative
1. **You shall not kill**	**Being angry, or saying, You fool!**	*Go, be reconciled*
2. You shall not commit adultery	Looking with lust	*Remove the cause of temptation* (cf. Mark 9:43ff.)
3. Whoever divorces, give a certificate	Divorcing involves you in adultery	(Be reconciled: 1 Cor. 7:11)
4. You shall not swear falsely	Swearing by anything involves you in a false claim	Let your yes be yes, and your no be no
5. **Eye for eye, tooth for tooth**	**Violently/revengefully resisting by evil means**	*Turn the other cheek* *Give your tunic and cloak* *Go the second mile* *Give to beggar and borrower*

42. Piper, "Love Your Enemies," p. 17.

43. Italicized items are repeated in the Sermon on the Plain or in other locations indicated in parentheses. Items in bold are those which I consider in my treatment in this chapter. Stassen, "Fourteen Triads," p. 296; *Kingdom Ethics*, p. 142. See also his discussion in *Just Peacemaking: Transforming Initiatives for Justice and Peace*, pp. 36-88.

6. Love neighbor and hate enemy	**If you love those who love you, what more is that than the Gentiles do?**	*Love enemies, pray for your persecutors; be all-inclusive as your Father in heaven is*
7. When you give alms,	Do not make a show like the hypocrites	But give in secret, and your Father will reward you
8. When you pray,	Do not make a show like the hypocrites	But pray in secret, and your Father will reward you
9. When you pray,	**Do not keep on babbling like the Gentiles**	*Therefore pray like this:* *Our Father . . .*
10. When you fast,	Do not be gloomy like the hypocrites	But dress with joy, and your Father will reward you
11. *Do not pile up treasures on earth (cf. Luke 12:16-31)*	*Where moth and rust destroy, and thieves enter and steal*	*But pile up treasures in heaven*
12. *No one can serve two masters*	*Therefore do not be worrying about food and clothes*	*But seek first God's reign and God's justice/righteousness*
13. *Do not judge, lest you be judged*	*By the measure with which you judge, you will be judged*	*First take the log out of your own eye*
14. Do not give holy things to dogs, nor pearls to pigs	They will trample them and tear you to pieces	*Give your trust in prayer to your Father in heaven*

Stassen's tightly argued contribution, considering other major scholarly efforts to understand the Sermon's structure, is most helpful, for his emphasis on the transforming initiatives puts the Sermon directly into the service of peacemaking. Loving the enemy, a key transforming initiative, is but one of fourteen clusters of thought in which Jesus goes beyond the traditional teaching, provides deliverance from the vicious cycle, and identifies concrete steps that make visible and functional his proclamation of the kingdom of God come and coming. Indeed, the cumulative effect of these fourteen triads provides "a transforming initiative of grace-based deliverance."[44]

44. Stassen, "Fourteen Triads," p. 308. Stassen also shows how this understanding modi-

It lies beyond the scope of purpose here to consider the numerous efforts to explain (away?) the appropriation of the nonretaliation and love of enemy commands.[45] These efforts to "narrow" the scope of appropriation are suspect because of the multiplicity of explanations and flawed in that they fail to note that the larger NT canon reflects the same moral exhortations appropriated to a range of social and political settings: in Jesus' own example during his Passion, in his parable of the Good Samaritan, and in Pauline and Petrine moral admonitions (see subsequent chapters). Further, peacemaking and love of enemies are related to one's identity as a child of God elsewhere also (Eph. 5:1-2; 1 Pet. 1:13-25; 2:21-24; 1 John 4:7-12; cf. Rom. 5:8-11 with 12:9-21). As Gardner puts it:

> . . . it is evident that the peacemakers Jesus blesses are not merely peaceful persons. Instead, they are those who work actively to bring peace or make peace. Taking their cue from God, whose love extends to friend and enemy (Matt. 5:45), they pursue peace with all persons. They work to restore wholeness in their relationships with others, whether with members of the church (5:23-24; 18:10ff.), or with hostile parties on the outside (5:38-48). Because those who make peace are acting as God acts, they show themselves to be the true children of God. Thus, Jesus says, God will claim them as his own in the age to come.[46]

Moltmann is correct, that loving enemies "is the only reasonable thing, if we are to ensure lasting peace on earth."[47]

---

fies and enriches the structural analyses of other scholars (Luz, Bornkamm, and Grundmann especially, pp. 300-307). His treatment of 7:6 is a major breakthrough by highlighting the Roman context for the sayings, not *giving* holy things to dogs (Gentile pagans) or pearls to pigs (Roman oppressors). This leads to the vicious cycle effect of getting trampled. The first two parts of the triad are "completed" by the transforming initiatives in vv. 6-12, where the verb *give* occurs six times.

45. Clarence Bauman's encyclopedic treatment of this effort within German scholarship, mostly twentieth-century, describes the varied attempts *(The Sermon on the Mount)*. More recently, with attention to wider western scholarship as well as selections from patristic and medieval writers, Dale C. Allison offers a helpful treatment, *The Sermon on the Mount: Inspiring the Moral Imagination*, pp. 92-106.

46. Gardner, *Matthew*, p. 97.

47. Moltmann, *The Way of Jesus Christ*, p. 131 (contra Allison, *Sermon on the Mount*, p. 101). Moltmann's discussion on messianic peace (pp. 127-36) is sterling.

Jesus' Teaching and His Conflict with the Pharisees

How does Jesus' command to love enemies correlate with Matthew's portrait of Jesus speaking harsh (violent?) words against the Pharisees? Many interpretations of "love of enemy" fail to correlate Jesus' teaching in these super-theses with Jesus' seemingly unloving speech against his opponents (Matthew 23, but also 8:10-12; 12:36-45; 16:4; 21:43). Are Jesus' teachings in the Sermon contradicted by his own words and actions?

Richard Hays describes the issue succinctly: "Matthew's text provides no clues about how this implacable hostility toward the traditional represen-tatives of Israel is to be integrated with Jesus' teaching concerning the love of enemies."[48] In his later chapter, "Anti-Judaism and Ethnic Conflict," Hays as-sesses Matthew's portrayal of Jesus critically, attributing to it a latent anti-Semitism that cannot be regarded as normative for Christian faith. Rather, Paul is a more reliable guide on this question. However, Hays also notes that Amy-Jill Levine, a Jewish Gospels scholar, disagrees, and holds that Matthew's judgment falls on the leaders, addressing issues of status and social inequality, rather than Judaism or the Jewish people as such.[49] Even so, one must ask how even this is compatible with love of the enemy.

Schottroff's emphasis on the need to resist evil through love that also

---

48. Hays, *The Moral Vision of the New Testament*, p. 109.

49. Hays, *Moral Vision*, pp. 422-24, 429-30. See Levine, *The Social and Ethnic Dimensions of Matthean Salvation History*. In a later article, "Anti-Judaism and the Gospel of Matthew," Le-vine addresses numerous issues that resist solution, most notably the identity of the socio-historical situation in which Matthew writes, and categorizes and assesses the dominant inter-pretations: internal prophetic polemic and critique; a Jewish Christian anti-Judaism, which, she notes, George Smiga labeled "subordinating polemic" in which Jesus in Matthean Christology replaces Torah and Temple; and Gentilizing anti-Judaism, which Smiga refines with "abrogating anti-Judaism." Her analysis is insightful and she locates herself between the second and third views. In the end, however, she finds she cannot "dismiss the question. Matthew's Gospel is, in my reading, anti-Jewish" (p. 36). In *Anti-Judaism and the Gospels*, ed. Farmer, pp. 9-36. In the same volume Philip L. Shuler (pp. 37-46) and Warren Carter (pp. 47-62) respond equally insightfully and contend that Levine's treatment is quite persuasive, but that other factors are to be considered also. Shuler argues that Matthew's positive portraits of Jewish people are so strong that he demurs on Levine's conclusion. Carter notes the importance of Sitz im Leben for both the writing of the Gospel — which we do not really know — and the reader, and proposes a revision of Levine's thesis: "*My fear is that parts of Matthew can be construed as anti-some-forms-of-Judaism by some readers at some times. My great joy is not all parts, not all Judaisms, and not by all readers*" (p. 62). Resolving this issue is most complex because we do not know Mat-thew's "religious location" in relation to Judaism. The matter is enigmatic, since Matthew is strongly pro-Jewish at points and also anti-Jewish, at least toward the religious leaders. But it is also pro-Gentile and anti-Gentile as well.

announces God's judgment wedges open an answer to this conundrum. It also suggests that Jesus fits squarely in the Hebrew prophetic tradition, which is noted for strong words of judgment. The majority understanding among Matthew scholars is that Jesus' "condemnation" of the Pharisees' actions must be seen as intra-Jewish critique, akin to that of all the Hebrew prophets (Isaiah to Malachi). Critique of certain Pharisees occurs also in later Jewish Talmudic literature, as in the text denoting seven types of Pharisees. In the first five types Pharisees are "cartooned" for their obsession to be known for their good works. They

> are the "shoulder Pharisee" who packs his good works on his shoulder (to be seen of men); the "wait-a-bit" Pharisee, who (when someone has business with him) says, Wait a little; I must do a good work; the "reckoning" Pharisee, who when he commits a fault and does a good work crosses off one with the other; the "economising" Pharisee, who asks, What economy can I practice to spare a little to do a good work? the "show me my fault" Pharisee, who says, show me what sin I have committed, and I will do an equivalent good work (implying that he had no fault). . . .[50]

The last two types are "the Pharisee of fear, like Job" and "the Pharisee of love, like Abraham. The latter is the only kind that is dear (to God)."[51] This caricature seems unduly harsh against Job. But the point here is that as long as Matthew 23 is understood as intra-Jewish critique, it fits into the stream of prophetic critique against religious leaders. It is not exceptional.[52]

---

50. JT *Berakoth* IX, § 7, f. 14b, line 48, and JT *Sotah* V. § 7, f. 29c. line 49. The texts with commentary can be found in Montefiore and Loewe, ed., *Rabbinic Anthology*, pp. 487-89.

51. Montefiore and Loewe, *Rabbinic Anthology*, p. 488.

52. Daniel Ulrich makes the same point, but adds to it by noting that Jesus' reproof of the Jewish leaders is in keeping with Matthew's emphasis on "reproving" *(elenchein)* elsewhere in the Gospel: to restore an erring brother in 18:15-20, and extends the teaching of Lev. 19:17-18, a text Matthew cites in 5:43; 18:15; 19:19; 22:39. Matt. 18:15 exhorts practice of the command in Lev. 19:17b (LXX), "reprove your neighbor." Seen in this light Jesus' sharp rebukes are intended to restore his fellow people. See Ulrich, "Did Jesus Love His Enemies?" pp. 158-160, 164-66. Josef Schreiner adds another consideration to this question, building on his point that in the OT Israel is nowhere called God's enemy. Thus in his concluding statement, he contends that if we say Jesus did not love, but rather showed hatred toward enemies (in Matthew 23 the Pharisees), then we would need to say the same of God, since in John the oneness between the Son and the Father means that those who hate Jesus hate the Father also (15:23). Schreiner is extending Rainer Kampling's earlier point that Jesus had enemies, people who hated him, but nowhere does the text indicate that Jesus hated them. Schreiner's point, based on his OT study, is that the enemies of the people *(Volkes)* are the enemies of God, and vice versa. See Josef Schreiner and Rainer Kampling, *Der Nächste — der Fremde — der Feind*, pp. 41, 80, 108. In Matthew since Jesus

This point has been developed in several thorough and competent studies.[53] Donald Senior sums up the point well: "Sharp and inflated language roundly condemning what are judged to be failures or excesses on the part of one's opponents was characteristic of such intra-Jewish debate and has precedents in the Bible and in extracanonical Jewish texts of this epoch."[54] The danger arises when such is lifted from its context and used by Christians against Jews. Such indeed violates the love command, and is an enemy-making action. Read as intra-Jewish polemic, Matthew 23 does not sanction ethnic hatred, and, specifically, not discrimination against Jews. The "woes" of Matthew 23 fall under the rubric of Jesus' prophetic word as judgment on his own people, and specifically the leaders, not all Israel. In keeping with the prophetic pattern of condemning sin among the people, announcing judgment even of exile, and then also hope for return, Graham Stanton proposes that Matt. 23:39, the last verse of the chapter, is to be understood not as judgment, but as an announcement of *hope and return.* Matthew 23 follows then the S-E-R structure, which Stanton shows is present in Jewish literature of the first centuries CE.[55]

Further, since Matthew emphasizes that Jesus came not to abolish the law, but to fulfill it (5:17), the severity of the judgment must be seen as a bold prophetic appeal that is grounded in his love for the leaders and the people. His sharp words aim to save the leaders from the destructive end of their misperception of moral values and current legalistic practices. In this respect the narrative is similar to earlier prophetic judgment against Israel's leaders such as Ezekiel 34.[56] Ezekiel is commanded to prophesy against the shepherds

---

does the will of "my Father in heaven," the same logic applies. What we say of Jesus' attitude to the Pharisees would score against Matthew's portrait of *God* also, contradicting what Jesus in Matthew says of the Father in 5:44-45.

53. Saldarini, *Matthew's Christian-Jewish Community,* especially chapter 3, pp. 44-67; Overman, *Matthew's Gospel and Formative Judaism,* especially pp. 141-49. Both authors argue persuasively against the notion that Matthew's Gospel reflects an ecclesial life-context of "post-parting" between church and synagogue, as had been held by numerous NT scholars. Rather we have in Matthew an inter-Jewish/Jewish Christian debate where "scribes and Pharisees" are very much part of the current conflict. In this way there is continuity with Jesus' own prophetic critique against Pharisaic practices summed up in the judgment: "For you tithe mint, dill, and cummin, and have neglected the weightier matters of the law: justice and mercy and faith" (23:23). Saldarini persuasively shows that the harsh condemnations of the chapter have precedents in the OT prophets.

54. Senior, *Matthew,* p. 31.

55. Stanton, *A Gospel for a New People,* pp. 247-55 (in his chapter on "Aspects of Early Christian–Jewish Polemic and Apologetic").

56. James Alison suggested this analogy in a presentation with Sandor Goodhart at the

of Israel because they were feeding themselves but not the sheep: "You have not strengthened the weak, you have not healed the sick, you have not bound up the injured, you have not brought back the strayed, you have not sought the lost, but with force and harshness you have ruled them" (v. 4). "Thus says the Lord GOD, I am against the shepherds; and I will demand my sheep at their hand, and put a stop to their feeding the sheep; no longer shall the shepherds feed themselves. I will rescue my sheep from their mouths, so that they may not be food for them" (v. 10).

N. T. Wright interprets Jesus' entire mission as an extended appeal, even in his death, to Israel to repent, to avoid the coming judgment. Only through heeding this appeal could Israel live in peace and avoid imminent catastrophe. In all this, Jesus' love for his own people was "uppermost, once more not simply as an idea, but as a reality."[57] Wright's interpretation of Jesus' life and death thus unites love and judgment at the deepest and most profound point — willingness to die for the people, as true Israel–Servant of God (Isaiah 53).

Did Jesus then fail as a peacemaker to his own people, since even his death did not lead to repentance and belief in his word and claims? The answer must be "yes" if 21:43 is read as descriptive or predictive fact: "Therefore I tell you, the kingdom of God will be taken away from you and given to a people *(ethnei)* that produces the fruits of the kingdom." But in keeping with Wright's understanding of Jesus' words of apparent condemnation, this pronouncement can also be read as a strong warning, coming as it does at the end of the parable of the vineyard's tenants. Jesus follows this harsh word with a pithy ominous maxim: "The one who falls on this stone will be broken to pieces; and it will crush anyone on whom it falls" (21:44). Again, is this to be understood as descriptive/predictive or as a last-ditch warning? The response of the chief priests and Pharisees is immediate: they perceive that he is talking about them. They want to arrest him but cannot because "they feared the crowds" (21:46). To the extent that one follows the narrative from within — not as facts about the outcome of the story — this threat of judgment is love pleading for conversion of mind and heart, for total change and turning back from exile to the heart of God. When read in this way, Jesus' prophetic judgment on Israel's leaders is not incompatible with the command to love

---

2002 meeting of the "Colloquium on Violence and Religion Conference on Judaism and Christianity in the Ancient World" at Purdue University. Goodhart interpreted John 8:1-12 through Jewish eyes with Jer. 17:13 as context, and Alison interpreted Ezekiel 34 through Christian eyes, with Matthew 23 as context.

57. Wright, *Jesus and the Victory of God*, p. 607, but see the larger context and then p. 639: "warning Jerusalem that [his coming] . . . would mean judgment for those who rejected him and his way of peace. . . ."

the enemy. Nor is it clear that Jesus or Matthew would have conceived Israel's leaders, even in their opposition, as enemies.[58]

The narrative concludes with Jesus' commission to make disciples of all nations, but this does not exclude continuing mission to Israel. The eleven commissioned on the mountain are themselves Jewish messianic believers. The Gospel narrative performs for God's covenant people (beginning with Abraham, 1:1) the same *good news* function that Second Isaiah performed, calling the people home from exile to God.

The Spirituality of the Sermon: How Not to Retaliate but to Love Enemies

Ulrich Luz has shown that the Sermon has a chiastic structure with several inclusions and correspondences in length (see p. 91 below), the Lord's Prayer forming the center:[59]

        a   5:1-2
            b   5:3-16
                c   5:17-20
                    d   5:21-48
                        e   6:1-6
                            the Lord's Prayer 6:7-15
                        e′   6:16-18
                    d′   6:19–7:11
                c′   7:12
            b′   7:13-27
        a′   7:28–8:1a

The prayer appears to be modeled after the Hebrew Kaddish prayer, which was recited two or three times a day. N. T. Wright reads the prayer against Israel's exodus and return from exile, enriching its depth of meaning.[60]

---

58. I have not considered here 27:24-25, what Hays calls the "chilling narrative detail: ". . . his blood be on us and on our children." First, this is not spoken by Jesus, so we have no way of knowing Jesus' own response. What Matthew intends is problematic. Is it part of the "shock call" to avoid coming disaster? Second, several interpretations have been advanced to argue that this is a cry of all the people *(pas ho laos)* for expiation of their sins. See my treatment of this proposal in *Israel's Scripture Traditions and the Synoptic Gospels*, p. 221, n. 58.

59. Luz, *Matthew: A Commentary*, vol. 1 (Minneapolis: Augsburg, 1989), p. 212.

60. In *Into God's Presence: Prayer in the New Testament*, ed. Richard N. Longenecker

The prayer consists of seven petitions: three "your"-directed, four "us"-directed, three of the latter for spiritual needs. In a few ancient mss. the prayer concludes with a doxology (traditionally used in most communions and similar to the closing of the Kaddish prayer; see 1 Chron. 29:11-13).

The Godward focus empowers the later petitions, as well as our living the ethic of the larger sermon. Sanctifying God's name makes possible love of the enemy.

> As God answers the petition to make God's name holy, such holiness comes to define those who are known by the name of the Father, Son, and Holy Spirit, and to empower them for the ethic of the sermon. Love of enemies, then, becomes possible, not on account of any human capacity for love or longsuffering, but rather because those who bear God's name are being "children of your Father in heaven."[61]

The prayer itself is bounded with instructions that make praying effectual: not heaping up empty phrases and forgiving those who trespass against us, infringing on our rights and crowding our space, literally or psychologically. By not attending to this instruction, we block the effectiveness of praying. In the language of the sixth Beatitude, our hearts are not pure in prayer. This hinders authentic spirituality.

Another key observation about this structural chiasm for the Sermon is the crucial parallel of 6:19-34 with the super-thesis of 5:21-48. In ch. 6 we are instructed to live with singleness of devotion; to lay up treasures not on earth but in heaven; not to have an evil eye of envy[62] but a simple, true eye; not to have divided allegiance by trying to serve two masters, but to trust in God for everyday needs. The significance of this parallel is that living the "greater righteousness" prescribed in the "super-theses" is one with shaping our lives by the single-mindedness of 6:18-34. With prayer at the center, trust in God empowers one to fulfill at least to some measure the "And I say to you . . . ," counsels toward perfection (5:48). As Stassen has demonstrated, the impera-

---

(Grand Rapids: Eerdmans, 2001), pp. 132-54. Boers's *Lord, Teach Us to Pray* contains useful commentary on the Prayer together with practical assistance in developing our own prayers in accord with this model. Another useful resource is Crosby, *Spirituality of the Beatitudes*.

61. Hinkle, "The Lord's Prayer," p. 102.

62. The "evil eye" was a common notion and was greatly feared in times contemporary to the New Testament (cf. Gal. 3:1-4). It was associated with cursing others, usually motivated by envy and consequent desire to wreak havoc and harm in another's life. A thorough study is John Elliott's "The Evil Eye and the Sermon on the Mount." See his extensive bibliography that shows the richness of literature on the subject.

tives by which we are to live are the transforming initiatives that go beyond the traditional teaching and deliver us from the enslaving vicious cycle.

Similarly, it is instructive to see "The Golden Rule" in relation to being salt and light to the world. By doing to others what we would have them do to us,[63] we become the fertilizing salt of the earth[64] and the light of the world. So also, the parables of the tree known by its fruits and the two foundations attest in different language to the same integrity and virtue that mark the Beatitudes.

Meditation on these different parts of the sermon, bathed with praying the Lord's Prayer, empowers one to live in accord with the other parts of the sermon. In a profound way the various aspects of the Sermon are interconnected. One cannot love enemies if the other parts of the Sermon are neglected.

What, Then, Is the "Greater Righteousness"?

Matthew's Gospel is identified often with the theme of the "greater righteousness," in deference to the key verse 5:20, "For I tell you, unless your righteousness exceeds that of the scribes and Pharisees, you will never enter the kingdom of heaven." The "super-theses" are then understood to illustrate how the moral attitudes and actions of Jesus' followers are to exceed the righteousness of the scribes and Pharisees. Further, v. 20 extends v. 17, "I have not come to abolish the law or the prophets; I have come not to abolish but to fulfill." As Allen Verhey puts it, in Matthew "the law holds."[65] However, as Richard Hays

63. The Jewish rabbinic parallel, attributed to Hillel, is in negative form, "What is hateful to you, do not do to your neighbor" (BT *Shabbat* 31a). For a wider background for the maxim, see J. H. Charlesworth, "Hillel and Jesus," pp. 19-20.

64. For a helpful article that explains "the salt of earth" as fertilizer (like potash), rather than table salt adding taste to food, see George Shillington, "Salt of the Earth." A similar interpretation was set forth earlier by Alan Kreider, "Salt and Light"; "Light"; see also "Salty Discipleship"; *Journey toward Holiness*, pp. 222-24, 238 n. 1. Kreider, through research into nineteenth-century farmers' cyclopedias learned that then in Britain salt in limited quantity was used as a fertilizer, a practice plausible also in the time of Jesus. The image thus calls for kingdom witness and growth, not a preservative of Christendom society.

65. Verhey, *The Great Reversal*, p. 83; *Remembering Jesus*, pp. 425-26. Verhey rightly stresses this point for Matthew but minimizes the significance of the novel dimension of Jesus' teaching on "nonretaliation" and "love of enemies." In *Remembering Jesus*, in discussing "Politics of the Law" he speaks of "a readiness to forgive and give (5:38-42)" and of "loving even the enemy (5:43-48)." He refers again to each in his discussion of ch. 18, on life within the community (pp. 428-29). But he only cites the phrases, without comment upon their radical signifi-

aptly says, Matthew combines the moral rigor of "A Communal Ethic of Perfection" with "The Hermeneutic of Mercy" in its portrait of Jesus and moral admonition.[66] These distinctive Matthean themes fit within the emphases above: Matthew's presentation of Jesus as the peacemaker and Jesus' call to his followers to be peacemakers, as children of their loving Father in heaven.[67]

I propose that "the greater righteousness" as moral achievement hinges on several features of narrative disclosure. First, at the beginning and end Jesus is God's presence with us — the bookends of Matthew. The Sermon on the Mount is bathed in the grace of God's presence. Second, as Peacemaker, Jesus subverts the Davidic notion of messianic rule by subjugating enemies. Rather, his kingly power is manifested in his healings and in his humble, meek kingship. Third, the possibility of his followers living the greater righteousness depends on grace-empowerment to do those things that Jesus teaches in the Sermon. Fourth, the empowerment for thinking, imagining, and doing depends on steeping oneself in the moral formation to which the entire Sermon beckons us. Fifth, Jesus' righteousness is greater in exposing the deeper heart-attitude that is also transgression of God's moral will: anger against a brother or sister, looking at a woman as a sexual object, rationalizing divorce with "good" reasons, and using oath-swearing to cloud integrity. Most distinctive is Jesus' command to love the enemy. In all these ways, the Sermon is more complete *(teleios)* in disclosing God's righteousness, love, and mercy.

An additional reality must be acknowledged. We need each other as Jesus' followers to attain Jesus' vision for the moral life. Though Leo Tolstoy called the individual qua individual to live the moral demands of the Sermon, Hauerwas says:

> I maintain that the Sermon on the Mount presupposes the existence of a community constituted by the practice of nonviolence, and it is unintelligible divorced from such a community. . . . I . . . suggest that the Sermon on the Mount constitutes and is constituted by a community that has

---

cance. Later he appeals to Romans 13:1-7 as the "*locus classicus*" for the Christian's responsibility to government (p. 440), and critiques J. H. Yoder's and Stanley Hauerwas's contributions (pp. 460-64).

66. Hays, *The Moral Vision*, pp. 97-101.

67. Matthew's frequent reference to God as Father, especially "your Father in heaven," used only when speaking to his disciples, not to the crowds, and derivative from his use of "my Father in heaven," has been well researched: Mowery, "God, Lord, and Father"; Marianne Meye Thompson, *The Promise of the Father*, pp. 105-14; Witherington and Ice, *The Shadow of the Almighty*, pp. 41-45.

learned that to live in the manner described in the Sermon requires learning to trust in others to help me so live. In other words, the object of the
Sermon on the Mount is to create dependence; it is to force us to need one
another.[68]

Being people of peace in personal, social, political dimensions is possible, but the formation process is long and often difficult. As in Mark, Jesus'
disciples in Matthew fail to grasp his teachings on discipleship, right up to the
end, expressed poignantly both in their striving for power (20:20-28) and by
one using a sword in Gethsemane (26:51). Indeed, this path to peace is not
confined to the realm of personal ethics but is immediately social and political as well, for Jesus and for us his followers.[69] This leads to a twofold statement that echoes through the ages, judging every epoch of history: "Put your
sword back into its place," and "for all who take the sword will perish by the
sword."[70] All Jesus' followers are beckoned to hear these words, to be hounded
by them so that the sword is not drawn from its sheath. Only then can we begin to attain the greater righteousness of loving our enemies,[71] praying for
our persecutors/abusers (Luke 6:27), and blessing those who curse us.

68. Hauerwas, *Unleashing the Scriptures,* p. 64. See similar emphases in Lohfink, *Jesus and
Community,* especially pp. 70-73; Hays, *Moral Vision,* pp. 304-6, 310 (point 10).

69. Yoder, *The Politics of Jesus.*

70. Further, Jesus says, "Do you think that I cannot appeal to my Father, and he will at
once send me more than twelve legions of angels?" It is clear that Jesus sees his death as the
means for God's will for his life-mission to be fulfilled. He trusted himself to his faithful Father,
and was vindicated in the resurrection as the faithful Son victorious over the powers of death.
The final commission to take the gospel to all peoples is a post-cross and resurrection declaration. The resurrection makes possible a new reality, presupposed by the Sermon, as it became
the catechesis for believers in the early church. The dialectic between the cross and resurrection
is essential for all Christian theology, be it Yoder's, Jenson's, or Moltmann's. Yoder has sometimes been criticized for making the cross central at the expense of the resurrection; Jenson has
been criticized for the opposite. Moltmann has maintained the dialectic well by focusing in his
first major book on *The Theology of Hope,* for which resurrection is an essential foundation. In
his second major book, *The Crucified God,* the cross is understood as core to the trinitarian relationship. See Bauckham's excellent exposition of Moltmann's theology, *The Theology of Jürgen
Moltmann.*

71. Alan Kreider has pointed out that Matt. 5:44, the command to love one's enemies, is
the most frequently cited verse from Matthew by the Church Fathers up to the time of Irenaeus.
The command itself is cited 17 times, as is the "This is my Son" declaration in the Transfiguration (17:5). But by expanding the count to include any part of 5:43-48, the number increases to
37, far higher than any other portion of Matthew. Kreider, *Worship and Evangelism in Pre-
Christendom,* p. 11, n. 6.

The Counter-Politics of Matthew's Royal Christology:
Son of David, Shepherd, Father

Peacemaking emphases are evident in Matthew's transformation of royal christology. The Gospel leaves no doubt that Jesus is King, a king specifically connected with God's promise to David (2 Sam. 7:13-14; Psalm 132, etc.). Elsewhere, I have argued that the titles "Son of David" and "Messiah-Christ" are treated with care in Matthew, in order to prepare for the climactic use of another preferred title in the passion narrative, "the Son of God."[72]

"Son of David," however, is used more often in this Gospel than in any other.[73] Its nine appearances make the point that Matthew intends his readers to see Jesus as heir to the promises made to David. Both the genealogy and the birth narratives stress this at the outset. But the title does not occur in the passion narrative; there Matthew uses "Son of God" to qualify and "shepherd" Jesus' identity as Davidic son.[74]

Three significant redactional themes are interrelated, and each connects to God's promise to David in 2 Sam. 7:13-14a: "*He shall build a house for my name, and I will establish the throne of his kingdom forever. I will be a father to him, and he shall be a son to me.*" The three themes are Matthew's distinctive use of the royal title "Son of David"; the second is his use of shepherd imagery, which, though present in Mark and Luke, is markedly important to Matthew; and Matthew's distinctive designation of God as my/your/our Father forty-four times. These three unique features in Matthew's christology, taken as a whole, function as a most incisive subversion of messianic hope based upon the "imperial" model.[75]

Of the six uses of the title "Son of David"[76] in the public ministry of Jesus,

---

72. Swartley, *Israel's Scripture Traditions*, pp. 198-203, 215-32.

73. Apart from the six uses cited in the discussion, the other three are: in 1:1, Jesus the Messiah's genealogy is of "the son of David"; Joseph, in 1:20, by whom Jesus born of a virgin is legal heir as "son of David"; and in 22:42 the Pharisees declare that the Messiah is to be "the son of David."

74. Swartley, *Israel's Scripture Traditions*, p. 225.

75. Warren Carter has developed the anti-imperial and counter-imperial emphases of Matthew. See Carter, *Matthew and Empire* and *Matthew and the Margins*. See also his article "Are There Imperial Texts in the Class?" Carter argues that the word *eagle(s)* refers to empires generically in Jewish and Greco-Roman literature, and here to Rome specifically. If 24:28 read, "Where the corpses are, there the eagles are also," his case would be more persuasive. He ably argues against identifying *eagles* with *vultures,* common in translation and commentary history.

76. Brian Nolan in his exacting textual study of Son of David in Matthew, sixty-five pages, fails to see Matthew's critique of the title. *Son of David* holds sway along with *Son of God* for Nolan, *Royal Son of God.* But see my discussion in *Israel's Scripture Traditions*, pp. 220-27.

both Galilean and Jerusalem, five are connected with Jesus' healing ministry (9:27-31; 12:22-24; 15:21-28; 20:29-34; 21:1-11; 21:14-16).[77] Of these in 21:1-11 Jesus is portrayed as the King coming into the holy city fulfilling the Davidic messianic hope. What is the significance of connecting Jesus as Son of David to healing? Mauser links the healings to the messianic expectation that the in-breaking kingdom of heaven would be marked by healing (Isa. 35:5-6; 61:1-2a). So Matt. 9:35: "Jesus went about . . . proclaiming the good news of the kingdom, and curing every disease and every sickness." In the midst of his catena of ten healing miracles (8:1–9:34), Matthew includes a "fulfillment" text: "This was to fulfill what has been spoken through the prophet Isaiah, 'He took our infirmities and bore our diseases'" (8:17). The point is clear also in Matthew 10, Jesus' missionary discourse to the twelve as they are sent out. It begins by stating that Jesus "gave them authority over unclean spirits, to cast them out, and to cure every disease and every sickness" (10:1). Later, Jesus commands, "As you go, proclaim the good news, 'The kingdom of heaven has come near.' Cure the sick, raise the dead, cleanse the lepers, cast out demons" (10:7-8a).[78] Indeed, Jesus responds similarly to John the Baptist's query: is Jesus really the expected Messiah?: "Go and tell John what you hear and see: the blind receive their sight, the lame walk, the lepers are cleansed, the deaf hear, the dead are raised, and the poor have good news brought to them" (11:4). Clearly, Matthew considers healing an identifying mark of the kingdom's coming and of Jesus' own identity as Messiah.

In light of this prominent association between healing and Jesus' messianic proclamation of the dawning kingdom, Matthew's use of the "Son of David" title in healing narratives qualifies, even subverts, the dominant metanarrative of a messianic "Son of David" who destroys enemies to gain peace. Of the many messianic portraits in the OT and the early Judaism,[79] a major stream portrays the Davidic Messiah establishing imperial rule in which enemies, especially Gentiles, are destroyed. Paul Yokota has studied Matthew's use of OT texts considered messianic in Judaism and makes a persuasive case

77. See Mauser, *The Gospel of Peace*, pp. 50-51. Mauser links the healings also to the inauguration of the reign of peace (Zech. 9:9-11). For fuller treatment of this topic see Christoph Burger, *Jesus als Davidssohn*.

78. Mauser treats this text in parallel with Luke 10:8-11 and notes that it follows the imparting of *peace* to the house if the peace is accepted (vv. 5-6); the healing is a concrete means of demonstrating that peace has come. Mauser says, "The gift of peace is an alternative way of speaking about healing and the closing in of God's kingdom. In other words, the peace offered by the missionaries is the same as the proclamation of the arrival of the kingdom of God with its resultant effect of healing" (*Gospel of Peace*, p. 55).

79. For the variety of portraits see the essays in *The Messiah*, ed. Charlesworth, especially Charlesworth's introductory article, "From Messianology to Christology: Problems and Prospects," pp. 3-35.

that Mattthew's Jesus chose different texts than those prevalent in early Judaism, with all its plurality, or reinterpreted key texts. For example, "Matthew accentuates Jesus as the non-violent and humble king. Early Jewish literature often envisages the royal Messiah as destroying the enemies of Israel by force, a picture derived from Gen 49:9-10, Num 24:17, Isa 11:1-5; Ps 2:8-9, and Dan 7:13-14. Matthew however does not *explicitly* cite any of these texts. . . ."[80]

But other notions of messianic expectation were present also. These other notions are those that Matthew selects and stresses. This selection and emphasis have the effect of subverting the political domination strand of hope connected with the Davidic Messiah and converting it to a fundamentally different, indeed peaceable messianic, portrait. Significantly, Matthew cites an extended Isaiah servant text (12:18-20, from Isa. 42:1-4, 9) to warrant Jesus curing all the sick in the great crowds that followed him (12:15). Further, these texts speak of the Gentiles as those who receive the messianic blessing (see below).

In addition to the healing narratives associated with "Son of David," other features expand the distinctive portrait of Jesus. As Mauser observes, the key text Matt. 9:35, which links kingdom of heaven with "curing every disease and every sickness," is followed immediately by portraying Jesus as the compassionate shepherd of the crowds who "were harassed and helpless, like sheep without a shepherd" (9:36).[81]

This shepherd image, Matthew's second distinctive theme, connects

---

80. Yokota, "Jesus the Messiah of Israel," p. 312. Yokota shows that a major stream of intertestamental texts draws on OT messianic texts to portray a coming Davidic Messiah who would rule in righteousness and in many of these texts an imperial messiah would rule, destroying enemies. The most prominent are:

- Gen. 49:10, cited in 4 Ezra 11-12 and 1Q28b;
- Num. 24:17, cited in Ps. 150, *Sib. Or.* 5, 4Q175, 4Q285, Jos. *J.W.* 6.312-14, and Bar Kosiba;
- 2 Sam. 7:11-14, 16, 26-29, cited in *Pss. Sol.* 17;
- Ps. 2:7, cited in 4 Ezra 13, *Pss. Sol.* 17, 1 *En. Sim.*;
- Isa. 11:1-5 cited in part in 4 Ezra 13 (though here the Lord is possibly the Warrior), 2 Bar. 36-40, *Pss. Sol.* 17, 1 *En. Sim.*, 1Q28b, 4Q161, 4Q285;
- Dan. 7:13-14, 22, cited in 4 Ezra 11-12, 4 Ezra 13, 1 *En. Sim.*

Both Micah 4 and 5 are cited in 1Q28b also with military, violent portraits of the Messiah's work. Bar Kosiba (CE 135), leader of the second Jewish revolt, is presented, of course, in accord with this tradition. Other texts, lesser in number, are cited to denote the Davidic Messiah, but not necessarily as one who violently destroys enemies, but rather judges righteously (*pace* Isa. 11:3-4): Amos 9 cited in 4Q174; Ps. 132 cited in Sir. 51 and Ps. 154; Ps. 2 in 4Q174; 2 Sam. 7 cited in Sir. 47 and 4Q174; and Gen. 49 cited in 4Q252. Most significant, Isaiah's Servant Songs cited in 1 *En. Sim.* at three different places portray the Messiah peaceably, even including Gentiles into the messianic kingdom.

81. The image, sheep without a shepherd, occurs in the OT for Israel: Num. 27:17; 1 Kgs. 22:17; 2 Chron. 18:16; Jdt. 11:19; Ezek. 34:5.

also to 2 Sam. 7:13ff. For God chose shepherd David to be the royal leader of Israel (2 Sam. 5:2; Mic. 5:2, 4-5a; Ps. 78:70-72). The last line in the Micah text describes this shepherd: "he shall be the one of peace."[82]

Matt. 2:6 explicitly designates the newborn babe, Jesus Messiah, as shepherd: "And you, Bethlehem, in the land of Judah, are by no means least among the rulers of Judah; for from you shall come a ruler, who will shepherd my people Israel." Mauser notes that this verse "is a combined quotation of Micah 5:2 and 4 [5:1 and 3, LXX] and 2 Samuel 5:2 ('It is you who shall be shepherd of my people Israel' spoken of David)."[83] Warren Carter uses the phrase, "Jesus will shepherd/govern my people Israel," an apt way to capture the double force, i.e., a caring gentle rule.[84]

The shepherd motif recurs throughout Matthew (2:6; 9:36; 10:6, 16; 14:14; 15:24, 32; 18:12-14; 25:32). In 9:36 Jesus has compassion on the crowd because "they were harassed and helpless, like sheep without a shepherd." J. P. Heil has persuasively argued that the Jewish Scriptures provide the inspiration for Matthew's shepherd portrait and that Ezekiel 34 in particular provides the entire semantic field for Matthew's varied uses.[85] The combined quotation of Mic. 5:2 and 2 Sam. 5:2 makes explicit that "the future Davidic leader is God's messianic shepherd and that the people of Israel are God's sheep," the express point of Ezek. 34:23: "I will set up over them one shepherd and he will shepherd (LXX poimanei) them, my servant David, and he will be their shepherd."[86] In Ezekiel 34 (and 37) God declares judgment on the shepherd-leaders of Israel because they are false shepherds, self-gratifying and not caring for the sheep. Other OT shepherd texts may be alluded to as well,[87] but the case for Ezekiel 34 (and 37) is strong. Paul Yokota cites numerous features in Matthew's use of shepherd that suggest Ezekiel 34 as his primary text source. Among these are: (1) The immediate context in Matthew 9 portrays Jesus teaching, preaching, and especially healing, reflecting shepherding (note Ezek. 34:4, 16: "strengthening the weak, healing the sick, and binding up the injured"). (2) As Matthew notes twice: Jesus is sent only to the lost sheep of the house of Israel (10:6; 15:24). (3) The reclining on the grass in

---

82. God too was envisioned as Shepherd of Israel (see Psalms 23, 80). The shepherd image was frequently used in the Ancient Near East as a royal image (cf. Isa. 44:28, for reference to Cyrus as God's shepherd).

83. Mauser, Gospel of Peace, p. 59.

84. Carter, Matthew and the Margins, p. 79.

85. Heil, "Ezekiel 34 and the Narrative Strategy of the Shepherd and Sheep Metaphor in Matthew," quoting p. 700.

86. Heil, "Ezekiel 34," pp. 699-700.

87. E.g., Jer. 3:15; 12:10; 22:22; 23:1-8; Ezek. 34:5-6; 1 Enoch 90:6; Bar. 7:13.

Matthew's feeding narratives echoes Ezekiel's emphasis on feeding the sheep with good pasture and lying down in rest (vv. 14-15). (4) In both feeding narratives (14:14; 15:32) Jesus has compassion on the multitudes (his flock?), an emotion congruent with a true shepherd. (5) Matthew presents Jesus' ministry as a restoration of Yahweh's people, and this matches the emphasis of Ezekiel 34.[88] To these points I would add that just as Matthew portrays Jesus as the messianic shepherd-king who calls forth peacemakers as children of God, so Ezekiel portrays God promising to make with his people a "covenant of peace" (34:23-25; 37:24-26; similarly Isa. 54:10). In both Ezekiel 34 and 37 God promises to be indeed the shepherd of the people bestowing manifold blessings of shalom, safety, and food in abundance. "My dwelling place shall be with them, and I will be their God, and they shall be my people" (37:27).[89]

Other texts that identify Jesus with a/the Shepherd are Matt. 10:6; 15:24; and 26:31 (the last quoting Zech. 13:7). Further, in the parable of the judgment of the nations (25:31-46), Jesus likens the "Son of man" to a shepherd who separates the goats from the sheep. The language of the parable also echoes the imagery of Ezek. 34. The parable of the lost sheep (18:10-14) combines the images of shepherd and father. The parable is framed by two uses of "my Father who is in heaven" (though the latter has as a textual variant "your Father"). The parable itself narrates how a man has a hundred sheep and, when one is lost, searches for the stray until it is found. Though shepherd is not used (rather *anthrōpos*), yet the focus on sheep implies a shepherd. The pericope joins the shepherd imagery, echoing 2 Sam. 5:2 and Mic. 5:2, 4-5a, with the Father-Son imagery (2 Sam. 7:12-14), which occurs here implicitly in "my Father" (vv. 10, 14 variant reading).

This father-son imagery of the parable anticipates the third major distinctive Matthean theme that connects with 2 Sam. 7:13ff., for Matthew frequently designates God as Father.[90] This Matthean distinctive has been developed fully by Marianne Meye Thompson and Julian Sheffield,[91] as well as by Robert L. Mowery earlier. Not only is the number of forty-four uses of *patēr*, "father," for God impressive, in contrast to Mark's four uses and Luke's seventeen, but as both Sheffield and Mary Rose D'Angelo[92] have shown, Matthew

---

88. Yokota, "Jesus the Messiah of Israel," pp. 170-72, 197-203.

89. See Lind's exposition of these texts in *Ezekiel*, pp. 273-80.

90. A fourth connection, not developed here but pointed out by Yokota (chapter 3, p. 71), is the Lord's promise to build a house for David and Matt. 16:18, where Jesus says, "I will build my church."

91. Marianne Meye Thompson, *The Promise of the Father*, pp. 135, 141-48, 152-54; Sheffield, "The Father in the Gospel of Matthew."

92. D'Angelo, "Abba and 'Father': Imperial Theology and the Jesus Traditions."

divests patriarchal notions by muting the role of earthly fathers in the narrative and replacing it with the pervasive and immanent presence of the heavenly Father.[93] Most significant is 23:9, "call no one your father on earth, for you have one Father — the one in heaven."[94]

The significance of this feature in Matthew, bluntly put, is to subordinate Jesus' royal lineage as "Son of David" to Jesus' identity as "Son of God" by repeatedly affirming God to be "my Father in heaven." This bold exchange subverts the royal Davidic promise of its imperialist trope, dominant in numerous messianic texts in early Judaism. These emphases, evoking the royal promise in 2 Sam. 7:13-14, provide strong literary and theological support for Warren Carter's thesis that although Matthew is not totally free of depicting a "future violent and forceful imposition of God's empire (13:41-42; 24:27-31)," he masterfully presents God's reign as a critical and subversive alternative to imperial domination. Matthew stresses, rather, "mercy not violence (4:23-25), service not domination (20:25-28)."[95]

As pointed out above in the discussion of the relation of 5:9-10 to 5:44-45, 48 Matthew's peacemaking and love of enemies, even when persecuted, mark identity as God's children and, therefore, God as their Father.[96] God as *Father* in 5:45, 48 functions as moral warrant for the conduct of God's children — literally "sons" to show the connection to the royal Davidic promise (*huioi tou patros* in v. 45 links to *huioi theou* in the "peacemakers" text of v. 9). Both Jesus' command to love enemies and his "performative" (i.e., calling into being) blessing on peacemakers mark the identity of God's children. In calling his disciples to become "sons of God" by becoming peacemakers (5:9) and loving the enemy (5:45) Jesus alludes to his own divine Sonship. Mat-

---

93. Matthew replaces patriarchy with paternity, as does the larger movement of Scripture. See Swartley, "God as Father: Patriarchy or Paternity?"

94. Carter notes not only that *father* in Matthew's social world setting "denotes religious, imperial, and social authority," but that the term was applied to Zeus, religious teachers, and also the emperor (e.g. the Roman senate called "Augustus the *Pater Patriae*, the father of the fatherland; Statius calls Domitian 'father of Rome' and 'of the world'"), in *Matthew and the Margins*, p. 454. In this respect Matthew's oft-used phrase "in heaven" — with Father and other uses as well, especially "kingdom of heaven" — may indeed represent what Jonathan Pennington has called "The Kingdom of Heaven against All Earthly Kingdoms" in his essay with that title. Thus Matthew's unique phrase "kingdom of heaven" is "a theme which serves to highlight God's universal sovereignty and to contrast the radical ethics of God's eschatological kingdom with those of the Roman Empire and other earthly kingdoms" (Pennington, p. 356).

95. *Matthew and Empire*, p. 176.

96. Matt. 5:16 draws on this notion also. The "good works" done by Jesus' disciples do not bear witness to their own goodness, but lead people to "glorify their Father in heaven." As children, they point to God.

thew's frequent uses of "Father" (2x; 11:25, 26), "the Father" (4x; 11:27b, 27c; 24:36; 28:19), "my (heavenly) Father (in heaven)" (15x; 7:21; 10:32-33; 11:27a; 12:50; 15:13; 16:17; 18:10, 19, 35; 20:23; 25:34; 26:29, 39, 42, 53), "your (pl.) Father (in heaven)" (14x; 5:16, 45, 48; 6:1, 8, 14, 15, 26, 32; 7:11 [10x in Sermon]; 10:20, 29; 18:14; 23:9), and "our Father" (6:9) disclose Jesus' personal identity as Son of God. All these uses speak of God in contexts where Jesus addresses his disciples and the crowds, which in Matthew are regarded as potential disciples.[97] God as Father (*my* Father) is first of all *Jesus'* birthright and prerogative. Derivatively, "*your* Father" occurs to denote Jesus' disciples whose character and conduct reflect that of the Father in heaven (5:16, 45, 48; 6:14-15; 12:50; 18:35; 21:31-32; 23:9; 25:31-36). Significantly, *my Father* and *your Father* join in *our Father* (6:9).[98] On the basis of his own filial relationship to God as Father, Jesus opens to his disciples the same relationship with God. Therefore they are to call no one father on earth (23:9).

This new relationship requires rethinking the very nature of the expected Davidic kingship. Becoming a new family of God (12:46-50, cf. 10:32-37; 19:29-30) means that questions like "Who is the greatest in the kingdom of heaven?" (18:1) and the sons of Zebedee's mother's demand, "Command that these two sons of mine may sit, one at your right hand and one at your left, in your kingdom" (20:21, RSV), reverberate Peter's Satanic temptation that Jesus denounced (16:22-23). To reflect Jesus' and the Father's nature, they are not to lord it over others, but rather become servants to one another and to all (20:26-27), feeding the hungry, giving drink to the thirsty, welcoming the stranger, clothing the naked, visiting the sick, and befriending prisoners (25:35-36).

Thus Matthew not only subverts the imperial domination mode, whether in Judaism's messianic hope or Gentile Roman rule, but he accentuates loving enemies, peacemaking, and good deeds done by the Father's children so that people glorify the heavenly Father (5:16). These behaviors are the identifying marks of God's reign inaugurated by Jesus.

97. For these data I am indebted originally to Robert L. Mowery for his speech and handout at the SBL meeting in Boston, 1987, "God the Father in the Gospel of Matthew." See now his companion essay: "God, Lord and Father," in which Mowery compares the uses of God, Lord and Father. Matthew is the only Synoptic Gospel to use *patēr* almost as often (44x) as God (51x); Lord occurs 18x to address God.

98. Cf. Thompson's comments in *The Promise of the Father,* pp. 111-13, 137, 162, approximating mine above. But neither Thompson nor Sheffield notes the dissonance between God as Father and the title Son of David, together with the triumphal notions associated with Jewish expectations of subjugating Gentiles (i.e., lording it over them) to fulfill the Davidic kingdom promise in 2 Sam. 7:13ff.

A Venn diagram portrays these three distinctive Matthean peaceable themes:

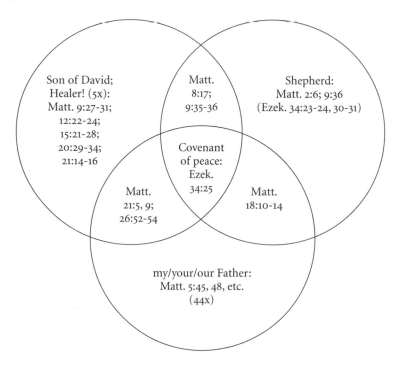

Matthew's Peaceable Kingdom
Jesus' Royal Identity in Matthew: Fulfillment of 2 Samuel 7:13-14

My use of the word *peace* in the center of this diagram connotes peace not in the narrow sense of its word usage, but denotes also the transformation of royal messianic hope. Such transformation toward peaceable living is signified by Jesus' teachings and his own manner of life, as portrayed in the three dominant themes of the diagram and their associative emphases that the Gospel narrates. My analysis of these distinctive Matthean emphases complements Warren Carter's contribution that reads Matthew as a counter-narrative to Rome's territorial imperial oppressive omnipresence, the *Sitz im Leben* of Matthew's church community. As he puts it:

> My reading perspective is that Matthew's gospel is a counter-narrative. It is a work of resistance written from and for a minority community of disciples committed to Jesus, the agent of God's saving presence and empire. The gospel shapes their identity and lifestyle as an alternative community.

It strengthens this community to resist the dominant Roman imperial and synagogal control. It anticipates Jesus' return when Jesus will complete God's salvific purposes in establishing God's reign or empire over all, including Rome.[99]

Carter develops his view of Matthew's distinctive moral emphases as a counter-narrative that empowers the community to live the Jesus lifestyle.[100] My emphases concur with Carter's portrayal of Jesus' moral teaching, but do not require his reconstruction of a localized marginalized community as such, though such lifestyle would marginalize believers throughout the empire to some degree. I examine Matthew's distinctive contribution against the backdrop, not so much of Rome, but of Israel's own messianic hopes. Matthew's extensive OT quotations attest his orientation to Jewish identity, consciousness, and messianic hope. The narrative fosters counter-identity to imperial messianic hope that does violence against enemies. Matthew grounds this emphasis in his christological portrait of Jesus.

While Matthew's primary focus is the transformation of dominant Jewish messianic hopes, this does not disallow narrative strategies that distinguish the Jesus-faith communities from the Roman imperial rule, as 20:25 makes pointedly clear: don't be like the rulers of the Gentiles. Also, Robert L. Mowery's contribution lends support to this notion of contrast-community to Roman rule. He shows that Matthew uses a unique form for "Son of God" *(theou huios)* at 14:33; 27:43, 54, the very form that occurs in titles for first-century Roman emperors — for five that together ruled nearly one hundred years.[101] Thus it is likely that for Matthew and some of his readers this distinctive form of this christological title in Matthew evoked Roman imperial rule.

99. Carter, *Matthew and the Margins*, xvii. I demur, however, on Carter's social reconstruction of Matthew's community, and his view that Matthew wrote from and for a small marginalized community in Syria. Here I find the arguments set forth in Richard Bauckham's *The Gospels for All Christians* more compelling. Further, I find Carter's social reconstruction of a small marginalized community to be helpful, but inconsequential to his excellent insights in his commentary. Those insights stand independently of the reconstruction.

100. See Carter's excellent 12-point summary in *Matthew and the Margins*, pp. 45-46. In his serial listing of fathers from Israel's past, he misses, however, the most important for Matthew, i.e., David.

101. Mowery, "Son of God in Roman Imperial Titles and Matthew." Mowery fails to mention, however, that 27:54, the climactic use, has textual variants that give pause to his conclusion: B D and ℵ*, with ἦν τοῦ coming between υἱός and θεοῦ, support the reverse order, as occurs in Mark 15:39. But since 14:33 and 27:43?are distinctive to Matthew, with the uncontested reading θεοῦ υἱός, it is likely that the same is the original in 27:54 also. Stassen's treatment of the puzzling verse of 7:6 in the Sermon also lends support to this context of Roman occupation and oppressor rule for understanding the Gospel.

Other strands of evidence in Matthew confirm my point that Matthew intends to subvert and transform the "imperial" domination emphasis in much of the Davidic messianism. One such is the role of Gentiles in the narrative, both in his Galilean ministry and also in his infancy and passion narratives. I have developed the point of Gentile inclusion for the Galilean ministry in an earlier book.[102] The key texts are three summary statements, evidence of Matthew's hand and purpose: 4:23-25; 9:35-36; 15:29-31. In each, Gentiles are either recipients of or co-participants in praise to Jesus as healer who does all things well. In the infancy narrative, the visit of the magi, who "observed his star at its rising,"[103] signals the inclusive Gentile stance of the book. This Gentile inclusion culminates in the Roman centurion's confession at the cross, unmasking and exposing the presumed imperial sovereignty.[104] The final scene on a mountain in Galilee (28:16-20) highlights both Jesus' royal kingship and the kingdom's inclusion of the nations (*ethnē*, Gentiles).[105] This scene also subverts Satan's power over the kingdoms of the earth, as offered to Jesus in the temptation. Dorothy Jean Weaver puts it, ". . . the Risen Jesus subverts the hegemonic claims of Satan altogether, *and by the same token those of the Roman emperor on Satan's behalf*, when he announces (28:18b), 'All authority in heaven *and on earth* has been given to me.'"[106] Or, as Carter puts it, "The center of the divine purposes is not Rome but the community that acknowledges God's reign . . . Caesar has power but God is sovereign."[107]

The clincher to this thesis that Matthew transforms the "Son of David" messianic hopes of political triumph by crushing Israel's enemies, notably the Romans, is his portrayal of Jesus' triumphal entry (21:1-16). Jesus enters Jerusalem in humility, riding upon the royal, but lowly donkey (1 Kgs. 1:38), thus enacting the fulfillment of the peaceable vision of Zech. 9:9-11. By quoting from the latter text to interpret the triumphal entry, Matthew repudiates the view of the Davidic Messiah as a military conqueror forcefully freeing Israel from political oppression, crushing the Gentiles. John Collins notes, "Zech 9:9 is never used as a messianic prophecy in the Scrolls or the Pseudepigrapha."[108] Matthew's choice to explicitly quote this text is most significant, since by doing so, he makes messianic what was not before so understood. Further,

102. *Israel's Scripture Traditions*, pp. 63-67.

103. "Star" carried messianic connotation. See Num. 24:17.

104. Dorothy Jean Weaver makes this point in "Thus You Will Know Them by Their Fruits."

105. See my discussion in *Israel's Scripture Traditions*, pp. 228-32.

106. Weaver, "By Their Fruits," p. 125.

107. Carter, *Matthew and Empire*, pp. 63-64.

108. John J. Collins, *The Scepter and the Star*, p. 206.

he does not quote those explicitly messianic texts in the intertestamental traditions that *expected military destruction of the enemies.*[109]

Dierdre Good, in her insightful study, *Jesus the Meek King,*[110] rightly holds that Matthew's significant portrayal of Jesus in the triumphal entry text as "meek" *(praüs)* is to be interpreted in light of 5:5, "Blessed are the meek . . . ," and 11:29, where Jesus describes himself, "I am meek and humble of heart."[111] In her thorough lexical study of *meek,* Good concludes that it belongs to "the category of positive moral qualities: what is good, kind, just, holy, perfect, humble, gentle, blessed, merciful."[112] In the political portrait in Hellenistic writings, the "ideal king" *learns* meekness through discipline in control and rejection of anger, which enables him to become a gentle, benevolent king. Further, meekness is a virtue that generally belonged to the female and slave roles in both Judaic and Hellenistic societies.

Good proposes that Matthew's presentation shares elements of the ideal king notion, but differs crucially in that Jesus' meekness is declared in a "revelational" context (11:25-27). Thus Jesus' meekness is one with his dependence on and obedience to his Father. This in turn harks back to his temptations where he refuses exercise of power and rejects Satan's enticements: to make stones into bread, to jump off the temple, and to possess the kingdoms of this world. Jesus' filial obedience to his Father means resisting any such presumptions upon his divine power as Son of God. Rather, he lives the model that he sets forth also for his followers, to be meek and humble in order to enter the kingdom (18:4). This disposition-virtue contrasts to the Gentiles' tyrant-lords who abuse their subjects (20:24-28), a teaching that just precedes Jesus' triumphal entry.

Good's contribution, however, must be supplemented, perhaps also tempered, by understandings of humility and meekness from the OT-Jewish tradi-

109. Collins says that in this text as in 4Q245, "this king will bring about universal peace, . . . apparently by military victory" (*Scepter and Star,* p. 207). But this misreads the text and fails to note the significance of Matthew quoting this text and *not those* in Yokota's list (see n. 80 above). Collins too treats these texts extensively. Numerous other OT texts bolster the Zech. 9 portrayal by their antimilitary imagery and emphases (Pss. 20:6-7; 33:16-17; 44:6; 46:9-10; 76:3; 147:10; Isa. 31:1-3).

110. Good, *The Meek King,* especially pp. 18, 26-27, 35, 70, 82, 92-93, 104-105. Good points out how this trait of Jesus was stressed in the *Didache,* by Ignatius, and by the desert Fathers. See also Mauser, *Gospel of Peace,* p. 52, for his excellent treatment of this emphasis.

111. New translations that use *gentle* for *praüs* in 11:29 and 21:5 obscure the significance of this emphasis on meekness by Matthew. Here note Warren Carter's excellent portrayal of Jesus' word about his *yoke* as "easy and light" in comparison to imperial uses of yoke in the Jewish literature of the time and the Roman world as well. See *Matthew and Empire,* pp. 122-23.

112. Good, p. 13.

tions. Klaus Wengst has persuasively argued that in this tradition humility is not a virtue attributed to a noble king but a condition of humiliation in which one stands in solidarity with the poor and oppressed.[113] Numerous texts portray the humble person in contrast to the oppressing rulers and wealthy, prosperous people. Those humble and meek, often associated with the poor *(anawim)*, do not strive to become rich and powerful but, casting their lot with the poor, trust in God for vindication. In light of this emphasis, Wengst understands 11:28-30 as parallel to Jesus' blessing to the poor in the first Beatitude. Jesus identifies with those who know the burden of slave-like toil, those who are exhausted from life's demands upon the poor. The "yoke" is not Pharisaic legalism, but Roman occupation and its economic oppression. Wengst writes:

> the two terms (πραΰς and ταπεινός) makes it evident that the former cannot be understood along the lines of the Graeco-Roman tradition, where πραΰς/*clementia* denotes the virtue of the ruler. It is not a matter of replacing a harsh rule with a humane one. πραΰς and ταπεινός stand side-by-side in the Septuagint as a translation of *'ānī wādāl*. This is a designation for the impoverished and humiliated who deliberately accept their situation, set their hope on God, withdraw from the complex of violence and practise a different form of justice and righteousness from those who rule by force. This connection is deliberately affirmed by the addition of the words "of heart" to "lowly."[114]

Must one choose between Good and Wengst on this matter, or *should* one? The portrait of the humiliated that Wengst presents accords with Jesus' teaching throughout Matthew, except the key fact that Matthew's Jesus does not shy away from royal identity. Rather, the babe born in Bethlehem, not Herod, is already and will remain the king of the Jews, even though as a babe Jesus is powerless and Herod exudes power, even to destroy all Bethlehem's infants. Further, given Mowery's study of the designation *theou huios* (son of God) as claimed by or ascribed to five Roman emperors, the exact same distinctive term-designation for Jesus three times in the narrative suggests that Jesus is proclaimed by Matthew as God's emperor as well. The climactic scene in 28:16-20 verifies the same.[115] Hence my judgment is that the triumphal entry in Matthew does not reject the notion of Jesus as messianic king, but

113. Wengst, *Humility*. Wengst bases his view on study of texts such as Amos 2:6-7; Isa. 11:3b-5; Zeph. 3:1b-13; Psalm 37; *I Enoch* 94:6–104:13; Prov. 15:33; Sirach 2:4-5; 3:17-20; 4:1-10; 7:11; 12:7, and several Qumran texts (1QH 5:20-22; 1QS 11).

114. Wengst, *Humility*, p. 39.

115. See my treatment of this in *Israel's Scripture Traditions*, pp. 228-32.

transforms it, utilizing both traditions of meaning for humility. The "ideal king" character is not achieved by some self-exertion or rivalry but by divine character and status that is God-granted to the one who hears at his baptism: "This is my Son, the beloved one" (3:17).

The triumphal entry has its interpretive climax in Jesus' cleansing of the temple, in which Matthew stresses Jesus' healing of the blind and the lame in the temple, and the outcry of the children's praise. Here in 21:16 Jesus quotes Psalm 8:2: "Yes; have you never read, 'Out of the mouths of infants and nursing babies you have prepared praise for yourself'?" For Matthew the response of the crowd in vv. 9-11 is ambiguous.[116] Yes, Matthew wants Jesus acclaimed "Son of David"; but he does not trust the crowd's acclaim, only the children's. Matthew's fulfillment-quotation of Zech. 9:9 interprets the entry as that of a peaceable, meek and humble king.[117] But since Matthew knows that the stories to follow do not show rejoicing, he substitutes for the first line of Zechariah 9:9, "Rejoice, greatly . . . ," a line from Isa. 62:11, "Say to the daughter of Zion." The change thus makes the entire quotation "an evangelistic challenge to unconverted Israel."[118] In this way the quotation stands in tension with the crowds' acclaim in vv. 9-11; it sets forth the moral character of "Hosanna to the Son of David." Indeed, the triumphal entry fits hand-in-glove with the Son of humanity's humble servanthood in 20:20-28.

By healing the blind and the lame in the temple, Jesus violated David's prohibition in 2 Sam. 5:8, which forbade the blind and the lame to enter the temple. In keeping with Matthew's earlier portrait of Jesus (twice quoting Hos. 6:6 that God desires mercy, 9:13; 12:7), Jesus is a minister of mercy. By ending the commerce of robbery, and healing instead, Jesus defines the proper cultic activity of the temple, even if it means revising the law of David — thus anticipating the "Son/Lord of David" riddle in 22:44. In Matthew the temple "cleansing" carries forward the prophetic vision of Isaiah 56 of the in-

---

116. Daniel Patte, *Gospel of Matthew,* pp. 286-88.

117. As Paul Yokota puts it in his study of Matthew's use of OT messianic texts, "While Zech. 9:9 is easily understood as a 'royal messianic' text, its messianic use is conspicuously absent in early Judaism. Matthew's use of Zech. 9:9 which describes a *non-military* ruler riding on (a) donkey(s), not a war horse, highlights the non-military nature of his messianic theology" ("Jesus the Messiah of Israel," pp. 268-69).

118. Gundry, *Matthew,* p. 408. Further, unlike Mark's rendering of Isaiah 56:7 as a rhetorical question, Matthew makes it indicative ("He said to them, 'It is written, "My house shall be called a house of prayer," but you are making it a den of robbers'"). It is thus a pronouncement on the will of God for the temple, a sharp contrast to its present functioning as "a den of robbers."

119. "Blind and lame" refers to the Jebusites in 2 Sam. 5:8. To exclude the "blind and lame" per se arose from misunderstanding. See Swartley, *Israel's Scripture Traditions,* p. 174, especially n. 58.

clusive messianic portrait of Jesus (Gentiles, foreigners, eunuchs) and the peaceable Son of David Messiah depicted in Zechariah 9. By challenging David's prohibition against the "blind and lame," Matthew's Jesus reverses David's policy against the enemy. Jesus, Son of David, the compassionate healer, welcomes the "enemy" into the temple.

For the blind and the lame, even Israel's Jebusite enemies,[119] salvation has now come to the temple! And the children (echo Ps. 8:2) acclaim it: "Hosanna to the Son of David." This is Matthew's version of Mark's "for all nations." Rather than exclude, Jesus welcomed and healed the lame and blind. He transformed a condition of enmity into a symbol and space of *shalom:* the enemy is welcomed into the holy place.

The portrait of Jesus as peaceable messianic king, transforming military, warrior traditions associated with a Davidic messiah, is compelling. Matthew has done well in portraying Jesus as a peaceable, meek, and humble king.[120] Jesus' response to the crowd that comes into the Garden of Gethsemane armed with clubs and swords and to Peter who struck with a sword the high priest's slave is his definitive stand against violence, even to defend himself (26:52-54). Three points disclose Jesus' stance: "All who take the sword will perish by the sword"; he could appeal to his Father to call a legion of angels to free him, but he refuses; he regards his stance as a fulfillment of Scripture. Jesus clearly distances himself from any violent, military way to achieve God's purpose. His restoration of Israel and gospel of peace for both Israel and the Gentiles are possible only by choosing the nonviolent way.

Matthew thus transforms the imperial messianic Son of David metanarrative with a counter "political" messianic narrative in which Jesus as meek king and savior shows the way to peaceable thought and life. Those who would disciple all nations, "teaching them to obey everything that I have commanded you" (28:20),[121] including peacemaking and love of enemies, are promised the blessings of the Beatitudes. Because Jesus knew God as "my Father," they, too, as God's children, address God as "Abba." They are assured of God's presence in Jesus, Emmanuel, "God with us" (1:23) "to the end of the age" (28:20b).

120. Some apocalyptic scenes (13:41-42; 24:27-31) are consummation-judgments that belong to the divine prerogative. They do not provide warrant for the moral practices of Jesus' disciples.

121. Dorothy Jean Weaver has shown well the integrated relationship between Matthew's mission emphasis and the peacemaking gospel in Matthew ("As Sheep in the Midst of Wolves"). See also my summary of Daly's *Christian Biblical Ethics* in Appendix 1. Daly makes the same point.

Ulrich Luz's Arrangement of the Sermon on the Mount (Matthew 5–7)

5:1-2
Situation

Framework

7:28–8:1a
Reaction of hearers

I: crowds, teach, ascend/descend . . . mountain

5:3-16
Introduction

Leading in/Leading out

7:13-27
Conclusion

I: kingdom of heaven
twice: 5:3, 10; 7:21
F: 5:3-10 3d person, 7:21-27
5:11-16 2d person, 7:13-20

5:17-20

Introit/Conclusion
of the main section

7:12

I: law and prophets

Main section

5:21-48
Antitheses

6:19–7:11
Possessions
judging, and
prayer

L: 59 lines in Nestle for each

6:1-6

6:16-18

Righteousness
before God

6:7-15

The Lord's Prayer
with frame

Correspondences:
I = inclusions
L = correspondence in the length of the sections*
F = other formal correspondences
Cf. also the frame 4:23–9:35 at Matt. 4:23-25, above p. 203 (in Luz)

*Correspondence in length is found elsewhere in Matthew, cf. (Luz's) introduction,
p. 38. . . . With the antitheses, the length of the antitheses 1-3 and 4-6 correspond
exactly, cf. (Luz's) introduction to 5:21-48, n. 1.

4 Mark: Gospel of the Way, Crucified Messiah

So Jesus called them and said to them, "You know that among the Gentiles those whom they recognize as their rulers lord it over them, and their great ones are tyrants over them. But it is not so among you; but whoever wishes to become great among you must be your servant, and whoever wishes to be first among you must be slave of all. For the Son of Man came not to be served but to serve, and to give his life a ransom for many."

MARK 10:42-45

This chapter consists of three main parts. In the first part I focus on Jesus' proclamation of God's reign as a battle against evil, as presented by Mark's Gospel (the same theme recurs in Luke; see Chapter 5). In the second part of this study of Mark I focus on Mark's strategic correlation between the nature of Jesus' Messiahship and the call to discipleship. Here Mark makes clear the nature of God's reign, both for Jesus as Messiah-Christ and for those who follow him. The final section builds upon the first two, focusing on the distinctiveness of Jesus' divine warfare and victory, and what this means in Mark's first-century setting of the emperor cult, in which emperors were deified as sons of God.

Jesus' Kingdom Gospel as Battle against Evil

Jesus' early ministry is a campaign of liberation in which Jesus as divine Warrior battles against the forces of evil under the control of Satan and the demonic powers. As Howard Kee puts it, Jesus is God's "agent who has come in the end time to defeat the powers of Satan."[1] After a brief introduction, Jesus appears in Galilee proclaiming the gospel of God, i.e., the kingdom of God has come near. Therefore, the time is fulfilled, and all are called to repent and believe in the gospel (1:14-15). The coming of the kingdom of God sets the tone of the gospel as a whole. Every event and saying in the Gospel is ultimately related to this narrative purpose.

This means that Mark's Gospel declares a counter-political message. A new vision of divine sovereignty and power emerges in the Gospel. It is thus no surprise that quite early in the narrative the power-brokers of Israel, Pharisees and Herodians, and later, chief priests and scribes emerge as the antagonists to Jesus' mission (3:6; 11:18; and the Jewish trial narrative). Jesus' actions upset the prevailing order, and raise signals of alarm early in the narrative. Thus the recurring query "who is this man?" creates puzzlement and narrative suspense.

But the divine warrior motif is signaled even before Jesus' public ministry, in the brief prologue of thirteen verses, especially in the two OT quotations (vv. 2-3) and in Jesus' temptation by Satan in the wilderness (vv. 12-13). Mark alone puts these two "way" *(hodos)* texts together in this manner, to strategically begin his Gospel.[2] His joining of these two quotations from Exod. 23:20 (Mal. 3:1) and Isa. 40:3 evoke two important streams of OT salvation tradition: divine warrior and return from exile. The first derives from God's promise to send an angel ahead of Israel to lead them to victory in possessing the land of promise. The second, from Isaiah, anticipates return from exile, in which God's making a way through the wilderness shows forth God's power to vindicate his suffering people. This announced return from exile is nothing less than the mighty display of God's sovereign, saving power, as declared in 40:9: "Get you up to a high mountain, O Zion, herald of good tidings *(gospel)*; lift up your voice with strength, O Jerusalem, herald of good tidings *(gospel)*, lift it up, do not fear; say to the cities of Judah, 'Here is your God!'"

In Chapter 1 we noted the significance of this verse as well as Isaiah 52:7 for understanding Jesus' proclamation of the kingdom in the Synoptic Gospels: "Here is your God!" is translated in the Isaiah Targum as "the kingdom

---

1. Kee, *Community of the New Age*, p. 36. This accords with the emphases of Brandenburger, *Frieden im Neuen Testament*, pp. 5-47; "Grundlinien des Friedensverständnisses im Neuen Testament," 25-54; Windisch, *Der messianische Krieg und das Urchristentum*; Kallas, *The Significance of the Synoptic Miracles*, pp. 38-76.

2. Matthew and Luke use them both at separate places in their narratives, and not as formal strategic openings of their Gospels.

of God will be revealed." In Mark, the combined quotations thus unite two powerful theological memories that become an essential core of the hope of the coming of God's kingdom (cf. Mark 1:14-15 and ch. 4). In these Exodus and Isaiah texts the divine warfare of the conquest is fused with the festal procession of Israel's trek through the desert/wilderness *(midbar)*, returning home from exile.[3] Both traditions brim full with God's royal, saving power and mercy for the covenant people, Israel. That Mark launches his Gospel with these emphases indicates that both the Exodus promise and the Isaian vision are to be recapitulated in this Gospel of Jesus Messiah, the Son of God.

The second tip-off is that Jesus' temptation by Satan is framed by God's declaration of Jesus at this baptism: "You are my Son, the Beloved; with you I am well pleased" (1:11), on one side, and angels waiting on Jesus, on the other side, as the closing line to the forty-day ordeal. Jeffrey Gibson's thorough study of Jesus' temptations contends that in every one of these testings *(peirasmoi)*, Jesus' faithfulness to his baptismal designation as Son, Beloved One, and Servant is tested, precisely whether he will be God's *peacemaker (eirēnopoios)* refusing vengeance against enemies or whether he will seek to secure the future through violence.[4] Just as the front-frame of Jesus' baptism accentuates Jesus' faithfulness to God as Son who will trust God for victory, and not take the battle against Satan and evil into his own hands, so the end-frame highlights God's faithfulness to Jesus in sending angels to minister to him. Jesus is God's Son *par excellence,* who endured temptations as a faithful Son (cf. Heb. 5:5-10). Once this encounter with Satan is seen in this light, the confrontation between Jesus and Peter (8:31-33) becomes crystal clear. Peter's Messiah does Satan's will; Jesus' *way* to messianic victory is God's will and way (see section below).

In Mark's first sustained portrayal of Jesus' public ministry (1:21–3:6), many of Jesus' deeds are acts of liberation: exorcisms and healings that free people from Satan's grip, as 3:22-27 makes clear. These deeds also free people

---

3. As Joel Marcus puts it, ". . . this theme of the festal procession to Zion has been fused with that of the holy war of conquest" (*The Way of the Lord*, p. 36). His context for this emphasis is observation of the use of *way* in 8:27–10:52 and the repeated use of *anabainei* ("go up") to Jerusalem in the passion-resurrection predictions. He regards *anabainei* as "a technical term for the festal ascent to the holy city."

4. Gibson, *The Temptations of Jesus in Early Christianity,* especially p. 110 and the summary of each chapter. Even "the testing" connected with the divorce controversy in ch. 10 involves the same issue, for to speak against divorce jeopardized Jesus' security under Herod's political control, since Herod notoriously violated the prohibition (pp. 285-87). For his own summation of part of his thesis, see Gibson's "Jesus' Wilderness Temptation according to Mark."

from social ostracism and challenge religious laws that fettered freedom. Jesus' pithy sayings, as in 2:10, 17, 28, his enigmatic riddles (2:19-22), and his parables (4:1-34) tantalize standard social expectations, threaten existing social order, and even harbinger revolution. Werner Thissen has shown persuasively that liberation permeates each of the five stories in 2:1–3:6.[5] This segment answers and also extends questions raised by Jesus' liberating deeds in the preceding segment of 1:21-45. Each story in Mark's narrative (1:21–3:6) accentuates various aspects of human liberation from some form of bondage. The section is aptly titled: Jesus, Liberator and Deliverer.

Exorcisms and healings are two of the most prominent types of Jesus' liberating actions. Mark's frontispiece for Jesus' public ministry is an exorcism in the synagogue (1:21-28; see also Mark's early summaries in 1:32-34; 3:7-12).[6] True to Mark's overall portrait of Jesus' kingdom power pushing back the darkness, Jesus at the outset of his public career confronts the demons and the Satan power they represent.[7] Exorcism, while common in the first-century world, has been marginalized from our modern consciousness — or its authenticity has been disputed — since such experience doesn't fit our modern world view of reason and scientific method.[8]

The exorcism is followed by Jesus' *second* liberating act of ministry, the healing of Peter's mother-in-law (1:29-31), releasing her from fever and illness. Then verses 32-34, a Markan summary that reports Jesus' evening activities of the same day, accentuate Jesus' healings and exorcisms.

Then, in the healing of the leper (1:40-45), a combination of the first, second, and fourth types of liberation occur. Howard Kee claims that the much disputed word "sternly charged" (1:43; *embrimēsamenos*) translates *ga'ar*, a Semitic term for exorcising demons.[9] Thus it is a demon that is thrown out of the

5. Thissen, *Erzählung der Befreiung.* The book as a whole develops this point.

6. Howard Clark Kee seeks to identify a communal setting for such emphases: "If one seeks for a *Sitz im Leben* for such a collection, the first in the series gives us a clue: it is a community in which Jesus is regarded as an agent who has come in the end time to defeat the powers of Satan." Kee, *Community of the New Age,* p. 36.

7. The next several pages draw from portions of my book *Israel's Scripture Traditions and the Synoptic Gospels,* pp. 50-59.

8. See Borg, *Jesus, A New Vision,* pp. 60-65; Twelftree, *Christ Triumphant;* Wink, *Unmasking the Powers,* pp. 43-50; Peck, *People of the Lie;* Finger and Swartley, "Bondage and Deliverance."

9. Key, *Community,* p. 36. Richard Horsley exposits this text in his chapter on "God's Judgment of the Roman Imperial Order" in *Jesus and Empire: "ga'ar/epitiman* refers to the decisive action by which God or God's representative brings demonic power into submission, and establishes the rule/kingdom of God and deliverance of Israel" (p. 100). Horsley interprets these exorcisms within his social analysis of the Roman domination of Israel, and regards the exor-

leper. But the healing of the leper is also an act of social inclusion, and it thus belongs also to type four below.

Jesus' liberating events continue in the next segment, for here Jesus forgives sins, his *third* powerful type of liberation (2:1-12). Forgiveness is here linked with power to heal. But forgiveness is God's prerogative only. Forgiveness of sins, therefore, might well be regarded as the ultimate expression of liberation in this narrative sequence.

Jesus' *fourth* type of liberating action is his own freedom from class and social status codes. He calls Levi, a tax collector, to be a disciple (2:13-14) and then eats with sinners and tax collectors (2:15-17). Jesus thus broke the bondage of human alienation that arose from class partitioning in social structure.

Fifth, Jesus chose not to fast according to custom because it was time to celebrate the dawning of the kingdom (2:18-21). Jesus paved a new path of freedom in religious ritual, replacing the ascetic practice of John's disciples with celebration.

The *sixth* strand of liberation strikes at the heart of contemporary Jewish identity defined by sabbath *halakah.* From the viewpoint of the Pharisees,[10] Jesus broke the sabbath law itself, twice in this section (2:23-28; 3:1-6). No offense could be greater. But from Jesus' view it was liberation on a most crucial point, for it raised the fundamental issue of the sabbath's purpose, bringing to the fore the exodus memory itself: does the sabbath mean keeping of laws or liberation from bondage? Jesus' penetrating declaration (2:27) and question (3:4) focus squarely on this issue.

The series of miracles in 4:35–5:43 resumes the exodus theme of liberation from bondage, intensifying the note already struck in the first section

---

cisms as indicating God's liberation of Israel (it happened in the synagogue!) from foreign oppression. This interpretation is reinforced by the reference to "Legion" in the Mark 5 exorcism of the Gadarene; "Legion" thus signifies the occupying Roman army. Myers, in *Binding the Strong Man,* interprets exorcisms similarly. I cannot agree with this interpretation (see my review of Myers's book in *Critical Review of Books in Religion.* While Horsley's sociopolitical analysis of the context of Jesus' ministry and message is important and a needed redress to treating the narrative as consisting only of theological or ethical ideas unconnected to political life-reality, this particular stream of interpretation is guilty of another "construct": imposing our modern Western failure to understand the spirit world on first-century texts that in their contexts surely referred to demonic spirit oppression. Otherwise, I concur with Horsley that it is important to "hear the whole story" of the Gospels, which means taking into account the sociopolitical life-situation in which Jesus spoke and the Gospel writers wrote. See his *Hearing the Whole Story.* Chapter 4 (pp. 79-104) of *Jesus and Empire* is a good concise description, more fully explicated in *Hearing the Whole Story.*

10. For discussion of the Pharisees' identification of the *halakah*'s authority with that of the Torah, see Goppelt, *Theology of the New Testament,* 1: 87-91.

(1:16–3:6). Numerous writers have noted that Jesus' rebuke *(epitimēsen)* of the wind and command to the sea (4:39) echo the tradition of the divine fight against the sea chaos in both exodus and creation.[11] The sea-chaos is viewed as part of the demonic power which the kingdom's power breaks and conquers. Then follows immediately Jesus' exorcism of the Gerasene demoniac, from whom he casts out a legion of demons. The next two healing narratives highlight Jesus' power to free from incurable illness and death itself. With this series of stories, culminating in the raising of Jairus's twelve-year-old daughter, the Gospel's narrative anticipates Jesus' own resurrection and victory over all the powers of evil.

As Kathleen M. Fischer and Urban C. Von Wahlde note in their study of this miracle catena, Mark chooses these four miracles in order to show forth God's mighty power in Jesus' ministry. In the stilling of the storm "Jesus is acting in ways similar to Yahweh in re-creating the harmony of the universe in reclaiming it from Satan." Then, in the exorcism (5:1-20) Jesus manifests divine power over personal possession by Satan. In the healing of the woman's incurable illness and in the raising of Jairus's daughter "the ultimate affliction of evil upon the world . . . is conquered." Further, they observe that

> the miracles are not simply demonstrations of divine power but are exorcisms, the means by which, in Mark's apocalyptic world-view, God's sovereignty over Satan reasserts itself. And this sovereignty controls all areas of life. Thus Mark presents a Jesus who has power greater than any human malady, a power from God which exerts itself to right the order of creation by expelling and controlling Satan's grip over man and the world.[12]

Jesus' liberation is comprehensive and complete. But the depth of its meaning is still a mystery, waiting to be unveiled in the narrative. Thus, Mark's crucial section, 8:27–10:52, unfolds the way of suffering and cross as God's necessary *(dei)* means to victory.

Until now this analysis of Mark's portrait of Jesus as Liberator has echoed, via analogy, the work of Moses. But the theology of the exodus affirms Yahweh, not Moses, as the actual Liberator, indeed as the Warrior who has triumphed gloriously (Exod. 15:1-3). Just as Yahweh-Warrior conquered through miracle, Mark depicts Jesus as God's Warrior attacking Satan's stronghold in

---

11. McCurley, *Ancient Myths and Biblical Faith*, pp. 58-61; Fawcett, *Hebrew Myth and Christian Gospel*, pp. 88-90; Mettinger, "Fighting the Powers of Chaos and Hell," 36; Kee, "The Terminology of Mark's Exorcism Stories"; *Miracle in the Early Christian World*, pp. 151-65.

12. "The Miracles of Mark 4:35-5:43," p. 15.

his exorcisms and healings (3:22-27). Jesus' method of subduing the enemy stands fully within the divine warfare miracle tradition:[13] *the word (of God) in and through Jesus is the power that smites the demons.* The exodus type behind Jesus' work is thus not Moses, but Yahweh. Hence, the push-and-pull of the narrative — "who then is this?" (4:41; 6:2) — is to see who Jesus really is, the Son of God (1:11; 9:7; 15:39), until now a secret to all humans in the narrative.[14]

Indeed, Mark depicts Jesus' ministry as "a cosmic struggle in history to inaugurate the eschatological reign of God."[15] The verbal exchanges between Jesus and the demons consist not of conversation, but of hostile shouts and orders. The demons recognize Jesus' divine power by calling him "Holy One of God" (1:24), "Son of God" (3:11), and "Son of the Most High God (5:7). These are but seductive efforts whereby the demons seek "to gain power over Jesus by using his secret, spirit-world name."[16] Always, Jesus hushes them up, for there is no common ground between the two opposing powers. Rather, a sharp contrast emerges: the demons are violent and destructive, seeking injury and death of the human person; Jesus' actions are liberating, restoring humans to tranquillity and communion with self and others. Hence in these confrontations, history discloses the cosmic struggle of "Son of God *versus* demon, Holy Spirit *versus* unclean spirit." Jesus' role, says Robinson, is "to enter this struggle on behalf of the true destiny of mankind and with his heavenly power . . . carry through to the victory, and to the life and communion that it brings."[17] This depiction of Jesus' ministry in Mark strikes the liberation chord at its deepest level.

Jesus' ministry culminates God's long battle-march against evil. Foster McCurley describes Jesus' ministry as God's triumph over primeval chaos, God's victory over chaos (and bondage) through Yahweh as Warrior and King in Israel's history, and Jesus as "The Son of God Versus Chaos."[18] McCurley considers Jesus' rebuke of the sea chaos (Mark 4:35-41) a parallel to Yahweh's rebuke of Satan in Zechariah 3 and to the earlier divine rebuke of primeval chaos (as in Ps. 18:15c). In rebuking and exorcising demons Jesus carries for-

---

13. Lind's *Yahweh Is a Warrior* is the best exposition of Yahweh's warfare as essentially miracle. True, many deviations from this model as set forth in Exod. 14:14 occur within Israel's history, but this does not change the essential nature of Yahweh's warfare.

14. Matera describes well this Markan literary feature: ". . . the reader enters the world of Mark's story with a knowledge that the characters within the narrative struggle to attain: Jesus is the Son of God" (*Passion Narratives and Gospel Theologies*, p. 52).

15. James M. Robinson, *The Problem of History in Mark*, p. 38.

16. Robinson, pp. 36-37.

17. Robinson, pp. 39, 42.

18. *Ancient Myths and Biblical Faith*, pp. 12-71.

ward God's purpose to establish sovereignty through victory over evil (cf. Pss. 76:5-6; 80:16; 104:7 for the Lord's rebuke and victory over the enemy).[19] Thus Jesus carries forward God's liberating actions in Hebrew Scripture.

Within this context of seeing Jesus' ministry as God's war against evil, Mark's prominent emphasis on "Do not fear, only believe" (Mk. 5:36) is immediately significant. It stands in the tradition of the "fear not" *('al tîrā')* divine warfare oracles, which function prominently in Hebrew Scripture.[20] The call to trust in Yahweh for defense is also a major feature of the Zion theology of Isaiah and the royal Psalms.[21]

While about one-third of Mark's Gospel, including such things as Jesus' rebuke of the sea chaos, reflects exorcistic emphasis, it is important also to note that Jesus' defense of his ministry to the religious leaders and his own family rests upon his authority and power to cast out demons (Mark 3:20-27). The Matthew/Luke parallel puts it sharply: "If it is by the Spirit of God ['finger of God' in Luke 11:20] that I cast out demons, then the kingdom of God has come upon you" (Matt. 12:28). This saying, part of the Beelzebul controversy, indicates clearly that Jesus' exorcisms were a key sign that the kingdom of God had come and that the Spirit of God was (and is) at work in Jesus Christ (so the extensive texts on this theme: 1:13, 22-27, 39; 3:11-12, 15, 23-30; 4:15, 35-41; 5:1-20; 6:7, 13; 7:24-39; 9:14-29). In addition to the prominent function of Jesus' exorcism in the synagogue, Jesus' exorcism of the Gerasene de-

---

19. McCurley, pp. 46-52. This theme of Jesus as holy warrior has been most fully developed in Bender, "The Holy War Trajectory."

20. Conrad, *Fear Not Warrior*. Conrad has shown the pervasiveness of this formula in much of the Hebrew Bible. Unfortunately, he does not include the Psalms; had he done so, the connection between God's cosmogonic victory in creation and Yahweh's victory in divine warfare would be more evident. These comments prompt a methodological issue: did Yahweh's victories in history provide the basis for the cosmogonic theology of triumph, or vice versa? Even though many texts present the primordial victory as the basis for assuring historical triumph, Israel's course of theological reflection likely developed in the other sequence.

21. Ollenburger, *Zion, City of the Great King*. Ollenburger shows, by his study of numerous royal Psalms and the Isaianic Zion theology, that Yahweh calls Israel to humble trust in and reliance on divine protection and security. Zion theology thus repudiates Israel's proud, boastful military alliances. Two doctoral dissertations on Mark contribute significantly to these themes in Mark. Using narrative criticism in his study of the Gospel, Christopher D. Marshall has shown that Mark's call to faith functions as a prominent narrative strand *(Faith as a Theme in Mark's Narrative)*. Herbert L. Swartz has shown that Mark's fear and amazement vocabulary functions in opposition to the call to faith; fear and amazement are unwanted substitutes, opponents of faith ("Fear and Amazement Responses"). While neither of these writers correlates his work with OT oracles of divine warfare, their composite contribution makes a new understanding of Mark possible: the call not to fear but to believe reflects Israel's tradition of accentuating the appropriate human role in God's fight against evil.

moniac (5:1-20), the Syrophoenician woman's daughter (7:24-30), and the epileptic boy (9:14-29) play significant roles in Mark's Gospel.

The healing of the demoniac extends the power of the kingdom to the Gentiles, the first clear excursion in Mark to the Gentile territory across the Sea of Galilee. This narrative has a sequel in a later border crossing. Jesus goes into the region of Tyre and Sidon, presumably for a period of rest (7:24). But immediately, a woman from that area, a Greek, finds him and begs him to cast a demon from her daughter. In this episode, the woman, through her clever persistence against Jesus' word that the children's bread should not be given to dogs, persuades Jesus to enlarge his borders for ministry. He complies, and thus extends God's delivering power beyond the borders of Israel again.

It is important to see that in Mark the crucial relation between those within and those outside of Israel is addressed carefully and forcefully. For this ministry outside Israel represents an important aspect of the divine warrior's victory. It shows that those in enemy-land are not to be destroyed (contra much in the older story), but that they have become recipients of God's mercy and salvation through the faithful Son, Jesus.

As bridge between this section and the next it is important to see in Mark's portrait of Jesus' Galilean ministry that Jesus goes forth in the royal power of God, as the Son-declaration from the royal Psalm (2:7) declared at his baptism. His anointing by the Spirit, descending as a dove from heaven, makes it clear that his ministry was empowered by the Lord God. Hence his power to heal and exorcize, his authority in his teaching, and his compassion for those who sought his healing. As Joel Marcus pens,

> Crucial for Mark are the depiction of Jesus blazing a new trail into the cosmos and the conviction that this trail is the way of the Lord, the highway along which God himself moves as the invisible but powerfully present comforter of the afflicted, liberator of the captives, and enlightener of the blind.[22]

The Messiah's Way of the Cross and Discipleship in Mark

Given the power that Jesus demonstrated in his "mighty deeds" of 1:21–8:26, it is little wonder that Peter would hope Jesus to be the expected messianic deliverer. Peter's confession of Jesus as Messiah comes at the beginning of a journey "on the way" from Galilee to Jerusalem (Mark 8:27ff.). Jesus questions the dis-

---

22. Marcus, *The Way of the Lord*, p. 45.

ciples, "Who do people say that I am?" The disciples' response? Some say John the Baptist, others Elijah, and yet others "one of the prophets." But Jesus presses for their perception: "But who do you say that I am?" Peter answers quickly, as if for the rest, and as if certain of what he says: "You are the Messiah" (8:29). What Peter says may be correct. Yet, just as quickly as Peter announces that Jesus is the Messiah, Jesus "strictly ordered" his disciples not to repeat Peter's answer to anyone — no one is to be told that Jesus is the Messiah.

If the inherent purpose of a "gospel" narrative is to bear witness to Christ, if the very aim of the apostolic mission authorized by Jesus is to proclaim Jesus as the Messiah, why silence the disciples in proclaiming this truth? It makes sense to rebuke and silence the unclean spirits that cry out, "You are the Son of God" (1:24, 34; 3:11-12; cf. 1:43) — what messiah would want to have his identity revealed by the opposing side? That might explain why the "scribes from Jerusalem" charged that Jesus' power and authority to heal is from Satan (3:22-27). But why silence your own followers to proclaim that Jesus is the Messiah? How is Israel to be restored and how are outsiders to receive salvation if the identity of the Messiah is not to be revealed by the Messiah's disciples? But, indeed this may be the wrong question. Rather, we should ask, what *kind* of Messiah is the apostolic mission to proclaim? We might just as well ask, Does Peter truly confess the Messiah? Or, rather, in saying (correctly) that Jesus is the Messiah, *what* does Peter confess? That is, which messiah does Peter confess? And is that the Messiah the apostolic mission is to proclaim? Is Peter's perception in his "confession" the reason he later denies Jesus? If so, his denials become his true confession, because through them he disowns the Messiah he hoped for, and by God's grace and Jesus' compassion comes to see just what *kind* of Messiah Jesus really is.

To correct Peter's fundamental misconception, reflecting that also of the other disciples, Mark presents a careful didactic structural design for this section of 8:27–10:52. The three prominent emphases are Jesus' messianic identity, in which expectations for Messiah are turned upside down. Jesus immediately, after Peter's confession and charge to silence, begins to speak about the Son of humanity who must suffer. This is followed with recurring passion-resurrection predictions that grate against long-standing messianic notions. Third, in each of three rounds of interaction that follow this pattern, Jesus teaches the way of costly discipleship.

These three emphases are tightly interlinked in three separate and structurally parallel segments (8:31-38; 9:31-41 or 50; 10:32-45). The entire section is framed by christological declarations which identify Jesus with royal messianic hope: Messiah in 8:29 and Son of David in 10:47-48. Jesus' identity, i.e., christology, is the context for the ethics that Jesus desires his disciples to understand.

This connection between christology and discipleship is strategic to properly understand what Jesus expects of his disciples in their moral commitment.

Within the larger Markan narrative this sectional framing of christological emphases is controlled by a most important Markan declaration of Jesus' identity, in three crucial events:

> Jesus' baptism, the voice from heaven, "You are my beloved Son" (1:11).
> Jesus' transfiguration, again a voice from heaven, "This is my Son" (9:7).
> The centurion's confession at the cross, "Truly this man was the Son of God" (15:39).

Jesus' self-identification as Son of Humanity (Man) appears to serve ultimately his identity as Son of God, but this truth is firmly linked to Jesus' dying as the Son of Humanity–Messiah who gives his life a ransom for many (10:45). As the Son of Humanity fulfills his mission in suffering and death he is rightly confessed as Son of God. In order to grasp the content of this crucial carefully crafted section, Mark 8:27–10:52, observe the following pattern:

passion-resurrection announcement	disciples do not understand	teaching on discipleship
8:31	8:32-33	8:34-38
9:31	9:32-34	9:35-50
10:32-34	10:35-41	10:38-45

Each of these three cycles follows the same sequential pattern, and each is connected to Mark's use of *way (hodos)*, which here in Mark is the way that leads to Jesus' suffering and death. The phrase "whoever will come after me *(opisō mou)*" in 8:34 connects the teaching and the cycle as a whole back to 8:27 where the section introduces Jesus as going "on the way" *(en tē hodō)*. In the center of the second cycle (9:33-34), the phrase *en tē hodō* occurs twice. The third cycle begins with the phrase, "As they were going on the way *(en tē hodō)*, Jesus was going before them" (10:32).

Mark uses the term *hodos* seven times in this section: 8:27; 9:33, 34; 10:17, 32, 46, 52. Matthew has two parallel uses and Luke only one.[23] Mark also uses the term twice in his introduction of the Gospel (1:2-3), thus linking together a prophetic text from Malachi with another from Isaiah, as noted above.

---

23. Matthew also has *en tē hodō* in 20:17b, which roughly but not precisely parallels Mark 10:32. Both Matthew (20:30) and Luke (18:35) use the phrase "beside the way" *(para tēn hodon)* in Mark 10:46c.

What is Mark's purpose in framing his Gospel with this opening and then also punctuating his narrative with this motif?[24]

Of the numerous explanations for this distinctive use of *hodos,* two emphases are crucially important. First, as Joel Marcus puts it: "The way is the way that the Lord leads; the disciples follow. The *hodos* of the journey section is not a "human way *to* the *Basileia* but rather . . . God's way, which is his *Basileia,* his own extension of kingly power."[25] Second, as Jesus leads (or *makes*) the *way* he teaches discipleship with sustained effort to assist his followers to also walk the way that he leads. The way *(hodos),* the symbolic frame for the section, embraces both the theological and ethical emphases. Here I disagree with Joel Marcus, who stresses the former and denies the second.[26] That *hodos* and discipleship are explicated within the context of Jesus' christological disclosure is both evident and striking. This does not mitigate Marcus's emphasis that the "journey" is not a human way to the Kingdom, but an extension of God's kingly power. Rather it joins together this important point with the intentional structural design of the section: the linking of christology with discipleship. Neither pole of this relationship is to be glossed over for the sake of the other. Further, it seems to be correct also, in view of the design of the book as a whole, to see this "way" emphasis as "signifying" transition in the nature of Jesus' ministry as Jesus journeys from Galilee to Jerusalem. Jesus therefore teaches the *necessity (dei)* of the Son of Humanity to *suffer,* for it is in Jerusalem, the destination of the journey, that this will take place (8:31; 9:31; 10:32-34).

This literary-theological *hodos* motif also connects the story of Jesus with the OT *way (derek)* motif,[27] thus echoing the important OT texts Exod. 23:20-23; Mal. 3:1; Isa. 40:3, and other *way (hodos)* emphases in Isaiah denoting Israel's new exodus, the Israelites' return from Babylon to Judea. The latter association, between Mark and Isaiah's new exodus, is the focus of Rikki Watt's significant study of Mark,[28] which draws on my earlier work in my dissertation and my article on this topic.[29]

24. Robert H. Gundry has challenged the widely held view that Mark has any special purpose in this strategic use of "way" *(hodos) (Mark,* pp. 40-42, 597, 1047). But he fails to assess properly the evidence, specifically the fivefold recurrence of *en tę hodǫ* and its close linking to Mark's emphases on christology and discipleship. Watts, *Isaiah's New Exodus and Mark* has rightly argued against Gundry's position (pp. 129-32).

25. Marcus, *The Way of the Lord,* p. 33.

26. Marcus, *The Way of the Lord,* pp. 33-36.

27. I have argued this in *Israel's Scripture Traditions and the Synoptic Gospels,* pp. 96-99, 102-11.

28. *Isaiah's New Exodus,* pp. 129-32.

29. Swartley, "A Study in Markan Structure," pp. 75-86, 163-190; "The Structural Function of the Term 'Way' *(Hodos)* in Mark's Gospel."

The way *(hodos)* of Jesus clearly includes suffering. Thus Jesus rebukes Peter, "Get behind me Satan!" (8:33), for Peter's refusal of suffering is Satan-inspired. Both Peter and Satan must be rebuked. The tempting from the religious leaders is also part of the same satanic trap (8:11; 10:2; 12:15); Jesus wins these "tests" by clear perception and declaration of God's will. The Satan power in the Gospels, according to Girard, protects, through the religious leaders and Jesus' adversaries, the system of hidden violence (see here especially Mark 8:29-33, where even Peter is the voice of Satan's thinking). Hence they accuse Jesus of casting out Satan by Satan's power (Mark 3:22). Jesus responds with the enigmatic question, "How can Satan cast out Satan?" (3:23).[30] The gospel story itself, Girard intimates, plays out an answer to Jesus' own question. They identified Jesus with Satan, and now Jesus' question becomes a riddle with double meaning: yes, they cast out the one they deemed to be Satan, but in truth the crucifixion cast out and down the power inspiring them to this action.[31] John's Gospel declares it baldly: "Now is the ruler of this world cast out" (12:31).

The Disciples' Responses

Immediately after Jesus' three announcements of his upcoming passion, the text clearly indicates that in each case the disciples do not understand what Jesus was talking about. In 8:32 *Peter rebukes (epitimaō) Jesus!* This is the same verb Jesus used in v. 30 in hushing the disciples to silence after Peter's confession. Peter knows what messiahs should do. Messiahs rule! They don't die!

But Peter is wrong and Jesus severely rebukes him. Jesus turns to Peter and says, "What you are saying is of satanic origin. It is not of God. Get behind me." This extends an earlier emphasis in Mark, from 3:20-27, where in the controversy over Jesus' source of power — whether Jesus is doing his

---

30. The title of René Girard's paper presented at the 1992 meeting of the American Academy of Religion, San Francisco, now published. See his book, *I See Satan Fall like Lightning.* Girard equates Satan with offense and scandal arising from rivalry. Violence that destroys all is averted by Satan maneuvering the scapegoat mechanism, with Jesus in the crucifixion. In that way Satan does cast out Satan.

31. Girard correlates this with a theory that evil contains its own self-governing structure. It eliminates the degree of chaos that would threaten its own survival. I doubt his interpretation here. Nonetheless, if one looks at it this way, the crucifixion of Jesus could be seen in accord with 1 Cor. 2:6-8. The rulers, here also seen as the intelligentsia, through whom evil worked, miscalculated. For they did not rid their system of this so-called Satan disrupter. The resurrection turned the tables, and thus the Christian gospel proclaims victory over the powers of evil. See later chapters for development of this topic.

work by God's power or Satan's — Mark makes clear that Jesus' exorcisms and miracles are God's work through Jesus, and not Satan's power. In light of that earlier controversy, Peter's — and the disciples' — failure to understand Jesus now becomes most crucial. On which side will the disciples be, when it comes to the ultimate crisis? This is why extended teaching on both the nature of Jesus' messianic identity and the way of discipleship is so strategic. The disciples in the following cycles of narrative seem to be unable to grasp the way of suffering, the way of the cross, which marks God's way for the Messiah, Jesus.

After the second announcement of Jesus' suffering, the disciples' response is sad non-response because of fear (9:32). "They did not understand the saying, and they were afraid to ask him." Little wonder that they were afraid to ask about the meaning in Jesus' second announcement since Peter had received such a sharp tongue-lashing on the first attempt. Rather than risk another scolding or face up to the agony of the predicted events, the disciples indulge in thoughts of imminent political pomp and prestige. As they walk on the way, leading eventually to Jerusalem (11:8, the last use of *hodos* in the sense of journey), they wonder, "Which one of us is going to be the greatest in the coming kingdom?" That is where their minds are; but Jesus' mind is fixed on the cross.

The same distance between Jesus and the disciples emerges again in the third cycle, in 10:32ff. In 10:35, right after the third passion announcement, James and John, the sons of Zebedee, come forward to Jesus and want him to do whatever they ask him, specifically, to promise them top seats in the coming kingdom. "Grant us to sit, one at your right hand and one at your left, in your glory." The disciples, in effect, are thinking and saying, "When you get that kingdom established, that kingdom that you've talked about in the parables and that's going to engulf the world, conquering even Rome, couldn't you somehow arrange it so that we'd get the left and right seats by your side?" Or, to modernize it, "Please promise to appoint one of us as Secretary of State and the other as Secretary of Defense, or as vice-president, if you prefer!" Clearly, the disciples still do not understand.

Jesus Teaches Discipleship

Mark's careful structural design correlated with his special emphasis continues. In each of the three cases Jesus teaches discipleship. In 8:34, 36-37, Jesus says, "If any want to become my followers, let them deny themselves and take up their cross and follow me. . . . For what will it profit them to gain the whole world and forfeit their life? Indeed, what can they give in return for their life?" The answer to the disciples' grasp for political power is the way of the cross. For Mark the cross is all-important to understand Jesus' teaching, his death and resurrection victory, and also the way of life to which Jesus calls his followers.

In the second cycle the teaching on discipleship begins in 9:35: "Whoever wants to be first must be last of all and servant of all. Then he took a little child and put it among them; and taking it in his arms, he said to them, 'Whoever welcomes one such child in my name welcomes me; and whoever welcomes me, welcomes not me but the one who sent me.'" In this case the disciples were vying for prestige among themselves, querying who would become the greatest. To correct them, Jesus takes a child into his arms and says they must be ready to receive and serve the needs of such little ones. In that society the child had no rights or power, no greatness.[32] The call to serve those without status and rights, including certainly the poor and handicapped today, is followed by severest judgment upon those who cause such to sin (9:42; in 10:14-15 Jesus calls all to become as children in order to enter into the kingdom). The section closes with Jesus commanding his disciples to be at peace *(eirēneuete)* with one another (9:50), and stop this destructive rivalry. Girard's view that rivalry leads to violence is pertinent here, for it highlights how rivalry and *skandalon* (*offense;* see vv. 42-48) are stumbling blocks to discipleship.[33]

In the third round, in 10:38-45, Jesus points the disciples to the role of the servant. In contrast to seeking for positions of rule and fame, Jesus calls his disciples to the cup of suffering and death (compare 14:36). Jesus calls his

---

32. Luke's wording of Jesus' teaching seems to verify this interpretation: "But not so with you; rather let the greatest among you become as the youngest, and the leader as one who serves" (22:26). "Youngest" denotes one who by definition is not great!

33. The theories of René Girard contribute to understanding the cross as a peacemaking event. In brief, Girard contends that the myths and art of culture generally, both ancient and modern, depict acts of violence in which some surrogate victim is sacrificed to "bleed out" the violence between rival parties. The violence itself stems from the growth of rivalry rooted in mimetic desire among humans, desire to be like one who is admired, who has taught what to value. Girard's theory holds that civilization itself is based on the animating power of this desire within and among humans, indeed upon a founding murder (Cain's murder of Abel). The sacrifice of an innocent victim effects peace between warring parties: witness Herod's and Pilate's enmity changed into friendship through their scapegoating of Jesus (Luke 23:12) and the Jews' collusion with the Romans in Jesus' sentence and death. The myths of cultures universally hide the violence, but Scripture, increasingly from OT to NT, exposes it. For that reason it is gospel. Scripture is unique among the world's literature since in it God increasingly sides with the victim: in the Bible, and the Gospels most clearly, we hear in the narrative the voice of the victim, and we identify with the victim.

followers to nonconformity from worldly thinking: "You know that those who are supposed to rule over the Gentiles lord it over them, and their great men exercise authority over them. But it shall not be so among you; but whoever would be great among you must be your servant, and whoever would be first among you must be slave of all. For the son of man also came not to be served but to serve, and to give his life as a ransom for many" (RSV). The call to be servant is rooted in what Jesus himself did. He was servant supreme, even giving his life for others. Verse 45 is rightly called the golden text of Mark's Gospel.

The Crux of Mark's Peace Theology

A closer look at the three cycles on passion and discipleship teachings helps us grasp the essential elements in Jesus' way-"conquest" theology *à la* Mark, as a paradigm for the way to peace.[34] It is clear that two opposing views of messiahship have locked horns. Peter's view is most likely the Maccabean model, in which the Messiah will crush the power of the enemy nations.[35] Jesus' view is the way of the suffering Son of Humanity. The call to take up the cross means nothing less than willingness to die, to be crucified, for the sake of Jesus' gospel (v. 38), i.e. the kingdom he proclaimed. It means losing one's life and not being ashamed of Jesus' gospel even though threatened with death (vv. 34-38).

The second opposition between Jesus' and the disciples' "conquest" theology appears in 9:33-34 where the disciples are quarreling over who is the greatest. While Mark does not narrate the substance of their dispute, it appears that the disciples were imagining themselves as part of a new ruling government of Palestine, and thus were discussing the ranking of each in the new administration. The third round of discussion in 10:37 makes this point

---

34. In this section I draw on portions of my work in *Israel's Scripture Traditions*, pp. 112-15.

35. It is striking that the various conceptualizations of evil in and behind biblical thought link war and military weapons to evil itself: in the "Watchers Myth" Asael (Azazel) gives to humans the knowledge of weapons for war (*1 Enoch* 8:1); the *nephilim,* who come from the union of gods and humans (Genesis 6), are Israel's later giant military foes; in the Isaiah 14 and Ezekiel 28 arrogant king traditions, which provide much of the later imagery for the devil, the kings are dethroned because of oppressive military power and self-deification; in the early *satan* tradition, Satan incites David to take a census for military enlistment. For extensive treatment of the origins of the conceptions of evil reflected in Scripture see Forsyth, *The Old Enemy: Satan and the Combat Myth*, pp. 44-191.

more specific. This time James and John ask for the top seats of power: one on the right and one on the left.

To these queries Jesus turns aspirations to greatness upside down. The identity images for life in the kingdom of God are child and servant. In the first case it means seeing a child, yes a child, as important. Ranked at the bottom of the pecking order in their social stratification, the child is precisely the one who merits care and love. To receive the child in "my name" is to receive me, says Jesus. And this Jesus is the one recently confessed to be Messiah and designated on the mountain by the divine voice "Son of God." To be with this great one is to re-vision greatness. The following paragraph puts into juxtaposition acts of power (exorcism) and humble service (giving a cup of water). Both are equally significant when done in Jesus' name! Harsh words of judgment fall on those who cause "one of these little ones who believe in me to sin." The cause of offense to the "little one" or to one's own spiritual welfare must be purged to enter the kingdom of God (v. 47; cf. "life" in vv. 43, 45). Drawing on the imagery of well-prepared salted sacrifices (Lev. 2:13), Jesus calls for the self to be purified of evil and ambitious desires, and for his followers to live peaceably with one another (vv. 49-50). To live *peaceably* with one another contrasts to the segment's initial portrait of the disciples disputing with one another over who is the greatest. To walk in the way of Jesus means giving up rivalry over greatness and passionately desiring relationships that do not offend others, but rather yield the fruit of peace (see Chapter 13 for further exposition on rivalry, in the context of R. Girard's reading of the Gospels).

Jesus' response in the third round penetrates even more deeply his messianic mission's transformation of "conquest" theology. Having presented the rigorous demands of the kingdom in relation to marriage, possessions, and family ties (10:1-31) and having reiterated again his impending suffering (vv. 32-34), Jesus now responds to the desire of James and John to be granted right and left side seats to him in glory. What exactly they had in mind is not clear, but the point of desiring to share in Jesus' future is clear. After questioning the intensity of their desire, Jesus promises them that they will share in the cup he will drink (see Mark 14:36) and the baptism with which he will be baptized, but their wish is not his to grant. The ten were indignant, presumably because they thought the two had gotten some edge over them. Then Jesus, calling them together, spoke words that sum up his kingdom way:

> You know that among the Gentiles those whom they recognize as their rulers (RSV; rule/*archein*) lord *(katakyrieuousin)* it over them, and their great ones *(megaloi)* are tyrants (RSV "exercise authority," *katexousi-azousin*) over them. But it is not so among you; but whoever wishes to be-

come great *(megas)* among you must be your servant *(diakonos)*, and whoever wishes to be first among you must be slave *(doulos)* of all. For the Son of Man came not to be served but to serve *(diakonēsai)*, and to give his life a ransom for many *(lytron anti pollōn)* (10:42-45).

Wengst points out that Jesus' opening words, "you know," summarize a long historical experience of an existing order of peace based on oppressive rule.[36] The text does not underwrite, but critiques the way things are. Jesus continues to teach the disciples that there is an alternative way. "Peace based on oppressive force is not what Jesus wants."[37] The peace of Jesus Christ is not the peace of the Empire. It is rooted in quite different attitudes and goals for life in community.

The verbal and grammatical terms linking these sentences are crucial. The first sentence speaks of political power and rule, denoted by verb forms of "to lord" *(katakyrieuō)* and "to exercise authority" *(katexousiazō)*; both verbs carry overtones of oppressive rule. Those who so rule are called *great people!* As Pilgrim puts it, "Mark provides a stronger critique [than Matthew] of those who rule when he states (sarcastically?), 'those who seem to rule [*hoi dokountes*, 10:42, RSV], lord it over others.' The NRSV unfortunately obscures this pointed remark ('those whom they recognize as their rulers')."[38] The second sentence is hooked to the first by the word *great*, and the word *great* is sharply redefined: to be great is to be servant! The point is reinforced by restatement, using the image of *first (prōtos)*, which here means "the head of things." The head must be the slave of all. The second and third sentences are linked by the crucial connective *For (gar)*, used with the intensive *kai*, which here is likely best translated *also* (as in RSV).

The effect is to put into parallel relationship the way of the Son of humanity and the way of his disciples. The service *(diakonēsai)* of the Son of humanity matches and is the ground for that of the disciples (who are called to be *diakonoi)*. Jesus and the disciples are indissolubly linked in this new version of greatness, indeed in a new *hodos*-"conquest" theology of thought and action. For the Son of humanity, this life-giving service has ultimate benefit: a

---

36. Wengst, *Pax Romana and the Peace of Jesus Christ*, p. 56. Wengst notes two other biblical texts that suggest Jesus critiqued the ruling order. In Luke 13:32 Jesus refers to Herod as a fox, which in context refers to Herod's wiliness. In Matt. 11:8 par. Luke 7:25 Jesus' words hold great respect for John the Baptist and present a commentary on the luxury of the powerful (p. 57). See also Horsley's description of the "whole story," the political reality that informs the plot of Mark (see n. 9 above).

37. Wengst, p. 56.

38. Pilgrim, *Uneasy Neighbors*, p. 61.

ransom for many. Whether this should be considered part of the parallel structure between Jesus and the disciples is debatable. While numerous aspects of the belabored exegesis of this saying lie outside the scope of this study,[39] the essential point is that Jesus' giving his life as a ransom means victory for the benefit of the many. While the element of substitution is present,[40] the overall context demands that we stress also the binding relationship between the Redeemer and the redeemed.[41] The redeemed, i.e. the followers of Jesus, are linked to Jesus as the servant-head who leads the ransomed into lives of servant-type living. Certainly this was one of Mark's primary aims in writing the Gospel: to set forth Jesus' life, death and resurrection as a call to and an empowerment for faithful discipleship.

39. Morna Hooker has argued that the phrase *lytron anti pollōn* does not have Isa. 53:12 as its background *(The Son of Man in Mark)*. If, however, we focus on Mark's portrait of Jesus as servant of justice akin to the servant in Isaiah 41–55, then the assessment of the textual similarity appears differently, which Hooker acknowledges. Hooker's scope of considerations is too narrow, not oriented sufficiently to the larger role of the servant in Isaiah. The vicarious suffering in Isa. 53:12 is not the starting point for the servant's role, which begins rather with faithful proclamation of God's justice and salvation to Israel and the nations (42:1-6; 49:1-7). Mark portrays Jesus' mission precisely in those perspectives.

The phrase may also have its background in the Maccabean martyr theology (see 2 Maccabees 7; *4 Maccabees* 6:26-30; 17:21-22). In accepting torture and death, Eleazar says, "Make my blood their purification and take my life as a ransom for theirs" (*4 Maccabees* 6:29). Similarly, "let our punishment be a satisfaction on their behalf" (v. 28). For an analysis of this tradition as background to the early church's view of atonement see Sam K. Williams, *Jesus' Death as Saving Event*, pp. 76-90, 165-202, 230-34; Pobee, *Persecution and Martyrdom in the Theology of Paul*, pp. 13-46.

40. Stott cites Mark 10:45 and the similar phrase in 1 Tim 2:6 in support of his emphasis on the substitutionary element of the atonement (*The Cross of Christ*, pp. 146-48, 177-79). While Stott and the exegetical tradition that stresses the "in place of, instead" meaning of *anti* are correct, the root meaning of *anti* as "face-to-face" should not be lost. Otherwise this teaching on the atonement tends to disconnect atonement from discipleship, a link that is fundamental to the Mark 10:42-45 context and to the nature of the Gospel narrative as a whole, in which Jesus' self-giving life and death function prototypically for discipleship. Goppelt has commendably emphasized this interconnection (*Theology of the New Testament*, 1:194-99). See also Taylor, *Atonement in New Testament Teaching*.

41. Albert de Mingo Kaminouchi also stresses this point, saying, "Christology and Christian ethics are tied together in v. 45. This connection between Jesus' specific service accomplished through his death and the service asked of every follower opens the possibility of participating in the redemptive mission of the Son of Man" (*But It Is Not So among You*, p. 152). Kaminouchi's study carefully reviews the debate on Mark 10:42-45 and the Isaiah background and contributes some new perspectives (such as the theme of *glory* framing both texts). He investigates also the Hellenistic background for the meaning of *lytron*. He argues that both backgrounds are instructive to understanding that *redemption* and *service* are intertwined. This too reflects the Isaiah servant songs theology (pp. 140-56).

Jesus' climactic instruction on the way *(en tę̄ hodǭ)*, set within the "conquest" (exodus) imagery of the Old Testament, leaves no doubt that Jesus is presenting a counter model of greatness for the ordering of social and political relationships. If entering and living within the kingdom are guided by this new empowering imagery, which subverts prevailing empire images, then the "way-conquest" tradition, which provided prominent imagery for this section of Mark's presentation of Jesus, has undergone significant transformation. The Divine Warrior Son of Humanity Messiah attains the victory, ransoming many, through suffering and death. It is notable that the inclusio images to Jesus' teaching in this section are *cross* (8:34) and *giving his life as a ransom* (10:45). Both point to suffering and death; and both point also toward gaining life and ransoming life. The way of the Messiah/Son of Humanity's own victory and the way of victory for his followers are bound together by the cross and resurrection.

Cross-bearing and servanthood are not substitutes for or bypasses around the task of overcoming evil. Rather, the section as a whole shows that God's victory comes in a most unsuspecting way: the way of self-denial, humble service and the very giving of one's life for others. This is the *way of Jesus. And there is also the resurrection,* a vital part of every passion prediction on the way. Jesus' *hodos* is not only a way to death, but a way also to God's victory. This victory is assured by Jesus' death as a "ransom for many." For Jesus and his disciples the way of faithful warfare was and is that of humble service, even unto death. Victory comes through God's vindication of the faithful.

Jesus' victory is achieved only through necessary suffering. The christological climax of the book in 15:33-39 makes the same point. For Mark any theology of glory, victory, or "conquest" is unthinkable apart from a *theologia crucis.* The transfiguration prefigures the "kingdom come in power," but the means of the "conquest" is *via dolorosa, en tę̄ hodǭ.* The transfiguration provides no bypass, but rather places within the Markan narrative and theology the tension and dialectic that greatness and victory arise from within humble service and suffering.

It is necessary *(dei)* for Jesus as the Son of Man to suffer. The Son of Man title appears to refocus the confession of Jesus as Messiah. Mark puts Messiah and Son of Man both parallel and in tension and connects both to an essential divinely willed pattern of suffering, death and resurrection. Drawing upon the apocalyptic genre, Mark links together the suffering Messiah–Son of Man with the victorious, triumphant Divine Warrior traditions. Jesus' exorcisms were signs of the victory to come, and the Gospel later discloses the ultimate triumph of the Messiah–Son of Man's victory: "you will see the Son of Man seated at the right hand of the Power, and 'coming with the clouds of heaven'" (14:62).[42]

Political Christology and Victory through Nonretaliation

Jesus' entry to Jerusalem (11:1-11) may be seen as God's holy warrior, Jesus, coming to reclaim the nation from its evil injustices and to reassert the sovereignty of God. The "way"/*hodos* motif that frames 8:27–10:52 occurs again in 11:8, thus suggesting that Jesus' revolutionary means of conquest will continue. The temple cleansing, as many writers indicate,[43] is a bold prophetic act in which Jesus showed his authority over Israel's most holy place. Jesus directed his action against two injustices: the economic exploitation (overcharging) in the selling of sacrificial animals (note that pigeons, the sacrifice of the poor, are especially mentioned), and the injustice of infringing on the worship of the Gentiles (note that "he would not allow any one to carry anything through the temple [court]"). Decrying this misuse of the temple, Jesus said, "This house which is to be a house of prayer *for all nations* you have made a den (hang-out) for robbers" (see Mark 11:17). Yes, Jesus moves into action, to stand against cheating the poor and crowding the Gentile worship space with commercial greed.

Jesus' cleansing of the temple is often used as a biblical argument to support the Christian's use of violence in war. This is a misuse of this incident and of Scripture. For Jesus' action was thoroughly prophetic, depending on the power of the word. Even though some translations of John 2:15 portray Jesus using the whip of cords against people, an alternative exegesis (reflected in NIV, NEB, GNB) takes the phrase "with the sheep and oxen" to be explanatory of the "all" *(pantas)* that Jesus drove out with a whip. Verse 16 supports this interpretation in saying that Jesus, after driving "all" out, spoke to those who had been selling the pigeons.[44]

---

42. For a scholarly analysis of the traditions that conjoin in Mark's presentation of Jesus as Warrior, see Stevens, "The Divine Warrior in the Gospel of Mark."

43. Lohmeyer, *Lord of the Temple,* pp. 40-51; Schweizer, *Mark,* pp. 14, 233-41; Gaston, *No Stone on Another,* pp. 474-75; Watty, "Jesus and the Temple — Cleansing or Cursing?"

44. In this alternative exegesis the antecedent of the masculine *pantas* ("all") is *boas* ("oxen"). The *te . . . kai* phrase then explains what "all" is meant: both the sheep and the oxen. Quite likely the people selling these animals also left the temple court, accompanying their capital investment, since v. 16 indicates that Jesus spoke only to those selling the doves. Since Jesus could not drive the doves out with a whip (a comic scene, had he tried!) he commanded the sellers to remove them. This confirms the alternative exegesis, for if the sellers had been the object

The temple event demonstrates Jesus' role as Warrior fighting against evil, and we must also note that the Gospels fully integrate this emphasis with another theme, Jesus the Servant. Jesus won the battle through his courageous stand for justice, his meekness in forgoing self-defense, and finally his humiliation in self-sacrificial suffering (10:45; 14:57–15:37; cf. Phil. 2:6-8). Fulfilling the peace theme of Zech. 9:9-10, Jesus rides upon a donkey, demonstrating that his victory is not by military means but by the longstanding model of quiet trust in God's sovereignty and power. Hence, the powers of evil expressed themselves not only in individuals who were oppressed by demonic powers, but also in the religious and political structures. The religious leaders and the political leaders became part of the satanic effort to detour Jesus from the course of his kingdom ministry.[45] Indeed, Jesus comes into Jerusalem as king, tripping all the lights of messianic hope. But the agenda of transforming those hopes and expectations now gets under way most seriously. Choosing a donkey signals that Davidic royalty will be redefined. Messianic hopes, high and feverish that day, will need to undergo the refiner's fire. The "coming kingdom of our ancestor David" (11:10) will become an upside-down kingdom because the King subverts the royal hope.

That the disciples were still on the wrong side of the event's meaning becomes clear by their actions later in the garden. When Jesus is arrested they make a brief, desperate, futile attempt to identify with him by defending his life with their own lives. But even this attempt only separates them further from Jesus. One of the disciples — likely representing all of them (he is named as Peter only in John's account) — draws a sword and assaults the high priest's servant (14:47). Interestingly, unlike in the other Synoptic accounts (cf. Matt. 26:51-52; Luke 22:50-51), in Mark Jesus does not rebuke his disciples for striking out in violence. It does not really require rebuke — the act of violence rebukes itself. For the act of striking out in violence to defend the Messiah from arrest reveals that the one who draws the sword does not truly know the Messiah he sets out to defend.

One cannot identify with the fate of the Messiah through violence, not even with violence that appears to be "justified" in the defense of the innocent. There is no "communion" between partaking of the bread and cup, sharing in the body and blood of Jesus, and drawing the sword, striking out in violence even on behalf of the One who is the Messiah. Indeed, drawing the

---

of the whip, those who sold the doves would have been driven out with the other merchants. For a detailed exegetical study supporting this interpretation of this text see Lasserre, "A Tenacious Misinterpretation: John 2:15." For similar exegetical emphasis see Macgregor, *The New Testament Basis of Pacifism*, pp. 17-18; Ferguson, *The Politics of Love*, pp. 28-30.

45. Finger, *Christian Theology: An Eschatological Approach*, 1: 291-98.

sword aims precisely at avoiding the suffering signified by the bread and cup, the suffering of the to-be-crucified Messiah. To identify with *this* Messiah entails willing solidarity in suffering and death. Solidarity with Christ crucified calls for rejection of the sword. To take up the sword in defense of the cause of the Messiah thus reveals one's own human weakness, one's own fear of suffering and death, and so betrays one's loyalty to the Messiah. To take up the sword is to abandon the suffering of the Messiah and so to abandon trust in the God who saves, the God unto whom Jesus surrenders his life: "yet, not what I want, but what you want" (14:36b).

What kind of king is Jesus? Peter's precocious confession and later denial focus the issue. Having left Jesus alone in his trial, Peter undergoes his own testing. Peter's distance from Jesus begins to widen at Jesus' arrest in the garden (14:53-54): "They took Jesus. . . . Peter followed at a distance." Peter follows "at a distance" from Jesus precisely because he cannot follow closely a Messiah that is arrested, a Messiah who is taken prisoner "as though a bandit" (14:48). Peter's denial of the Messiah on trial begins in his dissociation from the Messiah that is "handed over," seized, arrested, and led away. It is not only Peter's dissociation from Jesus — *none* of the twelve, *none* find themselves able to associate with one arrested as a criminal, an enemy of the people, a rebel against the regime (14:50): "All of them deserted him and fled." Denial is rooted in disloyalty: what Peter later confesses by word, he first discloses in action. Peter's desertion shows that it is now clear to him that Jesus as Son of Humanity will suffer and die; hence his distant following of Jesus. This reveals that Peter does not know "this man," so different from the Messiah Peter expected.[46]

Mark presents yet another window to view Jesus' triumph through the cross, a Roman centurion's confession of Jesus as Son of God. This confession too, like Peter's, has political connotation. Under the aegis of the book's title, "The beginning of the gospel of Jesus Christ / Messiah, Son of God," the narrative unfolds on the human, historical plane the identity of Jesus as precisely the Messiah, and with a/the Son of God perspective. In some sense there is a cat-and-mouse relation between the two titles and identities. For the reader, Jesus is first disclosed to be Son of God at his baptism (1:11), with the accompanying portent of the heavens split asunder, the Spirit as a dove descending upon him, and a voice speaking from the heavens. Later in the narrative demons cry out that he is the Son of God (3:11), and Jesus commands them to silence. Then Peter confesses Jesus to be Messiah (8:29), followed shortly with a mountaintop transfiguration of Jesus in which Jesus' three inner circle disci-

---

46. I have adapted material in the four preceding paragraphs from Darrin Belousek's unpublished passion meditation.

ples see him in dazzling white clothes and hear a voice speaking from the overshadowing cloud, "This is my Son, the Beloved; listen to him" (9:7). Later, in Jesus' trial before the Jewish leaders, when questioned: "Are you the Messiah, the Son of the Blessed?" Jesus answers, "I AM, and you will see the Son of man seated at the right hand of the Power, and coming with the clouds of heaven" (14:62). As John Donahue aptly puts it, drawing on Ernest Best, "the titles *Christos* (Messiah) and Son of God 'chase' each other through the Gospel, and here the chase ends."[47]

In the Roman trial narrative, Jesus is identified as "King of the Jews" six times: queried so first by Pilate (15:2), rejected as such by the Jewish crowd incited by the Jewish leaders (9, 12), mocked as "King of the Jews" by the soldiers (18) and crucified under the *titulus*, "The King of the Jews" (26); while he was hanging on the cross, the chief priests and scribes taunted him as "King of Israel" (v. 32). This sequence of six Messianic bashings is ironic, in that while the narrative presents the title in rejection or mockery, yet the author intends the reader of the narrative to see the truth of what was denied and contemptuously flouted.

The same occurs in the centurion's confession, "Truly, this man was the Son of God" (15:39). Quite possibly, the Roman soldier spoke this jeeringly: such a man, dying on the cross, yea, Son of God, to be sure! But the narrator of the Gospel intends the reader to hear it differently and truly. Indeed, the centurion uttered a true confession. For this is the treasure of the Gospel: the One who did not retaliate against the evil plots of the leaders, but willingly offered himself as suffering servant, in accord with God's purpose (the *dei* of 8:31; 9:31; 10:32), is the *true Son of God.*

Several additional scholarly contributions help us see the full impact of this narrative *gospel,* for *good news* it surely is, for the first readers and for us today. It offers humans a way out of the spiral of violence that besets our history, politics, and even religion. Robert Tannehill's study of the narrative christology of Mark provides a helpful contribution. Tannehill regards the Son of God disclosures in 1:11; 9:7; and 15:39 as markers in the narrative progress toward fulfillment of the divinely given commission of 1:11 (even signaled perhaps in the book's title).[48] The entire narrative may be seen then in terms of opponents and helpers who either seek to obstruct or assist Jesus' self-disclosure and his fulfillment of God's commission to him. This functions then as the narrative plot, the muscle that drives the narrative to its culmination.

---

47. John R. Donahue, *Are You the Christ? The Trial Narrative in the Gospel of Mark,* p. 91; Best, *The Temptation and Passion: The Marcan Soteriology,* p. 95.
48. Tannehill, "The Gospel of Mark as Narrative Christology."

Robert Beck views this narrative as a "nonviolent story" that contrasts to popular narratives that play out the myth of constructive or redemptive violence. In contrast to the dominant universal myth of gaining peace and security through superior violence, whether in novels like those of Louis L'Amour or any nation's arms superiority, Mark narrates the mission of One who refused to retaliate against violence used against him.[49]

Mark's drama scripts a story of nonviolent resistance against the oppression of hierarchy symbolized by the temple commerce. Jesus' prophetic resistance in this his first action in Jerusalem speeds the plot announced already at the end of Act 1: The Pharisees and Herodians collude on how to kill him (3:6). This pivotal Act 5 "sorts out" the course of the disciples in the drama. Because the prior teaching about Jesus' way of the cross was not understood, it is clear that they will not journey with him to his cross. They "are stranded and vulnerable to the designs of his enemies."[50]

Beck employs the commonly accepted six sectional divisions of Mark and narrates them as six acts. In his plot analysis of Mark, Beck regards the temple cleansing to be the pivotal narrative act (Act 5) in the six-act drama that leads to the cross. Titled "The Temple Action as the Narrative Climax," Jesus' initiative to confront injustice in the temple action initiates what could lead to a spiraling of violence. While the religious leaders seek to trap Jesus (11:27-33; 12:12-40), they are not immediately able to denounce him publicly in order to take him. The traps set for the Son snap back on their own fingers. That the aura of the narrative hangs under a cloud of potential violence is made clear by the three uses of *lēstēs* (bandit, robber, insurrectionist) in the narrative: Jesus, in his temple confrontation accuses the temple-keepers: "Is it not written, 'This house shall be a house for all nations'? But you have made it a den of *robbers*" (11:17, quoting Isa. 56:7 and Jer. 7:11); "Have you come out with swords and clubs to arrest me as though I were a *bandit (or better, insurrectionist)*?" (14:48); and ". . . with him they crucified two *bandits (again, insurrectionist),* one on his right and one on his left" (15:27). The intended meaning in these three uses may differ, for *robber* best connotes Jesus' accusation of the temple-keepers. Jesus unmasks the covert economic and religious violence in the temple demonstration. In the second instance he defends himself against the perception of him as an *insurrectionist.*[51] In the third, both the leaders' perception of Jesus as a

---

49. Robert Beck, *Nonviolent Story: Narrative Conflict Resolution in the Gospel of Mark.*

50. Beck, *Nonviolent Story,* p. 108; see the summary-analysis of Beck in McKay, "God's Covenant," pp. 24-26.

51. Josephus identifies numerous rebel leaders with the term *lēstēs.* For a list of such rebels and texts in Josephus see Evans, *Mark 8:27–16:20,* p. 425.

threat to their order and the scene of Jesus crucified with the *lēstai* suggests again the *insurrectionist* meaning.

Beck analyzes this "nonviolent narrative" with Gene Sharp's paradigm for nonviolent movements to overcome evil: the three-step progression of confrontation, repression, and nonretaliation.[52] In Mark Jesus refuses to retaliate in kind against the plotting of the leaders to kill him (3:6; 11:18; 14:1-2), but he suffers the repression that comes against his temple confrontation that publicly exposed the evil of blocking Gentiles from free access to worship God. Even though faced with violence against him and threatening death, Jesus refuses to retaliate.

Beck is right to regard Jesus' response to the repression against him an action that interrupts the spiral of violence. During his trial Jesus is mostly silent, willing to undergo a martyr's death, in submission to his Father's will (14:36). But Beck's title for Act 5 is misleading, for it locates the narrative *climax* with the temple episode. It fails to emphasize that the peaceable, nonretaliatory action of Jesus is truly the narrative climax![53] For precisely in following the story to this end do we see the vindication of Jesus' *way,* clearly cast in 8:27–10:52. Further, God vindicated Jesus in the resurrection (16:6); thus the proclamation of the *gospel,* cross and resurrection, determines the key symbols of Christian faith. I propose then that the temple confrontation is not the narrative climax. Rather, the climax is Jesus' death prompting the split temple veil and the centurion's confession, confirmed and vindicated by Jesus' resurrection.

This understanding of the Gospel becomes crucially significant when one queries what Mark as author intended his Gospel to achieve for his first and later readers. Clearly, Jesus' teaching and pattern of response to his accusers provide a model for Jesus' followers in the circumstances of threatening or actual persecution (13:9-13). Quite possibly this reality occasioned in part Mark's writing of the Gospel.[54]

52. Beck, *Nonviolent Story,* pp. 116-17. Beck draws on Sharp, *The Politics of Nonviolent Action,* vol. 3, part 3. Sharp's model differs significantly from Horsley's in that Horsley's last step is revolt or revolution rather than nonretaliation. In each the initial confrontation of nonviolent resistance is response to injustice, though injustice is spoken of more explicitly by Horsley than by Sharp. See Sharp, 118; Horsley, *Jesus and the Spiral of Violence,* pp. 33-58. Horsley, however, is describing the cycle as it occurred in first-century Palestine, as his subtitle indicates. To see Jesus' nonretaliation against this background of periodic revolt in the first century highlights Jesus' distinctive way of response, and his teaching in Matt. 5:39-42 as well.

53. Beck's title for Act 6, "The Agon and the Nonviolent Plot Resolution," is fine, but my point is that this should be regarded as the narrative climax, especially when one correlates the plot with the Gospel's leitmotif of christological disclosure, as will be evident in what follows.

54. Ralph P. Martin identifies also as a crucial factor the need for a Gospel that functions

But other related purposes, both political and Christological, are also evident in the emphases of the Gospel. Craig Evans identifies the purpose of the Gospel as a counter political claim, arising from Jesus as *Son of God*. As in Matthew, so in Mark, the significance of the confession of Jesus as *Son of God* cannot be fully grasped apart from knowing what that title conveyed in first-century Palestine, especially by 62-75 CE, the range of dates proposed for its writing. Evans identifies ten features associated with the deification of Rome's emperors, of which five such reigned during most of the years of the first century. Of these ten features, seven are present in Mark. These are:

The good news proclamation. Good news designated the emperors' proclamations of victory in war or the birth of a royal son. Mark's use of the noun *gospel/euangelion* seven times (1:1, 14, 15; 8:35; 10:29; 13:10; 14:9) is unique; each is associated with the person of Jesus and in 1:14-15 with the proclamation of the kingdom of God (10:29 follows Jesus' discussion with the twelve on how hard it is to enter into the kingdom).

Omens and prophecies. I have already mentioned several terrestrial signs at Jesus' baptism, transfiguration, and crucifixion — and for the latter *darkness* from noon until 3:00 p.m. is to be included also. Prophecies are present as well: 14:30 fulfilled in vv. 66-72; 14:58, even though by false witnesses, for the risen Jesus is the new temple, as implied by the "in three days" motif, echoing his own prophesying in the passion and resurrection predictions; and 14:62, mocked by his accusers sarcastically retorting "*Prophesy*" (v. 65) after he just did and right before another a previous prophesy is fulfilled (Peter's denial).

Hailed in divine terms. The sequence of declarations of Jesus as Son of God (1:11; 9:7; 15:39), even by demons (1:24; 3:11), count here from a narrative point of view. Also, the twofold disclosure from Jesus' lips as I AM (*Egō Eimi* in 6:50; 14:62), echoing Exod. 3:13-15, is most significant.

Healings. See the first part of this chapter.

Seated or standing at God's right hand. Again, the above commentary on 14:62 shows the prominence and importance of this feature in Mark. As Evans puts it, "It is not Caesar who sits next to God, . . . it is Jesus" in Mark's Gospel.

Libations in honor of the emperor; in Mark of Christ. The Last Supper words of Jesus include, "This is the blood of the covenant, which is poured out for many" (14:24).

---

as a handbook for the Gentile mission *(Mark: Evangelist and Theologian)*. Mission to the Gentiles figures significantly in Jesus' crossings of the Sea of Galilee, his excursion to Tyre and Sidon, and his cleansing of the temple, as well as in 13:10 and 14:9. See Malbon, "The Jesus of Mark and the Sea of Galilee"; "Galilee and Jerusalem: History and Literature in Marcan Interpretation"; Swartley, *Israel's Scripture Traditions,* pp. 39-43; *Mark: The Way for All Nations,* pp. 169-71, 187, 200-201.

Post-mortem deification. The first such acclamation is the word of the centurion, "Truly, this man was the Son of God," the very acclaim granted to deified emperors. Though not further made explicit in Mark, the same is inferred from the good news of the young man in the tomb, "He is not here; he has been raised." The anticipated gathering of the disciples with Jesus in Galilee points also in this direction.[55]

The significance of these crucial features of Mark's Gospel, from Evans's masterful presentation of evidence, makes a counter-claim to that of the emperor cult. From the beginning title to the centurion's acclaim the reader in the Roman world encounters Jesus as an opposition candidate to the deified Roman emperor. Despite Jesus' shameful death, and indeed by means of it, Jesus is true Son of God, humanity's true triumphant Savior and Lord.

To use such political language may strike one as strange, since Jesus taught so clearly the way of the cross, self-denial, humble service, and readiness to give up all for the kingdom. Exactly the point! As Donald Kraybill aptly entitles his book on Jesus, *The Upside-Down Kingdom*,[56] so it is. Mark's Gospel, as shown at the beginning of this chapter, utilizes divine warfare traditions, and transforms them by Jesus' surprising victory through his acts of deliverance, confrontation of evil, and nonretaliation. Hence Beck rightly regards Mark's Gospel as nonviolent narrative conflict resolution.

The ultimate battle against Satan and evil occurs in Jesus' agony in the garden, where he asks for the "cup of suffering" to be taken from him. But he also knows that the final victory will come *through* suffering, as he spoke in the passion and resurrection predictions. The triumph of the liberation from the powers of evil comes finally in Jesus' dying on the cross and God's vindication of him as faithful servant in raising him from the dead (16:5-7). Jesus' peaceable liberating encounters against evil, climaxing in Jesus' voluntary suffering and death, effect peace, the peace of the cross.[57]

Mark takes traditions of violence that permeated Israel's messianic hopes and transforms them into victory that comes via self-donation in the way of the cross. "Entering into the promised land" is transformed into "en-

---

55. Evans, *Mark 8:27–16:20*, pp. lxxxix-xciii. The three features of deified emperors (and all three do not apply to any one emperor — see Evans's exacting evidence, pp. lxxxi-lxxxix) are: the notion of triumph in celebration of the emperor, confession of Caesar as Lord, and the emperor's advent *(parousia)*. Evans points out the presence of these features in other NT writings, e.g. the last in Matthew and all in Paul or post-Pauline writings.

56. The same applies to John Howard Yoder's *The Politics of Jesus*.

57. Harrisville provocatively suggests that Mark was written as a commentary on Paul's hymn in Phil. 2:5-11 *(The Miracle of Mark)*. The fuller NT witness is clear that peace comes through what Jesus has done in his life and death, culminating in the cross (Eph. 2:13-17).

tering into the kingdom of God." The means and end of this is through the nonviolence of not retaliating against evil, but rather healing the sick, releasing people from Satan's grip, teaching the way of humble service, refusing the mindset of those who "seem to rule" over others, standing up for the rights of the Gentiles to worship God freely, and trusting in God's power to deliver even through death.

The gospel narrative indeed presents Jesus as a peacemaker who did not avoid evil's power and manifestations in this world. He did not settle for the peace of the system of violence, nor did he offer an easy peace that hides its head in the sand. Rather, coming in God's name and the power of the kingdom commissioned to him to confront Satan and his works (Mark 3:22-29), he not only confronted the powers of evil but liberated people — and one day all creation — from its oppressive powers. His climactic act, voluntarily taking the form of a servant unto death, enabled him to confront and endure death victoriously, and release, by God's resurrection power, "all those who through fear of death were subject to lifelong bondage" (Heb. 2:15).

This *is* the good news of the *Gospel*. Two more great reversals occur. Jesus is raised from the dead, vindicated as God's triumphant *Son*. Further, he calls his scattered disciples to gather again in Galilee to receive their apostolic, missionary mandate. From Galilee, not Jerusalem, God's *gospel/euangelion will radiate* to the whole world.[58]

---

58. For fuller exposition see Swartley, *Israel's Scripture Traditions*, pp. 39-43, 269-77.

5   Luke: Gospel of Joy, Salvation, Peace, and Praise

But the angel said to them [the shepherds], Do not be afraid; For see [behold] — I am binging you good news of great joy for all people: to you is born this day in the city of David a Savior, who is the Messiah, the Lord. . . . And suddenly there was with the angel a multitude of the heavenly host, praising God and saying, Glory to God in the highest heaven, and on earth peace among those whom he favors.

LUKE 2:10-11, 13-14

When he came to Nazareth, where he had been brought up, he went to the synagogue on the sabbath day, as was his custom. He stood up to read, and the scroll of the prophet Isaiah was given to him. He unrolled the scroll and found the place where it was written: "The Spirit of the Lord is upon me, because he has anointed me to bring good news to the poor. He has sent me to proclaim release to the captives and recovery of sight to the blind, to let the oppressed go free, to proclaim the year of the Lord's favor."

LUKE 4:16-19

Of all the NT literature Luke excels in presenting the story of Jesus as *gospel-announcing (euangelizomai)* of a new God-human relationship that brings salvation, joy, peace, and praise. A statistical analysis of the number of uses of these words makes the point:

"Save/salvation" *(sōzō/sōtēria):* verb used fourteen times (6:9; 7:50; 8:12; 9:24 (2x); 9:56; 13:23; 17:33; 18:26, 42; 19:10; 23:35, 37, 39; the noun, five times (1:69, 77; 2:30; 3:6; 19:9); and "Savior" *(sōtēr)*, two times (1:47; 2:11).

"Joy" *(chara):* used eight times (1:14; 2:10; 8:13; 10:17; 15:7, 10; 24:41, 52), with only one parallel in Mark and two in Matthew.

"Peace" *(eirēnē):* used fourteen times (1:79; 2:14, 29; 7:50; 8:48; 10:5-6 [3x]; 11:21; 12:51; 14:32; 19:38, 42; 24:36) with only one parallel use in Mark (5:34 par. Luke 8:48) and another parallel use in Matthew (10:34 par. Luke 12:51). Luke thus has twelve distinctive uses, with two of these occurring in narrative events also reported in Matthew and Mark (Luke 11:21 [the same event in Matt. 12:29; Mark 3:27]; Luke 19:38 [the same event in Matt. 21:9; Mark 11:10]).

"Praise" *(aineō):* used four times (2:13, 20; 19:37; 24:53), with no parallels in Matthew and Mark. Further, "praise" in Luke has two other companion words, "glorify" and "bless." These also merit notice, for they form a triune ethos of jubilant response to God's marvelous salvation work in Jesus Christ.

"Glorify" *(doxazō):* nine uses (2:20; 4:15; 5:25, 26; 7:16; 13:13; 17:15; 18:43; 28:47), with only one same parallel in Mark (2:12) and Matthew (9:8), though Matthew uses the verb distinctively three times (5:16; 6:2; 15:31)

"Bless" *(eulogeō):* thirteen times (1:28, 42, 64; 2:28, 34; 6:28; 9:16; 13:35; 19:38; 24:30, 50, 51, 53). Three parallel uses occur in Mark (Mark 6:41 par. Luke 9:16; Mark 11:9-10 par. Luke 19:38; Mark 14:22 par. Luke 24:30); Mark also has one other use (8:7), not in Luke. Matthew has five uses, with three uses parallel to Luke and Mark (Matt. 14:19; 23:39; 26:26); one use parallel to Luke (Matt. 21:9 par. Luke 13:35); and one distinctive use (Matt. 25:34).

Remarkably, Luke strikes a mood in his Gospel that beckons us to hear afresh his presentation of Jesus, for in Luke Jesus' coming into this world and forming a new community means salvation, joy, and peace come from heaven to earth and also praising, glorifying, and blessing ascend to heaven. Gary Yamasaki has shown that "salvation" and "peace" reinforce each other in the wonderful "Christmas" text, Luke 2:10-14, quoted above.[1] His study of both terms as they are used in 1:47, 79 and 2:11, 14 indicates that for Luke "the concept of salvation is tied to the concept of peace." The shepherds experience both as they hear first the joyful announcement *(gospel)* of the angel, and then joined by the *praising* heavenly host. In examining Mary's song of *praise* together with Zechariah's in ch. 1, Yamasaki persuasively proposes that three important elements of OT *shalom* are announced: *material* well-being for the lowly in Mary's song; *political* well-being — deliverance from enemies (also in Zechariah's); and *spiritual* well-being, for a mighty *savior* (1:69) will bring *forgiveness of sins.*[2]

In this context of the announced "*Shalom* for the Shepherds," from the viewpoint of "audience-hearing" of the Gospel (Yamasaki's method of analy-

---

1. Yamasaki, "Shalom for Shepherds."
2. Yamasaki, "Shalom for Shepherds," pp. 154-55.

sis), listeners hear these hopes in the angel's and heavenly host's *gospel* announcement. Hence, "peace is stipulated as a resulting state for those experiencing God's salvation. To put it another way, God bestows salvation on the people in the form of peace."[3] Since *peace* occurs so frequently and in distinctive portions of Luke, the topic merits special study.

Jesus' Gospel of Peace *(Eirēnē)* in Luke

In order to discern Luke's intentions in presenting Jesus' gospel of glad tidings of great joy (2:10) as the good news of peace (see Luke's designation as such in Acts 10:36), we examine each of Luke's twelve distinctive uses of peace.[4]

Luke 1:79: "to give light to those who sit in darkness and in the shadow of death, to guide our feet into the way of peace."

The *eirēnē* phrase carries a threefold significance: (1) it functions as the conceptual and literary climax to Zechariah's hymn, exalting the Lord God for Israel's now appearing *salvation,* redemption from "our enemies"; (2) it stands, however, in poetic parallel to a phrase which unites Israel's redemption to the giving of light to "those who sit in darkness," plus several previous phrases of distinctively universal outlook; and (3) it concludes and climaxes the entire series of Lukan annunciation hymns, setting at the same time the mood for the birth of the Savior child. Luke's use of *eirēnē is* clearly strategic, presaging fulfillment of Israel's messianic peace hopes, e.g., Isaiah 2:1-4, where swords are beaten into plowshares.

Luke 2:14: "Glory to God in the highest heaven, and on earth peace among those whom he favors!"

Heralding peace on earth because of God's limitless benevolence, this use sums up the divine commentary regarding the significance of Jesus' birth. Just as *eirēnē* was the last word of the human annunciation of Jesus' coming (1:79), so *eirēnē* is a key word in the divine commentary on the event of Jesus' birth. The preceding pericope of angelic announcement (vv. 10-12) clearly places the *eirēnē* text within Israel's tradition-hope of a Messiah-Savior, a king par excellence who, like Yahweh of old, will bring salvation to God's people. The text, however, does not limit the Messiah's peace to Israel, but envisions peace on earth among people everywhere.

3. Yamasaki, "Shalom for Shepherds," p. 155.

4. This portion is adapted from my "Politics and Peace *(Eirēnē)* in Luke's Gospel," pp. 26-29. The recent book (which appeared too late to come into my discussion) by Joseph A. Grassi, *Peace on Earth,* makes a good contribution to the topic, but does not analyze all of Luke's uses in context or show the relationship of peace to justice (the subject of his earlier book on Luke).

The text also culminates the angelic announcement to the shepherds: "And the angel said to them, 'Be not afraid; for behold, I bring you good news *(euangelizomai hymin)* of a great joy which will come to all people; . . . Glory to God in the highest, and on earth peace *(eirēnē)* among those with whom God is pleased'" (Luke 2:10, 14). These verses link *gospel* and *peace,* and v. 11 connects both to the royal tradition, for the baby born is of the "house of David."

Luke 2:29: "Master, now you are dismissing your servant in peace, according to your word. . . ."

While this use of *eirēnē* may be considered somewhat formulaic (cf. Gen. 15:15), its strategic function in Luke's birth narratives gives it crucial significance: the word itself is part of a unique prophetic oracle inspired by the Holy Spirit (vv. 25, 26, 27). Simeon, a man whose only credentials are his piety (v. 25) and his waiting for Israel's consolation *(paraklēsis),* can die in peace because Israel's hopes are now going to be fulfilled through the birth of this child Jesus, the Lord's Christ. The parallel themes to peace in the oracle are the appearance of God's salvation which shall be "a light for revelation to the Gentiles" and a glory to Israel. The death of God's servant *in peace* rests upon the certainty that God's now appearing consolation will have salvific significance both for the Gentiles (mentioned first!) and for Israel, thus fulfilling the universalistic messianic hopes of Isaiah 40ff. Thus any notion of vindicating Israel's hopes in nationalistic and exclusivist categories is repudiated.

Luke 7:50: "And he said to the woman, 'Your faith has saved you; go in peace.'"

This occurrence of *eirēnē* comes at the end of Luke's distinctive story of Jesus and the sinful woman, a story told in the context of a controversy over Jesus' authority and the negative response of the religious leaders. The story itself illustrates positive response, the love of the sinner forgiven much. The phrase "go in peace," climaxing discussion on Jesus' authority, occurs in conjunction with the woman's forgiveness and salvation. However, because this phrase, like 2:29, is somewhat formularic (cf. 8:48), it has limited significance when assessing Luke's editorial purposes.

Luke 10:5-6: "Whatever house you enter, first say, 'Peace to this house!' And if anyone is there who shares in peace, your peace will rest on that person; but if not, it will return to you."

Three uses of peace *(eirēnē)* occur here in Luke's distinctive account of Jesus sending out the seventy to proclaim the good news of the kingdom of God. This text, together with those in Luke's infancy chapters, is highly significant for assessing Luke's purpose. It is placed close to the beginning of Luke's special section known as the Journey Narrative, and thus serves as the first bookend matching the bookend of peace texts in 19:38-42, coming at the end of Luke's special section.

If one regards 9:51-62 as introductory to the section, then the first and last narratives in the section (10:1ff.; 19:28ff.) are laced with Luke's peace accent. The word occurs three times in 10:5-6, including the phrase "son of peace," and twice again in 19:28-42. Each occurrence is crucial and strategic both in Luke's literary design and theological intention. In the mission of the seventy, which prefigures the church's later mission to the Gentiles, the first word of address is "Peace be to this house." If a "child of peace" is there, the door will be open; you shall enter, heal the sick and say, "the kingdom of God has come near you" (v. 9). If the peace is refused, it "shall return to you" and you shall wipe off the dust of your feet against them and say, "Nevertheless, know this, that the kingdom of God has come near" (v. 11).[5] A peace response becomes the criterion by which the people receive the kingdom of God or condemnation. Certainly this emphasis, heading up Luke's special section, carries forward his narrative intentions in 2:14 where the angelic choir heralds the meaning of Jesus' birth as "glory in heaven" and "peace on earth."

Four features of 10:5-6 in its larger context are significant:

1. The message which the seventy take to the people is introduced by a greeting of peace *(shalom/eirēnē)*: "Peace be to this house" (v. 5).

2. The one who receives the gospel is called "a son or child of peace" (v. 6). This echoes Jesus' Beatitude, "Blessed are the peacemakers, for they shall be called the sons/children of God" (Matt. 5:9; cf. 5:48).

3. The gospel-peace message is further defined as "the kingdom of God" which has come to them (vv. 9, 11), regardless whether they accept or reject it.

4. On the basis of Jesus' statement in v. 18, "I was seeing Satan fall like lightning from heaven," it is clear that this kingdom peace gospel is one of ultimate power. It carries with it the power to overthrow the forces of evil. It extends and fulfills the long march of God's victorious battle against evil through Scripture.

The three uses of *peace (eirēnē)* in this text thus indicate that:

The gospel in its essence and distinguishing feature is peace;
Jesus' purpose in his mission is to identify and gather children of peace.[6]

---

5. Further, the seventy are "sent *(apesteilen)*," the same word used for Jesus' mission in 4:18, 43; Jesus sends the seventy out before his face *(pro prosōpou autou,* 10:1). While the favorite Lukan verb *euangelizomai* does not occur here, the same activity is carried forward by the seventy under the gospel salutation, "Peace be to this house."

6. William Klassen regards this phrase "son of peace" to be a unique and most significant

The peace gospel is God's way in Jesus and his followers to subdue evil. This missionary imperative to all nations (the seventy symbolizes the worldwide mission) extends the gospel as a gospel of peace.

Luke's purpose is to show that this gospel found its way to Rome, took root there, and began to do its work amid the greatest world empire known to date. The kingdom-gospel brought by Jesus is God's reign of peace; it will be victorious. It shall embrace all peoples. As Isaiah saw it, "All peoples shall see the salvation of the Lord" (Isa. 52:10).

Indeed, this text is linked with the themes of the seventy disciples healing the sick, proclaiming the dawning of the kingdom, and finally rejoicing that even the demons were subject to them in the name of Jesus (10:17). This leads to Jesus' astounding declaration, "I was seeing Satan falling like lightning from heaven." Clearly and dramatically, Luke presents Jesus the Savior (1:47; 2:11) as the one whose gospel of peace overthrows the powers of evil, indeed Satan himself. Victory over Satan and the demons is also a major theme of Luke, as I have shown elsewhere.[7]

Luke 14:32: "If he cannot, then, while the other is still far away, he sends a delegation and asks for the terms of peace."

This use of peace *(eirēnē)* occurs in a story told to illustrate the Gospel's emphasis on the call to discipleship. In the illustrative story, peace functions as the alternative to war, but the story itself commends neither war nor peace. It rather illustrates the necessity of counting the cost when taking up the cross of Jesus.

Luke 19:38, 42: "'Blessed is the king who comes in the name of the Lord! *Peace* in heaven, and glory in the highest heaven!' Some of the Pharisees in the crowd said to him, 'Teacher, order your disciples to stop.' He answered, 'I tell you, if these were silent, the stones would shout out.' As he came near and saw the city, he wept over it, saying, 'If you, even you, had only recognized on this day the things that make for *peace*! But now they are hidden from your eyes.'" (I cite the paragraph to show the connection between the two uses.)

These Lukan uses of peace *(eirēnē)* occur close to the end of Luke's special section (most scholars place the end at 19:44). Jesus' entry into Jerusalem (vv. 28-38) occurs in Matthew and Mark also, but Luke adds two *eirēnē* declarations. The first concludes the triumphal entry chorus, sung by a great crowd

---

expression, close in meaning perhaps to a "son of Torah." The phrase thus denotes dedication to the way of peace, the giving of one's life in service to its cause (cf. "peacemaker" in Matt. 5:9). See Klassen, "A Child of Peace"; "The Novel Element in the Love Commandment of Jesus."

7. Swartley, *Israel's Scripture Traditions,* pp. 85-87.

of Jesus' disciples, according to Luke. The phrase, "Peace in heaven and glory in the highest heavens," climaxing the chant, may be intended as earth's antiphonal response to heaven's declaration in 2:14, "Peace on earth among those of good will." It is clearly a Lukan emphasis; only Luke puts the *praise* (!), including "Blessed is the king who comes in the name of the Lord!" on the lips of disciples, people who have responded positively to Jesus. Some of the Pharisees, however, want Jesus to rebuke his disciples for greeting him with their outcry, "Blessed is the King who comes in the name of the Lord! Peace in heaven and glory in the highest." Jesus answers, "I tell you, if these were silent, the very stones would cry out" (19:38-40, RSV). Then as Jesus draws near to the city, he says, "Would that even today you knew the things that make for peace! But they are hidden from your eyes." Luke is saying that earth must cry out and acclaim Jesus king of peace. If earth's people of good will do not acclaim Jesus as king of peace, the stones will cry it out.[8]

Then Jesus laments over Jerusalem. Jesus weeps over the city because it does not know on this day, the day of Jesus' entry, what brings *peace*. The city does not recognize its king of peace and hence faces judgment and destruction. Failure to recognize and understand peace is the criterion against which Jesus judges Jerusalem, the cornerstone *(Jeru)* of peace *(shalom)*. Specifically, judgment comes because the people failed to "recognize their opportunity when God offered it" (v. 44; so also in 10:10-15). This then provides the context for Jesus' cleansing the temple, a prophetic act calling for the justice of God's peace. The passion narrative, opening with this emphasis, thus depicts the rejection of the king of peace. The structural function of these two *eirēnē* texts, closing off Luke's special section, underscores the prominence that Luke assigns to *eirēnē*.

Luke 24:36: "While they were talking about this, Jesus himself stood among them and said to them, 'Peace be with you.'"[9]

God's mission of peace, and not the people's rejection of it, triumphs. The resurrected Lord, upon appearing to the eleven gathered disciples, says, first of all, "Peace be with you!" In view of Luke's preceding peace emphasis,

---

8. Might Jesus be saying that *the stones will cry out "Peace" since you do not*? It is possible that this aphorism reflects the same notions that appear in later rabbinic writings where "the unhewn stones" ("stones of perfection," *šelemuṭ*) prescribed for building in Deut. 27:6 are several times called "stones that bring peace" *(šalom)*. See Urbach, *The Sages*, pp. 370-71, 597.

9. This occurrence of *eirēnē* is textually problematic. While most manuscripts include the *eirēnē* blessing upon the disciples, some mss. (D and the early old Latin mss.) lack the phrase. Since the addition can be explained by influence from John, the RSV omitted it, but the NRSV includes it (the ms. evidence for the phrase includes 𝔓⁷⁵ ℵ B and many early translations). Since also the use of *eirēnē* is characteristic for Luke, it certainly is original.

the phrase must be considered more than a customary greeting in this context. The words signal the triumph of the incarnation's purpose according to Luke. Peace comes to earth in the Messiah, born as Bearer of peace (2:14), proclaimed as Lord of peace (10:5 6), and rejected as King of peace (19:38-42). The worldwide mission of peace (signaled in 10:5-6) triumphs through the risen Jesus, who reassures his disciples that *eirēnē* remains.

Peace Texts That Occur Also in Matthew and Mark

Luke 11:21: "When a strong man, fully armed, guards his castle, his property is safe."

This use of *eirēnē* is similar to that of 14:32, discussed above. The word peace occurs within a story-image that illustrates Luke's main point, i.e., that Beelzebul's house (palace) is not *in peace* because God's kingdom, coming in Jesus, is stronger than Beelzebul. In this illustrative metaphor, *eirēnē* denotes security or safety. While the range of meaning for *eirēnē* is illustrated both here and in 14:32, these uses do not contribute directly to Luke's purposes elsewhere to show that the good news of Jesus is an *eirēnē*-event.

Luke 19:38. This distinctive Lukan use of *eirēnē* contributes indeed to Luke's purpose to connect the mission of Jesus to peace (see above on 19:38, 42).

Occurrences of "Peace" with Parallel Textual Uses

Luke 8:48: "He said to her, 'Daughter, your faith has made you well; go in peace.'"

Jesus' word, *go in peace,* to the daughter healed of a hemorrhage functions as a word of blessing. Peace is here associated with physical health, connoting wholeness and salvation. In Luke 7:50 the phrase is associated with forgiveness of sins. Because the phrase is an exact parallel to Mark 5:34, it may be that little special Lukan significance can be attached to it. But, on the other hand, from a Lukan narrative standpoint it does add to the emphasis of his other clearly distinctive uses of *eirēnē*. In this context it then connotes not only physical and spiritual health, but healed relationships socially. For the woman can now function as a full and respected member of her family, kinship, and community groups.

Luke 12:51: "Do you think that I have come to bring peace to the earth? No, I tell you, but rather division!"

This use of *eirēnē* appears to directly contradict Luke's efforts elsewhere to describe the significance of the gospel with *eirēnē*. But several factors preclude outright contradiction. The saying occurs in a larger section that advances Luke's teaching on Jesus' call to costly discipleship (cf. 14:32). Further, *eirēnē* is used in a metaphorical saying that illustrates the effect of costly discipleship upon family relationships. Luke may have felt the potential contradiction between this saying and his special emphases elsewhere, since Luke's version of the Q saying tones down the sharpness of Matthew's by at least three significant changes: *dokeite* instead of *nomisēte* (both mean "think," but with different nuances); *dounai* ("give") instead of *balein* ("cast" or "bring"): and, most significant, *diamerismon* ("division") instead of *machairan* ("sword"). With these changes, Luke protects the word from any notion that the gospel allows the use of the sword against enemies; he clearly assigns to it the meaning of division among household members that the gospel brings.

In sum, then, the twelve distinctive *peace* texts in Luke, with the exception of 14:32, serve the purpose of showing that Jesus in his proclamation of the kingdom of God announces and incarnates the gospel of peace *(eirēnē)*. Other Lukan themes connected to *eirēnē* in these texts belong to Luke's larger repertoire of special emphases: redemption from oppression, light to the pagans, forgiveness of sins, blessings to the outsiders (Gentiles, a sinner, women), a "yes" to those of good will, God's announced peace (2:14) empowering the disciples' peace-gospel as the hallmark of the missionary growth of the kingdom and the distinguishing character of the Jesus community, acceptance of God's purposes in the Messiah Jesus (and conversely, judgment upon those who reject the peace of the Messiah), and receiving the peace of Christ's presence.

It is important to note that Luke's distinctive occurrences of *eirēnē* occur at structurally strategic places in the Gospel's narrative. Three uses occur in Luke's infancy narratives (1:79; 2:14, 29) and thus set the mood of peace expectancy: the announced coming one will bring *eirene* as a new and unprecedented historical reality.[10] A second structurally strategic cluster comes close to the beginning and end of Luke's special section (10:5-6; 19:38, 42). Jesus' teachings on discipleship that leads to the kingdom of God are framed by peace emphases. And conversely, when *eirēnē* is refused, judgment follows

---

10. For this reason I do not agree with J. Massyngberde Ford, who in her otherwise most insightful book regards Luke's first three chapters as resonant with Judaism's expectation of a militant Messiah, while, beginning with Jesus' ministry in Nazareth, the opposing, peaceful view of messiahship begins to unfold. See her provocative study *My Enemy Is My Guest*. Otherwise, her view of Luke's portrait of Jesus provides corroborative support for mine.

(10:10-12; 19:43-46). Jesus' *eirēnē* thus brings crisis, a point clearly expressed in 12:51. The third structurally crucial occurrence is 24:36 where peace is the resurrected Lord's self-identifying greeting to his disciples.

These uses together make it clear that for Luke peace *(eirēnē)* expresses the very heart of the gospel. Further, his continuing uses of *eirēnē* in Acts corroborate this point (especially 7:26; 9:31; 10:36; 15:33). In these instances, *eirēnē* describes reconciliation, the advancement of the gospel, breaking down barriers, and celebrating the unity of the church.[11] Clearly, *eirēnē* essentially describes the mission of Jesus in Luke's double volume on Jesus and his Spirit.

Two Distinctive Corroborating Features

In discussing Matthew's call to not resist one doing evil against you, but rather to love the enemy, we noted that Luke's moral instruction on these points occurs in a different order (Luke 6:27-36). Luke accentuates Jesus' command to love enemies by putting it first *and* last in the series.[12] The first utterance is followed by "do good to those who hate you, bless those who curse you, pray for those who abuse you," which explicates that love for enemies is to be expressed through positive action to transform enmity into caring relationship. After four focal instances illustrating positive action,[13] Luke enunciates a warranting principle, "Do to others as you would have them do to you" (v. 31). This is followed by discounting love shown only to those who love in return (v. 32), which further accentuates the priority of the love of enemy command. A chiastic analysis readily shows this to be the center reinforcing the beginning and ending command:

> a   But I say to you that listen, Love your enemies, do good to those who hate you, bless those who curse you, pray for those who abuse you.

11. John R. Donahue has called attention to this emphasis in Luke-Acts as well; see his article "The Good News of Peace."

12. Scholars debate whether Luke's or Matthew's version more closely represents what Jesus said. While this point lies outside the scope of my study, most scholars argue that Luke's version is closer to Jesus' actual words since Matthew clearly has a didactic formula and pattern shaping 5:21-48 (the six supertheses). Wink, however, argues for Matthew as the more authentic (see his article cited in Chapter 3 above).

13. Luke does not include Jesus' saying on "going the second mile." Further, Jesus' command to give both coat and shirt (NRSV) is not portrayed as a lawsuit, as it possibly is in Matthew.

b   If anyone strikes you on the cheek, offer the other also; and
from anyone who takes away your coat do not withhold even
your shirt. Give to everyone who begs from you; and if
anyone takes away your goods, do not ask for them again.

c   Do to others as you would have them do to you.

b′   If you love those who love you, what credit is that to you?
For even sinners love those who love them. If you lend to
those from whom you hope to receive, what credit is that to
you? Even sinners lend to sinners, to receive as much again.[14]

a′   But love your enemies, do good, and lend, expecting nothing in
return. Your reward will be great, and you will be children of the
Most High; for he is kind to the ungrateful and the wicked. Be
merciful, just as your Father is merciful.

While Luke does not have Jesus' beatitude of blessing on the peacemakers,
his moral instruction in this teaching exemplifies the action of the peacemaker.
Even more clearly than in Matthew, Jesus' commands in Luke not only highlight the appeal to the character of the heavenly Father, but also demonstrate
consistently positive actions. There are no *non* commands, whether nonresistance or nonviolence. Both indeed may be implied, but the stress falls on the
priority to do good, bless, pray, offer, give, and lend. The only negatives occur in
oppositional phrases to the positive ("do not withhold even your shirt" and "do
not ask for them [goods] again"). Grasping Luke's distinctive emphasis in Jesus'
words here reinforces his larger portrait that Jesus comes as peace proclaimer
and doer, despite those verses that seem to contradict (12:51 discussed above).

A second important feature of Luke's account is the sword sayings Jesus
spoke to his disciples at his arrest (Luke 22:36b, 38; 22:49-52).[15] While these
sayings appear to contradict a *peace (eirēnē)* interpretation of Jesus in Luke,
yet close examination of the flow of the narrative here in Luke indicates that
Luke's Jesus is sheathing the sword, not calling for its use. His command to go
buy a sword is a graphic way of announcing the imminence of hostile circumstances.[16] Further, v. 37 gives a reason for the saying, to fulfill Scripture, specifically, the Isaiah 53:12c saying, "he was counted among the lawless."[17] That

14. This admonition is similar to two in B, but still a bit different. With this one, Luke too
has five "focal instances." But strikingly, four of them deal with property or money, a theme
widely recognized as dominant throughout Luke's Gospel.

15. The Matthean parallel, Matt. 26:52-53, is discussed in Chapter 3 above.

16. I. Howard Marshall, "New Testament Perspectives on War," p. 127.

17. Jean Lasserre combines these two points and rejects the literal meaning, saying that
twelve swords would not have been enough, let alone just two (*War and the Gospel*, pp. 37-45).

both these statements contain as closure the sharp declarations "It is enough" (*hikanon estin* in v. 38b) and "No more of this" (*eate heōs toutou* in v. 51b) indicates that Jesus wanted his disciples to face up to their impulses, and then decisively counter them. The scene about to unfold, with temple police coming out with swords and clubs, does call, from the natural instinct to self-defend, for swords to ward off the opponent. I. H. Marshall suggests 22:38b be translated, "Enough of this,"[18] indicating Jesus' reprimand of their "sword" type thinking.[19] Jesus' sharp rebuke against the use of the sword makes the point: sheath the sword, it will do no good.[20] His healing the high priest's slave's ear demonstrates his mission and manner of ministry. Put sharply, Jesus came to heal precisely what the sword devastates. Jesus' interchange with his disciples is a vivid simulation that shows the futility of the sword.[21]

From the standpoint of narrative analysis these "sword" texts grate against the larger peace *(eirēnē)* emphasis of Luke's Gospel. In this way the sword is exposed and repudiated. Noteworthy also is Luke's placement of Jesus' teaching that contrasts the servant way of the disciple with that of "the kings of the Gentiles" at the beginning (22:24-27) of this section of interchange on the *sword*. The fuller narrative thus "corrects" any notion that use of the sword would be fitting to Jesus and those who follow the "one who serves" (22:27c).

18. Marshall, "New Testament Perspectives," p. 127. Richard J. Cassidy says that Jesus' forgiving those who crucified him settles the question of what Jesus intended. *Jesus, Politics, and Society,* pp. 45-47.

19. Hubert Frankemölle interprets this differently, saying that Luke, writing after the destruction of Jerusalem, "is not seeking to justify the use of force in itself but rather shows understanding for those who used force to defend themselves in an emergency." Nonetheless, in Jesus' further responses and actions "it is made clear that Jesus expected no salvation by the sword, nor from the freedom struggle of the Zealots, and that peace cannot be achieved through the sword" ("Peace and the Sword in the New Testament," p. 224, revised edition, pp. 203-4). I doubt that Luke intended to give such a double message.

20. For fuller exposition of these texts in Luke 22 see my article "War and Peace in the New Testament," pp. 2322-24.

21. Hays gives a similar interpretation in *Moral Vision of the New Testament,* pp. 334-36. I summarize his view in Appendix 1 below. Kümmel also says of these sword texts: Matt. 10:34 par. Luke 12:51 "says nothing else but that Jesus' coming produces a division among people according to their attitude toward Jesus," and in Luke 22:35-38 the "word 'sword' can only be used in a figurative sense." It cannot be used to portray Jesus as a political governing Messiah but shows that "only obedience to God is decisive" (Kümmel, *Theology of the New Testament,* pp. 65, 73). See also my treatment in *Slavery, Sabbath,* pp. 122, 254. Schertz, "Swords and Prayer," proposes that Jesus' prayers on Olivet, at the center of the 22:31-62 chiasm, points to Jesus' own struggle with the sword. Perhaps, but if so, with it is a "both-and," since Jesus' disciples are highlighted at the beginning and end of the prayer paragraph.

Luke's Peace and Political Stance

Given Luke's distinctive emphasis on peace *(eirēnē)*, how is this emphasis to be understood in relation to the political stance of the Gospel? Competing theses have been advanced regarding Luke's political stance and intentions. Many New Testament "Introductions" describe Luke as a Gospel written to show that the Christian gospel is non-political and poses no threat to the empire. This view arises from Hans Conzelmann's influential work *The Theology of St. Luke,* which highlights the favorable depictions of Roman soldiers and Jesus' innocence before Pilate at his trial. Jesus' conflicts are with the Jews, not Roman rulers.[22] Richard Cassidy's and John Howard Yoder's books on Luke, however, emphasize other features in Luke's Gospel. Cassidy shows numerous times when the political authorities are not represented positively. Jesus refuses to defer to the political authorities, both Jews and Romans, as follows:

> In a derogatory remark, Jesus calls Herod (Antipas) a fox (13:31-33).
> The conflict between Jesus and the chief priests is great (19:47; 20:19), and during his trial Jesus responds first sarcastically (22:67-68), and then noncommittally (22:70).
> Jesus speaks of Pilate's massacre of the Galileans (13:1-3).
> The tax dispute puts God's claims in tension with, perhaps opposition to, Caesar's (20:21-25; 23:2).
> Jesus speaks of the behavior of the kings of the Gentiles as exactly what his followers are to refuse, and not to emulate in any way (22:24-27).
> Jesus says his disciples will be persecuted by kings and governors (21:12-15).
> Though Pilate declares Jesus not guilty three times, yet Pilate "gave the verdict" (23:24) for Jesus' execution and put the inscription over the cross, "This is the king of the Jews" (23:38). He also had jurisdiction over the body (23:52).[23]

Cassidy also describes Jesus' social stance as cutting against the grain of Rome's values. Five major emphases of Jesus in Luke's Gospel voice these values:[24]

22. See my article "Politics and Peace," pp. 18-20, for a fuller presentation of Conzelmann's views.

23. Cassidy, *Jesus, Politics, and Society,* pp. 50-79.

24. The following summary of Cassidy and Yoder is drawn, with modifications, from my article "Politics and Peace," pp. 21-24.

1. Jesus shows concern for the poor, the infirm, the women, and the Gentiles. Mary's Magnificat introduces Jesus as one who will vindicate the poor, send the rich empty away, and dethrone the mighty (1:52-53); John's preaching also calls the people to share their extra coats with those who have none (3:11). Jesus himself associates his mission with the social themes of Isaiah (Luke 4:18-19) which emerge later as the distinctive features of his ministry (7:22-23). This emphasis marks Jesus' preaching also: he announces blessing to the poor (6:20-21) and woe to the rich (6:24-25). Luke's Gospel regards Gentiles favorably (4:26-27), showing a universal outlook but not endorsing the status quo. It also gives special place to women, showing again its socially revolutionary character (7:11-17, 36-50; 8:2, 43-48; 13:10-13).

2. Jesus takes a clear stand against riches and criticizes the rich. He speaks against accumulating possessions (12:15-21) and counsels to live simply (10:4; 12:22-24). He instructs the rich to give to the poor (12:32-34; 16:9; 18:18-23) and repeatedly warns the rich against the destructiveness and perils of riches (8:14; 16:15, 19-31; 18:24-25; 21:1-4). He praises those who gave up possessions (7:25, 36-50; 19:8-10).

3. Jesus speaks and acts against practices of oppression and injustice (18:1-5; 20:9-19, 45-47). By affirming new personal and social identity for women, he takes a stand against structural oppression (8:1-3; 10:38-42; 16:18).

4. Jesus calls for social relations to be based upon service and humility (9:47-48; 14:7-11; 17:7-10; 20:46-47). Further, Jesus specifically identifies service and humility as characteristics that mark off his followers from the kings of the Gentiles "who lord it over them" (22:24-27). The model of kingdom behavior stands opposed to the empire model.

5. Jesus takes a stand against violence; his teaching encourages nonresistance (6:27-31). While speaking negatively of violence, he calls his followers to the way of repentance and forgiveness (17:3-4). Sayings that contain imagery of violence are best explained otherwise and do not alter this prevailing ethic (12:49-53; 22:35-38).[25] Jesus calls for the things that make for peace (19:42-44) and regards those who come with swords as inappropriately responding to his ministry (22:47-51).[26]

John H. Yoder's seminal work, *The Politics of Jesus,* advances a view of Luke that is a precursor to and corroborates Cassidy's view of Jesus' social stance. Yoder's thesis is that Jesus' ministry, from beginning to end, was socially, economically, and politically revolutionary. This provides no basis for the notion that Luke's presentation of Jesus and Christianity is intended to

---

25. See my treatment of these in Chapter 2 above and in *Slavery, Sabbath,* pp. 250-55.
26. Cassidy, pp. 20-49.

convince Rome that the Jesus movement is politically benign. Yoder's theses are (with additional comments of my own at several places):[27]

1. The annunciation texts and John's preaching (Luke 1:46ff., 68ff., cf. 3:7ff.) interpret the messianic advent in starkly socio-political images and hopes; e.g.

> he has put down the mighty from their thrones
> and exalted those of low degree;
> he has filled the hungry with good things
> and the rich he has sent empty away (1:52-53).

The birth narrative of chapter 2 also accentuates the political features of Jesus' coming: Bethlehem, David's city; "peace on earth"; and the liberation hopes of Simeon and Anna (cf. Matthew's report of Herod's fear and his massacre of babies).

2. Jesus' commissioning and testing (Luke 3:21–4:14) merge the themes of kingly enthronement (Psalm 2) and suffering servanthood (Isa. 42), on the one hand, and then show, on the other, that this unique commission is tested in the three temptations by empire models of economics, politics, and religion.

3. Luke introduces Jesus' ministry in the Nazareth synagogue with Jesus' jubilean sermon of Isaiah 61 (Luke 4:16-20). Jesus' messianic mission is described in expressly social terms:

> a   To *preach good news* to the poor,
>   b   To proclaim *release* to the captives,
>   c   And recovering of sight to the blind,
>   b′   To send forth the *oppressed in release,*
> a′   To proclaim the acceptable year of the Lord.

This great text of liberation outlines the mission of Jesus around five powerful declarations, with Luke's great word for *gospelize (euangelizomai)* at the head of the list. This specific textual arrangement with italicized key words highlights the recurring use of *release* in b and b′. By dropping one line of Isaiah 61:1, "to bind up the brokenhearted," and inserting one line from Isaiah 58:6, "to let the oppressed go free *(release),*" Luke puts special stress on the theme of *release,* a point that further substantiates Yoder's thesis.

Since the text begins with the anointing of the Servant Jesus, a kingly

---

27. John Howard Yoder, *The Politics of Jesus.* The following summary is of his chapter 2.

messianic act and symbol, the theme of gospel is linked directly to the reign of God. Jesus is anointed by the Spirit for his royal identity, first publicly in his baptism, and now again to begin his mission. Hence the liberating activity of *gospelizing* is the work of God's reign manifest in Jesus' deeds, words, death, and resurrection.

Holding that "the year of favor" refers to "the year of jubilee," Yoder argues that Jesus' mission is clearly presented as "a visible socio-political, economic restructuring of relations among the people of God."[28]

4. Jesus' sermon on the plain (Luke 6:12ff.) spells out in detail the socio-economic consequences of his Nazareth address. Having already established a new social reality in the Twelve, Jesus' teaching supported by his action enunciates an ethic of a new order. Rooted in God's boundless love even for rebellious sinners (6:35-36), Jesus' ethic is strikingly different from natural-law behavior (6:32-34).

5. When Jesus fed the multitude bread in the desert (9:1-22), the crowd wanted to make Jesus their welfare king. But Jesus withdraws and begins to teach that suffering and cross-bearing are essential components of God's kingdom. His withdrawal is not retreat but a renewed messianic commitment: "The cross is beginning to loom not as a ritually prescribed instrument of propitiation but as the political alternative to both insurrection and quietism."[29]

6. Jesus' teaching on the cost of discipleship (12:49–13:9; 14:25-35), framed by awareness of violent political events (13:1-9, 31ff.), instructs followers on the difficult experiences that arise from joining the new community of *voluntary* commitment: division within families and forsaking aspirations to greatness (22:25ff.). To form a new community with such distinctive lifestyles "constitutes an unavoidable challenge to the powers that be and . . . [introduces] a new set of social alternatives."[30]

7. Jesus' epiphany in the temple (19:36-46) depicts Jesus' kingly authority and incites the hostility of the chief priests to his messianic act and claim in cleansing the temple. This leads to a sequence of confrontations between "two social systems and Jesus' rejection of the status quo" (19:47–22:2).

8. The final episodes in Jesus' public ministry (22:24-53) show Jesus' last renunciation of messianic violence. He rejects a Zealot-like kingship by refusing to allow his disciples to defend him with the sword; though able to do so, he does not call twelve legions of angels to deliver him (Matt. 26:53).

28. Yoder, p. 39 (1994, p. 32).
29. Yoder, p. 43 (1994, p. 36).
30. Yoder, p. 47 (1994, p. 39).

9. Jesus' execution and exaltation (Luke 23-24) contain numerous political accents: traded for Barabbas, an insurrectionist, Jesus is crucified as a Zealot leader and "King of the Jews"; the irregularities of the trials accent the threat that the Jewish and Roman authorities felt Jesus to be; and in the post-resurrection narrative, Jesus' disciples still express their long-cherished hope that he will redeem Israel (24:21).

Yoder concludes this sketch of the social, economic, and political significance of Jesus' mission in Luke by declaring that "Jesus was in his divinely mandated prophethood, priesthood, and kingship, the bearer of a new possibility of human, social, and therefore, political relationships."[31]

Yoder follows up this sketch with an even more detailed analysis of the jubilean features of Jesus' mission *à la* Luke. He relates various teachings of Jesus in Luke to the four prescriptions for the year of jubilee (Lev. 25): (1) leaving the soil fallow, (2) the remission of debts, (3) the liberation of slaves, and (4) the return to each individual of his family's property.[32]

Yoder's portrait of Jesus as God's Jubilean prophet-Messiah bringing God's reign into concrete historical expression, together with those themes identified by Cassidy, clearly document that Luke is not a pawn of Rome's pacification policies. Rather, Luke develops a view of Jesus and the movement he began as an alternative social force in society. But Yoder does not sufficiently contextualize Luke's jubilee. For as Yoder intimates when he says that Luke 4:24-30 does not follow up on the emphasis of 4:18-19, something is missing in his pursuit of a rather literal application in Luke's Gospel. As I have argued elsewhere in critique of Yoder, Luke has his own program of contextualizing jubilee's meaning for his time and setting. I excerpt here a section from my article,[33] in which I ask if there are additional ways of thinking about the Jubilean theme that, if explored, would further support the Lukan Jubilee portrait of Jesus. Such possible emphases are:

> 1. Luke's recurring statements of blessings to the poor and stern warnings toward the rich. Almost all of chapters 12 and 16, the end of 18, and the beginning of 19 treat this theme. This emphasis has been widely recognized by New Testament scholars. What a congenial theme to the Jubilean platform!
>
> 2. Luke's frequent emphasis upon the important role of women in the Gospel drama: Elizabeth, Mary, Anna, the women from Galilee included

---

31. Yoder, pp. 62-63 (1994, p. 52).

32. This section summarizes chapter 3 of Yoder's *Politics of Jesus*.

33. For context and fuller treatment see my "Smelting for Gold: Jesus and Jubilee in John H. Yoder's *Politics of Jesus*" (quoting from pp. 294-96).

among Jesus' disciples, Martha and Mary, and the women at the tomb. Although the role of women is not an intrinsic part of the Old Testament Jubilee theme, the emphasis upon women in Luke's Gospel may be viewed as an expression of Jubilee justice and concern for equality.

3. Luke's strong emphasis upon Jesus' acceptance of sinners, outcasts, and outsiders. Note especially Luke 7:36-50[34] and all of chapter 15. Jubilee means that the forgiven prostitute and prodigal have a future in Jesus' messianic kingdom and community, a concrete fulfillment of the synagogue address. Precisely at this point the connection between the two parts of Luke 4:16-30 is apparent, since the Gentiles in 4:24-30 are, from a Jewish point of view, outcasts and outsiders. This point contrasts sharply to the use made of Isa. 61 in the Qumran community, where vengeance on the outsiders — the part not quoted from Isaiah (61:2b) by Jesus in Luke — is the main emphasis in 11QMelch.[35]

4. Luke's clear intent is to highlight the ministry of Jesus as "gospelizing," a literal translation of *euangelisasthai* in line *a* of the Nazareth synagogue reading. This *euangel* verb occurs 25 times in Luke-Acts to stress the spread of the gospel under the leading of the Holy Spirit. This evangelistic shower of blessing demonstrates too that Jesus' messianic kingdom breaks racial and national boundaries. In Acts it includes Samaritans, Gentiles, of whom one was Ethiopian. The main story line tells of the gospel's spread through Asia Minor, Macedonia, and finally to Rome. Luke-Acts is aptly titled, "From the Temple to Rome."[36]

5. Luke strongly emphasizes the gospel's *release* of people from Satan's power, and that occurs explicitly throughout both volumes. The feature has generated extended study of Luke's portrayal of the gospel's deliver-

34. James A. Sanders, "Sins, Debts, and Jubilee Release" (Evans and Sanders, eds., *Luke and Sacred Scripture*, pp. 84-92), develops at length this point that Luke makes of the woman's anointing something quite different from what occurs in the other three Gospels. Luke wants it to be a Jubilee manifesto. In the inner core of the story the verb *echarisato*, from *charizomai*, meaning "freely remit or graciously grant," occurs twice. The latter part of the story stresses the importance of forgiveness (verb forms of *aphesis*) and the pronouncement of forgiveness ("Your sins are forgiven," v. 48).

35. J. Massyngberde Ford rightly proposes that Isa. 61:1-3 serves as the textual heart of both 11QMelch and Luke 4:16-21, though Luke differs from 11QMelch in that he does not portray the vengeance function in the use of the text ("Reconciliation and Forgiveness in Luke's Gospel"). James Sanders ("From Isaiah 61 to Luke 4," Evans and Sanders, eds., *Luke and Sacred Scripture*, p. 101) puts it provocatively: "Is it not possible that Jesus might have used the *Essene second axiom as a foil* against which he gave his prophetic understanding of the judgements and grace of God in the End Time — and thereby so deeply offended some of his compatriots (was not *dektos* [accepted] in his own *patris*)."

36. See Swartley, *Israel's Scripture Traditions*, pp. 78-80.

ance from Satan's powers and specifically magical powers (Acts 8, 12, 16, 19). I have treated this theme in Luke elsewhere and Susan Garrett has studied it more broadly in Luke-Acts.[37]

Specific citations make the point. When John the Baptist in prison sends messengers to Jesus to ask if he is the one to come, or shall we look for another, Luke precedes Jesus' answer with, "Jesus had just cured many people of diseases, plagues, and evil spirits, and had given sight to many who were blind" (7:21). Hence, Jesus' healing and exorcisms attest to his messianic mission.

Likewise, Luke's summary of Jesus' mission in Peter's sermon celebrating the gospel's inclusion of Gentile Cornelius is that God's message of "preaching (*euangelizomenos!*) peace by Jesus Christ" consisted of Jesus going "about doing good and healing all who were oppressed by the devil, for God was with him" (Acts 10:36-38).

In Paul's final defense speech to King Agrippa, Paul sums up his mission, as portrayed by Luke, with these words, as God's commission to him, "I will rescue you from your people and from the Gentiles — to whom I am sending you to open their eyes so that they may turn from the power of Satan to God, so that they may receive forgiveness of sins and a place among those who are sanctified by faith in me" (Acts 26:17-18).

These texts are crucially placed in Luke's two-volume work and are interpretive of the Nazareth synagogue sermon in Luke 4:18-19 on the Sabbath.[38] Their emphases are not immediately socio-political or socio-economic (though might become such as in Acts 19). Lack of attention to this in Yoder renders Yoder's exposition of the jubilee proclamation reductionist, by Lukan standards.

These five points, taken together,[39] constitute a fuller portrait of the Jubilee mission of the servant Messiah. The significance of these exegetical observations means that Yoder's presentation of Jesus' jubilean mission needs to be qualified and broadened. Yoder's portrait of Jesus needs to be

---

37. Garrett, *The Demise of the Devil: Magic and the Demonic in Luke's Writings;* "Exodus from Bondage"; Swartley, *Israel's Scripture Traditions,* pp. 85-88.

38. Often overlooked is the Sabbath setting for this text. Jubilee is inherently related to Sabbath liberation, as Lowery, *Sabbath and Jubilee,* helpfully shows, including present-day appropriation of these important biblical themes.

39. A sixth point might be Luke's Jubilee emphases in the song of Zechariah in 1:68-79. Robin J. Dewitt Knauth presented a paper at the 2002 SBL meeting (*SBL Abstracts* S23-53, p. 183) arguing this point. The paper argues that following Cyrus's edict to permit captive Israel to return to the land, major reinterpretation of the Jubilee legislation occurs, emphasizing hope for restoration and eschatological hope, so clearly enunciated in Zechariah's song as in the process of fulfillment.

qualified by recognizing that for Luke Jubilee is broader in appropriation than Yoder shows it. Also, that while Matthew and Mark may be cited to bolster this stream of emphasis, neither Gospel develops a Jubilee motif *per se.* Yoder thus misses the opportunity to join Luke in stressing those themes that portray the contextualization of Jubilee into a wider theological, ethical, and spiritual — even personal — dimension. Not all of what Luke regards as fulfillment of Jubilee is socio-political or economic. "Release" from the devil's oppression (Acts 10:38) is personal and spiritual to the core.

Thus, Yoder's goal to show that Jesus is relevant to social ethics resulted in a Jesus-portrait that "screened" out important spiritual emphases of the Jubilee theme that Luke indeed intended to present.

This critique of Yoder does not mean that Luke's Jubilee is not political. It is, as the above study of *eirēnē* has shown. For Luke's *salvation-gospel* neither courts nor condemns Rome or the contemporary nations of this world. Nor does it give its main energies to aid or block the imperialistic pacification programs, of which the Pax Romana was a grand model. Rather, the new humanity of Christ's body welcomes people to become "children of peace," freed from the tyranny of the powers in whatever personal, national, socioeconomic, political, or ideological guise they manifest themselves.[40] This new humanity, in contrast to the dominant cultural power structures, expends its primary energies building communities of faith, hope, love, and peace. Further, Luke presents Jesus as a *Savior* who cries out in lament: if only you would know those things that make for peace (Luke 19:42). Long after Rome's imperial rule ends, the gospel of the Nazarene, the crucified and resurrected One, endures.

Peace and Justice

That Luke is not a political apologetic for the Pax Romana, as Conzelmann argued, is further demonstrated from his attention to justice, actually true justice that transcends the "just" pretenses of the religious leaders and comprehension of the political rulers. While much attention has been given to Luke's social ethic of jubilee and justice generally, no one, as far I know, has examined carefully Luke's recurring use of justice *(dikaios/dikaiosynē/*

---

40. See my essay, "Politics and Peace," pp. 33-35. On this topic see also Anna Janzen, *Der Friede im lukanischen Doppelwerk vor dem Hintergrund der Pax Romana.* Janzen argues that Luke reflects some of the good elements in the Pax Romana, such as the "benefactor" convention of the rich assisting the poor, but Luke is not a political apologetic.

dikaioō) as one of his special interests and emphases.[41] Yet this is of great importance, since the confession that the centurion makes of Jesus dying on the cross is not "Truly this was the Son of God," as found in Matthew and Mark. Rather, in Luke the centurion declares, "Truly this was a *just* man."[42] It is important to ask how Luke's treatment of *justice/righteousness* (*dikaios* and its adjectival and verbal forms) functions in the Gospel, and how his emphasis on true justice is related to his *peace* proclamation noted above. In the infancy narratives, those people who participate in and welcome the manifestation of the Christ-child are described as *righteous/just (dikaios)* people: Zechariah and Elizabeth in 1:6; the child to be born, John the Baptist will turn "the disobedient to the wisdom of the just," in 1:17; Simeon was righteous and devout, in 2:25. This humble *righteous/just* piety is honored by God to create the halo of holiness over the birth of One who will make all things new.

In Luke's journey narrative the verb, noun, or adjective forms of justice (*dikaios, dikaioō, ekdikeō, ekdikēsis*) occur twelve times, and none have parallels in either Matthew or Mark. Four texts either call for justice (12:57) or designate someone or some group as just:

> the resurrection of the just in 14:14;
> the ninety-nine righteous in 15:7 — which has a sarcastic edge to it;
> and the tax collector for his prayer of contrition who was "justified rather than the other," the Pharisee, in 18:14.

A second group of four uses occur in the parable of the Unjust Judge. Twice the woman pleads for justice (18:3, 5) and twice Jesus assures the listener that God will grant justice (18:7, 8). Here God's own character is the standard that defines justice.

Another four uses, most indicative of Luke's narrative purpose, describe specific persons or groups who pretend to be righteous or seek to justify themselves. These are: the lawyer in 10:29; the Pharisees in 16:15; likely Pharisees again in 18:9 who "trusted in themselves that they were righteous"; and

---

41. An excellent article on justice in biblical thought is John R. Donahue's "Biblical Perspectives on Justice." Even though he has a brief treatment specifically on Luke (pp. 106-8), he does not take up Luke's distinctive *dikaios* terms and their significance. Likewise, Joseph A. Grassi's helpful study of justice in the NT does not present a systematic treatment of Luke's uses and emphases as I show here. See Grassi, *Informing the Future: Social Justice in the New Testament.*

42. The NRSV translation "*innocent* man," is not correct. The redactional emphasis of Luke is on *just* or *righteous* people, as this section will demonstrate, not on *innocent* people. The notion of innocence as a leitmotif of ch. 23 is not supported by close analysis of the text. It is a modern concern read back into the text.

the scribes and chief priests in 20:20 in setting the tax trap. Note the similarity among the last three verses:

Luke 16:15. "So he [Jesus] said to them, 'You are those who justify yourselves *(dikaiountes heautous)* in the sight of others; but God knows your hearts; for what is prized by human beings is an abomination in the sight of God.'" This follows the Parable of the Unjust Steward, and introduces still another perspective from which the parable might be interpreted, i.e, the Pharisees' reaction to the view of money presented in this parable!

Luke 18:9. "He also told this parable to some who trusted in themselves that they were righteous *(eisin dikaioi)* and regarded others with contempt." Then follows the parable of the Pharisee and the tax collector.

Luke 20:20. "So they watched him and sent spies who pretended to be honest *(hypokrinomenous heautous dikaious einai)* in order to trap him by what he said, so as to hand him over to the jurisdiction and authority of the governor." This tax trap, by those playing the hypocrite role, serves as partial basis for the charges put on Jesus as he is turned over to Pilate by the multitude-mob in 23:2, instigated by the "chief priests and scribes" (20:19; 22:2).

These counterfeit portraits of justice provide a narrative foil for the Gospel's climactic christological confession, "Truly this was a righteous man," in 23:47, a bold alternative to Mark and Matthew. Thus in Luke's theology, Jesus, like God, emerges as the standard of true justice.

In an earlier study of the relationship of Luke's Journey Narrative to the sequential emphases in Deuteronomy,[43] I point out the justice parallels:

> Deut. 16:18-20 and Luke 14:1-14. In Deuteronomy God commands Israel to appoint judges to render just decisions and then calls for justice: "Justice, and only justice, you shall pursue, so that you may occupy the land that the LORD your God is giving you." In Luke 14:1-14 Jesus promises a reward "at the resurrection of the just" to those who host banquets the Jesus way — inviting in the poor, the maimed, the lame, and the blind.
>
> Deut. 24:6–25:3 and Luke 18:1-8. Deuteronomy contains numerous injunctions against oppressive treatment of the poor, the resident alien, the orphan, and the widow; 24:17 uses the word *justice (mishpat):* "You shall not deprive a resident alien or an orphan of justice; you shall not take the widow's garment in pledge." Luke's justice text describes a widow pleading for justice until the "Unjust Judge" gives in and decrees justice.

43. See *Israel's Scripture Traditions,* pp. 151-53.

Beyond these specific connections, Luke's pervasive emphasis on social justice matches Deuteronomy's. In two parables, The Rich Fool in 12:16-20 and The Rich Man and Lazarus in 16:19-31, Luke warns against wealth's blinding of people to the kingdom's call and its justice. These parables are distinctive to Luke and warn against the dangers arising from the apparent gap between rich and poor in the churches of his time and locality. Indeed, Luke's travel narrative includes not only these two parables, but Zacchaeus's giving half his goods to the poor (19:8), other teaching on almsgiving (11:41; 12:33), and a strong emphasis against wealth throughout chapters 12 and 16.

John Donahue summarizes Luke's special contribution: "Luke presents Jesus in the form of an OT prophet who takes the side of the widow (7:11-17; 18:1-8), the stranger in the land (10:29-37; 17:16), and those on the margin of society (14:12-13, 21)."[44]

In light of the contemporary urgent need to correlate peace with justice, Luke creatively and profoundly speaks to our needs as well as those of his time. The meaning of justice in both Deuteronomy and Luke is not to be confused with the Greek notion of rendering to every one his or her due, but must be understood in parallel to mercy as shown in God's covenant relationship to Israel. Seeing the needs of the poor and marginalized, it responds with compassion. As Lind puts it, "Both justice and mercy arise out of the covenant relationship of God and people." Further, Israel's "law is an expression of that [mercy and justice] norm."[45] Just as law and justice show the design of life within the people's covenant relationship with God, so the Gospel's portrayal of Jesus proclaiming peace and justice reflects also the good news of the kingdom and its pattern for life. It is the way of the Jesus community. It calls people to stop feigning justice, i.e. pretending to be righteous, but to actually live the way of God's kingdom, brought near in Jesus. Failing this, God's justice means judgment, for God's peace and justice confront and overcome evil.

Luke's inclusion of several narratives about Samaritans demonstrates also his interconnection with peace and justice, as God's gospel way in Jesus Christ to overcome enmity and evil. The lawyer by seeking to justify himself (*dikaiōsai heauton*, 10:29) draws forth Jesus' parable of the Good Samaritan.[46] In the face of God's love commands (10:25-28), the lawyer seeks self-justification. In contrast, Jesus' parable shows love compassionately aiding

44. Donahue, *The Gospel in Parable*, p. 175.

45. Lind, "Transformation of Justice: From Moses to Jesus." Lind's latest book, *The Sheer Sound of Silence and the Killing State*, is a close exegetical study of capital punishment in Scripture and exemplifies the transformation trajectory.

46. For description of the Samaritans and exposition of this parable see Donahue, "Who Is My Enemy?"

not only an unknown neighbor, but a known enemy — and the hands of love are those of a Samaritan! The narrative shifts from the question, "who is the neighbor whom I am commanded to love?" to another, "am I a loving neighbor even to the enemy?" To be such a neighbor ensures one of eternal life, and it does not test with evil intent the Teacher of truth and life. The Good Samaritan story climaxes Luke's first segment in his Journey Narrative, which is thus framed by the Samaritan theme, for in 9:54 the disciples wanted to rain fire down upon a Samaritan village because of its rejection of the journeying prophet Jesus (cf. 2 Kgs. 1:10, 12). But Jesus rebuked *(epetimēsen)* them (9:55), thus expelling their evil desire.

This first segment (9:51–10:37) of Luke's central section thus develops the theme of the gospel's overcoming of evil through its proclamation of peace in deeds of love, even to the enemy, in contrast to the lawyer who seeks to justify himself as righteous on some other ground. This story of the lawyer and the Good Samaritan parable against the context of the seventy sent out on a peace mission that marks Satan's downfall demonstrate that as people receive the kingdom's gospel of peace, Satan falls from his throne of power. Enemies are saved from death through love that risks life for life. The gospel of peace and love has conquered.

Since the mission of the seventy appears to be a narrative follow-up to Jesus' sending messengers ahead to Samaritan towns (9:51-53, 56), another point, blending the two above, comes also into view. The two themes, the peace of the kingdom and the "conquest" of evil, are developed in the narrative by actions that are located squarely in the territory of the religious and sociopolitical enemy, the despised Samaritans.[47] Rather than eradicating the enemy, as was the goal of Joshua's conquest narrative in the earlier story — in a similar location — the new strategy eradicates the enmity. Samaritans receive the peace of the kingdom of God (see also Luke's Samaritan emphasis in his near-end inclusio for the Journey Narrative in the cleansing of the ten lepers [17:11-19]). Instead of killing people to get rid of idolatry, the attack through the gospel is upon Satan directly (Luke 10). Instead of razing high places, Satan is toppled from his throne![48]

---

47. The entire segment of 9:51–10:37 thus has Samaria as its geographic context.

48. Hence the root of idolatry is plucked from its source (see Deut. 18:9-14 for the rationale, i.e. idolatry, for destroying the people in the promised land).

Jesus' Christological Identity as Messiah of Peace

As might be expected, the distinctive themes noted above shape the particular christological portrait of Jesus in Luke's Gospel. To be sure, the wider christological accents of Jesus' identity, as appear also in Matthew and/or Mark, are present in Luke: Davidic kingship, messianic prophet, Son of man, and Son of God. But what emerges as distinctive, virtually unique, is Jesus' identity and role as Savior and Lord (cf. Acts 5:31) and Righteous One (cf. Acts 3:14), with both toned by emphasis on Jesus as God's holy servant (cf. Acts 3:26; 4:30).

While Luke frequently identifies Jesus with Davidic royalty (1:27, 32, 69; 2:4, 11; 3:22 and, in triple tradition, 18:38-39; 20:41-44; through Acts also), show-ing the fulfillment of God's promise to David (2 Sam. 7:14), Luke qualifies this tradition by associating it with *Lord* (2:11; Acts 2:36; 10:36). *Lord* universalizes royalty by connecting Jesus' Davidic certification and authority to reign with Jesus' resurrection and heavenly exaltation — at the right hand of God (Acts 2:33-36). In the triumphal entry and passion narrative nothing is made of the Davidic pedigree (the list of Davidic kings is absent from the genealogy in ch. 3 also). This suggests that Luke seeks to universalize Jesus' royal authority.

The point is especially evident in his use of "Savior" and "Lord." While Luke designates Jesus as Savior *(sōtēr)* only twice (2:11; Acts 5:31), his pervasive emphasis on the verb *save (sōzō)* and related terms *(sōtēria, diasōzō)* indicates his extensive interest in this portrait of Jesus, as shown above.[49] Mary begins her Magnificat by rejoicing in God her "Savior" (1:47). Zechariah's Benedictus is punctuated with *praise* that the Lord God of Israel is now bringing "salva-tion" to his people (1:69, 71, 77). John the Baptist's proclamation of the dawn-ing new age ends its Isaianic burst with "all flesh shall see the salvation of God" (3:6). And Zacchaeus is glad to hear Jesus' word, "Today salvation has come to this house" (19:9). While the verb is used often for healings, as in Matthew and Mark, it also has the meaning of salvation as restored relation with God, freed from sin (9:56; 13:23; 19:10; throughout Acts also). In the pas-sion narrative, the rulers of Israel, the soldiers, and the unrepentant criminal mock Jesus' *power to save* (23:35-39). The title Savior envisaged the Messiah bringing salvation that delivers from Roman domination, but the Gospel's use of this title transforms its meaning.

The Greco-Roman world knew of both divine liberators and protectors (Zeus, Athena, etc.) and political saviors (the Ptolemies, Seleucids, Pompey, Caesar, Augustus, etc.). Luke's terminology thus connects to the thought-

---

49. See also I. Howard Marshall, *The Gospel of Luke*, pp. 95, 112, 419, 715, 716.

world of the Gentiles and Rome's imperial rule.[50] Not only does Luke portray Jesus' royalty and role as Savior (and even Benefactor), but his pervasive call to repentance has economic and political consequences, since it yields a counter blessing, salvation, joy and peace to that which Rome's emperors promised.[51] Rejecting both the Roman imperial and Maccabean models of peace gained through war and violence, Jesus comes to establish peace and justice, not by crushing the enemy through violence, but by transforming understandings of *salvation* and *peace.*

"Lord" also has a long tradition in the Hebrew Scriptures, with the LXX rendering the sacred Tetragrammaton as *kyrios.* Not only does Luke use "Lord" to refer often to God (33 times in Luke, 51 in Acts, according to Schneider's lists),[52] but Luke alone of the Synoptics also frequently uses "Lord" to refer to Jesus (42 times in Luke; 50 in Acts).[53] For Luke, "Lord" establishes Jesus' identity and role as *Savior-Ruler* in universal categories. Jesus the Messiah's lordship is analogous to God's (some mss. report the disciples worshipping Jesus in 24:52).[54]

Luke's use of "Son of Humanity" is also plentiful. In the passion narrative distinctive uses, associated with suffering, appear in 22:48 and 24:7 (cf. the traditional Synoptic use in 22:22). The most significant use showing Jesus' royalty is Jesus' final word to the Sanhedrin: "But from now on the Son of

50. Luke's preponderant use of *Lord* puts Jesus' royalty in competition with what people in the Greco-Roman world assigned to the emperors, first to Augustus in 12 BCE (cf. Festus's reference to Nero as his Lord, Acts 25:26).

51. In a presentation at the 2004 Society of Biblical Literature meeting, Guy D. Nave, Jr., stressed that Luke presents Jesus in both his titles and message as a counter-claim to the imperial view of blessing, salvation, and peace in that the call to repentance demands a change of values. Service replaces dominion. See Nave's abstract, "It's Time for a Change! Examining the Lukan Demand for Repentance within the Context of Roman Imperialism," *AAR/SBL Abstracts 2004,* pp. 347-48.

52. Schneider, *Lukas, Theologe der Heilsgeschichte,* pp. 214-15. This is from his 1980 essay, "Gott und Christus als *kurios* nach der Apostelgeschichte." The counts of Schneider's lists (pp. 216-17) are mine.

53. Of those in Luke, sixteen occur in narrative, eighteen in direct address *(kyrie),* and eight in direct address referring to Jesus, e.g., "mother of my Lord." Of these forty-two uses, seven occur in the passion narrative. In 22:33 Peter addresses Jesus as Lord. In 22:61a,b Jesus is referred to as Lord in the narrator's story of Peter's denial. In 22:49 the disciples, in dialogue with Jesus about the swords and their use, address Jesus as Lord. In 24:3 the women at the tomb ask about the body of the "Lord Jesus" (in some mss.). And in 24:34 the two Emmaus travelers report to the disciples, "The Lord has risen indeed." Schneider's conclusion from Luke's use of "Lord" is that it was a self-understood title for God and Jesus among the people to whom Luke wrote, and thus Luke could readily use it. Nonetheless, it is also clear that Luke in many of his special uses intends to accentuate this dimension of Jesus' identity.

54. Schneider, *Lukas,* p. 225.

Man will be seated at the right hand of the power of God" (22:69). Luke stresses that Jesus' enthroned position with God as Ruler takes effect now in the events of the passion. Seated at the right hand of God as Son of Humanity, Jesus assumes the prerogative of lordship.

Luke complements his portrayal of Jesus the jubilean prophet as Savior and Lord with Jesus as the suffering Righteous One.[55] In this tradition the "poor" *(anawim)* were identified with the righteous, who often suffered in this world, believing that God would be their vindicator. The Righteous One also suffered as martyr. Both themes, the poor and the righteous martyr, permeate Luke-Acts. Luke specifically identifies Jesus as "the (Holy and) Righteous One" (Acts 3:14; 7:52; 22:14).

As noted above, Luke boldly departs from Matthew and Mark in saying that the centurion *glorified* God and then declared, "This man was righteous" (or, a righteous one). In light of Luke's clear intention to identify and portray Jesus as the Righteous One three times in Acts, the centurion's confession should be rendered similarly, "the Righteous One."[56]

This strategically placed declaration by the centurion matches Luke's portrayal of Jesus generally: born within the circle of righteous, devout, and humble folk (1:6, 38; 2:7-20, 25, 36-38), advocate of the righteous poor whom God will vindicate (note 18:1-8) and announce blessing upon as well, and friend of those made to be outcasts by the supposedly righteous (see 5:32 in context). Further, just as Luke arranges an antiphonal chorus singing *peace* at Jesus' birth and entry into Jerusalem, so he also has arranged antiphonal acclamations of "glory to God" at Jesus' birth (2:14, 20; cf. 2:9) and death, through the centurion's *glorifying* of God upon *seeing* what had taken place (23:47),[57] thus fulfilling Isaiah's vision, "the glory of the Lord shall be revealed, and all people shall see it together" (Isa. 40:5). Between these first and last bursts of worship, moreover, Luke's emphatic depiction of humans *glorifying* God in the face of Jesus' deeds of compassion and justice is not lost in the narrative (5:25-26; 7:16; 13:13; 17:15, 18; 18:43; 19:38).[58]

---

55. Ruppert, *Jesus als der leidende Gerechte?* pp. 1-38; see also Wis. 2:12-22; 5:1-5, where the suffering righteous one is described in language akin to Isaiah 53.

56. The anarthrous grammatical form matches that of *huios theou* in Mark and Matthew, except that *dikaios* could be either a predicate adjective or predicate nominative.

57. Dennis D. Sylvan relates this point to his proposal that Luke seeks to portray Jesus' death as participating in the piety and worship of the temple. The torn temple veil precedes Jesus' prayer, "Father, into Your hands I commit my spirit." Then the centurion glorifies God. See Sylvan, "The Temple Curtain and Jesus' Death in Luke."

58. The refrain continues in Acts, especially on Gentiles' lips (4:21; 11:18; 13:48; 21:20). Luke also accentuates Jesus' participation in divine glory (9:31-32; 24:26; Acts 3:13).

Clearly, Luke's portrayal of Jesus as the Righteous One, interacting strategically in the narrative with emphasis on Jesus' royalty, discloses an important christological Lukan conviction: Jesus' royalty rises gloriously from the common terrain of mangers, shepherds, fisher-folk, widows, rejected prophets, and, most significantly, the humble, suffering righteous ones whose lives are gently held by the hands of God. For such ones, God is a God of help, salvation, and resurrection power, exalting the Righteous One to the right hand of Power, as Christ and Lord. No other royalty does Luke know.

Luke links to his designation of Jesus the Righteous One the term *archēgos,* meaning Author, Guide, Head, Leader. This one, whom you "killed and God raised up," God vindicates as the rejected Righteous One. Luke's uses of "child-servant" *(pais)* to designate Jesus (Acts 3:13, 26; 4:27, 30) draw on the Isaiah *ebed Yahweh* tradition and make a similar point. God glorified his servant/*pais* whom "you handed over and rejected in the presence of Pilate" (3:13).

In light of these Lukan christological emphases, Luke's twofold identification of Jesus with the righteous sufferer (in the centurion's confession and by Jesus' last cry in 23:46, the cry of the righteous sufferer in Ps. 31:5) must be seen as a conscious effort to transform the royalty tradition at its very heart. It is not a matter of choosing one against the other but of recognizing, rather, that both dwell together in the Lukan Gospel's christology. Jesus is Messiah-King, royal Son of God and Lord as well as rejected Prophet and suffering Righteous One (who is also the "servant of the Lord"/*ebed Yahweh* in Acts). The centurion's confession (23:47) thus displays the Lukan prism through which Jesus' royalty is refracted. In the light of Jesus' humble royalty, the centurion rightly *glorifies* God, therewith joining the lowly shepherds (2:20) to form a *glorifying* inclusio to frame Jesus' earthly life in this world. This inclusio complements the peace inclusio of 2:14 and 19:38. Thus we return now to Luke's special ethos of salvation, joy, peace, and praise, all for the glory of God.

Salvation, Joy, Peace, and Praise for the Glory of God

Luke's special gift orders his story of Jesus around the ethos of praise, blessing, and glorifying God. The celebrative mood represents the lowly people's response to *salvation,* in all its earthy fullness: material, political, and spiritual. This response arises precisely from the soil of the humble people who on earth laud God's shocking surprise of disarming grace: a Messiah-King born in a manger in a stable by Mary, who has sexual relations with no man! What royal claim could such a one ever have in this world?

Luke turns all things upside down. The "garment of praise, joy and glory" drapes over Luke's Gospel as a shroud of beauty, subverting death by resurrection and thus culminating the salvation and peace of the gospel of the kingdom. Paul Minear has suggested a direct correlation between "glory in heaven" and "peace on earth," in Luke's thematic intentions: "the more glory the more peace, and the more peace the more glory."[59] Similarly, Minear correlates the seventy's rejoicing that their names are written in heaven (10:20) with their *shalom-eirēnē* shout to the homes they visited; joy in heaven matches the peace, joy and wholeness experienced on earth (15:7, 10, 20-24).

This distinctive emphasis connects and adds to Israel's rich heritage of glorifying God in praise. This is ubiquitous in the Psalms but recurs often in the prophetic literature, as well as history and poetic portions of the canon. David Reid rightly connects this unique ethos of Luke's Gospel to Israel's heritage of worship and praise. Luke "establishes that continuity in the praise of God: the community who praised God in times past, in the ministry of Jesus, in response to the proclamation of the good news."[60] Indeed, this praise of God unites all the stages of Luke's salvation history (16:16) and carries the "purposes of God right into the present."[61] In Luke the gospel story begins and ends in the temple, the center from which praises to God arise. Note Luke's unique ending: "And they worshiped him, and returned to Jerusalem with great joy; and they were continually in the temple blessing God" (24:52-53).

At the same time Luke sets the Jesus story within the empire (2:1; 3:1) and thus introduces through the Jesus message and mission the Pax Christi, an alternative to the Pax Romana. Even more specifically, the Pax Christi praises the God of Israel who has become the Savior God for all peoples: Jews, Samaritans, and Gentiles. The Eirene Goddess of the Pax Romana has been eclipsed by the God of peace that, though rooted in a particular covenant history, is now spreading to all people through Jesus, and will soon be planted also in Rome through the sequential missionary endeavors of Jesus' apostles (in the story in Acts).

By introducing the peace motif prominently at the beginning and ending of his Journey Narrative (9:51–19:44), Luke want his readers to see that Jesus' entire mission was one of bringing peace.[62] The multitude of disciples that followed Jesus as he descended the Mount of Olives to enter Jerusalem

59. Minear, *To Heal and to Reveal*, p. 50.
60. Reid, "Peace and Praise in Luke," p. 79.
61. Reid, "Peace and Praise," p. 79.
62. John Donahue, "The Good News of Peace," suggests that we read the Lukan journey narrative as "a path to peace."

"began to praise God joyfully with a loud voice for all the deeds of power that they had seen, saying, 'Blessed is the King who comes in the name of the Lord! Peace in heaven and glory in the highest heaven'" (19:37-38). This shout of "Peace in heaven" is clearly an antiphonal response to 2:14 in the larger Lukan narrative.

The proclamation of the heavenly host is now complemented by the shout of the multitude of disciples. Earth answers heaven. It is urgent that the praise be given, for when the Pharisees try to hush it, Jesus says, "If they don't shout it, the very stones will cry it out" (my rendering). Luke's narrative exclaims: Jesus comes as king announcing and inaugurating peace. A vast multitude of followers responds, affirming peace (19:38). But the outcry may also indicate an abortive dimension: the peace has not been welcomed by all on earth. Hence, in sharp contrast to the mood of the praising multitude, Jesus laments over Jerusalem and pronounces judgment: "If you, even you, had only recognized on this day the things that make for peace! But now they are hidden from your eyes" (v. 42). The harsh words of judgment upon the city end with the sad explanatory comment: "because you did not recognize the time of your visitation from God" (v. 44). Thus the section ends. God has sent divine peace through Jesus, but the response pattern has been full of surprises. Those with standing invitations to the banquet have refused; those previously barred from the banquet have accepted.

But not all are ready to come to the banquet celebrating God's peace with praise. Donahue points out an arresting parallel between Israel's Holy War regulations in Deuteronomy 20 and Luke's Great Banquet parable in 14:16-24.[63] The excuses of the guests invited first to the banquet echo the same reasons why male Israelites were exempted from responding to the call to Holy War in Deuteronomy 20, as follows:

Deuteronomy war exemptions	Luke's banquet excuses
built a new house	bought a piece of land
planted a vineyard	bought five yoke of oxen
engaged to a woman	just married a wife

The parallelism is striking indeed. The first are property excuses; the second, work excuses — the oxen tilled the vineyard; and the third, marital obligation. Donahue observes that in OT and later Jewish literature the feast of the messianic age is inaugurated by great violence and war to crush the enemies.

---

63. Donahue, *Parable*, pp. 140-46. This connection is also one of the correspondences cited by C. F. Evans in his parallels between the Lukan travel narrative and Deuteronomy.

Indeed, in Luke Jesus tells this parable in response to earlier banqueting instructions (14:7-14) and in response to the exclamation in v. 15, "Blessed is anyone who will eat bread in the kingdom of God." Jesus' Great Banquet parable comes next and ends with the words, "For I tell you, none of those who were invited will eat of my banquet" (v. 24)!

Luke's portrayal of Jesus, says Donahue, departs from the standard Jewish eschatological anticipations in that "he omits those violent elements . . . normally associated with the eschatological banquet."[64] Luke's Jesus takes the parable into a second dimension in which substitute guests are invited: the poor, the crippled, and the lame — precisely those who in the Qumran literature (1 QM 7:4-6; 1QSa 2:5-10) were excluded from the expected messianic banquet.[65] Even after these ritually unclean people are gathered into the feast, a third invitation compels more to come from the highways and hedges. Luke accentuates the inclusiveness of the kingdom banquet, depicting Jesus' journey as God's gracious offer of peace, an offer rejected by those earlier called, but now accepted by those formerly barred from the banquet. By replacing "holy war" with "holy banquet" Luke shows Jesus as Savior-Messiah of nonviolence and peace.[66]

A detail in the narrative of the Triumphal Entry especially intrigues the reader: "the whole multitude of the disciples began to *praise* God *joyfully* with a loud voice for all the deeds of power they had seen, saying, '. . . *Peace* in heaven and glory in the highest heaven!'" (19:37b-38). Who were all those people in the multitude who sang the *joyful praises of peace?* Some, but probably not many, from Jerusalem joined in the choir (vv. 41-44). In light of Jesus' journey progressing from Galilee through Samaria and this judgment on Jerusalem, the composition of this multitude likely included a swelling crowd that followed Jesus, the journeying guest to the promised banquet. For these the *saving gospel* of the kingdom has come, bringing *jubilee-justice* and *joy, salvation* and *shalom, peace* and *praise!*

64. Donahue, *Parable,* p. 142.

65. Donahue, *Parable,* p. 144.

66. Luke does not spare description of the reality that many refuse the offer. In *Israel's Scripture Traditions* I cite Luke's sequence of harsh words of punishment to those who reject the offer of peace and praise (pp. 142-43).

6 Acts: God's Strategies
for Peace in the Church

Therefore let the entire house of Israel know with certainty that God has made him both Lord and Messiah, this Jesus whom you crucified.

ACTS 2:36

You know the message [God] sent to the people of Israel, preaching peace by Jesus Christ — he is Lord of all.

ACTS 10:36

Acts continues Lukan theological emphases: the proclamation of the kingdom of God, the presence, directing, and empowering of the Holy Spirit, the gospel's confrontation of the powers of evil, and peace *(eirēnē)* and justice. Two new emphases appear also: the expansion of the gospel from Jerusalem through Judea, Samaria, Syria, Cilicia, Asia Minor, Macedonia, and finally to Rome via Paul's arrest and imprisonment. The other striking new feature is that miracles and signs are now done "in the name of Jesus."[1] Jesus is the One exalted to God's right hand, declared both Lord and Christ (Acts 2:36), and this new post-resurrection reality shapes the entire narrative of Acts. In light of these new emphases the Lukan *euangelizomai* (gospel-proclamation) occurs *fifteen* times in Acts (over half of Luke's twenty-five uses). It continues to be strategic, evoking the Isaiah 52:7 prophetic oracle, which Luke undoubtedly considers messianic. Indeed, the full Isaiah LXX phrase *euangelizomenos*

---

1. For a helpful exposition of this motif and its significance in Acts see Thurston, *Spiritual Life in the Early Church*, pp. 34-43.

eirēnēn, is now linked to Jesus Christ, *dia Iēsou Christou,* and occurs in Peter's historic speech, on the occasion of the first Gentile's reception into the church, presumably without circumcision (Acts 10-11, in 10:36). This text is crucial to Acts' gospel-peace emphasis, and we examine it at length in this chapter.

Luke's leading themes are artfully interwoven in the gripping narrative: the key term *kingdom of God* occurs strategically in relation to the spread of the gospel in the specific sequential phases outlined in Acts 1:8, in response to the disciples' inquiry as to when the post-resurrection Jesus would restore the kingdom to Israel. The answer: "It is not for you to know the times or periods that the Father has set by his own authority. But you will receive power when the Holy Spirit has come upon you; and you will be my witnesses in Jerusalem, in all Judea and Samaria, and to the ends of the earth." In 1:3, the risen Jesus appears to the disciples during the forty days between resurrection and ascension with "many convincing proofs" and speaks "about the kingdom of God." This sets the agenda for the entire book. The strategic recurrences of *kingdom of God* then appear throughout the Acts drama, with the first major geographical breakthrough occurring with Philip's gospel-proclamation (five verbal forms of *euangelizomai* in ch. 8: vv. 4, 12, 25, 35, 40) in Samaria and to the Ethiopian eunuch. In 8:12 *euangelizomenō* is linked to *kingdom of God (basileias tou theou):* "But when they believed Philip, who was proclaiming the good news about the kingdom of God and the name of Jesus Christ, they were baptized, both men and women." The kingdom has leaped the first enemy-border hurdle! This is indeed a peacemaking story even though the term *eirēnē* does not occur here. The story is included in the summary statement of 9:31 that does include *eirēnē,* that we examine later.

Then in the third phase of the 1:8 outline, "to the ends of the earth," the gospel makes its way through Paul's call to "gospelize" the Gentiles through Asia Minor, where *kingdom of God (basileian tou theou)* occurs in 14:22 to sum up Paul's and Barnabas's mission in the first journey through Asia Minor, after they returned to the churches to encourage the believers in their new-found faith (14:22-23). Indeed, many entered the kingdom through tribulation, the persecution that beset the young churches.

The next phase, fulfilling the 1:8 design, develops as Paul and Silas in the next two journeys take the good news of the kingdom into Macedonia: Philippi, Thessalonica, Beroea, Athens, and Corinth and then return again to Ephesus, where in 19:8 *kingdom of God (basileias to theou)* occurs again. Here Paul "argues and pleads" about the kingdom of God. Then in 20:25 "preaching *(kēryssō)* the kingdom" occurs to describe to the Ephesian elders what he has been doing throughout his ministry journeys. Finally, when Paul arrives in Rome, his same vocational focus continues, even while prisoner. He testifies to and preaches the kingdom of God (28:23, 31). It is no coincidence that the book ends with that emphasis, for clearly Luke intends to frame as a bookend theme (inclusion) his second volume with the leitmotif also of the first volume, the *kingdom of God* (Acts 28:23, 31).

Acts and Its Political Stance

Since Acts is framed by the *kingdom of God* motif, and the swift spread of the gospel throughout the Roman Empire occurs often with Roman rulers aiding the cause of the apostolic witness, the issue of whether Acts is a political apologetic (*à la* Conzelmann) is as crucial, even more so, for Acts as it is for Luke. George Edwards sums up the Conzelmann case:

> According to the Jewish accusers [in Acts] Paul and the Christians are subversives (Acts 17:6-7; 24:5), but the charges are rejected by Roman officials (16:38-39; 18:12-17; 19:35-41; 23:26-30; 25:23-27; 26:30-32). It is clear from this that the political apologetic in Luke-Acts is programmatic.[2]

While this point and even wider textual evidence than here cited are significant, more recent studies have challenged this interpretation. As indicated for Luke's Gospel above, so here in Acts there is extensive textual evidence that contradicts this thesis. As I have argued elsewhere[3] it is more correct to hold that Luke's use of *eirēnē* does not confirm Conzelmann's thesis nor does it confirm the one part of Cassidy's counter-thesis that Luke contains a significant anti-Roman critique. Rather, Luke's purpose is to portray an alternative community with its own kingdom-gospel-*eirēnē* agenda that is inherently neither pro- nor anti-Roman. Conversely, this position allows for both negative and positive portraits of Rome and its provincial rulers.[4]

While the purpose of this chapter on Acts is broader than this issue, to be sure, yet this issue must also figure into the discussion. The larger purpose is to examine the seven occurrences of *eirēnē* in Acts and attend specifically to

2. Edwards, "Biblical and Contemporary Aspects of War Tax Resistance," p. 114. Edwards makes his comment in relation to Luke's account of the tax text (Luke 20:20), in which he sees a heightening of "the Jewish defamation of Jesus as an insurrectionist" (also in 20:26; 23:2, 5, 18-19, 23, 25).

3. Swartley, "Politics and Peace *(Eirēnē)* in Luke's Gospel."

4. For a treatment that shows both sides, see Mauser, *The Gospel of Peace*, pp. 84-89, and also Chapter 5 above on Luke.

how they interact with the larger thematic emphases noted above and the political stance of the book as well. Moreover, this chapter will examine several features that mark out this new growing kingdom movement, noting how these features contribute to understanding the spread of the kingdom gospel as a gospel of peace.

Uses of "Peace" *(Eirēnē)* in Context

Of the seven uses of *eirēnē* in Acts, four are in contexts where the Lukan theology of the church as God's people is the controlling perspective for understanding the meaning of *eirēnē*. The other three uses are in contexts where peace receives its connotation by the political peace of the empire, the Pax Romana. The purpose of this section is to sort out these different but complementary usages within the book, and to grasp what Luke as author is seeking to portray by lacing his story of the expanding gospel with these uses of peace.

Ecclesial

The *eirēnē* texts that pertain to the realm of God's people, called "church" in Acts, are:

> 7:26: The next day he came to some of them as they were quarreling and tried to reconcile them [*into peace*], saying, "Men, you are brothers; why do you wrong each other?"
>
> 9:31: Meanwhile the church throughout Judea, Galilee, and Samaria had *peace* and was built up. Living in the fear of the Lord and in the comfort of the Holy Spirit, it increased in numbers.
>
> 10:36: You know the message he sent to the people of Israel, *preaching peace* by Jesus Christ — he is Lord of all.
>
> 15:33: After they had been there for some time, they were sent off in *peace* by the believers to those who had sent them.

These four texts occur in roughly the first half of the 28 chapters. The second set will cluster roughly in the second half. Joseph Comblin, in his study of these texts in Acts, holds that these four uses cited above are telling of Luke's theological purpose. They show that Luke uses *eirēnē* to describe the reconciliation of Jews and outsiders in Christ: Moses, among two Hebrew brothers (7:24-26); Jews, with Samaritans who have come into the kingdom (9:31); Gentiles, who have received salvation (10:36); and finally adopting an apostolic decree that assures the ongoing unity, just jeopardized, of Jews and Gentiles in Christ (15:33). This is the mystery of the church (Eph. 3:3-6) which stands as testimony to the empire, a *Pax Christi* that achieved what the *Pax Romana* could never do.[5] Extending Comblin's contribution, I propose that Luke's uses of *peace* in the first half of Acts be put into dialectic conversation with the uses of peace in the second half to ascertain how the ecclesial peace is related to the peace of the empire, if at all. We shall first examine the significance of the uses in both sets of occurrences and then return to this point, guided in part by Mauser's fine contribution.

7:26   This use of *eirēnē* in Stephen's speech is striking because it interprets Moses' action in Exodus 2:13 in a manner not presented in the Hebrew text or Septuagint (which Luke follows). In the Exodus text, it simply says that Moses "saw two Hebrews fighting" whereas Acts 7:26 says, "he appeared to them as they were fighting and sought to reconcile them into peace." Most translations fail to translate *eis eirēnēn,* so that most English readers could not even know it occurs in the text. Of the dozen translations I consulted, only the NASB, the sixteenth-century Rheims translation, and the Amplified Bible enable the English reader to recognize the double emphasis, on both reconciliation *(synēllassen)* and peace *(eirēnēn).* By appearing redundant, Luke emphasizes his intention: don't miss the point! But translators regularly have!

Further, Exodus 2:13 indicates that Moses "said to the one who was in the wrong, 'Why do you strike your fellow Hebrew?'" In Acts 7:26 Moses addresses both as culpable, "Men, you are brothers. Why do you wrong each other?" By these differences Luke takes this event and portrays Moses as a peacemaker among his fellow Hebrews.[6] Moses is thus presented as reconciler

---

5. Comblin, "La Paix dans la Théologie de saint Luc," pp. 439-60. There have been few studies of the significance of Luke's use of "peace" in Acts. Until Mauser's *The Gospel of Peace*, Comblin's article was distinctive on the subject. Mauser's contribution (chapter 5, pp. 83-103) is most important. This chapter reflects at many points my debt to his work.

6. This emphasis is not extended to Moses' action one day earlier, when he struck down the Egyptian. Here he is not a peacemaker. In 7:27-29 Moses is accused by the Hebrew in the wrong of killing the Egyptian and then flees for his life. His peacemaking role between the two Hebrews does not "reshape" the entire story. In fact, it makes it more evident that Luke is introducing into the narrative the theme "reconcile to peace" *(synēllassen autous eis eirēnēn).* Whether Luke has access to other Greek or Aramaic versions of the text which may have included this cannot be ruled out, but it is unlikely, given the wider evidence of Luke's freedom to construct the narrative in such a way as to advance his theological purposes. None of the extant Targums contain such an emphasis, although Targum Psuedo-Jonathan on Exod. 2:13 takes the freedom to name those fighting as Dathan and Abiram (see Numbers 16). Targums often "tele-

between hostile parties and works to bring unity between two men fighting with each other.[7]

As Mauser suggests, it is not difficult to see in these changes an effort to present Moses in a role analogous to that of Jesus. Some other similarities in Luke's portrait of Moses are:

> Moses "performed wonders and signs" (7:36), and Luke has already spoken of Jesus as "a man attested to you by God with deeds of power, wonders, and signs that God did through him among you — as you yourselves know" (2:22).
>
> God sent this one, Moses, as a "ruler" *(archonta)* and "liberator" *(lytrōtēn,* 7:35). Climaxing Peter's great sermon, Jesus is declared Lord *(kyrion)* and Messiah *(Christon).* In 5:31 Jesus is confessed as the Leader *(archēgon)* and Savior *(sōtēra).*

These parallel portraits of Moses and Jesus in both *ruling/leading* and *saving/liberating* indicate that Luke regards Moses as a type of Jesus, the One who is our peace. Moses' role as reconciler thus anticipates later similar uses of *peace* in the narrative, in bringing together alienated parties: Jew and Samaritan; Jew and Gentile; and the factions in the Jerusalem Conference.[8] Thus the occurrence of *reconcile* and *peace* in this text reflects Luke's (and Paul's) theology of the work of Jesus Christ.

To be more precise for Acts, this is Luke's theology of the Holy Spirit leading God's people, the leitmotif of Acts as a whole. Through the gift and power of the Holy Spirit, Peter declares Jesus as Lord and Christ (2:36). Stephen's sermon is inspired by his witness to Jesus' Lordship. He becomes the first martyr for the faith. His final words attest to a Lukan typology between Stephen and Jesus: "Lord Jesus, receive my spirit'" (7:59// Luke 23:46, "Father, into your hands I commend my spirit") and "Lord, do not hold this sin against them" (7:60//Luke 23:34, "Father, forgive them for they do not know what they are doing").

---

scope" time and "persons," so that characters in one text that morally match those in a similar text may have their names repeated in the latter.

7. In Rabbinic writings Moses also is known for his mediating role, especially between Israel and God: "Why, then, did Moses merit that his countenance should shine, even in this world, with a light destined for the righteous in the next world? Because . . . he was ever striving, yearning, watching to establish peace between Israel and their Father in Heaven." *Tanna debe Eliyahu,* ed. M. Friedmann (Vienna, 1902), p. 17, cited in Montefiore and Loewe, *Rabbinic Anthology,* p. 543.

8. Mauser, pp. 97-98.

Within the first phase of the Acts narrative, Luke has told the story of the church's beginnings with the account on peacemaking, both in Stephen's rehearsal of the salvation story, in his interpretation of Moses' role, and in Stephen's forgiving attitude toward his enemies, his final martyr witness. That Stephen emerges in the narrative from the appointment of seven deacons — Stephen is named first (6:5) — settling an earlier dispute in the church is also significant. The entire narrative in chs. 2–8 may be viewed as resolving problems and transforming conflicts in the early church:

> *internal* (2:43-47): meeting the needs of the poor (see also 4:32-37)
>> *external* (4:1-31, resulting from a great miracle and Peter's bold powerful preaching in ch. 3):[9] clash with political leaders in Jerusalem; Peter and John imprisoned
> *internal* (5:1-11): deception within community; Ananias and Sapphira
>> *external* (5:12-42): even stronger clash with political leaders. See 5:29!
> *internal* (6:1-7): resolving conflict between Hebrew and Hellenist widows over food distribution
>> *external* (6:8–8:3): severe clash with political leaders, Stephen's martyrdom

All these obstacles are resolved by the empowerment of the Holy Spirit and the new community's commitment to the Lordship of Jesus Christ. The first part of Acts shows conflict, to be sure, but also God-given directive and Holy Spirit empowerment to resolve those conflicts, within and from without. Set in this context the specific emphases on reconciliation and peacemaking in Stephen's sermon make quite clear the point that God's new gospel in Jesus Christ marks a new way of life, in which peace is the goal and peacemaking is the means.

9:31   The second Lukan peace text occurs in one of six of Luke's summary statements, all of which describe the advancement of the kingdom gospel through the *preaching of the word*.[10] Kingdom growth through preaching

---

9. Both demonstrations of power are "in (through) the name of Jesus." This recurring motif is both the literary unity of these chapters and the source of the apostles' boldness. The preaching centers on Jesus Christ and his life, death, and resurrection. In the apostle's bold praying, Jesus' death, carried out by Jewish religious leaders and Roman political authorities ("both Herod and Pontius Pilate, with the Gentiles and the peoples of Israel," 4:27), is the outworking of God's sovereign purpose to save all people (cf. 3:18). Note also in Acts 4:25b-26 Luke's quotation of Psalm 2 stating the prophetic decree that Jesus' death would involve Gentiles, kings of the earth, and "the rulers" gathering together to conspire against the Lord's anointed.

10. David W. Pao regards the recurrence of this motif, "the word of the Lord (God)," in

the word of God carries forward Jesus' promise in the "design text" (1:8) of the book in six stages of geographical expansion. The six texts are as follows:

6:7   "The word of God continued to grow. . . ." This comes after the church survived initial persecutions in Jerusalem and internal difficulties, the last of which was the complaint of the Hellenist (Greek-speaking) widows against the Hebrew (Hebrew-speaking) widows. The appointment of seven deacons immediately precedes this summary text.

9:31   "Meanwhile the church throughout Judea, Galilee, and Samaria had *peace* and was built up. Living in the fear of the Lord and in the comfort of the Holy Spirit, it increased in numbers." While "word of God" is not used in this summary statement, the growth and welfare of the church are clearly in view. The statement comes at the conclusion of Saul's dramatic conversion and call, and that in causative (?) sequence to Stephen's stoning, with Philip's *proclaiming the good news* in Samaria and into Ethiopia sandwiched between Stephen's martyr sermon and Saul's conversion.

12:24   "But the word of God continued to advance and gain adherents." This text is placed at the end of the section in which Cornelius, the first Gentile convert, is received into the messianic faith community through Peter's vision and voice from heaven (chs. 10–11). The end of ch. 11 harks back to the persecution that took place over Stephen and narrates how the effect of it spread the gospel as far as Phoenicia, Cyprus, and Antioch. At Antioch the reception of the gospel was exceptional: a great number of Hellenist Jews became believers and there the disciples were first called Christians (11:26). When news of this success reached Jerusalem, Barnabas was sent to minister to them. He is highly praised for his leadership, and he soon goes to Tarsus to seek Saul to assist in the ministry at Antioch. The chapter concludes (11:29-30) by describing the relief gift sent from Antioch to the believers in Jerusalem suffering from a famine, sent by Barnabas and Saul.[11] Chapter 12 then narrates a devastating persecution by King Herod Agrippa I, killing the apostle James and arresting Peter. Peter's miraculous release, followed by Herod being struck down by "an angel of the Lord" amidst his boasting pomp, is the immediate context for the summary statement. But all the events contribute to this phase of the church's growth and well-being.

15:35, with 16:5   "Paul and Barnabas . . . taught and proclaimed the

---

Acts as one major strand of evidence that Acts is shaped by the new exodus theme of Isaiah 40–55 (40:1-9; 45:22-24; 55:10-11; also Isa. 2:3, where "the word of the LORD [goes forth] from Jerusalem"); the phrase occurs in Acts over twenty times. See Pao, *Acts and the Isaianic New Exodus*, chapter 5.

11. See discussion below in this chapter and in Chapter 7 on the relief gift and its relation to the peace of the early church.

word of the Lord. . . . So the churches were strengthened in the faith and increased in numbers daily." The context is the resolution of the serious conflict at the Jerusalem Conference as a result of Paul's belief and practice on his first missionary journey — not to require circumcision for Gentile converts. But the events leading up to this major conflict and historic resolution are the numerous experiences of Paul's first missionary journey throughout Asia Minor, preceded by Peter's own conversion on the matter of Gentile inclusion (chs. 10-11). Peter's dramatic reorientation regarding Gentile inclusion (Cornelius) together with Paul called as "a light to the Gentiles" (13:46-47; cf. 18:6) so that God's salvation extends to the ends of the earth (quotation from Isa. 49:6) are the foundational factors necessitating the Jerusalem Conference in ch. 15. The rift between Paul and Barnabas and Paul's accommodation-decision to have Timothy circumcised are placed between the two halves of this summary.

19:20   "So the word of the Lord grew mightily and prevailed." This statement comes at the end of Paul's second and third missionary journeys in Macedonia and Asia Minor, concluding with Paul's ministry in Ephesus. He is now ready to head toward Jerusalem. However, his leaving is delayed by the uproar instigated by Demetrius, the silversmith. The summary statement also functions to affirm the work of Paul and his coworkers in Asia Minor as a whole (chs. 16-19).

28:31   ". . . proclaiming the kingdom of God and teaching about the Lord Jesus Christ with all boldness and without hindrance." This concluding text fulfills the Acts 1:8 design: the kingdom has advanced through Judea and Samaria and now is rooted in the capital of the empire, Rome. The phrase, proclaiming (kēryssōn) the kingdom of God, is metonymic with "word of God" used in other summaries.[12] Luke has completed his story, with the entire narrative-history guided and empowered by the Holy Spirit, in direct fulfillment of Jesus' promise. Paul has weathered three major trial and defense episodes covering at least two-three years and God has brought him to Rome, the place from which he will disseminate the gospel to the ends of the earth, thus fulfilling the narrative purpose and divine destiny of the gospel (1:8).

In this context of the book's design and purpose, the occurrence of the word *peace* in the summary statement of 9:31 is strategic, both in its enhancement of the structural design and for understanding Luke's intentions by his use of peace (eirēnē). The verse itself cites the geographical regions to which the gospel has so far spread: Judea, Galilee, and Samaria. The immediate con-

---

12. Had Pao examined Luke's use of both kēryssō and euangelizomai and their occurrence in Isaiah 40–55 LXX, he could have strengthened further his thesis.

text is the conversion of Saul, persecutor of the messianic believers. As a consequence, the church now has peace, and is built up; "living in the fear of the Lord, and in the comfort of the Holy Spirit, it increased in numbers" (9:31).

By describing the condition of the church — a singular use that regards all congregations as one church — with the word *peace,* Luke is eulogizing the developments up to this point. Despite adverse circumstances the gospel's advancement continues under the missional empowerment of the Holy Spirit. Even though there will be more hurdles to jump, what has transpired already is phenomenal! In this section, Stephen's stoning, a blow to the movement, was "trumped," as it were, by the conversion of the chief adversary. The one who led out in the harassment and persecution of the messianic believers is now converted, and the church has peace — no small accomplishment.

Saul's conversion is so familiar a story that its theological and moral significance is often overlooked. Saul was a man of violence, persecuting and killing those who adhered to "The Way" sect of Judaism, followers of Messiah Jesus. Struck down by a blinding light on the road to Damascus, Saul's violence (cf. 1 Tim. 1:13) was confronted and transformed. Speaking out from this heavenly light, Jesus addresses this violence, "Saul, Saul, why do you persecute me?" (9:4-5).[13] From this dramatic encounter of both conversion and call to "bring my name before Gentiles and kings and before the people of Israel" (9:15; 26:17-18), Paul becomes the clearest first-century voice for peace and peacemaking, giving his life to unite formerly alienated peoples, and exhorting those caught in divisive rivalry within the newfound congregations to seek peace with one another (Rom. 14:19; 1 Thess. 5:13; 2 Cor. 13:11).

The use of the term *peace* in this summary statement is not a wasted word, in view of the violence Saul has just perpetrated onto the Way followers. Strategically, it functions as a stopper to one kind of historical experience for the believers and opens the way for another, the beginning of the gospel's extension to the ends of the earth. Two miracles immediately occur, both of which lead many to come to faith: Peter heals Aeneas at Lydda and Dorcas at Joppa. What then follows is the marvelous "conversion" of Peter regarding acceptance of Gentiles, indeed, Roman centurion Cornelius' admittance into the new community of Jesus. Rendering a theological account of that stupendous breakthrough sparks the next use of "peace" in Peter's sermon.

10:36 The crucial function of this text must be seen in the whole of Peter's sermon, 10:34-43. The key phrase in 10:36, "preaching peace by Jesus Christ — he is Lord of all" has already entered our discussion in both Chapters 1 and 4. Its significance is threefold. First it is a quotation from Isaiah 52:7

---

13. See the excellent article on this by Mary Schertz, "Turn in the Road."

(LXX): *euangelizomenos eirēnēn* linked here to *dia Iēsous Christou*. This is one of the Isaianic texts announcing that God's good news of peace will be heralded to and embraced by those at "the ends of the earth" (Isa. 52:10; cf. Acts 1:8).[14] That Peter draws on Scripture matches what had just been said: "You know the word that he sent to Israel." This is the word, and this is its fulfillment: Gentile Cornelius has come by the power of the Holy Spirit to believe in Jesus as Messiah, and this is the fulfillment of the promised messianic peace.

Second, "peace" is the object of "preaching the good news" *(euangelizomenos)*. The joining of Jews and Gentiles into one messianic fellowship is *peace.* The boundaries drawn for centuries are overcome by a new oneness that unites rival ethnic parties by joining diverse peoples into a common faith. This does not mean that ethnicity is done away with. Rather, it means that a new and more powerful reality transcends the differences and creates a new messianic identity, to which the ethnic diversities richly contribute. Peace between formerly separated and alienated peoples is the fruit of preaching the gospel; it is the coming of the kingdom of God that preoccupied the query of the disciples in 1:6, which 1:8 answers.

Third, this new reality has been brought about through Jesus Christ, and "This one is Lord of all" *(houtos estin pantōn kyrios)*. The Lordship of Jesus Christ, declared in 2:36, is now reaffirmed precisely at this point where Jews welcome Gentiles into the household of faith. Overcoming the divisions arising from life in this world of nations, races, and tribes attests to the Lordship of Jesus Christ. That Cornelius is a representative of the empire, not normally esteemed by Jews, should not be missed. With all the sociological and political significance this development entails, Cornelius's conversion symbolizes Rome, with the Pax Romana it sought to achieve, kneeling before the lordship of Jesus Christ. Something greater than even Solomon or the Roman Empire has come into historical existence.

From here forward in the history of this early church, the incorporation of Gentiles into the new faith community will occupy center stage in the unfolding drama. While Saul (Paul) is first converted — transformed from a man of violence to a messianic peacemaker — and called to head a mission to the Gentiles, it is Peter who welcomes the first Gentile into the hitherto all Jewish Christian faith community and proclaims the theological rationale for it. That

14. Pao in *Acts and the Isaianic New Exodus* could strengthen his thesis considerably by attending more to the significance of Isa. 52:7-10 in his otherwise helpful proposal. It would help to move from "possibility" to "probability" for his theses, as called for by G. K. Beale in his "Review Article."

Paul and Peter share together in this momentous paradigm shift — two historic episodes — is of no small significance. For, despite whatever tensions, even rifts, develop between Paul and Peter, or between the Petrine and Pauline communities, there is an underlying unity, made possible by the power of the Holy Spirit. The end of the narrative accentuates that "the Holy Spirit fell upon all who heard the word" (10:44). Further, the "circumcised believers who had come with Peter were astounded that the gift of the Holy Spirit had been poured out even on the Gentiles" (v. 45). This is why Peter's sermon begins with "Truly, I perceive that God shows no partiality" (RSV, v. 34).

Peace has been newly redefined by this event. In the next chapter on Paul, it becomes clear that a key emphasis in Paul's theology is peace, and this pertains to this Jewish-Gentile unity through the work of Messiah Jesus. It is a culmination of *shalom* in its journey of denoting relational well-being, between humans and their covenant God, and among humans as well.

15:33   This text refers to Judas and Silas, emissaries from Jerusalem to Antioch, being sent home to Jerusalem by the believers in Antioch. Judas and Silas appointed as official representatives from Jerusalem joined Paul and Barnabas to report the "findings" of the Jerusalem Conference to the church at Antioch. In the flow of the narrative, since the last use of *peace* in 10:36, the first great threat to the unity of the church, whether Gentiles can be admitted without first becoming Jewish through circumcision, was met and dealt with in an amicable manner. In reaching this solution, four elements played a crucial role:

> God testified by bestowing on Gentiles the Holy Spirit.
> Paul and Barnabas narrated signs and wonders that God did among the Gentiles.
> Peter recounted how God looked favorably on the Gentiles.
> James, brother of Jesus, who was now recognized as leader among the Jewish Christians, cited OT Scripture, Amos 9:11, a text that anticipates the rebuilding of the fallen booth of David so that all peoples will seek the Lord, even the Gentiles (Acts 15:15-17a).

James's pronouncement of fulfilled prophecy clinched the decision to welcome Gentiles without circumcision. Nonetheless, four points of Jewish law were set forth (vv. 20, 29) that were to be heeded and kept by the new believers: abstain from things polluted by idols, from fornication *(porneias)*,[15]

---

15. *Porneia*, used frequently in the NT, connotes a range of sexual relations outside the marriage bond of husband and wife.

from whatever has been strangled, and from blood.[16] Beyond this, "it seemed good to us and to the Holy Spirit to lay no further burden than these essentials" (v. 28). These decisions were communicated to believers in Antioch, and it was those believers who sent Judas and Silas home to Jerusalem in *peace*. The word is then not simply a farewell wish, but also conveys the notion that the divisive issue had been satisfactorily resolved, and the church in Antioch remained united with and in *peace* with the church in Jerusalem. Whew! No small accomplishment!

Peace in the World of the Pax Romana

> Acts 12:20: Now Herod was angry with the people of Tyre and Sidon. So they came to him in a body; and after winning over Blastus, the king's chamberlain, they asked for a *reconciliation (eirēnē)*, because their country depended on the king's country for food.
>
> Acts 16:36: And the jailer reported the message to Paul, saying, "The magistrates sent word to let you go; therefore come out now and go in *peace.*"
>
> Acts 24:2: When Paul had been summoned, Tertullus began to accuse him, saying: "Your Excellency, because of you we have long enjoyed *peace*, and reforms have been made for this people because of your foresight."

I presented in Chapter 5 on Luke the scholarly interpretations of Luke's political stance, and I described the Greco-Roman Pax Romana in Chapter 2. Together, these provide the context for understanding these three uses of *eirēnē*. In light of these texts and others, Richard Cassidy says of Christian mission and presence in the Roman world, "In a word, while Luke's Christians very evidently adhere to Jesus' teachings concerning 'the things that make for peace,' they hardly manage a peaceful entry into the world controlled by Rome."[17] Cassidy identifies the three main arguments that have been advanced to argue for Luke's pro-Roman political apologetic in Acts, and then presents evidence from the text to counter those arguments. I summarize this in two columns, to show the argument and the counter-evidence,[18] as follows:[19]

16. The order in v. 29 differs from that of v. 20. In v. 29 *porneias* occurs last.

17. Cassidy, *Society and Politics in the Acts of the Apostles*, p. 144.

18. Cassidy, *Society and Politics*, pp. 96-135.

19. E. Franklin earlier demonstrated that many of Conzelmann's claims for a political apologetic are unconvincing. See his *Christ the Lord*, pp. 137-38.

Pro-Roman Apologetic	Counter-Evidence
1. Christians are law-abiding and harmless.	
• disruptions are fomented by Jews	• but Rome too would see Paul as "agitator"
• Roman officials exonerate Paul (note Gallio, Festus, Herod Agrippa II)	• though Rome would not perceive Paul as against them, yet not as one contributing to the *pax* of the empire, either
2. Paul esteems his citizenship and cooperates with Roman officials.	But Paul is certainly not typically orthodox Roman citizen: *Jesus,* not Caesar, is Lord!
• takes pride in citizenship, "by birth"	• but Paul is reluctant to disclose citizenship and speaks of it only in private, not public
• defers to authorities, gives respect	• but portrays Felix desiring a bribe, and Felix and Festus seeking to be rid of the "case"; Paul lectures on justice, self-control, and judgment, and Felix is "alarmed" (24:25)
• appeals to Rome for "justice"	• but the text does not say that he expects justice, the decision was forced on him by the situation, and the text is silent on the final outcome
3. The Roman system is portrayed favorably.	not true, in any explicit sense
• legal, military, and economic institutions positive	• but the two Roman governors misconduct the case
• shows Roman "justice": Gallio; Claudius Lysias brings Paul before the Jerusalem Sanhedrin	• though an army official, Cornelius is portrayed positively, yet no blanket praise of system
• roads, harbors developed by Romans	• no explicit praise for these, just used

In addition to these considerations, Cassidy identifies other features in Acts that damage the argument that Acts is a pro-Roman political apologetic.

First, early in Acts Peter's and the apostles' political allegiance is clearly evident: 2:36; 4:19-20; 5:29 (we must obey God rather than any human, be it Jewish or Roman authority). Second, Luke's "narrative consistently shows the apostles and Paul obeying and witnessing to God's word without regard of concerns, even harsh reactions, of the political authorities."[20] Third, the narrative as a whole shows a great amount of turbulence and public controversy. Officials could only deduce that Christians had a "penchant of becoming embroiled in controversy." Fourth, if Luke intended a political apologetic, he hardly would have mentioned that one of the disciples of Jesus was a Zealot (1:13; "Simon, the Zealot").[21]

The alternative theory that Acts develops an "ecclesial apologetic" as developed by Walaskay[22] — Luke presents the empire favorably to encourage fellow Christians to adopt a positive political stance toward authorities — fares no better. The same counter-evidence described above counters this thesis as well. Rather, Luke's purpose in Acts is to encourage believers in their allegiance to Jesus and witness before kings and governors.[23] Thus Luke's primary goals were: first, to write out of his personal allegiance to his Lord and strengthen believers in their allegiance and, second, to shape the conduct of believers in their daily interactions with people generally but especially with government officials in accord with the gospel and specifically to provide models for their own "Christian witness in their trials before Roman officials."[24]

Mauser considers the portrait of Roman authorities in Acts also. His assessment overlaps in part with Cassidy's in that he presents the same evidence of Roman misconduct in Paul's trials, noting especially the flogging of Paul and Silas in prison (ch. 16), and Felix's delay in dealing with Paul, in hopes he might receive some bribe. The entire narrative of Acts 21–26 shows interminable delay and gives "the impression that the mills of Roman justice

20. The structure of Acts may indicate that the two previous martyr accounts (Stephen and James), occurring near the end of the first two geographical transitions (as per 1:8), in 7:54-60 and then 12:1-3, presage Paul's own martyrdom as part of the climax of the gospel coming to Rome. The structure together with Luke's ending the story narrating Paul's future may be taken to imply his martyrdom. For the historical evidence in support of Paul's death as a martyr in Rome, see Bruce, *The Spreading Flame*, pp. 139-46.

21. Cassidy, *Society and Politics*, pp. 140-55.

22. Walaskay, *"And So We Came to Rome."* Walaskay maintains that Luke sought "to aid the Christian community in its understanding of the workings of the empire so that the church may begin to develop a dialogue with local magistrates . . . and not feel intimidated by untrue accusations nor anxious about being dealt with unfairly" (p. 58).

23. Cassidy, *Society and Politics*, pp. 156-79.

24. Cassidy, *Society and Politics*, pp. 159-60.

grind very slowly indeed."[25] Indeed Luke does not whitewash Roman authorities in Acts!

Of key significance in Cassidy's argument are Luke's strong emphasis on the "kingdom of God" — which is not portrayed in other-worldly terms — and his depiction of Jesus as Lord, a claim not framed to win favor with Rome. As is true of Jesus' attitude toward the rulers as portrayed in Luke's Gospel, so also in Acts Paul's conduct before Roman officials does not show him especially deferential to them, nor are they portrayed in complimentary light in some cases, nor does Paul flaunt his Roman citizenship as having particular importance, but he uses it on several occasions only as a last resort.[26] Given the long list of trial narratives stretching from Acts 5 to Acts 26, it is clear that Luke's primary purpose is to prepare his readers to witness courageously before officials.

At the same time, the positive portrait of Rome cannot be denied. Cornelius is presented in a most positive light (ch. 10), and the proconsul Sergius Paulus likewise becomes a full believer (13:7-12). Overall, Paul's conduct, especially his appeals, shows a fundamental trust in Rome's due process of law. Gallio's deft judgment (18:12-16), and later Festus's (25:18-19) — that what Paul is accused of is an intra-Jewish haggling over law and does not score as offense against Rome — represent due process in the Roman legal system. Festus articulates the point of due process clearly in addressing King Agrippa and Queen Bernice. He says that he told the Jews in Jerusalem "that it was not the custom of the Romans to hand over anyone before the accused had met accusers face to face and had been given the opportunity to make a defense against the charge" (25:16). Later Festus says to Agrippa, "it seems to me unreasonable to send a prisoner without indicating the charges against him" (25:27). Indeed, Paul is declared innocent of charges three times by Roman officials: by the Jerusalem tribune, Claudius Lysias, in a letter to governor Felix (23:26-29); by Festus in addressing King Agrippa (25:25); and in the joint discernment of Festus and Agrippa (26:31). But Paul had already appealed to Rome, and thus to Rome he had to go (25:11-12). Later Agrippa says, "This man could have been set free if he had not appealed to the emperor" (26:32).

With this positive portrait of Roman law and Roman officials, we would expect that the use of *eirēnē*, in so far as it describes the *pax Romana*, would also render a positive portrait, as it indeed does in the latter two occurrences, at least on first impression. The three occurrences, with brief commentary, are:

25. Mauser, *Gospel of Peace*, pp. 92-93 (quoting p. 93).
26. Cassidy, *Society and Politics*, pp. 83-116.

12:20   A delegation from the cities of Tyre and Sidon is sent to request *peace* from King Herod Agrippa II. We do not know what circumstances led to this request, but the incident is evidence of deterioration in relations between the king and his subjects. Some commentators associate the petition with Herod's edict concerning grain import against the two cities. In that case, "peace" would mean lifting the boycott.[27] If indeed this was the case, then it must be noted that Herod's action does not put Rome in a favorable light, since Herod, though partly Jewish, represents Rome. Be that as it may, the clear intent of the narrative is to show God's judgment upon the pompous king (vv. 20-23). Because we can only conjecture the circumstances behind the "peace" appeal, it is not possible to draw anything concrete about the significance of "peace" in this use. By including this incident in his narrative, Luke augments the negative portrait of King Herod.

16:36   Ordered by the magistrates, the Philippian jailer releases Paul and sends him off with the word, "Go in peace." As Mauser points out, this is a Semitic phrase, and as such hardly fits the lips of a Roman jailer, even though just freshly converted to the faith (16:29-34).[28] Rather, we should understand the phrase within the context of what Roman law provides as part of the *Pax Romana*. Mauser's paraphrase of its meaning is, "Depart in the security of an official act of the city authorities, and in the liberty provided you by recourse to a good and well-functioning law that has the strength to right previous wrongs."[29] Paul, however, does not accept such an easy release from the jailer, but counters with a plea for greater justice: the wrong against us merits more than just a clandestine release. Paul is not satisfied until the Roman magistrates come and apologize for the public flogging and throwing them, Roman citizens (i.e., Paul and Silas), into prison.

If Mauser's interpretation of this use of *eirēnē* is correct, Paul's response casts a shadow over the jailer's role, and certainly over that of the magistrates. None of the Roman officials acted with integrity in words and actions that matched due remorse for their offenses against Paul and Silas. If *eirēnē* is to be understood in this "security of the law of the Pax Romana" sense, then the word sticks in the throat, since it was too easily used. Paul's response judges the "*eirēnē* assurance" as inadequate, not good enough, and wants more, a personal apology that restores the relationship of the magistrates to Paul and Silas with the integrity that *eirēnē* should have. Thus the query: is Paul hold-

27. Mauser, *Gospel of Peace*, p. 99, is inclined to accept this interpretation.
28. Mauser, *Gospel of Peace*, p. 91. Mauser also says that Luke would hardly have lapsed into this error since he elsewhere is careful to let Romans say what Romans say, and Jews say what Jews say.
29. Mauser, *Gospel of Peace*, p. 92.

ing the Roman *eirēnē* accountable to the fuller notion of peace, derived from the Hebrew *shalom*? Since the jailer is now a believer, this would serve as his first catechetical lesson as to what "peace" really is. Peace involves restoration of relationship, possible only when misdeeds are duly acknowledged. An element of "repentance" is thus needed for "peace" to be effectual.

24:2   In this use of *eirēnē* Tertullus, a lawyer, addresses Roman governor Felix to present the case against Paul on behalf of Paul's antagonists in the Jerusalem Jewish hierarchy. It begins with the usual diplomatic flourish of such speeches of the time.[30] Tertullus's opening praises governor Felix, "Your Excellency, because of you we have long enjoyed peace, and reforms have been made for this people because of your foresight. We welcome this in every way and everywhere with utmost gratitude" (24:2-3). Although there is a hollow ring in such a flattering eulogy since Felix was not known for any great accomplishments,[31] he nonetheless represents the *Pax* of the empire that began with Augustus's determination to extend the rule of peace to all the peoples under imperial governance. So Felix is heir to this legacy, and Tertullus's words fit into the larger imperial self-image, which it sought also to disseminate. But as Wengst's analysis of the Pax Romana has shown,[32] the truth of the "peace" is the suffering of many subjugated peoples. Thus one can only wonder how much of this "truth" entered the minds of the people, including Paul's accusers, as they heard this flowery address. And what are Luke's intentions in narrating this phrase, "we have long enjoyed peace"? Does Luke expect his readers to hear it without dissimulation? Or is there an ironic twist here also? Since the speech is made against Paul, it seems that it must be heard as disingenuous. And once again, what reads off as praise of the Pax Romana is underneath a dig, a critique of its claims and achievements.[33]

---

30. Veltman, "The Defense Speeches of Paul in Acts." Veltman begins with the stated assumption that Luke constructs the speeches and then shows that they confirm to stylistic literary features that mark such speeches in the Roman world. Conformity of style does not prove or disprove whether Luke constructed them or utilized reliable sources from the tradition.

31. As Mauser notes, both Josephus (*Antiquities* 20.141-44) and Tacitus (*Histories* 5.9; *Annals* 12.54) "severely censure his personal conduct and his handling of the affairs of the province" (p. 90).

32. See Chapter 2 above. Mauser too presents the "underside" view of the empire's "peace" (pp. 84-89).

33. For positive features of the Pax Romana, see Anna Janzen, *Der Friede im lukanischen Doppelwerk*. Janzen argues that Luke reflects some of the good elements in the Pax Romana, such as the "benefactor" convention of the rich assisting the poor, but Luke-Acts is not a political apologetic. Quite likely the church reflected some of the cultural patterns of the empire, especially those of benevolent quality. I do not discount this point, but the peace of the Way community and the empire's peace differ.

However, the narrative as a whole portrays the Pax Romana as serving the cause of Pax Christi, even though its claims to efficiency, due legal process, and justice are exposed and found wanting. In this there is an interrelation between the two contexts: the growing expanding church that experiences peace in its deeper sense and meaning and the Pax Romana that boasts of its peace achievements. I propose that Acts subverts the claims of the Pax Romana by letting them "play" a role in the narrative, only to show the limited nature and insubstantiality of the peace of the Pax Romana. The *peace* that is stronger and deeper is that found in the nascent Way community, even though beset by numerous conflictual situations, internal and external.

Peace with Justice

Luke's use of the term "justice" in Acts, continuing an emphasis we examined in the Gospel (Chapter 5 above), further supports this interpretation. Key texts are Acts 3:14; 7:52; and 22:14, where Jesus is identified in titular form as "the Righteous One." This accords with the Gospel's christology, which also portrays Jesus as "the Righteous One" and carries this forward into Jesus' post-resurrection identity. Jesus is the One who trusts humbly in God, obeys the divine will, and is vindicated by God (an emphasis on the righteous one found in many Psalms).[34] In four other places in Acts, *dikaiosynē* is used in contexts where the salvation-message is extended or presented to Gentiles (10:35; 13:10; 17:31; 24:25).

In 24:25 Paul speaks frequently to Governor Felix of justice, and thus Luke puts justice into direct conversation with Roman political power. It is a justice linked to self-control (virtue ethic) and future judgment (theological belief), thus showing essential interconnection between gospel witness and justice. Amid all the debate about Luke's view of Israel, the Jews, "Jewish Christianity" (which some say is anachronistic for Luke), Rome, the law, and the temple, one thing is clear: the people *(laos)* of God, a key term throughout Luke-Acts denoting the true people of God and including Jew and Gentile, is marked by *dikaios/dikaiosynē*! Acts 10:35-36, in summing up Jesus' mission, links together *dikaiosynē* and *eirēnē*, thus marking God's *laos*, whether Jew or Gentile, to be of distinctive moral character. In this respect Luke has only one people of God: that clearly is the point of 10:35. And this people is a people for whom justice and peace are the hallmark. Salvation in Luke takes on a strong

---

34. Psalms 5, 25, 26, 31, 43, 54, 64, 71, 94, 109, 140, and 142.

ethical tone.[35] Thus both Jewish and Gentile officials refuse *dikaios/ dikaiosynē* and *eirēnē,* and both Jewish people and Gentile people accept them. Both Jew and Gentile share in the culpability of Jesus' death (Acts 4:26-29); both likewise are beneficiaries of its salvific gift: God's righteous salvation bringing peace.

In the crucial text Acts 24:25, where Paul discusses with Felix the issues of "justice, self-control, and the coming judgment," the Roman official's portrait can be deemed both positive and negative. On the one hand, he is willing to hear Paul on the sensitive issue of justice. But the text also states a baser reason for his frequent conversations with Paul on justice: Felix was hoping for a bribe. Because he did not receive one, he left Paul in prison in order to do the Jews a favor. Quite clearly, in Luke's presentation, Felix falls short of the *dikaios* that characterizes Jesus and his people *(laos).* Felix's successor Festus is presented in much the same light (25:9). Paul's forthright appeal of this case to the emperor (v. 10) is also ambivalent in negative or positive valence. It would appear to regard the emperor as one who would vindicate his cause, but such never is reported in Acts. The delay of the trial in Acts 28 and inference of final martyr death (see above) is the narrative conclusion. Also the closure to King Agrippa's and Governor Festus's hearing, "This man could have been set free if he had not appealed to Caesar" (26:32), hardly gives Roman law a tribute for justice. The statement does not show Roman legal process to be Paul's friend. While on the one hand it comes as an acquittal from Rome's mouth that Jewish charges will not stand under Roman law, at the same time it inferentially acknowledges that Rome will condemn. Thus the viewpoint of the narrative is not consistent in presenting either a pro- or anti-Roman bias. It cuts both ways. And this is part of the larger story. The narrative puts Roman officials in poor light far too often (Herod in Acts 12, Festus and Felix in Acts 24–26, cf. Pilate in Luke 13:1-2) to make a pro-Roman thesis tenable. Indeed, the Conzelmann view cannot stand, and we must conceive anew just what Luke-Acts announces about the faithful people of God, the *laos,* in its understanding of peace and justice, and its relation to the empire.

The challenge is to seek new categories for describing Luke's view of the gospel's stance in relation to world power. Indeed, there is a strong liberationist and transformational emphasis in both volumes. And it arises always from the side of the gospel's own agenda and its encounter with diverse peoples.

---

35. François Bovon has suggested just this point in "Studies in Luke-Acts: Retrospect and Prospect," in his discussion of Luke's use of the OT, which contrasts to allegorical use in *Barnabas's* repudiation of the Jews as belonging to God's *laos.* See also Bovon's earlier work "Israel, die Kirche und die Völker im lukanischen Doppelwerk."

None of the prevailing models of gospel and politics fit the Luke-Acts reality. Hence, we need a conceptual transformation to grasp the reality of Luke's narrative as it presents the gospel's course in Palestine through Jesus and amid the Roman world. Might it be identified as "an alternative subversive messianic establishment of true righteousness/justice and peace"? Perhaps Luke intends to present Jesus as the fulfillment of both the Jewish messianic hope of true righteousness and peace (Isa. 11; *passim*) and the pregnant Greco-Roman hope for a millennial age of peace, which as Virgil's *Fourth Eclogue* anticipated, would be inaugurated by a miraculous birth of a royal son.[36] In this coming age, now announced as come in Jesus Christ, shalom finds expression in the new *laos* community of the Spirit, in which a fundamental reversal of values guides the community into bold witness in the name of Jesus, proclaiming the gospel to the ends of the earth, not being intimidated by the political authorities (Jewish or Roman), and seeking to turn the world upside down (note the accusation in 17:6b from ruffians in Thessalonica framed by Jewish opponents) not through any violence but by the bold public proclamation of the kingdom-gospel of peace. The members of this Way community also cared for each other in every way, as we shall see below.

Luke's story of the gospel's expansion into the world depicts also encounter with the demonic in the magic of the day (Simon in 8:9-24; Elymas [Bar-Jesus] in 13:6-12; and a slave girl fortune-teller in 16:16-18) and in idolatry as well (in Athens in 17:16-31 and in Ephesus in 19:23-41). These confrontations portray the peace-gospel challenging the economic systems dependent upon these magical and idolatrous practices, the intellectual philosophical worldview built upon multiple gods and goddesses — and this linked into the

---

36. See Helmut Koester's 1991 SBL address, in which he describes this Greco-Roman hope ("Jesus the Victim," especially p. 11). The vision for this eschatological hope is developed in Virgil's *Aeneid* and includes two notable features in relation to the NT Jesus-kingdom account: the birth of a divine child and fulfillment of "the promises and the righteousness of the primordial time." Koester's article as a whole is oriented to cursory assessment of historical Jesus research efforts and findings. He notes the diverse eschatological portraits in the NT witness and settles in on the fact that regardless of what Jesus proclaimed about eschatological fulfillment, he died a victim, not a victor. It was left to his followers "to design a new order of the world in which the victim is vindicated" (p. 9). This rather skeptical treatment, which ignores resurrection as historical vindication, regards critical inquiry as having established that Jesus called for (and lived) a reversal of values: serving others rather than lording it over them, loving one's enemy as the only possible response to hostility, welcoming people from all nations to the eschatological banquet, and saying that the poor, hungry, and mourners will inherit the kingdom (p. 15). On the basis of these criteria we are to understand our world, thus continuing to proclaim the kingdom of God as "the utopia of a new community, a new political order, and indeed a new world" (p. 15).

political as becomes evident in the story of Paul's preaching that undermines the god/goddess business of Demetrius in chapter 19. Paul and Silas's imprisonment in Philippi and the mob's uproar in Ephesus have nothing to do with Jews inciting the opposition. Rather, local citizens of Rome's Pax Romana are threatened by the proclamation of this gospel precisely because it calls for a new life order under the sovereign lordship of Jesus Christ. Economically, culturally, and politically, the gospel means stop fashioning god-images out of wood or clay but own the crucified and risen Jesus Christ as God's revelation of God's self and reckon with the truth that a day of reckoning, judgment, is coming. The peace of this gospel is revolutionary, for it ends one world and begins another. No longer does ethnic identity lead to rivalry. No longer does economic livelihood depend upon magic and idolatry. No longer does the political life of the community acknowledge Caesar as Lord. A new world begins where Jesus the vindicated Righteous One is Savior and Lord, where the Holy Spirit turns old Babel into Pentecostal multi-ethnic fellowship love, and where the new kingdom-peace-gospel turns all things upside-down, overcoming internal and external conflicts, transforming violent Saul into a gospel peacemaker, welcoming Cornelius into the Way community, and seating people formerly hostile to one another at the Lord's banquet table.

Expressions of Peacemaking in Community Life

One of the foremost expressions in the peacemaking dynamic of this new Pax Christi is the practice of mutual aid in the community embracing both richer and poorer people. We have noted above how economic challenges faced the community on two occasions: in Acts 2 and 4 those with resources sold what they had to care for the poor; in Acts 6 the church ordained deacons to oversee the distribution of material aid to care justly for those in need when complaints arose about unequal distribution to the Hebrew and Hellenist widows.

In his social world study of early Christianity, John Gager identifies as the key to the movement's survival, growth, and success "a single, overriding internal factor," namely, "the radical sense of Christian community — open to all, insistent on absolute loyalty, and concerned for every aspect of the believer's life. From the very beginning, the one distinctive gift of Christianity was this sense of community."[37] Assessing the nature of this experience of

---

37. Gager, *Kingdom and Community: The Social World of Early Christianity*, p. 140. See also Lohfink, *Jesus and Community* for a fuller description of the outworking of this new reality in formation of community.

community, Walsh and Langan rightly assert that an essential part of this sense of community depended on the willingness of Christians to aid the needy and on the teachings of the Christian church on the right use of material goods.[38]

Community and mutual aid: these were the twin pillars of early Christian life and the key to its survival and growth. The Holy Spirit's role in the formation and sustaining of this community, as well as the empowerment of the living, reigning Jesus Christ enabled this community to survive and grow. This social expression of the new Christ-Spirit reality, a community of love caring for another economically, attests to what Paul declares as a "new creation: everything old has passed away; see, everything has become new" (2 Cor. 5:17).

The two prominent New Testament models of sharing economic resources in Acts were those of "having goods in common" (Acts 2:44-47 and 4:32-37) and the churches that Paul helped to found collecting money for the poor in Jerusalem. These models, while not necessarily prescriptive for today, do provide normative characteristics for Christian practice of mutual aid. Both are anchored in the experience of *koinonia,* which had its origins in Jesus and his ministry.[39]

An essential practice in the Pauline mission was mutual care of one another, expressed in material aid as will be discussed also in Chapter 7. Paul so highly valued this expression as proof of the newly achieved unity in Jesus Christ that he willingly gave his life for the cause, despite prophetic declaration that he would encounter arrest and imprisonment in Jerusalem (Acts 21:7-14). Paul says, ". . . I am ready not only to be bound but even to die in Jerusalem for the name of the Lord Jesus Christ" (v. 13b). Paul regarded his relief gift to Jerusalem as the crowning achievement of his apostolic calling to give proof that Gentile and Jewish messianic believers are really, truly one in Jesus Christ, peace-fellows through the blood on the cross of the Lord Jesus Christ. The relief gift expressed the peace of the cross concretely, in mutual care for one another. The emphases in Romans 12 and 15 and 2 Corinthians 8–9 show how intrinsic this mutuality was to the nature of the missionary gospel.[40] By taking the relief gift to Jerusalem and encountering opposition there, leading to his arrest and eventual imprisonment in Rome, the goal of · the missionary vision of Luke-Acts is achieved. Paul preaches the kingdom of God in Rome, the capital of the empire.

38. Walsh and Langan, "Patristic Social Consciousness," p. 112.

39. Here see my article, "Mutual Aid Based in Jesus and Early Christianity," especially pp. 21-24.

40. This feature of early Christian community will be discussed more fully in Chapter 7.

This radical commitment to mutual aid was (and is today) mission with body and flesh, the gospel wrapped in the skin of loving care for one another. This is an important learning from Paul for Christian churches in the twenty-first century. It is an essential part of the gospel of Jesus Christ and the mission of the church.

"The Way" Identity of the Early Christians

The designation of the followers of Jesus in Acts as those belonging to "The Way" is not without significance in view of the believers' commitments to peace. The background for the early Christians' designation of themselves as those of "the way" was their self-perception as *disciples* of Jesus. The occurrence of *mathētēs(ai),* therefore, in Acts 6:1, 2, 7 and 9:1, 10, 19 should be regarded as foundational to their *hodos*-self-designation.[41] It is therefore quite possible that Jesus designated his own disciples with way-terminology. Indeed, "the way" motif plays an important role in Mark in relation to the disciples' learning the way of discipleship. That way meant giving up expectations of messianic royal power and, instead, taking up the cross, hearing Jesus' words of his imminent suffering and death, and then his crisp, virtually brusque "Follow me."

The use of *hodos* in Acts should be connected with Luke's phrase *en tę̄ hodǭ* in describing Jesus' encounter with two disciples on their walk to Emmaus. The same phrase with much the same meaning occurs in Acts 9:17, 27; and 26:13 to denote Paul's journey on the way/road. The image of walking in the way is foundational to the early Christian's self-understanding. Not only did the resurrected Lord speak with the disciples "in the way" (Luke 24:32, 35), but Paul's own vision of the resurrected Lord and conversion from violence to peace happened *en tę̄ hodǭ* (Acts 9:17, 27; 26:13).

In addition to these uses in Acts *hodos* occurs eight times: in the absolute use *(hē hodos)* in 9:2; 19:9, 23; 24:22 and the construct form in 18:25, 26; 22:4; and 24:14. Whereas 18:25 and 26 are modified by *of the Lord* and *of God* respectively, 22:4 is modified by *this* and 24:14 with a relative clause. The phrase *way of salvation* in 16:17 seems to carry a narrower meaning. These uses point up two important connections. First, the absolute use designates the followers of Jesus as a sect within Judaism. Second, the construct phrases

---

41. Repo, *Der "Weg" als Selbstbezeichnung des Urchristentums,* pp. 29-32. As Repo puts it, "Der Jüngerbegriff steht natürlich durch Vermittlung des Nachfolgegedankens auch in Verbindung mit dem Motiv der Wanderung."

hark back to the moral uses of *the way* and the eschatological use of *the way of the Lord* in the OT.[42] Certainly, Isaiah 40:3, basic to the Qumran Covenanters' identity (1QS 8:3-4) and to the introduction of the Gospels' announcing John's and Jesus' coming, figures strategically into the formation of community identity. *The Way* designates the early Christian believers as the elect of the end time, participating in God's long promised messianic salvation.

The motif appears also in Heb. 9:8 and 10:20 to designate a pilgrim people, who look to the future city of God. These motifs of pilgrimage, messianic fulfillment, and costly discipleship all intertwine in marking the Way identity of the early believers, first called Christians in Antioch (Acts 11:26). As followers of the Way they are people of God's peace; their commonwealth is not on this earth (see Phil. 3:20-21). They hope for the consummation of God's peace that God's new kingdom order on earth has begun.

---

42. The use of *hodos* in Qumran is significant also. Some scholars, including Repo, hold that John the Baptist mediated the Qumran *hodos* usage and community identity into early Christianity. For more on this see my doctoral dissertation, "A Study in Markan Structure," pp. 179-83, 263-65.

Jesus Makes the Covenant of Peace
(Retrospect and Prospect)

In each of the Synoptic Gospels Jesus, in his last meal during Passion Week, makes a (new) covenant with his disciples. This Passover meal celebrates God's delivering Israel from Egyptian bondage. What Jesus does and says about himself at this meal makes it memorable beyond Passover. Jesus makes a (new) covenant at this meal, fulfilling Israel's hope for ending exile and renewing covenant (Zech. 9:9-11; Jer. 31:31-34). Jesus' words at the Supper "mark his death as the inaugural event of covenant renewal,"[1] extending God's salvation purpose. Jesus speaks of his broken body and shed blood that announces his imminent death as having redemptive significance, for it is *broken* and *poured out for many* (in Luke, *for you*).

While wording differs slightly among the accounts, the core meanings of this ritual known as Communion, Lord's Supper, *Agape* Feast, or Eucharist are clear.[2] One aspect of this ritual's significance, however, is often overlooked. The (new) covenant that Jesus makes with his disciples also fulfills Ezekiel's prophecy, where the Lord God says, "I will make with them a covenant of peace" (34:25; 37:26; cf. Isa. 54:10).

My comments on the Lord's Supper focus on the peacemaking signifi-

---

1. Green and Baker, *Recovering the Scandal of the Cross,* p. 43. Green and Baker helpfully explicate the multiple atonement images in the NT versus emphasizing only the "penal" theory (see especially chapters 2-4, pp. 35-115). See also Driver, *Understanding the Atonement for the Mission of the Church.*

2. In keeping with the festive and solemn elements of Passover, the Communion celebration includes joyful, festive, and solemn remembrance elements. It was indeed formative of community-identity and fellowship *(koinōnia).* See Eleanor Kreider, *Communion Shapes Character* for discussion of these dimensions, especially the Agape meals, known also as Love Feasts (pp. 34-43).

cance of the Last Supper, in which Jesus' broken body and poured-out blood create enduring covenant relations between Jesus and his followers, as a covenant of peace.[3] I consider also the second- to fourth-century church's Eucharistic liturgy, specifically its import for peacemaking.

NT scholars have mined the four Eucharist texts (Matt. 26:26-29; Mark 14:22-25; Luke 22:17-20; 1 Cor. 11:23-25)[4] to assess the degree of authenticity (whether spoken by Jesus or developed by the early church). Paul's text, written in the 50s of the first century, is the earliest account, but that does not mean his wording preserves most closely the authentic words of Jesus. Paul's account concurs with Luke's in several wordings, especially in the phrase, "new covenant in my blood." But many scholars regard Matthew and Mark to be closer to the authentic words of Jesus. Other issues surface as well: was the Last Supper a Passover or a *chaburah* (fellowship) meal, which only later was identified as the Christian Passover? To what extent was the Lord's Supper meal similar to or distinct from the many other meals and banquets which characterized Jesus' ministry? Jesus' open commensality is one of the bedrocks in "historical Jesus studies" (notably Crossan and Borg). Moessner's study of Luke, *Lord of the Banquet,* shows the importance of meals in Jesus' ministry.[5] It is beyond my purpose here to examine these matters. John Koenig provides a recent and excellent synopsis and treatment of the issues.[6] The older classic work of Jeremias merits consideration as well.[7]

The purpose of this discussion focuses on aspects of the Lord's Supper

3. The texts to consider are numerous. Since one author wrote both Luke and Acts, we ask: do the meals in Acts 2 and 4 that celebrate the coming of the Spirit (Pentecost) connect theologically to the Last Supper and thus also celebrate the covenant of peace? Anticipating Chapter 7 below, how do Paul's words about the Lord's Supper in 1 Corinthians 11 shed light on the peacemaking significance of the Lord's Supper? Similarly, in John's Gospel does Jesus' discourse after the feeding of the five thousand in John 6 signify eucharistic intention, since the "words of institution" do not occur in John after the supper (see 13:2)?

4. Other relevant texts are John 6 together with John 2:1-12; 10:1-18; 13–17 (after the meal Jesus speaks twice about peace, which he bestows on his disciples); 19:34 (from Jesus' side flowed "water and blood," a distinctive Johannine phrase that likely echoes baptismal initiation and eucharistic observance: see 1 John 5:6-8); the daily meal practices in Acts 2:42, 46 (cf. 20:7, 11); and possibly 2 Cor. 4:15 with its reference to *eucharistia*, for here the "increase in thanksgiving" (Eucharist?) expresses the result of the grace *(charis)*-inspired mission.

5. Moessner, *Lord of the Banquet.* Another relevant study, focusing on inclusion of women at the meals, is Corley's *Private Women.* According to Corley, such inclusion of women was not unique to the Jesus movement, but reflects practices of Hellenistic Judaism in the Greco-Roman world. She contends that of the Synoptics Matthew is the most revolutionary in its inclusion of women, especially in their status and roles at the meals.

6. Koenig, *The Feast of the World's Redemption,* pp. 3-44.

7. Jeremias, *The Eucharistic Words of Jesus.*

that relate peacemaking and reconciliation to correlative emphases within the respective Gospels or Paul. None of the texts *explicitly* connect the Supper to *peace* and *reconciliation,* though the church in the second and third centuries did so (see below). All four texts connect Jesus' ritual action to making a *covenant* sealed in *my blood,* and the Gospel texts connect the ritual action to the anticipated consummation of the *kingdom of God* (in Matthew, *Father's kingdom*). The ritual action of *breaking the bread* is followed by the pronouncement, *this is my body.* Similarly, the ritual *taking up the cup* is accompanied by *this is my blood;* Matthew and Mark then say, *poured out for many,* while Luke reads *poured out for you.* Luke and Paul both speak of the *covenant* as a *new* covenant, and also identify the ritual as a memorial by the phrase *in remembrance of me.* Luke also presents a puzzle in that the cup ritual occurs twice, both before and after the bread ritual.

The key features of this Supper that mark it a memorable peace-making act are:

1. The ritual action itself, *breaking* the bread and *taking* the cup that is *poured out for many (you), dramatizes* Jesus' teaching his disciples the way of the cross, serving others, and humbling oneself to enter the kingdom. In these ritual actions Jesus embodies and culminates what he said and did in his ministry. Now it is visually concretized: Jesus gives himself "a ransom for many" (Mark 10:45) / "for the life of the world" (John 6:51). *Jesus,* who he is and what he did, *means* self-donation. Luke arranges Jesus' teachings on discipleship to accentuate this point. He places the disciples' dispute about greatness immediately after the Supper event, provocatively positioning the question, "Who is greater, the one who is at the table or the one who serves?" in the context of the Supper itself. Moreover, he adds a distinctive word of Jesus that speaks of conferring on them a kingdom because they stood with him in his trials, and thus they "may eat and drink at my table in my kingdom."

By this distinctive compositional design Luke highlights Jesus' teaching on status reversal that Mark and Matthew in their structure develop differently (see Chapter 4 for Mark's distinctive structural design in 8:27–10:52). Matthew like Mark locates the same three rounds of Jesus' discipleship teaching during his movement from Galilee to Jerusalem (16:21-28; 18:1-5; 20:20-28). This teaching turns upside-down the dominant cultural notions of greatness and power by employing the images of cross, child, and servant. Jesus' ritual action at the Last Supper, with his interpretation, *seals* the meaning of his ministry: he willingly faces suffering and cross, values the lowly, and gives himself as a servant to others, to ransom many (Mark 10:45).

2. Jesus' recurring reference to *cup* in his earlier teaching on discipleship

is now concretized in dramatic symbol. In response to the ("mother of the," Matt. 20:20) sons of Zebedee's (Mark 10:35) request to be granted seats on the right and left of Jesus in his kingdom (Matthew) or glory (Mark), Jesus asks, "Are you able to drink the cup that I will drink?" and he says further, "You will indeed drink my cup, but to sit at my right and my left, this is not mine to grant." The *cup* metaphor occurs again in Gethsemane, when Jesus prays, "Abba, Father, remove this cup from me; yet, not what I want, but what you want" (Mark 14:36 par. Matt. 26:39 and Luke 22:42). Clearly, the *cup* symbolizes Jesus' approaching suffering and death at the hands of the imperial powers (cf. its use in Ezek. 23:31-34 in context of vv. 23-24; Jer. 49:12). Thus, when Jesus *takes the cup* in the Last Supper and then says it is *poured out for many (you)*, it is clear that when the disciples drink of the cup they will participate in Jesus' sufferings (Col. 1:24; Phil 3:10). God's purpose is achieved not through revolt against the oppressors, i.e., fighting evil with evil, or any other means to obtain God's kingdom peace. In partaking of the cup, the disciples commit themselves to walk the way Jesus walked, trusting in God for vindication against the persecutors (see Chapter 9 below).

For this reason, in expositing Mark (see Chapter 4 above) I said (and the same can be said for Matthew and Luke) that there is no "communion" between partaking of the bread and cup, sharing in the body and blood of Jesus, and drawing the sword, striking out in violence even on behalf of the One who is the Messiah; that drawing the sword aims precisely at avoiding the suffering signified by the bread and cup, the suffering of the to-be-crucified Messiah; that identifying with *this* Messiah entails willing solidarity in suffering and death; that solidarity with Christ crucified calls for rejection of the sword; that to take up the sword is to abandon the suffering of the Messiah and so to abandon trust in the God who saves, the God unto whom Jesus willingly gives his life: "yet, not what I want, but what you want" (14:36b).

3. Both phrases *poured out* and *for many* echo the latter lines of Isaiah 53:12. As such they evoke the sacrificial emphasis of Isaiah 53 and indirectly the larger servant-obedience and justice themes of the servant songs (see especially Isa. 42:1-4). Pointing certainly to Jesus' own death, these Eucharistic words remind us that Jesus' body- and blood-*covenant* calls us likewise to servant-living and sacrificial self-giving for the welfare of others, contributing to the shalom of our communities. Peter Lampe sees this as what is meant in Paul's phrase "proclaiming the Lord's death until he comes." Christ's death is proclaimed not only by the *sacramental acts* and the liturgical *words*, but "by means of our giving ourselves up to others. Our love for others represents Christ's death to [*sic*, for?] other human beings. Only by actively loving and

caring for others does the participant in the Eucharist 'proclaim' Christ's death as something that happened for others."[8]

Matthew's *for the forgiveness of sins* is striking since it occurs only in Matthew, even though both Mark and Luke emphasize *forgiveness* as one of Jesus' core teachings. All three Synoptics include the early portrait of Jesus as one with authority to forgive sins (Mark 2:10; Matt. 9:6; Luke 5:24; cf. 7:49; 24:47). Forgiveness of sins is at the heart of the Lord's Prayer (Luke 11:4; Matt. 6:12, "debts"), and sayings on forgiveness (humans to humans and God to humans) follow the Lord's Prayer in Matthew with parallel in Mark (Matt. 6:14-15; Mark 11:25-26; cf. Matt. 18:21-35). In Mark this command to forgive follows judgment on the temple; it appears to be intended as an alternative mediatory *practice* to those of the temple and its priestly efficacy. Jesus' blood poured out for many for the forgiveness of sins recalls Moses' making of the covenant with a blood sacrifice for the atonement of sins (Exod. 24:6-8). Matthew's care to show that Jesus fulfills the covenant-law and the prophets likely motivates his explicit expression: ". . . this is my blood of the covenant, which is poured out for many for the forgiveness of sins" (cf. also 1:21 where the son is named Jesus, since "he will save his people from their sins)."[9] In Luke also Jesus says from the cross, "Forgive them, for they know not what they are doing" (23:34).[10] Israel's restoration is through Jesus' blood-covenant, which atones for, indeed forgives, sin.

4. All three Gospels relate the ritual action and covenant saying to *kingdom of God*. In this *kingdom* saying Jesus extends the core theme of his ministry's proclamation: repent, for the kingdom of God is at hand. Luke's placement of the saying, "I tell you that from now on I shall not drink of the fruit of the vine until the kingdom of God comes" (22:18), *after* the first taking of the cup and *before* the breaking of the bread and second taking of the cup, indicates its importance (the *final* word placement of *kingdom of God* in Matthew/Mark has the same effect). Virtually all commentators accentuate the eschatological significance of this meal in light of this saying.[11] Luke's parable of the great banquet also links *meal* and *kingdom:* "Blessed is anyone who will eat bread in the kingdom of God" (14:15). Further,

---

8. Lampe, "Eucharist," p. 45.

9. OT sacrifices were not solely, or even mostly, for atoning sin. See Green and Baker, *Recovering*, pp. 47-49.

10. While reliable textual witnesses attest to both this word's exclusion and inclusion, I include it here since most Greek and English Bibles include it in the text, often in brackets.

11. Jeremias make the point that Jesus' own abstinence from the cup is striking and accentuates his anticipation of the kingdom coming. He also proposes that Jesus' abstinence explains the early Christians' fasting before the Eucharist, contrary to Jewish Passover practice. See *Eucharistic Words*, 124-25.

When Jesus says of the Passover meal, "I will not eat it until it is fulfilled in the kingdom of God," in the context of having just said, "I have eagerly desired to eat this Passover with you before I suffer," it is clear that Jesus regards his suffering — and this meal commemorating his suffering — as a participation in and an anticipation of the consummated kingdom of God. The same point reappears in 22:28-30 where Jesus links "those who have stood by me in my trials" with conferring on the disciples what the Father "has conferred on me, a kingdom" and then declares, "so that you may eat and drink at my table in my kingdom." While this pericope begins with the disciples sharing "in my trials," it ends with the disciples sitting "on thrones judging the twelve tribes of Israel." This, in turn, is set in the context of Luke's unique placement of the disciples' dispute on greatness (22:24-27). Jesus speaks of "the kings of the Gentiles [who] lord it over them; and those in authority over them [who] are called benefactors" — usually older wealthy patrons. But Jesus says it shall not be so among you. The greatest must become like the youngest, and the leader as one who serves. He then identifies himself as one among them who serves and calls them into his example. Hence, in order to participate in the banquet of the kingdom, their values must undergo major transformation:

> Chief Benefactor (a term Luke's readers understood) = Most Willing Servant;
> Host for the Kingdom Banquet = Suffering Journeyer, Rejected Prophet;
> Messiah = suffering Son of humanity, lowly Savior.[12]

Consistently, Luke's banquet theme reverses culturally dominant power positions and roles. Jesus' willingness to die on the cross, the humiliated rebel's death, images memorably this central teaching and action of Jesus' ministry. Paul's great hymn confessing that Jesus emptied and humbled himself (Phil. 2: 5-11) emphasizes the same point (cf. 1 Cor. 2:2; Gal. 6:14; 2:19c-20). Jesus crucified, his death, is *one* in meaning with Jesus' life. In both his life and death Jesus' way is God's upside-down kingdom.

While Paul does not use *kingdom* language for the Supper account, he does stress its eschatological significance, linked specifically to Jesus' suffering and death: "proclaiming the Lord's death until he comes." While for Jesus and the first disciples the anticipated resurrection of Jesus may be viewed as the time-fulfillment of this saying, or Pentecost in light of the kingdom

---

12. Swartley, *Israel's Scripture Traditions,* pp. 238-39. Luke's prominent *banquet* theme culminates in this meal (see pp. 132-34, where I interact with Moessner's *Lord of the Banquet*).

emphasis in Acts 1:3, 6-8, Paul likely has the Parousia in mind. These expectations of the coming kingdom, anchored clearly in the cross and resurrection, accord with the proclamation of the present Lordship of Jesus Christ (evident in Peter's proclamation in Acts 2:23, 33-36 and Paul's great hymn in Phil. 2:5-11). The cross, culminating Jesus' life and teaching, and the resurrection are the means of God's victory over evil, establishing Jesus as Savior and Lord.[13] In the context of emperor claims to dominion and divinity, Jesus' royalty declarations unmask and subvert imperial hegemony, emphases that permeate NT literature.[14]

The *kingdom* emphasis of the Lord's Supper intensifies the royalty theme developed in the Gospels (see Chapters 3-5). A Roman soldier acclaims Jesus as royal Son of God (Matthew/Mark) in the face of his suffering on the cross for the sins of those who crucified him. In Luke the thief on the cross who exclaims, "Jesus, remember me when you come into your kingdom," hears Jesus' promise "Truly I tell you, today you will be with me in Paradise" (23:42-43).

Another striking connection between the royalty motif and Jesus' self-donation occurs in John 6. After Jesus fed the five thousand ("he took the loaves, and when he had *given thanks,* he distributed them . . ." [v. 11]), the people wanted to make him king (6:15), but Jesus eluded them. After the boat-ride when Jesus walks on the water and discloses his identity, "I AM" (v. 20), the ensuing discourse revolves, first, around Jesus' feeding of the multitude and Moses' manna which Jesus says was sent "by my Father who gives you the true bread from heaven" (v. 32b). This bread, Jesus says, "comes down from heaven and gives life to the world." The discourse proceeds to Jesus' self-disclosure, "I am the bread of life" (v. 48), and culminates with Jesus' shocking pronouncements in vv. 51 and 53-57, in which John discloses Jesus as the messianic "Prophet-King," as Wayne Meeks has amply shown.[15] The tradi-

---

13. Failure to see that the cross-event accords with God's salvation purpose is a major weakness in both René Girard's thought and in J. Denny Weaver's *The Nonviolent Atonement.* Acts 2:23 and 4:24-28 cannot be read any other way. Girard's emphasis on the cross unmasking human violence is important, but inadequate in light of the numerous NT salvation-emphases centered on the cross. The issue of violence and nonviolence in relation to atonement may function as an ethical decoy that lures us from speaking what is most important about atonement: through the cross God *and* Jesus Christ in self-donation make peace between humans and God and between humans and humans. See Weaver, *Nonviolent Atonement,* and Hans Boersma, *Violence, Hospitality, and the Cross: Appropriating the Atonement Tradition* as point and counterpoint. See also Chapter 14 below for my discussion of God and violence.

14. For correlating this theme with imperial reality in our world today, see Walsh and Keesmaat, *Colossians Remixed.*

15. Meeks, *The Prophet King.*

tions of the prophetic act of "eating the scroll" (Ezek. 3) and the royal act of feeding the people as a good shepherd-king (see Chapter 3 above and John 10:1-18) converge in Jesus' giving himself for the life of the world.[16] Strikingly, in precisely the context of God's raising up one true shepherd, "my servant David" as shepherd-king (cf. Ps. 78:70), Ezekiel 34 says, "I will make with them [faithful Israel] a covenant of peace" (vv. 23-26).

5. In Chapters 1, 3, 4, and 5 I have shown the integral relation between royalty emphases in each of the Synoptic Gospels and various peace and peacemaking emphases. In the Last Supper narratives the kingdom (royalty) emphasis is intertwined with Jesus' making of the covenant and Jesus' ritual actions and solemn words of institution. Insofar as this ritual action *symbolically* dramatizes[17] the entire ministry (words and deeds) of Jesus' life and is at the same time the *means* whereby Jesus *makes* a (new) covenant, this covenant extends the peace, peacemaking, and justice-teaching of his ministry.

A similar point is exemplified also by Paul's account of the Last Supper. Paul cites the Supper-tradition to correct a rupture in the peace of the community. Paul laments the church's divisions and factions (1 Cor. 11:17-19), which are now "acted out" in the common meal. The wealthier members of the church, who apparently come first and bring choice foods, eat much of the "potluck" meal before the poorer members arrive (all this in advance of the Eucharistic observance) and thus "humiliate those who have nothing" (v. 22).[18] The observance of the Eucharist itself thus brings judgment upon them, resulting even in illness (vv. 29-30). Clearly in this malpractice of the Meal and Eucharist, the peace (shalom) of the church is ruptured. Paul's intervention is a corrective, in order to restore the peace of the congregation. It is striking that this Epistle concludes with an injunction to "Greet one another with a holy kiss" (16:20, known later as the "kiss of peace").

---

16. Whether John 6:48-58 is Eucharistic (John's form of the institution of the Lord's Supper lacking in John 13) has been much discussed, with scholars arguing both pro and con. This issue is separate from whether it is sacramental. While extended discussion lies outside the scope of my study, I concur with those who emphasize that this text intends to express strongly the incarnation theme of the Gospel. Further, the Eucharistic meaning, whether intended or not, was readily understood by the church, as is evident in the *Didache* and Justin Martyr. Some of the many pertinent sources are Brown, *The Gospel According to John I-XII*, pp. 284-93; Dunn, "John VI — A Eucharistic Discourse?"; Anderson, *The Christology of the Fourth Gospel*, pp. 110-36; Moloney, *The Gospel of John*, pp. 217-26; Keener, *The Gospel of John*, 1:679-91.

17. See here the good discussion of the meals by Bonnie Thurston, *Spiritual Life in the Early Church*, pp. 47-48.

18. For the correlation between the Greco-Roman *eranos* (potluck) meal and the phrase "own dinner" *(idion deipnon)* see Lampe, "The Eucharist: Identifying with Christ on the Cross," 38.

6. In the early church of the second to fourth centuries the celebration of the Eucharist[19] explicitly connects the ritual to making peace with one another. The second-century *Didache* says, "Each Lord's day of the Lord, once you are gathered together, break bread and do the Eucharist, having first confessed your faults, so that your sacrifice might be pure. And any having a quarrel with another, let that one not gather with you until they are reconciled so that sacrifice may not be defiled" (14.1-2). Justin Martyr's several references to Eucharistic celebrations (*1 Apologia* 65–67) are framed by instructions to deacons to distribute funds to the needy (widows, orphans, sick, prisoners, foreigners or refugees). In keeping with Paul's valuing the relief-gift to the poor in Jerusalem as a priority for his mission, such aid to the poor makes economic shalom a companion, if not prerequisite, to celebrating the Eucharist.

Both the *Didascalia Apostolorum* (ca. 230) and the *Apostolic Constitutions* (a late-fourth-century Syrian "Church Order") regard participation in the Eucharist as re-enacting Christ's peacemaking death as reconciliation with God (and God's reconciliation with humans). Alan Kreider's study of these two documents contends that both "church orders" present "a remarkable vision of the church as a culture of peace."[20] The bishop, in these orders, is to shepherd the entire congregation into peace, make sure the brothers and sisters are at peace with one another, and thus ensure that God's people will be "'light and peace' to all people."[21] His study identifies four peacemaking processes in both orders: (1) the sermon or homily, which admonished the brothers and sisters to be at peace with one another, based upon Matthew 5:23-24; (2) the liturgical gesture, expressed in the *Didascalia* by the deacon's loud declamation, "Is there perhaps a man that keeps some grudge against his fellow?" as the bishop stands to pray (this may have prompted also the exchange of the holy kiss) — such persons are then expected to settle matters between them; (3) the "bishops court" which provided a method for reconciling antagonists; and (4) a process of purgation and restoration.[22] The *Apos-*

---

19. The designation of the Lord's Supper as the Eucharist appears to be derived from the *Didache* since it introduces the breaking of the bread by "We give you thanks (*eucharistoumen*) . . ." (*Didache* 9:2-3). If 2 Cor. 4:15 is indeed a reference to the Lord's Supper by means of the term *eucharistian*, usually translated *thanksgiving*, then we have a connection already in Paul (see Koenig, *Feast*, 241-42).

20. Alan Kreider, "Peacemaking in Worship in the Syrian Church Orders," 190.

21. Kreider, "Peacemaking," p. 179.

22. Kreider, "Peacemaking," pp. 180-81, 190. The "bishops court," a "dispute resolution process," has been identified and discussed in Taylor Burton Edwards, "The Teaching of Peace in Early Christian Liturgies" (M.A. thesis, Associated Mennonite Biblical Seminary, 1997), p. 39.

tolic Constitutions is more formalized than the *Didascalia,* evident in the second stage of the process where the deacon in the *Constitutions* loudly exhorts all "to examine their conscience about the peaceableness of their relationships" — hence the reconciliation happens in the mind and heart.[23] Nonetheless, the liturgy served the cause of peacemaking internally to qualify the community to witness to peace to outsiders. Eleanor Kreider describes the event:

> The communion service with its prayers, its kiss of peace, and its symbolic memorial feast comprises what we refer to as "unitive rites" of the church. This simply means that the service is altogether about reconciliation and unity, both with God and with one another. The purpose, the process, and the effects are unitive.[24]

The "kiss of peace" came prior to the bishop's final doxology preceding the partaking of the holy bread and wine. The bishop said: "The peace of God be with you all" to which the people responded, "And with your spirit." The "verbal exchange of peace is in essence the final liturgical act before reception of the body and blood."[25] With this double emphasis on peace, in the kiss and the pronouncement, both interpersonal peace and peace with God are essential to celebrating aright the Eucharist. The community's worship thus calls forth a life of reconciliation and peace. Eleanor Kreider regards the placement of the kiss of peace in the third and fourth centuries to be theologically fitting:

> Because of its strategic location between the two components (synaxis and eucharist) of the Lord's Day service, this was not a surprising development. And there were sound theological reasons behind it. Peace, reconciliation, and unity were of the very essence of the church's life; without them communion would have been a sham. Bestowed by the Spirit

---

23. Kreider, "Peacemaking," p. 185.

24. Eleanor Kreider, *Communion Shapes Character,* p. 110.

25. Burton-Edwards, "The Teaching of Peace in Early Christian Liturgies," p. 70. The "peace of God" is offered to the catechumens before their dismissal and also before the faithful partake of the holy meal. The *Canons of Hippolytus* "excluded from the mysteries" a Christian soldier who took life "until he has been 'purified by a punishment, tears, and wailing.'" How widespread and for how long such abstinence from the Eucharist was required is not clear, but also "in the West, Councils and penitential documents . . . excluded soldiers who killed from the eucharists for varying periods." Basil of Caesarea counseled abstaining for three years (*Ep.* 188.13). See Alan Kreider, "Military Service in the Church Orders," 426-27. For historical analysis of how Communion was practiced, with varying understandings, see Eleanor Kreider, *Communion Shapes Character,* especially pp. 19-96.

and experienced in prayer, their liturgical expression — which pointed forward to the eucharist — was the holy kiss.[26]

In later Christian practice of the Lord's Supper, several traditions expressly connect it to peacemaking and reconciliation. John Rempel has shown this in his study of the Lord's Supper as understood in the christologies of Balthasar Hubmaier, Pilgram Marpeck, and Dirk Philips. Rempel's conclusion states, "Anabaptism teaches that communion is the surpassing expression of reconciliation of Christians with God and with each other."[27] More recently, the Methodist communion liturgy states, "Christ our Lord invites to his table all who love him, who earnestly repent of their sin and seek to live in peace with one another."[28]

The kiss of peace as practiced in the NT churches[29] and the early church, reflected in Eucharistic liturgies, is a rite of peacemaking. Practiced in proximity to the Eucharist in early church liturgy, it "has reappeared in twentieth century eucharistic worship. Why not!" says Eleanor Kreider. She says further, ". . . the kiss (greeting) of peace is important because it reminds us and dramatizes for us a central truth about the Christian faith, about Jesus' work of *shalom*, peace. Jesus is the Lord of peace. We are to be his people of peace."[30] Exchanging the "peace of Christ" greeting, preceding or following the Eucharist, also links peacemaking to Communion observance.

7. The covenant the Lord Jesus made with his disciples, and all who later have chosen to become his disciples, has many layers of meaning. Its celebration is rich, comprises themes of remembrance (memorial), a substitution-dimension in *for many (you)*, forgiveness of sins (Matthew), fellowship (*koinōnia*), eschatological hope for the full consummation of the kingdom, and renewal of peace with God and with fellow brothers and sisters in the faith. From this holy ritual, the community of faith is empowered to become a presence and voice of peace and reconciliation to the world.[31] It testifies to the unity of the church, and as such fulfills Jesus' prayer, "that they may be completely one," as "the Father and I are one" (John 17:23b; 10:30).

---

26. Eleanor Kreider, "Let the Faithful Greet Each Other: The Kiss of Peace," p. 34.

27. Rempel, *The Lord's Supper in Anabaptism*, p. 226.

28. Smith, "Eucharistic Faith and Practice," 8.

29. Kreider, "Kiss of Peace," pp. 29-49; Phillips, "The Ritual Kiss in Early Christian Worship." For the social significance of the kiss in the NT churches see Klassen, "The Sacred Kiss in the New Testament."

30. Kreider, *Communion Shapes Character*, p. 110.

31. For Koenig the Eucharist is "co-missioning for the world's redemption" (*Feast*, pp. 217, 249-59).

Finally, in the benediction of Heb. 13:20-21, "the God of peace who raised the Lord Jesus" is joined to "the blood of the eternal covenant" as the means by which God equips believers to do his will:

> Now may the *God of peace,* who brought back from the dead our Lord Jesus, the great shepherd of the sheep, by the *blood of the eternal covenant,* make you complete in everything good so that you may do his will, working among us that which is pleasing in his sight, through Jesus Christ, to whom be the glory forever and ever. Amen.

7 Paul's Peace Interpretation of Jesus Christ

Therefore, since we are justified by faith, we have [or let us have] peace with God through our Lord Jesus Christ, . . . For if while we were enemies, we were reconciled to God through the death of his Son, much more surely, having been reconciled, will we be saved by his life.

ROMANS 5:1, 10

Do not repay anyone evil for evil, but take thought for what is noble in the sight of all. If it is possible, so far as it depends on you, live peaceably with all. Beloved, never avenge yourselves, but leave room for the wrath of God; for it is written, "Vengeance is mine, I will repay, says the Lord." No, "if your enemies are hungry, feed them; if they are thirsty, give them something to drink; for by doing this you will heap burning coals on their heads." Do not be overcome by evil, but overcome evil with good.

ROMANS 12:17-21

But now in Christ Jesus you who once were far off have been brought near by the blood of Christ. For he is our peace; in his flesh he has made both groups into one and has broken down the dividing wall, that is, the hostility between us. He has abolished the law with its commandments and ordinances, that he might create in himself one new humanity in place of the two, thus making peace, and might reconcile both groups to God in one body through the cross, thus putting to death that hostility through it. So he came and proclaimed peace to you who were far off and peace to those who were near; for through him both of us have access in one Spirit to the Father.

EPHESIANS 2:13-18

Paul, more than any other writer in the NT canon, makes peace, peacemaking, and peace-building central to his theological reflection and moral admonition. Various scholars have proposed differing "centers" for Pauline theology. Each is intriguing in its own way: i.e., justification by faith (Luther and Bultmann); Paul's apostolic self-consciousness (Fridrichson), with focus on mission to the Gentiles (Munck, Cullmann, Stendahl); "in Christ" mysticism (A. Schweitzer, and E. P. Sander's emphasis on "participation in Christ"); God's manifestation of "righteousness" in Jesus Christ (Käsemann); God's (apocalyptic) triumph in Jesus Christ (Beker); or the church as the body of Christ (Schnackenburg, who regards Ephesians as Paul's "crowning" contribution).

But none of the theological or ethical treatments of Paul over the last century has proposed *peacemaking* as integral.[1] The closest proposal is Ralph Martin's, who puts reconciliation at the core of Pauline theology and ethics.[2] Martin frequently speaks of "peace and making peace" in his discussion of key "reconciliation" texts (2 Cor. 5:17-21; Col. 1:15-23; Rom. 5:1-11; Eph. 2:11-22). He regards "peace" as basically a synonym to reconciliation. On occasion, however, he also follows, if ever so briefly, the path of peace into ethical pareneses.[3] But he nowhere observes the distinctive Pauline title for God,

---

1. C. K. Barrett's masterful presentation of Pauline thought, *Paul: An Introduction to His Thought,* mentions peace only several times. In commenting on Rom. 5:9-11 he says, "Reconciliation means that by a creative act of love one of two parties makes peace . . ." (p. 98). In discussing the role of "The Holy Spirit and Ethics," he refers to Rom. 14:17, where "righteousness, joy, and peace in the Holy Spirit," rather than haggling over food laws, are the purpose and mark of the kingdom. But nowhere in his otherwise quite comprehensive presentation do Paul's peace texts receive comment with peacemaking language present in the discussion. Barrett's treatment in this regard is typical, not atypical. J. D. G. Dunn in his 734 pages on *The Theology of Paul the Apostle* has only one entry on peace in his subject index. It occurs in his comment on Rom. 5:1, in which he says justification "means God bestowing the blessing of peace on those who were formerly enemies (5.10)." He then rightly says that "peace" here has not the Greek non-war meaning but is filled with "the richer Hebrew concept of *shalom*" (p. 387). J. C. Beker, in *Paul the Apostle,* is similar, but more substantive in his brief incisive but undeveloped comment: "Reconciliation symbolism stresses the contrast between enmity and peace, hate and love (cf. Rom. 5:1-12; 8:31-39; 2 Cor. 5:14-21). The basic metaphors are 'reconciliation,' 'peace,' 'love' *(katallagē, eirēnē, agapē)*" (pp. 257-58). H. Ridderbos, in 562 pages in *Paul: An Outline of His Theology,* has a five-page section (§32) titled "God's Reconciling Activity in Christ: The Peace of God." He mentions peace a few times but shapes his discussion around reconciliation and its relation to justification (pp. 182-86). Ridderbos's fuller treatment is due likely to his inclusion of Ephesians as Pauline, whereas Dunn and Beker do not include Ephesians.

2. Martin, *Reconciliation: A Study of Paul's Theology.*

3. See especially the following pages in Martin for this treatment of peace: pp. 93, 117, 121-24, 139-52, 168, 172, 186, 190, 197, and 229 ("peace" is not an entry in Martin's subject index,

"God of peace." Since "God of reconciliation" does not occur as a title, one might query whether "peace" should take primary position, with reconciliation the coordinate, thus in converse order of priority to Martin's proposal.

In this treatment of Paul's theology and ethics I seek to show that the concept-cluster of peace, peacemaking, and peace-building is prominent in Pauline writings. Indeed, peacemaking plays a strategic role in any of the above proposals, even though the point is not explicated and peace is not mentioned. For example, *justification* by faith leads to peace with God and peace between groups formerly at enmity. Proposals that claim *mission to the Gentiles* as central to Paul's thought inherently stress peacemaking between the Jewish Christian and Gentile Christian church members. The dual focus on God's *manifestation of righteousness* and the *faithfulness* of the Messiah Jesus embraces both the vertical and horizontal dimension of peacemaking. Both Schweitzer's "in Christ" *mysticism* and Schnackenburg's emphasis on the *church* imply elements of peacemaking, personally and corporately experienced.

The following six topical sections, with their respective features and emphases, demonstrate the centrality of peace, peacemaking, and peace-building in Paul's theological and ethical contribution to Christian theology.

Peace Terminology

Peace *(eirēnē)* occurs 44 times in Pauline and deutero-Pauline writings. Ten of these are in Romans (1:7; 2:10; 3:17; 5:1; 8:6; 14:17, 19; 15:13, 33; 16:20)[4] and eight in Ephesians (1:2; 2:14, 15, 17, 17; 4:3; 6:15, 23).[5] The distribution over the

---

though he lists it under and in relation to "reconciliation"). In several instances Martin moves beyond using "peace" as an important companion term to "reconciliation," and observes its use in a wider range of instruction: "The call of Paul's gospel was to live 'in peace' (1 Cor. 7:15; 14:33; 2 Cor. 13:11; Rom. 12:18; Col. 3:15; 1 Thess. 5:13)" (p. 229; cf. pp. 93, 152, 168, 186, 190 — all uses that have a wider connotation than "reconciliation"). Martin's thesis would be stronger had he proposed the center of Paul's theology to be "peace and reconciliation." His work is an important contribution. See pp. 1-3 and pp. 232-33 for the statement of his proposal.

4. This list does not include the phrase "gospel of peace" in 10:15, following RSV and NRSV and the Greek text of Nestle-Aland. The more reliable core of manuscripts ($\mathfrak{P}^{46}$ א* A B C 81 1881) omit it; however, א² D F G Ψ include it. Though the case for its inclusion cannot be totally ruled out, the strong Alexandrian ms. evidence for omission is decisive. Internal evidence attests likewise; a scribe knowing the Isa. 52:7 line could easily add *eirēnē*.

5. The remaining occurrences are: four each in 1 Corinthians (1:3; 7:15; 14:33; 16:11) and the Pastorals (1 Tim. 1:2; 2 Tim. 1:2; 2:22; Tit. 1:4), three each in Galatians (1:3; 5:22; 6:16), Colossians (1:2, 20; 3:15), Philippians (1:2; 4:7, 9), 1 Thessalonians (1:1; 5:3, 23), and 2 Thessalonians (1:2; 3:16 [2x]); two in 2 Corinthians (1:2; 13:11), and one in Philemon (v. 3).

full range of Pauline epistles is impressive, especially in light of the fact that other claims for "centrality of emphasis" in Paul occur in only some but not all of the writings.[6]

Moreover, the case for Paul's major emphasis on peacemaking is based not on vocabulary count alone. Rather, the notion of making peace between humans and God and between formerly alienated humans is so central to the core of Pauline doctrinal and ethical thought that it is impossible to develop a faithful construal of Pauline thought without peacemaking and/or reconciliation at the core. While peace terminology is most always present in a sustained theological discussion, the discussion itself may lack the term but involve at its heart the concept of bringing formerly alienated parties together, whether humans with God (or vice versa) or humans with humans. Such a text as Romans 1:16–4:25 is a classic example. The Pauline portrayal of all humanity, both Gentiles and Jews, as sinning and falling short of God's glory (3:23) and therefore needing God's righteousness and justification is inherently a peacemaking exposition, but the term peace or peacemaking as an action of God does not occur until 5:1. The occurrences of *peace* in 2:10 and 3:17 have different connotations, though 3:17 contrasts the "no peace" of sinful humanity to the new peace to be announced. This summary, "Therefore, since we are justified by faith, we have peace with God through our Lord Jesus Christ," leads immediately into another sustained exposition of salvation in and by Jesus Christ that speaks about reconciliation (5:10-11), dying to the old self and being made alive in Christ (ch. 6), agonizing over "the law of sin" that prevents doing the good law of God, and then rejoicing in freedom through Christ (7:1–8:5), but does not speak of *peace* explicitly until 8:6, "To set the mind on the flesh is death, but to set the mind on the Spirit is life and peace." For this reason, it is essential to see the peace-vocabulary in relation to Paul's exposition of the manifestation of God's righteousness, justification of humans by faith (perhaps by Jesus' faithfulness), or oneness in the body of Christ.

---

6. The high count of occurrences of "peace" in both Romans and Ephesians strengthens the case for Pauline authorship of Ephesians. The case is different for the Pastorals even though the term occurs there. It is not used there in the theological sense of the work of Jesus Christ effecting peace with God or between formerly alienated groups of humans. It is used, rather, three times in greetings and once in ethical parenesis: "Shun youthful passions and pursue righteousness, faith, love, and peace, along with those who call on the Lord from a pure heart" (2 Tim. 2:22). This moral admonition sounds like vintage Paul in its triad of faith, love, and peace, but the clearly authentic Pauline epistles do not have this exact combination (cf. 1 Thess. 1:3 and 5:8: faith, love, and hope; 1 Cor. 13:13: faith, hope, and love; Gal. 5:22: love, joy, peace; Rom. 15:13: "May the God of hope fill you with joy and peace in believing"; and 2 Cor. 13:11: "live in peace, and the God of love and peace will be with you").

The Essential Relation of Peace to Justification/Righteousness and Reconciliation

Justification and righteousness in both noun and verb forms translate the same Greek words: *dikaiosynē* (noun) and *dikaioō* (verb). Grasping the significance of this point means overcoming the unfortunate dichotomy between the personal and corporate (social and political) dimensions of God's making humans righteous. It is all too common for Christians to translate these words as either *justice* or *righteousness* and to block out the component that counts less in their personal ideology. The *justice* folk say little about *righteous* living, and the *righteous* living folk discount justice. It is imperative that this bifurcation cease, and that God's peace-loving folk embrace both dimensions of meaning in this term. In the classroom, to make the point I have at times used the terms *righteousfication* and *justiceness*, to overcome the splitting that has occurred across the ecclesial spectrum. Christopher Marshall, in the context of examining both Paul's and Jesus' teachings as consistent with "restorative justice" rather than "retributive justice" for law-offenders, has shown in his careful study of the topic that justification cannot be closeted to personal piety and relationship with God, but that justice for penal practice should be shaped by the theological understanding of God's justification of sinners, transgressors, the ungodly (Rom. 5:6-8) with intent to restore fellowship. This means that restorative justice flows from understanding justification by faith; it is God's way of restoring sinners to relationship. The aim of atonement is redemptive solidarity, not penal substitution.[7] Marshall's contribution helps to not only grasp the full meaning of *dikaiosynē* and *dikaioō*, but it also shows that this central doctrine in Paul is socially and politically relevant. Specifically, it means reconsidering retributive punishment of criminals. Christians, restored into relationship with God through justification by faith, are

---

7. Christopher D. Marshall, *Beyond Retribution*, pp. 38-69. Marshall does not, however, uncritically accept J. Denny Weaver's case for nonviolent atonement that separates the cross from God's will and rejects substitution completely. See Marshall, "Atonement, Violence and the Will of God: A Sympathetic Response to J. Denny Weaver's *The Nonviolent Atonement*," *MQR* 77 (2003): 69-92. I agree with Marshall that Weaver is correct in saying that the *cause* of Jesus' death lies with the powers of evil manifest in human violence but wrong in denying that God has anything to do with Jesus' death on the cross (Marshall, p. 82). The textual evidence for God's involvement in the cross is overwhelming, as Marshall documents. Weaver's denial refuses the important theological claim that salvation is effected through God's/Jesus' self-donation. In this refusal he undermines a basic connection between salvation and ethics (as, e.g., in Mark 10:44-45), a point he otherwise adamantly affirms. Also, with Marshall, it is impossible to take the NT witness on atonement seriously, and discount completely "substitution" (Marshall, p. 89). This does not mean we must concede to the dominance of either the satisfaction or penal theories of atonement.

morally obligated to extend the nature of God's justification into modes and goals of legal process dealing with criminal offense.[8]

Paul's gospel *(euangelion)* indeed proclaims that God's work in Jesus Christ has wrought peace with God (Rom. 5:1),[9] even when humans were God's enemies (Rom. 5:10). Salvation makes peace between previously hostile peoples, namely, Jews and Gentiles. Peace with God and peace with fellow-humans, even enemies, are twin gifts of Jesus Christ. In Colossians *peace* takes on a cosmic dimension in which all creation is recipient through the blood of the cross (1:20). Similarly, Paul declares God's redemptive purpose: "as a plan for the fullness of time, to gather up all things in him, things in heaven and things on earth" (Eph. 1:10). As the vicar in Great St. Mary's in Cambridge, England, put it: Paul's inclusive vision of uniting all things in Christ contrasts to John the Baptist's preaching in which "the ax is lying at the root of the trees" (Luke 3:9) and judgment is imminent in the dawning of the kingdom that the Coming One is about to bring.

Paul, rather, gives his life to an ever expanding vision of the inclusiveness and universality of the gospel. While "hell" appears in the Gospels, especially Matthew, it is strikingly absent in Paul, though he does speak of everyone giving an account of deeds done at the "judgment seat of Christ" and pronounces that those who persist sinning will not enter the kingdom of God (1 Cor. 6:9-11).[10] On the whole, however, Paul's theological emphasis is bold and robust in its inclusive and universal scope. The vicar cited Romans 5:12ff., with v. 18 summing it up, "Therefore just as one man's trespass led to condemnation for all, so one man's act of righteousness leads to justification and life for all." This *all* is Paul's universalism, and in Romans 11:26 it is used also for Israel, "And so all Israel will be saved."[11] However, it must be noted that Paul shifts back and forth in this Romans 5 section between *all (pantas)* in vv.

8. Marshall pioneered in introducing VORP (the Victim-Offender Reconciliation Program) into the justice system in New Zealand and was granted an award in early 2004 by Britain's Princess Anne. VORP, a form of justice-reconciliation, was begun in Kitchener, Ontario, by Dave Worth and Mark Yantzi and then in Elkhart, Indiana, by Howard Zehr in the 1970s. For a description of the program, see Zehr, *Changing Lenses,* pp. 158-74. See also Lederach, *The Journey toward Reconciliation* for Lederach's wide experience in ecclesial and international conflicts and his biblical and theological reflections.

9. Whether the text should read "we have peace" (indicative) or "let us have peace" (subjunctive), reflecting a textual variant, is discussed well and fully by Erich Dinkler in "*Eirēnē* — The Early Christian Concept of Peace," pp. 182-83 (1992 edition, pp. 99-101).

10. These texts of judgment I add to the vicar's homily to show both dimensions in Paul's theology.

11. A key issue here is whether "all Israel" refers to all the Jewish covenant people or to Jews and Gentiles who believe in the Messiah, with Paul redefining Israel.

12, 18 and *the many (hoi polloi)* in vv. 15, 19. Further, *pantas* is in the accusative, with *eis* signifying destination, indicating that *all* are affected by one man's sin and one man's righteousness. *Hoi polloi*, however, is in the nominative and describes the actual result: *many* will be made righteous. Paul is not speaking of individual persons as such. He uses *all (pantas)* to make the point that Gentiles as well as Jews are included in God's salvation purpose. Segal's commentary on Romans 11:26 interprets Paul's view correctly and succinctly:

> Although Paul polemicizes against his enemies [Segal has already dealt with Paul's vituperative language in Galatians], he does not exclude either Christians or Jews from the saved. All Israel is saved, he says, in typical Pharisaic manner (*pas Israēl sōthēsetai* [Rom. 11:26]). It is clear, however, that they will not be saved until they are transformed spiritually.[12]

What Paul affirms is a twofold gospel reality: that *all*, both Jews and Gentiles, are recipients of God's saving righteousness manifest in Jesus Christ, and that by God's grace those who receive this gift will be transformed and liberated from enslaving sin. This twofold reality is the salvific substance of peacemaking in Paul. Peace is the fruit of this all-encompassing regeneration, both personally and corporately. Most all of Paul's writings reflect this peacemaking breakthrough, peace with God through Christ and peace between former enemies.

Accordingly, it is not surprising that *apostolic mission* is at the center of Paul's vocational self-consciousness. Thus Munck, Cullmann, and Stendahl rightly propose a missional vision at the heart of Pauline thought. For Stendahl this is rooted in Paul's *call* to be the apostle to the Gentiles, in which peacemaking between Jews and Gentiles forged the doctrine of justification by faith.[13] In this interpretation justification by faith has an inherent social dimension. Indeed, peacemaking is also inherently part of this central passion

---

12. Segal, *Paul the Convert*, p. 160. Segal earlier developed Paul's view of expected transformation for both Gentiles and Jews as they became members of the new Christ body. Although Jews could accept the Messiah without "converting," by continuing their religious practices and seeing in the Messiah the fulfillment of these practices, Paul was "converted" to the priority of Gentile admission into the messianic faith. Segal regards the Acts 15 resolution as a compromise, affirming both models of Jewish Christianity. But for both types of Jewish Christians, as well as for Gentile Christians, Paul's expectation for continuing transformation into the image of Christ holds (pp. 11-12, 146, 214, where Segal sums up these two ways for Jews to become Christian). I believe Segal is correct from an Acts 15 and total first-century Jewish Christian reality, but I doubt that both models ever coexisted harmoniously in the same congregation. The conflicts over food laws in Romans (and possibly over eating food offered to idols) demonstrate the tension. In such cases, Paul sided with the Gentile and Jewish "converts."

13. Stendahl, *Paul among Jews and Gentiles*, pp. 1-40.

of Paul. Peace between God and humans is inextricably linked to the Gentile mission, for it is a peace brought about not by "works of the law" and "apart from the law itself" (Rom. 3:20-22).[14]

Prior to Stendahl's thesis asserting "call, not conversion" as a key to understanding Paul,[15] Marcus Barth defined justification as a "social event." The "works of the law" separated peoples, erecting "the dividing wall, that is, the hostility between us [Jews and Gentiles]" (Eph. 2:14-15). But the salvation event is, from God's side, a gift of grace (Eph. 2:8) and, from the human side, actualized through faith engendered by and responding to the prototypical faithfulness of Jesus Christ.[16] As Toews puts it, "The basis of the Christian life is the faithfulness of Jesus. Believers are those who live out of that faithfulness."[17] What this means is that Christ's faithfulness precedes and is the basis of the faith and possibility of the faithfulness of the believer. As Toews explicates:

> The structure of faith in Romans 3:21-26 is in concentric circles. Paul deliberately distinguishes the faith of Jesus from the faith of the believer. Both are necessary, but one is prior and the other responds. One is corporate — it is for all humanity, Jews and Gentiles; the other is individualistic — it is "my" response to what is prior to and greater than "my faith." The circumference of the circle is dependent on the center, but the center is not dependent on the circumference; the faith of Christ continues to manifest the righteousness of God in the world and to redeem human beings even if I choose not to respond in faith.

14. See the careful treatment of this in Toews, *Romans,* pp. 93-94, 101, 413-15.

15. Segal rightly disagrees with the "not conversion" half of Stendahl's thesis. Rather, Paul's commission is linked closely to his conversion, but not identical to it, nor can it replace it (pp. 5-8, with commentary on conversion *passim*).

16. For the view that Gal. 2:16 (2x), 20; 3:22; Rom. 3:22, 26; Phil. 3:9 (cf. Eph. 3:12) mean "through the faithfulness of Jesus Christ," see Hays, *Faith of Jesus Christ,* especially pp. 139ff., 247ff.; see also the revised 2002 edition for Hays's summary of the history of scholarship on the issue, pp. xxi-lii, and the 1991 SBL exchange on the "faith of/in Jesus" by Hays and Dunn, pp. 249-97. The same articles, "PISTIS and Pauline Christology: What Is at Stake?" by Hays and "Once More, *ΠΙΣΤΙΣ ΧΡΙΣΤΟΥ*" by Dunn, also appear with a response by Paul J. Achtemeier in *Pauline Theology,* vol. 4, ed. Johnson and Hay, pp. 35-92. Other important articles on the topic include George Howard, "'On the Faith of Christ'"; Luke T. Johnson, "Rom 3:21-26"; Barth, "The Faith of the Messiah"; Hooker, "*ΠΙΣΤΙΣ ΧΡΙΣΤΟΥ*"; Matlock, "Even the Demons Believe." Toews in his 2004 commentary on Romans persuasively argues for "faith of Jesus Christ." He examines the linguistic factors, issues in the scholarly debate, and undertakes a textual analysis of each occurrence of the phrase (*Romans,* pp. 108-13). Most significant, he shows how this interpretation coheres with Paul's larger argument in Romans 1–4 and 9–11.

17. Toews, *Romans,* p. 106.

Romans 3:21-26 is about gift, the gift of God's end-time, world-transforming righteousness to all humanity. It is not primarily about reception; only one phrase concerns reception, "to all the ones believing." God in Christ is graciously, freely, making righteous all people apart from any ethnic identity and its symbols of peoplehood.

David Ingles wrote a song in 1976 entitled "The Faith of Jesus." The lyrics read:

> I live by the faith of the Son of God, justified by the faith of Jesus. Looking from above with his eyes full of love is the way our Father sees us. But he only takes the view of me and you through the righteousness of Jesus, redeemed by the faith of the Son of God, justified by the faith of Jesus.[18]

Two other points follow from this interpretation of justification. First, the key emphases of Romans, the manifestation of God's righteousness in the faithfulness of Jesus and the justification of the ungodly, both reinforce the bookend emphases of Romans — "to bring about the obedience of faith" (1:5; 16:26). In both citations the Gentiles are specifically mentioned but not dissociated from "yourselves," Jewish Christians. Hence, second, both Jews and Gentiles have equal access to God through the faithfulness of Jesus; both have access to the one and same Spirit (Eph. 2:16-18). Thus Barth, Stendahl, and Volf[19] make the point that justification is a social event. Paul's doctrine of justification is the theological basis for the uniting of Gentiles and Jews into the common bond of messianic community. As Barth puts it:

> Justification is a social event. It ties human to human together. Justification by works would segregate people because each person would select his/her own arbitrary criterion of good works. Justification by grace, however, brings people together in reconciliation, even those of alien background, like the Jews and Gentiles.[20]

This inclusion of the Gentiles fulfills God's promise to Abraham: "in you all the families of the earth shall be blessed" (Gen. 12:3). Through justification by faith God's blessing to Abraham is extended not only to blood de-

---

18. Toews, *Romans,* pp. 112-13. A key point in the "faith of Jesus" construal is that it marks clearly Jesus Christ's role in the justification process. To use an old phrase from Willi Marxsen in relation to historical Jesus debates: "Jesus is the first [Christian] believer." Without the faith of Jesus there is no faith for the community. Not only are the two distinguished, the faith of Jesus and the faith of the believer, but the former is the precondition of the latter.

19. See Volf, "Social Meaning of Reconciliation."

20. Barth, "Jews and Gentiles," p. 241.

scendants, but to the Gentiles as well (Gal. 3:14).[21] The social dimension is evident particularly in Romans 14–15 and 1 Corinthians 8 and 10, where the relationships between the weak and the strong are discussed. In 11:17-18 a similar concern for different groups within the community arises when partaking the Lord's Supper. The social dimension applies to the union of Jews and Gentiles, rich and poor, free and slave, and male and female, since all have been joined together into the one messianic body.

The social meaning of justification, socio-political to the core, inherently links this key emphasis in Pauline thought to peace and peacemaking, as John H. Yoder declared, showing the logical consequence to be refusal to take another human's life, "It is the Good News that I and my enemy are united, through no merit or work of my own, in a new humanity that forbids henceforth my ever taking his life in my hands."[22] Aware of the negative emphasis much Protestant interpretation has put on law for the sake of justification by grace through faith, Perry Yoder structures his *shalom* exposition to put a chapter on law after one on atonement. Influenced by E. P. Sanders,[23] Yoder argues for a positive function of law, as the instrument of justice. It maintains the justice of God's justifying, atoning work, in the service of shalom.[24]

Were justification based upon human achievement of any type it would be a division-creating doctrine. But because it is, first and foremost, founded on the faithfulness of Jesus Christ *(extra nos)* and then upon our receiving by faith his salvation work for us (the numerous *hyper* statements for atonement formulas), the ground is level, and all come to salvation in the same way, the very way in which Abraham too was counted righteous, ". . . he believed the Lord, and the Lord reckoned it to him as righteousness" (Gen. 15:6).[25]

Dinkler specifies the central role of Christ in Paul's peacemaking manifesto:

> This passage . . . [Eph. 2:14-18], which posits enmity and peace to be antithetical, marks the crucifixion of Christ as a turning point. It declares Christ to be the bringer of peace, the one providing access to God as well

21. Barth, "Jews and Gentiles," p. 255.

22. John Howard Yoder, *The Politics of Jesus*, pp. 231-32 (1994 revised edition, p. 224).

23. Sanders, *Paul and Palestinian Judaism*.

24. Perry B. Yoder, *Shalom: The Bible's Word for Salvation, Peace and Justice*, pp. 71-84. In this respect his view is similar to that of Dunn, who argues that the two patterns are more similar than Sanders perceives; see Dunn, "The New Perspective on Paul."

25. Toews regards the key emphasis to be not Abraham's faith as such but Abraham's trust, "faithing" *God* that leads Paul to appeal to Abraham, in accord with Jesus' own faithfulness (*Romans*, pp. 120-24, 375-80).

as creating a new unity for those once separated in this world and living as enemies, objectively speaking. The *dual element* of the passage is:

1. Peace and reconciliation are tied to Jesus Christ in such a way that the cause for peace is anchored in the blood of Christ, in his crucifixion. Peace is constituted through the cross, and at the same time the crucifixion with its offensive character as *skandalon*[26] is interpreted as peace.

2. Peace as the abolition of enmity carries two dimensions of meaning, though with no clear separation between them: the reconciliation affects the *God-human* relationship, giving the reconciled person free access to God; and it leads to the *unity in the church* of those separated, thus tearing down the walls of enmity. This joining together of peace as gift of God in Jesus Christ to the believers, which grants them access to God, with peace as humanity's unity of racially separated peoples in the body of Christ, is constitutive, that is, foundational to the understanding of *eirēnē*.[27]

Paul goes even further in declaring peace as God's gift in Jesus Christ. Dinkler puts the point forcefully, showing how Paul correlates his declaration with OT texts and messianic anticipations:

Thus far we have ignored a statement resulting from the use of the OT text, Isaiah 52:7. In Ephesians 2, v. 17, it does not say "And so he came and became the peace . . .", but rather: ". . . and proclaimed peace. . . ." There is the following progression of statements:

v. 14 Christ is our peace.
v. 15 Christ brings peace.
v. 16 Christ reconciles the enemies in one body with God.
v. 17 Christ proclaims peace.

With this last verse, the borrowed inner structure of the *shalom* sayings in Deutero-Isaiah becomes quite evident. Jesus Christ, who is the peace, now proclaims himself and the cross event as peace.[28]

---

26. Repeatedly in the beginnings of Christian theology the concern is to take away from the death of Christ on the cross its element of offense and to see it as salvation. That is the intent of Ephesians 2; Col. 1:20; 1 Cor. 1:18ff.; 2 Cor. 5:14ff.; and Rom. 5:1-11. The theme is the cross, whereas *peace* is an interpretation of the cross of Christ (see Dinkler, cited below).

27. Dinkler, "*Eirēnē*— The Early Christian Concept of Peace," pp. 95-96. Martin Dibelius sees here an elaboration of the theme of the cosmic reconciliation of the universe in Col. 1:20. Dibelius, *An die Kolosser, Epheser, an Philemon*, p. 69 in *Epheser*.

28. Dinkler, p. 96. Dinkler points to another of his articles where he notes that "there is a similar line of thought in 2 Cor. 5:18-21," "Die Verkündigung als eschatologisch-sakramentales Geschehen." Compare also Acts 10:36.

In Ephesians 2:14-17 Paul draws on Isaiah, just as Jesus and the Gospel writers also did. Paul sums up Jesus' life and work by joining two Isaiah texts, 52:7 and 57:19. *Christ proclaims peace* is from the rich Isaiah declaration, "How beautiful upon the mountains are the feet of the messenger who announces peace" (Greek *euangelizesthai eirēnēn*, Hebrew *mebasser shalom*). This oracle continues by describing further this messenger as the one "who announces, who says, to Zion, 'Your God reigns.'" It concludes with the universal vision: "all the ends of the earth shall see the salvation of God" (52:10b).

Likewise the phrase, "peace to those far and near," denotes Isaiah's universal vision that breaks forth elsewhere in his oracles of the future (42:6; 49:6; 52:10 as well as here in 57:19). For Paul this peace phrase fits beautifully his own experience of God's expanding kingdom gospel of peace manifest through his apostolic work and mission. So he uses the Isaiah texts to authorize the new peace reality: Gentiles, *those far,* and Jews, *those near,* have been made one in and through the peace of Christ. The Christ-kingdom gospel breaks down the dividing wall of hostility, destroys the enmity, and creates one new humanity, thus making peace.[29]

Stuhlmacher's exegesis merits special notice also. Concurring with Dinkler and Yoder Neufeld, it emphasizes the Isaiah-tradition as the heart of the text:[30]

> On the basis of the catchword *eirēnē* it [Eph. 2:13-17] combines three passages of Scripture, Isa. 57:19 (vv. 13 and 17), Isa. 9:5-6 (v. 14) and Isa. 52:7 (v. 17). The way the passages are connected is thoroughly Jewish in form. The "peace" announced to the far and the near in Isa. 57:19 is brought about by the Messiah who is called the "prince of peace" (Isa. 9:5-6) and that in such a way that the Messiah, in accord with Isa. 52:7, appears as the proclaimer of peace for the far and near. The combined references of Isa. 57:19 and 9:5-6 to the Messiah as well as the messianic interpretation of Isa. 52:7 occur in Jewish texts. Our letter writer is apparently aware of the possibility of a messianic interpretation of this kind, except that he now uses it christologically. For him "the far" and "the near" of Isa. 57:19 are

29. For insightful exposition of this text see Yoder Neufeld, *Ephesians,* pp. 106-37; "For He Is Our Peace." See his five-panel chiastic structure (pp. 217-19):

    a   vv. 11-12
        b   v. 13
            c   vv. 14-16
        b' v. 17
    a' vv. 19-21

30. This same view is taken by Mauser, *The Gospel of Peace,* pp. 152-53.

the Gentiles and the Jews; the *eirene,* the salvation of God presented in Christ's atoning work; the Messiah referred to in Isa. 9:5-6 and 52:7 is Christ himself; and the fulfillment of the promise in Scripture is given by the work of creating peace and reconciliation through Christ, work that established the church out of Gentiles and Jews.[31]

For Paul the work of Christ fulfills the grand vision and compelling hope of Isaiah 9:6: As the promised son upon whose shoulder the government will rest, Jesus is revealed to be the "'Wonderful Counselor, Mighty God, Everlasting Father, Prince of Peace.' Of the increase of his government and of peace there will be no end, upon the throne of David, and over his kingdom, to establish it, and to uphold it with justice and with righteousness from this time forth and for evermore." As Messiah, Jesus fulfills the divine promise to David. His reign is through the gospel of peace.

The meaning of the cross as overcoming and ending the hostility between the Jews and formerly alienated Gentiles lies at the heart of Paul's gospel proclamation. In Galatians he fiercely rebuts those who "pervert the gospel," daring to say, "Let that one be accursed." The protasis is "if anyone proclaims to you a gospel contrary to what you have received." Thus Paul stops short of cursing any person or persons. In ch. 3 he queries whether the Galatians themselves have been bewitched, that due to a curse they veered so quickly away from the gospel he taught them.[32] Paul's peace blessing at the end of Galatians is reserved for those who "follow this rule" and they are identified as "the Israel of God."[33] The *rule (kanōn),* in the sense of measuring rod, is his gospel testimony: "May I never boast of anything except the cross of our Lord Jesus Christ, by which the world has been crucified to me, and I to the world. For neither circumcision nor uncircumcision is anything, but a new creation is everything!" (Gal. 6:14-15).

Reconciliation is the outcome of God's peacemaking event through Jesus Christ, incarnating God's love for enemies. "All this is from God, who reconciled us to himself through Christ and has given us the ministry of reconciliation: that is, God was in Christ reconciling the world to himself, not counting their trespasses against them" (2 Cor. 5:18-19). Although this text does not use the word *peace,* the firm connection between peace and reconcil-

---

31. Stuhlmacher, *Reconciliation,* pp. 234-35 (*Versöhnung,* pp. 187-88).

32. Bruce W. Longenecker, "Until Christ Is Formed in You."

33. What/whom does Paul mean by "the Israel of God"? Most likely he is referring to both Jewish and Gentile messianic believers who, as Segal put it, are in the process of spiritual transformation. Paul identifies himself and the congregation as within Israel. There is no hint here of "parting" between Jews and Christians.

iation in three other important texts (Rom. 5:1-11; Col. 1:15-22; Eph. 2:14-18) makes this text integral to the discussion as well. Martin rightly regards the two terms as synonymous,[34] and demonstrates the parallel thought in Romans 5:1-11:

> . . . the interpretative sequences in both instances are given in a matching way:
>
> Justified
> yet 'we have *peace* with God' (v. 1)
> Justified
> yet 'we are *reconciled* to God' (v. 10) (emphasis mine)
> Each explanatory and corrective sentence[35] is then followed by a phrase with an identical preposition:
> verse 1: 'through *(dia)* our Lord Jesus Christ'
> verse 10: 'through *(dia)* the death of his son'[36]

Similar parallel emphases are present in Ephesians 2:14-18 and Colossians 1:18-22. In light of the parallel between reconciliation and peace, 2 Corinthians 5:17-21 belongs to this topical scope. It is important because it clearly states that the task of believers to be agents of reconciliation is initiated by, grounded in, and empowered by God's own initiative of reconciliation in Christ Jesus. This is highlighted in the following chiastic analysis of the text:

a   In Christ, *new creation* (old passed away; all become new)!
   b   All this is from God, who reconciled us to himself through Christ,
      c   and has given us the ministry of reconciliation;
         d   that is, in Christ God was reconciling the world to himself, not counting their trespasses against them and

---

34. *Reconciliation*, p. 139.

35. Martin is here referring to the claim in v. 1 that we have been justified by faith and to the claim in v. 9 that we have been justified now at the cost of his blood. The "yet" completes the thought to show the result. Reta Halteman Finger has a helpful structural layout of the text in "Reconciled to God through the Death of his Son," p. 189.

36. Martin, p. 141. Elsewhere (p. 152) Martin says that while reconciliation is the concomitant of justification, it is a larger term. He contends that justification does not stand alone but leads to the new reality of reconciliation, vertically and horizontally, and Paul deliberately chose this emphasis to connect to Gentiles, thus indicating the overcoming of former barriers (pp. 153, 186, 190). I would include "peace" in this formulation as a twin to reconciliation.

    c′   entrusting the message of reconciliation to us. So we are
         ambassadors for Christ, since God is making his appeal
         through us;
  b′ we entreat you on behalf of Christ, be reconciled to God
a′   that we might become the righteousness of God.[37]

Each unit of the chiasm includes some form of the word "reconcile"
(*katallassō*). This analysis makes clear that reconciliation is God's initiative. It
specifies, first, middle, and last that *God's* act in Christ reconciles humans to
God (not God to humans by pacifying divine wrath) and that reconciled-to-
God humans are then enlisted into the ministry of reconciliation. As such,
humans are ambassadors *for* or *in behalf of (hyper) Christ's* work of reconciliation, and God makes his appeal through us humans. Again, the appeal itself,
"be reconciled to God," is grounded in "on behalf of *(hyper)* Christ." God,
Christ, and Christian believers work together at the task, to *reconcile* people to
God. This marvelous declaration of God's, Christ's, and our mission is
bounded by statements that orient us, first, to the declaration that "in Christ
there is a new creation." This radical new reality means we know Christ no
longer from a human point of view. Rather that way of knowing Christ has
passed away; a new way of knowing has come. All things are new. Second, the
end-frame points to the work of Christ, who knew no sin, but became sin for
us in dying on the cross,[38] "so that we might become the righteousness of

---

37. See this same chiasm in Shillington, *2 Corinthians*, p. 127. Shillington has an excellent
discussion of this passage, setting it within the wider letter context.

38. The phrase "became sin for us" is shorthand for a fuller idea. Three different meanings
are possible: people treated Jesus as a sinner as a result of who he was and what he did (witness the
Gospel accounts), especially identifying with tax collectors and sinners; Christ identified with sinful humanity in his incarnation (see Rom. 8:3); and Christ became a sacrifice for sin. Though Martin regards the third preferable, echoing Isa. 53:10 (*Reconciliation*, p. 96), the case for the first with
fuller explication and then as an essential part of the second and the third is stronger. Jesus was
considered a law-breaker and thus a sinner, and he was crucified for the same. But because he indeed was not a law-breaking sinner, he thus "condemned sin in the flesh" through his death (Rom.
8:3), as was manifested in his resurrection, in which believers become participants (Romans 6;
Phil. 2:7-11). Thus Rom. 8:4 flows smoothly from 8:3 with "so that the just requirement of the law
might be fulfilled in us. . . ." Christ's righteousness now becomes gift to us to fulfill righteousness,
because he bore our sin — the sin of crucifixion and all our sins — on the cross. Such a death
would indeed be sacrificial, in two senses: in the Girardian sense of Jesus becoming the scapegoat
to bleed out the violence of humans, and in the sense that the death has effectual benefit for others
in enabling a new creation. But since Scripture exposes the violence and the scapegoat system and
sides with the victim, violence and sin are doomed, stunned by the cross and routed by the resurrection. This power is appropriated in the believers' life via the "new creation" (2 Cor. 5:17), so that
they are able to renounce violence and "become the righteousness of God."

God" (cf. 1 Pet. 2:24). That believers stand justified through Christ is foundational for the calling to reconciliation.[39] The task is rooted firmly in God's
initiative in Christ. All Christian peacemaking efforts must never lose sight of
this important feature for their identity and long-term empowerment.

The cosmic goal of God's salvation in Jesus Christ is to reconcile all things
to God's self "by making peace through the blood of his cross" (Col. 1:20). God's
peacemaking is anchored fully in the cross of Jesus Christ, who disarmed the
powers (Col. 2:15; see Chapter 8), forgave sins (Col. 1:13-14; Eph. 1:7), and united
formerly alienated parties, Jews and Gentiles, in common access to God.

Romans is aptly understood as a "Friedensmemorandum," as Klaus
Haacker has suggested. Haacker places Paul's peace teaching in a dual setting,
the general political ferment that occasioned Romans 13:1-7 (Claudius's edict
of 49 CE expelling Jews — and Jewish Christians — from Rome), and the tensions between Jews and non-Jews, especially as they surfaced in the Christian
churches.[40] Given this political context, the Pauline effort to unite Jewish and
Gentile Christians into one bond and body in fellowship and love was no
small undertaking. For not only did Paul contend with tensions arising from
Jewish practices and beliefs in relation to admitting Gentiles into the community, but the Roman political responses to either group, Jewish or Christian,
also played an unpredictable role. If Jews were ostracized, it would affect the
Christian community composed of both Jews and Gentiles. Or, if Christians
were ostracized and not granted the Jewish *religio liciti* status, it would affect
the whole congregation.[41] In Paul's time threats or actions of harassment or
persecution from the empire would come toward the Jewish side of the congregation. But this reality made Paul's "calling" and vision for a unified
church of Jews and Gentiles even more difficult to fulfill. That it did happen is
no small miracle, with the peacemaking power of the cross of Jesus Christ
ever more strategic, as well as readiness on both parts of the congregation to

39. Martin's treatment of Rom. 5:1-11 emphasizes reconciliation as more effectively communicating the meaning of God's salvation in Jesus Christ than does justification for Gentiles
(pp. 138-39, 150-51, 153-54 — the term connected with the Gentile world whereas the language of
"justification/guilt/acquittal" did not); in 2 Cor. 5:17-21 reconciliation leads to "the *righteousness*
of God in us" (pp. 94-96, 108-10).

40. Haacker, "Der Römerbrief als Friedensmemorandum."

41. Some commentators see this tension behind the reprimand in Revelation to the
church at Smyrna, "those who say they are Jews and are not," in that Gentile Christians under
threat of persecution resorted to claiming Jewish identity to gain *liciti religio* standing. John
Yeatts gives four different understandings of this accusatory phrase in Revelation (*Revelation*,
p. 61), including Mark Bredin's proposal that Jews might be concealing their identity to avoid
paying a tax that was viewed as support of emperor worship. See Bredin, "The Synagogue of Satan Accusation in Revelation 2:9."

suffer for the faith. That reality tones Paul's letters, beginning with the earliest: "And you became imitators of us and of the Lord, for in spite of much persecution *(thlipsei)* you received the word with joy inspired by the Holy Spirit, so that you became an example *(typon)* to all the believers in Macedonia and in Achaia" (1 Thess. 1:6-7).[42]

This meaning of the cross, ending hostility between humans and God and between formerly alienated peoples, is most significant since the cross has become also the wedge of division and hostility between Christians and Jews in later times, in subsequent centuries. Scholarly contributions on "the parting of ways" between Christians and Jews vary considerably,[43] but most scholars agree that until the fall of the temple and possibly even through to the end of the first century it was common for Christians to maintain Jewish identity, and Jews would not necessarily disassociate themselves from messianic believers, since "Christians," so-called, saw themselves within the diversity of Judaism.

Seventh Day Adventist interpretation of the history regards the second century as the boundary-defining period since Christians then ceased to observe the Sabbath and anti-Judaism began in the Church Fathers.[44] Influenced then by

---

42. For discussion of each of Paul's imitation texts, with many speaking of suffering or affliction of some type, see Chapter 13 below.

43. For an insightful article on this issue, see Bauckham, "The Parting of the Ways: What Happened and Why?" Bauckham writes about the same time and independently of Dunn's second volume on the topic, which consists of papers presented at the second Durham-Tübingen Research Symposium (Dunn, ed., *Jews and Christians: The Parting of the Ways*). See Dunn's earlier related *The Partings of the Ways between Judaism and Christianity*. Bauckham objects to the current trend of speaking of diversity in Judaism as though it were the same as the diverse denominational groups in Protestantism. In fact, most first-century Jews were not members of any given party or ideological group, but were still Jews. Rather than locate the nascent Christian "Way" group as simply another sect amid the diversity, it would be more accurate to see its relationship to Judaism through the lens of the Samaritans' and Qumran's faith-claims, in that both communities espoused loyalty to the four "pillars" Dunn marks out as belonging to "common Judaism" (E. P. Sanders's term): temple, monotheism, election, and Torah, with the Samaritans identifying the temple with the Mount Gerizim shrine and rejecting Jerusalem's and Qumran separating from the Jerusalem temple because of its corrupt priesthood. Christianity differed too in its view of the temple, regarding Christ and the new community as the temple's eschatological fulfillment. Jews regarded Samaritans as "uncircumcised Gentiles," which led to divergent self-identities. Thus, "the case of the Samaritans shows how a Jewish group's self-identity could remain completely at odds with other Jews' identification of them. Samaritans asserted their identity as Israel just as strongly as Jews denied it to them" (Bauckham, p. 140). Outsiders did not always honor the distinction, for "Hegesippus includes Samaritans in his list of seven Jewish parties (*apud* Eusebius, *Hist. Eccl.* 4.22.7)." Bauckham proposes that the significance of the differences between Jews and Samaritans and between Jews and Qumran sheds light on the formation of distinct identities between Jews and Christians.

44. Adventists see this as "the fall of the church"; see Bacchiocchi, *From Sabbath to*

the Sun Cult, Rome instituted Sunday as the day of rest and worship.[45] The specific day — which one? — then became a defining identity factor. Others see the boundaries not clearly defined until much later. John Howard Yoder argues for no necessary cause for such a "parting." "Fuzziness" continued in differentiation of identity until the time of Constantine, when Christianity took the helm of power and began persecuting Jews as a minority group (earlier, Christians maintained their minority group identity by fostering good-will relations with the peoples around them, just as Jews did in their Diaspora existence).[46]

The issue is complex and none of the many explanations close all the gaps. Sources on the subject are limited, and those that we have show diversity. Daniel Boyarin has approached the topic through the window of examining Jewish and Christian experiences of martyrdom in the early centuries. He cites Rabbi Eliezer from the sixth century who at the price of death refused to disassociate himself from Christians.[47] This comes as a surprise to those in the scholarly guild who regard the division complete, with firm identity distinctions already set in the first, second, third, or fourth centuries. Clearly, the matter calls for ongoing reflection and continuing investigation into all sources available, Talmudic and Christian. One writer's views, such as the second-century anti-Judaism of *Barnabas,* cannot become definitive for the subject.[48]

Sunday, pp. 268-69. This differs significantly from Anabaptist streams of interpretation that point to the fourth century's Constantinian influence as "the fall of the church."

45. Under Roman pagan influence of the Sun-cult worship, Christians adopted Sunday as their official day of worship, authorized by leadership in Rome (Bacchiocchi, pp. 211, 310-12, citing Thomas Aquinas).

46. John Howard Yoder, *The Jewish-Christian Schism Revisited.* Collected texts in Williams, *The Jews among the Greeks and Romans: A Diaspora Sourcebook,* would seem to corroborate this view. Texts Williams cites from the third and fourth centuries indicate some peaceful, helping interactions between Jews and Christians, but by 397 CE the texts reflect a Christian triumphalism that "justifies" Christians burning synagogues or converting them into churches, with coerced baptism of the Jews (see especially pp. 157-59).

47. Boyarin, *Dying for God: Martyrdom and the Making of Christianity and Judaism,* pp. 36-50.

48. One might take up here the problem texts, such as the Johannine reference to "the Jews" (see Chapter 10) or Matthew's scathing denunciation of "the scribes and Pharisees" (see Chapter 3) or Paul's own harsh words in 1 Thess. 2:14-16. Segal's treatment of 1 Thess. 2:14-16 is helpful. He holds that the persecution Paul is speaking of (cf. 1:6-7) is coming from hostile Gentiles. Paul builds a typology by referring to earlier experience where Jews in Judea, including Jesus' relatives and friends, persecuted believers. The deaths in the community (4:13-18), a major problem for the church, may have been caused by persecution. Paul draws on "the martyrdom of the saints, who keep God's law, that most often raises the issue of resurrection in Jewish tradition (see Dan. 12:2, 2 Macc. 7). Paul relies on Jewish tradition, albeit in a hostile way, to answer their questions" (pp. 161-62). In this ironic way Paul introduces Jewish apocalyptic into the Gen-

Is Equality Loss of Identity?

What is here described as Paul's great achievement, the "one new humanity" through Jesus Messiah, is problematic for Daniel Boyarin.[49] Boyarin contends, based on his reading and interpretation of Galatians, with 3:28-29 as pivotal, that Paul's universal vision of equality and inclusion results in loss of particular identities: Jews as Jews, women as women, etc. Noting that Pauline texts have often been used "as props in the fight against liberation of slaves and women as well as major supports for theological anti-Judaism," Boyarin says:

> I am going to argue here that Paul need not be read this way, indeed, that his texts support, at least equally well, an alternative reading, one that makes him a passionate striver for human liberation and equality. I will further claim that this very passion for equality led Paul, for various cultural reasons, to equate equality with sameness, and that despite what I take to be the goodness of his intentions, his social thought was therefore deeply flawed.[50]

This flawed strategy shows itself in Paul's "allegoresis" (Boyarin's term) whereby earthly Jerusalem is devalued in preference for the heavenly Jerusalem; likewise, flesh is devalued and spirit is valorized. Paul's theology privileges the univocal and the universal. Boyarin objects to this and pleads for the hermeneutical value of *midrash* over allegory, and the freedom of minority identities to continue and not be threatened out of existence by some "superior" cultural "melting pot" that homogenizes differences into western dominant culture, in which imperial power pressures sub-groups to conform. Boyarin objects to insisting on any special value acceded to particularity, as

tile world, specifically to Gentile believers. The typology of Jewish persecution with its resurrection hope thus serves to vindicate the oppressed and generate hope for those who died (*Paul the Convert*, pp. 162-63). However this text is understood, it cannot compete with the clarity of Romans 9–11, which clearly regards the Jews as God's covenant people, with covenant and promises unbroken. Gentiles are branches grafted into the olive tree, the Jews. For treatment of this important text see Munck, *Christ and Israel;* Davies, *Jewish and Pauline Studies*, pp. 123-63; Watson, *Paul, Judaism, and the Gentiles*, pp. 160-74; John Piper, *The Justification of God*. An excellent brief treatment is that of E. Elizabeth Johnson, "Romans 9–11: The Faithfulness and Impartiality of God," and the response by Douglas Moo, "The Theology of Romans 9–11." Toews, *Romans*, pp. 237-94, has an excellent fuller treatment on Romans 9–11.

49. Boyarin, *A Radical Jew*. On this question of race and identity in Paul, see Buell and Hodge, "The Politics of Interpretation," which argues for a reading of Paul that preserves ethnic identities, even power differences, though all are one in Christ (p. 249). It contains also an up-to-date analysis of literature on the topic.

50. Boyarin, *A Radical Jew*, p. 9.

well as to desire for universality. Though both are necessary, both are problematic. Returning to this issue at the end of his book, Boyarin assesses the value of ethnic identity differently when the ethnic group is in a minority cultural position versus when it is the dominant culture and then exercises power territorially. If a people of strong ethnic identity achieve hegemonic status, then Paul's move toward leveling the diverse entities, but without "his universalizing, disembodying solution," is important "to develop an equally passionate concern for all human beings." Boyarin then proposes that a synthesis to this dialectic must be found, "one that will allow for stubborn hanging on to ethnic, cultural specificity but in a context of deeply felt and enacted human solidarity." He then points to the conditions of the Diaspora as best achieving the model he espouses.[51]

While Boyarin's reading of Paul accentuates dangers in Paul's equality-universalist emphasis often overlooked by most commentators, it does not reflect adequately on Paul's "blessing" of diversity and differing identities, ethnic or gender-related. Examples of such occur in Paul's discussion of spiritual gifts (1 Corinthians 12–14) and differing states of being (slave or free, married or unmarried in 1 Corinthians 7). One can also read Paul as desiring that specific cultural and gender identities of Jew and Gentile, male and female (e.g., 1 Corinthians 11, where distinction and freedom are both affirmed), be preserved and valorized in the messianic community. Thus Boyarin's claim that Paul privileges the univocal and universal is one-sided. His proposal for managing the dialectic between two important opposing and necessary impulses is helpful, indeed essential in order to avoid the horrible wars of ethnic cleansing and prejudices leading often to persecution of minority groups by dominant cultures.

"God of Peace"

Paul frequently employs the phrase, "God of peace." Numerous writers have observed this virtually unique phenomenon and have made brief, insightful contributions.[52] The phrase occurs seven times in Paul, once in Hebrews, and only once outside the NT, in *Testament of Dan* 5:2.[53]

51. Boyarin, *A Radical Jew,* p. 257. Yoder, in *The Jewish-Christian Schism,* shares this view, which I also hold.

52. Hastings, *The Christian Doctrine of Peace,* pp. 15-16; Delling, "Die Bezeichnung 'Gott des Friedens' und ähnliche Wendungen in den Paulusbriefen"; Klassen, "The God of Peace: New Testament Perspectives on God"; Mauser, *Gospel of Peace,* pp. 105-9.

53. The text here reads: "Each of you speak truth clearly to his neighbor, and you will not

Four occurrences are in benedictions:[54]

1 Thess. 5:23: May the God of peace himself sanctify you entirely; and may your spirit and soul and body be kept sound and blameless at the coming of our Lord Jesus Christ.

2 Thess. 3:16: Now may the Lord of peace himself give you peace at all times in all ways. The Lord be with all of you.

Rom. 15:33: The God of peace be with all of you. Amen.

Phil. 4:9: Keep on doing the things that you have learned and received and heard and seen in me, and the God of peace will be with you.

Two more are in assurances or promises:

Rom. 16:20: The God of peace will shortly crush Satan under your feet. The grace of our Lord Jesus Christ be with you.

2 Cor. 13:11: Finally, brothers and sisters, farewell. Put things in order, listen to my appeal, agree with one another, live in peace; and the God of love and peace will be with you.

The seventh is a moral pronouncement:

1 Cor. 14:33: . . . for God is a God not of disorder but of peace.

Paul's frequent use of the appellation "God of peace" is most significant, as Mauser points out. "God of hope" occurs only once (Rom. 15:13) and "God of love" only once — in conjunction with "God of peace" (2 Cor. 13:11). Other similar phrases accentuating divine attributes while absent in Paul occur in Jewish literature: "the God of faithfulness" (Deut. 32:4, literal), "the God of truth" (Isa. 65:16, literal), and "the God of glory" (Ps. 29:3).[55] Mauser rightly notes that Paul's choice of this term likely reflects Jewish piety expressed in the *shalom* benediction[56] and that other characteristics of God's

---

fall into wrath and troublemaking, but be at peace, holding to the God of peace. Thus no conflict will overwhelm you."

54. The occurrence in Hebrews is also in a benediction (13:20).

55. Mauser, *Gospel of Peace*, p. 105. In the manuscript form of the book (p. 133) Mauser identified also "the God of wisdom" (*1 Enoch* 63:2; Josephus, *Antiquities* 11.64) and "the God of righteousness" (1QM 18:8; Tob. 13:7).

56. Here we note Paul's frequent use also of grace (*charis*) in salutations. For discussion of the origins of this usage, see Mauser, *Gospel of Peace*, pp. 107-8. Toews, influenced by Judith M. Lieu's article "'Grace to You and Peace,'" regards the "grace and peace" salutation as "a specifically Pauline creation" (*Romans*, p. 42).

activity are not so privileged. Note also that nowhere does "God of wrath" or "God of judgment" occur as titles for God in Paul.[57] In light of the prominence of "God as Warrior" in the OT (Exod. 15:3), it is striking that no such appellations for God are found in Paul or any other NT writer. Yet, Paul uses martial imagery (see Chapter 8 below). The favored status of "God of peace" for Paul is a key to his larger theology, for his central doctrinal emphases are much associated with peacemaking.

The *God of peace* appellation has not received the attention in Pauline theology that it merits.[58] If indeed this is Paul's creation as it appears to be, then we have an indicator of Paul's distinctive view of God, as one who bestows and assures peace (in the benedictions) and also as the "God of peace" who "will shortly crush Satan under your feet" (Rom. 16:20).[59] While it may appear that this "God of peace" text breathes a different spirit from the others,[60] the notion that the God of peace is also the God who delivers/rescues *(rhyomai)* believers from divine wrath (1 Thess. 1:10), from evil (2 Tim. 4:17-18), persecution (3:11), and "wicked and evil people" (2 Thess. 3:2) lies at the heart of Pauline theology.[61] In the same Thessalonian epistles the "God of peace" blessing occurs twice (1 Thess. 5:23-24; 2 Thess. 3:16). For Paul, the

57. Mauser, *Gospel of Peace*, p. 106.

58. In view of the distinctiveness of this appellation and its frequency of occurrence, it is inexplicable to me that major works on Paul's theology completely overlook it (e.g., Beker's and Dunn's).

59. It is striking that the verb *(syntribō)* in Rom. 16:20 is the same as in the LXX translation of Exod. 15:3, where "God of war" in the Hebrew text becomes "God crushes war" — an astounding reinterpretation! But Pss. 46:9; 76:3-6 set a textual theological precedent (likewise LXX Isa. 42:13; Hos. 2:20). Judith 9:7 and 16:3 use the precise words of LXX Exod. 15:3. See Klassen and his wider discussion of Paul's "God of peace" texts in "The God of Peace."

60. Jewett, "The God of Peace in Romans," regards Rom. 16:20 as a later interpolation. Paul's authentic uses "are marked by inclusiveness and collegiality" (p. 191), but 16:17-20 sounds a different note — an anti-heretical spirit akin to the Pastorals, says Jewett, in opposition to that of 15:33. Even if from holy war tradition, 16:20 is a "fighting text," and must be non-Pauline (it contains seven *hapax logomena*), contends Jewett. But is Paul only "inclusive and collegial" in Romans, as Jewett represents him (e.g., in 1:18–3:20), let alone in the Corinthian correspondence, Galatians, and Philippians 3? Further, in 16:20 believers do not crush Satan: God does! Whether vv. 17-19 are Pauline lies outside the scope of my treatment, but 16:20 is certainly Pauline, given that the appellation is virtually uniquely Pauline, excepting Heb. 13:20. It does not occur in later deutero-Pauline writings.

61. See Elias, "Jesus Who Delivers Us from the Wrath to Come," especially pp. 123-24, and his commentary on these texts in *1 and 2 Thessalonians,* especially pp. 47-50, 53-54. Elias cites similar notions in other Pauline texts. To "crush Satan" is complimentary to this list of *rhyomai* texts, focusing God's deliverance in judgment of Satan, the symbolic, personalized "head" of evil. Both are apocalyptic in genre and at home in Paul.

"God of peace" blessing and delivering from evil/crushing Satan cohere. The former could not exist without the latter.

2 Cor. 13:11 contains both the moral imperative "live in peace" and the blessing of the "God of love and peace" being with you. Here a synergistic relation between God's empowerment and human responsibility occurs. Though not specifically articulated, the interplay between human action and God's initiative is implied in all the benediction blessings; so also in Paul's call to the chaotic Corinthian congregation to conduct their services in "order and peace" (1 Cor. 14:33). This complementary relation between God's grace initiative and the human ethical imperative characterizes Paul's theology, as has been widely discussed as the relation between the indicative and imperative in Pauline theology and ethics.[62] This feature of Pauline ethics manifests itself not only in the pattern of, e.g., Colossians' and Ephesians' structures, where the first half roughly is indicative and the second half imperative, but also in Philippians 2:1-12 where the great hymn of Christ's condescension for the human salvation is framed by ethical admonitions, with the close (v. 12) exhorting recipients of Christ's salvation-work to "work out your own salvation with fear and trembling." God's gift of salvation-peace is thus matched by the human responsibility to "work it out," to do those things that manifest the new life of peace with God and peace with one another.

A similar pattern occurs in the great 2 Corinthians 5:17-21 reconciliation text put above in chiastic form. God is the initiator of the reconciliation and Christ mediates it to humans. But the hymn reaches its climax with a purpose, so that "in him we might become the righteousness of God." If then we apply this pattern of thought to Paul's distinctive "God of peace" appellation, we can expect that this character description of God will be refracted in the whole of Paul's ethics. And so it is, as we will see. Paul's gospel, from beginning to end, is a gospel of peace and reconciliation.

Love and Peace as Ethical Virtues to Pursue and Cultivate

At several points in the above discussion, love was mentioned together with peace, in the title "God of peace," and in both the fruit and gifts of the Spirit. In this section it is essential to link them explicitly, for they are both foundational in Paul's exhortations for the moral formation of believers. They are

---

62. Of the many good treatments of this point, see Furnish, *Theology and Ethics in Paul*, pp. 207-41.

both also prominent in the Hebrew Scriptures as formative for the moral life. Jesus' summation of the law appeals to two commandments in his own Scripture, Deut. 6:4 (the Shema) and Leviticus 19:18 for love of God and love of neighbor respectively. Matthew's final comment in this pericope is "On these two commandments depend all the law and the prophets" (22:40; see Chapter 3 above). In both Testaments, love is primary, and peace plays a supportive secondary role. This may be seen in Eph. 4:1-16, in speaking of the Spirit's gifts, where in vv. 2 and 15 love frames the admonition. Similarly, in 1 Corinthians the great love chapter, ch. 13, forms the heart of Paul's moral catechesis on spiritual gifts. While peace is mentioned in both texts, as noted above, love plays the primary role.

The primacy of love as the highest of virtues is present not only in NT writings, but also in rabbinic writings. In two sources[63] seven classes of Pharisees are mentioned (see Chapter 3 on Matthew 23 for fuller discussion); the class that is most noble is "the God-loving Pharisee, who is like Abraham."[64] Even the "God-fearing Pharisee, who is like Job" is not commended to the same degree. In this classification one who seeks "peace" is not considered, but the permeation of *shalom* throughout Hebrew Scripture (see Chapter 2) certainly makes "peace" a corollary to love.

In Paul's writings believers are exhorted to fulfill the command to love the neighbor and to pursue peace. William Klassen has done a careful study of the "pursuit of peace" texts in Paul.[65] Believers are admonished to be at peace with one another and to seek/pursue peace (Rom. 12:18, quoting Ps. 34:14; 1 Thess. 5:13; 2 Cor. 13:11; 2 Tim. 2:22; cf. Heb. 12:14). Klassen has grouped the texts by categories, as follows:

God of Peace:	*Christ as our Peace:*	*The Peace of God:*
Rom. 15:33; 16:20;	Eph. 2:14;	Phil. 4:7;
1 Cor. 14:33; 2 Cor. 13:11;	*peace of Christ:* Col. 3:15	*peace from God:*
1 Thess. 5:23; Phil. 4:9;		1 Tim. 1:2; 2 John 3
Heb. 13:20		

63. JT *Berakoth* 9.7f.14b, line 48 and JT *Sotah* 5.7f.29c, line 49. The texts with commentary can be found in Montefiore and Loewe, *Rabbinic Anthology,* pp. 487-89.

64. Montefiore and Loewe, p. 488.

65. Klassen, "Pursue Peace: A Concrete Ethical Mandate (Romans 12:18-21)," with categories and diagram of texts on p. 197.

Ethical Admonition:

Let us have peace with God:	*Let us have peace with each other:*	*Live at peace with all:*
Rom. 5:1	Mark 9:50c; 1 Thess. 5:13; Rom. 14:19; 2 Cor. 13:11;	Rom. 12:18; Heb. 12:14
	Keep the bond of peace:	
	Eph. 4:3;	
	Pursue peace:	
	2 Tim. 2:22; 1 Pet. 3:11;	
	Heb. 12:14; Rom. 14:19	

If the top layer represents the theology of peace, the second tier draws out the ethical implications: "Be at peace with God, with fellow believers, with all people, even with outsiders." By stating that the nature of both God and Christ is peace, the ethical mandate to pursue peace finds its strongest theological and incarnational anchor.

Indeed, believers are called to peace (1 Cor. 7:15), and as members of one body are to make "every effort to maintain the unity of the Spirit in the bond of peace" (Eph. 4:3-6). Further, the peace of God is power that "guards your hearts and your minds in Christ Jesus" (Phil. 4:7). Peace also characterizes living for the service of God (Romans 12–15 and parallel thought in 1 and 2 Corinthians). A key text that shows the interrelation of love and peace in Paul's moral exhortation is Col. 3:12-15, where love and peace play strategic motivational roles in moral parenesis. Love is the crown of the previous five virtues. The peace of Christ ruling the hearts of the believers (v. 15) follows immediately. The last phrase, "in the one body," echoes Paul's "one body" metaphor in Corinthians and anticipates the fuller *peace* exposition of Eph. 2:14-18, where *one* body and *peace* are central.

The third love command, love of enemies,[66] integrates love and peace. This is especially evident in the many exhortations regarding response to enemies. In these texts peacemaking is appropriated to the sphere of life in which believers relate to enemies and need directive on how to respond to evil. Paul's moral admonition is fully in keeping with Jesus' teaching. 1 Corinthians 4:12b-13a puts it: "When reviled we bless, when persecuted we endure, when slandered we conciliate." Gordon Zerbe sums up a fuller list. He identifies as passive responses:

---

66. It is disputed whether this is unique to Jesus. William Klassen contends in *Love of Enemies: The Way to Peace* that it was significantly present in Judaism prior to Jesus. But the examples he cites support moral exhortation to nonretaliation more than, explicitly, to love of enemies. Perhaps it is more correct to say that the command is focused and intensified by Jesus.

(1) "not repaying evil for evil" (1 Thess. 5:15a; Rom. 12:17a);

(2) "not taking vengeance for oneself" (Rom. 12:19a);

(3) "not cursing" (Rom. 12:14);

(4) "forbearance" (Phil. 4:5; 1 Thess. 5:14; 1 Cor. 13:4; Gal. 5:22; 2 Cor. 6:6);

(5) "endurance" (1 Cor. 4:12; 2 Cor. 11:20; cf. Col. 3:13; 2 Thess. 1:4; Rom. 12:12; 2 Cor. 6:4; 1 Cor. 13:7; cf. Rom. 5:3-4; 2 Cor. 1:6);

(6) not litigating (1 Cor. 6:1-8);

(7) "not reckoning evil" (1 Cor. 13:6).

Active responses include:

(8) responding with good/kind deeds (1 Thess. 5:15b; Rom. 12:17b, 20-21);

(9) "blessing" (Rom. 12:1.4; 1 Cor. 4:12);

(10) "conciliating" (1 Cor. 4:13);

(11) "being at peace" (1 Thess. 5:13; Rom. 12:18; cf. Gal. 5:20, 22);

(12) "forgiving" (2 Cor. 2:7-10; Col. 3:13);

(13) "loving" (1 Cor. 13:4-7; cf. 2 Cor. 6:6; Rom. 12:9; 1 Thess. 3:12).[67]

Rom. 12:14-21 is especially important, because it not only articulates these points in compressed instruction but also stands in continuity with how believers are to respond to political authorities (13:1-7), a topic to be discussed further in the next chapter. Here belongs, however, an analysis of the basic moral exhortation of how believers pursue the good and respond to evil, key words that tie together Romans 12 and 13. The *major* theme of Rom. 12:9–13:10 is how one is to respond to *evil* (recurring 8 times: 12:9, 17[2], 21[2]; 13:3, 4, 10). The moral parenesis begins with "Let love be genuine" (12:9) and ends with "Owe no one anything, except to love one another" (13:8). Shun *evil,* do *good* recurs in multiform expression:

1. Hate (stay clear of) evil *(to ponēron),*
   but hold fast to the good *(tō agathō)* (12:9).
2. Bless those who persecute you,
   bless and do not curse (12:14).
3. Repay no one evil *(kakon)* for evil *(kakou),*
   but focus on good *(kala)* in the sight of all (12:17).
   As much as possible, make peace *(eirēneuontes)* with all (12:18).
4. Do not be conquered by evil *(kakou),*
   but conquer evil *(kakon)* with good *(agathō)* (12:21).

67. Zerbe, "Paul's Ethic of Nonretaliation and Peace," pp. 179-80.

5. Be subject to the authority(ies), who is (to be) a terror to evil *(kakǭ)*,
   not to good *(agathǭ)* (13:3);
   he is God's servant to you
   unto the good *(agathǭ)* (13:4).
6. If you do evil *(kakon)*, fear,
   for the servant avenges God's wrath *(orgēn)* against evil *(kakon)* (13:4).
7. Be subject therefore not only to avoid wrath *(orgēn)*
   but also for the sake of (keeping a good) conscience (13:5).
8. Pay what is owed *(opheilas)*;
   owe *(opheilete)* no one anything but love *(agapan)* (13:7-8).
9. Whoever loves *(ho agapōn)* fulfills the law (13:8b);
   and love *(hē agapē)* for the neighbor
   does not work/promote evil *(kakon)* (13:10).
10. Love *(agapē)* thus fulfills the law. (13:8-10).

Note also the contrast between the works of darkness and the armor of light, 13:12. Peacemaking, doing the good, and loving the neighbor and enemy are the Christian responses to evil; avenging evil is forbidden to Christians, for vengeance *(ekdikēsis,* 12:19; *ekdikos,* 13:4) belongs to God and the authorities, who are servants of wrath *(orgē,* used three times in 12:19; 13:4, 5).

In his writings more broadly Paul's use of the love of the neighbor command figures significantly into his moral exhortation as the basis for moral formation.[68] Twice Paul adduces the love of neighbor command as a persuasive force to either proscribe or prescribe behavior. In Romans 13, love of neighbor is induced to sum up the last six of the Ten Commandments and to warrant the counsel to "owe no one anything, except to love one another." This follows his parenesis on the believer's relationship to government and particularly whether or not the believer should pay taxes. Verses 8-10 appear to broaden the discussion to include Christian behavior in society generally, both in motivation and goals.

Paul again appeals to the love command in checking unbridled freedom among the Galatian believers after he has argued fiercely for freedom in Christ Jesus. Such freedom, however, can lead to self-gratification, and hence it must be regulated by the command, "through love be servants of one another" (5:13). Again, to warrant the exhortation, Paul cites the love of neigh-

68. Here I disagree with Richard B. Hays in his exclusion of love as a focal criterion for moral judgment, as he develops it in *The Moral Vision of the New Testament.* Granted it can be used as an abstract principle malleable to the interpreter's or ethicist's purposes that in the end subvert the textual intentions (as he argues regarding Reinhold Niebuhr), but the command widely used in the NT (though not in all parts of the NT canon) is an important moral criterion.

bor command. He thus opposes antinomian conduct, libertinism, and fleshly individualism. These attitudes and behaviors do not build, but rather destroy the community, the very opposite of the intent of the love commands.[69]

Peace-Building in the Community of the Spirit

One of Paul's main purposes in his epistles is to edify the nascent Christian communities, amid conflicts and growth pains of communities of great diversity. Segal's treatment of this feature in Paul's letters is most insightful; it shows how Paul's goals for transformation in the communities of faith, as well as his exegesis, were rooted in his own conversion glory *(kabod)* experience.[70]

Paul's peace-building vision and praxis are explicitly expressed in three key aspects of the role of the Holy Spirit in personal and communal transformation. First, the impact of justification on the role of the law in Christian living (Romans 5–7) is twofold: (1) Christ Jesus sets us free from the law of sin and death by condemning sin in the flesh (Jesus' living and dying in the life of flesh) so that "the just requirement of the law might be fulfilled in us" (Rom. 8:4); (2) as a consequence, believers are freed to set their minds not on the things of the flesh, but on the things of the Spirit, which leads to *life and peace* (Rom. 8:6). This important fruit of God's work in Christ heads Paul's exposition of the Spirit of God dwelling within believers, which in turn enables the identity-forming cry, *Abba,* assuring them they are children of God (8:9-17).[71]

Then follows the robust hope in God's redemption of all creation, now groaning for its release, which in turn empowers believers in their sufferings (8:18-25), assuring them that the Spirit ministers to them by praying for them in their weakness (8:26-27). More promises follow: God works for good for the believer in all things (v. 28); in accord with God's foreknowledge and sovereign purpose believers live toward the goal of being more and more conformed to the image of the Son (cf. 2 Cor. 3:17-18); and the believers' calling leads to justification and glorification (Rom. 8:28-30). Finally comes the grand finale, that since God is for us, nothing can be against us, and indeed nothing in all heaven and earth can separate us from the love of God in Christ

69. Helpful studies of the love command are Furnish, *The Love Command;* Perkins, *Love Commands;* and the collection of essays by Schottroff, et al., *Essays on the Love Commandment.*

70. Segal, *Paul the Convert,* pp. 58-71. On moral transformation see also Bruce Longenecker, "Until Christ Is Formed in You," and Barclay, *"Christ in You."*

71. For good treatments of the significance of the *Abba* address in prayer, see Luz, *Matthew 1-7,* pp. 375-77; Thompson, *The Promise of the Father,* chapter 2 (though all is relevant).

Jesus our Lord (8:31-39). What more can be said? Where else in all God's creation is there a grander vision of shalom for God's people? This pastoral homily, or shining *(kabod)* theology, is from start to finish a shalom-building gift to all believers. Treasured over the centuries, this gift has empowered Christian believers as they journey through life's trials and death's valley toward the promised land of God's final rest and peace.

This *peace,* shalom in its fullness, is God's gift in the justifying-sanctifying work of Christ Jesus. This life-gift of shalom frees us from living in the "flesh" (here a close parallel to "world" in John).[72] It attests to our true identity and builds hope amid our groaning with all creation and promises God-with-us throughout this life, whatever its trials, and into the life to come. Paul links this new life with the "kingdom of God" in 14:17, declaring that it consists not of "food and drink but righteousness and peace and joy in the Holy Spirit." The gospel Paul fervently preached links kingdom of God and peace with the gift and fruit of the Spirit.

Thus, a *second* emphasis of the Spirit's peace-building among believers identifies peace as one expression of the fruit of the Spirit. As developed in Chapter 2, the meaning of peace *(eirēnē)* in the NT carries forward some of the iridescence of *shalom* in Hebrew Scripture. Peace comes third, next to love and joy, in Paul's ninefold fruit of the Spirit ("love, joy, peace, patience, kindness, generosity, faithfulness, gentleness and self-control," Gal. 5:22-23). Each is rich in meaning.[73] Paul appeals to the fruit of the Spirit in Galatians in a context similar to Romans 8:1-12, where life in the Spirit is contrasted to "the works of the flesh" (Gal. 5:16-21). Here the works of the flesh are many separate enslaving powers, in contrast to the unitive fruit of the Spirit. The works of the flesh are destructive of life; the fruit of the Spirit is the elixir of life, forming a person into the image of Jesus Christ.

In Galatians this text cautions believers in their freedom from the yoke of slavery, from, that is, pursuing "works of the law" as a means of God's justification. With the fruit of the Spirit Paul "fences" the newly freed believers from fleshly indulgence (v. 13). He evokes the scriptural commandment, "You shall love your neighbor as yourself" (v. 14; Lev. 19:18). Through love the believers become servants (slaves) to one another. Rather than "bite and devour" one another, they are to build each other up in faith, and not allow fleshly desires to rule their lives.

Peace, as fruit of the Spirit, is not in this case a moral duty or obligation.

72. See Barrett, *Paul: An Introduction,* pp. 69-74, for a well-nuanced treatment of Paul's multi-level meanings in his use of *sarx* ("flesh").

73. For an enriching study of the fruit of the Spirit, see Kenneson, *Life on the Vine.*

The emphasis is not so much on peacemaking, though this is the implicit goal in the entire parenesis. Rather, peace here describes the demeanor of the human spirit and the character of the believer. Peace thus becomes an experienced attribute of the believer's life as one welcomes and yields to the presence and power of the Spirit. Along with the other eight qualities peace is a virtue that is first a gift (i.e, one *receives* the Spirit), and also a task (*Gabe und Aufgabe*, as Karl Barth put it). That task believers undertake by the power of the same Spirit. After listing numerous works of the flesh, Paul warns believers not to do such deeds since they prevent one from inheriting the kingdom of God. Paul does not *command* the fruit of the Spirit, as though it were within human capacity to embody it. Rather, he regards the fruit as *flowing* from the Spirit in one's life. The subtle sub-text, however, is that believers are to emulate these virtues in their character.

Third, the gifts of the Holy Spirit foster peace-building in the congregation (Rom. 12:3-8; 1 Cor. 12-14; Eph. 4:7-16).[74] In Romans and Ephesians the gifts are enumerated in contexts of assumed congregational health in their use. But in 1 Corinthians Paul admonishes the community in its tumultuous experience with spiritual gifts, especially "speaking in tongues." First and foremost is the "rule" that if one speaks by the Spirit of God one does not curse Jesus, for it is by the Holy Spirit that one confesses that Jesus Christ is Lord (1 Cor. 12:3). Subsequent criteria are recognition and respect of the diversity of gifts, with one Lord, one God, and one Spirit who enables and is honored by them (12:4-11); the one body with many members, each of which is to be valued (12:12-30); love among members as the more excellent way, a deciding factor (12:31–13:13); and the building up of the community as well as consideration for outsiders listening in ("building up" [*oikodomēn*] occurs three times in 14:1-32, in vv. 5, 12, 26). The climax of this discussion appeals to peace: "for God is not a God of disorder but of peace" (v. 33). Clearly, *peace* functions here in a climactic relation to Paul's threefold emphasis on *building up*. Peace is a virtue for community relations, as well as for personal life, as is all the fruit of the Spirit.

In Ephesians Paul prefaces his appeal to the gifts of grace (4:7) with an injunction "to maintain the unity of the Spirit in the bond of *peace*" as well as reminding the believers they were called into "one body and one Spirit, . . . one Lord, one faith, one baptism, one God and Father of all . . ." (4:3-6).[75]

---

74. In Romans 12 the call to live peaceably with all (v. 18) comes in the flow of admonitions that begin with discerning rightful use of the Spirit's gifts of grace. I am inclined to see a break between vv. 13 and 14, so that the injunction in v. 17 pertains to relations with those outside the community of faith and is not intrinsically related to the "gifts of grace" discussion.

75. The similarity in thought-logic to 1 Corinthians 12–14 lends credence to the proposal that Paul is author of both epistles, which I am inclined to accept for other reasons also. The

Paul's plea to maintain the unity of the Spirit as the context for understanding and valuing God's gifts of grace in vv. 7-16 is strikingly similar in character to his treatment in 1 Corinthians. Peace-building is both a condition for understanding the nature of the gifts and for the functioning of the gifts as well. If that criterion is violated, then grave questions arise as to how the exercise of the gift is the work of God's Spirit.[76] The gifts of the Spirit in Ephesians are designated as gifts of grace (4:7) and are here also for the building up *(eis oikodomēn)* of the community (4:12, 16), an identical term to that in 1 Corinthians 14.

In Romans 12 the list of gifts, though quite different, is rooted in God's grace also, thus charismatic (from Greek *charis,* which means "grace"). It is unfortunate that the term charismatic has received negative connotation, due to misuse of the gifts. For the word itself is as precious to the life of believers as is "steadfast love" *(chesed),* so dominant in Hebrew Scripture. Indeed, the LXX often chooses *charis* to translate *chesed.* From this perspective a related feature of the early church communities merits notice.

Gifts of Grace and Mutual Aid among Believers

In Romans 12, the last three gifts of grace are expressions of sharing: "he who contributes, in liberality; he who gives aid, with zeal; he who does acts of mercy, with cheerfulness" (v. 8, RSV).[77] When these acts of mutual care for one another are seen as part of the *charis*-empowerment of the church, then Paul's appeal for mutual sharing of financial resources in 2 Corinthians 8–9 comes into focus as a related peace-building action among the communities. The entire appeal is rooted in God's or Jesus Christ's act of grace toward us. Forms of *charis* occur eleven times (8:1, 4, 6c, 9, 16, 19; 9:8, 11, 12, 14, 15), two of which are the compound form, *eucharistia* in 9:11, 12. Paul speaks of this relief

---

proposal that Ephesians was intended as a circular letter is persuasive, explaining well the text variant *en Ephesō*. Further, Eph. 3:1-13 can hardly be understood credibly apart from Pauline authorship. These outweigh, in my judgment, the several significant differences in theology between Ephesians and Paul's other letters. Here I differ with Yoder Neufeld, whose discussion of the matter is illuminating (*Ephesians,* pp. 24-28, 341-44).

76. There is significant evidence of *glossolalia* in other religious groups as well, especially in the Dionysius Cult prominent in Delphi, across the isthmus from Corinth.

77. The translation is markedly different in the NRSV: "the giver, in generosity; the leader, in diligence; the compassionate, in cheerfulness." While *proïstamenos* can indeed mean "leader" ("one who leads"), as well as "one who gives aid" in a deacon-type ministry, the cluster of financially related terms here would argue for the RSV interpretation.

gift also in Romans 15 and "grounds" it in "the grace given me by God" (v. 15) and prays that this "offering of the Gentiles may be acceptable, sanctified by the Holy Spirit."

Later Paul describes the effort more explicitly: "At present, however, I am going to Jerusalem in a ministry to the saints; for Macedonia and Achaia have been pleased to share their resources with the poor among the saints at Jerusalem. They were pleased to do this, and indeed they owe it to them; for if the Gentiles have come to share in their spiritual blessings, they ought also to be of service to them in material things" (Rom. 15:25-27). This mutuality, or mutualism as Justin Meggitt describes it,[78] arises from the peace-bond within the communities of faith, especially between the Gentile and Jewish Christians, central to Paul's understanding of justification and reconciliation as the essential core of God's saving work in Jesus Christ. Mutual care for one another is not only an important manifestation of the gift of grace within Paul himself and in the community, but also evidence that the formerly alienated people are now one in Jesus Christ, who is their peace (Eph. 2:14). Meggitt identifies two characteristics of this mutual sharing:

> Firstly, it was aimed at promoting *material well being*. It was initially undertaken to achieve a tangible end: *the relief of the economically poor in the Jerusalem church*. . . . Secondly, it was thoroughly *mutual* in its character. *It was in no sense an individual or unilateral undertaking for any of those involved.* Paul emphasises that *all* the members were contributors as, indeed, were *all* the communities (we hear of no exceptions). It was not intended to be the work of a few wealthy members or congregations.[79]

Meggitt further rightly notes that such assistance, because it was *mutual,* would be expected to be returned when and if the situation of need were reversed. This is a true expression of care for the purpose of sustaining *shalom* in its fullest sense in the communities of faith.

Paul so highly valued this expression as proof of the newly achieved unity in Jesus Christ that he willingly gave his life for the cause, despite prophetic declaration that he would encounter arrest and imprisonment in Jeru-

---

78. Meggitt, *Paul, Poverty and Survival,* pp. 157-64. See also my article, "Mutual Aid Based in Jesus and Early Christianity." For monograph studies of Paul's collection for the poor in Jerusalem, see Nickle, *The Collection;* Georgi, *Remembering the Poor.*

79. Meggitt, *Paul, Poverty and Survival,* p. 159. Meggitt's thesis as a whole, argued on the basis of careful study of primary sources on the economic realities of the first century, is that Paul and the churches he founded belonged to the ninety-nine percent of the population, the poor; they shared generously from their limited means. This fits with Paul's profuse appeal to "grace" in 2 Corinthians 8–9.

salem (Acts 21:7-14). Paul says, "I am ready not only to be bound but even to die in Jerusalem for the name of the Lord Jesus Christ" (v. 13b). Paul regarded his relief gift to Jerusalem as the crowning achievement of his apostolic calling, to give proof that Gentile and Jewish messianic believers are really, truly one in Jesus Christ, peace-fellows through the blood on the cross of the Lord Jesus Christ. The peace of the cross expressed itself concretely in mutual care for one another.

The peace of Jesus Christ expressed itself also in the community's care for the poor and despised of the *plebs urbana*. Not only did the Christian community practice mutual aid among its own members, but it sought also to alleviate the horrific socioeconomic poverty conditions of the empire.[80] Early Christianity witnessed to Jesus Christ's victory over the powers by means of the church's incredible practice of charity and mutual aid. The Roman world treated human life with contempt in many instances, allowing especially female infants to die. Rodney Stark, from his sociological study of early Christianity, says, "We've unearthed sewers clogged with the bones of newborn girls." The early Christians "had to live with a trench running down the middle of the road, in which you could find dead bodies decomposing."[81] Christians did not install sewer systems, but they did speak against infanticide; they cared for each other and for the weak in a society that otherwise blinded itself to human need. Though agnostic in his personal stance toward Christianity, Stark is convinced that the early Christians made a striking difference in their world, by standing for life over against death, caring for each other, and valuing women and children, granting them dignity and worth that manifested God's kingdom values amid an immoral degenerate social order.[82]

---

80. For a description of how dire these conditions were, see Meggitt, *Paul, Poverty and Survival*, pp. 41-73.

81. Interview with Rodney Stark, "A Double Take on Early Christianity," in *Touchstone* 13/1 (January-February 2000): 44, 47. For fuller treatment, see Stark, *The Rise of Christianity*, especially his sections on "Epidemics," pp. 76-94, and "Urban Chaos and Crisis," pp. 147 62. In the latter he says that outside "on the streets [were] mud, open sewers, manure, and crowds. In fact, human corpses — adult as well as infant — were sometimes just pushed into the street and abandoned" (p. 154). Stark also describes the Christian communities as caring for each other through networks of support and doing much to alleviate the plight of sufferers during plagues and amid horrid urban conditions. Yet their survival rates were higher than those of the general population.

82. "Double Take," p. 47.

8 Paul:
Victory over Evil, Including
the Principalities and Powers

He disarmed the rulers and authorities and made a public example of
them, triumphing over them in it.

COL. 2:15

He himself is before all things, and in him all things hold together. He is
the head of the body, the church; he is the beginning, the firstborn from
the dead, so that he might come to have first place in everything. For in
him all the fullness of God was pleased to dwell, and through him God
was pleased to reconcile to himself all things, whether on earth or in
heaven, by making peace through the blood of his cross.

COL. 1:17-20

Stand therefore, and fasten the belt of truth around your waist, and put
on the breastplate of righteousness. As shoes for your feet put on whatever
will make you ready to proclaim the gospel of peace. With all of these,
take the shield of faith, with which you will be able to quench all the
flaming arrows of the evil one. Take the helmet of salvation, and the
sword of the Spirit, which is the word of God.

EPH. 6:14-17

To grasp adequately Paul's view of God's great peacemaking event in and
through Jesus Christ, we recap in brief a fundamental OT view of evil (Heb.
*ra*ʿ). While war in the OT interrupted the reign of peace *(shalom)* among

God's people, *shalom* is a much broader concept than simply the antonym of war.[1] Shalom cannot be understood apart from Israel's understanding of the Yahweh war that establishes and maintains creation order against chaos (Exod. 14:14; Psalms 29; 68; 89:7-18).[2] This chaos is expressed at many levels of human life and is close in meaning to evil *(ra')*, which God's sovereign redemptive work combats in history, especially through the faithful life of the covenant people. In light of this OT perspective, this chapter begins by identifying Paul's understanding of evil, and describes how God's victory in Christ Jesus is connected, directly and dynamically, to God's triumph over evil.

Paul's writings powerfully proclaim God's triumph through Christ over all the powers of evil, through which we, upon acceptance of Jesus Christ's work for us, have peace with God (Rom. 5:1) and receive Christ's peace, which unites former alienated peoples (Eph. 2:14-17). Paul's epistles first and foremost celebrate and proclaim the gospel of Jesus Christ, "the power of God unto salvation" (Rom. 1:16-17). God's salvation in Jesus Christ is *the* power that delivers us from "the dominion (or authority — *exousia*) of darkness and transfers us [in]to the kingdom of his beloved Son, in whom we have redemption, the forgiveness of sins" (Col. 1:13-14). By the power of this gospel alone humans can be delivered from the bondages of sin, evil, devil, and demons — manifested in many forms: be it personal oppression/possession or structural, systemic manifestations of demonic power. Deliverance from the powers of evil is the precondition and gift of our peace with God and fellow humans.

How Paul Understands Evil

Paul speaks of evil power in five ways.[3] The *first* is Satan or the devil. A most striking text occurs at the end of Romans where Paul calls believers to be wise about what is good, and guileless about what is evil (*akeraious*, "simple" or "harmless" in KJV): ". . . then the God of peace will soon crush Satan under your feet" (16:20). Notably, this pronouncement combines the unique NT term "God of peace" with the crushing of Satan's power. This brief jubilant declaration unites two major trajectories in biblical theology: God the Warrior and God the Peacemaker. They also meet in the life of the person and the believing

---

1. Though war is not an antonym of shalom (in 2 Sam. 11:7 David asks Uriah about the *shalom* of the war), shalom is usually absence of war, often by negotiated peace treaties between nations (Deut. 20:10-12; Josh. 9:15; 10:1, 4; Judg. 4:17; 1 Sam. 7:14; 1 Kgs. 5:12).

2. Ollenburger, "Peace and God's Action against Chaos in the Old Testament."

3. Compare four in Finger, *Christian Theology*, pp. 322-33.

community when the power of Satan is crushed by the power of God through Jesus Christ. In this way God triumphs over evil and establishes peace.[4]

Paul's letters speak of Satan or the devil numerous other times as well. The incestuous man is to be turned over to Satan for the "destruction of his flesh but in order that his spirit might be saved in the day of the Lord Jesus" (1 Cor. 5:5). Many texts speak of the believers' resistance against Satan (Eph. 4:26-27; 1 Cor. 7:5; 2 Cor. 2:11; 11:14; 12:7; 1 Thess. 2:18). The ways of Satan are deceitful; he masks himself as an "angel of light" (2 Cor. 11:14) and with deceitful designs seeks to get an advantage over the believer (2 Cor. 2:11). Paul speaks of Satan hindering the missionary team from visiting the Thessalonians (1 Thess. 2:18; if this refers to persecution, it is thus an instance of Satan working through political powers). Also, the believer is to give no place to the devil, by not letting the sun go down on his or her anger (Eph. 4:26-27). Paul proclaims God's victory in Jesus Christ as power and gift that delivers us from the works of Satan, or the devil, so we can know and enjoy the peace of Christ ruling in our hearts and uniting us in the one body (Col. 3:15), which we are in and through Christ. As the hymn writer puts it: "There is no other way; there is no other hope. Salvation full, salvation free, must come alone through Thee [Christ]!"

A *second* type of evil power(s) in Paul's epistles is his several uses of the word *demons*. Paul speaks of demons four times, but all in only one textual admonition, where he warns believers against idolatry (1 Cor. 10:20-21). Echoing the OT connection between idolatry and demon power (see the diagram on p. 226), Paul draws a parallel between the Israelites' worship of idols (10:6-13) and the Corinthian believers' potential idolatry through participating in cultic meals dedicated to pagan gods (10:14-22). Paul asserts, "you cannot partake of the table of the Lord and the table of demons" (v. 21). While in 8:5ff. Paul said pagan gods/idols have no real existence,[5] in 10:14-22 he does

---

4. William Klassen connects this text to the missionary proclamation of peace in Luke 10 ("The God of Peace: New Testament Perspectives on God," p. 129):

> There is a similar juxtaposition of joy, victory, fall of Satan, and "treading under foot snakes and scorpions and all the forces of the enemy . . ." in the commissioning of the disciples in Luke [10:18ff.]. They return having retained their identity as children of peace and this causes Jesus to become exuberant (Lk 10:21). . . .

> Paul like his fellow Jewish apocalyptic writers sees peace coming through the conquest of evil, the conquest of Satan, a conquest which is intimately related to the faithfulness of believers. But at the same time it is God, the God of peace, who destroys evil.

5. "Real" occurs rarely in English Bible translations, and no Hebrew or Greek word is readily translated with it, though the notion is at home in Greek thought. Translators intro-

not fudge the point that demons, nonetheless, exert functional power. He recognizes their power and calls Christian believers away from their influence: "I imply that what pagans sacrifice they sacrifice to demons and not to God. I do not want you to be partners with demons. You cannot drink the cup of the Lord and the cup of demons. You cannot partake of the table of the Lord and the table of demons. Or are we provoking the Lord to jealousy? Are we stronger than he?" (10:20-22). Paul's view here concurs with a commonly held prophetic understanding in the OT, as expressed both in Deuteronomy 32:17 and Psalm 106:37. What Israelites worshiped when they worshiped idols was not a god, since only the Lord God is truly such, but demons, an anti-God power.

Romans 1:18-23 indicates that Paul believed that human wickedness blinded people to truth, resulting in their making idols as substitutes for the God they do not know, indeed cannot know through reason or nature because of their wickedness. In light of the OT connection between idolatry and the demonic, it is likely that Paul linked the two in the same way. Daniel Patte explicates Romans 1:18–3:20 to explain how humans on the basis of partial revelation (creation, even law) establish notions of righteousness that reify limited knowledge. In this situation sin is defined, but actually from a stance of idolatry, so that "Jesus the crucified" is regarded within the sin structure. Only at the point when it is recognized that God manifests himself in the crucified and resurrected Jesus is "the logic of the idolatrous system of convictions . . . broken up and the power of the idolatry . . . destroyed. . . . 'Jesus crucified and raised' contradicts the logic of the idolatrous system."[6]

Paul's proclamation of the gospel of Jesus Christ, the revelation of the true God, is itself an exorcistic power, since at the name of Jesus every knee shall bend and every tongue shall confess Jesus' lordship (Phil. 2:9-11). While this confessional exclamation may be understood as an anti-imperial text

---

duced it here in the RSV (8:4). In the NRSV "really" is supplied. Both translations put the phrase *ouden eidōlon en kosmō* in quotations, suggesting that Paul is quoting what his opponents said. The RSV translates it as "an idol has no real existence" and the NRSV "no idol in the world really exists." The phrase is difficult to translate since it lacks a verb and also has no adjective ("real") or adverb ("really"). The quotations around other phrases in vv. 1 and 4 are translators' proposals also. Whether Paul is quoting what opponents said is difficult to establish. If the RSV and NRSV are correct, then we cannot know from this text whether Paul thought idols did or did not have (real) existence. Rom. 1:18ff. indicates that Paul believed idols have functional existence and exert power, even power to blind (1:19, 23). This provides rationale for assigning the statement in 8:4 to opponents. C. K. Barrett says, "Paul does not say that they do not exist, only that they are 'no gods'; not exactly 'anti-gods' but not to be described by the word 'God' as a Jew would understand it" (*Paul: An Introduction to His Thought*, p. 58).

6. Patte, *Paul's Faith and the Power of the Gospel*, pp. 284-86 (quotation from p. 286).

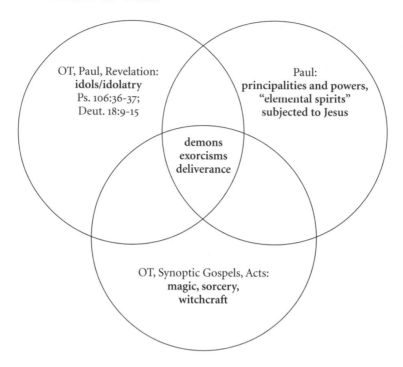

Biblical theological context and language for demons and evil spirits/powers
The gospel's triumph over magic, demons, and powers; the bold confidence
of early Christians; early Christian catechetical rituals, including exorcisms

(Caesar is not Lord), it functions also as power against the evil spirit world
and "the principalities and powers" as well. All the anti-God powers represented in the diagram above, regardless of nomenclature, are subject to the
power of God Almighty manifest in the gospel revelation of Jesus Christ.
Since these anti-God powers are at work in politics and ideologies alienating
humans from one another, empowering rivalry and violence, the gospel of Jesus Christ is both a "deliverance" power from these rival powers and an alternative political reality. The "assemblies" Paul began in numerous cities, which
he called *ekklēsiai,* were alternative identity-shapers and power influences to
the "assemblies" of the Greek *polis* (city-state).[7]

A *third* way in which Paul speaks of evil is in the categories of sin, flesh,
and death. The evil impulse of "the flesh" (Rom. 7:5-18) is in opposition to
God's Spirit (Rom. 8:3-9; Gal. 5:16-18, 24; 6:8). Through the impulse of the

7. On this see the work of Richard Horsley and Dieter Georgi, specifically Horsley, *Paul
and Empire,* p. 8.

flesh, the law itself becomes an occasion for humans to sin and come under the power of death (Rom. 7:5-25). Indeed, Romans 7 reflects a deep psychological despair — fanned by a sin, flesh, law syndrome — which can be overcome only by deliverance through Jesus Christ. Paul frequently calls for a "putting off" of the old and a "putting on" of the new. That which is to be put off are the sins of the flesh; that which is to be put on is the fruit of the Spirit (Gal. 5:16-23; Col. 3:1-17; Eph. 5:25-32).[8] Most important, Paul declares this new life in Christ Jesus as making possible two great achievements. First, because of God's gift in "sending his own Son in the likeness of sinful flesh, and to deal with sin," not only is sin condemned but "the just requirement of the law . . . [is to] be fulfilled in us, who walk not according to the flesh but according to the Spirit" (Rom. 8:3-4). Second, by living according to the Spirit believers "set the mind on the Spirit," which leads to "life and peace" (8:6). Later in Romans Paul makes clear that this peace is of both vertical and horizontal dimensions. Paul recapitulates God's great peacemaking achievement in Christ with the "Therefore" of 12:1 and then explicates the pursuit of peace with others in Christ (internally) and then with those outside the community of faith, even with enemies (12:17-21; see below for exposition).

A *fourth* face of evil appears in the forces that lie behind pagan religions and philosophies, as well as behind the law considered as a means for self-justification. Paul speaks of being redeemed from under the law and freed from "the elemental spirits *(stoicheia)* of the universe" (Gal. 4:3, 8-9; see also Col. 2:8, 18-23). These structures and rituals were powers that dominated life and thus destroyed freedom. For the Jews it was the law — not the law itself, but the works of the law as a means of salvation. For the Greeks the *stoicheia* consisted of astrological fate and fortune, powers governing the cycles of nature, imparted secret knowledge, and certain beliefs about how the cosmos is held together.[9]

From these texts we gain a basic understanding of idolatry itself. Structures that are deemed good and that provide the basis for the natural or social order that enables life (for the Jews, the law) are turned into ultimate values, ends in themselves, and thus elevated to powers over one's life, and then wor-

---

8. Paul nowhere calls any of these sins demons; yet his overall theology is such as to recognize that demonic power works through sin and preys upon human weakness.

9. Ulrich Mauser's analysis of "the rudimentary elements of the world" *(stoicheia)* in Colossians is pertinent here. He contends that the word likely refers to the four primary elements of Epimenides, fire, water, air, earth (*The Gospel of Peace,* pp. 143-44). In order not to offend these powers, the Colossian Christians thought it necessary to engage in various ascetic and ritual practices. By so doing they honored these powers as gods and undermined the all-sufficiency and supremacy of Jesus Christ.

shiped as gods.[10] In Romans 1:18ff. Paul describes the process of this pattern: through sinful impulses humans fail to see God's revelation in nature and therefore turn to idolatry, worshiping the creation and creature instead of the Creator. Hence, "God gave them over" — repeated three times (vv. 24, 26, 28) — to the course and consequences of their wickedness. Only the power of the liberating gospel can free humans from this chain of sin. Indeed, Jesus "gave himself for our sins to deliver us from the present evil age" (Gal. 1:4, RSV). Through release from the power of these elemental forces governing and oppressing life, believers claim a new freedom and identity: children of God who know God as loving Abba, father/mother who intimately cares for us in our deepest needs (Gal. 4:3-6; cf. Rom. 8:12-17). In this loving, intimate relationship, a Christ gives peace grounded in a child-parent relationship, a peace that the world cannot take away (cf. John 16:33). Nothing in all creation can separate us from the love of God that is in Christ Jesus our Lord (Rom. 8:37-39). This love surpasses understanding (Eph. 3:19); indeed, the peace of God, which likewise surpasses understanding, guards (keeps) our hearts and minds in Christ Jesus (Phil. 4:7). Here peace and love function similarly; both surpass understanding, just as love is a greater power than knowledge (1 Cor. 8:1-3; 13:2ff.).

The *fifth* way, related to the fourth, that evil expresses itself is identified through a variety of terms denoting types of *rulership:* principalities, powers, dominions, thrones, etc. While these powers have a positive function within the world outside Christ — restraining evil as agents of God's wrath (Rom. 13:4 reflects the OT link between the wrath of God and the demonic; cf. 2 Sam. 24:1 with 1 Chron. 21:1), they readily become instruments of the demonic. Indeed, these powers crucified the Lord of Glory (1 Cor. 2:6-9).

The Principalities and the Powers

A comprehensive view of the "powers" texts in the NT, however, shows that the powers may be viewed positively as well as negatively. Further, numerous texts speak of God's conquest of the powers through the work of Jesus Christ. The "powers" texts thus fall into three different streams of thought, as follows. I classify them as (1) negative, (2) positive, and (3) normative. By normative I mean that those texts speak theologically of Christ's victory over the powers and thus disclose how Christian believers stand in relation to the powers. The authority of the believers, as declared in Ephesians 1:18-22, derives from their

10. For sustained description of this process see Patte's exposition of Paul's faith convictions in Romans 1–8 in *Paul's Faith and the Power of the Gospel,* pp. 256-87.

Three Views of the Powers

Negative	*Positive*	*Normative*
Matt. 4:8-10 (Luke 4:6-8): Satan over kingdoms	Rom. 13:1-7: ordained-ordered by God; servant of God's wrath, reward good, punish evil	Col. 2:15: God in Jesus disarmed, made public display of, triumphed over the powers
Eph. 6:11-12: world rulers of present darkness	1 Tim. 2:1-4: prayers for kings, peace abound, enable gospel to spread	Eph. 1:19-23: by resurrection power Jesus reigns over all rule, authority, power, and dominion
Revelation 13: the "beast," the servant of the dragon (12:9)	Tit. 3:1: be submissive, obedient for good work	Eph. 3:10: the church witnesses to the powers
1 Cor. 2:6-8: rulers ignorant of Jesus	1 Pet. 2:13-17: be subject to and honor emperor	1 Pet. 3:22: the powers under the feet of exalted Jesus
1 Cor. 6:4: least esteemed by the church	In all above, Christians are to be subject to the authorities. Further, Roman law is a friend to Paul (Acts 18:12-17; 22:22-29; 25:23-27; 26:32).	1 Cor. 15:24-26: the powers rendered powerless
Mark 10:42: rulers of this world "lord it over"		Romans 8:35-39: no power can separate us from God's love in Jesus Christ
Luke 13:1-3: Pilate's massacre		Eph. 6:12-18: the believers' warfare is against the powers
Luke 13:31-33: Herod–fox		Col. 2:10: Christ is head over all rule, authority
Mark 13:9-13: persecution of Christians, martyrdom of apostles		

relationship to the victorious Jesus Christ, seated at God's right hand, with all powers put under his feet. The vindicated, resurrected Jesus is exalted and given "the name above every name" to which every knee will one day bend and "declare that Jesus Christ is Lord" (Phil. 2:9-11; cf. Acts 2:36). This exalted Jesus Christ is also the crucified one who, "though he was in the form of God

. . . humbled himself and took the form of a slave, being born in human like-ness" (Phil. 2:5-8).

For this reason the texts in the third column on page 229 are normative. They manifest the reality of God's kingdom come and coming in the reign of Jesus Christ (so also 1 Cor. 15:24-27).

From these diverse descriptions of the powers it is clear that political powers may be viewed both negatively and positively in their functions. In light of the first two columns it is impossible from a New Testament point of view to hold either that the powers are positive, or that they are negative in es-sence. The powers are not intrinsically good or evil, but may be *either* good or evil depending upon how they function, in accord with either God's purpose in creation or, as a result of their rebellion against God's purpose, their fallen state. This state is described in Scripture only mythically and allusively, but nonetheless profoundly (Gen. 6:1-4; Isaiah 14; Ezekiel 28; Jude 6-7; and espe-cially the "watchers myth" in *1 Enoch*). The responses and deeds of humans actualize in historical existence either God's good angelic rule over humans and the universe or the horrifically evil "anti-creations" of the fallen angels and their powers, empowered often by demonic spirits. Thus the goodness or evil of the powers as we know them is dependent upon whether the people and/or the policies are responsive to God's will or Satan's conniving.

A key question here is whether the powers are simply what people make them to be or whether they have ontological standing. Can they in their rebel-lion and "fallenness" be described as evil, apart from evil human impulses? If this is the case, then when we speak of rulers as oppressive, we point to some-thing more than the evil that infects humans and/or corporate structures in a systemic manner. The reality of evil is beyond any person(s) at their helm. It is in the "structures" as such, but also beyond the structures. Their fallenness links back to the Satan power described above.[11]

In light of the other four ways of perceiving evil in Pauline thought, three declarations about the powers are true: the power of Satan is ever ready to enter the people and systems, thus functioning as the causative force of the evil; people in the structures make decisions that operationalize Satan's sinis-ter goals; and the structures as structures may become dominated by evil and

---

11. Here my view of Satan differs from Walter Wink's as described in *Unmasking the Powers*, pp. 9-40. While his treatment overall is very helpful, to connect the actualization of Sa-tan to "our (human) choices" (p. 32) is not adequate, in my view. Our choices may opera-tionalize Satan's power within or over us, but Satan's power is also prior to these choices. Hence the phrase "stand against the wiles of the devil" in Eph. 6:11. The very notion of temptation as portrayed in the NT presupposes an "other" power outside ourselves that seeks to make us choose against God/Christ.

thus become also structures of domination over human life, germinating and multiplying evil by nature of their impersonal, complex, and "super-human" functional reality.

Theologically, christologically, and ecclesiologically, the third stream is most important, since it presents Jesus' victory over the powers and guides Christians' understanding of their position, authority, and witness in relation to the powers. The core claims of these texts are:

> 1 Cor. 15:24-27: Every authority, rule, and power has been put in subjection to Christ; when Jesus hands over the kingdom to the Father, they will be stripped of all power.
>
> Col. 1:15-16, 20: The powers, in all their variant expressions, owe their origin to God's creative work through Jesus Christ as agent of creation, and are included in the ultimate reconciliation of all things in Christ.
>
> Col. 2:10, 15: Jesus is head over the powers (v. 10). God disarmed them by making a public exposure of them (i.e., of how they operated in the cross), and thus triumphed over them in Christ.
>
> Eph. 1:19-23: The exalted Lord Jesus Christ now reigns far above all rule and authority. All such powers are subject to Christ for the sake of the church, to enable it to fulfill the spread of knowledge of God and radiate his love to all (3:17-19).
>
> Eph. 3:9-10: The call of the church includes witness to the powers of the manifold wisdom of God in uniting formerly hostile parties in Christ.
>
> Eph. 6:12-18: Believers must take a stand against the strategies of the powers to trick, deceive, and defeat us. The armor of resistance is the same as God's in his long battle against evil.
>
> Rom. 8:35-39: Nothing in all God's creation, not even the powers, can separate believers from the love of God which is in Christ Jesus our Lord.
>
> 1 Pet. 3:22: All angels, authorities, powers are subject to Jesus Christ who is in heaven, at the right hand of God.
>
> Rev. 18:2b, 10c: "Fallen, fallen is Babylon the great. . . . For in one hour your judgment has come."

Scholarly study of this stream of emphasis has turned up numerous interpretive issues, some of which I identify here.[12]

---

12. For fuller analysis, see Swartley, "War and Peace in the New Testament." See also

1. Are the powers benign (Carr),[13] or adversarial to God's purposes (most writers)?

2. Are the powers to be demythologized and relegated to a primitive worldview (Bultmann) or viewed as spirit powers, super-intelligent demons opposing God's purposes, often associated with idolatry (Arnold, O'Brien)?[14]

3. Are the demonic powers to be understood in terms of and virtually identified with socioeconomic-political structures (Berkhof, Yoder, Tambasco, Wink),[15] and/or should these structures, systems, and institutions be understood in both inner and outer dimensions, invisible and visible, to ascertain their spirit "personality" (Tambasco, Wink)?[16]

Marva J. Dawn's excellent and accessible treatment of the various interpretations of the "powers" in *Powers, Weakness, and the Tabernacling of God*, pp. 1-34.

13. Carr, *Angels and Principalities*.

14. Arnold, *Ephesians: Power and Magic; Powers of Darkness*. Concurring with Arnold, O'Brien sees no need to demythologize this view, for we confront the same reality today, and the faithful church is called to vigilance against these powers through appropriating Christ's victory through prayer and the word of God. O'Brien, "Principalities and Powers," pp. 141-47.

15. Berkhof, *Christ and the Powers;* John H. Yoder, *Politics of Jesus*, pp. 135-214 (1994 edition, pp. 134-211); Tambasco, "Principalities, Powers and Peace"; Wink, *Naming The Powers; Unmasking the Powers*.

Marva Dawn analyses Jacques Ellul on this matter. She points out that in his earlier writings (*The Ethics of Freedom*, 1976) Ellul said that even after scrutinizing every dimension of political power, "we have still not apprehended its reality; [rather] *another power intervenes and indwells and uses political power, thus giving it a range and force that it does not have in itself.*" But she notes that later (in *The Subversion of Christianity*, 1986) Ellul identifies six great evil powers that the Bible speaks of: "Mammon, the prince of this world, the prince of lies, Satan, the devil, and death," which are characterized by "their functions: money, power, deception, accusation, division, and destruction. . . . There is no infernal world or hierarchy of fallen angels with superimposed eons. There is nothing behind it. We are told about powers that are concretely at work in the human world and have no other reality or mystery." Dawn observes that Ellul seems to have shifted his view. See her article "The Biblical Concept of 'the Principalities and Powers': John Yoder Points to Jacques Ellul" (quoting pp. 175, 184). In my judgment, Ellul's earlier and later views need to be seen as one whole, with the earlier informing the latter. Four of the six great powers Ellul speaks of are spirit-beings and cannot be exhausted by "their functions," which he identifies correctly!

16. Two more issues are: 1) whether Rom 13:1 assumes a double dimension, i.e., spiritual powers and human rulers (Cullmann, *The State in the New Testament;* Morrison, *The Powers That Be;* Yoder, *Politics*), or one decides in each use which of the two levels of meaning is intended to the exclusion of the other (Campenhausen, "Zur Auslegung von Röm. 13," and the further listing in Morrison, *The Powers*, p. 40; also Stott, *God's New Society*, pp. 267-75); and 2) whether Christ's victory over the powers makes them subject to the lordship of the exalted Christ and thus effects a change in their status (Berkhof, Yoder), or the effectual benefit of Christ's victory has for its locus believers only, while the scope of its effect extends only eschato-

The Christus Victor view of the atonement emphasizes Jesus' binding and plundering the demons' powers.[17] In Paul's writings, the death and resurrection of Jesus means cosmic victory over evil spiritual powers.[18]

How should we understand the powers today? In a sermon at Associated Mennonite Biblical Seminary, Metropolitan Paulos Mar Gregorios[19] of India spoke on Col. 1:15-20 under the title, "The Comprehensiveness of Christ." The Metropolitan put it well:

> I think the people of Colossae did not live in our kind of secular world. They could understand many things which we cannot understand — like thrones, powers, principalities, authorities. These are lost to us, but for the Colossians these were important concepts because in the prevailing culture of that time . . . the belief was that there were other beings besides ourselves in this cosmos — visible as well as invisible. We don't believe that. Our secular civilization tries to teach us that whatever is open to our senses is all that there is. . . . But that is not what the Colossian people believed. They believed in a whole hierarchy of beings surrounding the human community.[20]

In a later dinner conversation on this subject a pastoral counseling professor said, "Granted there are these various phenomena that we must consider." Gregorios incisively cut into the sentence, "Not phenomena, but *beings*." The incident exemplifies how steeped we are in our scientific worldview and how prone we are to reduce all reality to the empirical. Even God-talk points only to function of belief, not to an actual Being, whose Word-Act determines the reality of the empirical, as traditional Christian faith holds.

---

logically to the powers (Morrison). For overall insightful treatment of the topic, see Caird, *Principalities and Powers;* Dibelius, *Die Geisterwelt im Glauben des Paulus;* Schlier, *Principalities and Powers in the New Testament.*

17. Thomas Finger proposes that second-century reflection on atonement as the "deception of the devil" did not speak of actual deception. The "disguise" was none other than Jesus' true servant nature, which the "powers" could not perceive — since it stands in opposition to their nature; *thus* they were deceived: "Satan and the powers then were deceived by Jesus. But not because he tricked them by appearing in some deceitful disguise. In Jesus, God came to humankind as he truly was: gracious, forgiving, seeking to win people by love and not by force." Finger, *Christian Theology,* 1:333.

18. Tambasco, "Principalities, Powers and Peace," pp. 118-19. For a treatment that develops continuity between the Synoptics and Paul, see Finger and Swartley, "Bondage and Deliverance: Biblical and Theological Perspectives," pp. 10-38.

19. Formerly known as Paul Verghese in his Mennonite affiliation and student days at Associated Mennonite Biblical Seminary.

20. From a copy of his sermon.

Thomas McAlpine identifies four main approaches historically in understanding the powers: [21] Reformed, which is transformational in objective; Anabaptist, which emphasizes the importance of the church as a contrast community to the powers;[22] and the Third Wave approach (Peter Wagner), which employs as its chief means in missionary strategy the binding of evil powers possessing territorial control.[23] McAlpine's fourth approach is sociological-anthropological, which is for the most part comparatively descriptive of evil as understood and dealt with in various societies in relation to differing worldviews. It is best, in my perception of this matter, not to choose among these views, but to recognize that each of the first three holds an essentially correct aspect of the whole. In the actual performance of these truths, the reverse sequence is usually appropriate: First, confrontation of the powers in missionary proclamation of God's salvation in Jesus Christ that frees people from the dominion of the powers (Col. 1:13-14), as is also demonstrated in Acts (see above). Second, communities of faith are formed whose lives are ordered under the lordship of Christ, and whose living contrasts with life ordered by the powers of the empire or nation-state. Third, a witness of Christian faith is given to the government powers that calls them to closer approximation of their highest held moral standards.[24]

The most explicit description of Christ's triumph over the powers is: he "disarmed the principalities and powers, and made a public example of them" (Col. 2:15). Ernest Martin illumines the structure of this text, showing a parallel pattern for 2:13-15. In Greek, in each verse, clauses a and c are participial; clause b is declarative, with the finite verb:[25]

21. McAlpine, *Facing the Powers: What Are the Options?*

22. A variant to this emphasis is advanced by Richard A. Horsley in his concluding chapter in *Paul and Empire,* p. 244. Horsley holds that in Paul's authentic writings (he excludes Colossians and Ephesians), the *archontes* are earthly political rulers (1 Cor. 2:6-8; 15:24-28; Rom. 13:3). Both *archē* and *exousia* refer to rulers in the Roman imperial system. The notion of some spiritual cosmic meaning results from "Christian scholarly mystification" influenced heavily by Paul's disciples' uses in Colossians and Ephesians (n. 4).

23. McAlpine's description of this category is too restrictive. It should include a broader use of exorcism in the ministry of the church. Peter Wagner's theory and strategy regarding territorial powers is only one emphasis, and a disputed one among scholars and practitioners of deliverance ministry. See Arnold, *Three Crucial Questions about Spiritual Warfare.* See also McClain, *Claiming All Things for God,* for ritual use of exorcism to free social and political systemic power from demonic control.

24. Even though this position is identified by McAlpine as Reformed, it is striking that Anabaptist John H. Yoder, in *The Christian Witness to the State,* develops both a theology and procedure for this approach. Positions 1 and 2 are not mutually exclusive.

25. Martin, *Colossians and Philemon,* p. 113.

a. when *you* were dead in your transgressions and the uncircumcision of your flesh,
b. HE MADE *YOU* ALIVE TOGETHER WITH HIM,
c. having forgiven *us* all our transgressions,

a. having canceled out *the certificate of debt* consisting of decrees against us and which was hostile to us,
b. HE HAS TAKEN IT OUT OF THE WAY,
c. having nailed *it* to the cross.

a. When he had disarmed *the rulers and authorities,*
b. HE MADE A PUBLIC DISPLAY OF *THEM,*
c. having triumphed over *them* through him.

The language of v. 15 evokes the scene of Emperor Vespasian and his son Titus (the general responsible for Jerusalem's destruction) leading Jewish captors, putting them on display, in the streets of Rome after the fall of Jerusalem (70 CE). The text emphasizes that the defeated powers have been publicly displayed. From a gospel point of view, the imperial powers are no longer victor. Christ is victor over the powers!

Building on the meaning of the middle voice of the verb, Philip Bender proposes that Jesus *stripped himself off from* the powers' power, this being the means of his divine warfare and victory, which in turn is a pattern for the contrast community.[26] This in itself is witness to the powers. In another important text (Eph.1:20-23) Christ is the head, the church is his body, and all the powers are put under Christ's feet. Paul regards the new Christian com-

---

26. Philip D. Bender proposes that the middle form of the participle *apekdysamenos* indicates that Christ, rather than directly attacking the powers, stripped off their power from himself, thus eluding their grasp and creating a new community of power independent of the powers. He sums up his work on this text as follows ("The Holy War Trajectory in the Synoptic Gospels and the Pauline Writings," p. 44):

> . . . in the context of *apekdysamenos* as "stripping off from himself," [Col. 2:15] suggests that Christ's warfare against the Powers consisted 1) of his obedience to God unto death, resulting 2) in the unmasking of those Powers as adversaries of God and humanity, leading 3) to their disarming through the stripping away of their power of illusion, which now 4) exhibits them as weak and humiliated captives. In Christ, the Powers have been "deglorified," through the exposure of their presumptuous and hostile claims. Relative to the power of God as evidenced by Christ in his rejection of their claims through obedience to God unto death, the power of the Powers now appears as "weak and beggarly" (Gal. 4:9). For Paul, Christ's stripping away of the Powers was his instrument of divine warfare and victory.

munity, composed of previously hostile parties, as God's witness to the principalities and powers, a demonstration of God's power over all other so-called powers (Eph.3:9-10). The frequent use of Psalm 110:1 throughout the NT, speaking of Christ's rule at God's right hand, further testifies to Christ's victory over the powers.[27]

The consummation also has consequence for the powers, but here emerge two emphases not easily harmonized. In some texts the picture is that of "destroying [or better, 'rendering powerless'] every rule and authority" (1 Cor. 15:24-28; cf. 2 Thess. 2:3-11), but other texts speak of a reconciliation of the powers to God's purpose (Col. 1:19-20; Eph. 1:9-10). Revelation (see Chapter 12) contains the same dual emphasis. What is crystal clear is Jesus' lordship over the powers. Indeed, *Jesus is Lord and Victor!*

The Believers' Relationship to the Powers

Walter Pilgrim's recent study of the NT writings on the Christian believers' views of their relationship to the powers presents three different models of relationship: subordinationist (Pauline), critical distancing (Jesus and the Gospels, Acts), and endurance of oppression and persecution (Peter and Revelation). While Pilgrim regards Rom. 13:1-7 as Paul's primary contribution to the subject and acknowledges that it is basically a call to a subordinationist stance, yet he makes six points of qualification. These are:

> 1. Romans 13 does not intend to provide a developed Christian doctrine of the state, good for all occasions. Paul's aims were more limited. He speaks first of all to the historical situation in Rome. . . . Most important, his primary purpose is to offer ethical instruction on proper conduct toward rulers, not a political theory on the nature of the state.
>
> 2. Romans 13 and the other loyalty traditions [he has discussed 1 Tim. 2:1-4; Tit. 3:1-2] cannot be used to give unqualified status to all earthly governments as somehow established by God nor is its corollary unconditional obedience. . . . Paul does not speak to the crucial issue regarding governments who oppose the good or do not resist evil. What if rulers betray their divine mandate for justice or fundamentally abuse or misuse their power? There is in Romans only a "deafening silence" on this question.
>
> 3. Paul elsewhere gives evidence that Romans 13 is not the whole of his attitude toward those who hold political office. For Paul and the early

---

27. Hay, *Glory at the Right Hand*, pp. 59ff.

church, there is only one sovereign Lord: "Jesus Christ is Lord" (1 Cor. 12:3; 8:5-6; Rom. 10:9; etc.). On coins and inscriptions, the ruling Caesar claimed to be *divus Augustus* (divine Augustus). Paul preaches another as God and Lord. . . .

Paul's own experience with Roman rule and the so-called *pax Romana* was decidedly mixed. Although a Roman citizen by birth, he often felt its harsh and cruel face. In 2 Cor. 11:23-33, Paul enumerates at some length his sufferings, beatings, tortures, stonings, imprisonments, banishment, and nocturnal escape over a wall. Both Jewish and Roman officials were responsible for these actions. . . . Paul could scarcely have been naïve about Roman justice.

4. For Paul and the early church, the Christian's true citizenship belongs in the kingdom of God (Phil. 3:20). . . . The government, as part of this present age, belongs to those structures that will one day pass away (1 Cor. 2:6). [Pilgrim cites 1 Cor. 6:1-8 as one passage where Paul seems to oppose Christian involvement in the structures of the state.]

5. Central to Paul's message is "Christ crucified" (1 Cor. 2:2; Gal. 3:1; etc.). . . the reference to a "crucified Lord" would constantly bring to mind the injustice of Roman power. . . . Neither Paul nor his hearers could be naïve or sentimental about the empire that nailed their Lord to the cross.

6. Finally, consider Paul's understanding of Christian suffering. He himself imitates Christ as one who bears in his body the "sufferings of Christ" (2 Cor. 4:7-11; Gal. 6:17; Rom. 8:17; Phil. 3:10). This suffering is a direct result of his faithfulness to the gospel and the cause of Jesus Christ. . . .

For the moment, Paul counsels acceptance of one's suffering for the sake of Christ. Here he is joined by the other New Testament writings advocating an ethic of obedience. But . . . this loyalty tradition constitutes only one stream of New Testament thinking regarding the state. Other voices, perhaps dealing with governments that have become increasingly the enemy of the church, will counsel forms of resistance quite different from this tradition.[28]

Pilgrim's treatment is most helpful and concurs generally with my own study of Romans 13 in relation to the issue of obligation to pay taxes that are used to finance the huge military operation of the U.S. government. As Pilgrim's last paragraph indicates, the topic of the believers' relation to government authorities, who in actuality often do evil, must consider the NT as a whole, not just Romans 13. Luise Schottroff's study of Romans 12–13, correlat-

28. Pilgrim, *Uneasy Neighbors: Church and State in the New Testament*, pp. 7-36.

ing it with Matthew 5:38-48 and Jesus' wider teachings is most helpful. Schottroff's view on the paradoxical and necessary relationship between Christian resistance and nonresistance is theologically and exegetically profound.[29] For her commentary on "love of enemy," see Chapter 3 above. In her Romans 12–13 study, "Make Room for God's Wrath: Romans 12:14-21," she identifies a sevenfold parenesis:

"Do not curse" (12:14)
"Repay no one evil for evil" (12:17)
"Never avenge yourselves" (12:19)
"Do not be overcome by evil, but overcome evil with good" (12:21)
"Leave it to the wrath of God" (12:19)
"Vengeance is mine" (12:19)
"If your enemy is hungry, feed him, . . .
      for by so doing you will heap burning coals upon his head" (12:20)

All of these admonitions are *peacemaking means to peaceable ends*. As Richard Hays succinctly puts it commenting on Romans 12, "There is not a syllable in the Pauline letters that can be cited in support of Christians employing violence."[30] Some interpreters take the last image of heaping burning coals upon the enemy's head as a form of violence or consigning to God's judgment, but as Fitzmyer, after examining the numerous interpretations, says, this action must concur with the spirit of the other exhortations, extending a loving response.[31] William Klassen proposed such an interpretation, appealing to an Egyptian ritual in which coals of fire carried upon one's head (in some sort of pan) symbolized penitence, conversion from wrong to right action.[32] Toews also regards this as congruous with the acts of kindness in this larger exhortation:

Such action [kindness] Paul explains with the strategic metaphor of *burning coals upon his head*, signifying that it will confuse the opponent. It is not clear whether the metaphor connotes judgment . . . or symbolizes contrition and repentance. . . . But the exhortation to act kindly is clear. Responding to evil with hospitality and kindness has a positive effect — it unsettles the enemy. The final counter-action uses the imagery of a Chris-

29. Schottroff, "Give to Caesar What Belongs to Caesar and to God What Belongs to God."
30. Hays, *The Moral Vision of the New Testament*, p. 331.
31. Fitzmyer, *Romans*, pp. 657-58.
32. Klassen, "Coals of Fire."

tian standing in the middle of a battle with the evil of the present age. Do not respond to the power of evil by using the means of evil, hostility or retaliation, but with the power of good.[33]

To what extent does this nonretaliation/acts of kindness stance extend to Paul's exhortations to believers in their relationship to the governing authorities (13:1-7)? While I have appealed to a situational understanding of this text with other writers,[34] Schottroff does not. She argues that Rom. 12:2 and 13:2 present a normative pattern. In 12:2 the believer is called "to resist": "do not be conformed" to this age/world; in 13:2, "not to resist." The same Greek word noted earlier in Matt. 5:39 and Eph. 6:13, *anthistēmi*, is used. The resistance, Schottroff says, is against Satan and the world. In principle the believer does not resist the powers that God ordained. But living out the former command often puts Christians in collision with the state powers, because in them the very Satan that Christians must resist is at work. Christians did not desire conflict with the empire, and even at times sought to avoid it, but their faithfulness to the command to "resist" brought them into conflict. "The root of the problem was their resistance against Satan and sin as the true rulers of

---

33. Toews, *Romans*, p. 312.

34. Swartley, "How to Interpret the Bible: A Case Study of Romans 13:1-7 and the Payment of Taxes Used for War," drawing on Friedrich, Pöhlmann, and Stuhlmacher, "Situation und Intention von Röm 13:1-7." It may be that this entire instruction of 12:14–13:10 was occasioned by a tax revolt brewing at the time Paul wrote his letter. Roman historian Tacitus tells us that Nero faced a growing tax revolt in his early years of reign. The government had levied two types of tax: the direct or fixed "poll" tax (Latin *tributa*, Greek *phoros*, RSV "taxes") and the indirect or commission tax (Latin *portoria*, Greek *telos*, RSV "revenue"). The direct tax was collected by government officials; the indirect was hired out to agents for the highest bid, a system which led to extortion and exploitation of the people. This generated a tax revolt. In his desire to please the people at the beginning of his reign, Nero was about to rescind the commission tax.

> His impulse, however, after much preliminary praise of his magnanimity, was checked by his older advisers, who pointed out that the dissolution of the empire was certain if the revenues on which the state subsisted were to be curtailed: "For, the moment the duties on imports were removed, the logical sequel would be a demand for the abrogation of the direct taxes" (*Annals*, Book XIII; *Loeb Classical Library*, vol. 153, p. 89).

Possibly the Roman believers thought they should join the revolt and protest the evil and unjust system. But Paul's word, and the gospel word, is: What is necessary for you is to not repay evil with evil, but rather to overcome evil with good. Be subject to the authorities and pay your taxes. Let love only rule your lives and let other people, those in God's wrath department, care for the necessary restraint of evil. Yours is a different vocation: freedom from the powers that enables you to respond to evil not with evil. You follow Jesus Christ who has subjugated the powers and who frees you to be free while in your subjection to the powers. Thus you participate in my victory, says the God of our Lord Jesus Christ.

this world."[35] Further, she contends that the "resistance of Christians against Satan is not the resistance of the powerless. God's power is on their side."[36] Living through this paradox is what gave the early Christians their freedom for everyday service to God, even in an uncongenial or hostile environment.

The bottom line in both Pilgrim's and Schottroff's work is: Christian believers take a stand against evil, the work of Satan and his hosts. This stand guides discernment of when not to resist (i.e., when to be subordinate) and when to resist (for which Revelation presents a model). This resistance never uses violence, military power, or armed revolution. Those models are inimical to Christian faith, according to Jesus and his followers, as exemplified through the first three centuries (see note 53 below). Paul exhorts believers to live in peace (*eirēneuontes* in Rom. 12:18), and nonretaliation against power, even imperial power, is foundational. As Michael Gorman puts it, "Nonretaliation is thus both a loving and witness-bearing activity."[37] It is resistance of evil, but through the power of love and deeds of kindness. But at the same time, Paul also speaks of resisting *(antistēnai)* or standing against evil (Eph. 6:13), which raises the issue of spiritual warfare.

The Believers' "Warfare" against the "Powers"[38]

On the topic of "spiritual warfare," one must immediately caution against the "crusader" image that impelled Christians through the centuries into horrific persecution of their "enemies." Beginning under Theodosius II's reign in the fifth century there have been recurring persecutions of Jews by Christians.[39] Such massacres are worlds away from what the NT means when it speaks about standing clothed with Christian armor against the "principalities and powers," or against the wiles of the devil (Eph. 6:11). In fact, to *resist* participation in such persecutions would have been a concrete and laudable exercise of "spiritual warfare." Such actions on the part of the Christian church "crucify" Christ. In fact, all war does, for it violates what Jesus consistently taught.[40]

35. Schottroff, "Give to Caesar," pp. 242-43.
36. Schottroff, "Give to Caesar," p. 244.
37. Gorman, *Cruciformity,* p. 248.
38. See Thomas Yoder Neufeld's excellent discussion of the "powers" in *Ephesians,* both in his discussion of Eph. 6:10-18 (pp. 290-316) and his essay on "Powers" (pp. 353-59).
39. For an overview of the horrible attacks on Jewish communities in the fifth century under Theodosius II see Hans Küng's encyclopedic work, *The Religious Situation of Our Time: Judaism,* pp. 153-54.
40. Here see my description of the pacifist/nonresistant position in *Slavery, Sabbath, War, and Women,* pp. 112-37.

Harnack has described well Paul's "warfare" texts:

We encounter immediately with Paul a number of warlike-sounding admonitions and images (1 Thess. 5:8; 2 Cor. 6:7; Rom. 6:13-14, 23; 13:12; Eph. 6:10-18), and we see that they have their origin in the images of the Old Testament prophets. This is particularly clear with the most extended allegory of this kind (Eph. 6:10-18). But even its detailed execution shows at once that virtually everything, the weaponry and the battle, is meant in a spiritual sense. It states expressly that it is concerned with the "gospel of peace." So the whole presentation is given the character of a lofty paradox, and the military element is neutralized.[41]

The use of warfare language is an issue that cannot be glossed over, however. Miroslav Volf in his brilliant *Exclusion and Embrace* deals responsibly and helpfully with this issue:

Is not the language of "struggle" and "combat" inappropriate, however? Does it not run at cross-purposes with nonviolence? Consider the fact that Jesus' public ministry — his proclamation and enactment of the reign of God as the reign of God's truth and God's justice — was not a drama played out on an empty stage, vacated by other voices and actors. An empty stage was unavailable to him, as it is unavailable to us. It was there only in the beginning, before the dawn of creation. On the empty stage of nonexistence, God enacted the drama of creation — and the world came into being. Every subsequent drama is performed on an occupied stage: all spectators are performers. Especially in a creation infested with sin, the proclamation and enactment of the kingdom of truth and justice is never an act of pure positing, but always already a transgression into spaces occupied by others. Active opposition to the kingdom of Satan, the kingdom of deception and oppression, is therefore inseparable from the proclamation of the kingdom of God. It is this opposition that brought Jesus Christ to the cross; and it is this opposition that gave meaning to his nonviolence. It takes the struggle against deception and oppression to transform nonviolence from barren negativity into a creative possibility, from a quicksand into a foundation of a new world.[42]

Indeed, it is crucially important to understand that the numerous NT texts that use warfare imagery do not negate the ethic of nonretaliation and love of enemy. In fact, the battle against the spiritual powers is the possibility

41. Harnack, *Militia Christi*, pp. 35-36.
42. Volf, *Exclusion and Embrace*, p. 293.

for not retaliating and not using violence to resist the enemy. Analogous to the theology of God as Warrior in the OT, God's prerogative makes it possible for humans to be nonviolent. Believers are called to trust in God's protection and provision.[43] Standing against evil by putting on the "truth, justice, peace, etc." armor of God may be understood then as the best antidote to waging military warfare, as the early church of the first three centuries so clearly understood.[44]

The martial imagery and conflict between good and evil in Pauline writings are the logical extension of Jesus' confrontation of the demonic power in the Gospels, portions that comprise about one-third of the narrative text of Mark and Luke. Wink's study of "power" language and reality in volumes 1 and 2 of his trilogy points in the direction of considering all this as one whole.[45] The personal and systemic, structural aspects are present in both the Gospels and the Pauline writings.

Eph. 6:10-20 is not alone in portraying Christian living as a battle against evil, whether "the powers," Satan, or the devil. Leivestad in *Christ the Conqueror* makes this point, treating Ephesians 6 together with numerous other "victory" texts (like Eph. 4:8-10) and the NT as a whole.[46] His work shows a strong stratum of unity in NT thought, and especially among the seven letters of Paul and Ephesians and Colossians.[47]

Indeed, if peace with God (Rom. 5:1-11) and among believers achieved by the cross (Eph. 2:1-22) is to be maintained, spiritual warfare must be considered an essential feature of the Christian life. For while Christ disarmed or "depotentiated" the powers, they are not abolished. The term *katargeō* in 1 Cor. 15:26 cannot be translated "abolished."[48] It is essential, therefore, to stand against the idolatrous presumptions of the powers, whenever and wherever they so manifest themselves.

The well-known call to Christian warfare in Eph. 6:10-18[49] emphasizes this point. The spiritual armor listed here is derived mostly from Isaiah, where it earlier described God's battle against chaos and evil. The list is as follows:

---

43. On this point, see Lind, *Yahweh Is a Warrior*. Note also the helpful study by Gregory A. Boyd, *God at War: The Bible and Spiritual Conflict.*

44. They prayed to bind the spirits that incite war: Tertullian, *Apologia* 32; Origen, *Contra Celsum* 8.68-75; Athanasius, *De Incarnatione* 52.4-6. Thus they argued they do more for the peace of the empire than the army does.

45. I agree here with Wink, *Naming the Powers; Unmasking the Powers.*

46. Leivestad, *Christ the Conqueror: Ideas of Conflict and Victory in the New Testament.*

47. James G. Kallas has made the same point through his numerous writings (see Bibliography, and for Paul especially *The Satanward View*).

48. Wink, *Naming the Powers*, p. 52.

49. This text echoes Ps. 18:1-3 in that God provides the resources for security and victory.

girdlebelt around waist	Isa. 11:5
breastplate of righteousness	Isa. 59:17
feet shod with preparation of the gospel of peace	Isa. 52:7
shield of faith	Isa. 7:9b
helmet of salvation	Isa. 59:17
sword of spirit	Isa. 11:4
Word of God	Isa. 49:2

The OT context of these metaphors indicates that this passage is an extension of divine warfare, in which God stands against evil and chaos, and vanquishes opposing powers. This is not military warfare; these are divine attributes mighty in power against all that challenges or defies God's sovereignty. The passage begins with key emphases that permeate the whole: "Finally, be strong in the Lord and in the strength of *his power*. Put on the whole *armor of God*, so that you may be able to stand against the wiles of the devil" (6:10-11). Most important in understanding this text and spiritual warfare is that it is *God's* battle; it is God's armor. Believers wear *God's* armor and only then are they/we able to withstand in the struggle, "not against enemies of blood and flesh, but against the rulers, against the authorities, against the cosmic powers of this present darkness, against the spiritual forces of evil in the heavenly places" (6:12-13).

This listing of the foes against which believers struggle clearly indicates that this is not a military battle, in which one group exerts its domination through war against another (nation, ethnic group, or ideological group). Clinton Arnold puts this spiritual warfare text into the context of the Ephesian believers' past religious allegiances to the Artemis cult, with its various forms of magic and astrology, and to other mystery cults, in all of which great fear of demonic powers played a major role.[50] Hence Christ's victory is a conquest of the powers; the believers are called to stand against them with the divine armor: "Victory over the 'powers' is not assured apart from the appropriation of the power of God. Failure to resist allows the devil to reassert his dominion."[51]

This text is prone to gross misunderstanding, unless set within Paul's larger emphasis on Christ's victory over the powers, as noted above, and informed by the divine warfare theology of the OT culminating in the NT kingdom-peace-gospel combating evil (see the chapters on Mark and Luke above). Only then can we understand rightly what it means to put on the ar-

50. Arnold, *Ephesians, Power and Magic*, pp. 14-41.
51. Arnold, *Ephesians*, p. 121.

mor of God. Often commentators note that all parts of the armor, except the sword of the Spirit, are defensive. The point is a good one to the extent that it guards against misconstruing this text as a call to some sort of Christian crusade. In this view, the sword, the word of God, is offensive, since it is the means of evangelism, of rescuing people from the bondage of evil and gathering them into Christ's kingdom.[52]

This view, however, merits careful reconsideration. While the weapons of armor, except the sword, are primarily defensive, yet the spiritual attributes they denote have both an offensive and defensive side to them.[53] A certain tension thus exists between the tenor of the metaphor (belt, breastplate, shoes, etc.) and the spiritual virtue or action to which it connects. Truth, righteousness, salvation, gospel of peace, and faith are powerful in confronting and disarming the enemy. In actuality, in the Christian life, the offensive and defensive blend together. When believers are empowered with these attributes derived from God's character combating evil, they synergistically extend the *divine* warfare. They are then stronger in their defense to withstand the evil one. The danger of stressing only the defensive stance lies in its fostering what Yoder Neufeld describes as becoming a church that keeps to itself rather than confronting evil. "The church's true existence consists of the active and bold actualization of gospel truth, justice, peace, and liberation in human relationships."[54] The active call to peacemaking, so clear in 2:13-17, is not to be lost but empowered in this call to arms, putting on only the divine armor, and *standing* against evil by these peacemaking virtues.

Further, the church as a body is called to this spiritual vigilance. While individual responsibility should not be pitted against the corporate, it "is much more in keeping with the gist of Ephesians to see this summons to battle directed to the church as a whole, to the body of Christ acting as a unified divine force."[55] Both the individual and the corporate/structural must be maintained in understanding the manifestation of evil. As Yoder Neufeld

52. Clinton E. Arnold represents well this view: *Powers of Darkness: Principalities and Powers in Paul's Letters,* pp. 154-58.

53. See Yoder Neufeld, *Ephesians,* for the same point. He criticizes both H. Berkhof and J. H. Yoder, saying they "downplay the offensive nature of the church's struggle much more than does Ephesians" (315).

54. Yoder Neufeld, *Ephesians,* p. 315.

55. Yoder Neufeld, *Ephesians,* p. 292. Yoder Neufeld contends that in Ephesians 6 God's work as Divine Warrior is "democratized" so that the church, the saints, participate with God in the battle against evil (see his earlier work, *"Put on the Whole Armor of God,"* especially p. 111). While the term "democratized" may mislead because of its several connotations, the corporate call of this divine armor passage is important, as is the point that it is *God's* armor that believers corporately wear.

puts it: ". . . the view of demonic forces affecting persons is vulnerable to underestimating the broad-ranging opposition to God's efforts at peacemaking. Likewise, however, a view of the demonic restricted to influences on institutions in society is just as vulnerable to underestimating how individual persons may be bound (e.g., Luke 13:16)."[56] This inclusive approach to what believers contend against is important in being vigilant against "the flaming arrows of the evil one" (Eph. 6:16). It is important also in that it bears witness to the full canonical portrait: exorcising demons in the Synoptic Gospels and boldly proclaiming Jesus' lordship over all powers (gods and goddesses, rulers and authorities, principalities and powers) in Paul.

In 2 Cor. 10:3-6 Paul states clearly the nature of Christian warfare, that the weapons are not military or worldly ("carnal," KJV) in nature. Just as Rom. 16:20, "The God of peace will shortly crush Satan under your feet," exhibits a startling blend of war and peace imagery, so 2 Cor. 10:3-6, put alongside Rom. 12:17-21, presents a similar complementary set of images, one of warfare and the other of peacemaking. Both seek to overcome evil with good. Eph. 6:10-18 set beside 2:11-22 features another similar striking blend of peacemaking and warfare-resistance. The metaphor in the armor of "feet shod with the preparation of the gospel of peace" (KJV), evoking Isa. 52:7, oft-used by NT writers, is itself a blending of peacemaking and warfare imagery. Put succinctly, the battle is one of peacemaking, not some anticipated result *(end)* of literal warfare, but rather "standing against" with the divine armor as the *means* to peace. Believers are enlisted, yes at baptism,[57] in the warfare of peacemaking.

The Peace of Jesus Christ and the Peace of the Empire

We have examined the relation of the peace of Jesus Christ in Luke and Acts to the peace of the empire. Here we consider the findings on this matter that arise from Paul's own writings. Klaus Wengst, whose contribution I summarized in Chapter 2, aptly presents the peace of Jesus Christ as an alternative to the Pax Romana.[58] The peace of Jesus Christ and the Pax Romana consist of two competing visions, ways, and realms of commitment, so that given certain religio-political situations arising from this inherent conflict, believers

---

56. Yoder Neufeld, *Ephesians,* p. 314.

57. Yoder Neufeld emphasizes this point: baptism is enlistment in this new creation army of love and peacemaking. See *Ephesians,* pp. 311-12, 316.

58. Wengst, *Pax Romana,* pp. 7-51. The difference between the two *peaces* is evident in the structure and argument of his book.

choose the peace of Christ. In doing so, they live within the structures of the empire but look to Jesus Christ as Lord, not to the emperor. Nor do they laud the peace that the empire enforces by its vast military presence in the many provinces. Early Christians refused participation in the military because their primary loyalty was to Jesus Christ as Lord, not to the Roman emperor.[59]

Wengst titles his Pauline section "Our Citizenship Is in Heaven" and describes how Christians were regarded by Roman authorities as "those alien and unadapted to the world." He notes two foundational points: Nero blamed the Christians for starting the fire of Rome, and because their leader, Jesus of Nazareth, was crucified, a degree of political suspicion and rebel attitude settled on the "Christians," a name given to the Jesus followers. He cites Paul's experiences of "in blows, in imprisonments, in tumults" and then takes up the phrase in 1 Thess. 5:3 "in peace and security," the slogan of the *Pax Romana*, which the early Christians considered an illusion, a sure sign of the "day of the Lord." Instead, they "await a Savior from heaven" (Phil. 3:20). This is Paul's only use of "Savior" (but cf. Eph. 5:23 and numerous uses in the Pastorals), which in its political context is also a rejection of the saviors "bound up with the Hellenistic kings and then also with the Roman emperors."[60] In this context, Wengst discusses Paul's teaching on subjection to the authorities (see above), the believers' peace with God (treated only briefly, in contrast to the empire's peace), and the call to overcome evil with good.

Recent studies dependent upon archeological data and sociological perspectives argue that the traditional approach to Paul which focuses on his gospel's relation to Judaism is too one-sided. Neglected in these efforts is the relationship of Paul to the Roman Empire. Paul's planting of "assemblies" *(ekklēsiai)* in numerous cities and his proclamation of Jesus as Savior and Lord are broadside critiques of the empire. Epigraphic data show that the Caesar-cult was strong during Paul's time, ubiquitous through statues in all

---

59. When defending themselves against the charge of disloyalty or treason, early Christians responded in such manner that faithfulness to Jesus' teaching to love enemies, refusal therefore to kill another human being, and resistance of worship of the emperor as part of the compulsory military vows were all part of one seamless rationale. See Brock, "Why Did St. Maximilian Refuse to Serve in the Roman Army?" For an insightful survey of the issue and literature, see David G. Hunter, "A Decade of Research on Early Christians and Military Service"; see also Swartley, "War and Peace in the New Testament," 2328, especially n. 133; "War." For a careful assessment of the bearing of the "church orders" (the *Apostolic Tradition,* the *Canons* of Hippolytus, the *Testament of Our Lord,* and the *Apostolic Constitutions)* on the reasons for the early Christians' refusal to participate in the military, see Kreider, "Military Service in the Church Orders." See also the important study of Heinz-Lothar Barth, "Das Verhältnis des Frühen Christentums zum Militär."

60. Wengst, *Pax Romana,* p. 79.

major cities and all coins.[61] Further, numerous festivals in many cities promoted emperor loyalty, if not outright worship. Moreover, the hierarchal honor-shame systemic structure of the empire[62] was threatened by Paul's egalitarian approach in receiving people of all classes into the *koinonia* that cared intimately for each other (see the list of names — Greek, Latin, and likely Jewish — in Romans 16). The evidence in Paul's epistles for this counter-imperial politics is often overlooked. To make the point that Paul must be understood as countering imperial power, Horsley rhetorically queries whether Paul's primary stance is against Judaism:

> Certainly, not in the earliest extant letter, 1 Thessalonians, where the emphasis falls on the coming (or the day) of the Lord Jesus, who will rescue the believers from "the wrath that is coming," while destruction will come upon those who trust in the Roman imperial "peace and security" (1 Thess. 1:10; 2:19; 3:13; 4:13-18; 5:2-3). Not in 1 Corinthians, where Paul opposes Christ crucified on a Roman cross not only to wisdom, but to "the rulers of this age, who are doomed to perish" and to "every ruler and every authority and power" whom Christ is about to destroy (esp. 1 Cor. 2:6-8; 15:24). Not in Philippians, where both Paul and the Philippians struggle against persecution by official and/or local opponents, but will attain martyrlike vindication, and whose real citizenship is in heaven, from which they expect the true "Savior" (Phil. 1:15-30; 2:14-18; 3:20-21).[63]

The textual emphasis for this approach to Paul is evident in three interacting topoi in Paul's writing, summarized well by Gordon Zerbe:

> (1) the underlying millenarian script in his letters [hence the prominence of Phil. 3:20-21 in this literature]; (2) the use of politically loaded words to describe liberation and deliverance (salvation), the Messiah, and Messiah's community; (3) Paul's own experience of arrest, imprisonment, torture, and eventually execution at the hands of the Roman *imperium*.[64]

Zerbe presents in short compass the extensive textual evidence supporting these themes and documents it into secondary literature, including a quota-

---

61. See Zanker, "The Power of Images."

62. See the accessible and quite comprehensive treatment by deSilva, *Honor, Patronage, Kinship and Purity.* For Paul especially see Chow, "Patronage in Roman Corinth," Garnsey and Saller, "Patronal Power Relations," and Gordon, "The Veil of Power," all in Horsley, ed., *Paul and Empire,* as well as Horsley's introduction to the section, pp. 88-95.

63. Horsley, *Paul and Empire,* p. 6.

64. Gordon Zerbe, "The Politics of Paul," quoting p. 85.

tion from N. T. Wright regarding believers awaiting "the Savior, the Lord Jesus, the Messiah" (Phil. 3:20):

> These are Caesar-titles. The whole verse says: Jesus is Lord, and Caesar isn't. Caesar's empire, of which Philippi is the colonial outpost, is the parody; Jesus' empire, of which the Philippian church is the colonial outpost, is the reality.[65]

This new emphasis in Pauline study does not repudiate the *new perspective* on Paul, in which Paul is understood more in *continuity with* than against Judaism, but it goes beyond the Paul-Judaism paradigm to call for a new paradigm in which Paul *versus* imperial power figures crucially in understanding Paul's theology, including key theological terms: gospel, justification, salvation, Jesus' lordship, and perhaps even faith.[66] Georgi contends that Paul in writing Romans chooses terms that clearly indicate that the gospel of Jesus Christ is an alternative social order to Roman imperial social structure:

> Furthermore, every page of the letter contains indications that Paul has very concrete and critical objections to the dominant political theology of the Roman Empire under the principate. By using such loaded terms as *euangelion, pistis, dikaiosynē, and eirēnē* as central concepts in Romans, he evokes their associations to Roman political theology. Monuments of this theology were familiar to his contemporaries throughout the Empire, both east and west. And everyone carried the flyers of this ideology about in the form of Roman coins. . . .
>
> The peace ideology of the Roman Empire had long been a force in Roman praxis and propaganda. It achieved worldwide recognition in consequence of the miraculous peace established by Augustus. The statistics of *eirēnē* in Paul suggest that he is looking for critical engagement with this ideology. In Romans, the theme of peace plays a more extensive role than anywhere else in Paul (or the remainder of the New Testament): the word *eirēnē* appears ten times, the expression "to have peace" once. There are

---

65. Zerbe, "Politics of Paul," p. 91. Quotation from Wright, "Paul's Gospel and Caesar's Empire," p. 173.

66. See here the two books edited by Richard A. Horsley, *Paul and Empire* and *Paul and Politics*, and Elliott, *Liberating Paul*. For an engaging, accessible read of Paul's mission in counter-dimensions to the Roman world and its imperial ubiquitous presence, see Horsley and Silberman, *The Message and the Kingdom*. The Pauline story begins with chapter 6 (p. 114); the counter-imperial emphasis is especially clear in chapter 7, "The Assemblies of the Saints," pp. 145-62, and again in chapter 9, "Storming the Kingdom," pp. 184-204.

also many words of related meaning: *dikaiosynē, charis, chara, oikodomē, zoē, elpis* ("solidarity, grace, joy, constructive activity, life, hope").[67]

In responding to this new contribution to Pauline studies, N. T. Wright acknowledges its merit, summarizing its enrichment to Pauline study and registering a few methodological reservations.[68] Wright comments anew then on several key Pauline texts: Romans 1:3-4; 9:5 together with 15:12; 1:16-17; and Philippians 3:20-21. In each he sees more clearly and sharply the political force of Paul's *gospel,* Paul's *christology,* Paul's *salvation-righteousness,* and Paul's alternative vision of "awaiting from heaven our *Savior (sōtēr),* the Lord *(kyrios)* Jesus, the Messiah."[69] All are alternative political claims to similar sovereignty claims of the imperial cult. The Roman goddess, Justitia, like the Caesar cult itself, was widely celebrated in every city where Paul took the alternative gospel of Jesus as Lord and king. To proclaim that in Jesus Christ God's justice is unveiled once for all time and people was a counter-Roman imperial claim.[70] Likewise, the preaching of the cross, through which "God has annulled the wisdom of this age and of the rulers of this age," declares how "God's justice [is to] be realized in a world dominated by evil powers,"[71] not through Roman Pax Romana, but through the manifestation of God's covenant faithfulness in Jesus Christ and the *ekklēsia* and their *koinōnia,* harbingers of a new world order.

Acknowledging the apocalyptic mode of some of Paul's peace emphases, Mauser puts the "peace and security" text of 1 Thess. 5:3 in juxtaposition with the assurance in Rom. 16:20: "The God of peace will soon crush Satan

---

67. Dieter Georgi, *Theocracy in Paul's Praxis and Theology,* pp. 83, 85. His work is especially important. The portion from which this is quoted, "God Turned Upside Down," appears in Horsley, ed., *Paul and Empire,* pp. 148-57 (quoting pp. 148, 150).

68. N. T. Wright, "Paul's Gospel and Caesar's Empire," pp. 160-64.

69. Larry Hurtado's monumental work on "Devotion to Jesus" *(Lord Jesus Christ: Devotion to Jesus in Earliest Christianity)* would be enriched if he considered also the imperial political significance of worshipping Jesus as Savior, Christ, and Lord. His treatment of "Lord" in "Early Pauline Christianity" completely overlooks this dimension (pp. 108-18).

70. Wright, "Paul's Gospel," p. 171. Wright links this also to Judaism's expectation of the Messiah.

71. Elliott, "The Anti-Imperial Message of the Cross." For fuller treatment, see Elliott, *Liberating Paul,* pp. 93-140. The political ugliness of the cross, central in Paul's gospel preaching, constitutes a strong critique of the empire's torturous means of squelching feared revolt. That the cross becomes the power of salvation is a "stumbling block to Jews and foolishness to Gentiles" (1 Cor. 1:23). It mystifies us moderns as well. Its power to unite diverse peoples then and now is both mystery and miracle! Recent ideological negativity to the "cross" as important to faith, since it supposedly legitimates torture, misses the anti-imperial function of its early proclamation. While it may make Christian faith appealing to the current cultural ethos, it is also appalling for any responsible hermeneutic of Paul's gospel proclamation.

under your feet." Paul claims the true apocalyptic peace as a sure reality and includes as opponents not only those who promise false peace, but especially those fomenting dissensions, deceiving believers, and serving their own bellies (Rom. 16:17-19; cf. Phil. 3:17-21; 1 Cor. 6:12-20). Mauser attends to the political significance of Paul's gospel mission and message, examining as well the inner-ecclesial tensions evident in Paul's letters.[72]

When we consider Paul's sufferings incurred in his apostolic mission (seen in his own letters), it is clear the Pax Romana was not the grantor of peace for Paul (2 Cor. 4:7-12; 6:4-5, 8b-10; 11:16-33). Paul's suffering for the gospel is astounding! While five of his eight cited beatings are by Jews, the others are apparently from mob crowds or Roman authorities. Paul's entire list of hardships transpires within the governance of the Pax Romana. He endures all this within the *peace (?)* of the Roman imperium *because* he gives his life to plant new kingdom communities whose social composition and economic care for one another cross-cut the imperial politics of the Roman world. To speak of believers as "one new humanity" (Eph. 2:15b) deconstructs Roman imperial power and constitutes a counter social, economic, and political order of life. From the gospel-*peace* perspective of Jesus Christ the pseudo-nature of Rome's peace is glaring. As Gorman aptly describes it:

> The peace over which the emperor presided was, for many others, oppression, nothing less than raw power. Imperial power meant the power to crush opposition, to expand borders, to colonize, to enslave, and to crucify. It is no wonder, then, that enemies of the imperial power developed and sometimes found expression in outright revolt, as in the Jewish war of 66-70 and the revolt of 135.[73]

In the context of this Pax Romana peace-through-oppression, Paul proclaims a counter-peace, a peace that repudiates domination over others, unites people of diverse backgrounds into the Christ-bond of peace, exhorts believers to welcome one another as brothers and sisters in Christ overcoming hierarchical societal structures marking the honor-shame culture, and commits his mission to reallocate monetary resources from the wealthier newly founded churches to help the poor in Jerusalem. This is Paul's alternative peace-gospel, a subversive power in the Roman Empire that promised and inaugurated a new order of society, birthing a new socioeconomic, political creation.

---

72. Mauser's treatment, like Wengst's, includes much of the new emphases of Elliott and Horsley, except that Horsley's work builds on his earlier sociological and social world analyses, as well as on that of other scholars like John Dominic Crossan.

73. Gorman, *Cruciformity,* p. 270.

All this derived not from Paul's genius, but from the transforming power of God beamed into Paul's life through the Damascus road experience. Only in God's covenant faithfulness and the gospel of Jesus Christ could Paul claim the *peace* that marks the messenger as truly proclaiming the gospel, the *peace* that will shortly crush Satan, the *peace* that unites former enemies and creates one new humanity, the *peace* that passes understanding and keeps the heart and mind centered in Christ Jesus, the *peace* that springs from the fruit of the Spirit, pledge *(arrabōn)* of the fullness of the new age, the *peace* and *life* granted by fulfilling the requirements of the law, the *peace* that witnesses to *kingdom* of God reality, and the *peace of the new covenant* that God established in manifesting divine faithfulness in Jesus Christ, proffering the gift of righteousness to all who believe.

Empowered by this gift of God's *peace,* effectual through Jesus Christ, Paul exhorts believers to live peaceably with one another, and so far as possible, live peaceably with all people outside the community of faith. Thus also he could write, "And let the peace of Christ rule in your hearts, to which indeed you were called in the one body. And be thankful" (Col. 3:15). Indeed, God's gift of *peace* in Jesus Christ enabled Paul to extend the blessing of the God of peace as his epistolary, theological, and ethical signature.

Addendum: The Pastoral Epistles

In these chapters on Paul, the Pastoral Epistles have been included on occasion in citing references to the topics of peace and the believers' relation to the powers. One additional feature, that extends the emphasis of the latter part of this chapter, merits comment. While the Pastorals have often been viewed as accommodating to the prevailing cultural ethic on such matters as the role of women, submission of slaves, and subordination to government, they nevertheless present Jesus Christ with christological titles that suggest the Pastorals functioned to strengthen believers in their stance against the imperial cult. Frances Young makes this point in her commentary on the Pastorals, drawing on Adolf Deissmann's classic *Light from the Ancient East.*[74]

Three features in the Pastorals contribute to the proposal that "there is a

---

74. Young, *The Theology of the Pastoral Epistles,* pp. 63-65; Deissmann, *Light from the Ancient East,* pp. 349-78. In his massive study *Lord Jesus Christ* Larry W. Hurtado makes the same point, drawing on Young (pp. 516-18). Though Hurtado mentions several times that Christian devotion developed in the context of the emperor cult (pp. 22, 75-76, 102), this is the only occasion in his book where early Christian devotion to the Lord Jesus Christ is presented in its obvious political import. Hurtado addresses this point more fully in a forthcoming book.

deliberate placing of the Christ-cult against the Caesar-cult."[75] First, the vocabulary of gospel/*euangelion* (1 Tim. 1:11; 2 Tim. 1:8, 10; 2:8), manifestation or appearing/*epiphaneia* (1 Tim. 6:14; 2 Tim. 1:10; 4:1, 8; Tit. 2:13) along with the verbal form *epiphainō* (Tit. 2:11; 3:4), and the verb appear/*phaneroō* (1 Tim. 3:16; 2 Tim. 1:10; Tit. 1:3) was used of royal announcements and appearances of kings and emperors. Second, the manifestation or appearance of Jesus Christ, both in his coming to earth and in his final role as judge, is linked to salvation/*sōtēria* (1 Tim. 6:14; 2 Tim. 1:10; Tit. 2:13) and to God-status and action: "the blessed and only Sovereign, the King of kings and Lord of lords" (1 Tim. 6:15) and the one who "abolished death and brought life and immortality to light through the gospel" (2 Tim. 1:10). Third, while Jesus Christ is clearly distinguished from God as the "one mediator between God and humankind" (1 Tim. 2:5), yet God and Jesus Christ are identified with the same divine titles and actions. The title Lord/*kyrios* designates Jesus in numerous uses (1 Tim. 1:2, 12; 6:3, 14; 2 Tim. 1:2, 8), but in a series of uses in 2 Timothy (4:8, 17, 18, 22) the referent is ambiguous, though in light of the 1 Timothy uses, it is likely again Jesus Christ. The title Savior is used of God (1 Tim. 2:3; 4:10; Tit. 1:3; 2:10), Jesus Christ (2 Tim. 1:10; 2:10; 3:15), and both together (Tit. 1:3; 2:13; 3:4-6). While "King of the ages, immortal, invisible, the only God" (1 Tim. 1:17) clearly describes God, the referent for "King of kings and Lord of lords," also associated with "immortality" (1 Tim. 6:15), is ambiguous. These titles, with their fluidity in identity and function in relation to God and to Jesus Christ, document binitarian Christian worship, as Hurtado argues.[76]

But, further, because the titles Lord/*kyrios* and "King of kings and Lord of lords" were used in the eastern empire for Roman emperors, and because the title Savior or "Savior of the world" "was bestowed upon Julius Caesar, Augustus, Claudius, Vespasian, Titus, Trajan, Hadrian, and other emperors in Eastern inscriptions,"[77] first-century believers in the Roman Empire would likely hear in these titles and functions of God and Jesus Christ a counter-claim to Caesar's authority over their lives.[78] Thus Young says,

> . . . this Saviour Christ is the true, universal Saviour, manifested according to the providential plan of the universal God who is Saviour of all, but

---

75. Young, *Pastoral Epistles*, p. 65.

76. Hurtado, *Lord Jesus Christ*, pp. 512-18.

77. Young, *Pastoral Epistles*, p. 64.

78. Similarly, when readers hear, "but when the goodness and loving kindness of God our Savior appeared" (Tit. 3:4), they would hear this too as a counter-claim to the patronage system of the empire's governance. For *goodness* and *kindness (philanthrōpia)* are ascribed to the true Savior, God/Jesus Christ, not the emperor.

this Lord demands exclusive loyalty, and is therefore not only the universal Saviour but the particular Saviour and Lord of those who entrust themselves to his plan. His 'epiphany' as the man Jesus Christ, and his return as Lord and Judge, rival the claims of Lord Caesar, Saviour of the world; and Christ's slaves and servants should not be ashamed of the chains they may have to wear as subversives in the Caesar's empire.[79]

In light of these descriptions of God and Jesus Christ in the Pastoral Epistles, the politically quietist view of the Pastorals, especially 1 Tim. 2:1-6b, must be reassessed.

The challenge for Christian believers living faithfully in the empire required them to recognize the rightful limited role of earthly kings and all those in high positions, and also to be clear about who is the King of kings and Lord of lords. For this reason their subordination, even obedience *(peitharchein)*,[80] to the "rulers and authorities *(archais kai exousiais)*" is conditioned by an extended purpose clause that speaks of readiness to do a good *(agathon)* work, speak evil of no one, avoid quarreling, be gentle, and show perfect courtesy to all (Tit. 3:1b-2). The optimal political situation is that these earthly rulers function under the sovereignty of the true Savior (God/Jesus Christ) of all people, performing their roles so that believers may live faithfully the Christian moral life and proclaim the gospel so that all may come to worship God, the King of all ages, and Jesus Christ, King of kings and Lord of lords. Hence, believers "wait for the blessed hope and the manifestation of the glory of our great God and Savior, Jesus Christ" (Tit. 2:13).

79. Young, *Pastoral Epistles*, p. 65.

80. This is the only use of a term meaning "obedience." The following purpose clause significantly qualifies that obedience. The widely used *hypotassō* verbs describe voluntary subordination to the authorities (see Yoder, *Politics of Jesus*, pp. 175, 181, 187, 193-214 [1994 edition, pp. 172, 177-78, 183, 193-211]).

9 Hebrews, James, and 1 Peter: Peace Commitment Tested

Hebrews, James, and 1 Peter[1] reflect settings in which communities of faith are experiencing tests and trials. In Hebrews some of the members have suffered imprisonment (10:34; 13:3). In each community setting the call to endurance and to accept suffering depicts the pattern of true Christian response.

Hebrews

The catalog of faithful sufferers in Hebrews 11 culminates in Jesus as the pioneer and perfecter of faith in 12:2. Exegetical work that draws significant peace teaching from Hebrews is sparse, though the texts discussed below speak specifically of peace.

King of Peace and Son of God

Heb. 7:1-3 is plainly christological in its use of *eirēnē*. As commonly recognized, it is a midrash on Gen. 14:18-20.[2] By joining this text to Ps. 110:4, "Thou art a priest forever, after the order of Melchizedek," the writer declares Jesus to be royal Son of God (Psalm 110) who is king of justice and peace. Dinkler be-

1. Portions of this chapter are adapted from my article "War and Peace in the New Testament."

2. See here J. W. Thompson, "The Conceptual Background and Purpose of the Midrash in Hebrews VII"; Kobelski, *Melchizedek and Melchiresa,* p. 117. See Kobelski, pp. 120-21, for proposed hymnic arrangements of 7:3 and for other verses in ch. 7 as well.

lieves the link between Psalm 110 and Isa. 9:6 might be assumed in that the latter identifies the royal son as "Prince of Peace." Thus Heb. 7:2, in identifying Jesus Christ as "King of Peace," echoing Isaiah's "Prince of Peace," together with Ephesians 2:14 confirms "the linkage between Christ and *eirēnē*, a link of historical bearing by its manifestation in the liturgy."[3] Hebrews' use of Gen. 14:18-20 parallels that of Philo, who also identifies Melchizedek as king of peace *(basileus eirēnē)*.[4] The two functions of Melchizedek, denoted in 11QMelch, are to execute divine vengeance on the wicked and bring good news to the pious.[5] But Hebrews' use of the Melchizedek tradition does not portray Melchizedek in the judgment-vengeance role.[6] Rather, the twofold emphasis falls upon the eternal order of the Melchizedek priesthood and his identification as "king of righteousness" *(basileus dikaiosynēs)* and "king of peace" *(basileus salēm)*.

Hebrews puts Jesus as supreme and eternal high priest into typological relation with Melchizedek, while Paul put Jesus into typological relation with Abraham. Abraham's faithfulness anticipated the faithfulness of Jesus Christ (see Chapter 7 above). That Abraham, the scriptural prototype of faith prior to Jesus' coming, bows to Melchizedek, king of righteousness/justice, vindicates the integrity of his faith-righteousness. Further this faith-righteousness stands in the service of shalom, as Abraham pays tithe and gives homage to Melchizedek, king of Salem. Jerusalem is the cornerstone *(Jerus)* of peace (shalom), and *Melek-tsedeq* (king of righteousness) rules through his royalty and priesthood in this holy city. Represented in and by Abraham, the person of true faith bows before and toward the vision of righteousness and shalom.[7] The author gives primary emphasis to the eternal priestly order. Intertwined with this theme are Jesus' learning obedience through his suffering to qualify

---

3. Dinkler, "*Eirēnē*— The Early Christian Concept of Peace," p. 103 (1992 edition, p. 184).

4. *De legum allegoria* 3.79. See Horton, *Melchizedek Tradition*, p. 158; Fitzmyer, "'Now This Melchizedek . . . ,'" p. 316; Kobelski, *Melchizedek and Melchiresa*, p. 118.

5. J. Massyngberde Ford says the same, though she does so when treating the Lukan text. She holds that Isa. 61:1-3 serves as the textual heart of both 11QMelch and Luke 4:16-21 ("Reconciliation and Forgiveness in Luke's Gospel"). Hebrews, like Luke, differs from 11QMelch in that it does not portray the vengeance function in the use of the text. See also Kobelski, *Melchizedek and Melchiresa*, pp. 123, 141.

6. Even though, as Kobelski argues, the Melchizedek tradition was associated with the Son of Man tradition in Daniel 7 and both were linked to Psalm 110 (*Melchizedek and Melchiresa*, pp. 130-41).

7. Several Psalm texts describe the moral cluster of *shalom-peace*. "Steadfast love and faithfulness will meet; righteousness and peace will kiss each other" (Ps. 85:10); "Righteousness and justice are the foundation of your throne; steadfast love and faithfulness go before you" (Ps. 89:14).

him for perfect priestly service (5:7-10) and the designation of Jesus/ Melchizedek as king of righteousness and peace (7:1-3).

Jesus Christ, however, is not only typologically linked with the priestly order of Melchizedek, but fulfills and supersedes Melchizedek's person and role in three important and unique ways. First, Jesus the perfect high priest became such in that he was tested in every respect like all humans, but did not sin (Heb. 4:15b). He thus is able to sympathize with all contrite humans, for whom he mediates and intercedes (4:15a). Therefore we are encouraged to "approach the throne with boldness, so that we may receive mercy and find grace to help in time of need" (4:16). Second, through his godly fear, his learning obedience through his suffering, he is appointed (5:5), designated (v. 10) "a high priest according to the order of Melchizedek." The author cites Pss. 2:7 and 110:4 to clinch Jesus' sonship (exalted *above* the angels, see Heb. 1:5-14) and his Melchizedek-order priesthood (ch. 7). Jesus' prayer and supplication to God, with loud cries and tears, his reverent submission, and his learning "obedience through what he suffered" qualify him for perfection in his priestly role. Thus he has become and is forever "the source of eternal salvation for all who obey him." Third, Jesus qualifies as perfect high priest as king of enduring Salem-peace in that having been vindicated by God who raised him from the dead, his priesthood endures "through the power of an indestructible life" (7:16c, again quoting Ps. 110:4 for authorization).

On this triple basis Hebrews 7; 8:1-5; and 9:11–10:25 laud the benefits of Christ's superior priesthood, especially in his becoming a "once and for all" sacrifice for human sin. This point is so significant that 10:5-7 quotes Psalm 40:7-9, which repudiates the divine mandate of burnt sacrifices for sin. The violence and sacred peace-making of the former sacrificial system are exposed and rendered superfluous through Christ's once-and-for-all death (cf. Psalms 50 and 51 for critique of animal sacrifices already in the OT).[8] Honoring Jesus' exalted sonship and perfect priesthood is the christological basis for peace and peacemaking in Hebrews. For though Jesus was "for a little while made lower than the angels" he is "now crowned with glory and honor because of his suffering and death" (2:9). He alone qualifies as "priest forever," the "king of righteousness" who has become "the cornerstone of peace" (Heb. 7:1-3).

In an insightful essay titled "'But We Do See Jesus,'" John Howard Yoder comments on Heb. 2:9-10, one of several NT texts utilized to demonstrate the particularity of the gospel's claims amid the relativism and pluralism of the larger world:

---

8. This point as formulated here arises in part from R. Girard's work on *Violence and the Sacred* (see Chapter 13 below).

Instead of claiming for the Son of Adam his place just *beneath* the angels, however, Messiah is declared to be *above* them at the Lord's right hand, appointed Son, reflecting the stamp of the divine nature, upholding the universe. Yet this cosmic honor was no exemption from human limits. His perfection is not a timeless divine status but was *attained* through weakness with prayers and supplications, loud cries and tears. Fully assuming the priestly system, as both priest and victim, once for all he ends the claim of the sacrificial system to order the community of faith, putting in its place a new covenant, a new universalized priestly order, an unshakable kingdom.

Yet this cosmic sovereignty is not a simple possession. Our contribution to proving or bringing about this sovereignty is our faithfulness to Jesus.[9]

A significant peace perspective emerges from these texts in Hebrews, for they craft a portrait of Jesus fulfilling OT messianic anticipations. The depiction of Jesus combines royal Son and mysterious priest Melchizedek: Jesus is declared Son *above* the angels, culminates Melchizedek-type priesthood through obedience and suffering, bringing not violence (the vengeance in 11QMelch) but the righteousness of peace, and consummates the sacrificial system through his own death, a sacrifice without blemish obtaining eternal redemption (Heb. 9:14).[10] In this extended midrashic christological portrait of Jesus (chs. 1–10) Melchizedek, who "resembling the Son of God . . . remains a priest forever," yields to Jesus, who by his tested, faithful obedience even unto death and his being raised to "an indestructible life," indeed remains forever as "King of righteousness/justice *(dikaiosynē)*, king of Salem, which means King of peace *(eirēnē)*."

---

9. John Howard Yoder, *The Priestly Kingdom: Social Ethics as Gospel*, p. 51.

10. In his discussion of "Atonement: Christ the Exception," John Milbank utilizes Hebrews to accentuate the gift *(donum)* character of Jesus' death, which stands unique in that "Christ's earthly self-giving death is but a shadow of the true eternal peaceful process in the heavenly tabernacle, and redemption consists in Christ's transition from shadow to reality. . . ." Milbank then speaks of the cleansing of the heavenly altar, which he takes to mean a cleansing "from the impurity of cosmic powers, which infect even the very portals of Godhead." Jesus' death "is a showing . . . of that utter ecstatic self-giving which is eternal life itself." Milbank ends his philosophical and theological reflection on this point, saying, "Therefore in pouring himself as an apparent oblation upon the heavenly altar — which is the upper terminus for the escalating smoke of oblation, not its basement origin in bloodletting — Christ in truth passes as peaceful gift-that-returns beyond this altar to the right hand of the Father" (*Being Reconciled: Ontology and Pardon*, pp. 100-101).

Pursue Peace

The exhortation in Heb. 12:14 to "seek peace with everyone" flows out of the larger context, in which Jesus is "the pioneer *(archēgos)* and perfecter *(teleiotēs)* of the faith." Though not directly linked in the text with Jesus as prototypical model, the injunction, among others, structurally connects to the catalog of faith heroes, culminating in Jesus Christ. 12:1-2 is discussed in Chapter 13 below, with other NT texts calling believers to imitate the Christ model, whether Christ directly or Paul as he reflects Christ.

But here it is important to note that the command to "pursue peace" is not without context. Immediately preceding it and following the faith/faithful recital is a lengthy paragraph on God's discipline of those God loves. This echoes the earlier emphasis on Jesus' own discipline as a faithful Son, which includes suffering. The last verse of that paragraph is: "Now, discipline always seems painful rather than pleasant at the time, but later it yields the peaceful fruit of righteousness to those who have been trained by it" (12:11). The same leitmotif associated with Melchizedek and Jesus as perfected high priest recurs here. Peace is in adjectival relation to righteousness/justice, but both are viewed as the fruit of discipline, which extends the important section on faith/faithfulness.

Verses 12 and 13 extend corrective admonitions to strengthen the weak-kneed and the lame, with the goal that they be healed. Then follows the moral injunction to "pursue peace," combined with quest for holiness. This contrasts to "defilement" of character through a "root of bitterness" or acting immorally as Esau did in despising his birthright. The peace of this text, combined with holiness, is best understood as a call to character formation (see Chapter 15 below). Lack of such leads to negative social consequences, exemplified by Esau's action.

The God of Peace

Similarly, the climactic God of peace benediction in Heb. 13:20-21, evoking the Pauline stamp (see Chapter 7 above), culminates the overall narrative emphases of Jesus' perfected priesthood bought by his blood and the call to shape one's character to do good and fulfill God's will. The particular christological points made in the benediction echo 2:14-16. There, the God of peace accomplishes salvation through Jesus' dying and God's resurrection of the Lord Jesus. Jesus through his death smites the power of death, the devil, and thus frees humans from lifelong bondage and fear of death. This strikes a liberation chord that is also Pauline. Moreover the image of the Lord Jesus as "shepherd of the sheep" is a rather unexpected twist — for one might expect an image of priesthood. Indeed, the two images coalesce in the next motif of "eternal covenant." The God of peace makes this covenant with a purpose: to enable people to do the good, to give them completeness (one definition of shalom), and to do what is pleasing in God's sight. All this is *through Christ,* King of righteousness, King of peace. To him belongs the glory forever and ever!

The "better covenant" theology of Hebrews is explicated within a distinct peace accent: Jesus is King of peace; people are called to pursue peace with everyone; and the epistle climaxes with a blessing from the God of peace.[11] Clearly, this book belongs in and contributes to the "covenant of peace" canon.

James

The key section on peace and war in James is 3:17–4:4. Dibelius and Greeven regard 3:18 as an isolated saying and then confine the significance of 4:1-3 to inner passions and communal strife. They believe that the terms *machesthe* and *polemeite* in v. 2 should be translated as "engage in conflicts and disputes" (as in NRSV) rather than as "fight and wage war" (RSV) and that they "do not refer to political or national conflicts." While the latter point is true in that the author is addressing issues in the faith community, yet the sense of "fight and wage war" should not be toned down. Dibelius and Greeven cite comparable uses in which the terms occur in relation to strife and quarreling,[12] among them *1 Clement* 3:2, which, however, uses *polemos* together with terms denoting insurrection or uprising (*akatastasia* and *aichmalōsia*). Further, despite their hedging,[13] the use of

11. That God is described with this distinctive Pauline appellation may argue for Pauline authorship, but if the Epistle was written by someone in Paul's school of thought, an explanation for such is ready at hand.

12. Dibelius and Greeven, *James,* p. 216. Most of the texts quoted in nn. 41 and 44 connect the two Greek terms to "civic strife, wars, conspiracies, and murders." "For all the wars of Greeks and barbarians between themselves or against each other, so familiar to the tragic stage, are sprung from one source, desire *(epithymia),* the desire for money or glory or pleasure" (p. 216, n. 41).

13. Dibelius and Greeven question whether "murder" *(phoneuete)* really fits the text (they acknowledge that there are no textual variants), when followed by the lesser offense of being zealous or envious *(zēloute).* Still further, the causal explanation of "neglect in prayers" in v. 3, they say, hardly fits the seriousness of wars and murders (pp. 217-18). Their reasoning misses some essential insights, which Luke Timothy Johnson in his NIB commentary perceives and emphasizes (see above). Girard's theory of generative violence readily explains the relation be-

phoneuete in Jas. 4:2 ("kill" in RSV, "commit murder" in NRSV) indicates war-action within the community. The RSV translation of *en tois melesin hymōn* at the end of v. 1 as "within your members" is a better translation than NRSV's "within you." Dibelius and Greeven unduly limit and distort the text.

In contrast, Luke Timothy Johnson perceives that "jealousy" or "envy" lies at the heart of James's analysis of the moral failure of the community. Johnson draws on the Greco-Roman moralist tradition to contend that "envy" was regarded as the most loathsome of all vices since it leads to other evils. Socrates, he notes, regarded envy as the "ulcer of the soul." Thus when "jealousy" *(zēlos)* and "envy" *(phthonos)* occur in 3:14, 16; 4:2, James diagnoses the "sickness" in the community marked by the arrogance of the rich and humiliation of the poor (chs. 2 and 5) as rooted not in a wisdom that comes from above but in the basest of human vices, envy.

As in the moral literature of the time, envy leads to "hatred, boorishness, faithlessness, tyranny, malice, hubris, ill will, ambition, and above all arrogance."[14] Arrogance is sharply reprimanded in 4:6, and manifests itself in slander and judgment of fellow believers (4:11-12) and taking life's decisions into one's own hands (4:13-15). Thus, James says, "As it is, you boast in your arrogance: all such boasting is evil" (4:16). As an antidote to the vice of arrogance, James calls for the virtue of humility and trust in God (4:6-10). The envy that empowers arrogance generates murder of those who stifle one's desire to possess (4:2; 5:5-6). As Johnson puts it, "Ultimately, envy leads to murder (4:2). Killing the competition is the ultimate expression of envy."[15] In his "Reflections" on 3:13–4:10 (his unit for analysis), Johnson says,

> This passage is a reminder . . . that the evil we experience in the world through social upheaval and violence and war and murder is not simply the result of inadequate social structures, but is above all the result of a diseased human freedom that has committed itself to a wisdom from below, which distorts reality — and which finds expression in social structures that make such distortions systemic. James's analysis of envy and the way it leads to murder is the most explicit and powerful in the New Testament, providing dramatic evidence for the earlier proposition that desire gives birth to sin; and when sin comes to full term it brings forth

tween envy and murder. The failure to *submit* to God in prayer, humbling oneself, seeds the ground for envy to arise. The sequence fits perfectly in Girardian analysis (see Chapter 13 in this volume).

14. Luke Timothy Johnson, "Letter of James," p. 211.

15. Johnson, "James," p. 211.

death (1:15). No analysis is more pertinent to contemporary North American culture, which is virtually based on the logic of envy. . . .

Because James attributes social disruption and violence to a disease of the human heart, he does not propose any healing for it except through a turning to God that is explicit and wholehearted. In an age when religious belief does as much to divide as it does to unite, James points to a way of thinking about social ethics that can be engaged by all those who regard human freedom as deriving from and responsible to the God "who gives to all generously and ungrudgingly" (1:5 NRSV).[16]

With this perceptive insight into this text, Johnson, however, fails to comment on the peace *(eirēnikē-eirēnē)* motif at the heart of this text, which provides the alternative vision for community life. It leads to the harvest of righteousness-justice (3:18) that precludes the envious, arrogant actions described in 4:11-12 and 5:1-6 (also 2:1-6). Indeed, the two opposing paradigms of life are categorized in James as "friendship with the world," which is "enmity with God" (4:4), versus "friendship with God," which reckons one righteous/just, the fruit of peace (2:23; 3:18).

Peter Davids also perceives continuity between v. 17 and v. 18 and the following verses in ch. 4 as well. He notes that 3:18 is joined to the preceding verses as a genuine conclusion, not simply by the hook-words, *eirēnikē-eirēnē*, and that it forms a transition to 4:1ff. on wars and fightings.[17] Indeed, v. 18 is linked to its context by both "fruit of righteousness" and "good fruit." Both sets of terms are descriptive of the wisdom from above. Moreover, the *eirēnē* of 3:18 stands in opposition to the "wars" and "cravings" of 4:1 and their recurrence in verbal form in 4:2. These terms, expressive of the fruit of wrong or evil desire (*epithymeite* in 4:2), contrast to the fruit of righteousness or justice of 3:18. This desire comes from "cravings" (*hēdonōn* in v. 1) and indicate love for the world that is enmity with God (in v. 4). Further, viewed within James's larger concerns about the tensions and injustices between the rich and the poor in chs. 2 and 5,[18] it is significant that the bearing of justice-fruit rests on two conditions: *sowing in peace*, i.e., peacefully (*en eirēnē*, instrumental of manner), *by those who make peace* (*tois poiousin eirēnēn*, instrumental of agency).[19] This close relation between justice and peace is thoroughly He-

---

16. Johnson, "James," p. 213.

17. Peter Davids, *The Epistle of James: A Commentary on the Greek Text,* NIGTC (Grand Rapids: Eerdmans, 1982), p. 155.

18. See here C. H. Felder, "Partiality and God's Law: An Exegesis of James 2:1-3," *JRT* 39 (1982-83): 51-69.

19. Dibelius and Greeven argue for a dative of advantage because they regard the instru-

braic; the two are certainly complementary (see citations of Pss. 85:10; 89:14 above).

Peace may be viewed as the fruit of justice (Isa. 32:17), but this text accentuates the other side of the dialectic, that justice-fruit comes about when those who seek to make peace pursue their goal in a peaceful manner. This link between justice and peace accords with Paul's treatment of justification and peace leading to reconciliation bonded to one's salvific experience.[20] While Davids's statement, "Peace in the community, then, is the sum of the matter of doing justice," is correct, the parenesis, when seen within the larger socioeconomic tensions in the community,[21] may be viewed as paradigmatic of war and peace impulses in the political and national realm, as Johnson describes in the above quotation. The vocabulary and analysis fit these dimensions as well, even though this text does not address explicitly this sphere of life.

The topic in the context of 3:18 is wisdom, wise speech, and control of the tongue. Immediately, the text calls for discrimination between two kinds of wisdom, that which is earthly, unspiritual, devilish, and that which is "pure, peaceable, gentle, open to reason, full of mercy and good fruits, without uncertainty or insincerity." In this respect the justice and peace emphasis of v. 18 partakes of the wisdom tradition.

Concern for pure speech recurs in Jas. 4:11-12. This command to not speak evil of another extends the earlier emphases in 3:9-10 ("cursing those made in the image of God") and the moral teaching on nonretaliation. Slander against a community member is forbidden for two reasons: it makes one a judge of the law and usurps God's role, for God alone is the judge over evil.[22] The pretension of judging someone as evil to correct evil is off-limits for those whose justice-fruit depends solely upon peace, in content and means. Thus 4:11-12 climaxes an oppositional chain of thought that began in 3:17. Justice pursued in peace by those who make peace marks true wisdom and stands in opposition to the cravings and desire that generate envy and lead to fightings (violence) and murder, oppression of the poor and wars, and idolatrous pride and slander.

---

mental to be redundant with the other phrase, but they miss the dual dimension of the instrumental, both manner and agency. Davids accepts the instrumental for both phrases, and regards it a tautology for rhetorical effect (p. 155), but this too fails to grasp the double qualification of the text.

20. It is correct for Johnson to identify "conversion as a continuing process" as the first theme under "Reflections" for this passage (Johnson, "James," p. 212).

21. For discussion of the rich and poor theme see T. B. Maston, "Ethical Dimensions of James," *SWJTh* 12 (1969): 33-34.

22. Davids, *Epistle of James*, pp. 169-70.

1 Peter

1 Peter's contribution to peace has received significant attention in recent literature. Jesus himself is the example: "For to this you have been called, because Christ also suffered for you, leaving you an example, so that you should follow in his steps" (1 Pet. 2:21). Jesus' nonretaliation command functions crucially in 1 Peter 3:9-17 (as in Rom. 12:14-21).[23]

In the last two decades 1 Peter has moved from being "a victim of benign neglect" in exegetical treatment to being a valued canonical contribution in its own right rather than simply another of a kind — either one of the general epistles or essentially deutero-Pauline in nature.[24] Several authors have addressed specifically the relation of Peter's use of the nonretaliation command to Paul's use, to Jesus' use in the Gospels, and to extra-canonical uses.[25]

Both John Elliott and David Schroeder contribute significantly to the socio-cultural background of 1 Peter. Elliott has persuasively argued that the recipients of the letter, in their status, are "a combination of displaced persons who are currently *aliens permanently residing in (paroikia, paroikoi) or strangers temporarily visiting or passing through (parepidēmoi)* the four provinces of Asia Minor named in the salutation (1:1)."[26] Because of their paralegal status and only semi-citizenry, their identity as the "elect and the holy," the spiritual household, and the people of God becomes significant (2:5-10; cf. 4:17).[27]

A key interpretive issue in 1 Peter centers on whether the counsel to subjection in the household codes is passive or resistant in some sense. This point gains significance in light of Peter's distinctive form of the code that heads the usual "slave-master, wife-husband" series with "the authority of every human institution" (2:13). Schroeder focuses his study on the nature of the household and argues for a potential revolutionary social situation by Christian members in the household. He rejects the "passive interpretation" of the house-

---

23. J. Ramsey Michaels puts these two texts in parallel columns, showing that 1 Pet. 3:8 has exhortations similar to Rom. 12:16a, 15, 9-10, 16b, in that order; 3:9 has parallels in Rom. 12:17a, 14. See Michaels, *1 Peter,* p. 174.

24. See the review of literature by J. H. Elliott, "The Rehabilitation of an Exegetical Step-Child: 1 Peter in Recent Research."

25. Klassen, *Love of Enemies,* pp. 57, 122; John Piper, *Love Your Enemies,* pp. 14-18, Zerbe, *Non-retaliation in Early Jewish and New Testament Texts.* Zerbe includes an extensive study of nonretaliation in early Judaism, pp. 34-173.

26. Elliott, *A Home for the Homeless,* p. 48.

27. While Elliott limits the terminological contrast to the sociological (*Home,* p. 49), the spiritual and eschatological dimensions are also part of the picture.

hold codes and argues that the nonresistance enjoined in the exhortations is a form of resistance within the "stations." A new order and reality is at work through obedience to God, as demonstrated by Christ, which enables humans to both nonresist and resist at the same time. Nonresistance is shown in subjection and nonretaliation when reviled or persecuted. Resistance occurs by doing good in the face of evil and by not allowing the evil to determine the moral standard or response.[28]

1 Peter's cardinal texts related to peace represent two different foci of moral admonition. The first citation speaks of believers' relation to government authorities, the first paired relationship in the household code series: humans to government, slaves to masters, and wives to husbands. The recurring moral admonition not to return evil for evil is expressed in different forms in 2:21-25 and again in 3:9-18. The texts are: 2:13-17, 21-24; 3:9-18 (cf. 4:12-18).

1 Pet. 2:13-17 differs significantly from Paul's similar exhortation in Rom. 13:1-7, a point recognized in varying degrees by commentators. Horst Goldstein, in focusing specifically on the text's relationship to Rom. 13:1-7, argues that the occasion for the text, unlike Romans 13, is disillusionment with the empire because of its intensified "Kaiserkult." Christians were increasingly maligned and blasphemed for their faith, with the threat of persecution as well. He thus argues for a late date, around the end of Domitian's reign. 1 Peter's parenesis is against two fronts: one of uncritical compensatory loyalty to Caesar and his officials in local Asia Minor — the text counters this by relativizing state authority by use of the term "every human institution" *(anthrōpinē ktisis)*, in contrast to Paul's "appointed by God" — and an enthusiasm which disparaged the functions of the political authorities and the obligations of citizenship. Peter, while relativizing the ruler's authority, also partially, at least, counters it by grounding Christian subordination in accountability to God — Goldstein takes *kyrion* (Lord) to refer to God — the "will of God." This will be a testimony among Gentiles that will lead them to glorify God (2:12).[29]

Subordination to the king and governors is treated as part of a larger

---

28. Schroeder, "Once You Were No People"; "The New Testament Haustafeln: Egalitarian or Status Quo?" Schroeder's articles are based on his doctoral dissertation ("Die Haustafeln des Neuen Testaments"). His doctoral advisor was Leonhard Goppelt, whose contributions are reflected in aspects of Schroeder's work (the influence was likely reciprocal). See my summary of Goppelt's *Theology of the New Testament*, vol. 2, in Appendix 1 below. The most exhaustive analysis of the social situation in which 1 Peter was written and of the history of its interpretation is Larry Miller, "Christianisme et société dans la première lettre de Pierre."

29. Goldstein, "Die politischen Paränesen in 1 Petr 2 und Röm 13."

network of other social institutional relations: slaves and masters, husbands and wives, and young and old (5:1-5). In each of these the community's testimony to unbelievers is of supreme importance, while at the same time Peter appeals for accountability to God, not to the conventional mores of social institutions per se. In 2:17, however, Peter departs from the Prov. 24:21 tradition by distinguishing between "honor" as the king's due and "fear" as God's due. If this verse has a chiastic structure, as Bammel has proposed,[30] then "honor everyone" stands in parallel to "honor the emperor," a point that puts the emperor among humans, not as one with divine status. It also shows an arresting relation between "love the family of believers" and "fear God." God is *above* all others, and is alone to be *feared,* a respect and submission that acknowledges divine sovereignty.

A translation of the phrase *anthrōpinē ktisis* is crucial to the interpretation of the text. Peter Davids challenges the translation "every human institution." In classical Greek *anthrōpinē ktisis* designates the created world and its creatures; *anthrōpinē* limits the creatures to the humans. The author is simply designating the names of significant people that believers must relate to in structures of authority: Caesar, governors, masters, husbands. The phrase, *dia ton kyrion,* refers to Christ as it normally does in the NT and thus anticipates 2:21-25. Davids regards this text as strongly relativizing the authority of government:

> It is because Christ, not Caesar, is Lord that one submits. It is not that people such as rulers or masters have authority in themselves. On the contrary, they are only creatures of God. But the Lord gave an example of submission and the Lord wishes his teaching to be spoken well of . . . , and therefore *for his sake* one submits. But this limits submission, for submission can never be to anything he does not will. These authorities are and always remain creatures — Christ alone is ultimate Lord.[31]

Regarding the larger section in which this pericope occurs, it must be noted that 2:11–3:17 differs significantly from the household code sections in Colossians and Ephesians. Michaels observes that the parenesis is framed so as to bear in mind that "the Christian community faces outward to confront Roman society." The "case" of 2:12, when outsiders speak about believers as evil-

---

30. E. Bammel, after considering various ways this verse has been viewed, suggests that it is a chiasmus, an a-b-b-a structure with "honor" in both terms ("The Commands in I Peter II.17").

31. Davids, *The First Epistle of Peter,* p. 99. Like Goldstein, Davids sees a distinction in the levels of obligation in v. 17: honor to the king, but fear to God (p. 104).

doers, begins a key motif, as the recurring use of "evil-doers" *(kakopoiōn)* in 2:14 indicates. Michaels regards 2:13-17 as a transition between 2:11-12 and the following household relations, so that the entire segment relates "the universal obligations of Christians to their fellow citizens" to "their particular obligations to one another," and it also relates "their obligations to the emperor and civil magistrates" to "their obligations to God." Verse 17 is a terse summary: respect to everyone, love for fellow believers; reverent fear for God, respect to the emperor. 1 Peter stresses the believers' freedom to choose their response (v. 16) and grounds its injunctions in a Christian rationale *(dia ton kyrion,* "for the Lord's sake," v. 13), anticipating vv. 21-24.[32]

Close analysis of 2:21-24 in the Greek indicates that parts of it have a poetic hymnic quality, signifying a basic catechetical function to nurture believers in the congregations. This factor increases the proposal of some scholars that 1 Peter served as a baptismal liturgy.[33] Mary Schertz has identified hymnic forms in these texts and has arranged the Greek text in a chiastic form that shows the same meter for matching lines in the chiasm.[34] She proposes a ring composition for 2:21-24, with v. 21a and v. 24e forming an eight-syllable inclusio containing rhyming aorist passives for line-endings *(eklēthēte/ iathēte,* "have been called"/"have been healed"). The center, v. 23b, contains only six syllables *(paschōn ouk ēpeilei).*[35] It stands as the mnemonic heart of this nonretaliatory pattern of response: "when suffering, he did not threaten."

A significant feature of this text is the "imitation" appeal to Jesus as pattern to shape believers' response to evil. The exhortation to "follow in his steps" *(epakolouthēsēte tois ichnesin autou)* has left a profound impression upon Christian thought and action. This is prefaced with the term "example" *(hypogrammos),* used only here in the NT, which literally means "the pattern that a child, learning to write, traces over."[36] The call is unapologetically to shape one's moral life, especially in response to persecution, abuse, and evil, after the pattern of Jesus Christ, specifically his response to his abusers in his

---

32. Michaels, *1 Peter,* pp. 122-24.

33. Most notably Cross, *1 Peter, A Paschal Liturgy.* David Bartlett considers this proposal in his *NIB* commentary, noting though that the only reference to baptism is in 3:18-21. Nonetheless, "much of the epistle plays on themes that are appropriate to new Christians, whether explicitly growing out of baptismal traditions or otherwise" (Bartlett, "The First Letter of Peter," p. 241).

34. Schertz, "Nonretaliation and the Haustafeln in 1 Peter," pp. 267-74. Schertz uses the Nestle-Aland Greek text (twenty-sixth edition) for this analysis.

35. Schertz, "Nonretaliation and the Haustafeln," pp. 268-69.

36. Bartlett, "The First Letter of Peter," p. 282. I discuss this text further in Chapter 13 when examining "imitation" in the NT.

arrest and crucifixion. But, as noted in earlier discussions, this is not simply a *non*-action, but is a positive antidote to evil's power and perversity.

1 Pet. 3:9-17 clarifies this. Among other numerous perceptive analyses, Schertz points out a rhyming pattern in 3:10-12, *kakou/dolon, kakou/agathon, eirēnēn/autēn*.[37] The second pair prescribes that one turn from evil and do good. The third puts a double accent on peace: seek *peace (eirēnēn)* and pursue it *(autēn)*. Vv. 10-12 cite Ps. 34:12-16a (LXX) to authorize the ethical injunction in v. 9 not to return evil for evil. Literary analysis of recurring motifs in this section demonstrates the dominance of the ethical opposition between good and evil and stresses positive action to overcome evil with good (this analysis strengthens Schertz's contribution[38]). Significantly, the terms "evil" and "good" (with variants of doing evil or good) recur in partial or complete "evil-good" opposition a dozen times between 2:12 and 3:17:[39]

> Maintain *good* conduct . . . so that when you are accused of evil-doing they will see your *good works* (2:12).
>
> Governors are to punish *evil-doers* and praise *good-doers;* by being subject and *doing good* you put to shame the *ignorance of foolish humans* (same word as in v. 13 to describe the *human* institution) (2:14-15).
>
> God approves enduring suffering for *doing good* but not for *sinning* (2:20; v. 23 as parallel thought, but with *not reviling* when reviled and *not threatening* when suffering).
>
> Wives are to be *good doers* and not *terrified,* presumably by *evil* treatment (3:6).
>
> Do not return *evil for evil,* but rather *bless* (3:9).
>
> He who sees *good* days keeps his lips from speaking *evil* (3:10).
>
> Turn away from *evil* and do *good* (3:11).
>
> *Seek peace and pursue it* (3:11).
>
> The Lord regards the *righteous* . . . but is against those doing *evil* (3:12).
>
> Who is there to do *evil* against you if you are zealous for the *good* (3:13)?
>
> When you keep a clear conscience when abused, those who *revile* you for *good* in Christ are shamed (3:16).
>
> It is better to suffer for doing *good* than for doing *evil* (3:17).

The permeation of this "good" *(agathos)* and "evil" *(kakos)* vocabulary indicates that this is the dominant theme of this particular text. That this termi-

---

37. Schertz, "Nonretaliation and the Haustafeln," p. 274.
38. Schertz, "Likewise You Wives," p. 78.
39. Swartley, "Method and Understanding for Texts and Disciples," pp. 115-16.

nology occurs in each of the five sub-units indicates also the author's intention, namely, that a particular kind of conduct, i.e., *doing good,* is called for in the context of others doing *evil* to believers. The text focuses, however, not on any of the institutions *per se,* but on the way in which the institutions and relationships express themselves. The situation envisioned by the epistle is that of believers experiencing evil in each relationship: believers from authorities, slaves from masters, and wives from husbands. The central unit (2:21-25) provides the model for Christian response and the last (3:13-17) a general warranting summary.

The moral admonition in the key text 3:9-17 is framed by Christ's own example in 2:21-25 and 3:18a-c: "For Christ also suffered for sins once for all, the righteous for the unrighteous, in order to bring you to God." In the related pericope in 4:13, the believers' sufferings are to be understood as "sharing Christ's sufferings" (*koinōneite tois tou Christou pathēmasin;* cf. Col. 1:24). While Peter appeals directly to Christ as the moral paradigm, he also punctuates this model with trusting God, the faithful Creator. Jesus' own suffering has similar ultimate warrant: "he entrusted himself to the one who judges justly" (2:23d). In light of the tendency to focus solely on Christ for this pattern of nonretaliation and suffering, it is important also to see its ultimate grounding in God. Erland Waltner points out that "God" (*theos*) occurs 105 times in 1 Peter, not a "distant reality" and "not only one to be worshiped (2:5; 4:11) but one who can be trusted (1:21; 4:19; 5:7) and also one to be reckoned with (1:17; 2:23; 4:5, 17) as the final arbiter and creator of justice."[40]

Since these believers lived in a social setting marginalized from the dominant communities, their response was also understood as a witness, even an *apologia.* As Waltner puts it,

> they are called to become the kind of loving community that practices forgiving love, that rejects retaliation, and that thus blesses others even as it experiences the blessing of its own calling. To be this kind of community is one dimension of the church's mission in the midst of a hostile society. . . .
>
> Out of their living hope, grounded on God's act of raising Jesus, not only salvation but nonretaliating, peacemaking love has become possible. Their mission begins with becoming a community of hope in the midst of a hostile world, a community of forgiving love in a violent world, and a community of witness and service in the midst of those who misunderstand, misinterpret, and mistreat them. They are not to remain silent or inactive in such a world but are to speak, to proclaim, to confront evil

---

40. Waltner, "Reign of God, Mission, and Peace in 1 Peter," p. 237.

with truth and love, even as they turn from it. They live and witness in a spirit and manner that is congruent with the nonretaliating, peacemaking love of Jesus Christ.[41]

In concluding his exhaustive study of the history of interpretation of 1 Peter and his interpretation of that history, Larry Miller contends that 1 Peter's response to its social situation is not simply one of adopting pragmatic strategies, as a minority group, for peaceful coexistence with the authorities and those who persecute. Rather, the prescribed response is first and foremost that of remaining faithful to the gospel of Jesus Christ and thus presenting a witness to society with transformative intention and effect. Their response was not violent revolution, nor passive subjection, nor endorsing the status quo of social conventions, but seeking good in the face of evil and mediating blessing even to those who abuse and persecute.[42] Indeed, these exhortations echo Jesus' nonretaliatory teachings in Matt. 5:38-42 and Luke 6:27-36.

The difficult and less than perspicuous text in 1 Pet. 3:18-22 also substantiates the moral teaching of 3:9-17, according to Mary Schertz's interpretation. The apparent digression of "preaching to captive spirits" is exemplary of the nonretaliatory Christ who overcomes evil with good: "In other words, the resistance the believers offer to evil by bonding in baptism and not repaying-in-kind is grounded in a hope that is, in turn, grounded in a cosmic reality. The nonretaliatory Christ, vindicated by God, won over the imprisoned spirits. Therefore the nonretaliatory readers, vindicated by God, will win over their opponents."[43] This elusive text then is one with the nonretaliatory ethic of 2:21-24 and 3:9-17 and extends this perspective to Jesus' victory over the powers of evil. Jesus is presented again as prototype, reinforcing the portrait of 2:21-24.

41. Waltner, "Reign of God," pp. 240, 247.

42. Larry Miller, "Christianisme et société," pp. 505-7, 514-24. In this respect, Miller's emphasis is similar to Schroeder's.

43. Schertz, "Nonretaliation," pp. 277-78; "Radical Trust in the Just Judge." This interpretation of 3:18ff. differs from most, but it fits best with the theme of its larger context. See Davids for a summary of five different understandings of Jesus' preaching to the spirits in prison and his own argument that it means Jesus proclaimed judgment to "the fallen angels, sealing their doom as he triumphed over sin and death and hell, redeeming human beings" (*1 Peter*, pp. 138-40, citation on p. 140). If this interpretation is correct, then this pericope's emphasis contrasts sharply to its context. The nonretaliatory spirit commended for Christians is vindicated, as it were, by Christ's judgment of evil. While this is not impossible, it is unlikely, for it breaks the function of Christ as moral prototype for believers, a point quite basic to 1 Peter as a whole, not only in 2:21-24, but again in 4:1-6. For Davids's excellent discussion of Jesus as moral paradigm, see *1 Peter*, pp. 108-9.

The related text in 1 Pet. 4:13-19 focuses specifically on suffering and willingness to suffer not "as a murderer, a thief, a criminal, or even as a mischief-maker." Rather, when suffering comes from standing true to the gospel, Christians are to "rejoice insofar as you are sharing Christ's sufferings." They will then "be glad and shout for joy when his glory is revealed." This interpretation of suffering has at its center a specific form of nonretaliation: "If you are reviled for the name of Christ, you are blessed, because the Spirit of glory, which is the Spirit of God, is resting on you" (4:14). The section ends with "let those suffering in accordance with God's will entrust themselves to a faithful Creator, while continuing to do good" (v. 19).

How then do we assess these teachings when faced with oppressive situations: humans degraded by government authorities, slaves beaten by masters, wives battered by husbands? The answer is difficult in light of this teaching. Schertz addresses this issue directly. She concurs with Schroeder's emphasis that the text plants revolutionary seeds within a firmly established hierarchical structure. But she also observes that the rhetoric of the text is readily supportive of oppression when believers not in the minority, powerless status in society use the text to legitimate hierarchical order and exert control over subjects.

How then do these texts bear upon the war and peace issue? First, they do not bless the social institutions that structure patterns of injustice.[44] By putting the Christ-tormentors paradigm between the slave-master and wife-husband injunctions — perhaps also at the center of a five-unit segment[45] — and then concluding the series with a homily on good and evil, the text acknowledges that evil and injustice occur within those structural relationships.

Second, the text provides a pattern of response to evil and injustice that might be called a "replacement strategy." Do good instead of evil, and thus

44. J. H. Elliott and D. Balch debate the function of the Domestic Codes. Balch argues that the entire book functioned to assimilate Christians into their social order; Elliott contends that the admonitions functioned to encourage Christians in their separate and somewhat alienated status in society. See Elliott, "I Peter, Its Situation and Strategy"; and Balch, "Hellenization/Acculturation in 1 Peter"; Let Wives Be Submissive, pp. 81-109. Elliott is more convincing, in my judgment.

45. Schertz proposes this in "Nonretaliation," p. 265; also in "Likewise You Wives," p. 80. But Ben C. Ollenburger dissents, contending that the text does not suggest that civil government, slavery, and patriarchy are evils to be suffered. Rather, "It is the entire community, living under imperial power — slaves, wives, and husbands — who are exhorted not to return evil for evil" ("Is God the Friend of Slaves and Wives?" p. 101). But, as noted above, the good-evil opposition permeates the entire complex (Swartley, "Method"). It does appear, however, that moral judgment of the institutions is not the concern of the text; the primary focus, rather, is the Christian response when evil is spoken against them or done to them.

seek peace and pursue it (3:11b). This double imperative calls for action; it can in no way be conscripted for passivity in the face of injustice and evil. But it is action controlled and limited by doing good and not defacing the Christian witness (3:10, 11a, 13, 16b).

Third, the text interprets suffering as having positive significance. To be sure, the ethical paradigm developed here assumes suffering as an essential part of Christian faithfulness (see 4:1-6). Suffering is interpreted by Christ's own model of suffering when threatened, the heart of the christological hymn as patterned by Schertz. In this precise way of response to evil, 1 Peter calls us to "follow in his steps" *(hina epakolouthēsēte tois ichnesin autou).*

Fourth, given the realities of the human condition, it is utopian to think that followers of Christ can live apart from structures and experiences of injustice, evil, and oppression. To fight such by rebellion against the structures or by war to defend human rights may be ways to seek to achieve greater justice, but it is not 1 Peter's answer. Rather, the alternative to revolt or war is the way of nonretaliation, suffering, and pursuit of peace that does good in the face of evil.

Fifth, 1 Peter also affirms God's vindication of the way of nonretaliation in declaring Jesus' triumph over the evil foes. Strikingly, after the somewhat obscure train of thought in 3:18-20, ch. 3 ends with a victory note: Jesus' resurrection, exaltation, and reign, with angels, authorities, and powers subject to him.[46] To this accomplishment the believer is linked by baptism, an appeal to God for a clear conscience. Baptism is understood in terms of moral identity with Christ, a distinctive way of pursuing peace when reviled, amid suffering, and in obedient hope in God. It is striking that this text, with leaps in thought, ends up by extolling Jesus Christ's relation to the powers, thus linking this baptismal text back to the topic of 2:13-17. Hence, again the book's function in addressing how believers relate to orders of power, and governing powers specifically, is high on its agenda.

For this reason 1 Peter is thus most relevant to contemporary Christian discussions. Benedikt Schwank rightly asserts that although 1 Peter has often been neglected in the discussion of NT views on the relation of Christians to the state, it is the clearest NT witness on this topic.[47] The Christians are admonished to be "as free" *(hōs eleutheroi)* in relation to the governing powers, but "as slaves of God" *(hōs theou douloi).*[48] Schwank holds that this rationale

---

46. My treatment of this text has been informed by both Schertz's work and that of Dalton, *Christ's Proclamation to the Spirits.*

47. P. Benedikt Schwank, "Wie Freie — aber als Sklaven Gottes," p. 5.

48. This judgment also concurs with Larry Miller's assessment in "Christianisme et société."

differs markedly from that in Romans 13, which regards the rulers as appointed ministers of God's governance over the secular order. Here, rather, one's subjection is the will of God and "on account of the Lord [Christ] *(dia ton kyrion),*" anticipating the prototypical function of Christ's conduct in the ring center, 2:21-24.

The designation of the Christians as strangers passing through *(parepidēmois),* stated immediately in the opening (1:1), and the author's locating of his writing "from Babylon" (5:13) reflect the status of Diaspora (Jewish) Christians in the empire. Schwank locates the writing of the book early, close to the time of the fire in Rome, suggesting that these conditions inform the tone and emphases of the book.[49]

Those who hold, however, that this epistle together with the other catholic epistles was written to counter revolutionary impulses among Christians in the empire are likely wrong.[50] For the recurring emphasis of 1 Peter's sense of political responsibility is expressed in doing good, staying free of evil, and maintaining a witness that glorifies God. Michaels rightly observes, after citing numerous parallels between 1 Peter and the Sermon on the Mount: "The ethical thrust of the epistle is to equate the radical command to love one's enemies with the doing of good in a variety of social situations in Roman society."[51] Davids describes well the emerging status of early Christians in the empire, their attitude toward Roman rule and order, and their discernment of moral boundaries that did not violate their primary loyalty to Jesus Christ:

> The Jews were aware that God controlled history and used even pagans to do his will. This did not mean that God approved of their means or would not punish them, but it did mean that they were not outside his purpose (Isa. 1:20; 5:23-29; 10:5-11; 45:1; Jer. 5:15-17; 16:3; 21:4-7; 25:9; 27:6; 43:10). As a result, even though the Jews in general believed that the Messiah would come and destroy their Roman rulers, they offered sacrifices and prayers for the Emperor (Philo, *Legatio* 157.355-56; Josephus, *Wars* 2.197; *C. Ap.* 2.77). Even Roman order was better than anarchy. Christians also followed this pattern, as Matt. 22:21, 1 Tim. 2:1-3, and Tit. 3:1 show. But, while due appropriate honor and rightly to be prayed for, the Emperor was human and therefore neither to receive blanket approval nor ultimate reverence, both of which were reserved for God alone. This bal-

---

49. If this is indeed the case, then the vocabulary of 4:12-18, "fiery ordeal . . . reproached . . . as a Christian . . . let him not be ashamed" *(pyrōsei . . . oneidizesthe . . . hōs Christianos . . . mē aischynesthō)* is especially striking.

50. Sleeper, "Political Responsibilty according to 1 Peter."

51. Michaels, *1 Peter,* pp. xlii-xliii.

ance made the church of the next few centuries refuse both revolution (e.g., the Jerusalem church fled Jerusalem rather than take part in the war against Rome in A.D. 66-70) and participation in the army; she would also both speak respectfully and appreciatively of Roman order, and refuse to give even a pinch of incense to the Emperor in worship (their equivalent of the practice of saluting the flag in the United States). Pagans would think them foolish for their obedience to law in general (which they often tried to avoid), and more foolish for their disobedience to the command to take part in a simple and relatively meaningless patriotic ceremony of worship. But it was that balance that Peter felt best expressed the truth to which Christians bear witness.[52]

1 Pet. 3:9-17, 18-22 was used extensively to empower martyrs, both in the early church and among the Anabaptists in the sixteenth century.[53] Erland Waltner illustrates this by narrating the stories of three early church women martyrs, Blandina, Perpetua, and her slave Felicitas, as well as three Anabaptist martyrs. The Anabaptists appealed often to these verses from this section of 1 Peter in support of their defenselessness before authorities, but also to witness to the authorities.[54] Entering the ark as Noah did was used as a model for *believing* the word of the Lord. One is thus saved in baptism through *believing* and *obeying*. Baptism is a pledge of faith that witnesses to a clear conscience and declares willingness to suffer and die for the faith through obedience rooted in confession of Jesus as Savior and Lord.[55]

For Peter, the believers' identity is that of "a chosen race, a royal priesthood, a holy nation, God's own people, in order that you may proclaim the mighty acts of him who called you out of darkness into his marvelous light" (2:9). For this reason, even in a hostile socio-political environment, believers live as Christ lived, not returning evil for evil, not retaliating when abused, but blessing in order that "you might inherit a blessing" (3:9). The epistle begins with the salutation, "May grace and peace be yours in abundance" (1:2d). It ends with the blessing, "Peace be to all of you who are in Christ (5:14b)." At the heart of the epistle is the noble calling, "turn away from evil, and do good; seek peace, and pursue it" (3:11).

---

52. Davids, *1 Peter*, p. 104.
53. The Anabaptists used 1 Peter also to articulate their doctrine of baptism.
54. Waltner, *1-2 Peter, Jude*, pp. 148-50.
55. Waltner, *1 Peter*, pp. 151-52. 1 Pet. 3:18-22 was cited frequently in Anabaptist Confessions of Faith and doctrinal writing to support believers baptism (Hubmaier, Marpeck, Dirk Philips, and the Hutterian brethren).

Addendum: 2 Peter and Jude

In both 2 Peter and Jude the salutation includes "peace" *(eirēnē)* — "may grace and peace be yours in abundance in the knowledge of God and of Jesus our Lord" in 2 Pet. 1:2. In the following paragraph a significant catalog of Christian virtues forms the life of Christian godliness (1:3-11). Indeed, these important virtues (faith, goodness, knowledge, self-control, endurance, godliness, mutual affection, and love) describe well the moral ingredients leading to maturity in Christian formation, and thus contribute to experiencing "grace and peace in abundance" (v. 2). Whether the author intends this link between the salutation and these virtues is doubtful. Rather, they stand in the service of vv. 3-4, specifically to attain a twofold goal: "escape from the corruption that is in the world because of lust, and . . . become participants of the divine nature" (v. 4b and 4c).

These verses will enter my discussion in Chapter 13 when I assess John H. Yoder's assertion that all NT moral admonitions related to imitation of Jesus Christ focus on suffering and humble service. These virtues may qualify that assertion. Likewise the emphasis "may become participants of the divine nature" introduces a formational goal that is rather distinctive, with perhaps the closest notion occurring in Ephesians 4:24 and 5:1.

The second occurrence of "peace" *(eirēnē)* is in 3:14: "Therefore, beloved, while you are waiting for these things, strive to be found by him in peace, without spot or blemish." It is unclear in what sense "peace" is used here. The context hardly connotes peace among brothers and sisters in an ethical sense. Rather, in light of the epistle's overwhelming concern to keep believers pure in the midst of a corrupt and degenerate world (in which people speak "bombastic nonsense" and are motivated by "licentious desires of the flesh," 2:18), the sense is more likely that of spiritual health: that is, "without spot and blemish" or "escape from the corruption of the world because of lust" (1:4b). This fits with the tenor of the epistle as a whole.

The Epistle of Jude contains much parallel, even repeated, language to the exhortation in 2 Peter. Both epistles describe in florid manner the degeneracy of people and society, seduced by heretical teachers who "pervert the grace of God into licentiousness and deny our only Master and Lord, Jesus Christ" (Jude 4c). The situation is so abominable that the mission of salvation is put in such stark terms as "have mercy on some who are wavering, save others by snatching them out of the fire; and have mercy on still others with fear, hating even the tunic defiled by their bodies" (Jude 23).

The well-known benediction "Now to him who is able to keep you from falling, and to make you stand without blemish in the presence of his glory with rejoicing, to the only God our Savior, through Jesus Christ our Lord, be glory, majesty, power, and authority, before all time and now and forever. Amen" also accentuates the purity and preservation of the saints from the falling away. Like 2 Peter, Jude's salutation includes "peace," but is otherwise quite distinctive among NT letters: "May mercy, peace, and love be yours in abundance" (v. 2). "Peace" is the one term of continuity with other epistolary greetings. It is Jude's only use of the term. Its sense of meaning is similar to that of 2 Peter's.

The uses of "peace" *(eirēnē)* in these two epistles do not connect to either christology or even salvation explicitly. Yet, at the same time, they implicitly describe salvation as living faithfully in a world of moral degeneracy. To live in peace and receive the peace of the salutations "in abundance" means cultivating a life of spiritual health, freed from morally degenerate seducement.[56]

---

56. For commentary on these epistles as a whole, see Charles, *1-2 Peter, Jude,* pp. 201-340; Bauckham, *2 Peter, Jude.*

10 The Johannine Corpus:
Conflictual Ethos and Alternative Community as Foundation for Peace

In this chapter I explore three interrelated topics pertaining to the distinctive ethos of the Johannine literature. First, I describe the nature of the conflictive reality that obtains in the three Johannine writings: Gospel, Epistles, and Apocalypse, even though with most scholars I regard the authorship and community of Revelation to be quite different from that of the Gospel and Epistles. Second, I investigate the nature and meaning of the Johannine literature as sectarian, with attention to its christological motivation grounded in the Father-Son relationship and, derivatively, in the Jesus-follower relationship. Third, I examine the mode of the community's witness to the world despite and precisely because of its conflictual relation to the world, addressing specifically the manner and extent of the peacemaking role of the love-community. In a fourth briefer section I take up the challenge and blessing: receiving and living the peace of Jesus Christ.

Granted, the analyses will vary significantly between the Gospel and Epistles, on one hand, and Revelation, on the other. At the same time, however, certain similar conflictual characteristics will be evident. For the second to fourth sections I say little about Revelation, since I will devote a subsequent chapter to Revelation.

The Conflict between Believers and the Hostile World

The Johannine corpus presents a special challenge to peacemaking as integral to the gospel of Jesus Christ. Nowhere in the Johannine writings (Gospel, Epistles, and Revelation) are Jesus' followers commanded to love their enemies. Nor is there any *explicit* emphasis on reconciliation of enmity relationships. Jesus' encounter with the Samaritan woman, however, exemplifies reconciliation in three important dimensions: racial, gender, and religious (see Chapter 11 below). Further, the "universalist" interpretation of Revelation implies reconciliation of enemy people in some way, even if only on the brink of eschatological consummation.[1]

Distinctively expressed in the Johannine writings, the community of the faithful confronts the world by its alternative ethic and lifestyle. In the Gospel and the epistles, *love for one another* is the identifying mark of the true Jesus community (John 13:34-35, etc.). In Revelation the followers of the Lamb testify to the lordship of Jesus Christ, setting themselves apart from those who follow and worship the "beast," symbol of the oppressive empire that persecutes and kills believers. The social and political situation forces a choice between rank idolatry in submitting to the deified emperor and humble obedience to and worship of God Almighty, who is victorious over evil through the slain Lamb. Hence, potential martyrdom is the umbrella of faithful witness in Revelation. As I summarized it in an earlier publication,

> The Johannine corpus contributes different but not contradictory emphases to other NT literature on peace. Peace is Jesus' bequest to his followers in the midst of a hostile world (John 14:27; 16:33). While peace and love in the Gospel are focused internally, within the community of faith, and Jesus' commands to love the enemy and not to retaliate do not occur, this model of communal life functions precisely so that all may recognize the disciples of Jesus (13:35). Both peace and love stand in opposition to the world's character. While both the Gospel-Epistles and Revelation portray hostile people and powers in the world that hate the believers, the believers are nowhere said to hate those who hate them. While they are instructed not to love the world — as the realm of evil — they are nowhere commanded to hate, nor are they portrayed as hating people in the world. In the Gospel-Epistles the victory over the evil ruler of the world is through Jesus, and the believers are protected from the evil one by abiding in love. God also loves the world (*kosmos* in the sense of the people of the world, not the realm of Satan's rule as *kosmos*, which is more frequently used in John) and seeks its salvation, and the believers — by implication — do so also.
>
> A strong conflictual atmosphere permeates all the Johannine writings. In Revelation the followers of the Lamb conquer the beast, the embodiment of evil, by their faithful testimony to the Lamb, who is already Vic-

---

1. See the summary of issues and scholars debating this view in Johns, "Leaning toward Consummation," pp. 258-61.

tor through his death and thus is Lord of lords and King of kings. The essential difference between the Johannine corpus and the Synoptics, Paul, and 1 Peter is that the former views reality comprehensively in moral dualities. Paul's view of the "principalities and powers" as both good and evil is collapsed in John into viewing the powers or "world" as evil. Christ is no less Victor (12:31-32), but the nature of the relationship between the Christians and these 'world' forces is an oppositional one. When evil and the opponents of the faith community are perceived in oppositional categories arising from the communities' social, religious, and/or political alienation, Jesus' commands to love the enemy and not to retaliate against evil do not fit the existential-life model. Rather, an alternative community of true love for another becomes the form of witness.

The stance of the early Christians toward the rulers and the powers, however, remains deeply christological and eschatological. Repeatedly, Jesus emerges as prototype, whether in the nature of his messiahship, his refusal to fight or retaliate during his trial, or in his victory over the evil powers as slain Lamb. . . . The consummation of Christ's reign will bring God's judgment of evil; then the messianic peace will prevail.[2]

The conflict between believers and the world is foundational in John's Gospel. But this is a derivative, not primary conflict-relation. To assess properly the conflict dimension in John's Gospel and Epistles, I propose four complementary dimensions: christological, ecclesial, moral, and political, and in that order of priority (though ecclesial and moral might be interchanged). The bedrock of the conflict is Jesus himself, who as the divine Logos comes as light into the world that loves darkness rather than light (1:4-5, 14; 3:19-21). Hence Jesus becomes a prototype of the believers' stance toward the world, the second duality dimension. For this reason, the christological dimension of conflict is intertwined with the ecclesial. People's response to Jesus, the Son, is the same as to the Father, since "The Father and I are one" (10:30; cf. 8:28b-29; 5:17-18, 30). Opposition to the Son is also opposition to the Father; believers are to be one as Jesus and the Father are one. No wedge can be driven between the Father and the Son, because they work, give life, and judge in concert.[3] Marianne Meye Thompson deftly summarizes the unity of the

2. Swartley, "War and Peace in the New Testament," p. 2388 (slightly adapted).

3. Thus Jesus prays that "those who will believe in me . . . may all be one. As you, Father, are in me and I am in you, may they also be in us, so the world may believe that you have sent me. The glory that you have given me I have given them, so that they may be one, as we are one, I in them and you in me, that they may become completely one, so the world may know that you have sent me and have loved them as you have loved me" (17:21-23).

Son and the Father, demonstrating that in John God's actions as Father "are distinctly and peculiarly concentrated toward and through Jesus the Son" and that "God's activity with relationship to the Son is all-encompassing . . . [expressing] God's life-giving powers and activity in past, present, and future." Indeed,

> The Father . . . loves the Son (5:20; 10:17; 15:9; 17:23, 26); shows the Son what he is doing (5:20); raises the dead and gives life (5:21); gives authority to the Son to have life (5:26) and execute judgment (5:27); gives his works to the Son (5:36); sent the Son (5:37, 38; 6:29, 39, 57; 8:16, 18, 26; 11:42); testifies to Jesus (5:37; 8:18); set his seal on the Son of man (6:27); gives true bread from heaven (6:32); gives "all" to the Son (6:37; 13:3; 17:2, 7); "draws" people to him and teaches them (6:44-45, 65); judges (8:16); instructs Jesus (8:28); is with Jesus (8:29); seeks Jesus' glory (8:50, 54); knows the Son (10:15); consecrated the Son (10:36); hears the Son (11:41); honors those who serve Jesus (12:26); glorifies his name (12:28); will come and "make his home" with believers (14:23); will send the Holy Spirit (14:26); prunes the vine (15:2); loves the disciples (16:27; 17:23); glorifies Jesus (17:1, 24); "keeps" what has been given to the Son (17:11, 15); and sanctifies believers in the truth (17:17).[4]

The world opposed to Jesus, therefore, will also be opposed to the Father. Thus in culminating his public ministry Jesus says, "The one who rejects me . . . has a judge . . . the Father who sent me has himself given me a commandment about what to say and what to speak . . . his commandment is eternal life. What I speak, therefore, I speak just as the Father has told me" (12:48-50; cf. 5:42-43; 8:42-43). A recurring motif in John's Gospel stresses the duality between Jesus who is "from above" and those who hear his word but refuse to believe, those "from below" or "earthly." Wayne Meeks's classic article on this theme drove home how central this duality is in John.[5] The Nicodemus story etches indelibly the point that that which is "from above" cannot be understood except by one who is "born from above" *(anōthen)*. This strong declaration buttresses the Father-Son oneness motif and also the duality between Jesus and the Son-rejecting world, which chooses darkness rather than light, even though "world" occurs also in the Gospel as the very object God loves and gave his Son to save (3:16-17), for which Jesus prays (17:21, 23) and gives his life (6:33, 51).

Another level of the christological conflict is between Jesus and Satan,

---

4. Marianne Meye Thompson, *The God of the Gospel of John*, p. 69.
5. Meeks, "The Man from Heaven in Johannine Sectarianism."

which explains, at least in part, the conflict between Jesus and the world. Though John's Gospel reports no exorcism, as do the Synoptics, it testifies to a cosmic exorcism, the judgment and casting out of "the ruler of this world": "Now is the judgment of this world, now shall the ruler of this world be cast out" (12:31); ". . . the ruler of this world is coming; he has no power over me" (14:30); and "the Advocate . . . will prove the world wrong about sin and righteousness and judgment: . . . about judgment, because the ruler of this world has been condemned" (16:8-11).

This same emphasis occurs in another time and place in Rev. 12:7-10: The ruler of this world and his cohorts are cast out of heaven and empower the beast and "another beast," likely the false prophet (ch. 13; cf. 19:20), which seek to deceive and plunder the believers. Because the battle is cosmic but focused in Jesus and Satan, the taproot of all duality in the Johannine literature is christological.

The Ecclesial Dimension

A second most evident conflict in the Gospel and Epistles is between the believers who belong to the Johannine faith community and the world; in Revelation, between the followers of the Lamb and the followers of the beast, thus connecting directly the ecclesial conflict with the political.

In the Gospel and Epistles, the duality between the believers and world is pervasive. Jesus declares, "If the world hates you, know that it hated me before it hated you" (15:18). Similarly, ". . . in me you may have peace. In the world you face persecution. But take courage; I have overcome the world!" (16:33). The peace that Jesus offers to his disciples is a gift that contrasts to the tribulation that the world gives (14:27). The opposition between Jesus and the world and between believers and the world occurs already in chs. 5, 7, and 8 but intensifies in the "upper room" discourse (see 14:17, 19, 22, 27, 30, 31; 15:18ff.; 16:11, 20, 33 [in vv. 21 and 28 "world" is used in the neutral sense]; 17:6, 9, 11, 13-19, 21, 25 [however, in v. 23, the Father *loves* the world, as in 3:16]). The same duality occurs in 1 John 2:15-17.

Another dimension of conflict in the Gospel and epistles is to be construed also at the ecclesial level. But the conflict is not with the world, but with rival religious groups (see especially 1 John 2:18-28). A split had occurred in the Johannine community prior to the writing of 1 John, and the group that broke off claimed apparently some type of sinless perfectionism or the opposite: sin does not break fellowship; sinning can be overlooked. John's faith community takes a decisive stance against both these views. Also, some anti-Christ claim of a "splinter group" appears in 4:1-2, holding that Jesus did not come in the flesh, but only *appeared* as such. This is evidence of proto-Gnostic influence upon the community in rejecting the Messiah's suffering and death.

A similar strand of opposition in the ecclesial dimension appears also in John's Gospel, but here the rivalry is between Johannine believers and the synagogue. Four texts indicate some form of expulsion (likely not permanent excommunication, as held by the Martyn-Brown-Rensberger thesis): John 9:22, 34-35; 12:42; 16:2. This reality results in scripting stereotypically some Jews, those who oppose Jesus and his claims, as "the Jews."[6] This opposition is

---

6. It is most difficult to understand the origins and rationale for this demeaning stereotype. The influential Martyn/Brown/Rensberger thesis connecting this to the *Birkat ha-minim* is most unlikely, since the "malediction" added to the "Eighteen Benedictions" postdates John's Gospel likely by several decades. The thesis would need to be revised to say that the conflicts of the Johannine believers with the synagogue extended over several decades and thus gave rise to the *Birkat ha-minim.* To me, Adele Reinhartz's alternative explanation is attractive: these passages "may have provided the Johannine community not with a direct reflection of their historical experience [with the synagogue] but rather with a divinely ordained etiology *in the time of Jesus* for a situation of separation which was part of their own experience" (*Befriending the Beloved Disciple,* p. 50). She considers four reading "positions" or stances: the compliant reader, the resistant reader, the sympathetic reader, the engaged reader. She rejects the first as impossible for herself, the second as unhelpful since it only hardens binary opposition, the third as muting the issues, and the fourth as most appealing, which engages the Beloved Disciple as "the other" and thus provides a model for constructive dialogue between Christians and Jews today. See also Reinhartz's article, "'Jews' and Jews in the Fourth Gospel" and the other fine articles in the same volume (*Anti-Judaism and the Fourth Gospel,* ed. Bieringer, Pollefeyt, and Vandecasteele-Vanneuville). For a fuller historical and theological context to reflect on this difficult issue, see John Howard Yoder's contribution together with Christian and Jewish responses in *The Jewish-Christian Schism Revisited,* ed. Cartwright and Ochs. Yoder's first essay, "It Did Not Have to Be" (pp. 43-68) argues that most first-century Christians (the "Nazarenes" or followers of the Jesus Way) were part of the pluriform nature of emerging Judaism. Many continued to worship with Jews in synagogues and continued to varying degrees practices of ritual and moral purity laws. Yoder contends that Christianity in the first three centuries and Judaism for most of the last 2500 years bear witness to a Jeremiah-type existence: make your home and witness in the circumstance of Diaspora. Only when Christianity became a state-church under Constantine and establishment and imperial in nature did it seal its cleavage with Judaism and resort to persecution of Jews. But for heirs of the radical reformation, this is not normative, nor is it so in post-Christendom free-church models. Of the many efforts to understand why John "typed" some Jews as "the Jews," I consider crucially helpful the contributions in Bieringer, et al., by de Jonge ("'The Jews' in the Gospel of John") and de Boer ("The Depiction of 'the Jews' in John's Gospel"). Their theses together credibly explain how in the narrator's intention the conflictual situation between Johannine Christians and "the Jews" is to be understood. De Jonge helpfully shows that the issues debated in John 5–10 are christological, precisely issues existing between the Johannine community and its theological opponents (note that "the Jews" is not

so strong that both "demonize" the other (8:39-59). This strand of bitter conflict does not portray Jesus' relationship to Judaism, for many incidents testify to amicable relationships with Jewish people. Most of the character "players" in the Gospel are Jews, including Jesus and his disciples. In 8:13 and 31; 9:13, 18 and 40 (cf. 11:45 and 47), Jesus' interlocutors appear first as Pharisees and then as "the Jews"; the two seem to be interchangeable, and are blended with the chief priests as the conflict mounts in the narrative (11:47ff.). John's Jesus, however, affirms continuity and solidarity with the law (1:17), even counting Moses as the climactic "witness" in his first round of "trial" defense in 5:45-47.[7] Moloney puts it rightly, "Whereas the Jews consider belief in Jesus a betrayal of the Law, Jn is tracing the Law back to its source and doing away with the opposition between the Law and belief in Jesus."[8]

With Revelation the landscape of ecclesial conflict changes considerably. Here the threat to the faith is not so much from faith groups with rival religious claims as in the Gospel and the Epistles, but more directly with the Empire, and believers are threatened, if not actually persecuted. Jesus himself is

---

used in 2:23-24, where one might expect it, and that Nicodemus [3:1-10; 19:39-42] is not identified with the stigma either). De Boer holds that actions, not ethnic or group identity as Jews, led to the conflictual, hostile language. Jews as a people or ethnic group are not the referents. Rather, only those who accuse, seek to kill and stone, and finally cry "crucify" are designated as "the Jews." One might blend these two theses but that would necessitate viewing the Johannine Christian heterodox opponents as still connected with the synagogue, which may, in view of Yoder's thesis, be correct. If we follow Reinhartz's preference for "engaged reading," this will mean not using "the Jews" or even fideistic exclusivism as enmity-creating language between Jews and Christians. The *Wirkungsgeschichte* of the text, the converging of the horizons of Jesus' history and the community's history, has generated an enormous problem in Jewish-Christian relations historically which require repentance and reconciliation. Collins, "Speaking of the Jews: 'Jews' in the Discourse Material of the Fourth Gospel," points out that Jews are spoken of only twice in the Gospel in Jesus' direct discourse: "Salvation is of the Jews" (4:22) and "as I said to the Jews, so now I say to you, 'Where I am going, you cannot come'" (13:33). The latter is connected to similar statements directed to "the Jews" in 7:33-34 and 8:21, but in those Jesus concludes with stinging words ("but you will not find me" and "you will die in your sins"); in addressing his disciples such do not occur. This connection collapses the narrative distinction between Johannine Gospel time and Jesus. Collins's treatment of "the Jews" in the passion narrative is also insightful. In addition to the essays in Bieringer, et al., see also the helpful essay by Rensberger, "Anti-Judaism and the Gospel of John," with the responses by Mark Goodwin and Thomas D. Lea in *Anti-Judaism and the Gospels.* See also n. 62 below and n. 23 in the next chapter on the issue of "the Jews."

7. See the engaging thesis of Andrew T. Lincoln that John's Gospel presents Jesus and his claims in the rubric of a defense trial, utilizing the "lawsuit motif" of the OT (*Truth on Trial,* especially pp. 73-81).

8. Moloney, *The Gospel of John,* p. 243. For the larger argument, see Pancaro, *The Law in the Fourth Gospel.*

introduced as *faithful martyr* (1:5). The terms for *witness* and *martyr* derive from the same stem *mart-* and permeate the entire narrative. At the center of the conflict stands the *slain, victorious Lamb* (Jesus Christ), opposed to the *dragon, beast, and allies.* Warfare, set in apocalyptic genre, dominates the book. The beast is empowered by the one cast down from heaven: the dragon known also as the devil or Satan (12:7-9). Thrown out of heaven, the beast makes war on the male child of "a woman clothed with the sun." Since "the earth came to the help of the woman; it opened its mouth and swallowed the river that the dragon had poured from his mouth" (12:16), the dragon pursues the other children, i.e., the followers of the Lamb. The dragon gives rise to the beast (12:18–13:1), who blasphemes God and makes war on the saints to conquer them (13:7). But the saints prevail because they testify to the one who has already conquered through his death, i.e. "the Lamb that was slaughtered" (13:8).

The Moral Dimension

The christological and ecclesial dimensions of duality opposing the world, Satan, and political powers shows itself clearly in the moral dimension as well. The Gospel strikes the moral chord immediately, in the duality between light and darkness. The Logos-Word (Christ) brings life and light into the world, and "the light shines in the darkness, and the darkness did not overcome it" (1:5). Jesus says about himself, "I am the light of the world. Whoever follows me will never walk in darkness but will have the light of life" (8:12). Upon meeting the man born blind and prior to his action to restore his sight, Jesus declares, "As long as I am in the world, I am the light of the world" (9:5). After the miracle and the ensuing conflict between Jesus and the Pharisees (vv. 12-15), later called "the Jews" (vv. 18, 22), Jesus proclaims, "I came into this world for judgment so that those who do not see may see, and those who do see may become blind" (9:39). Jesus' final appeal, culminating his public ministry, extends the light-darkness contrast, calling people to believe his works and his message as credentialed by God or to continue in darkness: "The light is with you for a little longer. Walk while you have the light, so the darkness may not overtake you. If you walk in the darkness, you do not know where you are going. While you have the light, believe in the light, so that you may become children of light. . . . I have come as light into the world, so that everyone who believes in me should not remain in the darkness" (12:35b-36, 46).

The light-darkness duality is of cosmic scope (as in 1:5; 8:12) and marks also the ecclesial experience (as in 3:19-21; 9:39: 11:9-10). 1 John begins by calling believers to walk no longer in the darkness, but to walk in the light (1:6-8).

Sin is cause or evidence of walking in darkness, and Jesus has come to free from sin. Similarly, believers are to love not the world, nor the things of the world (2:15). And believers are protected from the evil one (Satan), since Jesus Christ has overcome the world (5:5; cf. 5:19). The moral dualities named in 1 John are virtually the same as those mentioned in the Gospel.

In Revelation the conflict is at once christological, ecclesial, and moral. When the apocalyptic genre is decoded, it is clear that the Christian believers of Asia Minor are in mortal threat from the Roman Empire and its blasphemy: religiously-morally, in deifying emperors and outlawing worship of the true God revealed in Jesus; politically, by persecuting the followers of the Lamb Jesus (see below); and economically, by "marking" the beast's devotees and not allowing anyone unmarked to buy and sell (13:16-17). Revelation celebrates the downfall of this blasphemous political power in the catastrophic judgment of ch. 18 ("Fallen, fallen is Babylon the great," v. 2), which also details Rome's economic opulence and religious-political arrogance.[9] The great Hallelujah chorus follows (ch. 19), declaring the final doom of the beast with its allies and God's triumph over evil. Then the new heavens and earth appear and the followers of the Lamb enjoy a new order of life — new Jerusalem with its paradisiacal felicities. Punctuating the end-narrative of the book is the clear command: "Worship God" only.

The Political Dimension

While the political significance of Jesus' ministry is evident throughout the Gospel narrative in numerous texts, especially 6:15 and 11:48,[10] the trial narrative portrays Jesus' identity and claims as political beyond expectation. Jesus is identified as "king" eleven times (18:33, 37 [2x], 39; 19:3, 12, 14, 15, 19, 21 [2x]). The portrayal of Pilate as a character is difficult to assess. The seven-scene "inside-outside" movement of Pilate, widely recognized by scholars, as well as the chiastic structure of the trial narrative, heightens the chameleon quality of Pilate's role. The chiastic structure of 18:28–19:16a portrays Pilate's vacillation between the inside of his headquarters, where he meets Jesus, and the place outside his headquarters, where he meets the Jews. Whether Pilate is

9. For the economic dimension of Rome's oppressive power, see J. Nelson Kraybill, *Imperial Cult and Commerce.*

10. "When Jesus realized that they were about to come and take him by force to make him king, he withdrew again to the mountain by himself" (6:15); "If we let him go on like this, everyone will believe in him, and the Romans will come and destroy our holy place and our nation" (11:48).

deemed diabolically calculating, sympathetic, or even to be pitied, his repeated shifting from one stage to the other dramatically symbolizes his predicament. He, like the Johannine readers, must take a stand regarding Jesus, and he will be judged by the stand he chooses.

The structure discloses both the thematic focus and the artistic quality of the narrative:

a   18:28-32   The accusation
      Pilate and the Jews *(outside)*
      "early in the morning"
      b   18:33-38a   The testimony — Pilate and Jesus on kingship
           Pilate and Jesus *(inside)*
           c   18:38b-40   The verdict — Pilate pronounces Jesus'
                  innocence
                Pilate and the Jews *(outside)*
                Pilate appeals to Jewish "custom"
                d   19:1-3   Pilate makes a spectacle of Jesus (mockery)
                     Pilate, Jesus, and the soldiers *(inside)*
           c′   19:4-8   The verdict
                Pilate pronounces Jesus' innocence
                Pilate, the Jews, and Jesus *(outside)*
                The Jews appeal to Jewish "law"
      b′   19:9-11   The testimony — Pilate and Jesus on authority
           Pilate and Jesus *(inside)*
a′   19:12-15   The sentence
      Pilate, the Jews, and Jesus *(outside)*
      "the day of preparation for the Passover . . . about noon"
Epilogue   19:16-22 The written testimony-inscription in three
                 languages
             Pilate, the Jews, and Jesus
             a hinge connecting the trial with the crucifixion[11]

Indeed, the irony of the seven-scene narrative[12] features Pilate and Jesus as central figures, with a quality of dialogue oriented to the monumental issues

---

11. I am indebted to one of my Gospel of John students, Wanda Stopher, for this structural depiction, as well as some of the content in the paragraph in the subsequent note.

12. Rensberger stresses both "the artful construction of the story" and John as "the supreme ironist among New Testament writers" (*Johannine Faith,* 91). While the trial narrative is replete with irony, one notable instance is the double irony in the Jews' request that Pilate release Barabbas instead of Jesus. First, the name Barabbas is translated literally "son of the father"

of the nature of kingship and the nature of truth. Pilate first shows disinterest (18:28-32), then curious engagement (18:33-40), then perfunctory action to appease, followed by "more fear" when he is told by the Jews that Jesus claimed to be Son of God (19:1-9), then political opportunism to shame the Jews when the Jews frame Jesus as a threat to Caesar (19:10-16). The stratagem hooks the Jews into ironically acclaiming — in contradiction to their near Passover confession that they have no king but God[13] — "we have no king but Caesar." Finally, both Pilate and the Jews ironically bear testimony — in Hebrew, Latin, and Greek with the title over the cross: "Jesus of Nazareth, the King of the Jews."[14] Interpreting the entire scene are Jesus the king's words to Pilate, "You would have no power *(exousia)*[15] over me unless it had been given to you from above; therefore he who delivered me to you has the greater sin" (19:11).[16]

The Gospel's portrait of Jesus is not that he is *apolitical,* but that he is *neopolitical,* transcending the disciples', the Jews', and Pilate's political categories, as in his response to Peter's use of sword against the high priest's slave (18:10). His response declares his nonviolent stance, "Put your sword back into its sheath. Am I not to drink of the cup that the Father has given me?" (18:11). Similarly, in Pilate's struggle to understand the Jewish charge that Jesus claims to be a king, he encounters words from Jesus that he cannot comprehend: "My kingdom is not from this world. If my kingdom were from this world, my followers would be fighting to keep me from being handed over to the Jews. But as it is, my kingdom is not from here."[17]

Pilate manipulates the entire drama so that the Jewish leaders are forced into an unbearable situation, declaring loyalty to Caesar, rather than to God who called them into a covenant relationship, whose first command jealously declared, "You shall have no other gods before me." Talbert describes it well:

(Lincoln, *Truth on Trial,* p. 130). The Jews request a man's release whose very name reflects the claim Jesus has made of himself throughout the Gospel, that he is the Son of the Father. But instead of the true Son of the Father, the Jews choose a bandit *(lēstēs).* Jesus is declared innocent of any charge of political insurrection, but his release is traded for the release of one who is guilty, who is a bandit.

13. See Meeks, *The Prophet King,* p. 77, for the pertinent Passover text.

14. Schlier quotes Augustine's comment on this, "Denn darum hat Pilatus geschrieben, was er geschrieben hat, weil der Herr gesagt hat, was er gesagt hat" ("Jesus und Pilatus nach dem Johannesevangelium," p. 74).

15. In the preceding verse Pilate used *exousia* twice to speak of his authority to release or crucify Jesus.

16. Swartley, "War and Peace," pp. 2367-68, adapted.

17. Meeks is likely right, in light of 6:15, that John depicts Jesus as Prophet-King, drawing specifically on Moses traditions (*The Prophet-King,* pp. 87-99).

Their words drip with irony. Instead of "May you be our king, you alone" (= eleventh benediction, *Eighteen Benedictions*), or "From everlasting to everlasting you are God; beside you we have no king, redeemer, or savior, no liberator, deliverer, provider, none who takes pity in every time of distress and trouble; we have no king but you" (=the hymn sung at the conclusion of the Greater Hallel by the high priests as part of the Passover Haggadah), Judaism's priestly leadership confesses, "We have no king but the Caesar."[18]

Pilate raises the question of truth, but cannot comprehend it.

Jesus' response to Pilate's question, "Do you ask this on your own, or did others tell you about me?" (18:34), overtly turns the tables and we recognize that the accused is actually the accuser, the one on trial is actually the judge. This established, Pilate is turned into witness, but must also choose for himself, what he will believe and testify regarding Jesus. That Pilate is actually on trial comes through clearly in his own question, "I am not a Jew, am I?" (18:35). Pilate here disassociates himself from the Jews, and yet we will notice in the narrative, his moving closer and closer into alliance with the Jews' purposes. Pilate will not be able to take a neutral stand in regard to Jesus. He will by his actions align himself with those who are opposing the one who reveals the truth.

Although Pilate tries to separate the politics of state from the politics of religion, this trial is of cosmic consequence. Jesus' terms of kingdom and kingship supersede any that Pilate can imagine. Jesus defines his reign in terms of truth, solidly anchoring the events of the trial and crucifixion in the context of this important Johannine theme. The painful irony is that the one who is "full of grace and truth" (1:14), who is the giver of grace and truth (1:17), who "is the way, the truth, and the life" (14:6) will be judged by untruth, sentenced by those whose words are true, but who know not the truth that they speak. The fact, that truth rightly judges, aligns Jesus' statement of purpose here, "For this I was born and for this I came into the world, to testify to the truth" (18:37), with his earlier words, "I came into this world for judgment so that those who do not see may see, and those who do see may become blind" (9:39).[19]

Immediately following Pilate's question put to Jesus as "king," "What is truth?" (18:37-38), Pilate goes again outside, faces the Jews, and pronounces

---

18. Talbert, *Reading John*, p. 241.
19. Stopher, "The Trial," pp. 7-8, altered.

the truth. This is the first of three times Pilate pronounces Jesus' innocence with the words, "I find no case against him." This is the truth, but in the rising clamor of the crowd to crucify Jesus — an all-against-one in a mob scene (*pace* Girard[20]) — truth is spurned and denied.

Finally, the chiastic structure discloses an all-important truth. Not only is Jesus king throughout the narrative, but the center (d) element presents Jesus clothed in purple and mocked as "king of the Jews." In John the one royally clothed carries his own cross on the day the Passover lambs are slain. This one is slain "to take away the sins of the world" (1:29). Condemned and crucified as a criminal, "lifted up" on the cross to draw all people to himself (12:32), and glorified through this ignominious death (12:27-28; 17:1-5), Jesus shatters all prevailing political conceptions. He does not rule with a sword, nor does his kingdom depend on imperial power. His politics are opposed to those of both the Jewish leaders and Pilate. Jesus combines religion and politics at depth-level so that his crucifixion on the cross (a death for political subversives) is glorification, a vindication of his royalty and the form of his exaltation.

The political dimension of the Gospel arises from and culminates the other three dualities: christological, ecclesial, and moral. Because the royal claims of Jesus are of universal scope, the figure of the crucified, exalted Prophet-King, saving people from their sins, including violence, sets forth a paradigm in which his resurrection brings peace that the world neither knows nor can take away (14:27; 16:33; 20:19, 21).

The epistles show little or no political dimension, since they consist of encouragement for the community internally. "The Jews" are not present.

Revelation, however, stands surely within the political mind and mold of the Gospel. Like the Gospel, it also presents an alternative rendition of Paul's proclamation of Christ's victory over the principalities and powers. Though present in apocalyptic genre, it declares with the Gospel, "now is the prince (ruler) of this world cast out (down)." Rev. 12:7-10 testifies to cosmic victory.

While Revelation utilizes a form of the Gospel's duality "from above" versus "earthly" in its alternating portrait of a scene in heaven followed by a scene on earth, the "predominant dualities," as Culpepper observes, "relate to the opposition between the false powers of earthly (Roman) authority and the true power of Christ. Christ is the lamb who was slain (5:6), while the em-

---

20. For an overview of Girard's thought see my "Introduction" and Marlin E. Miller's "Girardian Perspectives and Christian Atonement" in *Violence Renounced*. For critique of Girard in relation to biblical studies see the other essays in the same volume and also McDonald, *God and Violence*, pp. 293-305.

peror (probably Nero or Domitian) is portrayed as the beast with a mortal wound (13:1-3). . . . In the end, the great harlot (Rome) who received power from the dragon (Satan) is overthrown, and those who worshiped the beast are destroyed by terrible plagues."[21] Culpepper also presents elements of ecclesial duality by noting that opposition between the Lamb and the powers intertwines with the conflict between the dragon (Satan) and the followers of the Lamb. The latter, who refuse to worship the beast, are conquerors through their faithful testimony, even unto death.[22]

The next chapter develops Revelation's political portrait more fully. As with Paul, Christ is victor over the powers of evil. Also, as with Paul, theologically the primary axis of relationship between Christian believers and these world powers is through Christ's own victory over the powers. The believers, even when threatened with death, appear never to regard themselves as victims, but as bearers of Christ's victorious power over all powers. The martyr is saint triumphant.

Indeed, as Culpepper notes in concluding his discussion of the "dualisms" in Johannine thought ("above and below, true and false, love and hate, good and evil, life and death, light and darkness, Christ and the devil"), "Christology, not dualism, is the real focus of each of the Johannine writings."[23] This concurs with the above emphasis that the dualities of ecclesial, moral, and political dimensions are rooted in the christological duality: the Logos brings the light into the world; darkness, while indeed it does exist in Johannine literature, has not, docs not, and will not overcome the light. While the theme is explicit in the Gospel and the epistles, it also emerges gloriously in Revelation: "the city has no need of sun or moon to shine on it, for the glory of God is its light, and its lamp is the Lamb. The nations will walk by its light, and the kings of the earth will bring their glory into it" (21:23-24).[24]

John as Sectarian

As noted above, a dominant trend in scholarship has regarded the Johannine communities as sectarian (the social location differs much between the Gos-

---

21. Culpepper, "An Introduction to the Johannine Writings," p. 24.

22. Culpepper, "Introduction," p. 24.

23. Culpepper, "Introduction," pp. 23, 24.

24. Except when quoting Culpepper I have avoided the terms "dualism" and "dualistic," using instead "duality" or "dualities" in order to guard against the notion of a dualism in which competing powers are equal, and even to avoid overplaying the notion of dualism in a more restricted sense. The Johannine literature is christologically, not dualistically, oriented.

pel and the epistles on the one hand, however, and Revelation on the other).[25] This analysis tends to regard these communities of faith as ethically deficient from a normative Christian point of view,[26] since making peace with the enemy does not appear to be an essential expression of the community's mission, whether in the Gospel, epistles, or Revelation. Other scholars have challenged this view and have argued that the peaceable vision is very much present in Johannine literature and that this is coherent with its view of its mission in the world.[27]

This distinctive Johannine emphasis, contrasting significantly to that of both the Synoptic Gospels and the Pauline literature, has been assessed in terms of sectarian identity and appropriated to contemporary challenges of living within a pluralistic world, most notably by David Rensberger, Robert H. Gundry, and Miroslav Volf, in complementary ways.

Rensberger has persuasively argued that the Johannine Gospel community was a sectarian community because of its social location, i.e., its expulsion from the synagogue as reflected in 9:22, 34; 12:42; 16:2.[28] Further, John's high christology is "directly related to the communal experience of the Christians for whom it was written"; and both together, while perhaps appearing to be "of no relevance to the social and political struggles of oppressed people,"[29] enable the community's witness to be a counter-cultural witness to the larger religious community and the social-political power of the world. As Rensberger puts it persuasively,

> Above all, the meaning of John's sectarianism is that *because it was sectarian* it challenged the world on the basis of the love of God and the word of

25. In this section I do not take up the sectarian nature of Revelation, even though that might be pursued. For brief overview of this, see Perkins's discussion of "sectarian isolation in Revelation" in "Apocalyptic Sectarianism and Love Commands."

26. This point is made succinctly by Meeks in "The Ethics of the Fourth Gospel," pp. 318-19, 322, 325. Nonetheless, leaning on Rensberger's contribution, Meeks affirms the need for the sectarian, counter-cultural stance as a welcomed inclusion in the canonical diversity, for it, despite its moral deficiencies, can empower the Christian church to a "subversive challenge to 'this world.'" This voice together with "the more accommodating, conversionist, or transformative modes of engagement with the world, represented elsewhere in the canon, can enable the Bible to guide and usefully to complicate — and not merely to decorate — Christian ethical discourse" (p. 325). For a helpful summary and response to Meeks's article, see D. Moody Smith, "Ethics and the Interpretation of the Fourth Gospel."

27. In addition to Chapter 11 below, see Johns, "Leaning toward Consummation." For a complementary masterful discussion of "universal election" in one set of texts in John's Gospel, see Culpepper, "Inclusivism and Exclusivism," pp. 101-2.

28. Rensberger, *Johannine Faith*, pp. 41-49.

29. Rensberger, *Johannine Faith*, pp. 119, 118.

God. No religion that sees itself as the backbone of a society, as the glue that holds a society together, can easily lay down a challenge to that society's wrongs. A cultural religion is all too readily told to mind its own business, because it *has* a business, a well-known role in maintaining society's fabric unmolested. It is the sect, which has no business in the world, that is able to present a fundamental challenge to the world's oppressive orders. Precisely because it sees itself alienated from the world, its commitment to the world's orders is attenuated, if not abolished altogether. Thus it is able to take a stand over against the world and to criticize that which the world holds most dear.[30]

Rensberger thus regards Johannine Christianity as a paradigm, sectarian though it be, for a faith community that is "set free to criticize the world's injustice and violence in the name of the world's Creator."[31] Here I would add, "Savior," since one of John's purposes is to set forth Jesus as the Messiah and Savior of the world (1:29; 4:42; 20:31).

Robert Gundry devotes an entire book to the sectarian nature and impulse of John's Gospel, appealing to it to address the alarming drift among evangelicals toward acculturation and accommodation to the world.[32] Gundry's work is important for it makes careful distinctions between what counts in John for and against sectarianism.[33] Most notably, John is thoroughly sectarian and strong in its evangelism at the same time, together with a clear emphasis upon election and a high christology, specifically a christology of the Word: because of its "high Christology of Jesus as the Word who, though not *of* the world, speaks volubly *to* it, John's sectarianism has sharpened rather than dulled the evangelistic thrust and usefulness — even today — of the Fourth Gospel."[34] Gundry drives home the sectarian nature of the Gospel by noting that Jesus does not pray for the world,[35] nor is he said to love it — only God does. Believers also are never said to love either the world or unbelievers.[36] Further the strong incarnational theology of John does not

30. Rensberger, *Johannine Faith*, p. 142.

31. Rensberger, *Johannine Faith*, p. 143.

32. Gundry, *Jesus the Word According to John the Sectarian*, especially the final chapter (pp. 71-94).

33. Gundry, *Jesus the Word*, pp. 66-70. See especially notes on pp. 37, 47-48, and the extended endnote, "The Sectarian Start of Christianity," pp. 110-13.

34. Gundry, *Jesus the Word*, p. 69.

35. Gundry, *Jesus the Word*, p. 60. While this is said in 17:9, I take this to refer to vv. 5-8, what Jesus wants those whom the Father gave him to know. Later, in vv. 21, 23 the world is very much in the purview of Jesus' prayer.

36. Gundry, *Jesus the Word*, pp. 58-59.

call for love for the world on the part of believers. "Rather, God loved it and Christ died for it in spite of its evil character. What comes out is the magnitude of God's love, not a partly positive view of the world."[37]

Miroslav Volf also sees the Johannine community as bearing a significant witness to the world. But he tempers both the notion of its sectarianism and the too easy conclusion that John's perceptual categories are dualistic.[38] He denies "dualism" as an accurate description of John's thought. He does this in view of the definition of dualism given by Ugo Bianchi, accepted generally by scholars of religion:

> As a category within the history and phenomenology of religion, dualism may be defined as a doctrine that posits the existence of two fundamental causal principles underlying the existence . . . of the world. In addition, dualistic doctrines, worldviews, or myths represent the basic components of the world or of man as participating in the ontological opposition and disparity of value that characterize their dual principles.[39]

On the basis of John's prologue and statements such as those in 3:16 and 12:32, as well as 17:21, 23, Volf denies that John is dualistic. Rather, John contains numerous dualities that are transcended and resolved by the all-encompassing and inclusive emphases within John, such as the Logos bringing life that is the light of all people (1:4c) and the true light that enlightens everyone (1:9). Hence, Volf argues,

> [M]oral opposition between good and evil as well as between their respective protagonists is as such not yet dualistic. "The simple contrasting of good and evil, life and death, light and darkness, and so on is in fact coextensive with religion itself and cannot be equated with the much more specific phenomenon of dualism."[40] We can speak of dualism, argues Bianchi, only when such dualities are connected with the opposite ontological "principles responsible for bringing the world and man into existence."[41]

---

37. Gundry, *Jesus the Word*, p. 63. As a result, Gundry says, "we must kiss goodbye to the incarnational argument for Christians' so-called cultural mandate" (p. 63). He thus refutes Robert Webber's "Christ-for-culture" appeal based on the incarnation (p. 63).

38. Here I utilize Volf, "Johannine Dualism and Contemporary Pluralism."

39. Bianchi, "Dualism," p. 506, cited by Volf, "Johannine Dualism," p. 191.

40. Bianchi, "Dualism," p. 506.

41. Volf, "Johannine Dualism," pp. 191-92. The quoted phrase is from Bianchi, "Dualism," p. 506.

Volf thus contends that John is not dualistic since God in Christ is Creator of all, and that the oppositional dualities within the text are within creation, ordered within the larger sovereignty of God. As he puts it,

> If we accept this definition of dualism, John's Gospel is clearly not a dualistic document. True, stable and firm oppositional dualities structure the text: above and below, heavenly realm and world, light and darkness, spirit and flesh, good and evil, truth and falsehood, God and Devil, children of God and children of the Devil. And yet, none of these dualities, singly or together, imply dualism. . . . John's Gospel starts with the affirmation that God through the Word *created* everything that is not divine (1:3). As a consequence, the creation as a whole can be properly described as "what is his [the Word's] own" (1:11). All the oppositional dualities within creation and between creation and God exist on account of God's creative activity.[42]

Volf thus regards John as not intrinsically opposed to pluralism, functional within creation, in which diversity and competing "truths" function. The dualities in the Gospel do not set the Johannine community in complete opposition to those around them. Thus Volf argues that John calls believers to be a particular kind of sectarians, those who do not see only black and white but who courageously name evil and also forgive and are willing to die for those who do evil.

Volf disagrees with Gundry's portrait of John's sectarianism on three interrelated points: (1) the community's relation to outsiders, (2) the nature of the community's boundaries, and (3) the character of its identity.[43] Because of John's strong emphasis on the mutual indwelling of the Father and the Son, it is not possible to contrast the Father's love for the world to that of the Son. The Son gives his life for the world (1:29; 6:51). The world is viewed in John not wholly in negative terms.

> After all, believers are explicitly sent into the world "*as*" the Son was sent by the Father (17:18; 20:21). Jesus embodied God's love for the world both in doing good — feeding the hungry (6:5-14), healing the sick (4:46-54; 5:2-9; 9:1-7, 11-27), giving money to the poor (13:29 by implication) — and ultimately in giving his life for the salvation of the world. By being sent as Jesus was sent, believers are commanded to do the same.[44] For Jesus and

---

42. Volf, "Johannine Dualism," p. 192.
43. Volf, "Johannine Dualism," pp. 204-10.
44. Here Volf disagrees with Meeks's claim that though John does present Jesus as the

for the believers to do all this *is*, in the relevant sense, to *love* the world in all but name — a world hostile to them, as John repeatedly underscores.[45]

Thus, for Volf, God's love and Christ's love for the world means that the world is not in oppositional duality to God. This fits with the Gospel's emphasis on outsiders. While the Johannine community had boundaries and needed boundaries for its identity, the boundaries were permeable. The identity of the believers in John's Gospel did not exclude others (10:16; 11:52); the community also welcomed into it those outside (i.e., the Samaritans and the Roman official in ch. 4). Further the boundaries are not clear-cut, for some persons and groups are portrayed in a gray zone: followers of John the Baptist, Nicodemus, Caiaphas, even the disciples at various stages in the story. And distinction is even made among Christians, between "apostolic Christians" (Petrine), and the Johannine Christians, according to Raymond Brown. Because the *goal* of Jesus' prayer in John 17 is the eventual salvation of the world and because of the strong emphasis on love in John — and the absence of law — together with the oneness of Father, Son, and those who come to believe, Volf holds that John "operates with a nonoppositional and inclusive account of personal identity" and that "this kind of identity lies at the heart of being itself, since it characterizes not only humans but the Creator of everything."[46] John's portrayal of the community, therefore, is not inimical to living within and witnessing effectively to a politically pluralistic world, even while affirming Jesus' words "I am the way, the truth, and the life; no one comes to the Father but by me." In the larger context of John, this statement has primarily a positive thrust, not an exclusionary one. Volf sees the power of Christian witness, even in John, as overcoming dualities:

> But God is not only the creator of all reality. God is also its redeemer. The aim of God's redemptive activity is to overcome oppositional dualities so

---

model for people to follow, Jesus is in fact not "imitable," "too alien to human weakness to provide a convincing model, too much 'the god striding over the face of the earth'" (Meeks, "The Ethics of the Fourth Gospel," p. 318).

45. Volf, "Johannine Dualism," pp. 204-5. Volf takes issue with Rensberger's speaking of "John's sectarian hostility toward outsiders" (*Johannine Faith,* p. 139). Volf distinguishes between critique of the world and hostility toward it. Critique can express love. Further, in John this critique, read by Rensberger and others as hostility, is directed specifically toward only some, not all, outsiders, those "seeking to harm Jesus and his disciples" (p. 215, n. 49). From a slightly different angle, I ask if portrayal of a hostile relationship, i.e., with the Jews, means that Jesus or his followers viewed them with hostility. Is that where John's emphasis falls? I don't think so. John rather portrays some Jews as "the Jews" who are hostile toward Jesus.

46. Volf, "Johannine Dualism," p. 208.

as to leave room in the whole of reality only for reconciled differences. By becoming flesh, the Word united itself intimately precisely to that which has alienated itself from God (1:14). Moreover, God loved the world which was opposed to him (3:16) so by becoming flesh the Word may also be "the Lamb of God who takes away the sin of the world" (1:29). The result is at least the partial transformation of oppositional dualities into non-oppositional ones: duality between God and world is transformed into communion between God and Jesus' disciples. As a consequence, oppositional dualities with the creation are overcome too: enmity between men and women is overcome in a community of equality among them, ethnic divisions between Jews and Samaritans, between Jews and Greeks, are bridged in a single community that worships God "in spirit and truth" (4:23). John's accounts of creation and redemption together undercut dualistic modes of thought.[47]

While Rensberger's, Volf's, and Gundry's contributions may seem to be at odds with each other, I see it otherwise. They are not mutually exclusive. Rather, they complement each other in helpful ways, in ascertaining the degree, nature, and purpose of John's sectarian character. Rensberger sees in its sectarian stance, with its focus on intra-community concern and clear boundaries, a strong counter-cultural witness against the dominant powers of religion and politics in the world. Gundry emphasizes John's clarity of boundary between the community of faith and the world, and — especially for evangelicals among the North American elite — a call to repent of accommodations to cultural pressures from the world, i.e., to keep the world out of the church! Volf wants us to see that in John the community-world boundaries are more permeable than often supposed and that narrative dualities are overcome in the overall theological perspective of the Gospel. John's particular sectarian quality does not discount it for meaningful life and witness in a pluralistic world.

In the mission of the church, in John's time and now, these three emphases may be just the ingredients needed to comprehend fully the essence and witness of the Johannine community in and to the world, and to provide a stance against which to appreciate John's peacemaking potential.

47. Volf, "Johannine Dualism," pp. 192-93.

The Johannine Mode of Peacemaking

In this section I seek to show that the sectarian[48] community as presented in John's Gospel and epistles is capable of and engages in peacemaking. Indeed, it has a surprising capacity (and resilience) to open its door to outsiders, and break down barriers erected by historical, sociological, and racial factors.

Numerous scholars have stressed that in John's Gospel believers are turned in upon themselves; some have used the language of "believers hating the world." But such emphasis receives no support from the text. Indeed, the "world" is hostile, and it will *hate* believers just as it hated Jesus (John 3:20; 15:18, 23-25; 17:14-16; 1 John 3:13). But, as has been widely recognized, John's Gospel emphasizes mission in its purpose and overall emphasis.[49] Hence Volf's contribution on the Gospel's stance or attitude toward outsiders fits well the Gospel's missional ethos. Granted, the community has clear boundaries, but that does not mitigate against a strong missional emphasis, as Gundry also claims.

John's pervasive emphasis on love for one another becomes the means of appeal to outsiders, an essential form of encounter with the world. Love for one another is the *mark* of the community (13:34-35; 1 John 4:21), *the* characteristic that draws people toward Jesus, as Jesus spoke about his own mission — "I will draw all people to myself" (12:32; cf. 3:14-16). In John's narrative world and community, love for one another makes peace within the community first of all. That peace includes the shalom of the neighbor in need, as extended homilies in 1 John make clear (3:14-18; 4:19-21). This love for the neighbor extends to its ultimate expression, laying down one's life for the brother or sister (1 John 3:16; 4:11 in context of Jesus giving his life as an atoning sacrifice and the model of the good shepherd in John 10:11-18; cf. 15:13).

Granted then, John is clear about love, even self-sacrificial love within the community, but does this then serve a positive or negative function in re-

---

48. One might legitimately ask whether the word "sectarian" is really meaningful for a first-century Christian group, since there was no established church to contrast it to. Also, is it meaningful in Western society today in a post-Christian culture that is profoundly pluralistic? The social order that prevailed when Weber developed his sect-church distinctions is largely eclipsed by new social and religious realities. Further, even "sects" vary significantly, so that only the barest sociological features serve as a common denominator. As Gundry points out, some sects, like Jehovah's Witnesses, have a low christology (p. 68), whereas John's Gospel, as well as some modern sectarian groups, has a high christology. Even among Mennonites, historically considered sectarian, one finds both high christology adhered to by some and a considerably lower christology adhered to by others.

49. See, for example, the bibliographical note (n. 7) in Erdmann, "Mission in John's Gospel and Letters," as well as Chapter 11 and its Attachment 2 below.

lation to the world, specifically those beyond the borders of the community? Church history is replete with models of both negative and positive expression. In times of war, when "enemies" play a role in determining personal or national response, it is quite possible that "love for one's own" may lead Christians to lay down their lives for their own but kill enemies. It is also possible that strong intracommunal love will lead the community to extend love toward the enemy and refuse participation in war (the typical just war and pacifist responses respectively). One cannot conclude, therefore, that strong intracommunity love militates against love for enemies. Moody Smith says that John's "love one another" (13:34) is "not just your neighbor, but also your enemy. . . . The synoptic Jesus' command to love your enemy (Mt. 5:44) is not contradicted."[50] But on what textual basis can we think that it may have positive effect for the enemies' welfare? Here, not only the important Samaritan encounter (ch. 4), but also the larger theological pattern of the Gospel's thought helpfully informs us.

First there is a strong love relationship between the Father and the Son, a mutual indwelling and interdependence. Both-as-one give as self-donation for the salvation of the world (John 3:16; 6:51). The model of shared love between Father and Son becomes a gift to the community (1 John 4:7-11, 16, 19), which the members of the community now express to one another. To answer the question whether love for one another extends to those outside the community, the model of God's love for the world set forth in the gift of the Son says *yes*. Because of John's deity claims about the Son, James A. Gustafson and Robert Gundry call John a "master narrative," but with different evaluations of such in John's Gospel, as well as the desirability and goodness of the sectarian ethos that master narratives represent.[51] Gundry's discussion is a rejoinder to Gustafson's criticism of master narratives that make exclusive claims as does John's christology. Gundry recognizes the point but is willing to accept the claim (bite the bullet and swallow the potato whole[52]).

A more significant outcome of regarding John as a master narrative, I suggest, is precisely its inclusivism, both social and theological. Culpepper has persuasively presented evidence for this in considering also texts that re-

50. Smith, "Ethics and the Interpretation of the Fourth Gospel," p. 111. Smith points out that the absence of "the Jews" in 1 John is good. This observation together with the perspective on "the Jews" I develop in n. 62 below names the enemy rightly: "heterodox Christians, who do not make the right confession about Jesus" (p. 111).

51. Gundry, *Jesus the Word*, pp. 66-68. Gundry here describes Gustafson's refutation of George Lindbeck's thesis that the future of Christianity lies with its sectarian expression, noting also Stanley Hauerwas's and Walter Brueggemann's self-positioning vis-à-vis sectarianism.

52. Gundry, *Jesus the Word*, p. 68.

flect exclusivism.[53] For his discussion of the Gospel's social inclusivism, Culpepper draws on Robert Karris's thesis[54] that John's emphasis on Jesus as the inclusive Messiah who embraces the outcast Samaritans (4:1-42) and the poor (12:5-8; 13:29) and heals the chronically ill (John 4:43–5:18, one a *Roman* official's son) is the impulse that generates "the Jews'" objections to Jesus' works. Except for the texts on the poor, the narrative sequence is striking: the tangle with "the Jews" comes immediately after these inclusive acts. In this thesis these acts and the arguments they generate lead eventually to "the Jews" putting Jesus out of the synagogue. Hence, social inclusivism, not exclusivism, represents the protagonist of the narrative. Similarly, John's theological inclusivism rests upon the narrative's recurring declaration of "universal election" (1:29, 36; 6:33, 51c; 12:32; 21:11 [the 153 fish likely symbolizes every known kind]; John's emphasis on "true worship" that transcends theological exclusivism; and the Samaritans' confession of Jesus as "Savior of the world," 4:42). A second pillar for this inclusivism is John's Logos theology that evokes the "universal" wisdom tradition and privileges the light-darkness imagery in which the Logos comes as the light of all people (1:4), the true light that enlightens every person (1:9). The Logos as agent of creation is also its purpose, goal, and end.[55]

The mediating connection between this primary universal strand and the exclusive emphases is what Culpepper calls "Fideistic Exclusivism." Only those who *believe* receive God's salvation gift intended for all (1:12; 3:16; 6:25-71; 20:30-31). Not only does failure to believe result in the exclusivist strand, but the narrative reflects also double predestination-type statements (most evident in 6:70-71; 12:39-40; 13:2, 27; 17:12), and christological exclusivism (10:1, 7-9; 14:6 and similar person-claims in 1:1, 18, 51; 3:13 expressive of the Gospel's high christology).[56]

Culpepper's contribution is ground-breaking in resolving what has been an intractable problem in understanding John, the relation between a strong inclusivism permeating the narrative alongside recurring strands of exclusivism. Culpepper privileges the inclusive over the exclusive, which may prompt Johannine scholars to rethink the sectarian thesis. To be sure, it means, as Volf puts it, John's community represents a particular form of sectarianism. Is it possible for a sectarian community to hold a theology that sets forth a vision of potential universal salvation? It may indeed require redefin-

---

53. Culpepper, "Inclusivism and Exclusivism," pp. 90-95, 100-105.

54. Karris, *Jesus and the Marginalized in John's Gospel*, pp. 105-8.

55. Culpepper, "Inclusivism and Exclusivism," pp. 90-95, 100-105.

56. Culpepper, "Inclusivism and Exclusivism," pp. 95-100.

ing sectarianism, delimiting it purely to sociological analysis (its original function), and acknowledging the possibility that a sectarian community's theological claims and vision, specifically its relation to outsiders, is at heart inclusive, not exclusive.

To pursue this line of thinking, the model of the mutual indwelling of the Father and the Son, specifically in their love binding each to the other, becomes the model for the community's love for one another and also for the world, because the chain of relational character is unbroken. As Volf points out, this mutual indwelling of love is on three levels: 1) intra-divine, 2) divine-human, and 3) human-human.[57] This love, divine in origin and revealed to humanity in Jesus giving his life for the world (6:33, 51; 12:23-24; 15:11, 16-18), is an incomparable gift and power, the muscle of the Johannine ethic (see 13:31-35; 15:9-17; 17:23-26; 21:15-19).

Jesus' encounter with Peter in 21:15-19 demonstrates the priority of love as the condition for following Jesus. "Do you love me?" (vv. 15-17) is the enduring question of the Gospel's Jesus to his followers. Only then can the community be anchored in love. Only when grounded in love for Jesus can Peter[58] and all followers "feed my lambs, . . . tend my sheep, . . . feed my sheep." And only then will intra-community love draw people to the gospel. As Rensberger has put it, "If we are prepared to envision faith and love as truly one [as is clearly said in 1 John 3–4], then we are prepared to expect that a call to love should be issued in the same historical context as the call to believe that Jesus is in God and God is in him."[59]

Combined with the dominant motif of "love one another" as the appeal of the gospel to those outside the community, thus ever expanding its horizons, Jesus' refusal to use violence even when threatened and arrested (18:11, 36) is the third pillar in John's triune strength for peacemaking. While John falls short of commanding love for enemy and uses bitter, hostile accusations against "the Jews," especially in 8:39-59, yet the Gospel lacks any command to hate enemies, as occurs in Qumran, for example. In "the abstract the Johannine form of the love commandment does not exclude love for them [enemies]."[60] While the historical and sociological circumstances of the community make such unlikely, love for one another does "envision the enemy and is a response to the enemy. It enables the community to stand its ground against its enemies, and to do so as disciples of Jesus the Messiah (John

57. Volf, "Johannine Dualism," p. 205.

58. Jesus' threefold question certainly evokes in Peter's memory his threefold denial. Thus, he "felt hurt" (v. 17c) as he recalled, likely in tears, his threefold denial.

59. Rensberger, "Love for One Another," p. 303.

60. Rensberger, "Love for One Another," p. 307.

13:35)."[61] Jesus' own model of refusal to use violence during his arrest and trial, fulfilling his love for his Father and for humanity, functions as moral imperative. Hear his sharp word to Peter to sheath the sword (18:11). Inspired by this model of not retaliating against enemies, the realism of love for one another as a means of drawing outsiders into the community, even enemies, extends to love for the enemy. No race, group, or gender is excluded, and certainly not Jews! The narrative indicates numerous times that many Jews believed (8:30; 10:42; 11:45; 12:42a; cf. 2:23).[62] The disciples, Martha, Mary, and Lazarus were Jews, as was Jesus.

In the context of this moral tripod: love for one another, drawing *all* people into the community through witness to Jesus as Messiah, and refusal to use violence, Jesus' bestowal of peace to his disciples gains meaning and power. The peace that Jesus promises and gives is not a peace that violence can or could bring. If it were, then Jesus and his followers would have fought the Jewish leaders and Roman soldiers who colluded to arrest and crucify him. If that had occurred, Jesus' climactic and significant final word from the cross, "It is finished," could not have been spoken. But, thanks be to God: the Father-Son love-purpose for humanity *is completed*, fully demonstrated.

The next chapter, a study of John's peace texts intertwined with the Johannine theme of mission, will show the horizon of peacemaking in John is as expansive as the mission of the community. If the Gospel calls all to believe that Jesus is the Messiah, Son of God, who gives eternal life (3:16; 12:50; 17:3), so also the Gospel calls all to inherit the Messiah's gift of peace, which transcends (and continues to value) religious, ethnic, and gender differences. The one introduced as "the Lamb of God who takes away the sins of the world" (1:29) commissions his disciples with authority to forgive sins, for "As the Father has sent me, so I send you (20:21c)."

---

61. Rensberger, "Love for One Another," p. 307.

62. Here Motyer's thesis, which I find compelling though not fully convincing, that John was written to persuade Jews to come to faith in Jesus as Messiah merits consideration. The negative portrait of "the Jews" functions as a foil to lead Jews to side with the "many" Jews that have believed. See *Your Father the Devil.* Sandra M. Schneiders correctly reminds us "that all those who accept Jesus in the Fourth Gospel, with the possible exception of the royal official in 4:46-54, are also Jews or, in the case of the Samaritans, originally Israelites. And a large segment of [the] Johannine community were also Jews by birth. Consequently, it is not Jewishness, in either its ethnic or its religious sense, that is the source of the conflict" (*Written That You May Believe,* p. 82).

Receiving and Living the Peace of Jesus Christ

Jesus' two statements promising bestowal of peace upon his disciples occur in the Upper Room discourse (chs. 13–17). The farewell speech conforms to the pattern found in numerous other Jewish and Greco-Roman documents.[63] The unity of the speech has been questioned by many, in light of the ending in 14:31, "Arise, let us go from here," and the disjuncture between 13:36; 14:5-6 and 16:5 on the recurring "where are you going" motif. Thomas Brodie sums up the scholarly debate on this matter, but goes beyond it to perceive a unity in these chapters that overcomes the notion that disparate materials are joined together or that 14:31 ends one speech, and chs. 15-16 duplicate it, and ch. 17 is tacked on as a farewell prayer.[64]

Brodie regards the speech as spiritual preparation of the disciples for the future, a spiritual-formation crash course. He sees a cleansing/purification/sanctification pattern that results in a changing meaning of the believers' life in the world:

> Stage 1, in chs. 13-14: cleansing — "the believer and the world's evil are in-termingled, and the task is to drive out the root of the evil." Here the foot-washing is interpreted as cleansing from sin.[65]
>
> Stage 2, in chs. 15-16: purification — "when the root of evil has been driven out and God is purifying the believer, there is a certain withdrawal from the world, a painful struggle to be free from all that chains the heart." This is accompanied by dual literary emphases: God's purifying and the hating action of the world: "a key function of the picture of the world's hatred is to highlight the idea that in following Christ, in drawing close to God, one must go through a stage of letting go of the world, a stage of separation, and one must place one's roots where they truly belong — in God. The world, feeling challenged or spurned, tends to feel resentment, and from this comes an antipathy, a hatred."
>
> Stage 3, in ch. 17: sanctification — "when one's identity in God has been firmly established, there is a return to the world — not as something

---

63. Talbert, pp. 200-202.

64. Brodie, *The Gospel According to John*, pp. 428-29. See also Moloney's discussion, which perceives an essential unity to the whole as well (pp. 370-71, 412).

65. This may be one aspect of its meaning, but the dramatic symbolism of servant humility is also surely a part of its meaning. Coloe proposes that it is also a household welcoming gesture. After noting five phases of action in the account that are typical of welcoming in the "tradition of the Greco-Roman banquet/symposium," she says: these phases of action "allow the foot washing to be seen for what it is — a gesture of welcome into 'my Father's household' (14:2)" ("Welcome into the Household of God," p. 414).

to be either exploited or idolized, but as something in which, despite its evil, one works for faith and understanding (. . . esp. 17:11, 15, 21, 23)."[66]

Brodie perceives a similar progression related to Jesus' two "peace" statements in 14:27 and 16:33 respectively. Jesus speaks in response to two complementary scenes: the emergence of the figure of the beloved disciple and his own giving of the new commandment, "love one another." In the first stage (ch. 14), as the disciples seek to respond, "trying to see and admit the divine presence, there is a related twofold conclusion: first, there is a picture of spirit-based peace (14:25-27b), and then there is a picture of all that threatens that peace (14:27c-31). . . . The overall picture of chaps. 14-15 . . . is of the development of a love, or of a love-related peace, which is present but threatened.[67]

In the second stage (16:4b-33) there are both a deepening of the "Spirit-led discernment of truth" and a change in the image of peace:

> . . . the believer now understands the Father's love directly (16:26-27) . . . the negative does not win; one is not alone and beaten. On the contrary, . . . the distress of the world, though very real, has been overcome, and in the presence of the Father there is a deep peace. Hence the final phrase: 'I have defeated the world'.[68]

A similar point occurs in 1 John 5:4b-5: "And this is the victory that conquers the world, our faith. Who is it that conquers the world but the one who believes that Jesus is the Son of God?" In John 13-17 there "is a gradual disentangling of the forces of good and evil": first, interwoven (betrayer in the midst); second, a division reasonably clear (Judas gone and Peter's denial foretold); third, clearly separated (chs 14-16); and finally, in ch. 17, "evil has been left aside." The whole discourse is about "Jesus' God-oriented battle against evil and the believer's consequent journey to God."[69]

Jesus' gift of peace is interwoven literarily with four recurring themes in the speech: the command to love one another, Jesus' going away, the promised gift of the Holy Spirit (five times in chs. 14-16), and preparation for the disciples to live in a hostile world that will persecute them. Further, the gift of peace flows out of the oneness, the mutual indwelling of the Father and the Son, a pattern shaping the farewell prayer as well, where Jesus first prays for himself (17:1-8), then for his disciples on the basis of the Father-Son mutual

---

66. Brodie, *The Gospel According to John*, pp. 429-33.
67. Brodie, *The Gospel According to John*, p. 434.
68. Brodie, *The Gospel According to John*, p. 435.
69. Brodie, *The Gospel According to John*, p. 435.

indwelling (9-19), and then for those who will come to believe on the basis of the disciples' witness (20-26). John 20:19-23 fulfills Jesus' promise of the Holy Spirit's coming and shows the inherent connection between Jesus' bestowal of peace and the gift of the Spirit (see Chapter 11). Indeed, "Jesus' gift of peace is 'from God,' a gift that the quantifiable and fragile peace produced by the politics of this world can never match."[70] Jesus' peace, rooted in the triple reality of the new creation (noted above), draws all people to the Gospel's gift of light, life, and love. These terms mark the Johannine theology, and provide the basic images for salvation and ethics. "Light" and "life" are concentrated in chs. 1–12, whereas "love" is concentrated in chs. 13–17, as follows:

Light: *phōs* 23x in chs. 1–12, the verb *phōtizō* 1x in 1:9
Life: *zōē* 32x in chs. 1–12, 4x in chs. 14–20, the verb
        zōopoieō 3x in chs. 5–6
Love: the verb *agapaō* 25x in chs. 13–17, 7x in chs. 1–12,
        5x in chs. 18–21
        the noun *agapē* 6x in chs. 13–17, 1x in 5:42
        the verb *phileō* 13x scattered throughout

Light and life, christologically-oriented, characterize the Johannine gift of salvation, and are thus concentrated in the Book of Signs (chs. 1-12).[71] Love is concentrated in the Book of Glory, especially chs. 13-17, and thus marks the ethical and communal identity of Jesus' disciples. Jesus' final encounter with Peter (21:15-19) makes the point with dramatic force and emotional intensity. Peter is called into the intimacy of relationship with Jesus that until now was exemplified by the Beloved Disciple. Now Jesus invites Peter into the love-bond that will enable him to truly follow Jesus. This love marks those who follow Jesus (13:34-35). In John it is grounded in the mutual indwelling of divine love that flows from the oneness of the Father-Son in self-donation. It is indeed a *gift* to the Jesus community whose watchword is: we love one another, because God first loved us (1 John 4:19). In John love is the womb of Jesus' covenant of peace.

---

70. Moloney, *The Gospel of John*, p. 410.

71. To grant eternal life is the Father's commandment to the Son in 12:50, the closing verse of the Book of Signs. For an excellent portrayal of the structure of John with the Book of Signs–Book of Glory division, see Burge in *The NIV Application Commentary*, p. 45.

11 Peace and Mission in John's Gospel: Jesus and the Samaritan Woman

Scholars have mined John's Gospel for its mission paradigms and theology, but little has been done to understand its peace emphasis.[1] Even though the word "peace" *(eirēnē)* is used more frequently in John than in Matthew and Mark, few researchers have studied the use of the term in the Gospel.[2] Two key texts in John blend emphases on peace and mission. The linking of these themes merits attention to their place in John's overall literary and theological purposes.

The first of the two peace and mission texts is John 4:1-42. In it, "peace" is not explicit; the term does not occur. Here the mission action, directed by the Spirit-anointed Jesus (1:32-34), is the foundation and possibility for peacemaking between alienated peoples, Jews and Samaritans. In the second text John 20:19-23, the *Sendung* text of the Gospel, *eirēnē* occurs twice (and again at the end of v. 26). This passage portrays peace as Jesus' gift that, together with receiving the Holy Spirit, foundationally empowers the disciples to carry out the mission charge.

The literature on mission in John is extensive, as Erdmann's recent article indicates.[3] An entire monograph has been devoted to the topic with its lo-

---

1. In "War and Peace in the New Testament," pp. 2365-69, I have discussed the secondary work on John's peace teaching.
2. Swartley, "Politics and Peace *(Eirēnē)* in Luke's Gospel." See also the analysis in Swartley, *Israel's Scripture Traditions,* pp. 134-39.
3. "Mission in John's Gospel and Letters."

This chapter is reprinted with several modications, by permission of the publisher, from *Beautiful upon the Mountains: Biblical Essays on Mission, Peace, and the Reign of God,* ed. Mary H. Schertz and Ivan Friesen (Elkhart: Institute of Mennonite Studies, 2004), pp. 161-81.

cus for research the text examined here, John 4:1-42.[4] Most recently Linda Oyer has completed a dissertation on the mission *Sendung* text of John, comparing it with Matthew's commission, 28:16-20.[5]

Although John 4 has received widespread attention for its mission impulse, few authors make the connection to the inherent peacemaking impact of the text. Ben Witherington's recent commentary on John is an exception. He comments, in criticizing the "target audience" emphasis in the church growth movement:

> The story of Jesus and the Samaritan woman is extremely potent to use as a tool for sharing the Gospel across socioeconomic, ethnic, and racial barriers and for exhorting Christians to get on with doing so. Jesus in this story not only rejects the notion that he shouldn't associate with Samaritans, he also rejects the notion that he shouldn't talk with a "strange" woman in public, and furthermore rejects the idea that one shouldn't associate with notoriously immoral people. Besides that, Jesus' act involves witnessing to a person that many of his fellow Jews would have written off as both unclean and theologically out of bounds, a hopeless case.[6]

But Witherington does not speak about the degree of enmity, historical and ethnic, that had developed between Samaritans and Jews over time. The potential of the text for peacemaking has not been sufficiently exploited.

Judith Gundry-Volf does pick up on the peacemaking dimension. She pairs the narrative about the Samaritan woman in John 4 with that of the Syrophoenician woman in Mark 7:24-30 and identifies them as paradigmatic for Christian mission-peacemaking:

> The Gospel stories of Jesus' encounters with the Samaritan woman (Jn. 4:1-42) and the Syrophoenician woman (Mk. 7:24-30; Matt. 15:21-28) can both be read as tales about the inclusion of the "other," about crossing the boundaries caused by ethnic, religious, social and gender otherness and bringing about a new, inclusive community of salvation. Exclusion is overcome in two radically different, but complementary models for dealing with a problem both urgent and complex in our own world. In John 4, the divine gift of the Spirit breaks down barriers between peoples and leads to reconciliation and fellowship. In Mark 7 and Matthew 15, human

4. Okure, *The Johannine Approach to Mission.*

5. Linda Oyer, "Interpreting the New in Light of the Old: A Comparative Study of the Post-Resurrection Commissioning Stories in Matthew and John" (Ph.D. dissertation, Catholic Institute of Paris, 1997).

6. Witherington, *John's Wisdom,* p. 124.

insistence on divine mercy, which is blind mercy, dramatically reverses a pattern of exclusion.[7]

Gundry-Volf thus identifies the contribution that this narrative of Jesus and the Samaritan woman makes to understanding the socio-ethical dimensions of the gospel: the good news of salvation is the breaking down of racial and cultural barriers. Mission and peacemaking are not two separate but linked ideas, but are in Scripture ontologically one, as other texts (Luke 2, Acts 10, Ephesians 2) explicitly show. As Krister Stendahl rightly perceived, what is usually regarded as Paul's conversion is his call to announce Jesus Christ's peace to the Gentiles and to make peace with the enemy.[8]

Literary Analysis of John 4:1-42

Peter Ellis seeks to unlock meaning in all units of John's Gospel by showing their concentric structure. His analysis of the John 4 narrative is as follows:

a   Jesus, *wearied (kekopiakōs)*, sits at the well (4:4-6).
    b   The Samaritan woman is *surprised* (4:7-18).
        c   Worship is in spirit and truth (4:19-24).
    b'   The apostles are *surprised* (4:25-34).
a'   Others have *labored (kekopiakasin)*, and you have entered into their *labor* (*kopon;* 4:35-38).[9]

This analysis highlights the connection between Jesus' *weariness* in *a* and the mission-*labor* in *a'*: both use the same verb root in Greek, though different grammatical forms and shades of meaning occur. The *surprise* element in both *b* and *b'* is also notable. Ellis's analysis, however, is fundamentally flawed because it does not include the final paragraph of the narrative (4:39-42), the climax, in which "many *Samaritans*" believe in Jesus and confess that he is "indeed the Savior of the world." One might rectify the deficiency in Ellis's analysis in part, at least, by beginning the analysis of the narrative at v. 3, so that verses 3-6 parallel verses 39-42 in the concentric structure, framing 4:4-38, as the real *a* and *a'*:

---

7. Gundry-Volf, "Spirit, Mercy and the Other."
8. Krister Stendahl, *Paul among Jews and Gentiles*, pp. 7-22.
9. Ellis, *The Genius of John*, pp. 65-66.

a   Jesus deliberately goes through *Samaria,* to the historic Jacob's
     well.
a'   The *Samaritans* come to believe that Jesus is the Savior of the
     world through the *Samaritan woman's testimony.*

This correction to Ellis's schema accentuates the mission element intended by the story itself. The center of the chiasm still focuses on the topic of the right place to worship, the issue that separated the Jews and the Samaritans at a fundamental level (see below). The topic of proper worship mediates the mission and peacemaking themes in that the alienating ideologies of cult are transcended by "spirit and truth" that knows no worship wars, specifically none of geography or edifice. Here also is a vital perspective: mission and peace are crucially linked to worship. This common worship of formerly alienated people testifies that mission and peacemaking are accomplished. Indeed, worship is often the first casualty in alienation arising from ethnic, gender, or racial barriers. We return to this point later, but register it here as arising from the text itself.

Utilizing A. J. Greimas's work on discourse structure and semionarrative structure, Hendrikus Boers undertakes a book-length structural and semiotic analysis of John 4.[10] After analyzing each pericope on a "need/preparedness/performance/sanction" grid with syntactic and semantic components, Boers explicates the whole text with the motifs of life, integration, and solidarity overcoming alienation and death.[11]

Arising from this structural semiotic analysis, Boers' commentary discloses a keen insight about how the story generates meaning at the deep structural level, overcoming factional security with human solidarity, and partisan salvation with universal salvation. Boers's analysis correlates the life-giving dimensions with Jesus' salvific initiatives and the woman's receptivity:

> What may be the most important thing to note is that Jesus' "engaging in discussion with the woman," and "staying with the Samaritan villagers" occurs under "life" and the value /obedience/, as well as under "integration" and the value /human solidarity/. That once more underlines the integrity — in the deep structure of our text — of life and integration, and of the existential value /obedience/ and the social value /human solidarity/. . . .
>
> The realization of worship of the Father in spirit and truth, in opposi-

10. Boers, *Neither On This Mountain nor in Jerusalem.*
11. Boers, *Neither On This Mountain,* p. 120. See here his semiotic structural diagram (Attachment 1, p. 321 below).

tion to either on this mountain or in Jerusalem, when the Samaritan villagers, having invited Jesus to stay with them, recognize him as the savior of the world, reinforces the integration of the values /human solidarity/ and /universal salvation/. These values, in turn, are integral to /obedience/ in the overall structure of the story. Everything that happens in it is a transformation of the value /obedience/ into a concrete figure of the story, represented at the most general level by Jesus "doing the will of the one who sent him and completing his work" for which the woman is his indispensable co-worker. . . .[12]

Boers's concluding emphasis is that we can recognize "all the figures in the story as transformations of values into concrete reality."[13] In short, the story *performs* transformation.

From another angle of analysis Gail R. O'Day, focusing on the Johannine narrative as revelation, appeals to this narrative to demonstrate that it not only mediates revelation, but *is* revelation. It not only reports Jesus as revealer, but also "allows the reader to *experience* Jesus' revelation for himself or herself."[14] The experience of revelation and transformation centers specifically in the mission of salvation, crumbling structures and prejudices of partitioning, alienation, and enmity. To understand this experience adequately, some investigation of the historical background to the key phrases in v. 9 is necessary:

> Woman: "How is it that you, a Jew, ask a drink of me, a woman of Samaria?"
> Narrator: "For Jews have no dealings with Samaritans."

The Historical Background: Sharpening the Meaning

One of the most demeaning and hostile representations of Samaritans comes from the lips of Jews in John's Gospel who say in accusing Jesus: "Are we not right in saying that you are a Samaritan and have a demon?" If John 4 seeks to show that Jesus transforms the enmity between Jews and Samaritans into salvation and solidarity in faith, the same Gospel narrator in 8:48 has Jewish lips voicing the prevailing hostility between the two groups: to Samaritanize is to demonize. The vitriolic interchange voices bitterest enmity.

---

12. Boers, *Neither On This Mountain,* pp. 119, 200.
13. Boers, *Neither On This Mountain,* p. 200.
14. O'Day, "Narrative Mode and Theological Claim."

This enmity developed and festered over centuries. Probably originating at the time of the exile of the northern kingdom (721 BCE), the hostility is clearly evident in the post-exilic period of Ezra and Nehemiah's leadership (ca. 464-438 BCE). The returned Babylonian Jewry regarded itself as the "holy seed" (Ezra 9:2) or faithful remnant (9:15), in contrast to those who had stayed in Israel, intermarried, practiced pagan worship, and thus become "unclean with the pollutions of the peoples of the lands, and with their abominations" (9:11). The Samaritans under Sanballat, the Persian governor, resisted Ezra and Nehemiah's program to rebuild the temple in Jerusalem (Neh. 6:1-14). Post-exilic Jewry sought vigorously to protect itself from this "pollution" by forbidding marriage to foreigners and building a wall around Jerusalem. Through these post-exilic decades and centuries, two contesting ideologies prevailed in Jewry: one more self-protective against outsiders (represented above) and another more inclusive of outsiders (Isaiah 52–53; 56:6-8; Jonah, Ruth).

The conquest of Alexander the Great and the rule of the Ptolemies exacerbated the tension between the two peoples. According to Josephus *(Antiquities)* the schism and separation arose when Alexander gave the Samaritans permission to build their own temple on Mount Gerizim.[15] Sirach (ca. 180 BCE) shows the depth of Jewish antipathy toward the Samaritans, whom they considered semi-pagan: "Two nations my soul detests, and the third is not even a people: Those who live in Seir, and the Philistines, and the foolish people that live in Shechem" (50:25-26). The Septuagint renders the last part: "those dwelling on the mountain of Samaria."

The final split between the Jews and Samaritans occurred during the Maccabean revolt (165 BCE) and was a consequence of the brutal destruction of Samaritans under John Hyrcanus (134-104). John's policy was to burn Hellenistic cities to the ground, but to extend sympathy toward circumcised peoples. Although Samaritans were circumcised, they fell under the axe destroying the pagan peoples. In 128 BCE John burned the temple on Mount Gerizim, and in 107 he destroyed Shechem. Little wonder that the Samaritans sought retaliation. In 6-9 CE some Samaritans scattered human bones in the Jerusalem temple during the festival of Unleavened Bread. About twenty years later, close to the time of Jesus' ministry in Samaria, an atrocity occurred against the Samari-

---

15. Scholars contest whether a temple was ever built because no archeological remains have been found, but Josephus narrates that the temple was burned under John Hyrcanus's rule. John R. Donahue notes that Menachem Mor, a respected scholar of this period, regards Josephus as reliable enough to accept his report that a temple was built and destroyed. See Donahue, "Who Is My Enemy?" p. 154, n. 21; Mor, "The Persian, Hellenistic, and Hasmonean Period," p. 16.

tans, apparently with Jews in cohort with Pilate. According to Josephus, a man persuaded a group of Samaritans to go with him to Mount Gerizim to view some sacred vessels preserved there. Some of the men in the group were armed and when Pilate forbade ascent of the Mount, fighting broke out and some Samaritans were killed or taken prisoner. Pilate then executed some of the Samaritan leaders, presumably blaming them for the "concocted uprising."[16]

Against this background of hostility, it is only natural that the two communities avoided contact, as John 4:9 explains: "for the Jews had no dealings with the Samaritans."[17] The shared beliefs of the two communities faded in importance, and differences were magnified. Both communities looked forward to the coming of an eschatological figure who would restore their community's autonomy, so they could live in peace and worship according to their beliefs. The Samaritans expected a Restorer *(Taheb)* to fulfill the prophecy of Deut. 18:18: a prophet like Moses would reinstate worship on Mount Gerizim with a new undefiled temple. Jews expected a messianic figure who would free them from Roman oppression and purify (or rebuild) the temple in Jerusalem so that they could worship the Lord in unhindered freedom (see Zech. 6:12; Mal. 3:1).[18] In John 4:25, the woman sounds more Jewish than Samaritan: "I know that Messiah is coming (he who is called Christ); when he comes, he will show us all things."

In addition to this history that bears on Jesus' encounter with a Samaritan woman, another religious and cultural enforcer figures into the situation. In Jewish and Samaritan custom, women were not to hold conversation with men in public. For a woman to do so would reflect negatively on her character, classifying her with the loose, immoral women.[19] This woman carries a moral burden or societal oppression of her own. She has had five husbands, and the man she is living with currently is not her hus-

---

16. This information comes from Josephus, *Antiquities* 18.4.1-2, §§ 85-89. I have used Donahue's "Who Is My Enemy?" in recounting this narrative of hostilities. Other secondary sources are cited by Donahue, p. 153. One of the more definitive studies of the Samaritans is by Mor ("Persian, Hellenistic"). See also other essays in the same volume and Schur, *History of the Samaritans.*

17. Some early mss. lack this clause (א* D it cop), but the evidence for its inclusion is comparatively much stronger (𝔓63, 66, 75, 76 א^a A B C K L W^supp Δ Θ Π *f*^1 *f*^13 28 33 565 700 892, etc.).

18. An Isaiah Targum on 53:5 says, "He will build the temple which was profaned for our transgressions and delivered up because of our sins." On this see Juel, *Messiah and Temple,* p. 181; Swartley, *Israel's Scripture Traditions,* pp. 158-70, 195.

19. Charles Talbert cites two primary rabbinic texts (m. *Pirke Aboth* 1:5 and BT *Kiddushin* 70a), advising against and forbidding a man to hold public conversation with a woman, even to greet a woman: "It is forbidden to give a woman any greeting" (*Reading John,* p. 112).

band.[20] Jesus in his prophetic role perceives this, discloses that he knows her situation, and yet continues to engage her in conversation in order that she and her fellow Samaritans, rejected as they were by Jews, might come to know him as "the Savior of the world." What a marvel!

For Jesus it is necessary *(dei)*[21] to go through Samaria. Why? To meet the woman at the well, initiate significant "salvation" conversation with her — in public — and welcome her to the living water. Even when her moral condition is mutually acknowledged, he continues to engage her in theological conversation about the proper place of worship, a key point in the racial enmity. The mission of Jesus is clearly depicted as shattering boundaries of religion, gender, and moral stigma. The movement of the text is from exposing the boundaries, to shattering and transcending them, to extending the living water of salvation, to welcoming the alienated community of Samaritans — not just the woman — into the solidarity of messianic salvation.

As Clifford W. Horn notes in a mission essay based on this text, this story is a model for cross-cultural communication. The meeting place is a well, a point of common human need, providing a natural opportunity for the encounter. In this narrative it is also a place of discovery. The woman discovers who Jesus is, and Jesus discovers receptivity in the Samaritans. Mission is accomplished in a simple but profound manner.[22]

20. Many commentators allegorize the Samaritan woman as representing the five religious idolatries that characterized Samaritan worship, as delineated in 2 Kgs. 17:24-41. For this view, building on the betrothal form of the narrative (cf. Genesis 24), see Sandra M. Schneiders, *The Revelatory Text,* pp. 190-91, who contends that the main point of the narrative is the "incorporation of Samaria into the New Israel . . . a 'wooing' of Samaria to full covenant fidelity in the New Israel by Jesus, the New Bridegroom." Another recent and novel interpretation argues that we should not ascribe to this woman the moral guilt of adultery, either literally or allegorically. Rather, she is not a loose woman or a type of something else, but a victim of levirate-type practices, forced economically to be attached to one man after another. Further, she is doubly victimized because her present partner will not give her marriage status; thus she is "stigmatized." For this view see Schottroff, "The Samaritan Woman." While these interpretations are engaging, the woman's climactic word to her townsfolk, "He told me everything I ever did" (4:39), gives one pause. Is this also part of the allegory, revealing the Samaritans' idolatries, or does it disclose her oppression, as in Schottroff's interpretation? The astounding element of the story is that the woman does not appear as a victim, nor as "morally loose" and crushed by her experience. In Jesus' encounter with her, she is first and finally a human being expressive of human dignity, a trusted hearer, and then the bearer of Jesus' salvation news.

21. Note that this term "it is necessary" (*dei* in Greek) occurs here climactically in a series of four uses: *it is necessary* to be born from above (3:7); *it is necessary* that the Son of Humanity be lifted up (3:14); *it is necessary* for Jesus to increase (3:30); and *it is necessary* for Jesus to go through Samaria (4:4).

22. Horn, "Communicating the Gospel Cross-Culturally."

John 4:1-42 and John 20:19-23

John 20:19-23 is here considered alongside 4:1-42 because it also contains a strong call to mission, "As the Father has sent me, so send I you." This missional charge is given under the umbrella of Jesus' peace-greeting. "Peace be with you" prefaces the commission (v. 21) and is distinct from the same word in the original greeting when Jesus first came and stood among the disciples (v. 19d).

It is striking, first, to note the verbal connection between 4:38 and 20:21. For the disciples, the significance of Jesus' encounter with the Samaritan woman is explicated in a brief homily concerning Jesus' vocational food: to complete the work of the Father and to call, or perhaps by calling the disciples to see the fields ripe for harvesting (v. 35d). The homily concludes by declaring Jesus' sending commission: "*I sent you* to reap that for which you did not labor" (v. 38a).

Expositions of John 4 regularly slight the impact of Jesus' encounter on the disciples, and understandably so. The narrative is constructed in such a way that interchanges the disciples and the woman in narrative space. When the disciples leave to buy bread, Jesus meets and talks with the woman. When the disciples return, the woman takes her water jar and goes back to the city (though v. 27 indicates that the disciples are astonished that Jesus is speaking with a woman). But the story does portray Jesus in dialogue with his disciples, indeed presenting a mini-discourse to them. The discourse clearly focuses on mission. For that reason, mission remains the primary focal point of John 4, which should thus be seen as the precursor to the sending text in John 20. If we consider John 3:16 and 20:21 together, we cannot maintain, as some scholars do, that John's Gospel represents a community turned in upon itself, with concern only for intra-communal welfare.[23]

23. While the text is clear that the world hates the believers, nowhere does it say that the Johannine Christians hate the world (to deduce this from 1 John 2:15 is not necessary). See Meeks's description of the ambivalence between hating and loving the world in *The Origins of Christian Morality,* pp. 58-61. Regarding the Johannine stance toward Jews, sometimes described as hatred (a judgment arising from the vituperative language used against "the Jews," most extreme in 8:48), Adele Reinhartz, a Jewish scholar, challenges the "consensus" that John's Gospel reflects the alienation of those excommunicated from the synagogue (9:22; 12:42; 16:2). She reminds us that ch. 11 portrays the Jesus community together with Jews. See Reinhartz, "The Johannine Community and its Jewish Neighbors." Further, 11:45; 12:42; and 2:23 clearly declare that "many" Jews, even the authorities, believed in Jesus. Thus the text does not show a uniform hostile relationship between Jesus and Jews. Granted, John's repeated use of "the Jews" in negative tone reflects hostile relations. It is incumbent upon us — for the sake of the salvation of all people — not to one-sidedly interpret the text and thus empower it to foster racist enmity or

Another intratextual connection is significant in grasping the peace dimension of 20:19ff. Talbert helpfully shows the integral connection between themes directed to the disciples in Jesus' farewell discourse and 20:19-23, as follows:[24]

I am coming back to you (14:18; 16:22).	Jesus came to them (20:19).
Peace I leave with you (14:27; cf. 16:33).	Peace be with you (20:21).
Then your hearts will rejoice (16:22).	Then the disciples were glad (20:20d).
As you have sent me, I have sent them (17:18).	As the Father has sent me, even so I send you (20:21).
If I go, I will send the Spirit to you (16:7b; cf. 14:17, 26; 15:26).	Receive the Holy Spirit (20:22).

Clearly, the gift of peace, which Jesus alone can give, is linked integrally to the sending theme in John's presentation of what Jesus has to say directly to his disciples.

The Holy Spirit (advocate, comforter, empowerer) is also a key player in the post-resurrection reality envisioned by the text. In 20:22 Jesus *breathes* the Spirit onto his disciples, as the empowerment for their task. As noted by numerous commentators, "breathe" *(emphysaō)* is a singular NT use and harks back to the LXX version of Gen. 2:7, where God breathed into the human the spirit-breath that made the human a "living soul." Is it too much to infer that in both narratives, Gen. 2:7 and John 20:22, the God-Jesus breath is the true source of true *shalom* and *eirēnē*, the peace of God's gospel manifest in Jesus Christ?

It is essential to locate Jesus' gift of peace within the context of John's larger conflictual ethos. Some commentators contend that the peace Jesus be-

---

anti-Semitism. To explain the situation by means of a specific historical situation, excommunication from the synagogue speculatively linked with the Jews adding the *Birkat ha-minim* "malediction" to the "Eighteen Benedictions," as Martyn proposes, does not alleviate the problem of the text. Rather, it unfortunately places the blame of the alienation on the Jews. It would be better, as Reinhartz proposes — and textually more responsible — to propose that the dual portrait of both hostile and amicable relationships between Jesus/the Johannine community and Jews is part of the Christian "community's ongoing struggle for self-definition rather than . . . an external, Jewish act of expulsion" (Reinhartz, p. 138).

24. Talbert, *Reading John*, p. 254.

stows on his disciples refers specifically to inner peace, which relieves anxiety and fear.[25] But the conflicts that bedevil the disciples in the entire narrative and the persecution predicted in the farewell discourse require a different conclusion. The conflictual reality exists in at least three dimensions: *cosmic,* in which Jesus and his followers are in combat with the prince of this world (12:31, where victory is triumphantly declared); *religious,* between Jesus and some — at times many — of the Jews; and *political,* where Jesus knows that his not-of-this-world kingdom will clash with the world empires (both Jewish and Roman authorities, see chs. 18-19). Given this context, it seems more correct to hold that the peace bestowed by Jesus on the disciples in chs. 14, 16, and 20 not only grants relief from fear and anxiety, but promises victory amid the tribulation of these conflicts. As Brandenburger and Foerster hold,[26] this peace belongs to the OT royal messianic hope, which anticipates victory over all evil. It is the eschatological victory — hence Jesus' triumphant word from the cross, "It is finished" (19:30). This word is spoken in the context of the trilingual proclamation of Jesus as king of the Jews — truth in irony.

The joining of the greeting bestowing peace and the commission in John 20 is significant, because the earlier two strands of emphasis, from John 4 and chs. 14 and 16, indicate that peace and mission in John's Gospel are cross-cultural and break racial boundaries.[27] The ripe fields (4:38) include Samaritans and others as well. John 4 goes on to portray the splendid faith of the Roman official, which brings Jesus' healing to his son. As a result, this man and his household become believers. In both cases, ethnic, religious, and national enmities are disempowered and transformed by the power of Jesus, the Savior of the world. The sending of 20:21, then, has the whole world as its horizon.

The authority bestowed upon the disciples in this "peace-breath-word" enables them to release people from sin's bondage, and to grant them freedom to live, and live abundantly (10:10b). As Marianne Meye Thompson has noted,[28] Jesus as the Son is one with his Father precisely in authority to give

---

25. Hesselink, "John 14:23-29"; Jeske, "Expository Article: John 14:27 and 16:33."

26. Brandenburger, *Frieden im Neuen Testament,* pp. 48-50; W. Foerster, "εἰρήνη," *TDNT* 2:400-402.

27. To what extent does this feature of the mission-commission set forth a normative conviction: that the mission charge stands under the umbrella of the peace greeting? Luke 10 bears eloquent testimony to this, in that the peace greeting of the seventy initiates and extends the gospel of the kingdom of God, with the result that the demons lose their power, since Jesus sees Satan falling from heaven like lightning when the disciples' mission is being accomplished (10:17-18). Paul, in Ephesians and more broadly, affirms the same point, as Yoder Neufeld's essay demonstrates: "'For He Is Our Peace': Ephesians 2:11-22."

28. Marianne Meye Thompson, *The Promise of the Father,* pp. 135, 141-48, 152-54.

life (5:26). This unity is also the foundation of the so-called high priestly prayer: "And this is eternal life, that they may know you, the only true God, and Jesus Christ whom you have sent" (17:3). This gift of God through Jesus is extended in 17:20 to all "those who will believe in me through their [the disciples'] word."

The specific part of the mission charge that gives authority to forgive or retain sins is significant also in relation to John 4. Nothing is said explicitly in John 4 about Jesus forgiving the woman's sins. The emphasis falls on the gift of living water so that she will never thirst again. This metaphor is never fully explained, but in John's overall narrative strategy it coheres with other salvation-giving metaphors describing the gift of salvation: born from above, bread of life, seeing clearly, branches abiding in the vine, and light of the world. All these metaphors illumine Jesus' offer of the gift of eternal life, which for John is not so much future as an experience here and now of newness and transformed living, liberated from sin (cf. 8:1-12). The overall tone of the Gospel narrative leads us to expect that the Samaritan woman was forgiven of her sins and thus received the gift of life that led her and her community to declare Jesus "Savior of the world."

Moreover, this particular confession of the Samaritan community has political significance, as does the trial narrative. Several authors have pointed out that "savior of the world" — in variant forms — was a title applied to Roman rulers from Julius Caesar to Hadrian. For Hadrian this precise form was used *(sōtēr tou kosmou)*. Craig Koester contends that the text intends to evoke in the reader imperial associations and, in keeping with David Rensburger's treatment of John 18–19,[29] to show that the Samaritan confession moves them beyond "a form of worship tainted by charges of idolatry to true worship of God, and beyond national identity defined by colonial powers to become true people of God."[30] Richard Cassidy likewise acknowledges the alternative political option, but also stresses another point arising from his extensive study of the theme of persecution in John, especially in Jesus' farewell discourse. Through this Samaritan confession and Jesus' teaching throughout the Gospel, John seeks "to encourage his readers not ever to be swayed or intimidated by the aggrandizing claims of the Roman emperors who styled themselves as saviors."[31] In my judgment, this point is correct, and it need not discount from, but may add to, Rensberger's contribution.

---

29. Rensberger, *Johannine Faith and Liberating Community,* pp. 87-100.

30. Koester, "The Savior of the World (John 4:42)," 667, 680.

31. Cassidy, *John's Gospel in New Perspective: Christology and the Realities of Roman Power,* pp. 84-85.

Precisely within this context of the Gospel's political realities, especially the certainty that believers will be persecuted by the world — i.e., the authorities (15:20; 16:33; 17:14-15; chs. 18–19; 21:18-19), the bestowal of peace (also in 16:33) and the sending charge to bear the presence of Jesus and the Father in the hating world take on new depth of meaning. The bearers of this unique mission of peace will be known by their love for one another (13:35), for their love incarnates God's love for the world (3:16), even though the world does not receive the one whom God sent (1:11; 5:40-44; 15:18-21). Within the fabric of the Gospel as a whole, the Samaritan woman together with her community and the community empowered by the commission represent the light of salvation, transformation, peace, and reconciliation in a world of hate, blindness, and persecution. Peacemaking is the mission; the mission is peacemaking — through the transforming power of the one who is the savior of the world.

4:1-42 and 20:19-23 in John's Larger Narrative Purpose

John 4:1-42 and 20:19-23 connect to the explicitly stated purpose of the Gospel: "that you may believe that Jesus is the Christ, the Son of God, and that believing you may have life in his name" (20:31). A tiny textual variant in this statement of purpose has generated much discussion. The manuscript evidence is divided between the present and aorist tenses for the word "believe" (*pisteuēte* or *pisteusēte*). If the present tense is considered original, then we might translate "continue to believe." The Gospel's purpose then is that of strengthening and deepening the faith of believers at a time when it is being tested. But if the aorist tense is accepted we would translate it "come to believe." Then the Gospel is intended to be unequivocally missionary in posture and purpose. Although a few strong and early mss. have the present tense (*pisteuēte*), the greater ms. support is for the aorist (*pisteusēte*). Because this reading has support from a wide geographical range in the early church,[32] it is clear that most of the early church understood the Gospel evangelistically (but this need not exclude the nurturing and spiritual formation functions of the Gospel).

The pervasive use of "sent" language in the Gospel, more than 50 uses of various forms of *apostellō*, presents strong internal evidence that the Gospel is to be understood in this evangelistic way. In her dissertation work on John

---

32. Textual support for the aorist πιστεύσητε is from all text types: ℵᶜ A C D L W X Δ Π Ψ *f*¹ *f*¹³ 33 565 700 etc. Syrˢ, ᵖ, ʰ, ᵖᵃˡ; support for the present πιστεύητε is 𝔓⁶⁶ᵛⁱᵈ ℵ* B Θ 892.

20:19-23, Linda Oyer tabulated and analyzed all uses of *apostellō* and *pempō* in John (see "Attachment 2," pp. 323-24 below). Her conclusions from this study emphasize that the Father's sending of the Son into the world to save the world is the predominant emphasis, and that Jesus' sending of the disciples is to be understood as extending the work of the sent one. Whatever view of mission we attribute to John's Gospel, it is clear that "having been sent" is the empowering muscle of mission, based in the prior action of the Father and the Son.

Andreas Köstenberger amplifies this point by showing that Jesus' work in John is viewed pervasively as the work of the sent one:

> bring glory and honor to the sender (5:23; 7:18),
> do the sender's will (4:34; 5:30, 38; 6:38-39) and works (5:36; 9:4),
> speak the sender's words (3:34; 7:16; 12:49; 14:10b, 24),
> be accountable to his sender (ch. 17),
> bear witness to his sender (5:36; 7:28 = 8:26),
> represent him faithfully (12:44-45; 13:20; 15:18-25),
> exercise delegated authority (5:21-22, 27; 13:3; 17:2; 20:23),
> know the sender intimately (7:29; cf. 15:21; 17:8, 25),
> live in a close relationship with the sender (8:16, 18, 29; 16:32), and
> follow the sender's example (13:16).[33]

Not only is the entire work of Jesus grounded in the Father's sending, but the mission of Jesus is often governed by a purpose statement that flows out of this reality, as Teresa Okure in her extensive study of mission in John, and specifically of John 4, describes:

> All the major statements on mission in the Gospel have or presuppose a purposeful *hina*-clause: Jesus is sent by the Father "so that" those who believe in him may have eternal life (3:15, 16) or "so that" the world be saved through him (3:17); he comes "so that" all may have life to the full (10:10). John the Baptist is sent "so that" he may bear witness to the light (1:7a, 8), that Jesus may be revealed to Israel (1:31) and that all may believe through him (1:7b). Though no purposeful clause is explicitly attached to the missions of the Holy Spirit and of the disciples, it is understood that the whole purpose of their witnessing mission to Jesus (14:26; 15:26, 27) is "so that" the world may believe that the Father sent Jesus (17:21, 23; cf. 16:13-

---

33. Köstenberger, "The Challenge of a Systematized Biblical Theology of Mission." See Köstenberger's monograph, *The Missions of Jesus and His Disciples according to the Fourth Gospel: With Implications for the Fourth Gospel's Purpose and the Mission of the Contemporary Church* (Grand Rapids: Eerdmans, 1998), pp. 107-11.

14; 17:17-20). Moreover, since their mission is portrayed as an integral aspect of Jesus' own mission, both necessarily share the same purpose.[34]

Commenting on 4:38, Okure says, "In the Johannine conception, every missionary endeavor of every age means essentially and fundamentally a harvesting, a reaping of the fruit of the work of salvation accomplished definitively by Jesus and the Father."[35] Köstenberger also notes that "the sending of the Spirit occurs with reference to the missions of Jesus and the disciples."[36]

The inclusion of the Samaritans in the Johannine community of faith, which John 4 affirms, demonstrates the mission of the Son, and also serves as a model for instruction to the disciples whom Jesus has *sent* to reap in fields ripe for harvest (4:38).

This mission emphasis of the Gospel serves further the attainment of Jesus' purpose as the sent one: to glorify God and to be glorified by God (17:1-5). In John, the mutual interdependence of Father and Son is depicted not only in the common *work* of giving life, mission, and love, but also in mutual *glorification*. The Son glorifies the Father, and asks also for the Father to glorify him "in your own presence" (v. 5a).

That the accomplishment of mission as the sent one is so crucial to the actualization of this glorification is demonstrated clearly in John 12:20-32. Until this point in the Gospel, the narrator paces and interprets Jesus' mission with the arresting phrase, "my hour has not yet come." But here in 12:23, the mantra changes to "the hour has come." Why so? What triggers the change is the news from Andrew and Philip that Greeks are there and wish to see Jesus. Jesus' way of "answering the door" is to announce strategic shift in ministry emphasis: "The hour has come for the Son of man to be glorified." Clearly, the cross is now in view in Jesus' teaching about a grain of wheat falling into the ground and dying in order to bear fruit, in his cry to be saved from this hour, in the voice from heaven that answers his announcement "I have glorified it, and will glorify it again," and in Jesus' pronouncement that "Now is the judgment of this world; now the ruler of this world will be cast out." The Greeks' coming to see Jesus rings the alarm on the sent one's clock. It sets in motion Jesus' glorification through death, so that "I, when I am lifted up, will draw all people to myself" (12:32).

---

34. Okure, *Johannine Approach*, p. 5.
35. Okure, *Johannine Approach*, p. 164.
36. Köstenberger, *Missions of Jesus*, p. 192.

John 4 in Worship and Catechesis for Mission-Peacemaking

Appropriating John 4 for the life of the church could take many turns. My students have noted that this narrative illumines many diverse ministry themes and challenges. They have suggested that it provides resources for:

> lifting women from oppression to apostolic witness,
> modeling counseling that is non-judgmental, inviting, and life-giving,
> a spiritual meditation on Jesus as the living water,
> a redemptive approach to divorce and remarriage,
> understanding dimensions of christology from prophet to Messiah to
>   Savior of the world,
> understanding the nature of true worship,
> evangelism and mission, and
> peacemaking and reconciliation.

All these are hermeneutically legitimate and empowering uses of this rich text. The last three, however, are not only explicit in the text itself, but connect directly to larger themes in the Gospel, as shown above. Further, the inter-linking of these three — worship, mission, and peacemaking — cuts to the heart of the gospel and the crucial dimensions of religious life. To probe still deeper, one might contend rightly that unless these three emphases are each vitally present in a community of faith, any one of the three may be arid, pre-tentious, or phony.

It is beyond the scope of this chapter to explicate each of these topics as they might shape contemporary church life. As indicated at the beginning of this chapter, Ben Witherington, in his commentary on John, speaks persua-sively to at least two of these dimensions in a way that edifies and calls the church to faithfulness:

> Finally, at the climax of the story Jesus is portrayed as the savior of the world, which means the savior of all races, ethnic groups, sexes, and ages, regardless of one's socio-economic status, health, or previous theological orientation. While it is true that no local church can be all things to all people, and that there is nothing wrong with sharing the faith with those sorts of people with whom one has various things in common, there is something wrong with an evangelism strategy that deliberately tries to avoid crossing lines, and ignores the mandate to reach out across social barriers as Jesus does in this story. We too easily forget that the commu-nity of Jesus is not intended to be a museum for a particular kind of

saints, but rather is to be a hospital for sick sinners in a broken and divided world full of hate, prejudice, and discrimination. If one is going to preach or teach this text adequately, it will be necessary to stress the intentionality of Jesus and of God in reaching across lines, and to stress the way Jesus enables even despised and disfranchised people like Samaritans and women to become disciples and able witnesses for the Savior of the world. The question becomes, is the food that satisfies Jesus also the food that satisfies us, or are we settling for the more material fare that the disciples brought back from town? The fields are ripe for harvest, but the laborers are few.[37]

Indeed, John 4, especially when it is understood within the larger narrative dynamic of the Gospel — especially 20:19-23 — is an exceedingly rich text instructing the church in holistic mission and peacemaking action.[38] It reminds us that the two themes are not two, but inherently one: without mission, there is no peace that reconciles and makes whole; without peacemaking, there is no mission that is authentic and worthy of the gospel of Jesus Christ. The sent one sends us, and beckons us to *go through Samaria,* offering the water of life that quenches the thirst of the human soul, and like an artesian spring, wells up unto eternal life.

Finally, the Johannine emphasis on glorification reminds us that both the mission and peacemaking emphases stand in the service of true worship of God. The chiastic structuring of John 4 puts worship in the center. The empowering *dei* of Jesus' journey into "enemy" land — sent from the heart of God — culminates in Jesus presenting the gospel to the Samaritans, who then confess Jesus as the Savior of the world. This opens up the new strategic breakthrough: the true worship and glorification of God, in which neither Jerusalem nor Gerizim is prescriptive. Rather, the one who came as the Light of the world, with authority to give life, inviting us to worship God in spirit and in truth, and empowering us to love one another, becomes for us living water, bread of life, model shepherd, peace-giver, and, climactically, "My Lord and my God!"

---

37. Witherington, *John's Wisdom,* p. 125.

38. A significant book appeared after this chapter was completed: *Through the Eyes of Another: Intercultural Reading of the Bible,* ed. de Wit, Jonker, Kool, and Schipani. Interpretation of John 4 is the book's textual focus and its twenty-seven chapters are written by people from six continents. John Riches's chapter is especially arresting in its query regarding the purpose of "Intercultural Hermeneutics," the title of his essay. "Is it to promote international peace and justice," or does it simply "create a particular quality of dialogue?" (p. 463).

Attachment 1. The Entire Semantic Component of John 4 on a Single Square

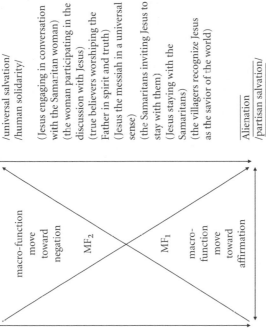

Death =
/sustenance/ =

Alienation
/partisan salvation/
/factional security/

(Jesus asking the woman for a drink of water)
(the disciples offering Jesus food to eat)

(Jesus passing through Samaria because he had to)
(Jews and Samaritans do not associate)
(Jesus a greater miracle worker than Jacob)
(Jesus a prophet)
(worshipping either on "this mountain" or in Jerusalem)
(Samaritans do not know what they worship, but Jews do)
(salvation is from the Jews)
(Jesus the messiah in a Samaritan sense)

$\overline{\text{Life}}$ =
/obedience/ =

$\overline{\text{Solidarity}}$
/universal salvation/
/human solidarity/

(the woman reminding Jesus of the impropriety of him, a Jew, asking her, a Samaritan woman, for a drink of water)

macro-function move toward negation
MF₂

MF₁
macro-function move toward affirmation

= Life
= /obedience/

Solidarity
/universal salvation/
/human solidarity/

(Jesus engaging in conversation with the Samaritan woman)
(the woman participating in the discussion with Jesus)
(true believers worshipping the Father in spirit and truth)
(Jesus the messiah in a universal sense)
(the Samaritans inviting Jesus to stay with them)
(Jesus staying with the Samaritans)
(the villagers recognize Jesus as the savior of the world)

(water of life = the woman witnessing about Jesus)
(Jesus' other food = engaging in discussion with the woman, and staying with the Samaritan villagers = doing the will of the one who sent him, and completing his work)
(the sower and the reaper rejoicing together in the fruit of the harvest)

$\overline{\text{Alienation}}$
/partisan salvation/
/factional security/

(Jesus ignoring the convention of nonassociation between Jews and Samaritans)
(worship neither on "this mountain" nor in Jerusalem)
(the villagers reject the woman's testimony)

= $\overline{\text{Death}}$
= /sustenance/

(the woman leaving her water behind)
(Jesus refusing the disciples' food)

Attachment 2. "Sent" in the Gospel of John

A = *apostellō*, P = *pempō*

Verse	Verb	Sender	One Sent
1:6	A	God	John the Baptist
1:19	A	Jews	priests
1:22	P	Jews	priests
1:24	A	Pharisees	priests
1:33	P	God	John B.
3:17	A	the Father	Jesus
3:28	A	God	John the Baptist
3:34	A	the Father	Jesus
4:34	P	the Father	Jesus
4:38	A	Jesus	disciples
5:23	P	the Father	Jesus
5:24	P	the Father	Jesus
5:30	P	the Father	Jesus
5:33	A	Jews	priests
5:36	A	the Father	Jesus
5:37	P	the Father	Jesus
5:38	A	the Father	Jesus
6:29	A	the Father	Jesus
6:38	P	the Father	Jesus
6:39	P	the Father	Jesus
6:44	P	the Father	Jesus
6:57	A	the Father	Jesus
7:16	P	the Father	Jesus
7:18	P	the Father	Jesus
7:28	P	the Father	Jesus
7:29	A	the Father	Jesus
7:32	A	priests	officers
7:33	P	the Father	Jesus
8:16	P	the Father	Jesus
8:18	P	the Father	Jesus
8:26	P	the Father	Jesus
8:29	P	the Father	Jesus
8:42	A	the Father	Jesus
9:4	P	the Father	Jesus

A = *apostellō*, P = *pempō*

Verse	Verb	Sender	One Sent
9:7	A		(*Siloam* = "sent")
10:36	A	the Father	Jesus
11:3	A	Martha and Mary	unnamed
11:42	A	the Father	Jesus
12:44	P	the Father	Jesus
12:45	P	the Father	Jesus
12:49	P	the Father	Jesus
13:16	P	general	
13:20	P	Jesus	disciple
13:20	P	the Father	Jesus
14:24	P	the Father	Jesus
14:26	P	the Father	Spirit
15:21	P	the Father	Jesus
15:26	P	Jesus	the Holy Spirit
16:5	P	the Father	Jesus
16:7	P	Jesus	the Holy Spirit
17:3	A	the Father	Jesus
17:8	A	the Father	Jesus
17:18	A	the Father	Jesus
17:18	A	Jesus	disciples
17:21	A	the Father	Jesus
17:23	A	the Father	Jesus
17:25	A	the Father	Jesus
18:24	A	Annas	Jesus
20:21	A	the Father	Jesus
20:21	P	Jesus	disciples

12   Revelation: Nonviolent Victory!
Faithfully Persevere in Prayer,
Praise, and Worship

Revelation, like John's Gospel, also presents a special challenge to the larger peace theology of the NT, but for different reasons. Loren Johns begins his study of the Lamb christology of Revelation by citing numerous writers who regard Revelation as morally deviant from NT theology as a whole. Sample such descriptions: "visions of a drug addict" (George Bernard Shaw), "the most detestable book of all [the] books in the Bible" (D. H. Lawrence), and from the highly respected NT scholar C. H. Dodd, "The God of the Apocalypse can hardly be recognized as the Father of our Lord Jesus Christ."[1] Mark Bredin, in his study of Revelation entitled *Jesus: Revolutionary of Peace*, cites an even longer list, including more NT scholars who regard Revelation as an aberration to the larger peace theology of the NT, among them Walter Wink, Marla Selvidge, M. Waldmann, R. Völkl, and even W. Barclay.[2]

---

1. Johns, *The Lamb Christology of the Book of Revelation*, p. 4. Johns cites further such remarks from these authors and similar statements from other writers, including Harold Bloom. Johns also connects the evocative power of the book with the David Koresh tragedy in Waco, Texas (1993) and the popularity of Hal Lindsey's books (pp. 5, 12, 150). The current popular "Left Behind" series by Tim LaHaye and Jerry B. Jenkins is the latest commercial fleecing of good-minded folks (see *Newsweek*, May 24, 2004, pp. 44-50) who, uninformed of the nonviolent lamb christology of Revelation, lack perspective to be critical of the series and its interpretation. For a helpful critique see Rossing, *Rapture Exposed;* Shuck, *Marks of the Beast*. Delegates of the Reformed Church in America annual General Synod declared the "Left Behind" books a "distortion of the biblical message" on June 8, 2004. The Synod also adopted a resolution against Christian Zionism, naming it an obstacle to peace in Middle East (*MWR*, July 8, 2004, p. 3).

2. Bredin, *Jesus, Revolutionary of Peace*, pp. 25-26. Throughout his work, Bredin compares the nonviolent resistance of Jesus and the believer-martyrs in Revelation to that of Mahatma Gandhi.

To understand Revelation and its rightful place in the canon that presents Jesus Christ and his followers as peacemakers, it is important to understand its apocalyptic genre and the historical context of its writing. Despite the demeaning of its ethical stance noted above, its central theology and ethics accord with other parts of the NT canon in its moral portrait of Jesus Christ. The purpose of this chapter is to show that this view represents the essential christological moral stance of Revelation.

Genre, Context, and Message

The nature of apocalyptic genre[3] is such that a literal reading of the text misses its purpose and prevents correct understanding of the literature. Apocalypticism began to flourish in Jewish writing in times of social and political crisis, most prominently in the OT books of Ezekiel, Zechariah, and Daniel. Numerous scholars regard apocalyptic writings to be rooted in the prophetic literature, though some see it as evolving from the wisdom traditions.[4] Prophetic literature calls the people to repent and usually offers hope for change and a better world within history. Apocalyptic literature looks to the edge of history, and anticipates a divine intervention that will inaugurate a new order, either on the historical plane or beyond history. Evil is rampant, but God will be victorious.

Scholars agree that apocalyptic literature is the voice of minority faith communities, whose position is often due to alienated social location,[5] who testify to their faith in coded symbolism that readers situated in a different time, place, or religious ethos may find hard to understand. While apocalyp-

---

3. See John J. Collins, *The Apocalyptic Imagination;* Rowland, *The Open Heaven.* Michael Gilbertson's study of Revelation and the theologies of Moltmann and Pannenberg shows how apocalyptic hope may be appropriated for an open future (Moltmann) or a consummated eschaton as universal history (Pannenberg) *(God and History in the Book of Revelation).*

4. See the eight essays on apocalypticism in Paul D. Hanson, ed., *Visionaries and Their Apocalypses.*

5. Paul Hanson's articles "Apocalypse, Genre" and "Apocalypticism" in *IDBSupp* helpfully distinguish between apocalypse (a *genre*), apocalyptic eschatology (dominant in specific communities), and apocalypticism (denoting a "symbolic universe" in which a community is alienated from the larger society). A particular group may not share all these features. Qumran was an apocalyptic community but produced no apocalypses, for example. Hanson also delineates three possible responses of the alienated community: withdraw to establish a counter-community based "upon a *symbolic utopian universe*"; become an underground movement within the larger society, with a *"symbolic subuniverse"* identity; or respond with violence empowered by a *"symbolic counter-universe"* (pp. 29-31).

ticism does not abandon the historical plane for divine action, it does anticipate a radical in-breaking of God into history and transformation of the present situation. The language is symbolic. Knowing as much as possible about
the social and political environment of the time when it was written aids understanding and interpretation. Revelation is indeed an apocalypse (its Greek
title is *Apokalypsis Iōannou*), and it must be read with an awareness of the nature of the apocalyptic genre, which regularly portrays end-time wars and
chaos preceding final victory.[6]

To grasp Revelation's message in its broad scope of theology, christology, ecclesiology, eschatology, God's sovereignty, and its call for faithful worship, I have poetically summed its drama of thought as follows:

Revelation's Mode and Scope of Faith-Proclamation

APOCALYPTIC	via multimedia projection on
	a cosmic screen
	the book of Revelation
	dramatizes
CHRISTOLOGY	how a bleeding Lamb
ECCLESIOLOGY	aids harmless saints
	to victoriously battle
	against militant horsemen and devouring beasts
	enraged for kill
	by a fierce dragon whose tail
	strikes down a third of the stars.
	In the midst,
	around,
	and above
THEOLOGY —	we see a *Throne!*
GOD'S SOVEREIGNTY	A throne — of God Almighty!
	The Lamb — with robe dipped in blood!
	The martyrs — those come out of great
ESCHATOLOGY	tribulation — in white robes!
	The Lamb's Bride
WORSHIP	The Lamb Hallelujah!
	The Throne Amen!

6. For an excellent treatment of the apocalyptic understanding of Revelation through
history, see Rowland, "The Book of Revelation," in *NIB*, vol. 12. Egon Brandenburger summarizes the apocalyptic themes in *Frieden im Neuen Testament*, pp. 23-24, also in "Perspektiven des
Friedens im Neuen Testament." For treating Revelation as opposition of God and Satan, see
Kallas, *Revelation: God and Satan in the Apocalypse.*

The historical circumstances that generated the Apocalypse were both experiences and threats of persecution of Christian believers by the Roman Empire. Virtually all contemporary scholars assign the time of Revelation's writing to the era of Domitian, on the strength of Irenaeus's statement (*Adversus haereses* 5.30.3). Current scholarship, however, disagrees that early Christians were programmatically persecuted, as earlier thought. Leonard Thompson argues for a "no persecution crisis." Adela Yarbro Collins proposes not an actual, but a "perceived crisis" about to fall upon the community of faith.[7] Marta Sordi, however, writing after Collins but before Thompson's major contribution, cites wide documentation for persecution under Domitian — from both Christian and pagan writers — and concludes: "I still maintain that the mere fact of there being so many individual reports of the persecutions having taken place makes it unreasonable to harbour any serious doubts on the subject."[8] Though Domitian likely never issued an all-out persecution of Christians, numerous local persecutions did occur,[9] and these may have been inspired mostly by social class conflict, with Christian believers alienated from the wealthy urban, often merchant, families that also were dominant in the Sebastos cult. Sebastos (the Greek for Latin *Augustus*) or Sebastoi (plural) designated venerated families who were recipients of sacrifice. Friesen in his careful study contends that the Sebastos temple cult at Ephesus (notable since this traditionally is the home of Revelation) differed from several earlier urban Sebastoi cults. This cult did not include among the Sebastoi "the corporate figures of Rome or the Senate." Rather, "the cult focused on the imperial family rather than on another corporate object of veneration." This means, says Friesen, that Domitian, and likely his wife Domitia, were worshiped in this cult's sacrificial practices.[10]

Certainly the anticipation, if not actual experience, of persecution was

---

7. Leonard Thompson, *The Book of Revelation: Apocalypse and Empire*, pp. 186-97; Adela Yarbro Collins, *Crisis and Catharsis: The Power of the Apocalypse*. Both authors hold, however, that conditions were such to marginalize the Christians and thus threaten their security. For a helpful survey of scholarly positions on this matter, and assessment of textual evidence, see Johns, *Lamb Christology*, pp. 120-27.

8. Sordi, *The Christians and the Roman Empire*, p. 45.

9. After examining the data testifying to regional persecutions and the scholarly diversity in interpretation, J. Nelson Kraybill rightly concludes that numerous local persecutions occurred. See *Imperial Cult and Commerce in John's Apocalypse*, pp. 33-36, 193-98.

10. Friesen, *Imperial Cults and the Apocalyspe of John*, p. 46. Friesen also points out that after Domitian's assassination the dedication inscriptions to Domitian were chiseled off the temple's bases and replaced with homage to Vespasian ("To Emperor *God* Caesar Sebastos *Vespasian*"). Vespasian was more revered, especially in the face of Domitian's impulsive violent actions.

well-founded in view of this cult practice of emperor worship and Domitian's unpredictable violence.[11] The evidence in Revelation itself for widespread persecution is also ambiguous, as Thompson's discussion indicates.[12] John's exile on Patmos and the specific reference to Antipas having been killed as a faithful witness (2:13) may indeed indicate that some form of persecution of Christians was a crucial part of Revelation's setting and causal motivation. That the writer locates himself in exile (one interpretation of 1:9) and that Rome is identified as "Babylon" are not without significance when judging the degree of the religious and political crisis. Jewish Christians knew the meaning of Babylon, its impact upon their communal security, and its threat to life. Several other texts may support martyrdom of saints (18:24; cf. 7:14; 16:6).

Walter Pilgrim proposes that Revelation's distinctive view arises from its historical context.

> The danger of intense persecution seemed right around the corner and the temptations from an idolatrous and corrupt culture on the move. . . . Under pressure from the political powers centering in imperial Rome, Revelation is written to resist the temptation to idolatry and compromise and to encourage believers to faithful endurance. This is Christian underground literature.[13]

Because of this historical reality Revelation portrays the believers' relationship and attitude to government authorities differently than does Paul, or even Jesus in the Synoptic Gospels. Regarding Revelation's view of government powers, Pilgrim perceptively says,

> The Apocalypse takes a position quite the opposite from that of Romans 13 and the loyalty tradition in the New Testament. Nor does its ethic correspond to that of the Gospel's depiction of Jesus' critical response to those in religious and political authority. In Revelation, the church and political powers are mortal enemies. Christ and Caesar are engaged in deadly combat, the classic New Testament example of 'Christ against Caesar'. There seems to be little room for compromise or accommoda-

---

11. For second- to fourth-century sources testifying to Domitian's megalomaniac actions and a good discussion of the evidence for incipient persecution, see Yeatts, *Revelation*, pp. 458-60. See also Beale, *The Book of Revelation*, pp. 6-9; Rowland, "The Book of Revelation," pp. 683-84.

12. L. Thompson, *Book of Revelation*, pp. 173-74. While Thompson chooses an interpretation of the texts that repudiates persecution, the same texts, he acknowledges, could be interpreted to support persecution.

13. Pilgrim, *Uneasy Neighbors*, p. 150.

tion. As we shall see, the Christian response toward the state in Revelation is not an ethic of subordination [as in Paul] or one of critical distancing [as in the Synoptic Gospels] but rather an ethic of resistance, even to the point of martyrdom.[14]

While Pilgrim is correct in this perception, it is of note that the Christian ethic in both Romans 13 and Revelation is essentially the same, as John H. Yoder argues in *The Politics of Jesus*.[15] Further, the Gospel of John is not to be contrasted to Revelation. As we have seen in Chapter 10, the distinction between Jesus and the believers, on one hand, and the world, on the other, is strong, matching the duality of light and darkness. The powers in John are portrayed, as in Revelation, as "of this world" (18:36) and as allied with the "prince of this world" (12:31). Jesus' victory through his death and exaltation in all the Johannine writings is victory over the powers: Satan, world, evil, or government authorities demonically inspired, as they appear in Revelation.

For this reason, the Christian community stands in a potential, if not actual martyr-death relationship to the empire. As Collins has shown, the believers' resistance is not that of the Zealots' violent resistance to Rome's oppression. Rather it is a non-resisting stance, "an explicit rejection of the militant option." Collins classifies the alternative as passive resistance, with two sub-types. One stance simply endures and waits for God's final battle against evil (Daniel). The other passive type (as in the *Assumption of Moses*) regards its resistance — even unto death — as synergistic with God's victory, hastening the coming of God's kingdom in its fullness. Martyrdom anticipates and participates in divine victory. Both passive types expect an eschatological battle when the Lord as holy warrior defeats and judges the powers of evil. Collins considers the phrase "those with him [the Lamb]" in 17:14, i.e., the "called and elect," as suggesting synergistic participation in the battle itself (cf. the 144,000 in 14:1-5 and 19:14, where "the armies of heaven" follow). Clearer, however, is the view that the death of the martyrs (6:9-11) functions synergistically to bring the final triumph closer.[16] Collins rightly sees a connection between Revelation's and the Zealots' critique of Rome; both protest the empire's horrific domination and demand for exclusive loyalty (e.g. the required "mark on the forehead" to buy and sell in 13:16-17).[17] The saints in Revelation, however, are nowhere portrayed as taking up arms against Rome; rather, they

14. Pilgrim, *Uneasy Neighbors*, p. 145.
15. John Howard Yoder, *The Politics of Jesus*, chapters 8, 10, and 12.
16. Adela Yarbro Collins, "The Political Perspective of the Book of Revelation," quoting p. 247; discussion extends to p. 249.
17. Collins, "Political Perspective," p. 252.

are portrayed as loyal followers of Jesus the Lamb in his death in 3:21; 12:11; and 20:4-6.[18]

I agree with Collins that Revelation depicts resistance of the second type, with the martyrs seeing their faithful endurance and death as participating in the eschatological coming of the kingdom. But more must be said: their role is not really passive. It has a fervent active component in the prayers of the saints and in their worship and praise of God. Bauckham's article on prayer in Revelation stresses this point, noting that the prayers (5:8; 6:9-10; 8:3-4) "are fully eschatological — that is, they are prayers for the coming of God's kingdom, for completion of God's purposes for his creation, for the fulfillment of all that God has promised . . . to perfect it [creation] by his own presence throughout eternity."[19] Further, the prayers of the saints have a place in in the Lamb's victory: "Revelation portrays the deaths of the martyrs as a kind of participation in the shed blood of the Lamb."[20] To discount prayer, praise, and worship in Revelation is to miss the heart of the book. Such action courageously counters the power of the powers, testifying even at the point of death that God is on the Throne. The saints nonviolently resist the imperial domination. As Hays puts it, "A work that places the Lamb that was slaughtered at the center of its praise and worship can hardly be used to validate violence and coercion."[21] Such praise and worship testifies to the true cosmic Sovereign, knowing that the arrogant earthly empire is doomed in God's judgment, and that the kingdom-empire of the Messiah-Lamb will endure forever.

Revelation and a Peace Ethic

From a NT canonical and theological perspective Revelation raises several crucial issues for peacemakers. The word *eirēnē* occurs only twice: in the liturgical introit in 1:4 and in the dismaying declaration of the rider on the red horse in 6:4 that he has been granted permission to take peace from the earth.[22] These two uses of "peace" disclose the narrative tension — and the

---

18. Collins, "Political Perspective," p. 254.

19. Bauckham, "Prayer in the Book of Revelation," pp. 252-53.

20. Bauckham, "Prayer," pp. 260-61.

21. Hays, *The Moral Vision of the New Testament*, p. 175. Hays quotes O'Donovan, "The Political Thought of the Book of Revelation," p. 90: "There is . . . something highly paradoxical about the picture of the Prince of Martyrs constituting himself the head of an army of conquest. It is an image which negates itself, canceling rather than confirming the significance of the political categories on which it draws."

22. In an early draft I used this phrase as a subtitle for this chapter. But the dominant em-

historical reality it reflects — of the book. As the recurring scenes of worship and praise to God burst forth throughout the narrative, it is clear that the "red horse" plague does not overcome the peace blessing. Rather, as in John's Gospel light triumphs over darkness, so in Revelation peace triumphs over war.

But warfare and judgment are writ large in the unfolding drama. Terms used seldom elsewhere in the NT appear quite frequently: twice the Lamb makes war *(polemēsō):* in 2:16 and in 19:11, where the warfare is linked with "judging righteously." Two words for wrath, *thymos* and *orgē,* are used ten and six times respectively, far more often than elsewhere in the NT, except *orgē* in Romans.[23] Also, numerous words from the *dik-* family are used, thus stressing the righteousness and justice of God *(dikaios* in 16:5, 7; 19:2; 22:11; *dikaioō* in 22:11; *dikaiōma* in 15:4; 19:8; and *dikaiosynē* in 19:11). The verb *avenge (ekdikeō)* occurs, however, only twice (6:10; 19:2) of its six NT uses.[24]

Even if circumscribed by the blessing of peace at the beginning and the new heavens and new earth at the end, how are the war-powered and wrath-dumping visions of the seer to be understood? How can a book filled with violent imagery contribute to peace and peacemaking? No easy answer is plausible, though, as David Barr has pointed out, much of the violence is the action of the empire-beast, though this too occurs within God's sovereign purpose.[25] Both the historical circumstances and the apocalyptic genre factor into this moral dilemma. The "holy war" tradition and imagery that often occur in apocalyptic literature make Revelation similar to the Qumran War Scroll in imagery and vocabulary. But the moral character of Revelation can be understood only as one perceives Revelation's transformation of the holy war tradition. As Barr puts it, "John consistently demythologizes the war — or perhaps more accurately, remythologizes the warrior with the image of the

---

phasis of Revelation lies not in the perpetration of this war-chaos, promulgated and symbolized by the red horse. This aspect of historical reality cannot negate the introit's bestowal of peace to the saints. This salutation extends the blessing (macarism) of 1:3 as the lector now addresses the churches, the suffering saints. The blessing form occurs seven times in the book and provides one of the clues for regarding Revelation as liturgical in nature and structure. See Vanni, "Liturgical Dialogue as a Literary Form in the Book of Revelation."

23. Greek *thymos* occurs a total of eighteen times and *orgē* thirty-six times, with twelve in Romans.

24. Noun *(ekdikēsis)* and adjective *(ekdikos)* forms do not occur in Revelation, but are used eleven times elsewhere, four in Luke-Acts.

25. Barr, "Doing Violence: Moral Issues in Reading John's Apocalypse," p. 104. I concur with Barr and Pippin *(Death and Desire: The Rhetoric of Gender in the Apocalypse of John)* that representing the beast Babylon (i.e., Rome) as a woman (17:18) is lamentable, even though we celebrate the downfall of violent imperial power.

suffering savior so that the death of the warrior and not some later battle is the crucial event."[26] This point provides a crucial perspective to key issues in the drama:

> What is the role of the Lamb and how is this related to the Warrior on the white horse of 19:11-16?
>
> What role do the saints play in the war and the victory?
>
> How are the wrath and vengeance of God to be understood in relation to the larger NT witness, especially John and 1 John, where the image of God as love predominates?
>
> Given the view of the empire that emerges in Revelation — as beast and stooge of Satan, from the perspective of the suffering believers — how shall these understandings of political power be evaluated and regarded by believers who live and work for justice and peace?

Loren Johns puts it well in his article on Revelation:

> The Apocalypse virtually seethes with images of blood and violence. To make matters worse, God and the Lamb often seem to be the source of the violence, sometimes to the accompaniment of cries of vengeance on the part of the saints. Is this an ethical vision? Let me be more specific. We know that John inherited a Lamb tradition from early Christian tradition as well as a divine warrior tradition, imagery he expressed in part by the figure of "the Lion of the tribe of Judah." The question is whether the book's great central image of Christ as the Lamb serves to control and interpret the other major themes, including the divine warrior and judgment imagery, or whether the divine warrior tradition ends up transforming, reinterpreting, or subverting the Lamb Christology.[27]

George B. Caird goes to the heart of these issues by rightly understanding the Lamb's, i.e. Jesus Christ's, victory as prototypical for his followers. Commenting on the Song of Moses in 15:2-4, Caird says, "because [God's] triumph [as at the Red Sea] has been won by no other weapons than the Cross of Christ and the martyr testimony of his followers, this song is also the song of the Lamb." And, in relation to the warrior on the white horse, after correlating his name, "Word of God," with his "sharp sword" in the tradition of Isa. 49:2; Heb. 4:12; and Eph. 6:17, ". . . the only weapon the Rider needs, if he is to

---

26. Barr, "Doing Violence," p. 101.

27. Johns, "The Violence of Revelation as a Theological Problem." The latter part is a quotation from his *Lamb Christology*, p. 151.

break the opposition of his enemies, and establish God's reign of justice and peace, is the proclamation of the gospel."[28] Indeed, it is "The Word of God" (19:13) that conquers evil, not only in Revelation but in OT prophetic and other NT literature as well. Patricia MacDonald expands this point and regards the identification of the rider on the white horse as "the Word of God" and the metaphor "sharp (two-edged) sword of his mouth" (1:16; 2:12; 19:15) as crucial to Revelation's theology. The Lamb's and his followers' victory is not by the military sword, but by the word-witness *(martyria)*.[29]

The Lamb christology combined with the faithful word-witness is the heartbeat of Revelation's distinctive contribution to peace theology. Loren Johns sums up his essay on Revelation 5, which sets the tone for his book:

> Our analysis of chap. 5 led us to conclude that the strategy of the Seer is to introduce the Lamb in chap. 5 in such a way as to underscore a central reversal in his apocalypse — a reversal in the conventional wisdom about the nature and function of power in the world. This reversal is set up with symbols clearly tied to the messiah, symbols like one from the tribe of Judah and the root of David. But there is a redefining of the *nature and method* of the messiah's victory. In the Apocalypse, the author draws from a multi-faceted mine of associations to the lamb in order to create a powerful new christological statement pregnant with ethical implications. Specifically, the power and authority — or worthiness — to unfold God's will for humanity are located in the readiness to die a witness's death. At the heart of this reversal lies an ethical intent; at the surface lies a Lamb Christology.
>
> The Lamb Christology predominates in this vision precisely because it expresses best the author's own understanding of the nature and importance of the death and resurrection of Christ for the question of how believers in the province of Asia are to express *their* resistance to evil. The theology of the Apocalypse can even be characterized as a theology of peace, with peace defined not as absence of conflict, but as an ethic of nonviolent resistance to evil. This ethic requires the assurance that the death of faithful testimony is really a symbol of victory — both for Christ and for believers who follow in his footsteps.[30]

The Lamb christology is indeed central to Revelation. The Greek term for lamb used in Revelation is *arnion*. Johns undertakes an exhaustive study

---

28. Caird, *The Revelation of St John the Divine*, pp. 198, 245.
29. McDonald, *God and Violence*, pp. 259-74.
30. Johns, *Lamb Christology*, 202-3; "Violence," p. 10.

of the OT background, noting the numerous Hebrew and LXX Greek terms for "lamb." From his study of five texts where *arnion* occurs,[31] he concludes that Revelation "represents Christ as lamb in order to represent the vulnerability that inevitably accompanies faithful witness. . . . Such vulnerability is no weakness; instead it proves triumphant over the powers of evil and exposes the weakness of violence."[32] Bauckham suggests that the lamb image in Revelation reflects the lamb *(amnos)* tradition of Isa. 53:7, the lamb led to the slaughter, a much more prominent emphasis in OT-NT theological reflection denoting both vulnerability and sacrificial imagery.[33] Indeed, if the martyrs are by their obedience unto death regarded as in some way nonviolently participating in or hastening the consummation of the Lamb's victory, decisively begun at Golgotha, then the sacrificial lamb imagery bolsters both the significance of their martyrdom and the triumph of the Lamb. As further support evoking sacrificial motifs, the saints' prayers are intertwined with "the altar" of "the slaughtered" and the shedding of "the blood of the saints."[34]

Whichever contextual meaning is in view — both in my judgment — Revelation clearly presents Christ as a defenseless lamb who suffers willingly to accomplish God's triumph over evil. The theology is similar to that of John's Gospel, in which death and exaltation are viewed as one: in being "lifted up" Jesus fulfills his commission to glorify God. The drama of Revelation is of the same moral fabric: through the Lamb's suffering and the suffering of the believers God's victory over evil is won.[35] The victory of the rider on the white horse whose only weapon is the sword that comes from the mouth (19:11-16) is one with the Gospel's triumphant cry of the defenseless Jesus, "It is finished" *(tetelestai,* John 19:30). "It is done" in Rev. 16:17 and 21:6 *(gegonen, gegonan)* is similar in meaning.

31. Jer. 11:19 (Hebrew *kebeš*); 50(27):45 *(ts'ire hatso'n);* Ps. 114:4, 6 *(bene tso'n);* Isa. 40:11 in Aquila *(telah); Psalms of Solomon* 8:23 (no Hebrew equivalent).

32. Johns, *Lamb Christology,* p. 204. Here Johns argues against Malina's view that the lamb is a symbol of force. See Malina, *On the Genre and Message of Revelation,* p. 101.

33. Bauckham, *Climax of Prophecy,* p. 215. Bauckham, in this crucial chapter of his book (pp. 210-37), proposes that Revelation is a Christian form of a War Scroll, with the intent of subverting violence by the witness of the suffering martyrs whose Redeemer-Leader is the slaughtered Lamb.

34. Bauckham, "Prayer," pp. 253-71. Bauckham astutely points out that Revelation speaks of two altars, the altar of incense (5:8 connected to 8:1, 3-5; 14:18) and an altar associated with slaughter and blood (6:9-11; 16:4-7). Reference to *slaughter* appears again in 18:24 and marks, of course, the definitive feature of the Lamb qualifying him to "open the scroll" (5:1-8). See Bauckham's diagram (p. 271) in the context of his persuasive discussion.

35. Quite strikingly, the anticipated battle of Harmagedon (16:16) never happens. Rather, the slain Lamb is the victor, and the battle need not be fought.

How is this nonviolent victory to be correlated with Revelation's emphasis on judgment, even vengeance? First, the vengeance in Revelation is akin to similar features in the OT in which God brings judgment on the pagan nations or Israel.[36] That such a role was envisioned for the expected Messiah is abundantly evident in the Jewish apocalypses, so it is not the cutting edge of the contribution of Revelation. Rather, the manner in which this war imagery is subverted becomes the distinctive contribution of the book. To make this point, William Klassen notes two distinctive features in Revelation. First, "the followers of the Lamb do not directly participate in the battle against the beast or the whore except that they are to remain faithful throughout life and in that way will conquer" and, second, the saints are at no place portrayed as enjoying forever the torture and destruction of the enemy, although there is indeed praise to God and the Lamb that the enemy has been judged and has fallen.[37] Klassen regards the cosmic disasters of the seals, trumpets, and plagues cycles as God extending opportunity and incentive to bring humans to repentance. John Wood, however, demurs on Klassen's attempt to rescue the book in this way from a portrait of God as vengeful. Wood suggests that Revelation's ethical character appears closer to that of the Qumran War Scroll than to that of First and Second Isaiah.[38] Yet at the end of his discussion he concedes significant elements of truth in Klassen's view, distinguishing between God's wrath judging evil and avenging enemies.[39]

The debate on these matters is extensive in the literature on Revelation. Most scholars agree that the believers do not participate in the battle, though not all agree on the believers'/martyrs' response to God's action, specifically vengeance, in Revelation. Klaus Wengst, for example, says, "The hope for the downfall of Rome is not free from a lust for vengeance . . . shown . . . by the desire for double retribution" (see 20:10, 13; 18:8).[40] Adela Yarbro Collins's judgment is: the "idea that God executes judgment does not exclude the human feeling of envy or desire for revenge."[41] Bredin categorizes interpreters' re-

36. Nor is this emphasis foreign to the Jesus of the Gospels. See the parables of judgment in Luke 19:11-27; Matthew 13:36-43; 18:23-35; 25. For a similar perspective in Paul, see 2 Thess. 1:6-10.

37. Klassen, "Vengeance in the Apocalypse of John," pp. 305, 309.

38. John A. Wood, *Perspectives on War in the Bible*, pp. 91-92.

39. Wood, *Perspectives*, p. 96.

40. Wengst, *Pax Romana and the Peace of Jesus Christ*, p. 127.

41. Collins, "Persecution and Vengeance in the Book of Revelation," p. 746. Collins also cautions against the potentially dangerous function of Revelation for communities of faith: its "call for vengeance . . . as an outlet for envy gives the book a tremendous potential for real psychological and social evil." But she also observes that it may serve us well also, "as a reminder to the privileged that the system which benefits them may be causing real hardship to others" (p. 747).

sponses into two differing positions.[42] One group (Yarbro Collins, Schüssler Fiorenza, M. Volf, and J. L. Coker) regard vengeance as God's prerogative, and the believers rejoice at this vengeance, which empowers their endurance as martyrs. Other interpreters (G. B. Caird, W. Klassen, J. Sweet, W. Harrington, R. Bauckham, and J. N. Kraybill) emphasize that the believers/martyrs do not rejoice because of God's vengeance or the enemy's destruction but over God's victory and consummation of salvation.[43]

In assessing the function of wrath and vengeance in Revelation, we have noted that the verb for *avenge (ekdikeō)* occurs only twice. In the first use, it occurs in a question put to God, "Sovereign Lord, holy and true, how long will it be before you judge and avenge our blood on the inhabitants of earth?" (6:10). God's answer, in keeping with Jewish belief in a predestined number of elect, is: until the number of martyrs is complete. The martyrs themselves have no role in the avenging, except to wait and trust. The interchange has the effect of strengthening the martyrs to remain faithful in suffering until it is God's time to avenge. And that God alone does. The inclusio surrounding the seven trumpets makes the same point: in 8:3-5 "the prayers of the saints" initiate the trumpet sequence of God's judgment on the wicked who do not repent and are accomplices to the beast; the end of the cycle in 11:15-18 depicts the elders, who head up the saints and martyrs, thanking God for his great victory and acknowledging the justice of God's wrath, even in destroying the destroyers of the earth. While *wrath (orgē)* occurs more frequently, as noted above, A. T. Hanson rightly contends that the function of God's and the Lamb's wrath in Revelation is not to mete out revenge and retribution but to lead people to repent, be reconciled to God, and thus be delivered from the powers of evil: Satan, the beast, and the idolatrous empire.[44]

The "bowls of wrath" cycle is similar in accent, though the structure differs. In 16:5-7, with the pouring out of the third bowl, an angel declares the justice of God in avenging (though the word is not used) the blood of the saints and prophets. The altar's response, presumably from the martyrs, is: "Yes, O Lord God, the Almighty, your judgments are true and just!" In the grand finale

42. It is not altogether clear whether Bredin is discussing here one or both of two related issues: 1) whether the saints-martyrs *desire* and rejoice in God's vengeance against the enemy, and/or 2) whether God in the final battle is portrayed as violent. In this chapter I focus the discussion primarily on the former issue; in Chapter 14 I will take up more directly the second issue.

43. Bredin, *Jesus, Revolutionary of Peace*, pp. 26-34. Bredin notes that Kraybill waffles on this point, at points siding with Adela Yarbro Collins, in that the drama of the book functions as catharsis of emotion for those about to face persecution (Bredin, p. 34; Kraybill, *Imperial Cult*, p. 205).

44. A. T. Hanson, *The Wrath of the Lamb*, pp. 159-201.

to all the cycles, the seals, trumpets, and bowls, the hallelujah choir celebrates both the downfall of Babylon (ch. 18) and God's act to avenge (19:2). The saints do rejoice over Babylon's downfall (18:20), and the loud voice of the great heavenly multitude includes the line, "he has avenged on her [Babylon] the blood of his saints" (19:2c). This declaration acknowledges God's victory as vengeance against the persecutors, not so much toward people as such, but toward the self-exalted idolatrous power of the empire. And certainly, the saints and martyrs do *not* execute the vengeance; it is God's prerogative. The saints and martyrs simply give thanks to and praise God that God has won the victory through the Lamb. Further, the believers' link to vengeance is not direct but only through submission to and trusting in God to accomplish his sovereignty.[45]

The "bowls of wrath" plagues in Revelation 16 serve four major purposes: to seriously warn Christians not to accommodate to the economic and political pressures of the beastly empire — not to accept its mark; to assure believers that the evil now unleashed in history is not independent from God's sovereignty but mysteriously serves its purpose; to grant time and opportunity for people to repent and "convert" from allegiance to the beast; and to show that "God's wrath, in hating and destroying evil, serves the purpose of cleansing creation" to prepare for the new heavens and new earth, the culmination of Revelation's gospel vision.[46]

For the persecuted believers the way of the Lamb's war is faithful testimony *(martyria)* to Jesus, defined as "the spirit of prophecy" in 19:10. This *martyria* (the word is used nine times: 1:2, 9; 6:9; 11:7; 12:11, 17; 19:10 [2x]; 20:4) puts one at risk of being killed as a martyr *(martys,* used five times: 1:5; 2:13; 3:14; 11:3; 17:6).[47] In this way the saints conquer *(nikaō,* 2:7, 11, 17, 26; 3:5, 12, 21; 21:7), just as the Lion (5:5)/Lamb (28x, see especially 17:14) has conquered and other brothers and sisters have already conquered (2:13; 12:11; 15:2), even though it is permitted for the beast to make war and conquer the saints (11:7; 13:7). Though the beast conquers the "testifiers" (11:7), the martyrs conquer the beast (12:11); though the beast conquers the saints (13:7), those singing the "Song of the Lamb" conquer the beast and its image (15:2-3). "The death and

---

45. For some of the ideas in this paragraph I am indebted to Gehman, "Rejoice O Heaven." The outpouring of God's wrath serves the cause of divine justice, as Schüssler Fiorenza, *The Book of Revelation: Justice and Judgment;* and Grimsrud, "Peace Theology and the Justice of God in the Book of Revelation," emphasize.

46. Grimsrud, "Peace Theology," p. 143.

47. Revelation 12:11 specifically and the drama of the book as a whole make the connection between these two words at the conceptual level. Hence the point that one leads to the other in Revelation is more than an etymological argument; it is embedded in the narrative use of the two words.

exaltation of Christ is now the means by which the dragon is cast down and provides a paradigmatic model for Christians. They too can defeat the dragon if they are 'washed in the blood' and are prepared to lay down their lives."[48]

A definite pattern of lock-step relationship marks Revelation's structure and theology. The death of Jesus is foundational for the believers' witness/ martyrdom; their faithfulness testifies to the Lamb's lordship over the church. But this lordship is not only ecclesiological, but anticipates the manifestation of God's cosmic lordship, in which the empires of the world become the empire of "his Lord and of his Christ." Prompted by Holtz's study of the centrality of 1:5-6 as foundational to the christological thought of Revelation,[49] I outline the structural sequences of the book in seven strophes, with each based on the Lamb prototype. Each strophe includes ecclesiological response and also the cosmic vision of God-through-the-Lamb's triumph, as follows. "Lamb" is used 28 times in Revelation and is the only designation for Christ in the narrative plot other than "Son of Man" in 14:14; other titles are used in the frames of the drama in chs. 1 and 22.

Punctuating the entire drama are great hymns of praise, often drawn directly from OT worship texts. For example, "the song of Moses . . . and of the Lamb" in 15:3-4 is a mosaic of Psalm texts, as Yeatts points out:

> Great and amazing are your deeds, (Pss. 92:5; 98:1; 111:2; 139:14)
> Lord God the Almighty! (Gen. 17:1; 35:11; Exod. 6:3; Ps. 68:14; Ezek. 10:5)
> Just and true are your ways, (Deut. 32:4; Ps. 145:17)
> King of the nations! Lord, who will not fear and glorify your name? (Jer. 10:6-7; Mal. 1:6, 11, 14)
> For you alone are holy. (1 Sam. 2:2; Pss. 99:3, 5, 9; 111:9)
> All nations will come and worship before you, (Ps. 86:9; Isa. 2:2-4; 66:19-21; Jer. 16:19; Mic. 4:2)
> for your judgments have been revealed. (Exod. 6:6; 7:4; 12:12; Ps. 98:2)[50]

---

48. J. Collins, *The Apocalyptic Imagination*, p. 213. See his Bibliography (pp. 251-74), especially his own works (pp. 254-55), for study of apocalypticism.

49. Holtz, *Die Christologie der Apokalypse des Johannes*. Holtz rightly says, "Every function of Christ [the Lamb] stands in fundamental connection to his atoning death" (p. 79). He holds that *arnion* connotes the Passover lamb and that the Lamb's atoning death is effective throughout the drama of the book (pp. 79-80) — in opening the seals (6:1), manifesting wrath (6:16), executing retribution (14:10), conquering evil (17:14; 12:11), giving water of life (7:17), disclosing the book of life (13:8; 21:27), appearing as leader and Lord of the church (14:1, 4; 15:3), and marrying the bride (19:7, 9; 21:9).

50. Yeatts, *Revelation*, p. 301. This song is sung with "harps in their hands" (see also 14:2). Might this, with Babylon's fall, be an echo reversing the "hung-up harps" in Psalm 137 (with thanks for the suggestion to Janeen Bertsche Johnson)?

Both the vocabulary and concepts are drawn largely from Scripture, which sustained the community amid its persecution. The Exodus plagues influenced especially the portrayal of the bowls of wrath. Psalms texts and the vision of God's sovereign presence and purpose set forth in Isaiah 40–66 influence the great hymns of Revelation. But at the heart of Revelation's structure and movement are three christological topoi (see the diagram on p. 340). The progression of the structure is consistently from the action of the Lamb, to the response-action of the faithful church, to the consequences for the cosmos and especially the world powers. Indeed, the believers' "life in the *basileia* provides power to live the resistance to evil *(hypomonē)* that is necessary in the time of *thlipsis.* (See 2:2-3; 13:10; 14:12.)" Further, in this drama of the saints prevailing against the beastly empire, "the prayers, the patience, the persistent resistance of the saints overthrow the powers of evil and bring God's kingdom into reality."[51]

God's Sovereignty and Worship: The Central Issue

Overarching the slain Lamb at the center of the book's christology, God and the throne (used 46 times) permeates the whole of Revelation. God's throne, symbol of divine sovereignty, extends over all else, as the heavens encircle the earth. The blaspheming idolatries of self-made emperor-gods are dwarfed as paltry preposterous powers. As Schüssler Fiorenza puts it, "The central question of these chapters [4-5] as well as of the whole book is: Who is the true Lord of this world?" The answer? "The author insists that the 'Lord' of the world is not the emperor but Jesus Christ who has created an alternative reign and community to that of the Roman empire."[52] Revelation forces a choice between loyalty to the "Herrschaft Gottes" and the "Herrschaft Roms," and the only Christian possibility for John is a decision against the political-religious power of his time.[53] The issue, as Vernard Eller emphasizes, is: whose mark will one bear and who will one follow, the *arnion* (Lamb) or the *thērion* (beast)?[54]

Hence, whom one worships is the central issue of the book and all the rest is stage effect creating a sharp silhouette — framed by the stark experiences of near past, present, and imminent suffering — for the urgent plea,

51. Barr, "Doing Violence," pp. 106, 108.
52. Schüssler Fiorenza, *Justice and Judgment,* p. 4; *Invitation to the Book of Revelation,* p. 72.
53. Schüssler Fiorenza, "Religion und Politik in der Offenbarung des Johannes."
54. *The Most Revealing Book of the Bible: Making Sense Out of Revelation,* p. 133.

Lamb-Throne Christology

	Death of Jesus (faithful unto death)	Lord of the church (ecclesiological)	Lord of the World (cosmic)
1:5a	the faithful witness (*martyria*)	the first-born of the dead	the ruler of the kings on earth
1:5b-7	loved us, freed us from sin by his blood	made us a kingdom, priests to God	coming on clouds; every eye will see him; all tribes will wail
1:18	I died	I live forever (chs. 2-3: address to the churches)	I have the keys of death and hades
chs. 4–5	Lamb slain (5:6, 9b)	worldwide kingdom of priests (5:9c-10)	cosmic acclaim and praise (5:12-14)
chs. 6–18	slain Lamb opens *seven seals,* showing the tribulation of the martyrs (6:1-8:1)	prayers of saints ascend while *seven trumpets* blow, climaxed by *victory* (trumpet 7 and song of the redeemed — 11:15-19) (8:2–11:19)	*seven bowls* of wrath poured out on the nations (16:1–18:24; see 17:15)
chs. 12–15	persecuted child (12:4b)	build theme of triumph through tribulation and victory of the saints (separation-judgment: 14:18 and 20:11-15); ch. 15	doom of the beast Babylon (13-14; 14:18-20)
ch. 19	rider with robe dipped in blood (19:13)	praise of redeemed multitude (19:1-8)	destruction of evil generals (19:17-21)
ch. 20		reign of the martyrs	destruction of evil itself (separation-judgment here and 14:18)
21:1–22:5	Lamb death no more	bride city of light	nations healed through tree of life and river of water
			eternal praise and triumph

sabbath of eternal blessedness

"Worship God" *(proskynēson tǭ theǭ)* in 19:10, repeated in 22:9. The verb *proskyneō* is used 24 times, far more often than in any other NT book. In eleven uses the recipients of false worship are demons, the dragon, and the beast or its image. In another ten God the Sovereign One or the Lamb is the rightful recipient of the saints' worship. The other three are to angels or humans to humans.[55] God and the Lamb alone are *worthy* of worship. John knows that the destiny of history is worship. Indeed, worship, an intrinsic aspect of the war and peace issue, lies at the heart of Revelation, as well as the biblical story as a whole (see especially Deut. 18:9-14). Precisely for this reason Revelation is dated to the reign of Domitian, for he certainly welcomed and likely promoted emperor worship beyond that of his immediate predecessors.[56] It explains why Revelation is doxological, affecting even its structure.[57]

55. For the evil forces: Rev. 9:20; 13:4 (2x), 8, 12, 15; 14:9, 11; 16:2; 19:20; 20:4; for worship of God or the Lamb: 4:10; 5:14; 7:11; 11:1, 16; 14:7; 15:4; 19:4, 10; 22:8. The two references to angels are in 19:10; 22:8; here the "seer" (John) is corrected: "Worship God!" The one remaining reference is 3:9 where those of the "synagogue of Satan" will be made to bow down at the feet of the faithful at Philadelphia.

56. According to Roman sources, around 86 CE Domitian requested his courtiers and poets to greet him as *Deus et dominus* (Suetonius, *Domitian* 4.4; 13.2; Dio Cassius 67.7; Martial 5.8.1; cf. 1.30.7; Frend, *Martyrdom and Persecution,* p. 213). While some scholars may doubt the veracity of the report in these sources, especially that Domitian requested such, yet Steven Friesen's findings from epigraphic evidence and the text of Revelation point in the same direction: "The group of thirteen inscriptions commemorated the dedication of a provincial temple in Ephesos for the worship of the Flavian emperors in 89/90 C.E. *during the reign of Domitian.* The texts come from bases of statues that were once displayed in the precincts of the temple of the Sebastoi" ("Myth and Symbolic Resistance in Revelation 13," p. 300, emphasis added). From this it is clear that the Sebastoi (seventeen elite men mentioned in the inscriptions) promoted emperor worship. The structure of Roman society with its Sebastoi cults meant that participation in civic responsibility was inextricably bound to emperor worship. Thompson's discussion of who is to be worshiped in his chapter on "Worship and Authority" is quite helpful, noting that John regarded Roman imperial authority as demonic (see Friesen, *Imperial Cults,* pp. 201-4).

57. Otto Piper, "The Apocalypse of John and the Liturgy of the Ancient Church." See also the worship resource below, which utilizes much of the text, privileging its seven choirs of praise. Howard-Brook and Gwyther, in *Unveiling Empire: Revelation Then and Now,* appropriately include in their insightful commentary a chapter (7) subtitled "Liturgy and Worship in Revelation" (main title "The Empire of the World Has Become the Empire of Our Lord and of His Messiah," pp. 197-222). The chapter consists of commentary on the anthems of praise to God and the Lamb and also includes a helpful analysis in chart form of the component-content of these hymns of worship with cross-references to OT texts (pp. 198-202). Both Bauckham, "Prayer," and Vanni, "Liturgical Dialogue," also perceive the centrality of worship features in Revelation. See also Ruiz, "Betwixt and Between the Lord's Day"; "The Politics of Praise: A Reading of Revelation 19:1-10," and Thompson on worship in Revelation (*Imperial Cults,* pp. 180-209, especially p. 199 for a chart depicting the progression of worship in Revelation 4-5).

Through worship of God and the Lamb, the church voices "One mighty NO to imperial Caesar and all his idolatrous works and ways!"[58] The "No" is to compromise, and precisely so in whom one worships. When the empire, the beast, demands worship, the Christian sings the songs of Revelation 4–5. Only God, the Almighty One and the Lamb, is *worthy* of praise. Revelation connects directly the economic and political abuses of the empire with both violence and misplaced worship. Neither arrogant Domitian nor any other world ruler in history may claim the honor and glory that belongs only to God Almighty. Political and economic policies that oppress and torture people and threaten the spiritual life of communities offend God's honor and stand under God's certain and coming judgment.[59]

The positive response from the church thus includes faithful witness, patient endurance, and resistance. The church is witness in its resistance. The believers' testimony may well culminate in and be magnified in martyrdom. This is the test for believers as it was for Jesus, *ho martys ho pistos* (1:5). "Patient endurance" *(hypomonē)* constitutes the core ethic in Revelation. "Rather than faith or love, *hypomonē* becomes the main Christian virtue in Revelation."

> Underlying *hypomonē* is the strong sense of reliance upon God, a willingness to wait with patience in the sure hope of God's fulfilling what God has promised. In Revelation this is the certainty that the future belongs to God, that the victory over Satan has already been won in heaven and on earth by virtue of Christ's death on the cross, and that soon the struggle will be over and the cosmos will belong to God and the Lamb and all the redeemed in the new heaven and earth.[60]

The apocalyptic focus on the cosmic battle heightens the reader's passion to resist the powers of evil. It does not encourage escapism, as often thought, but provokes confidence toward active resistance. Pilgrim rightly says,

> This is underground literature meant to create faithfulness to God and the Lamb in times of harassment, suffering, and persecution. This is resistance literature that defies the emperor and his propaganda machine, and unmasks the illusions of power and invincibility as the "great lie." This is subversive literature that refuses to say yes to the imperial cult and proclaims

58. Pilgrim, *Uneasy Neighbors*, p. 166.

59. See Bredin, *Jesus, Revolutionary of Peace*, p. 137, and D. E. Oakman whom he quotes ("The Ancient Economy and St. John's Apocalypse," *Listening: Journal of Religion and Culture* 28 [1993]: 200-214). The same emphases permeate Kraybill's contribution and that of Howard-Brook and Gwyther.

60. Pilgrim, *Uneasy Neighbors*, p. 166.

another as "Lord and Savior." This is martyr-producing literature that models bold and unflinching commitment to God and the Lamb, regardless of cost. This is revolutionary literature that creates counter-communities of Christian resistance in the midst of the enemy's domain.[61]

Christian resistance — not returning evil for evil, but a willingness to suffer for the cause of Jesus Christ, echoes the central theology of other parts of the NT. What Revelation adds is the central figure of the slain Lamb. The paradoxical image of victory through suffering love forms the heart and soul of Revelation's christology. Suffering love marks the authentic followers of the Lamb. Pilgrim notes, however, that:

> The Apocalypse adopts a stance toward the state that is radically different from the two other New Testament traditions. Here we find an understanding of the political structures as demonic, historical embodiments of injustice and evil. In response, the church is encouraged toward an ethic of uncompromising resistance.[62]

What Revelation contributes to an understanding of peace is that even when peace is taken from the earth, Jesus' followers receive the blessing of "grace and peace" and confess with heart, soul, and strength that God is sovereign, is alone the one to be worshipped, knowing that through their faithful endurance God's victory will shine forth after the present chaos ends and mighty "Babylon" is fallen. It also makes clear the interrelationship between evil spiritual powers and earthly rulers (see Chapter 8 above) and the role of believers to trust God for the warfare and the victory. The believers' refusal to comply with Rome's demands, committing themselves instead to suffer persecution and death, is their passive resistance; their proclamation of God's sovereignty through prayer, praise, and worship and their identification with the Lamb's war are their means of active resistance.[63] Most distinctive is the model of the Lamb as paradigmatic and normative for believers, a model in which one gives one's own life rather than taking another's and in which the power of the word, cross, and song of praise assures the fall of mighty Babylon, symbol for all deified political power.[64]

61. Pilgrim, *Uneasy Neighbors*, p. 170.
62. Pilgrim, *Uneasy Neighbors*, p. 178.
63. As Bauckham puts it, "Revelation offers a different way of perceiving the world which leads people to resist and to challenge the effects of the dominant ideology." *The Theology of the Book of Revelation*, p. 159.
64. Swartley, "War and Peace," 2374. On this, see Ellul's perceptive comments in *Apocalypse: The Book of Revelation*, pp. 92-98.

John Yeatts connects the dynamic of the book to what brought an end to apartheid in South Africa.

> Allan Boesak recalls that black South Africans made freedom songs central to their struggle. He says that "the struggle is inconceivable without them." They sang as they marched into the face of police and army troops. They sang in prison "songs of defiance and faith and freedom," songs which often made the oppressors nervous and aggressive. Their songs paralleled the hosts of heaven who sang:
>
>> Worthy is the Lamb who was slain, to receive power and wealth and wisdom and might and honour and glory and blessing!
>
> Young black Christians in South Africa danced around a police vehicle and sang:
>
>> It is broken, the power of Satan is broken!
>> We have disappointed Satan, his power is broken. Alleluia![65]

Yeatts concludes by quoting from the 1630 Anabaptist Articles of Christian Doctrine (Amsterdam) asserting faith in the coming of Christ and its attendant bliss.[66]

> Finally, we believe also, that our Saviour Jesus Christ, forever blessed, shall visibly come again in the clouds, like as He ascended before . . . glorious and magnificent, with the power and glory of all His angels. . . . Then shall the blessed of God abound in heavenly joy, so that with angelic tongues and heavenly voices they will begin to sing with all the saints of God the new song, giving unto Him who sitteth upon the throne, and unto the Lamb, praise, honor, glory, and blessing, forever and ever. Amen.

To grasp adequately the heart-pulse of Revelation, we join the exiled John in his Lord's Day (1:10) worship service, joining in the choirs of creatures, elders, and angels. For the destination of history is worship. The following liturgy is taken directly from Revelation, with the swelling *worship* in seven acts of John's Lord's Day visions.

---

65. Yeatts, *Revelation*, pp. 119-20.
66. Yeatts, *Revelation*, pp. 433-34.

THE SERVICE OF WORSHIP

For this half-hour service you will need nine voices:
  John, the worship leader
  the narrator
  male and female angel voices
  male and female elders' voices
  the voice of Jesus
   the voice of God
  "a loud voice"
A trumpeter can be used if one is available. John lines out the hymns of praise by phrases. Sections of the congregation are assigned to be creatures (denoted by 1), elders (2), and angels (3). In hymns where "all" is specified, all three groups speak together what John lines out.

Processional

John or choir of nine voices above: Grace and peace to you from him who is, and who was, and who is to come. (1:4b)

God's voice: I am the Alpha and the Omega who is, and who was, and who is to come, the Almighty. (1:8)

John: I, John, your brother and companion in the suffering and kingdom and patient endurance that are ours in Jesus, was on the island of Patmos because of the word of God and the testimony of Jesus. On the Lord's Day I was in the Spirit, and I heard behind me a loud voice like a trumpet. (1:9-10)

Loud voice: Write on a scroll what you see and send it to the seven churches. (1:11a)

Voice of Jesus: Do not be afraid. I am the First and the Last. I am the Living One; I was dead, and behold I am alive for ever and ever! And I hold the keys of death and Hades.

Write, therefore, what you have seen, what is now and what will take place later. The mystery of the seven stars that you saw in my right hand and of the seven golden lampstands is this: The seven stars are the angels of the seven churches, and the seven lampstands are the seven churches. (1:17b-20)

Act I

Narrator: In Act I, the glorified Jesus addresses the seven churches (chapters 2–4). The exiled apostle hears the message of the revealed Jesus to the seven churches. Each message is a call to faithfulness and perseverance in the faith. Each call and admonition ends with a promise.

John: (Read messages to Pergamum and Philadelphia.)

Pause before chapter 4

John: After this I looked, and there before me was a door standing open in heaven. And the voice I had first heard speaking to me like a trumpet said: (4:1a)

Loud voice: Come up here, and I will show you what must take place after this. (4:1b)

John: At once I was in the Spirit, and there before me was a throne in heaven with someone sitting on it. And the one who sat there had the appearance of jasper and carnelian. A rainbow, resembling an emerald, encircled the throne. Surrounding the throne were twenty-four other thrones, and seated on them were twenty-four elders. They were dressed in white and had crowns of gold on their heads. From the throne came flashes of lightning, rumblings and peals of thunder. Before the throne, seven lamps were blazing. These are the seven spirits of God. Also before the throne there was what looked like a sea of glass, clear as crystal. (4:2-6a)

In the center, around the throne, were four living creatures. and they were covered with eyes, in front and in back. The first living creature was like a lion, the second was like an ox, the third had a face like a man, the fourth was like a flying eagle. Each of the four living creatures had six wings and was covered with eyes all around, even under his wings. Day and night they never stop saying: (4:6b-8)

1: Holy, holy, holy
is the Lord God Almighty,
who was, and is, and is to come. (4:8b)

John: Whenever the living creatures give glory, honor and thanks to him who sits on the throne and who lives for ever and ever, the twenty-four elders fall down before him who sits on the throne, and worship him who lives for ever and ever. They lay their crowns before the throne and say. (4:9-10)

2: You are worthy, our Lord and God,
to receive glory and honor and power,
for you created all things,
and by your will they were created
and have their being. (4:11)

Act II

Narrator: In Act II the slain Lamb appears as the one who holds the destiny of history (5:1-14). We now worship the one who emerges from the right hand of the one seated on the throne, the one worthy to open the scroll.

John: Then I saw in the right hand of him who sat on the throne a scroll with writing on both sides and sealed with seven seals. And I saw a mighty angel proclaiming in a loud voice: (5:1-2a)

Angel: Who is worthy to break the seals and open the scroll? (5:2b)

John: But no one in heaven or on earth or under the earth could open the scroll or even look inside it. I wept and wept because no one was found who was worthy to open the scroll or look inside. Then one of the elders said to me: (5:3-5a)

Elder: Do not weep! See, the Lion of the tribe of Judah, the Root of David, has triumphed. He is able to open the scroll and its seven seals. (5:5b)

John: Then I saw a Lamb, looking as if it had been slain, standing in the center of the throne, encircled by the four living creatures and the elders. He had seven horns and seven eyes, which are the seven spirits of God sent out into all the earth. He came and took the scroll from the right hand of him who sat on the throne. And when he had taken it, the four living creatures and the twenty-four elders fell down before the Lamb. Each one had a harp and they were holding golden bowls full of incense, which are the prayers of the saints. And they sang a new song: (5:6-9a)

1, 2: You are worthy to take the scroll
  and to open its seals,
  because you were slain,
  and with your blood you purchased people for God
  from every tribe and language and people and nation.
  You have made them to be a kingdom and priests to serve our God,
  and they will reign on the earth. (5:9b-10)

John: Then I looked and heard the voice of many angels, numbering thousands upon thousands, and ten thousand times ten thousand. They encircled the throne and the living creatures and the elders. In a loud voice they sang: (5:11-12a)

3: Worthy is the Lamb, who was slain,
  to receive power and wealth and wisdom and strength
  and honor and glory and praise! (5:12b)

John: Then I heard every creature in heaven and on earth and under the earth and on the sea, and all that is in them, singing: (5:13a)

All: To him who sits on the throne
   and to the Lamb
   be praise and honor
   and glory and power,
   for ever and ever! (5:13b)

John: The four living creatures said, (5:14a)

1: Amen, (5:14a)

John: and the elders fell down and worshiped. (5:14b)

Congregational hymns: (Select what fits, such as "Behold the Glories of the Lamb," stanza 4, or "Let the Whole Creation Cry," stanza 1.)

Act III

Narrator: In Act III the martyrs disclose the meaning of history (chapters 6–7). As the seven seals are opened each opened seal describes an aspect of the tribulation of God's saints and martyrs in history. With the fifth seal there is an outcry from the martyrs from under the altar:

Two elders: How long, Sovereign Lord, holy and true, until you judge the inhabitants of the earth and avenge our blood? (6:10)

John: Then each of them was given a white robe. and they were told to wait a little longer, until the number of their fellow servants and brothers who were to be killed as they had been was completed.

I watched as he opened the sixth seal. There was a great earthquake. The sun turned black like sackcloth made of goat hair, the whole moon turned blood red, and the stars in the sky fell to earth as late figs drop from a fig tree when shaken by a strong wind. The sky receded like a scroll, rolling up, and every mountain and island was removed from its place.

Then the kings of the earth, the princes, the generals, the rich, the mighty, and every slave and every free man hid in caves and among the rocks of the mountains. They called to the mountains and the rocks, "Fall on us and hide us from the face of him who sits on the throne and from the wrath of the Lamb! For the great day of their wrath has come, and who can stand?"

After this I saw four angels standing at the four corners of the earth, holding back the four winds of the earth to prevent any wind from blowing on the land or on the sea or on any tree. Then I saw another angel coming up from the east, having the seal of the living God. He called out in a loud voice to the four angels who had been given power to harm the land and the sea.

Angel: Do not harm the land or the sea or the trees until we put a seal on the foreheads of the servants of our God.

John: Then I heard the number of those who were sealed: 144,000 from all the tribes of Israel. (6:11–7:4)

Pause

John: After this I looked and there before me was a great multitude that no one could count, from every nation, tribe, people and language, standing before the throne and in front of the Lamb. They were wearing white robes and were holding palm branches in their hands. And they cried out in a loud voice: (7:9-10a)

2: Salvation belongs to our God,
who sits on the throne,
and to the Lamb. (7:10b)

John: All the angels were standing around the throne and around the elders and the four living creatures. They fell down on their faces before the throne and worshiped God, saying: (7:11-12a)

3 Amen!
Praise and glory
and wisdom and thanks and honor
and power and strength
be to our God forever and ever.
Amen! (7:12b)

John: Then one of the elders asked me: (7:13a)

Elder: These in white robes — who are they, and where did they come from? (7:13b)

John: Sir, you know. (7:14a)

Elder: These are they who have come out of the great tribulation; they have washed their robes and made them white in the blood of the Lamb. (7:14)

Act IV

Narrator: In Act IV God is victorious in history: the seven trumpets blow (chapters 8–10).

John: With the opening of the seventh seal, there is silence in heaven for about half an hour.

Silence one to three minutes

John: Then seven trumpets are given to the seven angels. With each trumpet blast, God's battle against evil rages more fierce and the victory blast more sure. With the seventh trumpet blast the victory cry bursts forth in full crescendo.

The seventh angel sounded his trumpet, and there were loud voices in heaven, which said: (11:15a)

3: The kingdom of the world
   has become the kingdom of our Lord and of his Christ,
   and he will reign forever and ever. (11:15b)

John: And the twenty-four elders, who were seated on their thrones before God, fell on their faces and worshiped God, saying: (11:16-17a)

2: We give thanks to you, Lord God Almighty,
   the One who is and who was,
   because you have taken your great power
   and have begun to reign. (11:17b)

John: Then God's temple in heaven was opened, and within his temple was seen the ark of his covenant. And there came flashes of lightning, rumblings, peals of thunder, an earthquake and a great hailstorm. (11:19)

Act V

Narrator: In Act V the struggle in history continues; God rescues the saints (chapters 12–14; 15:2-4). Another picture of God's combat against evil emerges.

John: A woman clothed with the sun bears a child whom the dragon seeks to destroy. After warring in heaven the dragon is cast down to earth, and I heard a loud voice in heaven saying,

Loud voice: Now have come the salvation and the power and the kingdom of our God,

and the authority of his Christ.
For the accuser of our brothers,
who accuses them before our God day and night,
has been hurled down.

They overcame him
  by the blood of the Lamb
  and by the word of their testimony;
  they did not love their lives so much
  as to shrink from death.

Therefore rejoice, you heavens
  and you who dwell in them!
  But woe to the earth and the sea,
  because the devil has gone down to you!
  He is filled with fury,
  because he knows that his time is short. (12:10-12)

John: The dragon then turns upon the seed of the child, making war on the saints through the beast. The faithful, those who conquer the beast and its image, are delivered.

One like a Son of man appears with a sickle in his hand to gather the harvest and throw the grapes into the great winepress of the wrath of God. As seven angels with seven plagues dispense the bowls of God's wrath, the saints, those who kept the commandments of God and the faith of Jesus, who had conquered the beast and its image, stood beside a sea of glass with harps of God in their hands.

They held harps given them by God and sang the song of Moses the servant of God and the song of the Lamb:

2: Great and marvelous are your deeds,
  Lord God Almighty.
  Just and true are your ways,
  King of the ages.

Who will not fear you, O Lord,
  and bring glory to your name?
  For you alone are holy.
  All nations will come
  and worship before you,
  for your righteous acts have been revealed. (15:3b-4)

Act VI

Narrator: In Act VI God judges evil: the seven bowls of wrath are poured out (15:1, 5–18:24).

John: God's wrath is poured out upon the harlot, the city set on seven hills, the great mother of harlots. The angel of the water testifies to the justice of God's judgment:

Angel: You are just in these judgments,
    you who are and who were, the Holy One,
    because you have so judged;
    for they have shed the blood of your saints and prophets,
    and you have given them blood to drink as they deserve. (16:5b-6)

John: And I heard the altar respond: (16:7a)

2: Yes, Lord God Almighty,
    true and just are your judgments. (16:7b)

John: The seventh angel poured out his bowl into the air, and out of the temple came a loud voice from the throne, saying, (16:17a)

Voice: It is done! (16:17b)

John: Then there came flashes of lightning, rumblings, peals of thunder and a severe earthquake. No earthquake like it has ever occurred since man has been on earth, so tremendous was the quake. (16:18)

Pause

John: After this I saw another angel coming down from heaven. He had great authority, and the earth was illuminated by his splendor. With a mighty voice he shouted: (18:1-2a)

Loud voice: Fallen! Fallen is Babylon the Great! (18:2b)
    Woe! Woe, O great city,
    O Babylon, city of power!
    In one hour your doom has come! (18:10b)

John: In one hour she has been brought to ruin! (18:10c)

All: Rejoice over her, O heaven!
    Rejoice, saints and apostles and prophets! (18:20a)

John: God has judged her for the way she treated you. (18:20)
    In her was found the blood of prophets and of the saints,
    and all who have been killed on the earth. (18:24)

Act VII

Narrator: In Act VII God's purpose triumphs; a new heaven and new earth appear, and God's dwelling place is with his people (chapters 19–22).

John: After this I heard what sounded like the roar of a great multitude in heaven shouting: (19:1a)

All: Hallelujah!
   Salvation and glory and power belong to our God,
   for true and just are his judgments.
   He has condemned the great prostitute
   who corrupted the earth by her adulteries.
   He has avenged on her the blood of his servants. (19:1b-2)

John: And again they shouted: (19:3a)

All: Hallelujah!
   The smoke from her goes up forever and ever. (19:3b)

John: The twenty-four elders and the four living creatures fell down and worshiped God, who was seated on the throne. And they cried: (19:4a)

1 and 2: Amen, Hallelujah! (19:4b)

John: Then a voice came from the throne, saying: (19:5a)

Angel: Praise our God,
   all you his servants,
   you who fear him,
   both small and great! (19:5b)

John: Then I heard what sounded like a great multitude, like the roaring of rushing waters and like loud peals of thunder, shouting: (19:6a)

All: Hallelujah!
   For our Lord God Almighty reigns.
   Let us rejoice and be glad
   and give him glory!
   For the wedding of the Lamb has come,
   and his bride has made herself ready. (19:6b-7)
   Hallelujah!
   Salvation,
   glory,
   and power
   belong to our God.

Congregational hymn, (if desired): "All Hail the Power of Jesus' Name"

John: Then I saw a new heaven and a new earth, for the first heaven and the first earth had passed away, and there was no longer any sea. I saw the Holy City, the new Jerusalem, coming down out of heaven from God, prepared as a bride beautifully dressed for her husband. And I heard a loud voice from the throne, saying, (21:1-3a)

Loud voice: Now the dwelling of God is with men, and he will live with them. They will be his people, and God himself will be with them and be their God. He will wipe every tear from their eyes. There will be no more death or mourning or crying or pain, for the old order of things has passed away. (21:3b-4)

John: He who was seated on the throne said, (21:5a)

God's voice: I am making everything new! (21:5b)

John: Then he said, (21:6a)

God's voice: It is done. I am the Alpha and the Omega, the Beginning and the End. (21:6b)

John: The angel said to me, (22:6a)

Angel: These words are trustworthy and true. The Lord, the God of the spirits of the prophets, sent his angel to show his servants the things that must soon take place. (22:6b)

Jesus' voice: Behold, I am coming soon! (22:7a)

Angel's voice: Blessed is he who keeps the words of the prophecy of this book. (22:7b)

John: I, John, am the one who heard and saw these things. And when I had heard and seen them, I fell down to worship at the feet of the angel who had been showing them to me. But he said to me, (22:8-9a)

Angel: Do not do it! I am a fellow servant with you and with your brothers the prophets and with all who keep the words of this book. Worship God! (22:9b)

John: Then he told me, (22:10a)

Angel: Do not seal up the words of the prophecy of this book, because the time is near. Let him who does wrong continue to do wrong; let him who is vile continue to be vile; let him who does right continue to do right; and let him who is holy continue to be holy. (22:10-11)

Jesus' voice: Behold, I am coming soon! My reward is with me, and I will give to everyone according to what he has done. I am the Alpha and the Omega, the First and the Last, the Beginning and the End. (22:12-13)

John: The Spirit and the bride say, "Come!" And let him who hears say, "Come!" Whoever is thirsty, let him come; and whoever wishes, let him take the free gift of the water of life. (22:17)

He who testifies to these things says, (22:20a)

Jesus' voice: Yes, I am coming soon. (22:20b)

All (congregational antiphon): Amen. Come, Lord Jesus. (22:20c)

John: The grace of the Lord Jesus be with God's people. (22:21a)

All (congregational antiphon): Amen. (22:21b)

Recessional

God's and Jesus' voices: I am the Alpha and the Omega, the First and the Last, the Beginning and the End. (22:13)

13 Discipleship and Imitation of Jesus the Suffering Servant: The Mimesis of New Creation

The Gospels and the New Testament do not preach a morality of sponta-
neous action. They do not claim that humans must get rid of imitation;
they recommend imitating the sole model who never runs the danger —
if we really imitate in the way that children imitate — of being transformed into a fascinating rival:

> He who says he abides in him ought to walk in the same way in which
> he walked. 1 John 2,6.

> On one side are the prisoners of violent imitation, which always leads
> to a dead end, on the other are the adherents of nonviolent imitation,
> who will meet with no obstacle. (René Girard, *Things Hidden*)[1]

In this statement Girard speaks of positive mimesis. But overall Girard says
relatively little about this,[2] although at numerous points he speaks of good

---

1. *Things Hidden since the Foundation of the World,* p. 430.

2. I consider this a neglected area in Girard's work and in writings on Girard. Raymund
Schwager has written briefly on it, but quite inadequately. He confines most of his remarks to
John's Gospel, emphasizing the significance of Jesus calling his disciples "no longer servants,
but friends," thus inviting them into full unity with himself and with God his Father. This
means renouncing selfish ambitions and striving to be like Christ and God in true love (*Must
There Be Scapegoats?* pp. 176-80). Michael Hardin has also utilized this theme in his analysis of
Maximus the Confessor's explication of growth into spiritual maturity ("Mimesis and Dominion: The Dynamics of Violence and the Imitation of Christ in Maximus Confessor"). More recently, James Alison has added significantly to this emphasis in his profound theological monograph, *Raising Abel: The Recovery of Eschatological Imagination.*

This chapter is reprinted, with some adaptation, from *Violence Renounced: René Girard, Biblical
Studies and Peacemaking,* ed. Willard M. Swartley (Telford: Pandora [now Cascadia], 2000), pp.
218-45, with permission from the publisher.

mimesis and occasionally commends Jesus as the good model.[3] Usually, Girard focuses simply on mimetic *desire,* which for him is desire that leads to rivalry. Thus, "Following Christ means giving up mimetic desire."[4] By this he means mimesis that is *generated by acquisitive desire.* But giving up either *mimesis* or *desire* is impossible. Rather, what is necessary is a double transformation: by transcendent provision we are given an object for mimesis whose very nature and action do not lead to rivalry when imitated, and through the empowerment of this one our human desires are transformed so that we will *desire* to imitate the nonrivalous, nonviolent Person.

In this chapter I seek to show that major strands of NT teaching are directed specifically to just this reality: transformation of desire that enables a positive, *non-acquisitive mimesis.* This study seeks to show how foundational and ubiquitous this idea is in the NT.

Further, I develop this thesis: that the NT use of imitation/discipleship language carries contextual emphases that prevent, even repudiate, *the mimesis of acquisitive desire.* Rather, this stream of NT parenesis (i.e., counsel, exhortation, instruction) sets forth another type of mimesis, one antithetical to the mimetic desire that generates rivalry and in turn leads to violence. The mimesis enjoined by the NT canonical literature is grounded in the Jesus cross event, an event that exposes violence and, from Jesus' side, manifests the freedom and power of new creation.

In developing this thesis, this chapter also sheds fresh light on the long-standing issue in biblical studies of the role of *imitation* in Christian character formation, a point in the modern debate initiated by Martin Luther's strong reaction to *imitatio Christi* because it threatened to undermine his central and precious doctrine of justification by faith alone.[5] Any effort to imitate Christ, says Luther, invites through the side door a works righteousness into the salvation experience and thereby mitigates God's grace and salvation *extra nos.*

Much Protestant exegesis has continued in Luther's footsteps, spurred

---

3. In his more recent writing Girard speaks more of this possibility and need. See his comments in "How Can Satan Cast Out Satan?" p. 128, and in the interview with Rebecca Adams, "Violence, Difference, Sacrifice: A Conversation with René Girard."

4. *Things Hidden,* p. 431.

5. This, however, is not the first time that *mimēsis* plays a crucial role in Christian theological dispute. Fodor, "Imitation and Emulation: Training in Practical Christian Judgment," observes that Augustine's controversy with the Arians hinged on whether the incarnate Son's being is a true mimesis or only a pale reflection of the Father. Further, the issue arises in describing the interrelation of Father, Son, and Spirit more broadly and is thus intrinsic to the disputed doctrine of *perichōrēsis* (Fodor, p. 40).

additionally by atonement theology that sets off Jesus' suffering and death as so unique in its salvific purpose that it disconnects discipleship from salvation. This produces lamentable moral results and invites through the side door the old acquisitive mimesis under the guise of protecting salvation. Consequently, the liberating gospel of peace is displaced by a self-serving redeemer myth. Further, one or both of these factors often play into exegetical comments that argue down the importance of NT *imitation/example* language.

The influential article by Michaelis in *TDNT* demonstrates the point. Disagreeing with Oepke and Larsson in their important and full-length studies of the topic,[6] Michaelis argues against any genuine imitation in Paul:

> First, there is simple comparison. The older example seems to be imitated, but there is no conscious imitation. This type occurs in 1 Th. 2:14 and 1 Th. 1:6. Then there is the following of an example. This use is found in 2 Th. 3:7, 9; Phil. 3:17, and Paul is always the example. Recognition of the authority of Paul is plainly implied in these passages, so that following his example carried with it obedience to his commands. In the third group obedience is predominant, so exclusively so in 1 C. 4:16 that the thought of an example is quite overshadowed, and in 1 C. 11:1; 1 Th. 1:6; Eph. 5:1 it is quite obvious that the main stress falls on the element of obedience. In this third group alone are Christ and God associated with Paul as authorities in relation to whom one must be a *mimētēs*.[7]

Given this reduction of *mimēsis* in Paul to a command-obedience paradigm, it is easy to see why Elizabeth Castelli, in her recent study of Paul's *imitation* language,[8] concludes that Paul's call/command to imitation functions to imprint the hierarchical structure of power on Christian thought and conduct. But, as Fodor points out, Castelli's wider study of *mimēsis* in Greek literature and her own caution against reduction of its meaning should have prevented her narrow conclusion.[9]

In view of this mimetic error in NT scholarship, one purpose of this chapter is to resolve this problem by fresh exegetical commentary on the *mimēsis* texts in light of Girard's theory. Indeed, if Girard's theories are correct, mimesis in the NT can be very bad news, given Castelli's thesis that it re-

---

6. A. Oepke, *Nachfolge und Nachahmung Christi*, pp. 853-69; Larsson, *Christus als Vorbild.*

7. *TDNT* 4: 671-72.

8. Elizabeth A. Castelli, *Imitating Paul: A Discourse of Power.*

9. Fodor, "Imitation and Emulation," pp. 47-48. Worth noting in this regard is that clearly in the thought and life of Ignatius (early second century), who profoundly emulates Paul, the concept of *imitatio Christi* is central. See Swartley, "The Imitatio Christi in the Ignatian Letters."

inforces a conservative hierarchical power structure. Or it might also be very very good news, if the call to imitation is securely linked with renunciation of *acquisitive mimetic* desire through Jesus' own model, so that the spiral of rivalry and violence is decisively broken.

If the Girardian thesis is correct that mimetic rivalry is the generative power behind the scapegoating mechanism that led to Jesus' violent death, and if Jesus' life-death breaks this spiral of violence empowered by rivalry — the thesis that I will argue, then it should be possible to show exegetically that Jesus' teachings on discipleship and the early church's teaching of imitation (later called *imitatio Christi*) are an antidote to aspirations of rivalry. They are analogous to Jesus' own refusal to play the mimetic game that feeds destructive impulses and leads to violence, sacralized under the guise of having made peace (a counterfeit to true peace). Further, if it is exegetically possible to demonstrate this point, then theological quarrel among biblical scholars about the relationship between discipleship and imitation in the NT will be resolved via a fresh perspective on the topic.

The first part of this chapter thus takes up Paul's and the wider NT use of imitation language and parenesis with brief expositional comment on the passages. The second part then examines the Gospel narratives that emphasize Jesus' teachings on discipleship — i.e., the call to follow Jesus. The third part of the article casts a still larger net in considering a wider set of *correspondence* and *identification* language. This will set the stage for final comments to clinch the thesis developed. In this way this study seeks to provide a fresh understanding of *imitation and discipleship* in the NT.

Methodologically, a word about the order of these three parts is necessary. The atonement is the precondition theologically and practically for all imitation "in Christ" and identification or correspondence parenesis. The potential of a new mimesis rests on God's inauguration of a new creation reality through the cross and, most significantly, the resurrection of Jesus Christ. Theologically, then, the three parts of this essay should be presented in reverse order.[10] But since the basic topic focuses on imitation and mimesis, I follow this order, building to the climax of the foundation of the new reality. Hence, to play on Girard's book title (see note 1), this essay is about "Things Designed (in Christ Revealed) before the Foundation of the World" (Eph. 1:4ff.).

---

10. For these comments about method and theological order, I am grateful for Diana Culbertson's written response to my paper at the Colloquium, which stresses that rebirth and daughter/sonship precedes imitation.

Analysis of Imitation Texts

1 Thess. 1:6-7   This text is crucially important for two reasons. First, it is likely the earliest extant Christian writing. Second, this early parenesis sets forth an identity mark by which the Thessalonian believers are assured of their authentic Jesus character. Daniel Patte, in his structural analysis and explication of Paul's letters, regards this second factor as most crucial. That these believers received the word in suffering marks them in *type* (*typon,* the word translated *example*). That they suffered like their Lord Jesus and like Paul and his coworkers before them (note the plural "us," referring back to "Paul, Silvanus, and Timothy" in the salutation)[11] marks them as genuine. It certifies and assures them that they belong to Jesus.[12]

En thlipsei pollē should be taken as an instrumental of manner, i.e., "with much affliction/persecution/suffering," denotes the manner in which they received the gospel. This *affliction* specifies the mimetic relationship (*mimētai* in v. 6a) to the Lord Jesus. There is, as it were, a double marking, first in *mimētai,* in that their experience stands in continuity with that of Jesus, and second, in *typon,* in that they become a type for others who likewise undergo similar suffering in receiving and living out the gospel.

1 Thess. 2:14   This text, standing in the tradition of the Hebrew prophetic critique, as Craig Evans has shown,[13] similarly denotes suffering (*epathete*) as the identifying mark of Christian experience. Here, as in 1:6-7, the Christians know who they are in relation to Christ in that they share his experience as victim. Their suffering certifies their character as those who did not mimetically counter-respond but experienced typologically the fate of Jesus.

2 Thess. 3:6-9   Again, as in 1 Thessalonians, the model to be imitated is not Paul alone but Paul, Silvanus, and Timothy, the leadership team. This appears to reflect the assumed pattern of Greek education, *paideia,* in which learners imitate the model of noble leaders.[14]

---

11. Castelli, in her effort to reduce imitation to a rhetorical strategy that utilizes Paul's position of power in a hierarchical structure in order to valorize sameness, resists the true import of this plural construction. Even though she recognizes it, she shifts back to the singular: "became imitators of me and of the Lord" (*Imitating Paul,* pp. 91-92, 95). Obviously, this first use of the concept in the plural, which puts imitation in a communal-type context, threatens her entire project.

12. Patte, *Paul's Faith and the Power of the Gospel,* pp. 134-40.

13. Craig A. Evans, "The New Testament and First-century Judaism" (see p. 3 for citation of this Pauline text).

14. Jaeger, *Paideia: The Ideals of Greek Culture,* 1: 310. For a wider survey of Greek literature, see Castelli, *Imitating Paul,* pp. 81-85.

Three features of this text are especially noteworthy: first, it begins with a command *(parangellomen)* that appeals to "tradition" *(paradosis)* for its authorization. In the universally recognized Pauline writings (2 Thessalonians is often considered deutero-Pauline), the appeal to tradition is associated with central tenets of the gospel (notably 1 Cor. 15:3; 11:1; cf. 1 Thess. 4:1-2). Second, this text reflects the hebraic *halakahic* concept of the moral life in its use of "walk" *(peripateō* in 3:6, NRSV "living"). On this basis we might question whether the NT concept of imitation is derived in part from the Hebrew tradition, in which "way" *(derek)* and "walk" *(halak)* are foundational to parenesis on the moral life.[15]

Third, of all the NT uses of imitation language, only this one is not linked to the conceptual field of love, forgiveness, servanthood, humility, and suffering. Work as such, avoiding idleness or unruliness, does not necessarily fit the paradigm to which the other imitation texts conform.

1 Cor. 4:11-16   This passage reflects Paul's conflictual relationship with some in the Corinthian congregation and comes at the end of a sarcastic outburst in which the Corinthian believers are "rich" and "kings," while Paul and company are spectacles of death. While *they* are wise, strong, and honored, Paul and company are fools, weak, and in disrepute. Clearly, here Paul is risking his "cool" for the sake of making clear that the gospel of Jesus Christ is not a *theologia gloria* but a *theologia crucis.* Literarily, these verses anticipate Paul's classic description of his sufferings for the gospel in 2 Cor. 4:6ff. (the "treasure in earthen vessels" text).

Just before his call to "imitate me," Paul uses the metaphor of father. This personalizing of his relation to the young believers explains the shift from the plural (vv. 8-13) to the singular (vv. 16-21). The father metaphor intends to convey intimacy and care, descriptive of his relation to the community. The profile of experience in vv. 10-13 clearly denotes personal deprivation, suffering, and abuse. When the father-image is blended with this list of hardships, the pattern that emerges is willingness to take on personal anguish because of caring love for others. Thus Paul voluntarily forgoes his own rights for the cause of the gospel and the welfare of the faith communities. This forms the model of attitude and action that Paul now calls the believers to imitate.

1 Cor. 10:31–11:1   The context of this summary depiction of Paul's effort to please others in order not to impede the gospel's salvific effect among both

---

15. See, e.g., Muilenburg, *The Way of Israel: Biblical Faith and Ethics;* Janzen, *Old Testament Ethics: A Paradigmatic Approach.* Janzen's use of the word "paradigm" is similar to the concept of a model that one follows.

Jews and Gentiles focuses on whether or not to eat meat offered to idols (ch. 8) and whether or not to participate in (cultic) feasts in the temple shrines of pagan gods (ch. 10). While his counsel on the former is yes and his command on the latter is no, the bottom-line principle is not to become a stumbling-block/scandal *(skandalon)* to another believer's conscience. That is, one deliberately avoids scandalizing another brother or sister *(scandalizō*, 8:13d; cf. *enkopēn* in 9:12b, NRSV "obstacle"). That this becomes the model to imitate is most provocative in view of Girard's extensive attention to the role of *scandal* in the gospel narrative.

Girard treats the point of *scandal* in numerous writings, most provocatively in his essay on Peter's denial in *The Scapegoat*[16] and in his 1992 AAR speech, "How Can Satan Cast Out Satan?"[17] In his essay on Peter, Girard claims: "The convergence of the content of the [Passion] narratives with the theory of the *skandalon* — theory of mimetic desire — cannot be fortuitous."[18] He observes that Jesus says to his disciples, "You will all scandalize yourselves because of me this night" (Matt. 26:31).[19] Earlier, he notes, Jesus had severely reprimanded Peter, "Get behind me, Satan! You are an obstacle in my path [you scandalize me]" (Matt. 16:23).[20]

Girard rightly contends that mimetic desire (a.k.a. Satan) drives Peter in both cases and that it causes Peter to be a scandal to Jesus and Jesus to be a scandal to Peter and the other disciples. This mimetic desire, of course, is *acquisitive desire,* the exact opposite of those desires and impulses that occur in the contexts of Paul's parenesis that exhorts believers to imitate him, Christ, and God. In my analysis of the Markan discipleship pericopes below, this contrast between the way of Jesus and the desires of the disciples will be further elucidated.

A surface reading of Paul's admonition to imitate him and Christ in the context of the Gospel's portrait of Jesus as a *skandalon* raises an apparent contradiction. Paul's self-denying actions have as their express purpose avoidance of scandal/offense that causes another to stumble. And he attributes this pattern to Christ, from whom he learned it.

---

16. *Scapegoat*, pp. 157-62.

17. See also his section "Beyond Scandal," in *Things Hidden*, pp. 393-431.

18. *Scapegoat*, p. 159. Girard then questions whether the Gospel writers fully understood this point. He thinks not, but that they simply repeated what Jesus said in all its mysterious detail, specifically the crowing of the cock (twice — mimetically — in Mark, but only once in Matthew and Luke). Without understanding the import of this, the story of the cock becomes a kind of miracle fetish, says Girard. On this, Girard is speculative, as he himself suggests (p. 160).

19. *Scapegoat*, p. 158.

20. *Scapegoat*, p. 157.

But the gospel story portrays Jesus occasioning scandal. The resolution hinges on two crucial points. First, in the Gospels the disciples' acquisitive mimetic desire is the real reason Jesus becomes a scandal. Second, Paul's concern in this text is that young believers are not scandalized by other believers. At the same time, this epistle begins by marking the gospel's proclamation as a *skandalon* to unbelieving Jews and as foolishness to refusing Gentiles (1 Cor. 1:23). Paul does not court the illusion that it is possible to strip the gospel of its scandalizing edge to those oriented to acquisitive mimetic desire.

Phil. 3:17-18   The context of this admonition is Paul's counting as loss his Jewish credentials and achievements, which he labels as "confidence in the flesh," and then he owns a righteousness based on the faith of Jesus Christ, a righteousness which is from God based on faith (3:9). What Paul then desires, as mark of this righteousness, is to know the power of Jesus' resurrection and to share in Jesus' sufferings, thus "becoming like him in death" (3:10). These twin points of analogous experience are pursued further in vv. 11-16. Then follows the language of imitation and example.

Clearly, given the preceding context of sharing in the sufferings of Christ and the immediately following reference to the cross of Christ, this use of *imitation* and *example* is oriented specifically to the cross and suffering. It is also striking that Paul completes this thought by pointing to a heavenly reward for this kind of earthly life (vv. 20-21). He then (4:1-2) addresses a conflict between two sisters in the community, Euodia and Syntyche, a manifestation of mimetic rivalry in the sisterhood. He speaks highly of their contribution to the missionary enterprise and is confident that this conflict can and will be resolved.

Phil. 2:5-11   Even though this text does not use either of the key terms, *imitation* or *type*, it clearly portrays the believers patterning their conduct after the suffering and obedience of Christ Jesus. Hence this important text takes its place in this list. Further, this text is joined to 3:16 by the similar exhortation "be of the same mind" (*touto phroneite* in 2:5 and *to auto phronein* in 3:16). The context of this foundational confession of Jesus' self-emptying and humbling to the cross is Paul's admonition in vv. 3-4 to put away conduct that proceeds from mimetic rivalry.

Eph. 4:32–5:2   Here, the longer context exhorts believers to put off old pagan ways of conduct and to put on the new clothing of attitude and action that accords with their having been re-created in the image of God (4:23). The admonition to imitate is linked not to Paul, or even to Christ, but to God (echoing the Sermon on the Mount's injunction to be perfect in indiscriminate love as God is, Matt. 5:44-48). This is a singular use of imitation in the NT; nowhere else are believers told to imitate God. The dispositions identified are: kindness, being tenderhearted, forgiving others, and loving, which is specifically linked then to Christ and his example in giving himself for us, as a fragrant offering and sacrifice to God.

This is one of numerous cases where the word "sacrifice" is used in a sense quite different from the Girardian use. A synonym might be costly gift or thank offering. In my judgment, Schwager is correct when he distinguishes different meanings in "sacrifice" as used in Scripture, not all of which can be reduced to a sacrificial crisis generated by violence.[21] Indeed, there is a distinct metaphorical use of the term (as Girard recognizes[22] and as can be seen in Pss. 50:14, 23; 51:17; Rom. 12:1; 1 Pet. 2:4-5; Heb. 13:15-16 — cf. the use of "offering" in Isa. 66:20 and Rom. 15:16). It is striking also to realize that Paul does not refer to Jesus' death as a "sacrifice" even though he has a wide repertoire of images for explicating the salvific meaning of Jesus' death.[23]

Other New Testament Example/Imitation Texts

1 Pet. 2:21-24   Although the Pauline terms for example/type *(typos)* and imitation *(mimēsis/mimeomai)* do not occur in these verses, similar ideas are present in Peter's distinctive vocabulary. The word for "example" *(hypogrammon)* occurs only here in the NT and carries the connotation of a sketch or imprint.[24] This idea is then joined to the memorable phrase "in his steps" *(tois ichnesin autou)*. Clearly, Jesus is set forth as a pattern that is to guide the formation of the believers' thought and conduct.

The content of the example is unambiguously the nonretaliatory conduct of Jesus when he was threatened and abused. Mary Schertz's chiastic and

21. On this see Schwager, "Christ's Death and the Critique of Sacrifice"; also North, "Violence and the Bible: The Girard Connection," especially pp. 8-10 and North's summary on this point on p. 26: "Sacrifice is inadequately equated with simple violence rather than 'self-deprivation for an ulterior goal.'" In *The Bible, Violence, and the Sacred*, Williams has a good survey of the various (anthropological) theories of sacrifice (pp. 14-20).

22. *Things Hidden*, p. 243; Adams, "Loving Mimesis," pp. 28-31. For an extensive critique of Girard's use and understanding of the word "sacrifice," see Chilton, *The Temple of Jesus*, pp. 15-42.

23. On this see McLean, "The Absence of an Atoning Sacrifice in Paul's Soteriology." McLean convincingly shows that *sacrifice* is not a category in Paul's explication of Jesus' death, even though metaphors of *redeeming, delivering, expiating, and dying–rising* abound.

24. In 2 Macc. 2:28 the word is used to denote the "outline" of a sketch that the artist fills in with detail. But the use by Clement of Alexandria (*Stromateis* 5.8.49) of a "master copy" that pupils use to imitate is more common. Thus Christ sets a pattern to be reproduced. See Bigg, *Epistles of St. Peter and St. Jude*, pp. 145-46. See also G. Schrenk, "ὑπογραμμός," *TDNT* 1:772-73.

stichometric analysis of this hymn shows that v. 23b forms the center, with six syllables: *paschōn ouk epeilei* ("when suffering he did not retaliate").[25] That this same parenetic emphasis occurs throughout the NT and forms a signifi-cant unity to the NT canon has been persuasively argued and demonstrated by William Farmer.[26] This injunction not to retaliate, i.e. not to repay evil for evil, is present also in two Pauline texts (Rom. 12:17-21 and 1 Thess. 5:15), al-though there it is not joined to *example* or *imitation* language. But it is con-gruous with and even provides theological foundation for Paul's other exhor-tations, as noted above.

Heb. 6:12; 12:1-3a; 13:7   While Heb. 6:12 and 13:7 use *imitate*, 12:1-3a em-ploys distinctive vocabulary to portray Jesus as a model by which believers form moral conviction and character. Here, in the context of the ch. 11 catalog of those who lived by faith — from Abraham onward — and did not see the promise fulfilled, Jesus is set forth as the leader or pioneer *(archēgos)* of the train of the faithful. The pilgrimage image of chapter 11 now shifts to that of a race *(agōn)* that lies ahead of the faithful. Immediately, this is linked to Jesus' own endurance of the cross and the hostility of sinners against him. This in turn is the motive or rationale for believers not to grow weary in doing good.

When this injunction to "look" — literally "fix one's eyes on" or "be glued to" (to use the modern colloquialism) — "to Jesus" is joined to the de-scription of Jesus as the "pioneer of the faith," a strong case for Jesus func-tioning as a model for the shaping of our desire emerges. But again, Jesus is linked to the cross, and only through it to an exalted position at the right hand of God. The short phrase, "disregarding the shame" (of the cross), ar-rests our attention on two counts. First, what does *aischynēs kataphronēsas* re-ally mean, especially when earlier versions translated it as "despising the cross"? Second, how does this meaning square with a Girardian interpreta-tion of Jesus' attitude toward the cross?

Although "despising" is the more natural translation, the NRSV transla-tors, apparently failing to see sense in this, took the less likely connotation "disregarding" the shame, i.e., putting up with the shame to move on to the

25. Schertz, "Nonretaliation and the Haustafeln in 1 Peter."

26. William R. Farmer proposes that the books that made it into the canon did so be-cause they nurtured and empowered Christians amid suffering. It is striking how prominent that theme is in virtually all the NT writings. See Farmer, *Jesus and the Gospel*, pp. 177-221. Farmer, after showing the correlation between emerging lists of books and persecution, con-cludes: "That the reality of Christian martyrdom in the early church and the selection of Chris-tian writings for the New Testament canon stand in some vital relationship to one another is as certain as anything that can be conjectured on this complex historical question" (p. 221). See also Farmer and Farkasfalvy, *The Formation of the New Testament Canon*, pp. 7-95.

next phase of exaltation (Phil. 2:5-11 *may,* but need not, be interpreted to concur with this meaning). The weakness of this solution lies in its tendency to "slide over or through" the cross to get on to glory. But this is hardly in keeping with the larger emphasis of Hebrews (as well as Paul's emphasis on *theologia crucis*).

The more natural meaning, "despising the cross," acquires special significance when informed by the Girardian understanding of the cross as exposure of human violence and the culmination of acquisitive mimetic desire against the innocent victim. The *shame* of the cross lies precisely in its function as death for criminals. To identify the *shame* factor in the experience is to expose its injustice, to say clearly that Jesus was killed as a criminal, and that this *shameful* action is one Jesus despised and despises today when human violence scapegoats the innocent. The good of Jesus' death — even the divine necessity *(dei),* therefore, does not justify or whitewash the violence. It was and is *shameful.* In this light, there is important reason to retain the older translation (KJV, RSV).

John 13:14-16   In John's Gospel account, Jesus memorializes the moral injunction to humble service in ritual enactment. The discourse in which we find this exhortation to follow Jesus' example *(hypodeigma)* concludes with denoting the mark of the disciples' identity: "By this everyone will know that you are my disciples, if you have love for one another" (13:35). Indeed, even though John's Gospel is distinctive in its account of Jesus' ministry, it too speaks the same voice as the Pauline imitation parenesis, the 1 Peter "example," the Hebrews "pioneer" of faith amid hardship, and the Synoptics' dramatic presentation of Jesus' repeated efforts to enable the disciples to see and walk a new way. This new way diverges decisively from that of acquisitive mimesis to willingness to suffer under the rejection and violence of humanity against the righteous One.

Mimesis in the Synoptic Passion Narrative

The convergence of the content of the [Passion] narratives with the theory of the *skandalon* — theory of mimetic desire — cannot be fortuitous.[27]

That same day Herod and Pilate became friends with each other; before this they had been enemies (Luke 23:12).

---

27. Girard, *The Scapegoat,* p. 159.

Girard gives considerable space to analysis of the passion narrative, since it shows well how the players in the story depict the mimetic rivalry: the disciples, Judas, the chief priest, elders, and scribes, the council, and Pilate and Herod. Even though crowds are initially favorable to Jesus, the religious leaders maneuver them to their side so that the story moves to the climax of "all against one," summed up deftly in Acts 4:27, "For in this city, in fact, both Herod and Pontius Pilate, with the Gentiles and the peoples of Israel, gathered together against your holy servant Jesus, whom you anointed. . . ."[28]

Here I will focus on Mark's central section, for there the two types of mimesis are starkly contrasted.[29] The same content and emphasis are present in Matthew and Luke as well, with slightly different accents. Mark's pre-passion section is carefully crafted, interweaving Jesus' teaching on the forthcoming passion (8:31; 9:31; 10:32-34) with depiction of the disciples' failure to understand (8:32-33; 9:32-34; 10:35-41), followed immediately by Jesus' teaching on cross-bearing (8:34-37), valuing the child (9:35-37), and self-giving service (10:42-45). This pattern of thinking contrasts sharply to the disciples' persisting acquisitive mimesis and rivalry: messianic rule by oppressive power — Peter voices Satan's thoughts (8:29-33); seeking prestige in the coming kingdom — "who is the greatest?" (9:33-34); and clamoring for top positions in the messianic cabinet (10:35-37).

According to Girard's analyses, the object of desire progresses in this section into ever greater specificity, with mounting rivalry and latent violence. Further, the second cycle of teaching is followed by an extended admonition (9:38-50) to avoid *scandalizing* little ones and to cut from one's life those *desires* that cause offense and stumbling *(scandal)*. The section ends (v. 50) with Jesus urging the disciples to be at peace with one another, possible only when they have repudiated their acquisitive mimetic rivalry and have learned to avoid the *skandalon*.

Probing to yet another level, Mark frames his journey section with the *hodos* motif, which echoes Israel's earlier journey to the land of promise, the movement from old life in Egypt's slavery to new life in the land promised as God's gift and their inheritance.[30] The theological significance of Mark's weaving of Jesus' announced passion and resurrection into the recurring exo-

---

28. A longer analysis of Girardian perspectives on this story is to be found in Girard, *The Scapegoat*, pp. 100-164; "How Can Satan Cast Out Satan?"; Williams, *The Bible, Violence, and the Sacred*, pp. 185-258; Hamerton-Kelly, *The Gospel and the Sacred: Poetics of Violence in Mark.*

29. See here Hamerton-Kelly, *The Gospel and the Sacred*, pp. 103-11.

30. My *Israel's Scripture Traditions and the Synoptic Gospels* develops broader theses on this point for each of the Synoptics' travel narratives (see ch. 4).

dus and way-"conquest" motifs is far-reaching. Many scholars have recognized that Mark's *hodos* is indeed the "way" of suffering. *Hodos* in 8:27–10:52 is not only Jesus' journey to Jerusalem, but it also marks both the *way* of Jesus in his passion and the *way* of disciples who follow him. It will be a way of suffering.[31] In this *hodos* narrative (8:27–10:52) Jesus concentrates his teaching on discipleship.[32] Indeed, Mark uses *hodos* as a hermeneutical tool to contemporize Jesus' past history so that Mark's readers — and we — can hear the call to follow on the way.[33]

From these three cycles on Jesus' passion and teachings on discipleship we can grasp the essential conditions of entrance into the kingdom of God, the goal of Jesus' *hodos* teachings *à la* Mark. In the first cycle Jesus as the suffering Son of Humanity-Messiah rebukes the disciples for their too eager acclaim of Peter's confession of Jesus as Messiah (*epitimaō* is used already in 8:30). In v. 32 Peter rebukes Jesus for speaking about suffering. Then in v. 33 Jesus sternly rebukes Peter and identifies Peter's thinking with Satan.

It is clear that two opposing views of messiahship have locked horns. Peter's view is most likely the Maccabean model, in which the Messiah will crush the power of the enemy nations.[34] Jesus' view is the way of the suffering Son of humanity, indeed the way of the Servant of the Lord (Isaiah 53). The call to take up the cross means nothing less than willingness to die, to be crucified, for the sake of Jesus' gospel (v. 34), i.e., the kingdom he proclaimed. It means losing one's life and not being ashamed of Jesus' gospel even when threatened with death (vv. 34-38; see further Chapter 4 above).

Concluding the second cycle, Mark juxtaposes acts of power (exorcism)

31. For discussion and documentation of this point, see Swartley, *Israel's Scripture Traditions*, p. 11, n. 50.

32. Again see Swartley, *Israel's Scripture Traditions*, p. 111 and notes 51 and 52 for documentation and discussion.

33. In this interpretation, *hodos* leads from Jesus' own history to the suffering experience of Christians in Mark's Christian community in the late 60s of the first century. See Reploh, *Markus — Lehrer der Gemeinde*, pp. 96, 107, 141, 222, 226.

34. It is striking that the various conceptualizations of evil in and behind biblical thought link war and military weapons to evil itself: in the "Watchers Myth" Asael (Azazel) gives to humans the knowledge of weapons for war (*1 Enoch* 8:1); in Genesis 6 the *nephilim*, which come from the union of gods and humans, are Israel's later giant military foes; in the Isaiah 14 and Ezekiel 28 arrogant king traditions, which provide much of the later imagery for the devil, the kings are dethroned because of oppressive military power and self-deification; in the early *satan* tradition, Satan incites David to take a census for military enlistment (1 Chronicles 21). For extensive treatment of the origins of the conceptions of evil reflected in Scripture see Forsyth, *The Old Enemy*, pp. 44-191.

and humble service (giving a cup of water). Both are equally significant when done in Jesus' name! Then the narrative takes up the topic of offense *(skandalon)*. Harsh words of judgment fall on those who cause "one of these little ones who believe in me to sin." The cause of offense *(skandalon)* to the "little one" or to one's own transformed desires must be purged for one to enter the kingdom of God (v. 47; cf. "life" in vv. 43, 45). Drawing on the imagery of well-prepared salted sacrifices (Lev. 2:13), Jesus calls for the self to be salted,[35] purified of evil and acquisitive desires, and for his followers to live peaceably with one another (vv. 49-50). This exhortation to peace contrasts to the segment's initial portrait of the disciples disputing with one another over which was the greatest. Walking in the way of Jesus means giving up rivalry over greatness and passionately desiring relationships that do not offend others, but rather yield the fruit of peace.

In the third round of *hodos* teaching, Jesus now responds to the *acquisitive desires* of James and John to be granted seats beside him in glory. What exactly they had in mind is not clear, but the point of their desiring to share in (their misunderstanding of) Jesus' future is clear. Williams comments perceptively on this matter and the effect this portrait of the disciples had on the early Christians:

> The mimetic desire and rivalry of the disciples and their corresponding inability to comprehend the call to Jesus as the Christ, Son of man, and Suffering Servant is the most difficult aspect of Mark for the Christian tradition to understand and assimilate. Surely, this depiction of the disciples was a scandal and a primary factor occasioning the writing of the Gospels of Matthew and Luke.[36]

After exposing the intensity of their desire, Jesus shocks them — subverting their assumptions — by promising them that they will share in the cup (of suffering) he will drink (see 14:36) and the baptism with which he will be baptized, but their wish is not his to grant. The ten were indignant — their own mimetic desire flashing — presumably because they thought James and John had gotten some edge over them.

In his subsequent teaching Jesus stresses a binding relationship between the Redeemer and the redeemed (10:43-45). The redeemed, i.e. the followers of Jesus, are linked to Jesus as the servant-head who leads the ransomed into lives of servant-living. Certainly this was one of Mark's primary aims in writing the Gospel: to set forth Jesus' life, death, and resurrection as a call to and

---

35. Might this be an anti-sacrificial pun?
36. *Bible, Violence, and the Sacred*, p. 225.

empowerment for faithful discipleship.[37] This discipleship is to consist of transformed desires so that the natural human acquisitive desire is refused in the name and power of Jesus as the Servant of the Lord who leads us into the new creation. Williams puts it well:

> I think Mark probably intends to say, in effect, "The human condition is such that only the price of the Son of man's suffering and death will have the effect of loosing the bonds of the sacred social structure, enabling human beings to see what their predicament is and the kind of faith and action that will bring liberation."[38]

The images of *hodos*-cross (8:34) and giving his life as a ransom (10:45) form an inclusio around Jesus' teaching in this section. Both point to suffering and death, and both point also toward gaining life and ransoming life. The way of the Messiah's victory and the way of victory for his followers are bound together by the cross and resurrection. The section as a whole shows that God's victory[39] comes in a most unsuspecting way: the way of self-denial, humble service, and the very giving of one's life for others.[40] This is the way of Jesus. Jesus' resurrection is indeed a vital part of every passion prediction on the way. Jesus' *hodos* is not only a way to death, but also a way to God's victory (note *proagein* in 16:7). This victory is assured by Jesus' death as "a ransom for many." For Jesus and his disciples the way of faithful warfare was and is that of humble service, even unto death. Victory comes through God's vindication of the faithful.

This emphasis lies at the heart of the model/imitation-pattern found in Luke-Acts, where Jesus' conduct before authorities inspires the persecuted in

37. This climactic instruction on the way *(en tē hodǭ)*, set within the "conquest" (exodus) imagery of the OT, leaves no doubt that Jesus is presenting a counter-model to *acquisitive desire and mimetic rivalry* for the ordering of social and political relationships. If entering and living within the kingdom are guided by this new empowering imagery, which subverts prevailing empire images, then the "way-conquest" tradition, which provided prominent imagery for this section of Mark's presentation of Jesus, has undergone significant transformation. The Divine Warrior–Son of Humanity–Messiah attains the victory, ransoming many, through suffering and death.

38. *Bible, Violence and the Sacred*, p. 224.

39. In the only exorcism in this section (9:14-30), Jesus sharply rebukes the disciples for their lack of faith. This story makes it clear that Mark's Jesus does not avoid the fight against evil. Cross-bearing and servanthood are not substitutes for or bypasses around the task of overcoming evil.

40. This accords with atonement theories that emphasize Jesus' humiliation and death as tricking the devil (cf. 1 Cor. 2:6-8).

their testimony to the gospel before rulers. I regard Richard Cassidy's thesis tenable: Acts serves the cause of strengthening allegiance to Jesus Christ and witness before political authorities. Luke's primary goals were, first, to write out of his personal allegiance to his Lord and strengthen believers in their allegiance and, second, to shape the conduct of believers in their daily interactions with people generally but especially with government officials, in accord with the gospel. Luke-Acts thus provides models for believers in their own "Christian witness in their trials before Roman officials."[41]

Revelation shows the same pattern. Believers are challenged to conquer the beast — the epitome of mimetic violence (2:7, 11, 17, 26; 3:5, 12, 21; 21:7) — just as the Lion (5:5)/Lamb (17:14) has already conquered and other brothers and sisters have conquered as well (12:11; 15:2). Hence the pattern of mimesis appears to permeate NT thought.

The Wider New Testament Perspective

In addition to this narrower scope of an imitation/discipleship pattern defining the manner in which believers relate to Jesus, a much wider set of language and concepts develops *correspondence* logic between the believer and Jesus as leader or prototype. John H. Yoder develops this correspondence logic around three main categories of thought.[42]

The disciple/participant and the love of God. Yoder quotes a series of texts that speak of believers sharing the divine nature: in light and purity (1 John 1:5-7; 3:1-3; 4:17); in holy living (1 Pet. 1:15-16, citing Lev. 19:2); and putting on a new nature and being constantly renewed in the image of its Creator (Col. 3:9-10; Eph. 4:23-24). To these might be added 2 Pet. 1:3ff., which explicitly speaks of believers sharing in the divine nature. Yoder then identifies numerous texts that enjoin believers to forgive as God in Christ forgave us (Eph. 4:32; Col. 3:13; Matt. 6:12 par. Luke 11:4; Matt. 6:14-15; 18:32ff.). To this list others might be added: Mark 11:25 and especially the Johannine form of the sending commission, John 20:23, although in these texts the correspondence is only implied. Yoder then focuses on Jesus' command to love indiscriminately, thus including the enemy, just as God is indiscriminate in sending sun and rain on the just and unjust (Matt. 5:43-48 and Luke 6:32-36).

The disciple/participant and the life of Christ. Here Yoder refers to being

---

41. Cassidy, *Society and Politics in the Acts of the Apostles*, pp. 159-60.
42. John H. Yoder, *The Politics of Jesus*, chapter 7.

"in Christ" (1 John 2:6 — many others in Paul could be cited[43]) and texts that speak of dying with Christ and sharing in his risen life (Rom. 6:6-11; 8:11; Gal. 2:20; cf. 5:24; Eph. 4:20-24; Col. 2:12–3:1). To this he adds "loving as Christ loved, giving himself" (John 13:34; 15:12; 1 John 3:11-16; cf. 4:4-10; and Mark 12:28ff. par.). Related to this, the next category is "serving others as he served" (John 13:1-17; Rom. 15:1-7; 2 Cor. 5:14ff.; 8:7-9; Eph. 5:22-28), and finally "subordination," where Yoder refers to another entire chapter under the title "Revolutionary Subordination," in which, through citation of the several *Haustafeln* texts, Yoder puts forward his thesis: "Sub*ord*ination means the acceptance of an *order*, as it exists, but with the new meaning given to it by the fact that one's acceptance of it is willing and meaningfully motivated."[44] Throughout the chapter Yoder shows how the appeal for subordination is rooted "in the example of Jesus Christ or in the nature of Christ as shared by the believer."[45]

The disciple/participant and the death of Christ.   To document his first major point that suffering with Christ defines apostolic and Christian existence, Yoder cites many of the *imitation/example* texts I cited above, as well as 2 Cor. 4:10; 1:5; Col. 1:24. His key text for documenting the point that believers are expected to share in the divine condescension and to give their lives as Jesus did is Phil. 2:3-14 (cf. Eph. 5:1 and texts cited above). Then Yoder focuses on suffering: suffering servanthood replaces dominion (Mark 10:42-45 par.); the believer is to accept innocent suffering without complaint (1 Pet. 2:20ff.; 3:14-18; 4:12-16; John 15:20-21; 2 Tim. 3:12; Phil. 1:29). Death is then viewed as liberation from sin's power (1 Pet. 4:1-2; Gal. 5:24), as the fate of the prophets (Matt. 23:34; Mark 12:1-9; Luke 24:19-20; Acts 2:36; 4:10; 7:52; 1 Thess. 2:15ff.), and as victory (Col. 2:15; 1 Cor. 1:22-24; Rev. 12:10-11; cf. 5:9ff.; 17:14). Yoder enumerates many actions, life-style features, and cultural particularities that believers are never told to emulate or copy, then concludes provocatively,

> There is but one realm in which the concept of imitation holds — but there it holds in every strand of the New Testament literature and all the more strikingly by virtue of the absence of parallels in other realms: this is at the point of the concrete social meaning of the cross in its relation to enmity and power. Servanthood replaces dominion, forgiveness absorbs hostility. Thus — and only thus — are we bound by New Testament thought to "be like Jesus."[46]

43. For a complete list see Schweitzer, *The Mysticism of St. Paul the Apostle*, pp. 123-27; Smedes, *Union with Christ*, especially pp. 55-135.

44. Yoder, *Politics of Jesus*, p. 175 (second edition, p. 172).

45. Yoder, *Politics of Jesus*, p. 180 (second edition, p. 177).

46. Yoder, *Politics of Jesus*, p. 134 (second edition, p. 131).

I suggest that Yoder's treatment and summary are perhaps reductionistic since the correspondence logic is extended to include other features of God or Christ in certain uncited passages,[47] most notably 2 Pet. 1:3ff., which correlates a string of Christian virtues with the goal "that you may become participants in the divine nature" (v. 4c). The constituent qualifications of this identification with the divine nature are the divine empowerment of life and godliness — to escape corruption through this world's lusts — and numerous virtues *(aretai):* faith, goodness, knowledge, self-control, endurance, godliness, mutual affection, and love.

The Pauline ethical injunctions introduced by "put off/put on" language carry forward the "new creation" reality into practical life and significantly interconnect to Girard's view of desire, and its causative relation to rivalry and violence. Below is a list of the vices in Col. 3:5-9 with parallels in other NT books.[48]

	Col 3:5-9	Rom 1	Gal 5	Eph 4–5	1 Cor 5	1 Cor 6	1 Pet 4:3	Rev 21:8
fornication		◆	◆	◆	◆		◆	
impurity	◆	◆	◆					
passion	◆	(◆)						
evil desire	◆	(◆)	(◆)			(◆)		
greed	◆		◆	◆	◆			
(idolatry)		◆	◆	◆	◆	◆		◆
anger			◆					
wrath	◆		◆					
malice	◆		◆					
slander			◆					
abusive (filthy) language			◆					
(lying)	(◆)		◆			(◆)	◆	

It is striking to see the prevalence of "evil desire" *(epithymian kakēn),* "greed" or "covetousness" (RSV; *pleonexian),* and "idolatry" *(eidōlolatria;* Galatians 5 also includes "witchcraft" [NIV] or "sorcery" [NRSV] = *pharmakia)* and that

47. Michael Griffiths selects a broader set of texts in his helpful work, *The Example of Jesus.*

48. From Martin, *Colossians-Philemon,* p. 163.

"anger," "wrath," and "malice" are close associates in a few texts. The argument that these lists have kinship to (perhaps origin in) Hellenistic usage does not detract from, but adds to the force of Girard's emphasis regarding the human condition. These vices that characterize the "old life," the life displeasing to God, are all interrelated aspects of what Girard identifies as acquisitive mimetic desire and its evil works. Especially noteworthy is the prominence of "covetousness" (or "greed") in this list (echoing Genesis 4) and its identification with idolatry (echoing Genesis 3) in both Colossians and Ephesians.

In contrast to this list, the virtues are "compassion, kindness, lowliness, meekness, patience, forbearing one another, and forgiving each other" (Col. 3:12-14; see p. 412). The ninefold "fruit" (singular) of the Spirit — "love, peace, joy, patience, kindness, goodness, faithfulness, gentleness, self-control" — is also a gospel description of the new life, in sharp contrast to the "works" (plural) of the flesh (Gal. 5:16-24). These vice-virtue lists in the NT epistles thus corroborate Girard's theses regarding the human plight.

But not only is the believer's life to be modeled ethically after virtues which flow from the new life in Christ, but the destiny of believers is connected to a process of change in 2 Cor. 3:17-18. Here the image that functions as the object of desire is the exalted Lord Jesus, who significantly (see ch. 4) is never detached from the suffering Jesus Christ. But this also means that the model of mimetic desire in the new creation is not only the Jesus of suffering, forgiving, and humble service, but also the exalted, vindicated Jesus, victorious over the powers of evil.

The fundamental conception in Pauline thought that unites believers to their Savior Jesus Christ is the "in Christ" stream of emphasis, so pervasive that entire epistolary discourses are shaped by it (Romans 6 and 8, Ephesians 1).[49] Paul also uses numerous *co*-constructions (with the Greek prefix *syn*): co-buried (*synetaphēmen*, Rom. 6:4), united with him (*symphytoi*, 6:5), co-crucified (*synestaurōthē*, 6:6), co-died (*apothneiskein*, 6:8), co-live (*syzēsomen*, 6:8), co-inherit, co-suffer, and co-glorified (all in 8:17). The grand climax to this co-participation language comes in Rom. 8:29: "in order that we might be conformed (co-formed, *symmorphous*) into the image *(eikonos)* of God's Son, in order that he might be the firstborn *(prōtotokon)* among many brothers and sisters."

This identification with Christ as model is so strong that in some texts

---

49. On this see Schweitzer, *Mysticism*, pp. 120-30; Smedes, *Union with Christ*, pp. 55-85; and the several treatments by Lucien Cerfaux: *The Christian in the Theology of St. Paul; Christ in the Theology of St. Paul;* and *The Church in the Theology of St. Paul.*

Jesus Christ is said to be (manifest) in the believers: the life of Jesus is manifest in our dying bodies (2 Cor. 4:10-12), Christ's sufferings abound in us (2 Cor. 1:5-7); Christ is glorified in my (our) body (Phil. 1:20); that Christ be formed in you (plural; Gal. 4:19); Christ in you (plural), the hope of glory (Col. 1:27); and that Christ dwell in your (plural) hearts by faith (Eph. 3:17a).

While this language, part and parcel of the massive "in Christ" emphasis, has generated much debate over whether this relationship is to be understood mystically — and if so, of what kind? — its obvious connection to the core emphases on *imitation/example/following Jesus* should not be missed. If there is a mysticism here, it is moral and mimetic at its core.[50] It is linked to desire and assumes that thought, conduct, and aspiration are governed by new desires. The point is put most sharply in Paul's exposition on the first and second Adam (Rom. 5:12ff.) and his depiction of the new Christ reality as a "new creation" (2 Cor. 5:17).

Grounded in the life, death, and resurrection of Jesus, this new reality makes possible "things destined (now revealed) before the foundation of the world." The person "in Christ" dies to the old *acquisitive mimetic desire* and lives by the power of a new mimesis, *imitating the pattern of Jesus Christ and seeking to be conformed to his image.* Jesus in the fullness of his work enables renunciation of the natural human desire for reward or glory.

This desire is "*cross*-fired," refined through transformation. Through this experience, solely possible through the *Pioneer* of the faith, we learn a new pattern of *mimetic desire*, one that leads not to rivalry and violence, but to building others up, avoiding scandal, preferring one another, empowering the other, and nonretaliation against evil in order that as members of the community of the new creation we break the spiral of violence and become the strands of yarn that by God's Spirit are knitted into the display of love, justice, and shalom.

Summary and Conclusion

A mimesis pattern lies at the heart of NT thought. Any theology or ethics of the NT should make this point foundational, but few do. Just as world culture generally manifests energy via mimetic desire, so life in the kingdom of God, the new creation, is animated and empowered also by a mimetic model. The key difference is that in the latter the lead model is the new Adam, precisely because he was tempted with the acquisitive mimeses in all ways such as we

---

50. For a survey of the various interpretations, see Smedes, *Union with Christ*, pp. 58-67.

are, but did not yield to the mimetic pattern that generates rivalry and violence. Jesus as faithful Servant of the Lord has opened up for us a new world of hope and potential; we are saved by his transforming of our desire. We seek then to follow in his steps and be conformed to his image.

Precisely in this context we can grasp anew the full significance of the gospel's declaration that "Christ is our peace" (Eph. 2:14) and that Christ is our reconciliation and entrusts to his followers the ministry of reconciliation (2 Cor. 5:18-20). Further, the pervasive NT teaching on love of enemy and nonretaliation against evil is the outworking of this new mimesis in an ethic for conflictual relations.[51]

Finally, I suggest that the evidence presented in this chapter witnesses analogically to the correctness of Girard's analysis of the human condition and culture. If indeed the life of Jesus' followers is so profusely and consistently described as a a relation between Jesus as *Model* and his followers as *imitators-disciples* in self-giving love, service, and suffering, then from the standpoint of this gospel revelation we can deduce also the nature and dynamic of the shadow-model that rules the world: acquisitive mimetic desire, rivalry, and violence (indeed the Genesis 3–4 depiction).

The element of sacrificial scapegoating that enshrouds the violence in a halo-lie cannot be adduced analogically from the evidence given here (though with more work on "atonement" in Mark 10:45; Eph. 5:2; Heb. 12:2; and Rev. 5:9, this may be possible also). However, the ubiquity and reign of the persecutors' myths might be inferred logically from the predominant suffering-martyr experience of the paracletic community. But as Luke-Acts testifies, the gospel witness of the believers exposes the persecutor's myth and manifests, in life and martyr-death, the proclaimed incarnation of the "gospel of peace" (Luke 10:5-9; Acts 10:36 quoting Isa. 52:7).

51. Some work has been done on these themes. See the three volumes in the Studies in Peace and Scripture series published in 1992: Mauser, *The Gospel of Peace;* Yoder and Swartley, eds., *The Meaning of Peace: Biblical Essays,* especially the essay by Erich Dinkler; and Swartley, ed., *The Love of Enemy and Nonretaliation in the New Testament,* especially the article by Luise Schottroff.

14 God's Moral Character as the Basis for Human Ethics: Foundational Convictions

This chapter addresses a topic that has passionately engaged Mennonite and Girardian scholars,[1] as well as all Jews and Christians who seek to be peacemakers for God in our world: how to understand Scripture as a unique resource for a peacemaking ethic. A persisting issue in both biblical interpretation and theological construction of a pacifist ethic presents a double challenge: how we understand the human role in combat of evil and whether God's character and actions serve as exemplary model for believers committed to peacemaking. This chapter addresses both dimensions of this issue, with greater focus on the latter. I propose an element of paradox in seeking to mediate between two persuasive poles of thought and acknowledge some ambiguity, even though my leaning on the matter is clear. This "positioning" on my part grows out of what will be discussed first, namely that the rationale for constraint in the human role to combat evil is based in God's right to vengeance and judgment. Here several foundational moral convictions rooted in Scripture require rethinking of conventional wisdom; after this section the greater part of the chapter focuses explicitly on the topic of the title.

A first fundamental conviction is that God does not need us humans to fight against human enemies to win divine victory. Here the work of Millard Lind in his groundbreaking book *Yahweh Is A Warrior* has been of enormous help in understanding warfare in Hebrew Scripture.[2] John H. Yoder's *The Pol-*

---

1. This chapter had its beginnings in my brief address to a combined meeting of the Colloquium on Violence and Religion (the René Girard group) and Mennonite scholars in November 2002 at the SBL annual meeting.

2. Significantly, David Noel Freedman wrote the Foreword (pp. 13-15), and John H. Yoder wrote the Introduction (pp. 17-19).

itics of Jesus and *The Original Revolution*[3] mediated Lind's theses to a much wider readership.

A recent article by Steven Nolt, interviewing Millard Lind, tells the story of the breakthrough giving rise to Lind's doctoral dissertation and later book. While spending a summer in Chicago reading Ancient Near Eastern texts on war, Lind says, "suddenly everything [about the biblical record of war] stood out in a new way against that Near East background."[4] Nolt writes, summarizing Lind's comments, sprinkled with quotations from Lind:

> Yes, Yahweh was certainly a warrior, but a warrior who "fought for his people by miracle, not by sword and spear." Military action was actually out of Israel's control and it relied upon faith rather than marshal [sic, martial] prowess or human strategy. Throughout the . . . [Hebrew Scripture] "this conviction was so emphatic that Israel's [human] fighting, while at times a sequel to the act of Yahweh, was regarded as ineffectual." In fact, disaster often struck when humans tried to take matters of defense into their own hands.
>
> The witness of the Hebrews pointed to a God profoundly different from the other deities, despite their surface similarities. Yahweh gave teaching [Torah] that was not a graceless law code, but was instead a way of life with the goal of shalom — holy justice, well-being, and right relationships.[5]

Owing to the influence of the Lind-Yoder thesis, corroborated by numerous scholars, we know that we humans need not take God's battle into our own hands, that we need not control history's outcome, and that we need not take revenge on our enemies. When we affirm this conviction, God relents punishment upon us, freeing us from the consequence that killing brings: violence recoiling back upon our own heads to destroy us.

My study of the Synoptic Gospels, *Israel's Scripture Traditions and the Synoptic Gospels: Story Shaping Story*,[6] demonstrates that the Gospel narratives, both in structural form and distinctive emphases, extend the same call to trust in God and in Jesus' power to win victory over evil in every manifestation.[7] Similarly, N. T. Wright rightly portrays the historical Jesus calling Israel to a third way, the way of peacemaking, based on the Scripture traditions

---

3. Especially ch. 4 of *The Politics of Jesus* and chapter IV of *The Original Revolution*.
4. Nolt, "Passion for the Prophets: Millard Lind Champions the Old Testament."
5. Nolt, "Passion for the Prophets."
6. Especially pp. 56-59, 67-70, 76-94.
7. This is especially prominent in the miracle stories and Jesus' teaching on discipleship.

in Isaiah 40-55[8] in order to avoid being crushed by the Romans.[9] Within Israel's traditions of hope and bliss for the future, Jesus comes as prophetic peacemaker. A great tragedy of history is that followers of Jesus' peace legacy have often relapsed, turning persecutor even against God's first covenant people who birthed Jesus, the Peacemaker, into this world.

For those who grasp aright the way of the suffering servant/Jesus-Savior as power to deliver us from our own pretensions to power and martial inclinations, God relents punishment. Then, our violence will not recoil upon our own heads.

A second foundational conviction comes with René Girard's discovery of Scripture's contribution to his unfolding insight into the mimetic desire/ sacrificial violence cycle. In James G. Williams's interview with Girard in *The Girard Reader* Girard says,

> The third great discovery for me was when I began to see the uniqueness of the Bible, especially the Christian text, from the standpoint of the scapegoat theory. The mimetic representation of scapegoating in the Passion was the solution to the relationship of the Gospels and archaic cultures. In the Gospels we have the revelation of the mechanism that dominates culture unconsciously.[10]

Girard's three-stage intellectual-literary discovery (first, mimetic desire and rivalry; second, the scapegoat mechanism; and third, the uniqueness of the Bible in exposing violence and God's siding with the victim) is complemented by a subsequent significant transformational experience, which might well be called Girard's "heart" conversion. Williams writes of this also in *The Girard Reader*. Through a scare with what he thought might be terminal cancer at age 35, Girard's "intellectual conversion" was now "totally changed."[11] Upon receiving word of relief from his cancer on the Wednesday before Easter, Girard immediately went to confession and began his religious life and pilgrimage. Moving from an atheistic deconstructionist stance, Girard came to see his contribution as a witness to faith, standing against the strongholds of intellectual and destructive negativity in academia so prevalent in the Western world. Girard opposes the bracketing out of religious truth in order to be neutral in scholarship, regarding such an approach as a hangover from nineteenth-century nihilism.

---

8. For an excellent exposition of Isa. 52:13–53:12, see Goodhart, "René Girard and the Innocent Victim."

9. Wright, *Jesus and the Victory of God.*

10. James G. Williams, *The Girard Reader,* p. 262.

11. Williams, *The Girard Reader,* p. 285.

John H. Yoder also zeroes in on the gospel, specifically Jesus, for an answer to violence. While doubting that Girard's theory of the etiology of violence "explains *all* the modes of bloodshed," he believes it does explain what Genesis 4 narrates, in both the mimetic rivalry surrounding the type of sacrifice that leads to Cain's murder of Abel and the sequel, Lamech's increase of vengeance. He notes that "eye for eye" is one form ("state" or "law and order") of limiting the ever-threatening spiral of violence, and the "sacrificial" response is another. Most significant is his statement:

> . . . if the phenomenon of violence is not rational in its causes, its functions, its objectives, neither will its cure be rational. The cure will have to be something as primitive, as elemental, as the evil. It will have to act upon the deep levels of meaning and motivation, deeper than mental self-definition and self-control. It will have to be *sacrifice*. There will have to be innocent suffering.[12]

Rehearsing the numerous forms in which the "eye for eye" mantra has come to be regarded as virtually "the notion of cosmic symmetry," he contends "it is not in the actual Hebrew jurisprudence, and not in the nature of God." While noting that Girard would say this perpetuation of violence "*is* the law of gravity," Yoder observes that explanations of "the *origin* of the phenomenon of reflexive vengeance" or regulatory proscriptions to control it are after the fact. He then declares:

> The response that is needed is then not a new way to *think* about it — what we might properly call a "theological critique" — but something to be done about it. The response is divine judgment, not an explanation, not an evaluation, but an intervention.
> The name of that intervention is "Jesus."[13]

Yoder then addresses how one interprets the meaning of Jesus and finds that it depends on whether one draws on a worldview that is sacrificial, juridical, political, or psycho-dynamic; another mode of description is Tolstoy's oversimplified poetic "breaking the chain." But the common base line in all these "is that the thing to do with violence is not to understand it *but to undergo it*."[14]

12. John Howard Yoder, "Theological Critique of Violence."
13. Yoder, "Theological Critique," p. 5.
14. Yoder, "Theological Critique," p. 5.

Later, Yoder correlates violence, the cross, and salvation in a memorable expression:

> Every major strand of the New Testament, each in its own way, interprets the acceptance by Jesus of the violence of the cross as the means, necessary and sufficient, of God's victory over the rebellious powers. Violence is not merely a problem to solve, a temptation to resist, a mystery to penetrate, or a challenge to resolve with a theodicy. It is all of that, but that is not yet the good news. The good news is that the violence with which we heirs of Cain respond to our brothers' differentness is the occasion of our salvation. *Were it not for that primeval destructive reflex, there would have been no suffering servant, and no wisdom and power of God in the Cross.*[15]

Girard and Yoder point us to the Jesus of the Gospels, who, fulfilling the Suffering Servant model of Isaiah 53, exemplifies by his nonretaliatory life and death that the cycle of violence, which crucified him, is broken. Jesus, therefore, is our salvation, hope, and moral compass guiding us to peace.

A third foundational conviction arises from a broadened understanding of the term *mimetic desire*. Girard's writings, except for his later ones, restrict the concept of mimetic desire to bad mimesis only. But in later writings, Girard acknowledges that there is also good mimetic desire.[16] My contribution, which examines the NT teaching on "imitation of Christ" as well as Jesus' teachings on discipleship, shows clearly that Jesus in his revelation of God presents a model of desire and imitation that does not lead to rivalry and violence.[17] This thesis is then taken up and developed more fully both theologically and philosophically by Jim Fodor, in his excellent article, which grounds both discipleship and imitation in the nature of the Trinity, proposing a "participatory model" for the joining of the two parts of this chapter's title: God's moral character and human ethical action.[18] Rebecca Adams, while affirming Girard's phenomenal breakthrough, proposes, however, a shift in the fundamental Girardian theory, so that a subject-subject mimesis is the truly primal

---

15. Yoder, "Theological Critique," p. 6. See also, in the same issue of *New Conversations*, García, "Reflections on Violence," and Goetz, "The Primordial Violence of God."

16. Upon receiving the *Violence Renounced* manuscript in order to write a response, Girard said in a telephone conversation, "Your essay is a breakthrough, the model of a new mimesis made possible by Jesus and the resurrection. I wonder why I didn't see and develop that myself." Then I began to realize how my own religious tradition had enabled me to contribute this perspective rather naturally.

17. "Discipleship and Imitation of Jesus/Suffering Servant: The Mimesis of New Creation."

18. "Christian Discipleship as Participative Imitation: Theological Reflections on Girardian Themes."

human reality, and thus the primal nature of mimesis is radically reconceived.[19] Whether such reality for human historical life can be sustained by appeal to the creation narrative, as she proposes, seems to me to be problematic, since Genesis 1–2 lies beyond the historical reality of Genesis 3–4 in which humans live. Can the subject-subject relationship truly be known and morally achieved apart from the work and empowerment of God in Christ, i.e., the "new creation" that proffers the new mimesis? If so, would not the NT teaching on discipleship, Christ's own nonviolent victory over evil, and the call to *imitatio Christi* be superfluous?

It is one thing to see this strong strand of self-renunciation in both discipleship and *imitatio Christi* in Christian Scripture, but quite another to live by it. What Paul calls the "old Adam" (Rom. 5:12-20) lurks ever close. Of two things I am convinced regarding this mimesis. First, it is achieved not by human effort, but by the transforming power of God, which for Christians is through Jesus our Savior and Lord.[20] An article by Robin Collins[21] contributes significantly to this emphasis and methodological concern.

Indeed, peacemaking is not based upon some prior divine grace apart from the covenant relationship with God and consequent empowerment, which for Christians is the work of Jesus as Savior, Peacemaker, and Reconciler. John Milbank makes this point persuasively in his critique of both Girard and Raymund Schwager. Exposing human responsibility for violence through the mimesis-rivalry-scapegoat theory is essential, but more is needed for deliverance of humans from this trap. Because "original sin" blinds us to its stranglehold over us, even precluding an adequate definition, "the irreplaceability of Christ's specific, concrete manifestation" is necessarily part of any adequate reflection on freedom from the old mimesis by the power of the new:

> "Jesus" — this set of stories, metaphors etc. — is necessary for the redemption, not just because he exposes the old practice and defines the terms of the new, but also because the particular way in which he does

19. "Loving Mimesis and Girard's 'Scapegoat of the Text': A Creative Reassessment of Mimetic Desire."

20. In response to my essay presented at a 1994 Conference held at Associated Mennonite Biblical Seminary on "René Girard and Biblical Peace Theology," Diana Culbertson expressed concern that my paper presented "imitation of Christ" as ethical obligation. Rather, it is the fruit of the transformed life dependent on Jesus Christ and his atoning work *extra nos*. I received her counsel gladly and hope the published form of my essay in *Violence Renounced* adequately responded to her critique.

21. "Girard and Atonement: An Incarnational Theory of Mimetic Participation."

this enacts and enshrines the *viability* of the new, forgiving practice, by virtue of its unique and universal "attractiveness."[22]

The reason "only God incarnate can end violence" is the "physical event of the cross" (which event is "elevated into a figure of meaning"). "Jesus is 'substituted' for us, because he becomes totally a sign, . . . transformed into a perfect metaphor of forgiveness."[23] All the NT metaphors for atonement "represent the actual *happening* of atonement as a meaning in language."[24] Further, for the sign to be effective in ending mimetic rivalry it must be not only "an enabling sign, but also a material reality . . . because it is the *inauguration* of the 'political' practice of forgiveness; forgiveness as a mode of 'government' and social being. This practice is *itself* continuing atonement."[25] The Eucharist celebrates the atonement as both a "once for all" sign and also as atonement continuously renewed. In more traditional theological language, the experiential reality of our justification and sanctification precedes and empowers our peacemaking. In this we learn to be what we have become in Jesus Christ, a participant in God's great shalom vision and purpose. The "in Christ" identity shapes our ethics, as both gift and task (*Gabe* and *Aufgabe*).[26]

I am convinced also that this new mimesis cannot be practiced adequately, in the sense of "practice" defined by Alasdair MacIntyre,[27] on an individualistic basis. The new identity of being "in Christ," or in the "faithful remnant" for Jews, is essential to living out the vision. Thus this new mimesis is corporately based; the individual achieves it only through the empowerment of the community, the Spirit, and the Scripture, a gift both of and over the community of faith.

The fourth foundational conviction, currently under debate, consists of our view of God's moral nature. Is God a God of violence (or wrath?), who uses violence to conquer evil, or is God to be understood as a nonviolent

22. Milbank, *The Word Made Strange,* p. 160.

23. Milbank, *The Word Made Strange,* p. 160.

24. Milbank, *The Word Made Strange,* p. 161.

25. Milbank, *The Word Made Strange,* p. 161. In his earlier work Milbank contended that Girard's contribution, significant as it is, does not go far enough. Girard "does not seem to think in terms of a positive, alternative practice, but only a negative refusal." Milbank explains that both "Anselm's 'idea' of atonement and Girard's 'idea' of Jesus' divinity . . . only make sense if they remind us that Jesus is significant *as* the way, the kingdom, the *autobasileia*." Milbank, *Theology and Social Theory: Beyond Secular Reason,* pp. 395-96.

26. See Stanley Hauerwas's helpful comments along these same lines in *The Peaceable Kingdom: A Primer in Christian Ethics,* pp. 87-94.

27. *After Virtue: A Study in Moral Theology,* pp. 187-96.

God? In *Must There Be Scapegoats?* Raymund Schwager points out that only rarely is God angry for no rational reason. In most of the 1000 instances where Hebrew Scripture speaks of "wrath," it refers to God's response to evil or violence done by humans, and, in a large number of cases, it is executed by actions of other humans. In the fourth type, people become victims of their own crimes. Violence recoils upon them (this too may be applied to God's anger executed through other humans). Thus Schwager proposes that in most, but not all, cases "wherever divine anger or divine vengeance is mentioned, one has in mind concrete deeds of human beings through which the perpetrators punish themselves."[28]

This is an important issue for peace-seeking theologians. In seeking to resolve this issue, I note two fundamental points. First, Millard Lind's insights on warfare are persuasive, to a large extent, because God bears the task of punishing evil and judging justly. Only God, and God alone, can be trusted to do right in executing wrath. Miroslav Volf makes the same point, and refers to Jewish scholar Henri Atlan's discussion of the relation between "God of violence" and "God of love." Atlan contends that a "'God who takes upon Himself the founding violence' is therefore not entirely love in relation to the world." Rather, "God of love" functions within "God of violence." To this Volf says "no." Violence, rather, is "an aspect of God's love." Volf agrees with Atlan, however, that "the best way to rid the world of the violent sacred is to retroject it onto a transcendence" and that by doing so we are able to prohibit human violence. Further, if God would not be angry at the injustice of the world, and act to punish it, then God would not be worthy of human worship.[29]

Second, as my colleague Ben Ollenburger has put it in our co-teaching of War and Peace in the Bible, the issue is whether we think of God's moral essence in symmetrical or asymmetrical relation to what is proscribed and prescribed for us humans. Are God's actions and prerogatives limited by the moral boundaries prescribed for human ethics? Ollenburger answers negatively: God's prerogative to execute wrath, to fight and war against chaos and evil, is indeed God's prerogative. Would we truly want it any other way? Otherwise, we reduce God to human standards or usurp the authority to do what God alone has the right and wisdom to do.

In the NT, texts like Matt. 5:43-48 ground "love of enemies" in the indis-

---

28. Schwager, *Must There Be Scapegoats?* pp. 52-70 (quoting p. 66). Using Girardian analytic, Schwager suggests that the notion "divine anger" may be a human projection of scapegoat fantasies onto the divine being. This is dubious, in my judgment, since "violence" is not projected in this way (see below). Girard's distinction between "myth" and "gospel" might also be considered, but this does not fully satisfy either.

29. Volf, *Exclusion and Embrace*, pp. 302-3.

criminate love of God, for the just and unjust alike. Further, Eph. 5:1 calls us to imitate God's own self in self-giving love. But numerous other texts in Christian Scripture attribute judgment, punishment, and vengeance to God, most notably Rom. 12:19, possibly 1 Thess. 1:10, and numerous parables. The parable of the nobleman-king and pounds in Luke 19:11-27 appears to include both Jesus and God in the act of vengeance. 2 Thess. 1:7-10 ascribes the same function to Jesus Christ, to be manifest at some eschatological time.[30]

When Nancey Murphy seeks to summarize and systematize John Howard Yoder's core thesis about Jesus, however, it is: "The moral character of God is revealed in Jesus' vulnerable enemy love and renunciation of domination. Imitation of Jesus in this regard constitutes a *social ethic.*"[31] Murphy's buttressing hypotheses regarding Yoder's thought further accentuate the same emphasis.

But Volf takes issue with such indiscriminate basing of human ethics in God's moral character, with direct reference to Yoder:

> The thesis about the correspondence between divine and human action rightly underlines that the fundamental theological question in relation to violence is the question about God: "what is God like?" — the God who "loves enemies and is the original peacemaker" (Yoder 1985 [*He Came Preaching Peace*], 104). . . . The thesis has, however, one small but fatal flaw: humans are not God. There is a duty prior to the duty of imitating God, and that is the duty *of not wanting to be God,* of letting God be God and humans be humans.
>
> Preserving the fundamental difference between God and nonGod, the biblical tradition insists that there are things which only God may do. One of them is to use violence.[32]

But on the other side of the debate, Girard argues for a *nonviolent* God. When speaking of Jesus' crucifixion, he says,

---

30. These textual choices leave Revelation aside, since its analysis merits treatment in its own right (see Chapter 12 above). But clearly, God's execution of judgment in wrath and vengeance is a major emphasis, though interconnected with repeated pleading for the people to repent, in order that God relent the judgment.

31. "John Howard Yoder's Systemic Defense of Christian Pacifism," p. 48. In an excursus Murphy proposes that Girard's contribution can explain an anomaly in Yoder's writings, failure to account for NT sacrificial atonement language in Jesus' significance for ethics. Girard's thesis, interpreting Jesus' violent death as a once-for-all sacrifice, functions as a rationale for prohibiting all further violence (pp. 56-59) and thus additionally confirms Yoder's view. See my review of *The Wisdom of the Cross* in *Theology Today* 57 (2000): 412-17.

32. Volf, *Exclusion and Embrace,* p. 301.

Jesus had to die because continuing to live would mean a compromise with violence. . . . Here we have the difference between the religions that remain subordinated to the powers and the act of destroying those powers through a form of transcendence that never acts by means of violence, is never responsible for any violence, and remains radically opposed to violence.[33]

Further, "A nonviolent deity . . . can only signal his existence to mankind by having himself driven out by violence — by demonstrating that he is not able to dwell in the kingdom of violence."[34]

Volf, however, disagrees with Girard, saying,

Girard takes too lightly people's tendency to remask what has been demasked when it fits their interests. Moreover, though Jesus was innocent not all who suffer violence are innocent. The tendency of persecutors to blame victims is reinforced by actual guilt of victims, even if the guilt is minimal and they incur it in reaction to the original violence committed against them. Demasking the scapegoat mechanism will not suffice.[35]

Toward the end of his volume, Volf waxes passionate and eloquent against the notion of a nonviolent God.

My thesis that the practice of nonviolence requires a belief in divine vengeance will be unpopular with many Christians, especially theologians in the west. To the person who is inclined to dismiss it, I suggest imagining that you are delivering a lecture in a war zone (which is where a paper that underlies this chapter was originally delivered). Among your listeners are people whose cities and villages have been first plundered, then burned, and leveled to the ground, whose daughters and sisters have been raped, whose fathers and brothers have had their throats slit. The topic of the lecture: A Christian attitude toward violence. The thesis: we should not retaliate since God is perfect noncoercive love. Soon you would discover that it takes the quiet of a suburban home for the birth of the thesis that human nonviolence corresponds to God's refusal to judge. In a scorched land, soaked in the blood of the innocent, it will invariably die. And as one watches it, one will do well to reflect about many other pleasant captivities of the liberal mind.[36]

33. Girard, *Things Hidden*, p. 213.
34. Girard, *Things Hidden*, p. 219.
35. Volf, *Exclusion and Embrace*, pp. 292-93.
36. Volf, p. 304. Volf also says, "A 'nice' [i.e., nonviolent] God is a figment of the liberal

Witness here George Hunsinger's entry into the debate. Hunsinger is not satisfied with Girard's *means* of arriving at the conclusion that God is nonviolent, though he agrees with that claim. He contends that Girard's view is coupled with an overly optimistic valuing of western cultural achievement, i.e., a gradual unmasking of the cultural mechanisms that conceal violence — through the power of Christianity in culture over the centuries.[37] Hunsinger, rather, seeks for a theological basis for God as nonviolent. Drawing on the contributions of Hans Urs von Balthasar, Thomas Torrance, and Karl Barth, Hunsinger sets forth a theology of the cross in relation to the trinity, which identifies God's nonviolence in terms of salvation activity and the oneness of the triune God. The cross that killed Jesus is the cross of God and of Jesus Christ, on which God self-manifests that judgment is executed through love. This is the revelation of the divine trinity, whereby we see how the nonviolence of the cross overcomes human violence.[38]

Jim Fodor develops this view at length by lodging, systematically and integrally, both nonviolence and Christian discipleship in trinitarian relationships.[39] Numerous other essays in *Violence Renounced* address the issue of God's wrath and whether God is to be described as violent or nonviolent.[40] Still others relate Christian discipleship to Jesus' own nonviolence, both in deed and teaching, but stop short of addressing whether God is to be viewed as violent or nonviolent. An important point not noted in current discussion is whether Scripture itself uses the term *violence* (Hebrew *hamas*) to describe God's actions (a point to be addressed below).

Contributions from various Mennonite scholars take opposite stands on this issue as well. Harry Huebner mounts a sustained and helpful argument against what he calls the "divine-human-moral-discontinuity-pacifism," held by many pacifists. Such a view, in brief, has the inner logical contradiction that while God exercises the divine prerogative to achieve justice through violence, humans may not do so. Humans are called to imitate Jesus Christ's nonvio-

---

imagination, a projection onto the sky of the inability to give up cherished illusions about goodness, freedom, and the rationality of social actors" (p. 294).

37. John H. Yoder critiques this "progressively precarious promise" as well. See his review of Girard's *The Scapegoat* (quoting p. 92).

38. Hunsinger, "The Politics of the Nonviolent God." Finger, in "Moltmann's Theology of the Cross" (Swartley, ed., *Politics of Discipleship*, pp. 77, 82-86), presents Moltmann's theology with similar emphasis, highlighting God's suffering and pain in Jesus' death.

39. "Christian Discipleship as Participative Imitation."

40. In *Violence Renounced,* ed. Swartley: Swartley, "Introduction," pp. 24-25; Marlin E. Miller, "Girardian Perspectives on Christian Atonement," pp. 36, 42, 44-45; Robin Collins, "Girard and Atonement," pp. 136-37; James G. Williams, "King as Servant, Sacrifice as Service: Gospel Transformations," pp. 192-96.

lence, even while holding that Jesus is the true and full revelation of God. The end result of such pacifism magnifies Jesus as the basis for ethics at the expense of God's moral character. It puts christology in tension with, if not in contradiction to, theology. Rejecting also what he calls the "divine-human-moral-continuity-non-pacifism" of Martin Luther and Balthasar Hubmaier, Huebner proposes a third view: a "divine-human-moral-continuity-pacifism," in which case the moral character of God is the basis of the discipleship taught by Jesus and the NT call to the imitation of Christ.

For this view he appeals to two Anabaptists, Hans Denck and Menno Simons.[41] In his sustained argument for the moral and theological integrity of this position, Huebner asks us to reconsider our understanding of both power and freedom. Drawing on Bonhoeffer and Schubert Ogden, as well as the MacIntyre and Hauerwas tradition of narrative ethics, Huebner makes the case that God's freedom and power are manifest in ways and means congruent with the divine character. The pervasive portrait of NT discipleship is evidence not only of Jesus Christ's character, but also of God's character, which Jesus discloses. Modern autonomous notions of power and freedom are erroneous from a Christian theological perspective. Freedom and power manifest character, not what is popularly conceived as individual desire. God's actions are covenant-determined, and that covenant is grounded in God's steadfast love and faithfulness. God's character shapes Christian ethics.

James Reimer, writing several years later, argues that God's character or moral nature cannot be limited to what humans are instructed to be and do.[42] As important as pacifism, perhaps more so, is the biblical command of anti-idolatry (recall Volf above).[43] Since humans are forbidden to make an image of God, we are also warned against limiting God's being and prerogative to

41. Huebner, "Christian Pacifism and the Character of God."

42. Reimer, "God Is Love but Not a Pacifist."

43. Sandor Goodhart made this same point in the 1994 Conference mentioned above, that anti-idolatry is more intrinsic to the core belief of Judaism than is proscription against violence (i.e., killing). Goodhart amplifies this view in "We Will Cling Fast to Your Torah," p. 15. In the same essay, responding to Girard's "Response" to the essays in *Violence Renounced* (pp. 315-18), Goodhart addresses the issue of the uniqueness of the Gospels' revelation of the sacrificial mechanism. Holding that Christianity speaks the same voice as Isaiah 52–53 on this matter, he proposes, however, that the resurrection of Jesus makes a difference (appealing to Girard himself, *I See Satan Fall like Lightning*, pp. 125, 189), with consequences for the uniqueness of the revelation of the violence-scapegoat mechanism (Goodhart, p. 16):

> He [Jesus] literally passed "through death" to show us the scapegoat mechanism to the end, something that did not happen in Isaiah 52–53. In light of the resurrection, all social structure, the entire scapegoating machinery, is revealed as delusional, a delusional quality we cannot see until we see the victim "after death" so to speak.

our moral prescriptions and proscriptions. But to address also the concern of Huebner above, Reimer distinguishes between two modalities of the trinity: the "immanent trinity" and the "economic trinity." The former defines the essence of God as God's divine love in "God's inner trinitarian relations"; the latter describes God's relation to creation and care of the world. God thus works in ways not entirely clear to us. Reimer concludes:

> God's means of achieving the ultimate reconciliation of all things are not immediately evident to us. God cannot be subjected to our interpretation of the non-violent way of Jesus. Our commitment to the way of the cross (reconciliation) is not premised on God's pacifism or non-pacifism. It is precisely because God has the prerogative to give and take life that we do not have the right. Vengeance we leave up to God. Anabaptists called this *Gelassenheit* — surrender to and trust in God. We do not avoid the reality of violence in ourselves and in our world, but we side with the dynamic power of peace and reconciliation which is mysteriously at work in the scrabble game of life, knowing that ultimately all things rest in God's providential and loving hands.[44]

While Huebner's and Reimer's contributions may appear to be at odds with each other, I believe they both contribute to a necessary holistic grasp of the mystery of God and God's being as the basis for human moral obligation. Further, the "truth" on both sides of this issue enables us to both "resist," i.e., fight against evil, and "nonresist," leaving wrath and vengeance to God. Thomas Yoder Neufeld, while not addressing the "violence/nonviolence" of God specifically, reminds us that "resistance and nonresistance" are both essential in faithful discipleship. Jesus modeled both.[45] Paul Keim speaks similarly: "When God's character is expressed in terms of a negative — 'nonviolent' — we may easily overlook the call for active, vigorous action in the world to alleviate suffering, to protect the dignity of human life in the face of daily humiliations and degradations, to stand in the breach, and to say 'No, over my dead body, no.'" He further warns that we may be driving with Jehu, claiming all is *shalom* when we do not know what *shalom* really is when we reduce the gospel to nonviolence.[46]

Several other Mennonite voices have weighed into the issue directly as well. In a collection of insightful essays, *Seeking Cultures of Peace*,[47] Denny

---

44. Reimer, "God Is Love," p. 492.
45. "Resistance and Nonresistance: The Two Legs of a Biblical Peace Stance."
46. Keim, "Is God Nonviolent?" pp. 30-31.
47. Enns, Holland, and Riggs, eds., *Seeking Cultures of Peace: A Peace Church Conversation.*

Weaver in brief compass argues his case made in *Nonviolent Atonement*,[48] a view we considered earlier in this volume, in light of Christopher Marshall's critique.[49] In similar vein, Ray Gingerich, in the Grimsrud and Johns volume, considers the image of a "Warrior God" (which he learned from Lind) a major problem. As he puts it, "If we hold to a violent God, in the name of justice, as being the one to rectify all things, we deny the way of the nonviolent cross of Jesus as being the revelation of God and the harbinger of God's new humanity."[50] His essay then calls for reimaging our notions of power, even God's power, so that it is consonant with Jesus' nonviolent love manifest in the cross.

On the other side, however, Scott Holland's most insightful counter-perspective in his essay "The Gospel of Peace and the Violence of God" argues persuasively that the gospel of peace depends on God's prerogative to exercise vengeance.[51] Influenced by his short-term teaching experience in northern Nigeria, which has seen a surplus of brutal war over the last decades, Holland came to see through dialogue with and identifying with his Nigerian fellow Christians' experience of loss (a widow and seven fatherless children, e.g.) that only the Volf and Reimer arguments make any healthy sense in such an environment. For those who think otherwise, I will not argue with them, he says, but ask them to walk with me through the village of destruction and loss, connecting with believers in deep grief. Further,

> I will ask them to lean into their feelings, not only into their properly tutored thoughts of pacifism, but into the inescapable feelings of shock, sorrow, anger, outrage, judgment, and perhaps even vengeance. These are

48. J. Denny Weaver, *The Nonviolent Atonement.* See also his "Violence in Christian Theology"; "Atonement and the Gospel of Peace." Weaver reads classical theological positions as more violent than those who advocate them. See the corrective article by Richard J. Mouw, "Violence and the Atonement." Mouw's corrective to John H. Yoder is instructive also. I agree with Mouw that some elements — I would say dimensions of significance — of Jesus' suffering on the cross are not imitable for Jesus' followers. At the same time, I believe Yoder is correct, for Jesus' sufferings are set forth in Scripture not only as an imitable paradigm. Believers are also said to complete (Col. 1:24) and share *(gnōnai koinōnian)* Christ's sufferings (Phil. 3:10), an emphasis appearing not only in Paul, but also in Peter, Hebrews, and Revelation in different language. The unique efficacy of Jesus' suffering for atonement, whether suffering God's wrath or vanquishing the principalities and powers, cannot be claimed for the suffering of Jesus' followers. What Jesus did he alone did! Thanks be to God! But in our faithful following Jesus we participate in, witness to, and make Christ's victory effectual in our history, within our particular social locations and cross-like tests and agonies.

49. See Chapter 7, n. 7.

50. Gingerich, "Reimaging Power: Toward a Theology of Nonviolence," p. 194.

51. Holland, *Cultures of Peace,* pp. 132-46.

feelings that come from souls conflicted by the paradoxical desire for love and justice, and emerge naturally from psyches throbbing from the bodily chemicals and emotions of human aggression, judgment, and justice. These are elemental passions.

What are we to do with these intense, inescapable feelings? We could address and release these tensions by reaching for a sword. Or we might instead find a deep theological therapy through reflecting upon a rather terrifying revelation. I propose the latter. As we consider this astonishing revelation, I propose that we ponder a very strange question as an exercise of deep theological therapy: could it be that a theopoetic acknowledgement of the violence of a Hidden God might indeed transform the aggressive energies in the human psyche, soul, and body into active and nonviolent expressions of peacemaking on earth?[52]

Holland has put together theology and heart in this analysis. It is only because God exercises divine wrath against evil,[53] even in self-donation in the atoning death of Jesus, that we can resist retaliation and live into the future to love the enemy, blessing those who curse us, and seeking to overcome evil with good.

Ben Ollenburger and Amy Barker's critique of Weaver's work on atonement objects to Weaver's dissociation of the cross from effecting salvation. Their article juxtaposes Mel Gibson's *The Passion of the Christ* with Weaver's discounting the significance of Jesus' suffering and death on the cross as essential for human salvation. The article examines the atoning meaning of the cross in light of the numerous references to God's wrath and judgment in both the OT and NT, on the one hand, and human sin, on the other. Citing Isa. 53:5, 7 and numerous NT texts such as 1 Pet. 1:19 and Rev. 5:9, their critique of Weaver's view is sharp: "To speak as if Jesus' death accomplishes nothing for the salvation of sinners, is to speak of something other than atonement — and of someone other than Jesus."[54]

In similar vein, but in the context of considering feminist theologies that tend to reject God-images of warrior, Lord, and such sovereignty referents, Catherine Madsen persuasively counters current tendencies to discount the necessity of the cross. She puts the issue in the perspective of human history, in which peace has been lost through humans turning away from God. Thus the story of salvation has at its heart God fighting against evil to restore

---

52. Holland, *Cultures of Peace*, p. 142.

53. See here the helpful article by Fretheim, "Theological Reflections on the Wrath of God in the Old Testament," though I do not agree fully with his critique of vocabulary analysis as a significant factor in this debate.

54. Ollenburger and Barker, "The Passion and God's Atonement."

peace. The image of God battling evil, even violence, is the blood and guts of the redemptive story, given the human condition.[55]

As developed in Chapter 3 above, Luise Schottroff's theological grasp of Jesus' love of enemy command points us in the right direction. In my judgment, hers is the best theological statement on the paradoxical and necessary relationship between these two emphases of God's nonviolent love as the basis for human morality and what Scripture says about divine wrath and judgment.[56]

> Matthew 5:38-41 . . . commands the refusal to retaliate as well as prophetic judgment of violent persons. . . . As imitators of God, Christians are supposed to confront the enemies of God with . . . [God's] mercies. . . . Loving one's enemy is the attempt to change the violent person into a child of God through a confrontation with the love of God. That is, love of one's enemy can be concretely presented as the prophetic proclamation of the approaching sovereignty of God.[57]

As noted earlier she identifies a sevenfold parenesis in Rom. 12:14-21:

> Do not curse (12:14).
> Repay no one evil for evil (12:17).
> Never avenge yourselves (12:19).
> Do not be overcome by evil, but overcome evil with good (12:21).
> Leave it to the wrath of God (12:19).
> Vengeance is mine (12:19).
> If your enemy is hungry, feed him, . . . for by so doing you will heap
>   burning coals upon his head (12:20).

Schottroff thus contends that this behavior breaks the spiral of human violence and grows out of "the assurance that God's judgment is just."[58] She summarizes her thesis by referring to a threefold behavioral ensemble: "This behavioral ensemble consisting of refusal to pay retribution, expecting prophetic judgment, and loving the enemy has its reason or its goal in the justice of God or in the sovereignty of God."[59] Hence, believers are free not to take revenge against evil because nonretaliation is a prophetic announcement of

---

55. Madsen, "Notes on God's Violence."
56. Schottroff, "Give to Caesar What Belongs to Caesar and to God What Belongs to God."
57. Schottroff, "Give to Caesar," p. 232.
58. Schottroff, "Give to Caesar," p. 235.
59. Schottroff, "Give to Caesar," p. 236.

God's sovereignty and judgment against evil. At the same time, Christians are enjoined to resist evil, both Satan and oppressive political structures. This behavior breaks the spiral of violence and grows out of "the assurance that God's judgment is just." This threefold response testifies to and manifests God's justice and sovereignty.

Schottroff's contribution mediates between Yoder's, Girard's, Hunsinger's, Gingerich's, and Weaver's contributions on the one side and Volf's, Reimer's, Keim's and Holland's on the other.[60] It also provides biblical theological foundations to integrate both Huebner's and Reimer's contributions.

The recent work of Patricia McDonald, *God and Violence,* provides a helpful perspective. While expositing those accounts of God's apparent violence in Scripture, she nonetheless asks us not to allow those stories to eclipse the more dominant image of God in care for the poor, the widow, and the orphan. God's grace and mercy are central emphases and we must guard against fixation on violence of God in Scripture. In some respects she points in the same direction as Girard, but then she also has a stinging critique of Girard's use of Scripture (forgetting perhaps that Girard claims not to be a biblical scholar or theologian, but that his expertise arises from universal cultural analysis, and as he puts it, his basic thesis is "banal" for those with ears to hear).[61]

A Biblical Perspective for Resolving the Paradox

A curious fact about the biblical data on this hotly disputed topic of the violence or nonviolence of God, whether in atonement theories[62] or as basis for pacifism, is that the textual uses of the Hebrew term *hamas* ("violence") seldom refer to *God's* violence against humans.[63] Rather, *human* violence is the

---

60. John Dear categorically describes God as nonviolent. See *The God of Peace: Toward a Theology of Nonviolence,* especially chapter 3 and his bald statement, "Jesus' God does not use violence" (p. 30).

61. McDonald, *God and Violence: Biblical Resources for Living in a Small World.* While the entire book makes this point, her Conclusions and appendix on Girard are especially pertinent (pp. 279-305).

62. Especially as argued by J. Denny Weaver, "Violence in Christian Theology"; *The Nonviolent Atonement.* Perhaps due to the effectual historical theology of Anselm's *Cur Deus Homo,* Weaver reads Anselm quite differently than does John Milbank (*Theology and Social Theory,* pp. 395ff.).

63. God is the subject of the verbal form *(hamas)* in Lam. 2:6: "God *has broken down* his booth like a garden," describing God's action against the temple (?) in devastating Jerusalem. In two nominal uses God is *possibly* implicated: in Job's speech (19:7, "Even when I cry out 'Vio-

basis or warrant for God's judgment and/or punishment. Of the eight verbal uses and sixty nominal uses, the referent is almost always human violence, either specific personal or corporate acts or the condition of society: oppression of the foreigner, fatherless, and widow or shedding of blood — murder or war (Jer. 22:3 includes both aspects; Gen. 49:5; Judg. 9:24; Ezek. 45:9; Hab. 2:8, 17; Zeph. 1:9; Ps. 72:14). Often *hamas* occurs in a general inclusive sense, likely with these connotations.[64]

A notable comprehensive use is "the earth was filled with violence" (Gen. 6:11, 13), which incites God's judgment to destroy humankind through the flood. The Psalmist cries out for salvation from and protection against the violent (Pss. 18:48; 25:19; 27:12; 140:4, 11; cf. 2 Sam. 22:3, 49). In several instances, violence boomerangs for self-destruction (Pss. 7:16; 140:9). The designation "violent person" occurs often in Proverbs (3:31; 4:17; 10:6, 11; 13:2; 16:29; 26:6; cf. Mal. 2:16). On occasion the NRSV translates *hamas* as "malicious" (Exod. 23:1; Deut. 19:16; Ps. 35:11), "mischief" (Ps. 55:10), or "stir up wars" (Ps. 140:2). In several uses "the law" and "the holy things" are said to be violated (Ezek. 22:26; Zeph. 3:4; Hab. 1:3-4). Sarah accuses Abraham of violence, for "wrong (NRSV) done to me," in the face of Hagar's contempt of her (Gen. 16:5). Striking is Isaiah's depiction of the Lord's servant of justice: "he had done no violence, and there was no deceit in his mouth" (53:9). In this range of uses several theological claims emerge: all violence is ultimately against the community and Yahweh; the righteous cry out to God for deliverance from the violent; and God is the just Judge who hears the outcry of the victims and will defend them.[65]

What is clear from this analysis of biblical texts and terms is that any speech about the "violence of God" is a "category fallacy." While the term "violence" occurs quite frequently in Hebrew Scripture (and much more rarely in the NT),[66] it does not denote God's actions against humans. Indeed, the

---

lence!' I am not answered; I call aloud, but there is no justice") and Jeremiah's outcry (20:8, "Violence and destruction!"; cf. Hab. 1:2).

64. For this section of my paper I utilize work now available also in my article on "Violence, Violent," in *The Westminster Theological Wordbook of the Bible.*

65. H. Haag, *hamas* in *TDOT* 4: 485-86.

66. *Bia* is used to denote use of force or violence four times in Acts (5:26; 21:35; 24:7; 27:41), but none are consequential for Christian ethics. The use of *diaseiō* in Luke 3:14 (NRSV "do not *extort money* from anyone"; RSV "rob no one by violence") is of Christian ethical significance since it proscribes violence to those who repent to prepare for the One coming. The use of *biazomai/biastēs* in Matt. 11:12 is problematic, since it connects Jesus' announced kingdom with violence: "From the days of John the Baptist until now, the kingdom of heaven has suffered violence, and the violent take it by force." Clearly, the sense is not that the kingdom brings or condones violence but that its coming sets up violent reactions by those who refuse or subvert its message; it also causes Satan's fall (Luke 10:1-20). A single use of *hormēma* occurs in Rev.

opposite is the case. God stands against violence, and violence is precisely that which ignites God's wrath and brings divine punishment upon humans. If we choose to call that violence and attribute it to God, we have slipped a step exegetically, failing to recognize a fundamental fact about Scripture: God "hates the lover of violence" (Ps. 11:5).

To attribute violence to God is a misnomer, a misplaced indictment from Scripture's point of view. Rather, judgment is what characterizes the sovereign, holy God[67] who punishes humans for sin and violence. God's redemptive acts stand in the service of bringing human violence to an end! Only then can God's shalom cover the earth as the waters cover the sea. To attribute violence to God is to undermine the moral character of God, God's redemptive purpose, and to confuse human perversity with the divine prerogative to establish justice and shalom by punishing human violence. To put it bluntly, God's vengeance, however executed,[68] stands against human violence. Scripture rarely speaks explicitly about God being violent or nonviolent, but depicts God as one who condemns human violence in order to establish divine justice and shalom.

Conclusion

Clearly, we have more textual work to do, biblical and theological, and perhaps philosophical,[69] before we further opine on this most important and difficult

---

18:21, where a "mighty angel" says, "With such violence Babylon the great city will be thrown down." The NRSV translates *hybristēn* in 1 Tim. 1:13, Paul's description of himself before conversion, as "man of violence."

67. Scott Holland's view presented above, with its critique of efforts to "cleanse" God or atonement from violence is accessible also in his "The Gospel of Peace and the Violence of God." Developing his views against the context of his pacifist commitment and his exposure to the recent ruthless slaughter in Nigeria's religious wars, Holland contends that God's holiness and hiddenness beckon us to the dimension of mystery (R. Otto) and asks whether "a theopoetic acknowledgement of the violence of the Hidden God might transform the aggressive energies in the human psyche, soul, and body into active and nonviolent expressions of peacemaking on earth?" He then cites a catena of texts from Revelation to make the point (pp. 480-81). I think it more accurate biblically to use another word here than "violence" to denote God's actions, but the point he makes is cogent. He concludes: "Could it be that because Yahweh is a Warrior, we can be a people of peace?" (p. 481).

68. See the provocative and fresh contribution of Christopher D. Marshall, *Beyond Retribution: A New Testament Vision for Justice, Crime, and Punishment.* Marshall makes a strong and persuasive case for restorative justice.

69. Anthony W. Bartlett's stimulating *Cross Purposes: The Violent Grammar of Christian Atonement* is an excellent sample of just such post-Girardian inquiry. He proposes understand-

topic. Wisdom suggests that at this point in the debate speaking of God as violent or nonviolent is best avoided, for it appears to be a misconceived duality in relation to God. Other language can be employed which respects the biblical theological discourse. Thus we note that beyond Schwager's 1000 instances where "wrath" is used in Hebrew Scripture, many texts speak of God as "punishing" human sin, e.g. Psalms 39 and 41; the terms "judgment" and "vengeance" are also pervasive (e.g., Pss. 98:9 and 94, applied in the context of rulers' accountability to God in 94:20). But, indeed, we must also certainly consider in depth the pervasive, never-ending refrain, "God's *hesed* endures forever," as in Psalm 136 and *passim*.[70] Note also that Scripture specifically says, "[God's] anger is but for a moment; his favor is for a lifetime" (Ps. 30:5).[71] God's love outlasts God's wrath. God's anger or wrath is an intrinsically necessary component of God's divine love and justice. If this were not the case, how would God bring about justice, given the reality of evil in this world? While recognizing that Scripture says *Yahweh Is a Warrior*, Millard Lind has said on numerous occasions that while God's punishment extends to the third and fourth generation, God's steadfast love extends to the thousandth generation (Exod. 20:5-6). Both God's steadfast love and God's wrath are part of an integral whole in the divine nature.[72] But this provides no biblical warrant for as-

---

ing the cross via the metaphor of "abyss." Four cardinal points that guide his geometry of analysis are *"abandonment, violence, philosophical postmodernism,* and *the gospel account of Jesus itself"* (pp. 18ff.).

> The compassion of the Crucified becomes the point at which the foundationless, unconditional gift of love transforms the mimetic faculty from hostile rivalry to a totally new movement of the self. Because it is sensed as foundationless, without ontological grounds or power, because it surrenders itself without remainder, abyssal compassion is able to undo the reserve of "selfish" (conflictual) identification with the other that in every case remains in relationship. The traditional word for this is *grace,* but the difference here is that it proceeds directly from the phenomenology of the cross and is decisively not the term of an economic redemption based on a cosmic exchange. The name *compassion* is suited to be at the core of this phenomenon because it evokes a double-sided event, an identification working from both sides. On the one it is a suffering-with and "mimetic" gift of self on the part of Christ, and then an answering identification on the part of the believer that is both the experience of forgiveness and the birth of love — a mutual passivity that is at once intensely active. (p. 39)

70. Of the many good works on this topic, see especially Sakenfeld, *The Meaning of Hesed in the Hebrew Bible.* The many texts that speak of God's faithfulness *(emunâ)*, righteousness *(ṣedaqâ)*, justice *(mišpat)*, and shalom count heavily in such discernment as well. See Pss. 85:10-13; 89:14; 97:2.

71. See here also Isa. 54:8-10; Sir. 5:6; 16:11; and Hosea as a whole.

72. See Tasker's classic article "The Biblical Doctrine of the Wrath of God." Perhaps too we need to learn from the Book of Job. Might God's answer to Job be the same to us? Confessing

cribing violence or nonviolence to God.[73] Be assured, "[T]he God of *peace* will soon *crush* Satan under your feet" (Rom. 16:20, RSV).

When we ground Christian ethics in the divine nature revealed in Hebrew Scripture and most completely in Jesus Christ, as my essay in *Violence Renounced* seeks to do, it is clear that God's wrath is not specified as that which believers are called to imitate. Rather, vengeance and judgment of evil are consistently deferred to God, with Jesus Christ as co-executor. Though I critique John H. Yoder for too narrow a list of specific virtues believers are exhorted to imitate,[74] yet the wider list I develop — utilizing 2 Pet. 1:4d-8, in which believers "become participants in the divine nature" — does not include wrath, judgment, or vengeance.

Such a conclusion may trouble, even offend us. Biblical revelation manifest fully in the gospel of Jesus Christ exposes the mimetic desire syndrome with its scapegoat and violence mechanism. But in doing so it carries with it an element of deep *offense* (see Girard *passim* on this point).[75] Hence our

---

that the ways of God are beyond our knowing and that God is free to be God, I conclude with Job's response, "I put my finger over my mouth, and am silent."

73. The summer 2001 issue of *Cross Currents* contains six articles that speak about the violence/nonviolence of God. This is a prime illustration of the "category fallacy" I discuss above, even though some of the essays argue for God's nonviolence based upon Jesus' life and death (J. Denny Weaver, "Violence in Christian Theology," pp. 150-76) or that God's violence, or better wrath, is essential to God's adequate response to evil — in response to feminist writings that reject core biblical teachings because they are deemed violent and produce violence (Madsen, "Notes on God's Violence," pp. 229-56). On this latter point, see my "Introduction" in *Violence Renounced*, pp. 26-28.

74. Yoder concludes his chapter on "The Disciple of Christ and the Way of Jesus" by asserting that there is "but one realm in which the concept of imitation holds" — and there in every strand of NT literature — "at the point of the concrete social meaning of the cross in its relation to enmity and power. Servanthood replaces dominion, forgiveness absorbs hostility" (*Politics of Jesus*, p. 134 [1994 edition, p. 131]). Gibson, *The Temptations of Jesus in Early Christianity*, largely substantiates Yoder's thesis by contending that in each of the eight testings (*peirasmoi*) in Mark and Q, Jesus' faithfulness to his baptismal designation as Son, Servant, and Beloved One is tested, precisely whether he will continue to be God's peacemaker (*eirēnopoios*) refusing vengeance against enemies or seek to secure the future through violence. On pp. 10-12 Gibson quotes Yoder and asks whether the testing of the early Christians in this sense occasioned the writing of Hebrews, even though it states that Jesus was tempted in all ways as we are (2:18; 5:2).

75. See here Girard's response to selected essays in *Violence Renounced*, pp. 310-11. Girard's latest book, *I See Satan Fall*, develops this point at length: Satan is manifest in the *skandalon*, but the gospel, by exposing the mimetic desire-rivalry-violence cycle, both occasions the *skandalon* — because of natural human resistance, of which Peter is the prime example in Mark 8:30-33 — and defeats Satan and his power over us. Let us therefore not *stumble* at the offense of the gospel or at the offense of this category distinction between God's prerogative and our obedience to those aspects of imitation of Christ and God set forth for us in Scripture.

"justification" of the Christian ethic of nonretaliation, peacemaking, and reconciliation may offend our sense of logical consistency, in that God is both our model for ethical behavior and yet retains divine prerogative to execute judgment in ways forbidden to humans.

My hope is that in our efforts to grapple with this issue we will not stumble over the problematic of "God's Moral Character as the Basis for Human Ethics." Thus we will not accuse God of what God hates about us humans: violence done to one another. Rather, let us look to Jesus for empowerment to stop the mimetic cycle of desire-rivalry-scapegoating that generates violence. Let us also thank and praise God for revealing Yahweh's Servant of justice, fully manifest in the incarnate Jesus, God's Son, to close the gap between human perversity and redeemed human potential. In this revelation, culminating in the cross and resurrection, we know the *sign* and *transformative power* enabling us to participate in the new mimesis.[76]

---

76. I am indebted to John Milbank for this distinctive way of speaking about the once-for-all and continuing significance of the atonement (see above).

15 New Testament Peacemaking in the Service of Moral Formation

In this Chapter I orient the topics of this volume on peace and peacemaking to Christian moral formation. I locate my methodology within two analytic contributions. The first is that of Johannes A. Van der Ven, in his *Formation of the Moral Self.* Van der Ven helpfully identifies alternative paradigms used to conceptualize how formation of the self occurs. The five paradigms are individualism, communitarianism, institutionalism, pluralism, and multiculturalism. The five are not mutually exclusive. For example, communitarianism and multiculturism could be combined, but each brings with it underlying assumptions that determine methodology. Van der Ven analyzes the strengths and weaknesses in each of these educational paradigms, and proposes yet another: *interactionism,* an approach that seeks to combine the "pole of the individual" with the "pole of the community and society."[1]

Van der Ven devotes his massive study to six modes of informal and formal education — informal: discipline and socialization; formal: transmission, cognitive development, clarification, and emotional formation.[2] These culminate in a final chapter on education for character. His section on "A Narrative Account of Character"[3] helpfully joins his contribution to wider discussions on the interplay between narrative, virtue, and character formation (MacIntyre, Hauerwas). Here I am interested in the formation not only of the moral self but also of the moral ecclesial community.

The second "locating" signal echoes the contributions of Charles Wood's *Formation of Christian Understanding* and Fowl and Jones's *Reading*

1. Van der Ven, *Formation of the Moral Self,* pp. 21-31.
2. Van der Ven, *Formation,* pp. 40-337.
3. Van der Ven, *Formation,* pp. 358-60.

in Communion.[4] First, a key point from Fowl and Jones: "the importance of moral rules is not *independent* of the formation of character in socially-embodied traditions."[5] Second, "The aim of Scriptural interpretation is to shape our common life in the situation in which we find ourselves according to the characters, convictions, and practices related in Scripture."[6] Scripture interpretation "is not only bound up with particular social contexts, but it is also related to the character of the interpreter."[7]

The canonical shape of Scripture is determinative also. I thus draw on the canonical NT's abundant testimony to peace/peacemaking emphases, with the conviction expressed by Charles Wood, "The principal aim of Christian understanding is the knowledge of God. The canon serves chiefly as the criterion of that knowledge. . . ."[8]

Within this methodological context I focus on NT peace texts that are formational of character. The noun *peace (eirēnē)* and the verb *to make peace (eirēneuō)* occur over 100 times. Other texts, while not using either word, are inherently related to peace/peacemaking as well.

To organize the range of textual witness evident in this study to peacemaking and associative emphases, I utilize the four modes of hermeneutic appeal to Scripture for moral formation, as proposed by Richard Hays: commands or rules, principles, paradigms, and symbolic world.[9] I shift his order, however, and start with symbolic world. Then I consider three basic paradigms and join principles to the paradigms, since I believe principles are embedded in or develop from paradigms or are derived from the symbolic world. Then I list "rules or commands," which may be considered principles also when viewed as normative moral guidelines.

Symbolic World Peace Perspectives

Here I consider five NT textual contributions as most significant: Jesus' seventh Beatitude, "blessed are the peacemakers"; Paul's unique title for God

---

4. Charles Wood, *The Formation of Christian Understanding;* Fowl and Jones, *Reading in Communion.* Both these works are influenced by the contribution of Stanley Hauerwas, especially his *Character and the Christian Life; A Community of Character;* and *The Peaceable Kingdom.*

5. Fowl and Jones, *Reading in Communion,* p. 10.

6. Fowl and Jones, *Reading in Communion,* p. 20.

7. Fowl and Jones, *Reading in Communion,* p. 103.

8. Wood, *Formation,* p. 112.

9. Hays, *The Moral Vision of the New Testament,* pp. 208-9. See also his discussion of the same in *New Testament Ethics,* pp. 32-33.

"God of peace"; NT imitation and discipleship texts; Paul's bold claim that "Christ is our peace"; and the Lamb's War in Revelation. Perhaps we should consider also a sixth: the shape and structure of the Synoptic Gospels' narrative portrait of Jesus' life, death, and resurrection (which I treat under "paradigm"). Hauerwas rightly contends that this "master narrative" forms identity for the early Christians:[10] "Jesus is the story that forms the church."[11]

1. I classify the Beatitude "blessed are the peacemakers, for they shall be called children of God" as an aspect of the symbolic world of the NT's contribution to Christian moral formation because I regard it not as a command but as a blessing to those who are peacemakers. The Beatitudes assume an ecclesial-eschatological context, and as such expound the character of the kingdom of God. They announce a reality that is *present* through the proclamation, life, death, and resurrection of Jesus Messiah. They describe and validate the new gospel-reality.

The Beatitude is thus an identity-forming declaration. It assumes the gift of the gospel's grace and it also calls forth *blessedness* for those who receive the gospel of the kingdom. Becoming and being a peacemaker draws on God's gift of grace. Within this context peacemaking is also a virtue for God's kingdom people, a value which believers cultivate and practice.[12] This Beatitude is conceptually linked to the love of enemy command, which occurs later (5:44) and thus connects with the "rule, command" form of moral instruction (see below and Chapter 3 for full discussion).

2. I include in the symbolic world the frequently used Pauline (plus Hebrews) "God of Peace" title because it connotes depth in symbolic world. The phrase occurs seven times in Paul, once in Hebrews, and only once outside the NT. See Chapter 7 for further discussion.

The favored status of "God of peace" is a key to Paul's larger theology, for it is intertwined with other peacemaking emphases. It is intrinsically related to imitation as a means of forming moral character (see below), a model that appeals both to Christ *(imitatio Christi)* and to God (Eph. 5:2). The "God

---

10. Hauerwas, *Peaceable Kingdom*, pp. 24-30 and especially chapter 5, "Jesus: The Presence of the Peaceable Kingdom," pp. 72-95, and *Community of Character*, chapter 2, "Jesus: The Story of the Kingdom," pp. 36-52.

11. Hauerwas, *Community of Character*, p. 50.

12. See here Glen Stassen's "Virtues of God's People," chapter 2 in Stassen and Gushee, *Kingdom Ethics*, pp. 32-54. Alasdair MacIntyre and Stanley Hauerwas are well-known advocates for virtue ethics. Kotva, *The Christian Case for Virtue Ethics,* provides a good explication of just why virtue ethics has returned in ethical discourse. He addresses matters of definition and need, theological links and biblical connections, and finally an appeal for ethicists and Christian believers to commit to virtue ethics.

of Peace" title, distinctive as it is, necessarily has formational impact on believers' moral identity. If God is a God of peace, then *we*, by our identity as God's children, are to be a people of peace.

3. The NT texts on *imitation*, together with the pervasive emphasis on discipleship, as presented and discussed in Chapter 13, form another stream in the symbolic world of the NT that authorizes peacemaking. A discipleship and imitation pattern lies at the heart of the NT. A theology or ethics of the NT should make this point foundational, so that students using such texts are formed morally and spiritually by this pattern of thought, which in turn should lead to *practices of daily formation in daily life*. Such practices will shape a person's character into the new creation mimesis, in exchange for the mimesis that leads to rivalry and violence. Jesus as faithful Servant of the Lord will become the model for belief and behavior. Participation in a community of faith that also seeks faithfulness in discipleship and new creation imitation of Jesus Christ will further strengthen the Christian formation of believers committed to this pattern and practice of spiritual discipline.

4. "Christ is our peace." The dominant contribution of Paul's mission and theology is the actualized eschatological vision of uniting formerly alienated peoples into one body in Jesus Christ. Paul's relief gift (Romans 15; 2 Corinthians 8–9) is the material embodiment of the symbolic world that Jew and Gentile are one in Jesus Christ. Here see my discussion in Chapter 7, in which peacemaking and reconciliation are seen as dominant themes of Paul's theology and mission. These are not only theological concepts, but expressive virtues as well. Paul gave his life for the vision of uniting alienated Jews and Gentiles into one body in Christ, with two risk-taking practical faces: a Jerusalem conference to settle differences and a last major trip to Jerusalem with a relief gift to show that Jews and Gentiles are one in faith and love. This is *practicing* the peacemaking virtue!

The union of believing Jews and Gentiles in one body in Christ was the "symbolic world" master narrative that formed Christian self-identity, corporately and personally in the Pauline churches. As Paul puts it, "And let the *peace of Christ* rule in your hearts, to which indeed you were *called in one body*, and be thankful" (Col. 3:15). Given the political context of churches mentioned in Paul's writing in which the socio-political dynamics of the Roman world structured society hierarchically, as Horsley has shown (see Chapter 8), the Pauline effort to unite Jewish and Gentile Christians into one bond and body in fellowship and love was no small undertaking. For the political context of Romans, add the recent expulsion of Jews under Claudius (49 CE). One can imagine the strain put on relationships between Jewish Christians and Gentile Christians in this new "household of God," as well as on Christian identity, continuity with the synagogue, and messianic conversations in that setting.[13]

Paul's "God of peace" benedictions thus symbolized a concrete ecclesial and moral reality: Christ is our peace, who has made us both one. The *cosmic* goal of God's peacemaking salvation in Jesus Christ was and is to reconcile all things to God's self "by making peace through the blood of his cross" (Col. 1:20). The peacemaking victory of the cross also has consequence for the principalities and powers, here specifically the ubiquitous Roman imperial presence. Believers are freed from its domination. In some texts Christ's victory is portrayed as "destroying [or better, 'rendering powerless'] every rule and authority" (1 Cor. 15:24-28; cf. 2 Thess. 2:3-11), but other texts speak of a reconciliation of the powers to God's purpose (Col. 1:19-20; Eph. 1:9-10). What is clear in both emphases is Jesus' lordship over the powers.

5. A fifth powerful metaphor for early Christians shaping their moral formation as peacemakers is the imagery from Revelation, commonly referred to as the Lamb's war. Here see Chapter 12, both the exposition of the key symbols in the text and the "Service of Worship." God has triumphed through the slain Lamb; the battle against evil and Rome's tyranny is won by no other weapons than the Lamb slain on the cross and the testimony *(martyria)* of his followers.

Revelation beckons us not to forget whom we worship. It calls us to confess with heart, soul, and strength that God is sovereign, is alone to be worshiped. The saints know that through their faithful endurance God's victory will shine forth like the sun (cf. Ps. 37:6) after the present chaos ends and mighty "Babylon" falls. "The central question of these chapters [Revelation 4-5] as well as of the whole book is: Who is the true Lord of this world?" Answer? "The author insists that the 'Lord' of the world is not the emperor but Jesus Christ who has created an alternative reign and community to that of the Roman empire."[14]

Revelation also makes it clear that when evil spiritual powers control and inspire the actions of earthly rulers the role of believers is to persevere in trust and worship of God. The believers' refusal to comply with Rome's demands, committing themselves instead to suffer persecution and death, is their passive resistance. Their proclamation of God's sovereignty through praise and worship and their identification with the Lamb's war are their means of active resistance. The Lamb is paradigmatic for believers, a model of

---

13. Here see Klaus Haacker's thesis that Romans was a *Friedensmemorandum* designed to address the polarizing forces of this political situation (see Chapter 7 above).

14. Schüssler Fiorenza, *Invitation to the Book of Revelation*, p. 72.

giving one's own life rather than taking another's. The power of the word, cross, and song of praise outlasts mighty Babylon, symbol for all deified political power.[15]

Paradigms (and Principles)

Numerous portions of NT Scripture could be cited as "peacemaking pillars" contributing to character formation. I mention here three basic paradigms.

1. The gospel narrative as a whole presents Jesus as a paradigm for peacemaking. The manner of his birth, with the angelic proclamation of "peace on earth" (Luke 2:14), and Jesus' pattern of behavior before the authorities in his passion are the bookends of the narrative of this peaceable Messiah. This depiction of Jesus is later echoed in the famous *kenosis*-hymn in Phil. 2:6-11; in the exhortation to "follow in his steps" (1 Pet. 2:21-23); and again in Hebrews, especially 2:9; 5:5-10; and 12:2. Jesus exemplifies the paradigm of faithful perseverance in suffering without retaliation. Foundational to the gospel pattern, this emphasis is the core motif in the symbolic world of the gospel.

Within this master paradigm are sub-paradigms. One is Jesus' sustained teaching to his disciples on *cross, humility,* and *servanthood* in Mark 8:27–10:52, a classic narrative exemplar. In this carefully crafted structure, Mark develops three interrelated themes: Jesus' messianic identity, with the focus on the Son of Humanity who must suffer; the recurring passion-resurrection predictions; and the subsequent recurring teaching on discipleship (see 8:31-38; 9:31-41 or 50; 10:32-45). See Chapter 4 above for discussion and explication.

Jesus instructs his disciples how they must live if they follow him on this way. The focal images for character formation are taking up the cross, valorizing a child, and living as a servant, in contrast to seeking power, prestige, and position. Concluding his teaching in Mark 9 Jesus commands to "make peace with one another." Drawing on the imagery of well-prepared salted sacrifices (Lev. 2:13), Jesus calls for the self to be purified of evil and ambitious desires, and for his followers to live peaceably with one another (*eirēneuete en allēlois,* v. 50d). This contrasts to the segment's initial portrait of the disciples disputing with one another over who is the greatest. To walk Jesus' way means giving up rivalry, seeking not to offend "the little one," and striving to live peaceably with one another.[16]

---

15. On this, see Jacques Ellul's perceptive contribution, *Apocalypse: The Book of Revelation,* pp. 92-98.

16. I have written elsewhere more extensively on this section of Mark. See *Mark: The Way*

While it is possible to extract principles from Mark's *hodos* teaching as well as from the paradigm stories of the good Samaritan and Jesus and the Samaritan woman, they are all better viewed as paradigms, set firmly within the gospel as narrative. This assures that moral principles will not be abstracted to bolster natural wisdom (generic moral values that do not conform to the cruciform gospel narrative). For the *hodos* teachings are embedded in the particular story and identity of Jesus in the Gospels. This roots the moral life christologically. It is inextricably tied to knowledge of God revealed in Jesus Christ.

2. The second master paradigm in the NT canon is that of Paul's extensive participation and correspondence parenesis for becoming Christian in character and conduct. I developed this at length in Chapter 13 by citing Paul's recurring use of *co-positioning* the believer with Christ. The co-identity with Jesus Christ and fellow believers enables us to learn a new mimetic pattern, one that leads not to rivalry and violence, but to building others up, avoiding scandal, preferring one another, empowering the other, and nonretaliation against evil in order that as members of the community of the new creation we break the spiral of violence and become the strands of yarn that by God's Spirit are knitted into the display of love, justice, and shalom.[17]

Jim Fodor's critique of Girard's theory speaks specifically to the issue of consequences for the moral life and character formation. Fodor regards Girard's theory of mimesis and generation of violence as too abstract and formal, not sufficiently consequential for understanding the role of mimesis in Christian formation. As he puts it:

> [Girard] does not take the care to elaborate in any great detail the positive, alternative practices, ways of life, or patterns of behavior enjoined by the gospel. But what is finally compelling, I would contend . . . is not the mere idea of nonacquisitive mimesis but how it is that one might become initiated in and apprenticed to a particular way of life that actually manifests non-acquisitive, nonviolent mimesis. In other words, unless and until non-acquisitive desire expresses itself in particular habits of attention, practices, patterns of behavior, and forms of worship and praise, it is hard for anyone to understand its character, let alone experience its power, be persuaded of its virtues, assess its merits, or gauge its veracity.[18]

---

for All Nations, chapters 7 and 8; *Israel's Scripture Traditions,* pp. 98-102, 111-15; and "Discipleship and Imitation," pp. 230-34.

17. Swartley, "Discipleship and Imitation," pp. 237-39.

18. Jim Fodor, "Christian Discipleship as Participative Imitation," pp. 249-50.

Fodor contends rightly that discipleship, peacemaking, participating in Christ, *kenosis,* or mimesis of God's love in love for neighbor and enemy must come to terms with the need for God's empowerment. The matter of *agent* is important. The human will, of one's own efforts, is not able to perform it:

> any model that separates the will from prayer, contemplation, and dispossession is woefully inadequate . . . the disciple is not first and foremost one who constructs herself or himself in the process of performance; if that were the case, the meaning of our actions would unavoidably and exclusively terminate in the will's success. Not only that, but given what Girard rightly describes as the competitive, Hobbesian-like character of unregenerate human life, any attempt to extricate ourselves from unredeemed human structures of desire would inevitably fail. We would remain trapped in a never-ending, downward spiral of animosity, conflict, rivalry, and violence.
>
> Discipleship, however, is grounded in God, not in our own will or desire. External autonomous achievement does not secure our status as Jesus' disciples. On the contrary, the disciple's adequacy or excellence or attunement to God lies, in its most determinative sense, outside the agent's control. Our actions, in the final analysis, are grounded in God rather than in our own desires. In that respect human acts of faithfulness always show more than the life of the agent: they show the character of the Creator.[19]

Fodor grounds discipleship in the trinitarian model of *perichoresis,* the model of God's own peaceable life as the basis of our peacemaking. The atonement in this context is the salvific grounding of our moral life. Echoing themes in my essay, Fodor says,

> With regard to Christian teaching on atonement, discipleship and imitation are inextricably linked with God's work of redemption in Christ. Without being bound to Jesus as the ransomed are bound to their ran-

---

19. Fodor, p. 256. The same sentiment is expressed by Marlin E. Miller in the same volume ("Girardian Perspectives and Christian Atonement," p. 45):

> A Girardian perspective highlights the God revealed in and through Jesus Christ as the God whose love is perfect, to use the word from Matthew 5. God's love is without violence and without limits. God calls human beings to a nonviolent mimesis: to accept God's forgiveness, to love one another, and to follow Jesus in life and in death. Jesus calls his disciples to follow him not only by his words but by his whole existence. Since his own desires and ambitions were focused on the will of the Father, he assigns the same goal to his disciples.

somer, without becoming friends of God in Christ, without actually taking up, participating in, being conformed to, and living out an atoning way of life, the whole point of the incarnation is thwarted. In other words, the incarnation is more than just the communication of the *idea* of reconciliation. The incarnation includes actual training and participation in particular peaceable relations and reconciling patterns of existence. It means learning a whole new *idiom,* a completely different set of skills and practices and language games.[20]

3. A third peace paradigm emerges in the Gospels' attitude toward government powers. While there are in the NT diverse portraits of the church's stance toward government powers, as Walter Pilgrim has shown[21] (see Chapter 8), from the stance of the Gospels as an "Ethic of Critical Distancing" to the more "Subordinationist Ethic" of Paul, it is clear that the Gospels and Paul creatively forge a vision of an alternative socioeconomic-political community. As Chapter 1 contends, Jesus fulfills Isa. 52:7, a text quoted or alluded to over a half dozen times in NT writings. Thus, the phrase "announcing good news of peace" *(euangelizomenos shalom/eirēnēn),* influences NT writers more than usually noted. Together with Isa. 61:1-2, quoted by Luke (4:18-19) for Jesus' platform address in the Nazareth synagogue, these two OT texts are strategic to the Gospels' overall theological and ethical emphases. See Chapters 1, 3, 4, and 5 for explication.

Healings, announcing the gospel, and the downfall of Satan are part and parcel of the gospel of peace. In Acts, Luke sums up the ministry of Jesus: "preaching the gospel of peace through Jesus Christ" (10:36, *euangelizomenos eirēnēn dia Iēsou Christou).*[22]

As the book of Acts further demonstrates, the community of Christ testifies to the kingdom of God spreading like strawberry runners, in diverse political, cultural, and economic settings. It breaks barriers that alienate and forms community such that the Pax Romana was never able to achieve. As the church lived through numerous faces of persecution, it nonetheless testified to God's peace as an enduring gift for shaping moral

---

20. Fodor, "Christian Discipleship," p. 264.

21. Pilgrim, *Uneasy Neighbors.*

22. The phrase also occurs in LXX form in Eph. 6:15 in the description of the Christian armor, "feet shod with the preparation of the gospel of peace," to thwart the wiles of the devil in the struggle against the principalities and powers, and specifically, the spiritual powers in heavenly places (referring to the demonic spirits that incite the powers). In some manuscripts, the full LXX phrase "preaching the gospel of peace" is used in Rom. 10:15 to describe the proclamation of the gospel messenger.

life and forming the corporate character of peacemakers. Acts testifies that by God's grace the kingdom of God takes root in diverse settings, even in the empire's capital city.

Thus the new creation, God's people of peace, has its own kingdom mission and agenda. It neither courts nor condemns Rome or the contemporary nations of this world. Nor does it give its main energies to aid or block the imperialistic pacification programs, of which the Pax Romana was a grand model. Rather, the new humanity of Christ's body welcomes people to become "children of peace," freed from the tyranny of the powers in whatever personal, national, socioeconomic, political, or ideological guise they manifest themselves.[23] This new humanity, in contrast to the dominant cultural power structures, expends its primary energies building communities of faith, hope, love, and peace.

Further, Luke-Acts shows us a Savior who weeps in lament: "if only you would know those things that make for peace" (Luke 19:42). It also presents a model of how to witness boldly to the powers. As Cassidy has argued, in Acts Luke's purpose is to encourage believers in their allegiance to Jesus to witness boldly before kings and governors.[24]

Indeed, the history of the faith of God's people, in both the older and younger covenants, witnesses to the survival and flourishing of God's people even amid the collapse of the nation. None of the Caesars of this world, monarchs, or presidents even of democracies is worthy to receive the honor, power, and glory that belongs to the Lord God alone. We can be subject to the nation's leaders, because our Liberator, whom we acclaim as Mighty Lord, is the Lord of hosts, Lord of the powers.[25]

23. See Chapters 5 and 6 above.

24. Cassidy, *Society and Politics in the Acts of the Apostles*, pp. 144, 156-79.

25. At this point one could appropriately address the concrete form that the church's witness to the powers might take in a North American context. But that is a topic for another place. The church's witness to government is rooted first and foremost in the sovereignty of God. Years ago John Howard Yoder developed a carefully considered model of the church's witness to government on issues of peace and justice. Writing in the era after the 1948 WCC General Assembly when the concept of "middle axioms" was introduced, Yoder used this concept as a bridge for the dialogue between the church and political powers in *The Christian Witness to the State*. See especially pp. 32-33, 72 for his use of the "Middle Axiom" through which the *agapē* norm is connected to the statesman through a "spring" tension that mediates general ideals such as liberty, equality, and human rights to the political reality. Yoder was careful to maintain an ecclesial identity in the witness and not to allow so-called political realism to accommodate moral principles held by the church into political quagmires that eviscerate the church of its moral distinctiveness. Further, the community of Christ, or Pax Christi, as Klaus Wengst calls it in *Pax Romana and the Peace of Jesus Christ*, p. 84, knows that its security is not in the political success,

Rules/Commands Derived from Symbolic World or Embedded in Principles

1. Jesus' command to "love enemies" (Matt. 5:44-45) identifies this moral behavior with identity, namely being "children of God." This command thus correlates with the seventh Beatitude, which promises "peacemakers" that "they shall be called children of God." *Being* peacemakers and loving enemies are thus intrinsically linked to God's moral character. Being children of God depends upon Jesus' disciples becoming and being peacemakers who love their enemies. Peacemaking marks those who follow Jesus and are children of God, *his* and *our* heavenly Father.[26]

To love enemies is beyond our human capacity, for our natural response is to retaliate against an enemy act. Rarely does one think of responding in such manner that might convert enmity into friendship! But this is the gospel of Jesus. The Sermon on the Mount stands as the frontispiece of Jesus' proclamation of the kingdom in Matthew. Since the love of enemy command is linked to God's moral character, the teaching is essential to the character formation of Jesus' followers. It is not superfluous to the gospel, but lies at the heart of the gospel.

Further, both the seventh Beatitude and the love of enemy command are connected to persecution, as Mauser has shown (see Chapter 3 above).

2. Correlative to Jesus' love of enemy command is the command not to "resist the evil one" and not to "repay evil for evil." Jesus' teaching appears also in Paul, who likewise unites commands to love the enemy and to not retaliate. The key text is Rom. 12:14-21 (1 Pet. 3:9 is similar). The command not to retaliate occurs also in 1 Thess. 5:13b, 15: "be at peace among yourselves. . . . See that none of you repays evil for evil, but always seek to do good to one another and to all."

Gordon Zerbe cites over thirty texts that witness to some form of non-retaliation, including not cursing, not litigating, forbearing, enduring, and being at peace (see Chapter 7). Several times in Chapters 3, 7, and 14 I referred to Luise Schottroff's perceptive treatment of managing dual loyalty, with

---

and certainly not in the military success, of the empire. Rather, its security and loyalty are in the lordship of Christ, which endures as empires rise and fall. Further, in Eph. 3:9-10, the church as a body is the demonstration of the manifold wisdom of God to the powers. This is the unified humanity described in Ephesians 1–2 and enunciated in Paul's apostolic mission (3:1-8). Here the Pax Christi becomes a model for the Pax Romana.

26. Hauerwas rightly regards this moral vision of being perfect as God is perfect as a command (as it is in Matt. 5:48 and 1 Pet. 1:16) for Jesus' followers to accept and perform, since the formation of the self has duration in time that enables growth and "practice" to become what God intends us to be (*Character and the Christian Life*, pp. 178-79).

Christ above Caesar.[27] She rightly perceives that refusal to retaliate and love of enemy are two sides of the same coin.

> Matthew 5:38-41 . . . commands the refusal to retaliate [and thereby announces] as well prophetic judgment of violent persons. . . . As imitators of God, Christians are supposed to confront the enemies of God with his mercies. . . . Loving one's enemy is the attempt to change the violent person into a child of God through a confrontation with the love of God. That is, love of one's enemy can be concretely presented as the prophetic proclamation of the approaching sovereignty of God.[28]

3. Paul exhorts believers to fulfill the command to love the neighbor and to pursue peace. See William Klassen's summary diagram of these "pursuit of peace" texts in Paul's commands and exhortations in Chapter 7.[29] Believers are admonished to be at peace with one another and to seek/pursue peace: Rom. 12:18; 1 Thess. 5:13; 2 Cor. 13:11; 2 Tim. 2:22; 1 Pet. 3:11; Rom. 14:19; cf. Heb. 12:14.

These repeated commands "to make peace" and "to pursue peace" also draw upon the symbolic world that describes God's own character and action. Peaceful relationships are desirable and possible because of what God has done: God loved us even when we were enemies, and acted in Jesus Christ to make peace with enemies (Rom. 5:10). As Ronald Sider put it: "One fundamental aspect of the holiness and perfection of God is that He loves His enemies. Those who by His grace seek to reflect His holiness will likewise love their enemies — even when it involves a cross."[30] This love of enemy command stands thus not as coercion, but as a privilege possible because we are children of God whose work in Jesus Christ is a paradigm for just this pattern of moral response. This is the character of the new person described in many and diverse ways in NT parenesis.

Indeed, believers are called to peace (1 Cor. 7:15); to "pursue what makes for peace and mutual upbuilding" (Rom. 14:19); as members of one body they are to make "every effort to maintain the unity of the Spirit in the bond of peace" (Eph. 4:3-6). Further, the peace of God is power that "guards your hearts and your minds in Christ Jesus" (Phil. 4:7; cf. 1 Thess. 5:23).

Another category, beyond those employed from Richard Hays's work, is that of Christian virtues. Admonition in Paul to cultivate (often in language

---

27. Schottroff, "Give to Caesar What Belongs to Caesar."
28. Schottroff, "Give to Caesar What Belongs to Caesar," p. 232.
29. William Klassen, "Pursue Peace: A Concrete Ethical Mandate (Romans 12:18-21)."
30. Sider, *Christ and Violence*, p. 26.

of "put on") them occurs frequently. Glen Stassen provides us with two important table-summaries on NT virtues. First, he presents a basic correlation between Jesus and Paul:[31]

Paul's virtues parallel the Beatitudes

Jesus' Beatitudes	*Paul's virtues*
humility and meekness	humility and gentleness
righteousness	righteousness
mercy	kindness, compassion, love, forgiveness
purity of heart	purity or goodness
peacemaking	peace, tolerance, unity, patience
suffering persecution for justice and Jesus' sake	endurance
(blessed are you)	joy

The similarity of emphasis is striking. Further, the emphases I listed above under commands or rules may also be considered virtues, for they are actions that flow from formation of character rooted in discipleship and imitation (as presented in Chapter 13). These are: loving enemies, not retaliating, blessing those who curse us, praying for those who persecute us, seeking to overcome evil with good, not avenging ourselves against one who does wrong but deferring to God's judgment, and reconciling with or forgiving one another when wrong is done. Most of these occur more than once in both the Gospels (Jesus) and Paul. Adding these seven to the seven above describes Christian character. Together they form a profile of Christian values and practices.

The profile is even richer in Paul's letters, in his admonition and encouragement. Stassen and Gushee present a listing of virtues that Paul exhorts believers in the churches to emulate (see p. 412). The base list is from Col. 3:12-17 (compare this to the table in Chapter 13, which also uses Colossians 3 for its base list of vices). As Stassen and Gushee indicate, other NT texts from the Pastorals and Peter's writings both concur with the list above, but also add a few:

31. Stassen and Gushee, *Kingdom Ethics,* p. 48. The following table and the table on p. 412 are taken from *Kingdom Ethics* by Glen H. Stassen and David P. Gushee, © 2003 by Glen H. Stassen and David P. Gushee, and used here with permission of InterVarsity Press, P.O. Box 1400, Downers Grove, IL 60515. www.ivpress.com

Virtues in Paul's lists[32]

Col. 3:12-17	Phil. 2:2-3	Eph. 4:2-3, 32	Gal. 5:22-23	Rom. 14:17; 15:4-5	2 Cor. 6:4-10
love	love	love	love		
compassion		compassion			
kindness		kindness	kindness		
humility	humility	humility			
gentleness		gentleness	gentleness		
patience		patience	patience		
tolerance		tolerance			
forgiveness		forgiveness			
	unity	unity		unity	
gratitude	like-mindedness				
wisdom					
peace		peace	peace	peace	
				righteousness	righteousness
			joy	joy in the Holy Spirit	joy
				endurance	endurance
				hope	
			goodness		purity
			faithfulness		understanding
			self-control		kindness
					patience

First Timothy 4:12; 6:11; 2 Timothy 2:22; 3:10: 1 Peter 3:8; and 2 Peter 1:5-7 advocate basically the same virtues that we have seen already: love five times, faith three times, righteousness twice, godliness twice, purity and purity of heart, endurance, perseverance, gentleness, peace, harmony, sympathy, compassion, kindness, humility, goodness, knowledge, and self-control. They would add faith to our list of those mentioned twice or more.[33]

32. Stassen and Gushee, *Kingdom Ethics,* p. 50.
33. Stassen and Gushee, *Kingdom Ethics,* pp. 48-49. Stassen and Gushee compare this list to Farley's in *In Praise of Virtue.* They note that "Farley does not note the extensive biblical theme of *peacemaking*" (Stassen and Gushee, p. 49).

This contribution by Stassen and Gushee, together with my analysis of "correspondence" and "imitation" language in regard to John H. Yoder's work in *Politics of Jesus* (see Chapter 13 above), profiles Christian character, formation, and living. One significant list overlooked by Stassen and Gushee is Phil. 4:8, which puts "truth" first, a new entry on the list above. This virtue is evident also in Eph. 4:15, where Paul enjoins believers to be "truthing in love" (a literal translation). Truth is a significant addition (see also Eph. 4:21, 25) and contrasts with "lies" at the end of the vice list in Chapter 13. Granted, Paul's phrasing of the virtues in the Philippians text is a bit different, since he sets the virtues in goal-type form: "whatever is true, whatever is honorable, whatever is just, whatever is pure, whatever is pleasing, whatever is commendable, if there is any excellence and if there is anything worthy of praise, think about these things." Nevertheless, they are generally regarded as virtues by commentators, and as a list resembling Greek virtue lists. Paul, however, connects them directly to Christ and God. The list is prefaced by: "the peace of God, which passes all understanding, will keep your hearts and minds in Christ Jesus" (4:7). It is followed by "the God of peace will be with you all" (4:9b). God as "God of peace" frames the virtue list. This feature itself is a stellar expression of the central thesis of this book: that God's children seek to be peacemakers because God is the "God of peace" whose love even for enemies transforms people through Jesus Christ into children of peace. This is the foremost truth that the NT invites us to believe and live.

Epilogue and Forward to Formation of Virtue

I loop back to the distinctive appellation "God of peace," virtually unique to the NT, and mostly in Pauline writings. The Gospels also make a similar point in both Luke and John, that the risen Lord greets his discombobulated followers with the greeting "Peace be with you" (see Chapters 5 and 11 above). This is the "frame" by which they know Jesus, the now vindicated one who foretold his passion and resurrection and called them to walk the disciple way.

Further, in Jesus' upper room discourse, the Gospel of John promises peace to Jesus' disciples such as the world cannot give (14:27; 16:33). This is prelude to the self-identity of Jesus in his post-resurrection greeting, with narrative repetition three times, "Peace be with you" (20:19, 21, 26). The first two uses preface Jesus' commissioning of his disciples to go forth to "bind and loose" people's sins. The third use prefaces Thomas's existential encounter with Jesus as "My Lord and my God." Luke likewise has the same greeting as preface to the meal in which Jesus discloses himself as the risen Jesus to his disciples gathered in response to the strange report of the Emmaus road episode.

These greetings culminate the Gospel narrative, which proclaims fulfillment of the messianic shalom. Jesus brings that peace, promising his followers, "Peace I leave with you." It remains with us as a gift of grace *(Gabe)* and a task *(Aufgabe)* for our vocation. As James says, the wisdom from above is peaceable; it bears the fruit of justice or righteousness that is sown in peace by those who make peace (3:17-18), i.e. it is virtue-making.

The connection between peace/peacemaking and the formation of virtue may be demonstrated in relation to each person of the Trinity, the "God of peace" in Phil. 4:7-9, "Christ of peace" in Col. 3:12-15, and "the Spirit of peace" in Gal. 5:22. These texts make clear the vital connection between the pervasive NT emphasis on peace and character formation, in the cultivation of the virtues that permeate NT writings, whether in the Beatitudes, Pauline exhortation, or the moral instruction of Jesus in the Gospels, such as in Mark 8:27–10:52. The connection is intrinsic to what formation in Christ (2 Cor. 3:18) and "Christ being formed in you" (Gal. 4:19) means for our lives today. As this study has shown, this formation is not limited to the personal sphere of life, but consists of the fostering of *shalom* in its iridescent dimensions; it is personal and corporate in all dimensions of life: material (economics), political, and indeed spiritual.

As Revelation and the "God of peace" benedictions have reminded us, worship consisting of prayer and blessing to God is a cardinal means of orienting our lives to ever increasing moral formation. Quite rightly, Nicholas Wolterstorff addresses the need to renew the authenticity of our worship and liturgy in his excellent contribution to spurring us toward the embrace of justice and peace.[34] A daily commitment to praying the Lord's Prayer — and meaning it — is a helpful beginning to put the quest for peace and justice into divine sovereign perspective. As noted in Chapter 3, the "Our Father" prayer forms the chiastic center of the Sermon on the Mount, reminding us that empowerment through such communion with God is strategic to living the *gospel-peace* of God's reign. For the heavenly Father grants the *blessing* to be formed as *peacemakers* bear the mark of God's children.

---

34. Wolterstorff, *Until Justice and Peace Embrace,* pp. 146-61.

Summary and Conclusion,
Reflections and Directions

Since Chapter 15 already presents a summary by appropriating main emphases from preceding chapters for Christian moral formation, here I carry forward that format for an outline-summary and then take up other concluding
emphases, both reflections and directions for future work.

1. I present the main themes of this study, carrying forward the modes
of hermeneutical appeal to Scripture proposed by Richard Hays, as utilized in
Chapter 15:[1]

> *Symbolic World Features from This Study:*
> Jesus' seventh Beatitude: "Blessed are the peacemakers"
> Paul's unique title for God as "God of peace"
> NT imitation and discipleship texts
> "Christ is our peace" who has formed Jews and Gentiles into one
>   body
> The "Lamb's War" in Revelation

Each of these points as developed in this study represents a worldview perspective. They also draw from the same basic conviction that Jesus and the
gospel he and his followers proclaimed inaugurate a new creation. Each point
requires a paradigm-shift in one's thinking and living. None of these world-
changing ways of thinking and living arises from human choice alone, but all
depend on God's gracious act of redemption of humankind through Jesus
Christ, his life, death, resurrection, and exalted reign at God's right hand.

---

1. Hays, *The Moral Vision of the New Testament*, pp. 208-9. See also his discussion of the
same in *New Testament Ethics: The Story Retold*, pp. 32-33.

415

Paradigms (and Principles):

The gospel narrative as a whole presents Jesus as a paradigm for peacemaking. This paradigm might also be considered another aspect of
the symbolic world of the gospel. From the angelic proclamation,
"Peace on earth" (Luke 2:14), to Jesus' pattern of behavior before the
authorities in his passion, to Paul's *kenosis*-hymn in Phil. 2:6-11, and
Peter's exhortation to "follow in his steps" (1 Pet. 2:21-23; cf. Heb. 2:9;
5:5-10; 12:2), this peacemaking pattern is a foundational paradigm of
the gospel.

A second master paradigm in the NT canon is that of Paul's extensive
participation and correspondence parenesis for becoming Christian
in character and conduct. The co-identity of fellow-believers with Jesus Christ ("in Christ") enables us to learn the new mimetic pattern
of the new creation that breaks the spiral of violence and valorizes
love, justice, and shalom.

A third peace paradigm emerges in the early church's attitude toward
government powers. While the NT presents diverse portraits of the
church's stance toward government powers, as we have seen in Chapter 7, it is clear that the Gospels and Paul creatively forge a vision of
an alternative socioeconomic-political community. As Chapter 1
contends, Jesus fulfills Isa. 52:7, a text quoted or alluded to over a half
dozen times in NT writings. Thus, the phrase "announcing good
news of peace" *(euangelizomenos shalom/eirēnēn)* influences NT
writers more than usually noted. Together with Isa. 61:1-2, quoted by
Luke (4:18-19) for Jesus' platform-address in the Nazareth synagogue,
these two OT texts are strategic to the Gospels' overall theological
and ethical emphases of peace and peacemaking.

Rules/Commands Derived from Symbolic World:

Jesus *commands* his followers to "love enemies" (Matt. 5:44-45). This
moral behavior is evidence of being "children of God," as in the seventh Beatitude. *Being* peacemakers and loving enemies mark those
who follow Jesus and are children of God, *his* and *our* heavenly Father.

Correlative to Jesus' love of enemy command is his command not to
"resist the evil one," not to repay evil for evil. Paul also unites commands to love the enemy and to not retaliate (Rom. 12:14-21; cf. 1 Pet.
2-3; 1 Thess. 5:13b, 15).

Believers are to fulfill the command to pursue peace. Klassen has shown
how pervasive the command to pursue or seek peace is in the NT
(see Chapter 7 above).

2. The aim of this book is to fill a lacuna in NT theology and ethics, as stated in the Introduction. Three test-criteria of the "missing" NT peace emphases in the twenty-five[2] volumes analyzed (see Appendix 1) are:

> Does the evident Lukan contribution to *peace* (and *righteousness/justice*) in both the Gospel and Acts show in these volumes? This is a distinctive feature of this sizeable part (ca. one-fourth) of the NT canon.
>
> Is Paul's distinctive appellation "*God of peace*" noticed and, if so, does it catch the author's attention enough to receive significant comment? It seems to me that "God of Peace" in Paul is an indicator as to whether writers of NT theology especially, and "ethics" as well, have done justice to Paul's *peace/peacemaking* theology. This distinctive Pauline appellation scores significantly in attesting whether the "theology" and "ethics" are on the *peace/peacemaking* nettle.
>
> As authors explicate the NT in relation to the OT, do they notice the extent to which Isa. 52:7 influenced both the Synoptic Gospels' and Pauline understandings of the kingdom-gospel of Jesus Christ?

The result for the first criterion is straightforward. *None* of the twenty-five authors pass this test-criterion. Some of Luke's peace texts, especially Luke 2:14; 19:42, are mentioned with comment, but none of the authors pursue the significance of Luke's full peace emphasis for its theological and/or ethical significance.

To answer the second, the "showings" are: C. K. Lehman refers to the "God of peace" benediction in Hebrews, but fails to mention Paul's frequent uses; Richard Hays cites 1 Thess. 5:23, not for the "God of peace" title, but for evidence of the expected parousia and judgment; Whiteley cites two "God of peace" texts to bolster other points in his discussion; Bultmann cites five "God of peace" references only, to bolster his point that "peace" is synonymous with salvation in its eschatological sense; and Leon Morris notes the "God of peace" appellation, citing all the references, as one of three outstanding NT descriptions of God. Though only briefly commenting on the significance of this Pauline contribution, Morris alone of the twenty-five writers passes this test-criterion. The other twenty-four writers failed this particular test point (perhaps Bultmann gets a low pass).

---

2. The count is higher if one includes those mentioned in notes such as R. E. O. White, Victor Paul Furnish, Joachim Jeremias, and A. M. Hunter and the works mentioned at the end of Appendix 1.

On the third test-criterion, four authors did well in utilizing Isa. 52:7 formatively for their explication of NT peace theology or ethics. Each in different ways, C. K. Lehman, J. C. Beker, Ben Wiebe, and Frank Matera appealed to the "gospel of peace" motif from Isa. 52:7 to accentuate the peace emphasis in Jesus' proclamation of the kingdom (see Appendix 1 summary). While three recognized the important influence of this text in their analysis of the Gospels, as Beker did for Paul, the other twenty-one failed this criterion.[3] One might hypothesize that if an author recognizes the influence that Isaiah 52:7 has upon NT thought, that author will formulate his "theology" or "ethics" with a significant *peace/peacemaking* accent.

3. Richard Hays makes a claim that many scholars would likely dispute: "With regard to the issue of *violence,* the New Testament bears a powerful witness that is both univocal and pervasive, for it is integrally related to the heart of the kerygma and to God's fundamental elective purpose."[4] My version of this claim is that the NT speaks univocally and pervasively of *peace/peacemaking* as one central feature of the gospel.[5] In differing parts of the NT other correlative emphases join this core theme, such as *reconciliation* in Paul and *love for one another* in John. In most strands, Johannine excepted, *love of enemies* is present. This is coupled with blessing those who curse, praying for those who persecute, and overcoming evil with good.

Fashionable in NT studies is the assumption and dominant claim that we can find only diversity, not any sort of unity, in the NT literature. This view applies to *peace* also. While recognizing the pervasive emphasis on peace in the NT, Hubert Frankemölle says, "there can be no suprahistorical, harmo-

---

3. That C. H. Dodd failed to include this text in what he describes as OT texts of messianic significance that form the substructure of NT theology is lamentable, as noted above in Chapter 1, since Dodd elsewhere articulates Jesus' proclamation of the kingdom gospel as setting forth a vision of life in which war and personal participation in war directly contradict kingdom principles. These principles are: the kingdom transcends all divisions among humans, God's unity for humans is not by coercion but by God's new creation that makes peace, divine charity offers grace and forgiveness, in God's love each person is one for whom Christ died, the cross signifies both participation in human suffering and power to re-create, and all humans are children of one heavenly Father. Dodd is clear that "war is fundamentally antagonistic" to the kingdom and that "war is evil. . . . we cannot Christianise it by taking part in it." See Dodd, "The Theology of Pacifism," pp. 10-13. William Klassen summarizes these points a bit differently in "The Eschatology of Jesus," pp. 86-87.

4. Hays, *Moral Vision,* p. 314.

5. Michel Desjardins sees this differently, as I indicated in Chapter 2 above, in his *Peace and Violence in the New Testament.* Among several weaknesses of his work, however, he does not examine exegetically whether images of violence or portrayals of violence are used in such a way as to authorize violence for praxis by Jesus' disciples. See my review of his book in *CGR* 17 (1999): 122-24.

nized New Testament concept of peace, but only conceptions of peace characteristic of individual writings."[6] While this is true to a considerable extent when one examines the differing historical contexts and literary purposes of the varied writings, yet substantial concurrence in meaning cannot be overlooked. For while four differing denotations in meaning for the word *peace* are evident (and one author may utilize one more than the others), this does not negate the claim for pervasive unity and univocal witness.

Paul, for example, clearly uses the term "peace" to describe both the restored relationship with God through God's gift of salvation in Jesus Christ and the making of Jews and Gentiles into one body in Christ, "breaking down the wall of partition," to use language from Ephesians. In these two senses, peacemaking is a synonym for reconciliation, and close in meaning to salvation. Further, "the peace of God" in Phil. 4:7 denotes power that protects from fear and anxiety to bring calm. It guards the heart and the mind in Jesus Christ. Fourth, since Paul uses the term "peace and security" to denote world political peace (1 Thess. 5:3), one might expect that his following "God of peace" benediction (5:23) is a counter-claim, even though its focus is certainly on bestowing peace upon the Thessalonian faith community, with a personal inner dimension for each believer. In this counter-claim believers know that the Pax Christi has effected what the Pax Romana could not achieve: the birthing of a new community that crosscuts prevailing cultural polarities (ethnic, status, economic, and gender: Gal. 3:28). In Luke's Gospel, peace clearly carries a world-political dimension in 2:14 and 19:42. At the same time, Luke's overall use of "peace" is holistic, embracing other dimensions of meaning as well.

The determination of which connotation is primary in each particular use is useful (see Chapter 2, especially my *eirēnē* diagram and Stuhlmacher's contribution, as well as Appendix 2). This does not lessen but intensifies the import of the fact that peace is pervasive in NT gospel proclamation and parenesis. Paul's uses of "the God of peace" in various literary contexts reflect multiple levels of denotation (cf., e.g., Rom. 16:20 with Rom. 15:33). By this multivalent peace the community of faith is established and empowered to live as a contrast community to the powers and their means of peacemaking through conquest and subjugation. Even though one denotation in meaning is more evident in a given use of "peace," the other denotations may also be alluded to. It is important that we do not piecemeal peace away.

My thesis complements Hays's claim by showing that the NT not only

---

6. Frankemölle, "Peace and the Sword in the New Testament," pp. 205-6 (1992 edition, p. 214).

consistently and pervasively renounces the use of violence, even to achieve our calculated justice, it presents also a positive calling for believers. It asks us not only to commit to nonviolence (nonretaliation and nonresistance to evil are more biblical terms), but it overwhelmingly enlists us in the service of seeking to overcome evil with good, to love the enemy, pray for the abuser, and be peacemakers.[7]

Another angle to this thesis is to recognize that refusal to participate in war, claiming to be a pacifist, and adhering to nonviolence are minimal expressions of the peacemaking task.[8] Stanley Hauerwas expresses this in reflecting on John Howard Yoder's contribution and anticipating dialogue with John Milbank. Hauerwas quotes Yoder from *Christian Attitudes Toward War, Peace, and Revolution* (p. 428), where Yoder defines Jesus' mission as political since Jesus speaks of all the sorts of things politics is concerned about, though his approach is consistently noncoercive. Then Hauerwas says:

> So Yoder is not a pacifist if by that you mean someone who assumes that pacifists know in advance what may and may not be violence. Of course Yoder assumes that Christians do not kill, but that is only to state what it means to be a pacifist in the most minimal fashion. The practice of peace among Christians requires constant care of our lives together, through which we discover the violence that grips our lives and compromises our witness to the world. If the church is not peace, then the world does not have an alternative to violence. But if the church is not such an alternative, then what we believe as Christians is clearly false. For when all is said and done, the question of peace is the question of truth and why the truth that is ours in Christ makes possible a joy and peace otherwise unobtainable.[9]

Once we instinctively think of the positive approach to peacemaking in the fuller dimensions spelt out above, then we will be able to overcome the cleavage between peace witness and evangelism, a dichotomy I lamented in the Introduction to this volume. Then, and only then, is it credible and imperative to say that the gospel is about peace and that peace/peacemaking is the gospel. If on the other hand, peace/peacemaking is re-

---

7. In my book *Slavery, Sabbath, War, and Women*, I outline systematically the biblical case for pacifism under five topical headings, most of which are positive-directed action (pp. 118-37). Each of the five points has numerous subpoints; together they provide a useful complement to this study.

8. Two excellent books on pacifism that not only treat the topic in the "non-stance" dimension but demonstrate positive action to overcome evil are Brown, *Biblical Pacifism*, and Sider and Keefer, eds., *A Peace Reader*.

9. Stanley Hauerwas, "Explaining Christian Nonviolence," p. 176.

duced to simply what we stand against, then it is a travesty to the gospel to make such a claim. Looping back to my quotation of Hauerwas in the Introduction together with the above, we are urgently beckoned to move from what he calls the "minimalist" to the "maximalist" understanding and commitment. This will also enable us to make the church in its corporate life a true peace church, and give witness to the same, in the same way that Ulrich Luz calls for regarding

> *the church as a sphere of action. In that the church incorporates love, that is,*
> *truly is the church, it becomes a peace factor in the world.* Concretely this
> means a reformation of the church in its leadership and its membership,
> so that it truly represents the cross of Christ in the world. That would be
> the decisive contribution of the church to peace.[10]

4. In every chapter of textual analysis above (Chapters 3-12) some aspect of the book's or author's theology related to "peace" *(eirēnē)* carried either explicit or implicit counter-imperial claims. Whether Matthew's or Mark's "Son of God" title applied to Jesus, Luke's uses of *eirēnē* with political connotation, Paul's dominion titles for Jesus Christ, John's portrayal of Jesus' encounter with Pilate, or Revelation's theological assault on the empire as the beast allied with the false prophet arrayed against God's people, the theological and ethical stance is similar: Jesus is Savior and Lord. Emperor and empire claims to dominion, divine status, or even Pax Romana grandeur pale, for God's people and kingdom will triumph in and through Jesus Christ, articulated memorably in Revelation 11:15 and chs. 18–19. We recall from Chapter 8 Wright's point on Paul that believers await "the Savior, the Lord Jesus, the Messiah" (Phil. 3:20):

> These are Caesar-titles. The whole verse says: Jesus is Lord, and Caesar isn't. Caesar's empire, of which Philippi is the colonial outpost, is the parody; Jesus' empire, of which the Philippian church is the colonial outpost, is the reality.[11]

Though each portion of the NT has its own genre and vocabulary, the essential point is the same: believers who become part of Jesus' new covenant of peace own a new Savior and Lord whose life, death, and resurrection open up new kingdom reality and a new creation. This new community is indeed a

---

10. Ulrich Luz, "The Significance of the Biblical Witnesses for Church Peace Action," p. 255 (1992 edition, p. 251).
11. Wright, "Paul's Gospel and Caesar's Empire," p. 173.

contrast community, as Gerhard Lohfink identifies it.[12] But it is also a counter-community in that its very existence critiques the dominant culture of the empire. When tested by the tax question, Jesus answered, "Give to the emperor what is the emperor's, and to God the things that are God's" (Mark 12:17). God's claim surpasses Caesar's; believers submit to God's Lordship, putting loyalty to God above loyalty to Caesar. Caesar's empire is temporal, certain to collapse, but God's rule through Jesus Christ endures. Using Matthew's language, reflecting perhaps Daniel's vision, the kingdom of heaven inaugurated in Jesus endures; earthly kingdoms crumble, but God's universal sovereignty is everlasting. Matthew's extensive teaching contrasts the ethics of the kingdom of heaven with those of Rome and all earthly kingdoms.[13] Hence, from the Galilean mountain, Jesus the royal Son sends his first disciples into all the world to "make disciples of all nations" (28:19a).

In this context Jesus' followers live as a peaceable witness to the principalities and powers of the manifold wisdom of God (Eph. 3:9-10), for the new creation in Jesus Christ knows divine power through servant living, love and forgiveness that ends enmity, and faithful obedience that triumphs even through martyrdom. Both Walter Wink's *Engaging the Powers* and George McClain's *Claiming All Things for God*, which narrates a liturgy of exorcism for evil structural action, exemplify patterns of bold witness to the powers.[14] Wink's chapter, "Prayer and the Powers," is excellent. As he puts it in his conclusion:

> Prayer that ignores the Powers ends up blaming God for evils committed by the Powers. But prayer that acknowledges the Powers becomes a form of social action. Indeed, no struggle for justice is complete unless it has first discerned, not only the outer, political manifestations of the Powers,

12. Lohfink, *Jesus and Community,* pp. 157-68. Lohfink demonstrates the effect of this stance in the early church's refusal of military service (pp. 168-76) and contrasts in life-praxis (pp. 176-80).

13. Pennington, in his paper "The Kingdom of Heaven against All Earthly Kingdoms," proposed that Matthew's distinctive "kingdom of heaven" is to be understood in contrast to all earthly kingdoms. It marks a qualitative difference from all earthly kingdoms, which Satan desired Jesus to co-rule (Matt. 4:8-9). Guy D. Nave and Gerhard van den Heever presented similar emphases for Luke and John respectively, since in Luke the call to repentance is exemplified by economic conversion (Zacchaeus) and political loyalty (Jesus is Savior), and in John Jesus' kingship is power above Caesar's and Jesus as Son of God subverts Caesar as *dominus Deus.* See summaries in *2004 AAR/SBL Abstracts,* pp. 347-48, 356, and 406.

14. Wink, *Engaging the Powers;* McClain, *Claiming All Things for God.* I do not wish here to privilege social exorcism at the expense of personal exorcism. Many good resources are readily available on the latter. See my bibliography in Johns and Krabill, eds., *Deliver Us from Evil,* but very few resources exist on utilizing an exorcist approach to dismantle powers of structural evil.

but also their inner spirituality, and has lifted the Powers, inner and outer, to God for transformation. Otherwise we change only the shell, and leave the spirit intact.

Prayer in the face of the Powers is a spiritual war of attrition. God's hands are effectively tied when we fail to pray. That is the dignity and urgency of our praying.[15]

Through prayer believers gain strength to live faithfully, even when the Powers persecute. Further, through prayer that binds the evil of the Powers and praises God for Jesus Christ's victory over Satan, sin, and death, the Powers are disempowered. The 1990 mass prayer gathering of 70,000 people in the St. Nikolai Church in Leipzig, East Germany, testifies to prayer's power, for it protected against the efforts of the USSR to squelch the freedom movement. The event exemplifies the power of faith in God to deliver and defend against powers that mask as sovereign. Only God is the Sovereign. In this world and history, though, God's sovereignty is often a contested sovereignty.

5. Ulrich Luz made an important point in his conclusion to an extended symposium study (twelve years) as described in his essay, "The Significance of the Biblical Witnesses for Church Peace Action."[16] From the beginning of the study the interdisciplinary group of participants identified three peace issues that they believed Scripture to address: poverty, violence, and oppression. In the course of the study they found it necessary to add a fourth dimension, which they described variously as "minimization of fear," of "sin," with "comfort" or "gaining of identity." Luz writes,

> It is no accident that in all the essays of this book the so-called "*inner dimension*" played a notable role. . . . In virtually all the studies it became clear that this inner dimension need not stand as a contrast to the outer dimensions of peace. Forgiveness of debt, the lifting of fear, experiencing comfort, and gaining of identity do not replace active expressions of peacemaking but rather enable them. It became evident that the "inner" and the "outer" are modern points of contrast, whereas in biblical anthropology they are integrated. . . . Outer needs, such as persecution, threats to religious freedom, or hunger can lead to a deeper experience of inner freedom. In the Pauline dialectic of cross and resurrection living, of suffering and of love, such thoughts have probably been most tightly formulated. . . .

15. Wink, *Engaging the Powers*, p. 317.

16. In the notes of this chapter Luz frequently refers to the studies by Jürgen Kegler, Peter Lampe, Paul Hoffmann, and Ulrich Luz in Luz, et al., *Eschatologie und Friedenshandeln*, pp. 195-214.

Based on these observations, it seems to us that perhaps it is time to raise serious questions not only about modern secular concepts but also about modern theological concepts, insofar as they tend to evaluate a theological effort purely or mainly on the basis of its ability to produce peace action and emancipation, to minimize outer oppression, violence, and want. Is it not true that often from the side of Christianity, a specifically Christian contribution to the peace problem (even if not the only contribution) is too quickly relativized or even negatively evaluated in a one-sided manner? Should not theology insist that the concept of peace be expanded to include an "inner dimension" for the sake of our total experience of living as humans?[17]

Further, the importance of these four dimensions does not stand in a lockstep linear order: the three outer dimensions are not resolved before the fourth inner expression of peace is realized. Rather, there is a dialectic relationship, whereby the inner empowers the outer, or the outer occasions need for the inner. This corrective, of course, does not mean down-playing the socio-political and economic dimensions of the peacemaking task. The major study that Luz summarizes began with precisely those dimensions of the peacemaking task, but the "surprise discovery" was that it missed initially an important dimension of peace as experienced by faith communities in both Old and New Testaments. In this "Decade to Overcome Violence," so designated by the World Council of Churches, it is most urgent that faith communities commit to the holistic peace mission. Thus, *trust in God* as the One who wills peace (*shalom* in its fullest sense) beckons us on. For indeed *peacemaking* is not simply done by human effort, but by the power of God's Spirit and living humbly under the Lordship of Jesus Christ. Otherwise, peace efforts soon wear down the best intentioned people. Jesus Christ is both our peacemaker-prototype and our living Lord who by his Spirit and Word empowers us. Peace is both *Gabe und Aufgabe,* both gift and task. Seen in this light, peacemaking unites us to God in sharing the divine mission, the *Missio Dei.*

6. Ulrich Mauser stresses the importance of recognizing that we receive peace as God's *gift,* "given as freely as the grace of God itself." Further, as the "Christian community *remembers* God's gift of peace" it also knows that "God's act of peacemaking is identical with the life, death, and resurrection of Jesus Christ."[18] This is important, because it is the whole story of Jesus that

---

17. Luz, "The Significance of the Biblical Witnesses," pp. 240-41 (1992 edition, pp. 237-38).
18. Ulrich Mauser, *The Gospel of Peace,* p. 168.

shapes and empowers the Christian peace witness. It is not only what Jesus taught, nor is it only his death. Either of these taken alone would yield no more than either a great prophet or another death of one deemed politically troubling.

The entire story, together with God's willed purpose in Jesus' death and God's resurrection of his faithful Son, is essential for maintaining the biblical peace manifesto. All of this, together with the full canonical exposition of what this peace means in concrete and varied situations of life, such as church conflicts for which Paul appropriated the peace of Christ, figures into the memory and narrative we affirm as God's peace gift to those baptized into the *koinōnia* of Jesus Christ's life, death, resurrection, and exaltation. As Peter puts it, he "has gone into heaven and is at the right hand of God, with angels, authorities, and powers made subject to him" (1 Pet. 3:22). The Christian church must revive the significance of both the life of Jesus, as witnessed by the Gospels, and ascension theology, as is pervasive in Acts, Paul, Peter, and Hebrews.

In order to recover the importance of Jesus' life and teaching, I propose three additions to the Apostles' Creed. After "born of the virgin Mary," I suggest: "Lived obediently to his Abba. Lived and taught love, peace, and forgiveness." This addition speaks of Jesus' relation to his Father and sums up crucial emphases in his teaching. The second addition follows immediately, summing up Jesus' deeds: "Healed the sick, cast out demons, forgave sins, raised the dead, confounded the powers." This would recognize liturgically that Jesus' life is one with his death in significance. The ascension is included in the Apostles' Creed, though Christian churches over the years have ceased observance of Ascension Day and thus tend to downplay the significance of Jesus' lordship claims. To express the theological significance of ascension, I propose that the phrase "triumphing over the powers" be added as a preface to "He ascended into heaven." Jesus Christ's triumph over the powers thus links resurrection and ascension. With these additions, the Apostles' Creed would testify more fully to the gospel and its import for faithful living.

I underscore also the importance of the "discipline of peace," as Mauser puts it, knowing that both "discernment" and willingness to commit to the "discipline of being radical" are important.[19] Hauerwas speaks of "honing the skills" to be peacemakers as well as "giving constant care" to the communal task of peacemaking (see above). Among the Christian practices described in the book edited by Dorothy Bass,[20] peacemaking — though missing — belongs. It is a Christian practice, the sort of thing one learns to do better by in-

19. Mauser, *The Gospel of Peace*, pp. 173-81.
20. Bass, ed., *Practicing Our Faith*.

tentionally practicing it. Such practice embraces one's spiritual disciplines, including prayer and meditation (and here good resources abound) as well as taking concrete action-steps, such as affirming peace positions as outlined by Mauser at the end of his last chapter.[21]

I affirm also the importance of what may seem to be *insignificant* initiatives, often called the small-step approach to peace. Such steps are to be valued as fruit of the gospel of Jesus Christ, not just humanistic efforts. Rudolf Schnackenburg puts this point well:

> The rule of God announced by Jesus is already begun. For in Jesus himself, in his person, and his actions, in his struggles, suffering and dying the meaning of the rule of God, what it can be and should be is clearly earmarked: service for others, love to the uttermost. And everywhere where people follow him in his way, a portion of God's rule is realized, the strength for peace grown, and peace emerges triumphant over all hatred, clash of weapons, and tumults of war. Whoever has once comprehended the absolute will of Jesus toward peace, which nourishes itself on the peaceful disposition of God, can and must affirm and receive all human, earthly, socio-political efforts toward peace, all small initiatives and large organizational measures. Out of the message of Jesus, that God will eventually grant humankind the last perfect peace, such a person will never be disillusioned or discouraged. This is the power of Christian peace efforts and peace work.[22]

When small steps or bigger steps are seen in this light, peacemaking efforts bear witness to the life, death, resurrection, and exaltation of Jesus Christ, the peace-pioneer and prototype who empowers us in peacemaking.

Glen Stassen has directed us on the right road, the kingdom road, in emphasizing the gospel's transforming initiatives (see Chapter 3 above). In his second *Just Peacemaking* book Stassen proposes ten peacemaking practices that he believes will serve the cause of peace for humans living together in this world.[23] These steps are developed in the three "Parts" of his book:

21. Mauser, *The Gospel of Peace*, pp. 186-88.

22. Rudolf Schnackenburg, "Macht, Gewalt und Friede nach dem Neuen Testament."

23. Stassen, ed., *Just Peacemaking: Ten Practices for Abolishing War*. The following ten points are the titles of the chapters by different authors in this book. Moltmann, in "Political Theology and Political Hermeneutics," helpfully identifies five dimensions of messianic peacemaking: "The struggle for economic justice. . . . The struggle for human rights and freedom. . . . The struggle for human solidarity against cultural alienation. . . . The struggle for ecological peace with nature. . . . The struggle for the meaning of life against apathy. . . ." In Swartley, ed., *Politics of Discipleship*, p. 47.

Peacemaking Initiatives; Justice; and Love and Community. The four initiatives in Part 1 are: (1) support nonviolent direct action; (2) take independent initiatives to reduce threat; (3) use cooperative conflict resolution; and (4) acknowledge responsibility of conflict and injustice. The next two in Part 2 seek to advance justice: (5) advance democracy, human rights, and religious liberty and (6) foster just and sustainable economic development. The last four in Part 3 seek to enhance community: (7) work with emerging cooperative forces in the international system; (8) strengthen the United Nations and international efforts for cooperation and human rights; (9) reduce offensive weapons and weapons trade; and (10) encourage grassroots peacemaking groups and voluntary associations. What the essays by different authors lack is the grounding of these practices in religious sanctions.[24] Stassen's article in *Must Christianity be Violent?* anchors these practices in biblical teachings,[25] appealing frequently to the texts I have discussed in this book.[26] He also helpfully illustrates how these initiatives, when practiced, have either resolved conflict or reduced violence, preventing war that threatened to develop.

Stassen's contribution serves the cause of world peace. Another setting for transforming initiatives is recounted by Mark Gornik in *To Live in Peace*. Gornik utilizes the vision of biblical shalom to address the urban challenge, thus seeking to bring good news to an economically and politically "broken place." His theological and sociological analysis is laced with personal life-experience in the New Song Community Church in Sandtown, Baltimore. Issues of justice and building community (headings in Stassen's book) are focused on seeking the welfare of the city, so that shalom and not violence, justice and not poverty, hope and not despair characterize the life of the people. Peacemaking means moving "Out of the Ruins" to "Singing a New Song."[27]

Another important step in building peace in our world is to recognize the importance of preventive measures, developing programs to reduce violence by creating environments that build peace. Such programs have proven

---

24. A further weakness of these ten points is that some are construed from western assumptions, especially that to "advance democracy" is an uncontested good. It would have been prudent for each writer to have had a dialogue partner from the non-western world.

25. Stassen explicates these practices with appeal to Scripture, especially Jesus, in "Jesus and Just Peacemaking Theory." For the biblical foundations of human rights, see Christopher D. Marshall, *Crowned with Glory and Honor*.

26. For group study rooting peacemaking in biblical study, especially the book of Romans, I commend Glen Stassen's *The Journey into Peacemaking*.

27. Gornik, *To Live in Peace: Biblical Faith and the Changing Inner City*. See especially chapters 3-5, which contain his exposition on shalom as the welfare of the city, strategies for rebuilding community, and the experience of the New Song Community.

effective: teaching conflict resolution in elementary schools, providing peace-building activities for junior high and high school youth, and even offering gun buy-back programs. The United States especially needs to examine its priorities: why can we afford to build new prisons but we cannot afford these educational components in our public schools? Three women with wide international and domestic experience in peace-building efforts have recently published a rich contribution in these areas of peacemaking challenge.[28]

7. As we commit to live toward and work for peace, we live indeed in a world dominated by "imitation" of aggression and inclination toward the spiral of violence. My comments in Chapter 9, discussing James, together with the significance of Girard's contribution (Chapter 13), mean that human culture outside the transformative power of the gospel is much empowered by envy, rivalry, and violence. For this reason my contribution in Chapter 13 is crucial in helping us see the importance of harnessing the power of mimesis in a different direction. This is possible only through fastening our eyes on Jesus, who broke the spiral of violence. The consistency of the NT's ethical stance of nonretaliation to evil is striking, for it presents the gospel's solution to the hegemony of generative violence in human culture. Nowhere does the NT condone use of violence by Christ's followers, even as a means to defeat evil. The cross exposes and condemns the violence of humans in putting Jesus to death.[29] The resurrection makes a new mimesis possible. The phrase from Heb. 2:9, "but we do see Jesus," linked to 12:1-2, where Jesus is the prototype

28. See the ground-breaking book by Holsopple, Krall, and Weaver Pittman, *Building Peace: Overcoming Violence in Communities*. This book developed from a Peace and Justice Collaborative of three educational institutions (Andrews University, Associated Mennonite Biblical Seminary, and Goshen College), which I initiated in 1998 when I was academic dean at the seminary. A similar book, lucid and helpful, is that by Lisa Schirch, *The Little Book of Strategic Peacemaking*. A helpful study resource is the biblical, theological study by Duchrow and Liedke, *Shalom: Biblical Perspectives on Creation, Justice, and Peace*, as well as the new and accessible studies by Ott, *God's Shalom Project,* and Kreider, Kreider, and Widjaja, *A Culture of Peace.*

29. I think it wrong to link the death of Jesus to divine violence, though I value the concern to counter any theological sanctioning of abusive behavior (see Chapter 10 above on the Father-Son solidarity in the life-giving purpose of the cross-event). I speak to this point in my Introduction to *Violence Renounced,* pp. 26-28. For a careful, helpful analysis of whether there is a credible, practicable connection between "atonement theory" and promotion of domestic abuse or violence, see Mouw's helpful article "Violence and the Atonement." An analogy to this question is whether the image of God as Warrior makes people warring in spirit and deed. Certainly for Mennonite writers it does not, though some think that such a God-image must be renounced in favor of a nonviolent God. See my Chapter 14 above, where I engage this issue. On atonement, I believe that there are both symmetrical and asymmetrical relationships between Jesus and his followers. See note 48 in Chapter 14 above.

and pioneer in the faith-obedience model, is a powerful image to inform and inspire his followers on their journey of discipleship "into his image."[30]

As we walk this journey, let us reflect often on these three provocative claims from Richard Hays:

> Those who are members of the one body in Christ ([Rom.] 12:5) are never to take vengeance (12:19); they are to bless their persecutors and minister to their enemies, returning good for evil. There is not a syllable in the Pauline letters that can be cited in support of Christians employing violence.

> With regard to the issue of *violence,* the New Testament bears a powerful witness that is both univocal and pervasive, for it is integrally related to the heart of the kerygma and to God's fundamental elective purpose.

> One reason that the world finds the New Testament's message of peacemaking and love of enemies incredible is that the church is so massively faithless. . . . Only when the church renounces the way of violence, will people see what the Gospel means. . . . The meaning of the New Testament's teaching on violence will become evident only in communities of Jesus' followers who embody the costly way of peace.[31]

Hays presents a clarion call to renounce violence, and to seek those things that make for peace. His incisive critique of his selected five theologians shows that he is not about to let us off the hook by employing other considerations that mute the NT witness on this important issue. I affirm Hays's nonviolence manifesto and call for the complement of positive peacemaking teaching and action as revealed to us by NT Scripture. Jürgen Moltmann, in his final word to churches in *"their service of peace,"* calls churches to the tasks of *"learning to love their enemies, . . . recognizing the real danger threatening the church . . .* [and] *becoming a peace church."*[32]

Let us live toward the vision of peace by the *means* of peace, claiming thus our identity as Abba's children, for God did not spare his own Son, but in mutual self-donation (Father and Son) bore the agony of death so that we might die to the old self and be raised by God's power to new life. A hymn text

---

30. Helpful resources written in a more popular vein include Augsburger, *The Peacemaker,* Egan's wide ranging expositional and meditative essays in *Peace Be with You: Justified Warfare or the Way of Nonviolence,* and Lehn's *Peace Be with You.*

31. Hays, *Moral Vision,* pp. 331, 314, 343-44.

32. Moltmann, "Following Jesus Christ in an Age of Nuclear War," in Swartley, ed., *Politics of Discipleship,* pp. 67-69. Similarly, John Stoner's movement slogan is "What would it mean if every churcher were a peace church?"

written by Menno Simons in 1552 (translated by Esther Bergen for the *Mennonite World Conference Songbook*, 1990) describes well the celebration of Christ's peace as believers gather.

We Are People of God's Peace[33]

Tune: Ave Virgo Virginum (Gaudeamus Pariter)D

We are people of God's peace as a new creation.
Love unites and strengthens us at this celebration.
Sons and daughters of the Lord, serving one another,
a new covenant of peace binds us all together.

We are children of God's peace in this new creation,
spreading joy and happiness, through God's great salvation.
Hope we bring in spirit meek, in our daily living.
Peace with everyone we seek, good for evil giving.

We are servants of God's peace, of the new creation.
Choosing peace, we faithfully serve with heart's devotion.
Jesus Christ, the Prince of peace, confidence will give us.
Christ the Lord is our defense; Christ will never leave us.

Finale

Now may the *God of peace*,
who brought back from the dead our *Lord Jesus*,
the great shepherd of the sheep,

by the blood of the *eternal covenant*,

make you *complete in everything good*
so that you may *do his will*,
working among us that which is *pleasing in his sight*,

through *Jesus Christ*,
to whom *be the glory* forever and ever.
Amen. (Heb. 13:20-21)

---

33. This hymn appears in the *Hymnal: A Worship Book* (Elgin: Brethren/Newton: Faith and Life/Scottdale: Mennonite Publishing House, 1992), number 407. Used with permission from the Mennonite World Conference.

Analysis of Important Contributions
to New Testament Theology and Ethics

This appendix focuses on the theme struck in the Introduction, the neglected and in some respects virtually *missing peace* in NT Theologies and Ethics. At the end it comments briefly on three key books on NT mission and social justice. It considers contributions to NT Theology and NT Ethics from roughly the last half century.[1] I examined the following sources, many influential in the field, listed here in alphabetical order:

Beker, J. Christiaan. *Paul the Apostle: The Triumph of God in Life and Thought.* Philadelphia: Fortress Press, 1980.
Bultmann, Rudolf. *Theology of the New Testament.* Vols. 1 and 2. New York: Scribner, 1951.
Caird, G. B. *New Testament Theology.* Completed and ed. by L. D. Hurst. Oxford: Oxford Univ. Pr., 1994.
Conzelmann, Hans. *An Outline of the Theology of the New Testament.* New York: Harper & Row, 1969.

---

1. I considered other books for inclusion but omitted them since their format and goal were not that of a NT theology or ethics. One is Gerhard Lohfink's insightful volume, *Jesus and Community: The Social Dimension of the Christian Faith.* While it is neither a theology nor an ethics of the NT, it could serve as an ethics of Jesus, especially in understanding the centrality of peacemaking and nonviolence in Jesus' teaching and his legacy for Christian community. "Peace," however, does not occur in its subject index. I also did not include some that fit the categories followed here: Joachim Jeremias's *New Testament Theology: The Proclamation of Jesus* has no subject index. It comes closest to the topics of this volume in a section on "Politics" (pp. 228-30), where Jeremias distinguishes Jesus from zealotry and violence, citing Matt. 5:38-44 and discounting the "anti-tax" charge in Luke 23:2 on the basis of the tax teaching in Mark 12:13-17. Similarly A. M. Hunter, *Introducing New Testament Theology:* "Peace" is not listed in the index, and the chapter on "The Gospel of the Kingdom of God" (pp. 25-51) speaks of grace and love, but not peace. For other works on NT theology or ethics, see also nn. 30, 36, and 37.

Daly, Robert J. *Christian Biblical Ethics: From Biblical Revelation to Contemporary Christian Praxis: Method and Content.* New York: Paulist, 1984.

Dunn, J. D. G. *The Theology of Paul the Apostle.* Grand Rapids: Eerdmans, 1998.

Goldsmith, Dale. *New Testament Ethics: An Introduction.* Elgin: Brethren, 1988.

Goppelt, Leonhard. *Theology of the New Testament.* Vols. 1 and 2. Grand Rapids: Eerdmans, 1981.

Hays, Richard B. *The Moral Vision of the New Testament.* San Francisco: HarperSanFrancisco, 1996.

Kümmel, Werner Georg. *The Theology of the New Testament: According to Its Major Witnesses Jesus — Paul — John.* Nashville/New York: Abingdon, 1973.

Ladd, George Eldon. *A Theology of the New Testament.* Grand Rapids: Eerdmans, 1974. Revised editions, 1984, 1993, rev. and ed. by Donald A. Hagner.

Lehman, Chester K. *Biblical Theology: New Testament* (vol. 2). Scottdale: Herald, 1974.

Lohse, Eduard. *Theologische Ethik des Neuen Testaments.* Stuttgart: Kohlhammer, 1988.[2]

Marshall, I. Howard. *New Testament Theology: Many Witnesses, One Gospel.* Downers Grove, Ill.: InterVarsity, 2004.

Matera, Frank J. *New Testament Ethics: The Legacies of Jesus and Paul.* Louisville: Westminster John Knox, 1996.

Morris, Leon. *New Testament Theology.* Grand Rapids: Zondervan, 1986.

Ridderbos, Herman. *Paul: An Outline of His Theology.* Grand Rapids: Eerdmans, 1975.

Schnackenburg, Rudolf. *The Moral Teaching of the New Testament.* New York: Herder and Herder, 1965.

Schrage, Wolfgang. *The Ethics of the New Testament.* Minneapolis: Fortress, 1988.

Stauffer, Ethelbert. *New Testament Theology.* London: SCM, 1955, 1963.

Verhey, Allen. *The Great Reversal: Ethics and the New Testament.* Grand Rapids: Eerdmans, 1984.

Verhey, Allen. *Remembering Jesus: Christian Community, Scripture, and the Moral Life.* Grand Rapids: Eerdmans, 2002.

Whiteley, D. E. H. *The Theology of St. Paul.* Oxford: Blackwell, 1964.

Wiebe, Ben. *Messianic Ethics: Jesus' Proclamation of the Kingdom of God and the Church in Response.* Scottdale: Herald, 1992.

Wiles, Virginia. *Making Sense of Paul: A Basic Introduction to Pauline Theology.* Peabody: Hendrickson, 2000.

2. The English version has no subject index.

Table of Subject Index Peace/Reconciliation Occurrences
(summarizing the data from an analysis of the subject indices)

Author/Title	"Peace" in subject index	"Peace" not in subject index	No subject index	Other*
Beker			X	
Bultmann	8x			REC 11x
Caird		X		REC 2x
Conzelmann	1x			REC 1x
Daly	4x			REC 10x LE 7x
Dunn	1x			REC 4x
Goldsmith			X	
Goppelt	3x			REC 10x
Hays	"peace churches" 1x pacifism/nonviolence 12x			
Kümmel	3x			REC 6x
Ladd		X		REC 12x; LE 2x
Lehman		X		
Lohse	7x ("Frieden")			
Marshall	27x			REC 22x
Matera		X		REC 4x; LE 6x
Morris		X		REC 3x
Ridderbos	20x +			REC ca. 50x
Schnackenburg	3x			
Schrage			X	
Stauffer			X	
Verhey, *Great Reversal*	6x + more in *Pax Dei* section			
Verhey, *Remem. Jesus*	pacifism 7x peace/shalom 10x pax Christi 3x pax romana 2x			REC 2x
Whiteley	1x			REC 2x
Wiebe	8x; "peacemakers" 1x			REC 3x; LE 2x
Wiles	15x; "shalom" 30x +			

*Index contains the term "reconciliation" (REC) or phrase "love (of) enemies" (LE).
Of the twenty-five cited works, four have no subject index, and five of those that do have a subject index do not include "peace" in it, even though the term occurs frequently in the volume. In only seven of the indexes does the term "peace" register more than six times.

Overall Analysis

(Throughout the discussion, peace in italics is my emphasis, even in quotations.)

While the above counts are based on data in Subject Indices, in numerous cases the work contains significantly more mention of *peace* and its related themes. In overall use, in "Theology" Chester K. Lehman, Ethelbert Stauffer, and J. Christiaan Beker come in for A or A-.[3] Most disappointing are some of the otherwise good and widely used contributions: in "Theology" those of Conzelmann (in Index: *peace*, once; reconciliation, once), Caird (*peace*, none; reconciliation, two; but *peace* occurs in his text at least eight times,[4] but with no integrating discussion of the theme; reconciliation occurs several times in speaking of believers, including Jews and Gentiles); Dunn (*peace*, once; reconciliation, four); Kümmel (*peace*, three times; reconciliation, six times), Goppelt (*peace*, three, but his contribution is much stronger than this; reconciliation, ten); Whiteley (*peace*, only once, but at least eight times in text[5]); in "Ethics," Schnackenburg (*peace*, three; reconciliation, none) and Schrage (neither *peace* nor reconciliation in index, but a significant contribution in his two-volume book).

While Ladd and Matera have more on *peace* than their indices show, they emphasize reconciliation (Ladd, twelve times with a chapter devoted to the topic; Matera, four times) and love of enemies (Ladd, twice; Matera, six times) more than *peace*. Ridderbos devotes a chapter of twenty-three pages to "Reconciliation," with a subsection of four and a half pages on "*Peace* with God." Marshall's volume has numerous occurrences of *peace*, but it is never the subject of discussion, as is reconciliation (at two places). How does one assess this diminished role of *peace* in these treatments? Why is emphasis on *peace* so sparse by leading NT theologians and ethicists, and what is the significance of this?

The strongest contributions on *peace* are Richard Hays's *The Moral Vision of the New Testament* and Allen Verhey's *The Great Reversal* and *Jesus Remembered*. *Peace* does not appear in Hays's index,[6] though it figures signifi-

---

3. Since this book is oriented to both NT theologies and NT ethics, this analysis excludes works specifically devoted to peace, such as Klaus Wengst's and Ulrich Mauser's, my own edited volumes, and numerous essays on the topic by scholars such as William Klassen.

4. Caird, *New Testament Theology*, pp. 113, 157, 182, 276, 364, 368, 369, 394.

5. Whiteley, *Theology of St. Paul*, pp. 30, 37, 139, 140 [3x], 160 [2x].

6. Hays told me he regrets that "peace" is missing, citing a fiasco in the indexing process. As the analysis below of his work shows, issues of peace and nonviolence head the list of moral concerns evident in his book.

cantly and vigorously in several extended discussions (Chapters 12, 14, and 17). *Peace* occurs only several times, however, in his descriptive, exegetical section in his "Part One." Verhey's earlier volume has six references to *peace* in his Index; the latter volume has ten for *peace/shalom*, seven on pacifism, and five for *pax Romana* or *pax Christi*. *Reconciliation*, however, occurs only twice.[7] See below for fuller analysis of all authors.

In these works as a whole *reconciliation* receives more emphasis than does *peace*. This may be understandable in light of the current cultural ethos and need, but the NT may redirect our thinking to help us see that *reconciliation* stands in the service of *peacemaking*, God's *shalom* project for humans and all creation.

Works in Which Peace/Reconciliation Contribute Significantly

Stauffer, Lehman, Beker, and Wiles treat *peace/peacemaking* emphases more significantly than do the other "Theology" authors. Hays, Schrage, Verhey, and Wiebe do the same for "Ethics," in ways that show this to be an important aspect of their contributions. Except for Wiles and Wiebe, which are limited in NT scope and not NT Theologies or Ethics *per se*, *peace* is not a subject of sustained discussion in even these best of the twenty-five currently used. While the term permeates the discussion in Stauffer and Lehman, these are older works no longer used. For this reason, even though the term *peace* abounds in numerous volumes, the current works as a whole reflect *the missing peace in New Testament Theology and Ethics*.

I examine the emphases of these eight contributions, and then analyze also the remaining authors.

New Testament Theologies

Ethelbert Stauffer, *New Testament Theology* While people say "*Peace, peace, when there is no peace*" (p. 71), history is really a struggle and battle against the adversary in a world characterized by enmity. Christ through his salvific work is "the future restorer of *peace* that has been lost to the whole creation" (p. 74).

---

7. I do not agree with Verhey's view expressed in *Remembering Jesus* that war and use of violence are justified in some cases. Nor does Verhey make the case that the NT authorizes such. Only when other values and factors are figured in, use of violence for self-defense may become a moral consideration and possibility.

A resistance fighter such as Simon Maccabeus may make *peace* in the sense of restraining chaos, but that *peace* is through violence to establish order.

Stauffer devotes an entire chapter to "The *Peace* of God." He uses *peace* as the most elementary expression to describe the new reality that God brings about for humans through Christ (p. 143). He notes the close link in Luke 10 between the gospel that the apostles are sent to proclaim and the gift of *peace* in Christ's name, and connects this to Luke 19:42; Rom. 3:17; and John 16:33. Indeed, *peace* is an essential element in mercy, grace, atonement, and justification that describes the "new situation brought about by the coming of Christ" (p. 144). *Peace* and reconciliation are together the fruit of Christ's work. Stauffer links Christ's gift of universal atonement to his work on Good Friday through which God makes the new creation. The gift of justification begins at one's baptism, the individual benefit of Christ's atonement. Together these comprise Paul's "motif of a state of *peace*," which "has its final expression in Col. 1:20ff. In view of the death of his Son and his blood that was shed, God reaches out the hand of reconciliation to those who were once his enemies, and on the cross concludes a universal *peace* (echoes in Eph. 2:16)" (p. 145). Stauffer sums up this section with a sequential grid: "At the very beginning . . . God's act of grace and forgiveness [that leads to] reconciliation and justification, there stands Christ, proclaiming *peace* on earth. At the end . . . there stands the idea of a *pax domini* (1 Thess. 5:23; Rom 1:7; 15:33). To Christ's *peace* we are called (Col. 3:15; cf. Isa. 9:6; 53:5) — that is the conclusion of Paul's doctrine of reconciliation and justification" (p. 146).

Peace emphases *permeate* Stauffer's work, with various types of amplification in a dozen subsequent sections of his book, including Christ as the universal *peace*maker and the reconciler of all (Col. 1:16, 20; 2:15).[8] The believers' eternal hope is the fulfillment of perfect fellowship with God's *peace* in Christ filling all things. "*The antiphony of universal history leads into a symphonic doxology.*"[9] *Peace* and exultation mark the culmination of history, as portrayed in Revelation 21–22.

Chester K. Lehman, *Biblical Theology,* **Vol. 2:** *New Testament*   Volume 1 of Lehman's two-volume work is devoted to the OT. His approach in volume 2 is thematic. *Peace* literally laces the pages, from citing the God of *peace* benediction in Hebrews 13:20 (p. 29) on to Melchizedek as "king of *peace*" (p. 451) to his

---

8. Stauffer, pp. 224-25.

9. Stauffer, pp. 228-31 (quoting p. 231). His chapters 57, 58, and 59 are titled "Universal Homecoming," "The New Created Order," and "The Final Glory of God" (pp. 222-31). Together they emphasize the universality of Paul's vision for salvation.

mention of the "grace and *peace*" greeting in Revelation 1:4-5 to introduce Christian hope (p. 484). Oddly, *peace* is not in his extensive subject index, but it recurs as a dominant theme throughout, likely subconsciously since Lehman writes as a Mennonite in a time when *peace*-teaching was prominent in the catechism and preaching of the church.[10] The count for uses of *peace* is thirty-three,[11] with key texts such as Isaiah 52:7 repeatedly referenced! Texts and emphases that ground his discussion are: Matthew 5:9; Luke 19:42; James 3:18; a series of Pauline *peace* texts on justification and reconciliation; numerous ethical imperatives "to be at *peace*"; and texts that celebrate the *peace* of God ruling or pleading for unity in the bond of *peace*.

Lehman's contribution is peculiar since *peace* is nowhere separately emphasized, but the *topic permeates* his treatment. His distinctive work represents how one's ecclesial tradition shapes the tenor of one's theological contribution. Emphasis on love of enemy (p. 167) and nonretaliation is also present, but neither is noted in the Index!

J. Christiaan Beker, *Paul the Apostle: The Triumph of God in Life and Thought*   For Beker *peace* is intertwined deeply with apocalyptic hope, and *peace* is a fundamental element of salvation. His treatment, unlike the two above, is limited to Paul, and in this respect departs from the grid used for this analysis. But his work, like Dunn's, is an extensive NT theological contribution. As with Lehman, Isa. 52:7 plays a key role in Beker's setting of the stage for *peace* emphases, but Beker's *peace* accent is much more intertwined with an eschatological perspective, i.e., *peace* is realized only partially in the present, with fullness awaiting future consummation. His treatment of *peace* is largely in the context of Romans, especially ch. 5 (pp. 257-58) and ch. 8 (p. 279). He holds that Paul's theology ever points forward to the goal of shalom wherein God's righteousness, inaugurated by Christ, is fully consummated. He stops short of identifying the two, even when discussing Colossians 1:19-20, which leaves a gap between the Christ event realized and that yet to be fulfilled in God's future cosmic reign (p. 359). Since for Beker, Ephesians is post-Pauline, the grand *peace* emphasis of that book does not show in his treatment, an unfortunate omission for purposes of this analysis.

---

10. Though published in 1974, his constructive thought on NT theology was formed from 1940 to the mid-1960s. I include this "biblical theology" because it is devoted to the NT. The term "biblical" does not mean that his work should be considered part of the biblical theology emphasis connected to Wright, Bright, Anderson, Minear, Childs, Ollenburger, and Martens. It follows a more systematic format with close attention to the biblical text, a type of Bible doctrine approach.

11. According to researcher Reuben Glick Shank.

Virginia Wiles, *Making Sense of Paul: A Basic Introduction to Pauline Theology*   Perhaps Wiles should stand first in this list, or even be put in a separate category, since it does what no other volume does. Though limited to Paul, Wiles's treatment provides a model of how NT Theology and Ethics might be done with *peace, shalom, reconciliation* integrating and shaping the entire contribution.

Chapter 2 begins with a subsection titled "*Peace on Earth*," with the first two paragraphs defining and explicating *peace* and shalom. To sample: "God's goal for the cosmos is shalom — *peace*. . . . Shalom is order; it is right-relatedness; it is wholeness. Shalom is the integrity of the whole — of the whole created cosmos, of everything that is" (pp. 24-25). In introducing Paul's major emphasis on "righteousness" one of Wiles's three definitions is: "God's righteousness is God's shalom-making activity" (p. 25). On the same topic, later she says, "Christ, in Paul's view, is the revelation of the gracious righteousness of God that will bring shalom to the entire cosmos" (p. 92). In discussing Paul on law, again *peace/shalom* is important: "If obeying the law is the way to attain this joy and this shalom, and if obeying the law is itself the experience of this joy and shalom, then obedience to the law is joy and *peace*" (p. 37). This cosmic vision of Paul's theological contribution is evident throughout. In discussing "Faith and Hope: 'Jesus Christ Is Lord,'" she says of this confession, "God has created the universe and intends to weave the whole of reality into an unbroken fabric of *peace*" (p. 128). In discussing Romans 5:1-5, her treatment of "*peace* with God" and "hope that does not disappoint" is related once again to Paul's anticipation that God intends "shalom for the whole of creation" so that personal experience of *peace* with God is viewed in the context of the wider messianic vision. The same occurs in her discussion of Romans 8:6: "To set our mind on the Spirit is to accept our status as creatures of this Creator. Herein . . . lies the key to life and *peace*" (p. 140). Finally her Glossary not only includes *shalom,* but shalom occurs in definitions for other terms: law, righteousness, slavery (pp. 153-54).

Her extensive treatment of Paul on *reconciliation* is at times intertwined with *peace/shalom* (pp. 109-11, 153), which is as it should be in Paul. The title "A Reconciliation" heads her discussion of "Spirit and Community: 'One Body in Christ'" (ch. 9; p. 110). Here she cites Eph. 2:13-18 (p. 111),[12] which unites *peace* and *reconciliation* textually. Wiles rightly emphasizes, that this reconciliation of Jews and Gentiles was a central emphasis in Paul's theology.

Clearly, this volume, though written at a basic level to introduce stu-

---

12. Wiles regards Ephesians as coming from the pen of an "early student of Paul's" (p. 110).

dents to Paul, stands alone among all the volumes I analyzed in that the crucial terms of this study *shape* Paul's theology. Unfortunately she does not include discussion of Paul's "*Peace* of God" appellation, a point that would further enrich her work.

Works on New Testament Ethics

Richard B. Hays, *The Moral Vision of the New Testament*   Hays's *Moral Vision* is a classic for its penetrating, succinct exegesis of selected NT writings; his hermeneutical model — especially the three focal images of community, cross, and new creation; and his perceptive treatment of five major voices in theological ethics, in the context of which he proposes his own set of normative proposals. But even more, his five thematic test cases take up the pragmatic task, and thus chart a path for ethical thinking on contemporary thorny issues.

Hays puts "renunciation of violence" *first* among the ethical issues "at the heart of Christian discipleship as spotlighted by the New Testament" (p. 313). Further, he says, "With regard to the issue of *violence,* the New Testament bears a powerful witness that is both univocal and pervasive, for it is integrally related to the heart of the kerygma and to God's fundamental elective purpose" (p. 314). Hence, the priority put on the issue of *violence* and *nonviolence* in Hays's work is clear — *peace* is sparse, however. This concern figures prominently into his entire Part III, "The Hermeneutical Task," and is implicit in his "Diagnostic Checklist" when he poses the "fruits test: How is the vision embodied in a living community? Does the community manifest the fruit of the Spirit?" (p. 213). *Peacemaking* is also implicit in his three focal images, for he describes "Community" as "a countercultural community of discipleship." His description of the "Cross" image contains many *peace-related* emphases, such as "self-giving love . . . correspondence to Jesus' example . . . the *imitatio Christi* as the way of obedience" (p. 197). These concerns permeate his analysis of the ethical methodologies of his five selected theologians/NT scholars (pp. 215-82).

Peace is slighted, however, in his "Part One" that treats major portions of the NT canon (perhaps because he saves it for his later discussions). Hays recognizes the importance, even primacy of *peace* and nonviolence in his treatment of Reinhold Niebuhr, Karl Barth, John Howard Yoder, Stanley Hauerwas, and Elisabeth Schüssler Fiorenza. In light of Hays's clarity about the priority of nonviolence and *peace* in "Part III" and his incisive comments against violence and promotion of *peace*making in chapter 14 ("Violence in

Defense of Justice") and again in his "Living the Text" section in chapter 17 ("Anti-Judaism and Ethnic Conflict"), it is surprising that *peace/peacemaking* and *reconciliation* receive only sparse comment in his "Descriptive" exegetical "Part One." Most of these comments occur in the sections on "Paul" and the "Developments of the Pauline Tradition" (which he treats before the Gospels). In Paul, verses citing *peace* are merely mentioned[13] while *reconciliation* is more theologically and socially developed.[14] But even for Paul the prominent *peacemaking* emphases of the biblical text are underdeveloped.

Hays's only reference to Paul's use of "the God of *peace*" benediction (1 Thess. 5:23) occurs in his discussion of the parousia and final judgment (p. 22); nothing is said of the significance of the title as such. In the context of discussing Paul's apostolic vocation in 2 Corinthians and also Paul's grounding his "bold claims . . . in his apocalyptic worldview," Hays describes Paul as "'an ambassador of Christ' (5:20) announcing a new order, announcing the apocalyptic message of the reconciliation of the world to God" (pp. 23-24). He notes also Paul's bold assertion that "the church is to *become* the righteousness of God: where the church embodies in its life together the world-reconciling love of Jesus Christ, the new creation is manifest. The church incarnates the righteousness of God" (p. 24).

Later, in discussing how Paul's eschatology shapes ecclesial ethics Hays addresses the type of weapons believers use in the battle "of God's new creation in an unwilling and hostile world": the church engages in cosmic conflict, but "not with weapons of violence — but with proclamation of the truth (cf. 2 Cor. 10:3-6)" (p. 26). The warfare of believers is fought not with weapons of violence (p. 65). In his discussion of the primacy of the cross in Paul, "a paradigm for the life of faith," he observes that Paul's salutation of *peace* links directly to "the Lord Jesus Christ, who gave himself for our sins to set us free from the present evil age . . ." (Gal. 1:3-4). But neither here nor elsewhere in his treatment of Paul is *peace* as such discussed. Briefly he focuses on *reconciliation:* "God is at work through the Spirit to create communities that prefigure and embody the reconciliation and healing of the world" (p. 32). Here Hays stresses the gospel's power to overcome social barriers between Jews and Gentiles. Later, in explicating Paul's moral logic for the life of the church, especially in the use of the gifts of the Spirit, Hays sums up his point: "Where God's Spirit is at work, Paul contends, the result will be *peace* and holiness, not moral anarchy" (p. 37).

In his treatment of the developing Pauline tradition (Ephesians), Hays

13. Hays, *Moral Vision*, pp. 22, 27, 37, 65, 67.
14. Hays, *Moral Vision*, pp. 24, 32, 63.

is more explicit on *peace* and reconciliation: "In the Church God has 'broken down the dividing wall' between Jews and Gentiles" (Eph. 2:14-16; p. 63). On the armor of God's weapons against the assaults of the evil one, the third piece is: "Shoes: the gospel of *peace!*" (6:10-20; p. 65). Hays notes also that 1 Timothy values "'a quiet and *peace*able life' for the community . . ." (1 Tim. 2:1-2); believers are to pray for *peace* to spread the gospel (p. 67).

Hays's treatments of Mark, Matthew, Luke-Acts, and John are incisive, and often pick up on cognate emphases of *peace*making, such as the servant way of the cross in Mark or the Jubilee vision of Luke-Acts, but direct discussion of *peace* is lacking. In discussing Matthew's Beatitudes, however, he includes "those who make *peace*" in a list of Jesus' blessings (p. 97). That Jesus' way stands against use of violence is clear throughout, and explicitly mentioned (p. 98).[15] Under the heading, "Communal Ethic of Perfection," Hays speaks of the Beatitudes that "pronounce Jesus' blessing upon . . . those who make *peace*" (p. 97). In two places he speaks of Jesus going beyond the Law in commanding love of enemies (pp. 96, 98). While he excels in discussing "the Hermeneutic of Mercy" and "Community of Discipline and Forgiveness," he does not connect these to the *peace*making theme. He cites key Lukan *peace* texts, but makes no attempt to show how *peace* is foundational to Luke's overall moral contribution.[16]

Hays addresses *peace, peacemaking,* and *reconciliation* head-on in "Part Four." Chapter 14 is a classic defense against use of violence in the cause of justice, and he makes a persuasive case for *peace/peacemaking* as the Christian means to justice and *peace*.[17] Here he focuses the question: "is it ever God's will for Christians to employ violence in defense of justice?" (p. 317). After a moving, lengthy quotation from Father George Zabelka, chaplain for the Hiroshima and Nagasaki bomb squadrons, Hays evokes Luke's account of Jesus weeping over Jerusalem: if only you would know "the things that make for *peace*" but they were hidden from your eyes (p. 319). Hays then takes up sustained comment on Matt. 5:38-48, in which *peacemaking and nonviolent enemy-love* are core emphases (pp. 319-29), even if *peace*making is mentioned

15. It is possible that I have missed some references to "peace" in this section. For future printings of the volume, I recommend that the results of a computer search for "peace" be added to the Topic Index.

16. See Swartley, "Politics and Peace *(Eirēnē)* in Luke's Gospel."

17. Hays's inclusion and discussion of the hermeneutical strategies of Reinhold Niebuhr, Karl Barth, John H. Yoder, and Stanley Hauerwas exemplify and enrich his overall contribution to understanding the gospel in the service of peace (pp. 215-66). Note especially his critical engagement with his Duke colleague Hauerwas (p. 259) from which we learn the distinctive strengths of both Hauerwas's and Hays's approaches.

only a few times. In his second section (Synthesis) of chapter 14, Hays shows similar teaching elsewhere in the NT, asserting that "the death of Christ is interpreted (by Paul) as God's *peace* initiative" (p. 330), quoting Rom. 5:8-10 in support.

Hays considers Luke's enigmatic text, "The one who has no sword must sell his cloak and buy one" (22:36b), and rightly concurs with I. Howard Marshall that this word is "grimly ironic," expressing metaphorically the intensity of opposition the disciples are about to face. It does not condone use of violence, as later verses make clear. The next verse (22:37) explicitly gives the reason for this saying: to fulfill Scripture, citing "And he was counted with the lawless" (Isa. 53:12). When Peter later uses a sword to cut off the high priest's servant's ear, defending Jesus, Jesus' response is clear and definitive: "No more of this!" (Luke 22:49-51). Further, Jesus' healing the ear clearly indicates that Jesus will have nothing to do with violent self-defense (p. 333).[18] Hays cites Hebrews, 1 Peter, and Revelation as bearing similar testimony, accentuating the believers' call to faithful suffering, rather than violently resisting or accommodating to the evil power's demands (pp. 331-32). Hays says clearly, toward the end, "that the reasons for choosing Jesus' way of *peace*making are not prudential . . . our reasons for choosing nonviolence are shaped by the New Testament witness, we act in simple obedience to the God who willed that his own Son should give himself up to death on a cross" (p. 343). The Chapter concludes with a short section, "Living the Text: The Church as Community of *Peace.*" Hays makes his point eloquently: "One reason that the world finds the New Testament's message of *peace*making and love of enemies incredible is that the church is so massively faithless. . . . Only when the church renounces the way of violence, will people see what the Gospel means. . . . The meaning of the New Testament's teaching on violence will become evident only in communities of Jesus' followers who embody the costly way of *peace*" (pp. 343-44).

In his concluding chapter 17 on Anti-Judaism, Hays returns to the *peacemaking* theme, quoting Ephesians 2:14-19 (with its four occurrences of *peace*) to accentuate that Jews and Gentiles are brought into one body, to be one new humanity in their life together, and to "'maintain the unity of the Spirit in the bond of peace'" (4:3). He rightly says, "the New Testament makes a compelling case for the church to live as a community that transcends racial and ethnic differences," whether in the United States or South Africa. He ap-

---

18. Hays comments also on other texts often used to support violence: Jesus' cleansing of the temple and soldiers in the NT. He rightly argues that neither provides normative moral guidance that would support use of violence (pp. 334-36).

peals finally to Col. 1:20: "to reconcile to himself all things . . . by making *peace* through the blood of his cross." This fulfills Isaiah's vision of God's people becoming "a light to the nations, that my salvation may reach to the end of the earth" (49:6) (pp. 440-41).

Hays regards Rom. 12:14, 16a, 17-21 as Paul's *key exhortation on peace making and love of enemy.* Acknowledging the role of governing authorities who "bear the sword to execute God's wrath (13:4)," Hays, however, asserts succinctly and categorically, "Those who are members of the one body in Christ (12:5) are never to take vengeance (12:19); they are to bless their persecutors and minister to their enemies, returning good for evil. There is not a syllable in the Pauline letters that can be cited in support of Christians employing violence" (p. 331).

Wolfgang Schrage, *The Ethics of the New Testament*   Among his many incisive comments on methodology in NT Ethics, Schrage cautions against succumbing to conventional wisdom and popular ideological pressures. After quoting Karl Barth on the same point, he says, "The conflicts over the *peace* movement today make the Sermon on the Mount topical for many, especially in its apparently irrational, utopian, and rigoristic injunctions that often seem out of place in the real world" (p. 9). Throughout his work, Schrage resists fudging the ethical challenge of Jesus' teachings. He acknowledges that their radical nature also creates division, not simply a pleasant *peace*: "Anyone who infringes on family obligations and property rights (cf. Matt. 8:22) does not in fact bring '*peace*' for the existing order but 'a sword' " (Matt. 10:34-35)" (p. 88).

In discussing Jesus' "Concrete Precepts" Schrage holds that Jesus' eschatological ethics radically challenged "the institutions and structures of the world," which are "provisional" in relation to the kingdom demand, whether that be his teaching on divorce and remarriage, possessions, or the state and use of violence (pp. 87-115). On "The State and Violence" Schrage says Jesus was not a Zealot. Commenting on Mark 9:35; 10:42-45, Schrage appeals to Jesus' teaching to refuse the existing models of social power and authority. Rather, Jesus' followers are "to renounce domination in a community of equals engaged in love and service (cf. also Matt. 23:8-9)." This teaching is "the expected eschatological reversal of the secular order into present conduct" (pp. 111-12).

That Jesus' political stance contrasts to Jewish resistance revolts is clear in the seventh Beatitude:

> . . . *peacemakers* are called blessed (Matt. 5:9). The "*peace*" referred to is of course not "*peace of mind*" but, as in passages like Rom. 12:18, *peace between individuals.* The dynamism and power of *God's peace* that comes

with the kingdom, which the disciples hand on as '*messengers of peace*' (Luke 10:5, 16), seek to be incarnate on earth in the *peacemaking* of the disciples. They do not utter threats. With mercy, *not violence*, they will attempt to take the battle line and trenches of this world and to surmount the walls of hostility, enmity, and distrust. That *peacemaking* cannot be limited to the private sphere is shown by the final macarism of the persecuted in Matthew (5:10-11). (p. 112)

On the "Tax Dispute," Schrage describes the divinity symbols of the emperor on both sides of the denarius, with the obverse depicting the emperor with the inscription "Emperor Tiberius, venerated son of the venerated God" and the laurel wreath symbolizing his divinity. The reverse, with inscription, "High Priest," depicted the emperor's "mother seated on a divine throne as the earthly incarnation of the heavenly *peace*" (p. 113). For Schrage, God and state do not have equal claims; rather, Jesus' teaching and practice, more than Paul's, downgraded the authority of the state, especially the claims of the emperor (pp. 113-14). Jesus' call to discipleship envisions new values and a new order. He says "there is no reason to doubt that Jesus, too, gave his disciples a share in his ministry and authority and sent them out as messengers and agents of *peace* (cf. Luke 10:5)" (p. 52).

Paul's commitment to *peace* continues some of Jesus' emphases, but also reflects a different Sitz im Leben in which the life of congregational communities is addressed. "The fruits of the Spirit listed in Galatians 5 are equally binding on all: love, joy, *peace*, patience, kindness, etc." (p. 180). In Philippians 4:5-7, Paul declares "the Lord is at hand (v. 5), inculcates the law of love (v. 5), and promises the *peace* of God (v. 7)" (p. 200). Christian love "not only changes hearts but also, by changing hearts, changes actions — not just 'in the Lord,' as in the case of common meals, the kiss of *peace*," expressive of community solidarity, but also "in the outward circumstances of earthly life" (pp. 214-15). At the same time, "Paul is well aware that the world as a whole is not too happy with the ultimate sovereignty of God, and Christians can live *peace*ably only so far as it depends upon them (Rom. 12:18). But this by no means vitiates the call to bear the reality of Christ into the domain of the world" (p. 204).

Paul's *peace* theology comes into sharp focus in calling believers of diverse ethnic and religious backgrounds into a common new life under Jesus' saving Lordship. In discussing Ephesians and Colossians, Schrage affirms,

Solidarity between Jewish and gentile Christians is especially important to the author. He uses it, for example, to historicize the traditional cosmic language of the *hymn to peace* in Eph. 2:14ff. The *pacification and reconcili-*

ation of the universe are documented on earth in the bringing together of Jews and Gentiles in one church. *Reconciliation* of the divine realm with the earthly realm also means *reconciliation* in the human realm. Salvation does not simply establish privately and inwardly the right relationship between the individual and God; it *brings peace to a broken world.*" (p. 251)

Schrage also comments on *peace* emphases in Hebrews and Revelation, noting that in Hebrews the command to "strive for *peace* with all (12:14) is probably limited to members of the Christian community . . ." (p. 327). Revelation, he holds, calls believers to acknowledge "that the sovereignty of Jesus begins here and now with the freedom of those who spurn the mark of the beast under the aegis of a *pax Romana* and bear witness that he who makes all things new is on the march" (p. 332). In the face of persecution, Revelation calls "for nonviolent, passive resistance . . . only the sword that issues from the mouth of the Word can conquer the enemy" (p. 346). Perhaps too, the Revelator sets forth a contrast model to the disaster of the Jewish War, offering this "pacifistic" response instead (p. 347).

While *peace/peacemaking* and reconciliation are never addressed discretely as topics, Schrage clearly values this emphasis in his treatment of NT Ethics.

Allen Verhey, *The Great Reversal*   In two separate volumes Verhey clearly identifies *peace*making as essential to his discussion of NT Ethics. His second (2002) volume has a broader focus than NT Ethics, but it is instructive on how current ethical issues are to be addressed in light of NT Ethics.

In *Great Reversal* Verhey identifies early on his view of Jesus as neither zealot nor escapist. This is clear in his comments on Jesus' temple entry, which he connects with Zech. 9:10 and its proclamation of "*peace* to the nations." His entry on a donkey signals humble, not Zealot, character, but his actions in the temple show that his approach is not "the pacifist prohibition of political power and coercion" but a "great reversal" to usual methods of political power (p. 31). "There is no political program in Jesus' teachings but there is a political posture, a posture that seeks God's intentions for political power. Such a posture seeks *peace* and judges the Zealot desire for revenge; it seeks justice and judges the Sadducean collaboration in exploitation and extortion" (p. 32).

In discussing Jesus' teaching on nonretaliation, Verhey points out that a positive counterpart occurs as well, especially as this is cited in NT writings more broadly: e.g., the injunction "to bless" or "seek to do good." With the prohibition not to return evil for evil, parallel positive short commands occur, often as participial imperatives: "'be at *peace*' (Gk. *eirēneuete,* I Thess.

5:13; Rom. 12:18 uses the participle; I Pet. 3:8 substitutes Gk. *homophrones;* I Pet. 3:11 cites Psalm 34:15; I Thess. calls for *peace* 'among yourselves'; Romans, for *peace* 'with all')" (p. 66). Later Verhey asserts that the Beatitudes "conform to the eschatological way of God" and are the central "character traits" for Christians. He explicitly highlights the blessing of "the *peacemak-ers*" (cf. Ps. 34:14) (p. 86; cf. also his comment on the seventh Beatitude on p. 42). Indeed, "The Christian community's 'surpassing righteousness' will be disposed toward reconciliation, not anger; toward purity, not lust; toward faithfulness, not divorce; toward truthfulness, not deceit; *toward peace, not re-venge*; toward uncalculating love, not reciprocity" (p. 87).

In treating Paul's contribution, Verhey appeals to Paul's handling of Onesimus with Philemon to make the point that Paul "does not separate the unity, equality, *peace* 'in the Lord' from the 'real world' of Philemon and Onesimus. The unity is eschatological, but is not docetic; it must have some 'fleshly' expression" (p. 115). Similarly, in dealing with divorce, "Paul advises the believer not to initiate divorce; but if the unbeliever initiates the divorce, his advice is to permit it, 'for God has called us to *peace*' (I Cor. 7:15)" (p. 118).

Verhey's fullest treatment of Paul's *peace* ethic occurs in his discussion of Ephesians, in the unity and new world creation of Jew and Greek becoming one new *peace* body in Christ. He begins his eloquent, perceptive paragraph acknowledging that "The principle developed in response to the crisis of war is '*peace*.' While the *pax Romana* crumbles, the author announces the good news and the requirements of the *pax Dei*." This includes God's creating "one new humanity . . . so making *peace*," exhorting believers to "maintain the unity of the Spirit in the bond of *peace*," making "the gospel of *peace*" an important part of the armor of God, where we might expect to find love. He ends the epistle with a subtle exhortation, joining "'*peace*' . . . with 'love' as the blessing of God (6:23)" (p. 125). Further, he regards the newness of roles in the Haustafeln as analogous to the newness of the one new humanity: "The Haustafeln of Ephesians stands as far from the conventional understanding of roles as the *peace of God* stands from the conventional hostility between Jew and Gentile" (p. 126).

Verhey, *Remembering Jesus*   In this volume Verhey is a step removed from his earlier closer treatment of the NT text (though he does refer to Jesus' entry into Jerusalem, with comments similar to those in *Great Reversal*). His discussion of *peace/peace*making arises in the context of addressing the current ethical use of violence in the cause of *peace*. His comments contain paradox, often a yes and a no. Jesus "consistently rejected violence as a messianic strategy. . . . He sought *peace*." But "*pacifism* is not the new *halakah*. Nevertheless, *peace, shalom*, is the new *haggadah*, the new story" (p. 415).

Christians will look for political alternatives to violence, alternatives that protect both justice and the neighbors while keeping the *peace*. They will be *peacemakers*, hungering and thirsting for justice; they will be justice-makers, hungering and thirsting for *shalom*. . . . They will not, however, reduce God's good future and the *shalom* it promises to the absence of hostilities. They will hope for — and already respond to — a future in which *justice and peace* "will kiss each other." (p. 416)

But on the same page, "Those who would follow Jesus need not, I think, require the absolute forswearing of force or coercion or even violence in the defense of *justice and peace*." Further, violence "is not God's cause. But sometimes, in this sad world, violence is necessary to *protect peace and justice*" (p. 417).

Not forgetting his earlier work, Verhey sprinkles his ongoing comments on Christians within the political order with pithy points from NT ethical perspectives:

"We remember Jesus and we know that *God's cause is peace . . .*" (p. 344).

"*Peaceful* coexistence with the established authorities was never an option for Jesus" (p. 422).

". . . bless the *peacemakers*, for in the *peace* they make there is a token of the *shalom* God promises" (p. 426).

He appeals to Matthew's binding and loosing, and discipleship, for a

"*politics of reconciliation and forgiveness*" (p. 429).

On Paul, more memorable one-liners occur:

"A *new international order of peace* [is] . . . fulfilled through the Gentile mission" (p. 433).

"Discipleship required a *politics of peaceable difference*" (p. 435).

In discussing Luke-Acts, Verhey notes Peter's summary of Jesus' mission as "preaching *peace*" (which also interprets the Peter-Cornelius story, focusing on welcoming Gentiles and the unity of former enemies). He speaks of this two-volume work as

"A Politics in Memory of a Universal Savior: Mutual Respect of Jew and Gentile" (p. 436).

Finally,

"Love for enemies is not inconsistent with a concern for maintaining justice and stability in the land" (p. 444).

Quite significantly, Verhey's two volumes appear at points to march to different drummers. While the first might lead one to regard NT teachings on *peace* and reconciliation normative for practices within the church and for believers in the world, the second reflects a Niebuhrian temperament, the need to adjust, even accommodate NT *peace* ethics to the constraints of life in a fallen, violent world (as though Jesus' and Paul's world were somehow different from ours!).[19]

19. On what appears as "double-speak" in this section of Verhey, student researcher Reuben Glick Shank comments:

> Verhey as a Reformed theologian-ethicist-biblical scholar betrays the weakness of a "narrative" approach. He strongly uncovers the motifs of peace and love for enemies precisely because of this narrative approach, but then as he deals with "managing," "government," this "sad world," and "ambiguities" he transparently presents the assumptions, worldview, and framework of a more classic Reformed and Lutheran system of thought (or perhaps most clearly Niebuhrian). In his entire treatment of theocracy (which grounds his thesis), he does not treat in any depth questions of the nature of "power" or even "God's power" or Jesus' power (and what that means for a "*theo*-cracy"!). Nor does he try to see critically and biblically in Jesus' way and word what the relations are between justice, peace, love, and power because these require a more systematic and "philosophical" approach to the powerful evidence for peace and justice that he presents narratively.
>
> Thus Verhey can say things that may appear entirely contradictory or completely ambiguous such as "hope for peace and justice" with a church politics of "discourse, deliberation, and discernment in memory of Jesus" and a politics of friendship, peaceable difference, reconciliation, forgiveness (opposed to a politics of coercion and oppression) while simultaneously broadly calling for "supporting, respecting, submitting, and participating in government" but only insofar as government is involved in justice for the weak, for the neighbor, and is not self-interested (all of which are vague and slippery political concepts). But since few (if any) governments of current nation-states exist unambiguously as such, then what? Or is he implying that one may participate in government as long as one remains within the arena of the "social services," but not in the realms of taxation, the military, and the presidency? Indeed, how do you discern how to participate when no institution (not even the church) is any more sin-free than any individual (indeed all our dominant governments and many of our institutions so far in Western history have *ultimately* been grounded in coercion and oppression, including the democratic nation-state)?
>
> Then again Verhey does not define government or church or their relationship — the Christian-world relation — in any real depth. Is this a result of not examining more closely the interpretation of power in the biblical texts? And what of the "powers and principalities" — how do they fit in his theocratic vision? Thus in the final analysis it appears that he says no more than: we should on the one hand seek to follow Jesus and be peaceful and on the other hand support the government, which will

Wiebe, *Messianic Ethics*   Wiebe's book of about 200 pages represents among all the ethics books a laudable concentration of the NT's *peace* and *reconciliation* ethic, but it is limited to the Jesus section of the NT canon.[20] He roots his Jesus and the kingdom focus by citing key OT texts: Isa. 9:6-7, "*Prince of Peace*. . . . Of his reign and of his *peace* there will be no end"; Isa. 11:1-10, "the establishment of *peace* in the earth"; Ezek. 37:24-28, to "live in his everlasting covenant of *peace*"; Zech. 9:9-10, "he shall command *peace* to the nations" (pp. 65-66; emphasis mine). These citations define Jesus' vision for his Messiahship. This messianic "*Prince of Peace*" vision included a universal horizon: "Moreover, in Yahweh's judgment upon Israel, there was a decisive universalizing of God's action; and this was true also for the *new order of peace* and righteousness anticipated from the Messiah. . . . Ultimately, it is not a question of the victory of one people over others, but the *peace* of all within the victory and blessing of God" (p. 67).

Looking briefly at Qumran's *peace* vision (1QS 4.7-9) that includes "healing, great *peace* in a long life, and fruitfulness, together with every everlasting blessing and eternal joy in life without end" as well as their dualistic view of future hope that consigns those in darkness and deceit to "everlasting damnation" (p. 77), Wiebe holds that the NT is universal in its vision for *peace*; quoting Moltmann, "God is revealed where 'his blessing, *peace*, and righteousness are fulfilled by him'" (p. 83). He cites also from 4 Ezra, that as in Isa. 2:1-5 a new Torah "would bring the nations to participate in the eschatological *peace* of God (cf. Isa. 2:1-5)" (p. 88).

Jesus' ministry is shaped by fulfilling Isa. 52:7-9 in which both "the *peace* and restoration of Israel" and the inclusion of the nations are reflected in Jesus' ministry (p. 103). The seventh Beatitude calls the Jesus follower to align oneself with "*peacemakers*" (p. 109). Matthew's "mercy paradigm . . .

---

occasionally have to use violence for justice. In short, the status quo is preserved alongside a discerning voice for a future peace and justice. His call for communal discernment in memory of Jesus is his strongest point, but in the end, in regard to peace and justice, which he does claim to be foundational to Jesus, he seems to be doing even less than J. H. Yoder's "prophetic witness" with its clearer church–government distinction (though he believes he is actually doing more), because other than a vacuous "justice" he gives no real critical Christian criteria for "managing" or participating in government, thus undermining his Christ-centered peace and justice and dualistically separating his politics of peace from his politics of justice. This of course is consonant with his dualistic *halakah/haggadah* divide.

20. In this respect, it is a good companion volume to Virginia Wiles's *Making Sense of Paul*. Both writers come from "historic peace church" backgrounds. And both volumes are written on a level accessible to university students and church lay leaders.

calls for love of enemies and for blessing on the *peacemakers*" (p. 109). Wiebe explicates this in the context of discussing "The community and the ethic of love," as well as the double love command. He addresses the contrary-sounding text, "not *peace* but a sword," which is to be understood in the context of Jesus' "Messiahship and the ethics of discipleship with its rigorous demands connected with following Jesus ('sword' thus describes the opposition and division that discipleship generates). Jesus' way is not a way of nationalistic power and authority, but the way of the cross, a powerful message that will be divisive and cause tension and suffering for disciples as well" (p. 152).

Wiebe does not treat the entire New Testament, but makes a strong case for the centrality of *peace* and *peace*making *essential* to Jesus' kingdom mission and message.

Contributions in Which Peace Occurs in Limited Theological or Ethical Roles

Rudolf Bultmann, *Theology of the New Testament,* Volume 1   Peace and reconciliation figure prominently in Bultmann, but not with social, political significance. Hence his work comes here rightly first in this second category. His uses of *peace* are mostly in cited texts, such as "God's '*peace*' exceeds all understanding" (Phil. 4:7) and "The *peace* of God . . . will keep your *hearts* and your *minds*" (Phil. 4:7) (pp. 211, 213). In Part II, ch. 4, in discussing man prior to faith under the topic "Mind and Conscience," *peace* (of God) is accidental to the topic: *nous* is mind/conscience and is understood in a strictly spiritualized, somewhat "contemplative" sense. Citation of *peace* texts continues: Rom. 14:19 (p. 226); Rom. 5:1 trans.: "Rightwised therefore by faith we have *peace* with God" (p. 274); and later, "we have *peace* with God = we are reconciled" and "'reconciliation' is a consequence of 'righteousness'" (p. 286). "God's 'reconciling' is His restoration of *peace* by no longer letting His 'wrath' . . . prevail" (p. 287). "Combined with '*peace*' (= salvation) in the greetings at the beginning or end of the epistles, 'grace' is that which God does and confers for salvation" (p. 291). He cites also the blessing, "the God of love and *peace* . . . be with you all" (2 Cor. 13:11; p. 292).

In Part II, ch. 5, "Man Under Faith," in a section on "The Righteousness of God," *peace* is seen in terms of the God-man salvific, spiritual relation as God restores *peace* through grace (pp. 281-85).[21] He quotes Rom. 14:17 and

---

21. "Enemies" are those who are enemies of the gospel or the cross of Christ (pp. 286-87).

"'*peace* here means 'salvation' in the eschatological sense, as Rom. 2:10; 8:6 (joined with 'life'!) indicate, or the wish at Phil. 4:7 or the formula 'the God of peace' (Rom. 15:33; 16:20; Phil. 4:9; I Thess. 5:23)" (p. 339).

Bultmann accentuates "God reconciled the 'world' to Himself . . . not counting their [the world's!] trespasses against them" (2 Cor. 5:19) and the "reconciliation of the world" (Rom. 11:15) (p. 255). For Bultmann reconciliation=righteousness: "All man can do is to 'receive' the reconciliation (Rom. 5:11)" (p. 286) and afterwards "be reconciled to God" (p. 287). Reconciliation of God implies that "*before* any effort of man God made an end of enmity (Rom. 5:10)"; thus there is yet more radical dependence on the grace of God (p. 287). But again little is said of any dimension of "social or horizontal reconciliation," an opportune unique context where Paul is emphasizing "release from sinning, release from the power of sin" (p. 287). Bultmann connects reconciliation to Jesus' sacrifice/blood (p. 295) and holds that the call "Be reconciled to God!" is "the call for faith or the challenge to give up one's previous self-understanding" = "proclamation of salvation-occurrence" (p. 301). Earlier in discussing Colossians 1:20, Bultmann stresses the divide between God and Man in the context of the Gnostic myth of the alienated cosmos.[22] "God has appointed an end for the cosmic disorder which originated in the primeval fall and through him has 'reconciled all things' (i.e. the universe) to Himself." "The cosmic '*peace*' bestowed by the work of salvation is still more radically Christianized in Eph. 2:14ff., which interprets the 'dividing wall of hostility,' which according to the Gnostic myth divides the earthly from the heavenly world, as applying both to the enmity between Jew and Gentile (v. 14) and to the enmity between God and man (v. 16)" (p. 176).[23]

---

22. In a discussion of *kosmos* as referring to the human historical situation (not a cosmological term) and the "sphere of human relationships," Bultmann gives examples of places where *kosmos* can be understood as humans in the "*quintessence of earthly conditions of life and earthly possibilities*" (p. 254), but again his focus is primarily on (transcendent spiritual) reconciliation of the God-human condition. He goes on to say that *kosmos* often represents what is under judgment by God and implies a "power" that "grows up out of [humans]" "constituted by that which the individual does and upon which he bestows his care." Thus *kosmos* becomes a "super-self" that enslaves and has dominion, ambiguously both God's creation and the realm of spirit powers in conflict and struggle (pp. 255-57).

23. In the context of Gnostic motifs and influences on NT theology, a key point for Bultmann is the framing of salvation history in a cosmic pattern of the Redeemer-God active in history and the whole cosmos needing to pay homage to the exalted one and we humans entering fully in history (in flesh and spirit) into this "eschatological occurrence." This may be the most radical "peace" statement in his book, though it is not very developed and still dominantly related to the death and exaltation of the Lord Christ (not to the living Life of Jesus). Also, for example, there is Bultmann's highlighting of church-body unity as the "inner unity of believers with each other and with the Redeemer" (p. 178).

Bultmann has an important section on "ministry of reconciliation" (p. 302), which is the "message (lit. 'word,' KJV) of reconciliation." But though he goes on to speak of the "union of believers into one *soma* in Christ," he doesn't work out what that means concretely in a social sense (pp. 304-5).[24] Bultmann is clear (as he reflects on Gal. 3:28 and 1 Cor. 7:17-24) that "the negation of worldly differentiations does not mean a sociological program within this world; rather, it is an eschatological occurrence which takes place only within the eschatological Congregation" (p. 309). But then paradoxically he says that one's self-understanding and one's conduct must be determined by the cross and Christ as one's Lord (p. 312).[25]

Bultmann, *Theology of the New Testament*, Volume 2   In this volume emphasis on eschatological existence continues: "Two characteristics of eschatological existence are 'peace' (εἰρήνη) and 'joy' (χαρά), terms familiar from tradition as descriptions of eschatological salvation (cf. Rom 14:17, etc.). *Eirene* is 'well-being' in the full sense of the Semitic word שלם (*shalom*) . . . '*peace*' is an eschatological possibility lying beyond all possibilities that are of this world" (pp. 82-83). Here *peace* appears as an eschatological and "*extra nos*" gift of faith ("seized as a reality by faith alone") not to be realized in this world where "trouble" is what believers will find.[26] Bultmann stresses "Christ's work of cosmic reconciliation" both between God and humans and within the *sōma* (organism) of which Christ is the head. This reconciliation is clear in Jews-Gentiles as one body (Eph. 2:11-22) (pp. 150-51). But in his chap-

---

24. His incarnational and imitation language still focuses more on the proclaimer-listener salvation-event through preaching *(kerygma)* than on the "salvation-process" of reconciliation with God and each other.

25. Reuben Glick Shank says at this point:

> I don't quite grasp any coherence to the relation between his eschatological and salvation-occurrence and daily living reflection. In the process of such a comprehensive biblical theology, while indeed he is presenting wonderful exegesis and contextual interpretation of texts (with fantastic nuggets to be found for sure), Bultmann, in his reconstructing of "believing self-understanding," is betraying biases of his dogmatic Lutheran tradition rather than presenting critical theological insights. While that may be no different from someone doing dogmatics reflecting his or her own background, the critical difference is that in systematics theological coherency is assumed and used as a critical self-evaluator. Of course the relationship between one's personal meta-narratives (or prime semantic lenses) and the details of the particular subjects one encounters is not a simple one. In Bultmann's exegesis his Lutheran dogmatic assumptions dominate his vision. This is most evident in his conclusions on Christian living.

26. The relation between Bultmann's Christian congregation and world-concept, together with his use of "Eschatological Congregation," is unclear.

ter on "Christology and Soteriology" (pp. 155-202) *peace* and reconciliation are totally absent. It is mostly a discussion of "between-ness," concluding with the importance of the proclaimed word of Christ (over against legalism and institutional sacramentalism).

In his chapter on "The Problem of Christian Living" (pp. 203-36) he again focuses on the between-ness and indicative-imperative question, noting the negative commands and lists of vices. On the positive side of sanctification, he mostly simply points toward general or philosophical or good bourgeois or family ethical standards with an occasional extra push toward asceticism. He does point out the high regard for the love command which he translates primarily into an attitude of brotherly fellowship in response to needs and troubles around one. He again clearly points out that Christians are not involved in some kind of economic or political program, dismissing the love-communism of Acts as an isolated instance; rather, more normative is the "collection" at worship services for charity (1 Cor. 16:1-4; p. 229). His relation to the state is pure Luther. He concludes with a critique of legalism vs. sin-grace-salvation, with no mention in the chapter on Christian living of reconciliation, *peacemaking*, or discipleship.[27]

G. B. Caird, *New Testament Theology*   Caird regards NT theology as a "historical discipline," "descriptive" in nature; further, "historical accuracy is the product of free discussion, honest criticism, and constant revision" (p. 4). Thus he invites a "conference table" approach (p. 18).

His *peace* emphases emerge in discussing Ephesians and "The Plan of Salvation": the vision that heaven and earth, i.e. the universe, "might be brought into a unity in Christ" (Eph. 1:9-10) (p. 40). Also, the barrier separating the Jew and Gentile having been broken down "provides the solid ground for confidence that God can in the end reconcile all the warring and divisive forces that comprise the human world (2:13-22)" (p. 41).

---

27. His final conclusion on Christian living for the Johannine corpus appears to contradict his earlier statements in volume 1 on "the unity of the eschatological and the ethical message of Jesus" and the "fulfillment of God's will [as] the condition for participation in the salvation of His Reign" (p. 20), as well as his claim that "these imperatives are clearly meant radically as absolute demand" (pp. 20-21). While he includes "peacemaking" (from the Sermon on the Mount) in the ultimate commandment of love, he regards this ultimate demand of love, i.e., the command of God, as an "eschatological ethic," not an ethic of "world-reform" because "it aims neither at the formation of 'character' nor at the molding of human society" (p. 19). The eschatological proclamation and the ethical demand simply bring the human "into his Now as the hour of decision for God" (p. 21). Thus for Bultmann Jesus' message appears to be limited to an eschatological and ethical critique of legalism alongside a cry of repentance in order for God to confront the human to create the crisis of self as sinner and thus discover dependence on God's grace.

Later, when speaking of end-time consummation, when the work of the antichrist is vanquished, he speaks of attaining a state of *peace*: "after the punishment and restoration of Israel, when through the redemptive activity of God the earth has attained a *state of peace*" (p. 113). In discussing Paul, he cites Romans 5:1 ("Now that we have been justified through faith, we are at *peace* with God through our Lord Jesus Christ . . .") to introduce his section on the "The Three Tenses of Salvation" (p. 118). "The Fact of Salvation" includes universal reconciliation, i.e., *making peace* (Col. 1:20). Human relationships are not mentioned here because Paul "*assumes* that those who are reconciled to God will be reconciled to one another." And "across every division of hatred, antagonism, distrust, and suspicion that separates human beings from one another, of which the division between Jew and Gentile in the early Church was the most pressing instance, he had 'made the two one'" (p. 157).

For believers, there is "a *peace* that surpasses comprehension," one sample of Paul's *hyper* (*sur*passing) normal expectation (p. 182). In discussing "The Imitation of Christ," to be viewed in the discipleship context of Mark 8:34, "Jesus is the leader of a national movement which, although itself *peaceful* and nonviolent, is certain to evoke violent resistance from those who see the national destiny in terms of security, prosperity, independence, and power" (p. 202).

The universal scope of God's salvation-purpose is clear in Colossians 1:16-20: "to reconcile all things by *making peace* through the blood of the cross." Here he addresses "The Redemption of the Powers," a point prominent in his earlier *Principalities and Powers* book,[28] but in this discussion he makes no explicit statement on *peace*, only on redemption of "heavenly powers" as part of the scope of cosmic salvation (p. 276).[29] He picks up this theme again when in discussing Jesus Christ's demolishing of the Jew-Gentile hostility (Eph. 2:14-16), he asserts "confidence in God's power to reduce all the warring forces of the universe to harmony" (p. 336).

Caird discusses "The Theology of Jesus" toward the end of his volume and holds that both C. H. Dodd's realized eschatology and the futurists who see "light and *peace*" only at the end are both wrong. Jesus' view includes present and future. In regard to *peace*, Jesus' word of judgment upon Jerusalem because it failed to recognize its day of visitation and "does not know those things that make for *peace*" (Luke 19:42) illustrates the present-future

28. Caird, *Principalities and Powers: A Study in Pauline Theology.*
29. Caird also asserts in this discussion that Paul toward the end of his life was more appreciative of the work of the governing authorities, as indicated by his statements in Rom. 13:1-7.

dimensions. Hence Jesus' message is that God's reversal of fortunes, in which God establishes his kingdom of *justice and peace*, is in process of fulfillment through Jesus' ministry. Hence in Jesus the prophetic vision of commanding *peace* to the nations is being fulfilled (Zech. 9:9-10; Matt. 21:5ff.; Luke 19:38) (p. 394). Further, Caird contends that "Jesus intends his teaching and his example to be rationally implemented, embedded in the ethos and in the institutions of the national life" (p. 416).

Robert J. Daly, *Christian Biblical Ethics*   As the subtitle, *From Biblical Revelation to Contemporary Christian Praxis: Method and Content,* indicates, this work seeks to assess the mandate of the NT moral teaching for contemporary praxis. While it could be judged that this book fits better in another category, like that of the Birch-Rasmussen volume,[30] its treatment of Scripture, and specifically in regard to the topic of this volume, *Covenant of Peace,* merits its inclusion here. Daly's work, which is a team effort in collaboration with James A. Fischer, Terence J. Keegan, and Anthony J. Tambasco as well as specific contributors L. John Topel and Frederick E. Schuele, seeks to speak a Roman Catholic voice on its subtitle topic. The most pertinent sections of the book are Chapters 1-3 of Part Two, on Luke's Sermon, Matthew's Sermon on the Mount, "The NT Love Command and Call to Nonviolence," respectively by Topel, Schuele, and Daly. Jesus' teachings on nonretaliation and love for enemies are clearly the focus of Schuele and Daly. Schuele contends rightly that the text itself should be the focal point, but we should be aware of assuming that the Bible is on our side or that what the text *means* is exactly what it *says.* He cites Grundmann's view favorably that the Sermon is "an eschatological-Christological proclamation of the will of God. That is, because it is proclaimed *now,* it has the power now to break through the demonic cycle of sin, revenge and isolation, by creating a new fellowship based on forgiveness, reconciliation, and *peace*" (p. 202). In summarizing findings sifted from other writers, he concludes that (1) "Christians *are bound* to live up to the practical demands. . . . They cannot dodge these demands. . . . (2) Christians are bound in principle by *all* the demands . . . taken to their practical conclusions. They cannot pick and choose. . . . (3) This . . . is possible because the Christian is living in a new age [i.e., the work of Jesus Christ] . . ." (pp. 206-7). He later formulates eight practical guidelines in which "literal" application is negated: he warns against legalism; weakness and failure should not lead to giving up; it is necessary to maintain relationship with Jesus as a disciple to do his will; we must recognize that some of the teachings are hyperbolic; we are to be aware that "different times make for different answers or emphases;" further, differ-

---

30. Birch and Rasmussen, *Bible and Ethics in the Christian Life.*

ent "calls are given to different individuals who share common discipleship" (this does not mean "two levels" of morality); and the NT witnesses are not identical in answers or approaches (pp. 208-09).

Daly's article continues by searching for faithful and mature response to Matthew 5:38-48 and Luke 6:27-36. His discussion considers the social world context of antiquity in which these commands might have been situated, drawing on the work of Luise Schottroff[31]: that of the "underdog" — no other response possible, the "renunciation of revenge by the powerful" as a way of keeping subordinates cooperative, or "the non-violent protest of the power-less" (pp. 215-16). But none of these situations fit the motivation of Jesus' commands. He notes that the same exhortations occur throughout the NT (Rom. 12:14; 1 Cor. 4:12-13; 1 Pet. 2:12, 23; 3:9, 16; 4:4, 14) and concludes with Schottroff that the motivation for such action cannot be explained by any of the social impulses above, but rather by the "desire of the powerless for the salvation of their enemies" (pp. 216-17; Schottroff, p. 24). This is an *active* and not a *passive nonresistance* so that when applied to politics it means not cooperating with evil. This is consistent with "the prohibition against resisting one who is evil" (p. 217). He believes too that the early Christians understood this to be the "relationship between non-violence and love": "It is an active, missionary, 'aggressive' love that makes sense of the whole picture." Further, this love command, even of enemies, logically fits with the command to "make disciples of all nations" (p. 218).

Other uses of *peace* occur in discussing 1 Corinthians 7 regarding separating from an unbelieving partner and living *peace*ably in any state (pp. 248-50). *Reconcilation* occurs when discussing 2 Corinthians 5:18-19 (p. 229). While *peace* shows in but a small slice of the book, discussion of non-retaliation and love of enemy, and what it means for Christian life, is substantial. The contribution would indeed be strengthened if the wider NT teaching on *peace* and *peacemaking* had been included as well.

Leonhard Goppelt, *Theology of the New Testament,* **Volume 1:** *The Ministry of Jesus in Its Theological Significance*   Throughout this volume the kingdom of God is central to Jesus' ministry. With this perspective dominant, it is surprising that *peace* and OT citations like Isaiah 52:7 are not picked up in his discussion. From Judaism's antecedents to salvation, Goppelt cites a pseudepigraphal text ". . . but with the righteous he will make *peace* . . ." from 1 Enoch 1:3-9 (p. 48). On the Beatitudes, Goppelt regards the last four (Matt. 5:7-10), like the first four, as effectual because of the blessing itself, not because of human accomplishment. Thus, Jesus' blessing the *peacemakers* "di-

---

31. Schottroff, "Non-Violence and the Love of One's Enemies."

rected one into an existence that was blessed, i.e., upon which even now was conferred life-fulfilling significance" (p. 125). But this is neither "Jewish righteousness" nor "Greek virtue." Rather, "those who become *peacemakers*" do so "because they desired God's will to have its way with them" (p. 126). The Beatitudes must be understood as the call to repentance and participation in the kingdom of God.[32]

Goppelt, *Theology of the New Testament*, Volume 2: *The Variety and Unity of the Apostolic Witness*   Set within the influences of apocalypticism and Pharisaism, Paul's gospel is Christologically focused, rather than on the kingdom of God. Promise and fulfillment provide the foundational motif for understanding the Christ-event. Hence Goppelt introduces the Christ hymn of Colossians 1:15-20 as a window into Paul's theology. Here Christ is the "Preexistent One as the Agent of Creation." Christ has an "enduring relationship to the cosmos." "For Greek thought that meant that he guaranteed the harmonious order; for biblical thought it meant that he upheld everything by giving shape and direction (Sir. 43:26, Heb. 1:3)." His work in redemption is "to reconcile *all things* to himself by making *peace* by the blood of his cross" (p. 77). Reconciliation means not only "*peace* of the soul" or "*peace* for a cloister," "but *peace* for the world." Justification leading to God-human reconciliation has "cosmic breadth" (p. 139).

Goppelt refers to Rom. 14:17 to highlight the work of the Spirit: "The presence of the Spirit brought 'righteousness, *peace*, and joy,'" the fundamental elements of God's end-time reign (p. 121). Reconciliation begins now through Christ: the "love of God" turns the "enemy of God" into the one who has "*peace* with God" (p. 138; Goppelt notes specifically that *peace/eirēnē* is used, not "expiation" as the result of Christ's work).

In discussing 1 Peter, in "Responsible Conduct in the Institutions of Society," Goppelt takes up both Paul's and Peter's injunction to subordination. He refers to 1 Cor. 14:40 as one text where Paul joins the concept of

---

32. Goppelt reflects on the Lutheran interpretation that "non-resistance and suffering injustice were required when the issue concerned oneself, and [that] resisting injustice was in order when the issue was a matter of one's neighbor" (p. 116). He notes that this view is expressed in the Lutheran "doctrine of the two kingdoms," that one is either obedient to the new commandment of love *or* the demands of the "natural order." Goppelt questions rhetorically whether it is ever possible to neatly separate the two, whether what concerns self does not also concern neighbor. See further his n. 20 (p. 116). Later, he refutes this view, arguing that "Jesus' demands were after nothing less than a transformation of the person from the very core, i.e., a total repentance" (p. 118). Nonresistance, "the demonstration of love for one's enemy . . . was always possible" (p. 119). But this remains only a sign of the kingdom's "present coming of the end-time reign of God" (p. 119). Further, "it always remained a sign beclouded by human failure" (p. 119).

taxis (order) "together with that of *peace*, i.e., with that of the *shalom* that God . . . willed and accomplished. *Shalom* was the right relationship of all people to each other, the relationship that meant prosperity and life for all" (pp. 168-69; cf. Rom. 13:4 where social order also serves *shalom*). "But the *peace* of God did not come through these orders *per se* but through the establishment of the eschatological dominion (Rom. 8:6; 14:17)." Thus, "the Christian bore an obligation to the particular historical forms of life and lived responsibly in them" (p. 169), i.e., "responsible and critical conduct within them" (p. 171; this includes the household codes). Nonetheless, "God" is the main standard of measure for discernment, not "social motifs or goal-oriented concepts such as love, *peace*, righteousness, or freedom" (p. 172). Further, the Christians' "vision was to penetrate the fog of ideology when the offer of *pax et securitas* was made (I Thess. 5:3): they were not 'to worship'. . . . There is always the tendency to turn politics into something final, to deify it. The task of Christians is to expose this tendency with the help of Rev. 13 and to resist it, and precisely when the tendency is trimmed with theology" (p. 191).

Goppelt's last section returns to the Gospels for redactional emphases. He notes Luke's emphasis on "Jesus; he who was born the *sōtēr* (Savior, Lk. 2:11), the One who brought *eirēnē* (*peace*, Lk. 2:14) on earth." Luke puts Jesus' birth "in the framework of contemporary history," to contrast or parallel what was also said of Augustus and the *Pax Romana* (p. 272). While Goppelt does not pursue Luke's full *eirēnē* emphasis, he begins well.

Goppelt's second volume, but not the first, makes one of the stronger theological contributions to understanding the NT contribution to *peace* and reconciliation. If volume 1 were as strong as is 2 on *peace*, Goppelt would be included in Group 1 above. In volume 2 he wrestles with the theological issues these emphases raise.

Werner Georg Kümmel, *The Theology of the New Testament: According to Its Major Witnesses: Jesus — Paul — John*   While Kümmel has numerous references to *peace*, mostly quotations of texts (though his Index cites only three — pp. 167, 204, 295), these texts don't shape the outline of his thought. For example, "Blessed are the *peacemakers*" (Matt. 5:9; cf. 5:45) is cited in his discussion of the Lord's Prayer, to illustrate the promissory nature of the kingdom of God and the eschatological petition addressed to God as Abba (cf. Luke 12:32) (p. 41).

Later he cites the "sword" texts (Matt. 10:34 par. Luke 12:49) and rightly makes the point: "this says nothing else but that Jesus' coming produces a division among people according to their attitude toward Jesus" (p. 65). In Luke 22:35-38 the "word 'sword' can only be used in a figurative sense." It cannot be used to portray Jesus as a political governing messiah but shows that "only obedience to God is decisive (Mark 12:33ff. par.)" (p. 73). Further, Jesus "demanded of his disciples service instead of the lordship customary among the Gentiles (Mark 10:42-43 par.)" (p. 73).

The *peace* text, Romans 5:1, is cited twice: once in the context of discussing atonement (p. 162) and second in the context of discussing justification by faith and the manifestation of God's righteousness on the basis of faith (p. 197), where other Pauline texts are also cited (Phil. 3:9; Col. 2:13-14). When discussing "Christ and the Spirit," he references two *peace* texts: "we have *peace* in Christ and in the Holy Spirit (Phil. 4:7; Rom. 14:17)" (p. 167).

On "Liberation from the Spiritual Powers" he says, "Through the cross and resurrection of his Son, God has disarmed the powers and 'made *peace* through him by the blood of his cross, on earth as in heaven' (Col. 1:20)" (p. 187). The same text is quoted again in a treatment of reconciliation, which is viewed mostly on the vertical axis (p. 200), but also specifies reconciliation of the universe (Col. 1:19-20). Reconciliation marks the end of enmity and of God's wrath: "Thus God has buried the enmity and made *peace*" (Col. 1:20; Rom. 5:1) (p. 204). In the context of treating the eschatological people of God, he cites "'*peace* be upon the Israel of God' (Gal. 6:16)" (p. 211).

Finally, in treating John, Kümmel cites the two key texts of 14:27a and 16:33a, commenting that "This does not mean a state of mind, but the certainty that Christ has overcome the world (16:33c) and that therewith the Christian who has *peace* in Christ (16:33a) is likewise delivered from the compelling power of the world" (p. 295). For John the meaning of Christ is liberation from death and this world. Jesus' admonition means that the disciples who despair have not yet grasped the reality of the gift of life: *peace*, joy, love (p. 295). Kümmel more directly exposits the meaning of *peace* in John than he does for the texts in Paul and the Synoptics, where the texts cited bolster other points.

George Eldon Ladd, *A Theology of the New Testament*   This tome of 719 pages contains numerous references to *peace* and reconciliation. They occur, however, almost totally in his Pauline sections. The several references from his Gospels section are in citations of OT prophetic texts pointing toward the ideal messianic king (Isa. 32:15 on p. 34; Zech. 9:9-10 and Jer. 22:4 in connection with Jesus' entry into Jerusalem on p. 135; and 2 Kgs. 20:19 citing "*peace* and truth" on p. 302). The Gospels as such, in their own emphases, appear disconnected from NT *peace* agenda.

In discussing Paul, Ladd emphasizes: "In Jesus Christ God has made known the mystery, i.e., the hidden purpose of his will to restore harmony to a disordered world (Eph. 1:9-10)," a sum of "the totality of the historical event of Jesus Christ and of apostolic interpretation" (p. 425). *Peace* is understood clearly as interpersonal and as an objective relationship to God (Rom. 12:17 cited on pp. 451 and 526). The kingdom of Christ belongs to an "invisible sphere" in which there is "subduing of everything hostile to the will of God." In this context "reconciliation among people who have been estranged" occurs as God's gift as well (here Ladd quotes Eph. 2:14-16, p. 498). He also holds that *reconciliation* is the correct translation of Romans 5:11, not atonement (p. 451). In his words, "Thus God's kingdom is not concerned primarily with physical things, necessary though they be, but with spiritual realities: righteousness and *peace* and joy — the fruits of the indwelling Holy Spirit (Rom. 14:17)" (p. 451). He stresses similarly that "we have *peace* through the blood of his cross" (Col. 1:20), in the context of discussing the "sacrificial aspect of Christ's death," with focus on the blood (p. 467).

In later discussion of "The Results of Reconciliation," Ladd emphasizes first that "God's wrath no longer threatens. . . ." *Peace* refers to an objective "relationship to God. We are no longer his enemies but the objects of his favor" (p. 497). Inward *peace* is unthinkable biblically prior to the outward "*peace* with God, the *peace* of reconciliation. *Peace* with God, therefore, is grounded upon the redemptive work of Christ" (p. 498). Second, Ladd speaks also of "*reconciliation among people* who have been estranged" for "those who are reconciled to God are to enjoy *peace* with one another" (p. 498). The Jew-Gentile hostility is removed: "The reconciliation of the hostility between Jew and Greek may be taken as representative of every sort of interpersonal hostility. In Christ there is *peace* among human beings" (p. 498).

Ladd also quotes Phil. 4:7 in discussing the mind *(nous)* (p. 526) and joins love and joy to *peace* in discussing Gal. 5:22 (citing also Rom. 14:17; 15:13). In this context, Ladd makes his most comprehensive *peace* statement: "*peace* is not primarily emotional tranquility but a term encompassing the salvation of the whole person" (p. 534). In this context of discussing "The New Life in Christ: The Lord is the Spirit," he refers also to the "gospel of *peace*" (Eph. 6:15 and Rom. 5:1), and says, "*Peace* is practically synonymous with salvation (Rom. 2:10) and is a power that protects people in their inner beings (Phil. 4:7) and that rules in their hearts (Col. 3:15)" (p. 534).

In a later short section where he addresses the universal goal of salvation (Col. 1:20), he says, "The goal of God's redemptive purpose is the restoration of order to a universe that has been disturbed by evil and sin" (p. 612). "The very cosmos, which has been rent by conflict and rebellion against God, will be restored to *peace* with its Creator" (p. 612). For "the universal reconciliation means that *peace* is everywhere restored" (pp. 612-13). But this does not mean a universal homecoming, for Paul is clear about judgment and punishment as well. Nonetheless, "The divine purpose is that people may be gathered in willing subordination to the divine rule, that in the end 'God may be everything to every one' (1 Cor. 15:28)" (p. 614).

Eduard Lohse, *Theologische Ethik des Neuen Testaments*[33]   *Frieden* appears seven times, but *Versöhnung* does not appear in the Index. Lohse also has an insightful section on discipleship *(Nachfolge Christi)* in chs. 3-4, including Jesus' command to love enemies. In ch. 7 he addresses the believers' relation to state-order. His seven citations to *peace* scatter over various topical foci. His first citation is to 1 Corinthians 7:15, where the call to *peace* occurs in relation to Paul's counsel allowing an unbelieving partner to separate (p. 26). The second reference is in his discussion of Matt. 5:23-24, Jesus' exhortation to be reconciled with a brother or sister before presenting an offering at the altar (p. 43). His third, and substantial, reference regards the nature of the Sermon on the Mount, whether it can be considered to be "eine *Friedensethik.*" He argues for the binding character of the Sermon's teachings, but notes their one-sidedness. While it demands obedience, it develops no political program (p. 47). It will function always as a call to repentance. It is not to be restricted to the private sphere, but to guide the everyday life of humans. As such it will serve the cause of reconciliation among humans and provide a foundation for *peace,* his fourth use (*Frieden zu stiften;* p. 51).

His fifth use occurs in his discussion of the fifth Barmen thesis regarding the Christian relation to the state. He argues the point that the state, according to Paul, is to be a power for just law and *peace* (pp. 87-88). His next use comes in his discussion of Christ uniting Jews and Gentiles, where he references both Ephesians 2:14 ("Christ is our *peace*") and 4:3 (the call "to maintain the unity in the bond of *peace*") (p. 98). His last set of uses (four on p. 98) refer to *peace* as a divine gift, which stands as the "*peace*maker" sign in the life-experience of the believers (Matt. 5:9). They are to implement this *peace* in all relationships so far as is possible (Rom. 12:18). Even though early Christians could not participate in political life, their *peace* life and action would have effect upon their environment, socially and politically. The catechism of the Sermon on the Mount serves this end as well (p. 133).

It appears that *peace* and its proper understanding is part of the NT theological task, as Lohse sees it. The comments above are sparse in his total treatment, but show a responsible effort to grapple with some of the NT *peace* texts and their significance. That *peace* and *peacemaking,* as well as *reconciliation,* are foundational or central in NT theological thought is not evident in Lohse's treatment.

33. For my review of this book, see *Critical Review* 1990, pp. 217-20.

Frank Matera, *New Testament Ethics: The Legacies of Jesus and Paul*
Though *peace* does not occur in the Subject Index, *reconciliation* occurs four
times and *love of enemies* six times. Matera describes his method as neither
diachronic nor synchronic, but a narrative approach to ascertain what the NT
writings tell us about the moral life.

Significantly, Matera describes the ministry of Jesus against the background of Isa. 52:7, the "good news" that "announces *peace*." This provides the
perspective for understanding God's kingship as linked to salvation, and the
perspective to understand Jesus (p. 17). "The Markan Jesus has not despaired
of God's help but neither are his last words a *peace*ful cry of submission"
(p. 34). In Matthew the Sermon on the Mount's "Blessed are the *peace*makers"
is one of the four more active Beatitudes, emphasizing positive action to
make *peace* (p. 45). Matt. 5:38-42 is a call to nonviolence, instead of retaliation; 5:43-48 commands love even for enemies (p. 46). At the same time, Jesus
does not bring *peace* (10:34) but blood, forgiveness of sins, and reconciliation
of humanity to God (1:21; 20:28; 26:28). Luke's platform for Jesus' ministry is
4:18-19, the gospel mission in summary form (p. 68). Luke accentuates love
for enemies (pp. 76-77): "One of the most distinctive aspects of discipleship
as presented in Luke's Gospel, however, is Jesus' insistence upon love for one's
enemies" (p. 90). In John, footwashing is important in that Jesus here provides the pattern for humble service (p. 104); this includes willingness to lay
down one's life for one's friends (15:13; p. 108).

Paul regards his life a model for reconciliation: "Through his apostolic
hardships, he is participating in Christ's work of reconciliation" (p. 157). The
fruit of the Spirit consists of three triads reflecting perfect harmony in community:

love, joy, *peace*,
patience, kindness, generosity,
faithfulness, gentleness, self-control (Gal. 5:22-23; p. 171)

These are followed by the exhortation to bear one another's burdens
(Gal. 6:2), expressing community solidarity. The mood of Philippians 1–2 is
that of "*peace* and joy" as opposed to harsh warning in ch. 3 (p. 175). Rom.
12:17-21 extends Jesus' teaching on love of enemies (pp. 197-200). In 14:17 the
kingdom of God means "righteousness, *peace*, and joy in the Holy Spirit"
(p. 204). Paul's vision of Christ's redemption is to reconcile all things, a cosmic vision (Col. 1:20; pp. 207, 211). Finally, in putting on the whole armor of
God (Eph. 6:10-20), "readiness to proclaim the gospel of *peace*" is an important part (p. 223). Humans, even believers, are not able to live the moral life

without God, and the church is God's fighting force. The moral life is to be lived in and with a community of disciples which is the church (p. 250). The moral life expresses itself in love for God, love for neighbor, and love for one's enemy, as well as in "mutual service" (p. 254).

This summary indicates that Matera's narrative reading grasps the emphasis of this volume, though the topics as such are nowhere identified for extended comment.

I. Howard Marshall, *New Testament Theology* Marshall includes *Peace* in his subject index, with twenty-seven citations and three of those listing two continuous pages. Clearly, *peace* figures into the work, but it is never the subject of discussion *per se*. *Reconciliation*, listed in the Index twenty-two times, is given more attention, including its use as a subject heading (for pp. 294-96). Here *peace* is mentioned as the fruit of reconciliation, but only in the sense of harmonious and *peace*ful relationships. In his discussion of "Justification by Grace through Faith," Marshall speaks of humans' relationship to God now "characterized by *peace* and not by wrath" (p. 310). Many of Marshall's uses of *peace* refer to the God-human relationship that salvation effects, as his summary chapter on Paul, "The Theology of the Pauline Letters," shows. After identifying reconciliation as the fourth main image in Paul's theology, which he notes some regard as "the central or unifying theme in Paul's theology," he explicates as follows:

> Reconciliation is the establishment of *peace* between two opposing or warring groups or individuals, and it may be achieved either by one party taking the initiative or by a third party intervening as a mediator to bring about *peace*. . . . Since Paul stresses that God in his grace sent Jesus his Son, it follows that Jesus is to be seen as the envoy of God bringing the offer of *peace* to his enemies rather than as somebody who has to persuade God and humanity to come together. . . . [Thus] God . . . was acting in and through Christ, offering *peace* to sinners and not holding their sins against them (2 Cor. 5:18, 19, 20, 21)." (p. 441)

Commenting then on Rom. 5:9-11, Col. 1:20-22, and Eph. 2:16-18, Marshall stresses that because of Christ's death humans are "now at *peace* with God" (Rom. 5:1). "God makes *peace* through the blood shed on the cross and thus reconciles all things to himself. . . . It is the death that makes *peace* and turns sinners into righteous" (p. 442). While Marshall assumes that this *peace* results in *peace* between former enemies, his emphasis falls on the vertical: those in enmity with God now enjoy *peace* with God (see also his discussion on pp. 369-70).

Hence, while *peace* is mentioned often, its role in his theology is limited mostly to texts on reconciliation where he addresses the God-human relationship. The term *peace* plays no role in the book's Conclusion that sums up the themes representing diversity and unity in NT theology (pp. 707-31).

Leon Morris, *New Testament Theology*   For Morris, *peace* does not occur in the Subject Index; *reconciliation* occurs three times. The *cross* is a central emphasis; he begins with Paul since his writings are earliest. In his first chapter, "God at the Center," in a section on "One Glorious God," Morris mentions a series of *peace* texts: "God of love and *peace*" (2 Cor. 13:11); "*the God of peace*" (Rom. 15:33; cf. 1 Cor. 14:33; Phil. 4:9; 1 Thess. 5:23). That *the God of peace* "will crush Satan under [our] feet" (Rom. 16:20) is an "active and new dimension to *peace*, . . . compatible with militant opposition to evil," as opposed to *peace* as a "quiescent state" (p. 26). In his second last paragraph of this chapter, Morris returns to *peace* emphases: "God is a God who delights to bless. He has called his people in *peace* (1 Cor. 7:15); '*The peace of God*' is with God's people (Phil. 4:7; Col. 3:15)" (p. 38). While he doesn't detail here what he means by "the *peace* of God," he lifts it up here in chapter 1, indicating its prominent place in Paul's thought.

Later, he cites "Grace to you and *peace* from God our Father and the Lord Jesus Christ" (Rom. 1:7) to illustrate that Christ and God are held together as one common source of *peace* (p. 42). Also, *the peace of God* (Phil. 4:7) and the *peace of Christ* (Col. 3:15) occur in a long list of functions to show that Paul "assigns a number of functions indifferently to God and to Christ" (p. 47). Morris cites Romans 5:1, Christ "brought *peace*," among numerous gifts of Christ's salvation, such as justification, redemption, etc. (the list is long, p. 51). Jesus' "death may be seen as effecting reconciliation (Rom. 5:10-11; 2 Cor. 5:18-20; Eph. 2:16; Col. 1:20), which is the same as making *peace* (Eph. 2:14-15; cf. Phil. 4:7). Morris regards "reconciliation" as distinctive to Paul but not dominant because it is not "widespread in the apostle's writings" (only 4 times and even with the addition of "*making peace*" references, it is still not frequent). "The concept still comes short of being dominant . . . neither should we minimize it" (p. 72). "*Reconciliation* is a personal category; it means the *making of peace* after a quarrel or a state of hostility" (italics mine). But he cautions against simply making it into a "process of people being reconciled" and points toward the more cosmic work of God manifest on the cross: reconciliation is "'through the cross' which killed the enmity (Eph. 2:16); *peace* was made 'through the blood of his cross'" (Col. 1:20). In this context he discusses sin and atonement, propitiation, and expiation (pp. 72-73).

Morris cites numerous Pauline texts that include *peace*: "The fruit of the Spirit is love, joy, *peace*, longsuffering, . . ." (Gal. 5:22-23; cf. Eph. 5:9);

"righteousness, *peace*, joy" (Rom. 14:17; cf. 1 Thess. 1:6) as marks of "Life in the Spirit"; and "the mind of the Spirit" which is "life and *peace*" (Rom. 8:6) (p. 76).

In a later section he returns to specific Gospel emphases. For Matthew, in a section on "Teaching about God" he notes that "It is the *peacemakers* who are to be called God's sons" (Matt. 5:9). This teaching is rightly joined to love of enemies who do as the Father does (5:44-45). This status as God's children, Morris links to Matthew's frequent use of Father, and the intimacy of Jesus' addressing God as "my Father" (pp. 119-20). In the Beatitudes we encounter the "absoluteness of Jesus and the reversal of values it involves (5:1-12)"; this includes the call to be *peace*makers (p. 138).

Luke's two-volume work is important here as well. Regarding the striking text spoken by Peter in the house of Cornelius (Acts 10:34-36) Morris writes in a section titled "The Christ" in his chapter "The God of Luke and Acts": "Peter referred to the word that God sent to the children of Israel, 'preaching *peace* through Jesus Christ   he is Lord of all . . .' (Acts 10:36). *Peace* is, of course, *peace* between God and man, but in the context of a message given in the house of a pious Gentile to whom God had given a vision there can be little doubt that there is also the thought of *peace* between people as widely divided as were Jew and Gentile. There is a comprehensive *peace*. And it is brought about by Jesus Christ, who is spoken of in this connection as 'Lord of all'" (p. 166).

Morris cites Luke 2:14, "*Peace* on earth," to make the point that Luke has a "wide vision," one in which people of all nations and races are included in the scope of salvation (p. 200).

Morris also notes Hebrews' witness to *peace*, where Christ is "a priest like Mechizedek" "king of Salem." "This man's name means 'king of righteousness' and his title means '*king of peace*' [emphasis mine]. Both point to Christ's work, but these thoughts are not developed" (p. 304).

Clearly, Morris's contribution does remarkably well in showing the *spread and significance of peace* as integral to NT ethics. But these many citations appear within long and comprehensive lists of topics that Morris is describing, and their force is often lost within the volume of emphases. To illustrate, his list of references to "God of *peace*" would indicate that Morris regards this as preeminent in importance, since it occurs on the second page of his first chapter (p. 26). But prior to this are longer lists of verse citations in two preceding paragraphs — verses attesting God's oneness and God's glory (a word occurring 77 times in Paul). It is telling that despite the many references to *peace*, the topic is missed in the Subject Index. It is difficult to assess the role *peace and reconciliation* play in Morris's *Theology*. On the basis of the number of citations, Morris belongs in the first group above. But his lack of explicating the theological significance of these citations and omitting *peace* in his Index lead me to place him in this second group. None of his many, many topical headings include either *peace* or *reconciliation*.

Herman Ridderbos, *Paul: An Outline of His Theology* Ridderbos devotes a twenty-five-page chapter to "Reconciliation." "Christ's Reconciling Activity in Christ. The *Peace* with God" is the first section (pp. 182-86). His Index refers to these pages under "*Peace* with God," but has no other entries on *peace*. Except for references in his next topical section, "Christ's Death as Atonement," he does not appear to integrate his discussion on reconciliation and *peace* with any other topics in his 562 pages of treating Pauline theology. In this one topical section, *peace* (*peacemaking*) occurs at least twenty times, and *reconciliation* fifty times or more (both noun and verb) in four and a half pages of discussion. He regards *peace* as the fruit of reconciliation, and regards them as close to synonymous. But almost all his discussion deals with reconciliation and *peace* in vertical dimension, the God-human relationship. At one point there is a fine exception, a broader view of *peace* in Paul:

> But the idea of *peace*, which for Paul repeatedly denotes the result of reconciliation, is not in conflict with such a conception of reconciliation ["objective" atonement], but rather forms its confirmation. For in Paul (as in the whole of the Scripture) "*peace*" refers not only or in the first place to disposition, but is the denotation of the all-embracing gift of salvation, the condition of *shalom*, which God will again bring to unrestricted dominion. It is the *peace* that is to reign when "the God of *peace* will soon crush Satan under the feet" (Rom. 16:20). It consists therefore as much in the pacification of the powers hostile to God as in the restoration of *peace* between Jews and gentiles, the *peace* of the Messianic kingdom, which is represented by Christ ("He is our *peace*") because he has reconciled the enmity between the two through his cross (Eph. 2:14ff.), and which stands in contrast to the wrath, indignation, tribulation, and anguish of the eschatological divine judgment (Rom. 2:9, 10). (p. 184).

In addition to this inclusion of the horizontal human arena of reconciliation and *peacemaking*, Ridderbos also speaks briefly of two other dimensions of *peace*: inner *peace* (referencing Rom. 15:13; Phil. 4:7) and *peace* as answering any judgment against oneself, thus settling "uncertainty or inner discord (Col. 3:15; cf. 2 Thess. 3:16)" (p. 186). As he begins his next section on atonement, he cites Eph. 2:13, then 2:14; and joins these two texts to Col. 1:20, so that the horizontal and cosmic also comes into focus, if ever so briefly (p. 186). "Reconciliation" as a chapter heading continues for another eighteen pages to discuss aspects of atonement doctrine: the relation between reconciliation and propitiation, and justification. Then he devotes a section to "Ransom" and another to "Adoption" and "Inheritance." In these extended discussions, *peace* is missing, thematically confined, it seems, to pp. 182-86.

Perhaps this lack of integrating *peace* into Paul's wider theological vision and emphasis is dictated by the format of the book: "An Outline of [Paul's] Theology." Similar to Morris, Ridderbos treats Paul's theology under discrete topics, in sequential fashion, and thus does not undertake a synthetic integration of how these topics are interwoven in Paul's writings.

Rudolf Schnackenburg, *The Moral Teaching of the New Testament* Though Schnackenburg cites only three references to *peace* in his Subject Index and *reconciliation* is not listed, both occur quite often in the text. *Love of enemies* occurs quite often, but is not listed in the Index, though both "love for God" and "love for neighbor" are listed. For Schnackenburg, the kingdom of God is closely linked with love, love, and more love, and this includes many references and discussions of love of enemies. Throughout there is a call to more vital discipleship, and the problems of eschatology and of dual loyalties to God and emperor figure largely into the discussion.

Regarding *peace*, he begins his discussion of "Jesus' Moral Demands" (Ch. 1) by referencing Israel's hope that God's gracious intervention into history would mean "renewal of the covenant" that would include "embracing the whole world," i.e. "'nations' will stream to Mount Sion; the *peace of Eden* will be restored; and a new heaven and new earth will appear" (p. 16). The kingdom of God is present in the Messiah, "but not yet present as the cosmic kingdom of *peace* and glory" (p. 19).

Schnackenburg gives considerable attention to "Jesus' Radicalism" expressed in the Sermon on the Mount, especially Matthew 5:38-48, and specifically nonretaliation and love of enemies. His way of making sense of this is to put it in context: "the eschatological hour of salvation has struck, Jesus has returned to the primordial will of God, unrestrained by the conditions and difficult circumstances of the world . . ." (p. 80). Thus the radicality of the divine commands, including "loving one's enemies," confronts us. He considers several "escape" interpretations,[34] but ends by saying "we must let the words of Jesus stand in all their severity and ruggedness" (p. 88).[35] We must also strive

34. For analysis of such efforts in mostly German scholarship, see Clarence Bauman, *The Sermon on the Mount: The Modern Quest for Its Meaning.* See p. 67 n. 45 above for Allison's work.

35. Schnackenburg notes also that "Acts of charity towards pagan fellow-citizens are demanded more than once in the Mishnah, but only 'for the sake of peace' (and thus from social good sense)" (p. 97).

for the "highest peak of love." The lofty moral goal of the Sermon on the Mount "consisting primarily in the attainment of salvation and of all the blessings of salvation promised by Jesus, is also a source of true happiness and *lasting peace* in the earthly life of men with one another" (p. 109).

Schnackenburg considers texts that may endorse a lower ethic (Luke 14:31; 16:1-7; 18:1-5), but holds it is "not Jesus' intention to put them forward as patterns for war and *peace*, social life and legal practice" (p. 111). But also, we should not characterize Jesus as "a *pacifist* in the political sense because of his commandment to love one's enemies," because "all these forms of radicalism are oriented towards this world," whereas Jesus is "wholly religious and moral." "Jesus never suggested that his precept of love is to lead to a *peaceful revolution*, to reform and renewal of this world" (p. 114). Jesus "called for *pacific dispositions* and love of enemies, but did not deal directly with the emergencies that may face a nation" (p. 121; emphases mine). At the same time Schnackenburg recognizes that Luke's emphasis stresses more the "social and earthly" (p. 129). He also notes that "The moral seriousness, fraternal love, chastity, *peacefulness* and ability to suffer, of Christians, contributed not a little to the triumph of Christianity, for in the long run their lesson was stronger than calumny and oppression" (p. 185). This comports with James's censure of "wars and contentions" within the communities (Jas. 4:1-12; p. 361).

For whatever reason, Schnackenburg does little with the *Pauline* teachings on *peace* and *reconciliation*.

D. E. H. Whiteley, *The Theology of St. Paul*   While it may be questioned whether this volume fits the grid, restricted as it is to Paul, I have included it since it is a *Theology* of Paul.[36] Its Subject Index cites one reference for *peace* (p. 140) and two for *reconciliation,* under *katallassein* (pp. 69-70, 132), but there are more occurrences of *peace* in the text. In discussing Christ's "victory over evil spirits at the cross," Whiteley cites Romans 16:20, "The God of *peace* will soon crush Satan beneath your feet" (p. 30). To document Paul's unitary view of man (sic), he cites "May God himself, the *God of peace,* make you holy in every part, and keep you sound in spirit, soul and body, without fault when our Lord Jesus Christ comes" (1 Thess. 5:23; p. 37). In discussing expiation and propitiation, he refers to the OT people who "offered burnt offerings and sacrificed *peace offerings* of oxen unto the Lord" (Exod. 24:5; p. 139).

In this context also he has a longer *peace* section where he claims

---

36. I also considered including Furnish, *Theology and Ethics in Paul.* But it has even less discussion pertinent to the focus of this volume. References to peace and reconciliation occur on pp. 148-51, but are subservient to his discussion of justification. Peace is not listed in the index, and reconciliation has only two references, pp. 148-49 and 205.

"*peace*" as one element of the right relationship between God and humans in covenant. Col. 1:20 follows the OT tradition of "the blood of the covenant" for establishing relationship. Also Eph. 2:13 and Eph. 2:17 are noted, "*Peace* to you who were far off, and *peace* to those who were near" referring to Isa. 57:19: "Christ by the blood of his cross established a relationship with God for Jew and Gentile alike which resembled but transcended that established through Moses on Mount Horeb." He cites also Zech. 9:10-11, "And he shall command *peace* to the nations. . . . As for you, because of the blood of my covenant with you, I will set your captives free from the waterless pit." His discussion in this section on "The Whole Work of Christ: the Death of Christ" with attention to expiation/propitiation as part of the covenantal relationship focuses mostly on the blood of covenant, not on *peace* (p. 140).

In discussing justification apart from the law, he notes that "The Jew might have applied the expression 'right relationship' to the *peace* (*shalom*) with God which he enjoyed by means of the covenant. This '*peace*' had been established by God on Mount Sinai with Israel as a whole . . ." (p. 160). Later he addresses the issue of universal salvation, considering the *peace* text of Colossians 1:20, and says that while it suggests universal salvation, we don't know what happens to the unfaithful (p. 273).

Contributions that Marginalize Peace and Reconciliation[37]

Hans Conzelmann, *An Outline of the Theology of the New Testament*   Only a few references to *peace* and cognate concepts occur in his 358-page treatment. He notes (p. 20) that at the end of time in eternal life violence will cease, with support from Slavonic Enoch 65 (represents Jewish apocalypticism). Then much later he declares "God's *peace* surpasses the [*nous*], the human capability of understanding (Phil. 4.7)"; par. to Bultmann. Also, "God is the reconciler," said in the context of atonement and eschatology (p. 180). "Divine power is

---

37. White, *Biblical Ethics*, might have been included in the above section or here, since it is mostly concerned with the NT, though it contains several good chapters on OT ethics. He has one subject index reference for peacemaking (p. 77), with a cross-reference to "military service," which has three page references. He discusses peacemaking in relation to Matt. 5:9, where he relates peacemaking in the church (Matt. 18:15-20) to the same theme. "Peace" does occur as he cites Paul's ethical injunctions (pp. 130-31). He has a section on "imitation of Christ" (pp. 192-93). A significant section, referenced from "military service," is his discussion of when and if it is permissible for a Christian to use violence in war as an alternative to "unresisting surrender to evil" (pp. 98-99). His next section, "The Kingdom and Social Legislation" (pp. 99-103), continues with a related discussion, noting that the Christian church plays an important role in affecting the moral tone of the wider society.

also the strength, love, *peace*, wrath of God" (p. 219). He uses the phrase "spirit of *peace*" in discussing Paul's response to the pneumatics dividing the community at Corinth (p. 259). His most significant statement is "Salvation can be described throughout the New Testament as '*peace*' (Rom 5.1; Phil. 4.7: the *peace* of God; Luke 2.14)" (p. 328). Further, "The 'mood' of *peace* is joy. . . ." "*Peace* and joy describe the eschatological condition in the world" (p. 328). In discussing John's Christology, he links it to "my *peace*, my joy," and notes that Jesus' "departure is the condition for establishing *peace*. This establishing of *peace* is more closely connected with the church than in other parts of the New Testament; *peace* is visible as love of the brethren . . . who are kept together through the world's hate and in precisely this way experience *peace*, as the spirit rules in the community and leads it into all truth" (p. 329).

J. D. G. Dunn, *The Theology of Paul the Apostle* See note 1 in Chapter 7 above. Despite Dunn's surprising lack of peace emphasis in a theology of Paul, he has several good sentences on peace, defining *eirēnē* as distinct from the Greek idea of peace, and extending the OT *shalom*. His notable comment (p. 387):

> If justification means God accepting the sinner ([Rom.] 5.8), it also means God bestowing the blessing of peace on those who were formerly enemies (5.10). "*Peace*" here is not to be restricted to the Greek idea of cessation of war, or to be merely spiritualized (inner calm). It will certainly include the much richer Hebrew concept of *shalom*, where the basic idea is of "well-being," including social harmony and communal well-doing.

Beyond this, in his exposition of numerous texts, *peace* does not figure into his discussion, though reconciliation does, on the same page and elsewhere.

Dale Goldsmith, *New Testament Ethics* In this more popular (and somewhat "centrist") account, the author seems to carefully avoid grounding *peace* or pacifism biblically, though he will occasionally speak of "wholeness." In speaking of salvation he quotes "God in Christ reconciles the world to himself" (2 Cor. 5:19) (p. 1). In introducing his thematic approach to ethics he uses the terms "Love. Justice. *Peace.* Obedience" (p. 4). In discussing Paul, he quotes Romans 14:19, "Let us pursue what makes for *peace* and for mutual upbuilding" (p. 45). He emphasizes that Jesus "continues to bring people to wholeness, to include them once again in fellowship with God and others" (p. 111). He mentions "love your enemies" (p. 114). For John the accent falls on the "mutually loving community" (p. 156). But, ironically, John is dismissed shortly, with the claim that his ethics do not focus "outwardly on questions of *peace and social justice*" (p. 166).

Other Works Related to the Topics of This Volume

Ralph P. Martin, *Reconciliation: A Study of Paul's Theology*   On Martin's helpful treatment, and his relating *peace* to *reconciliation,* see Chapter 7 above, notes 2, 3, 34, 36, 38, 39, and the chapter's discussion matching those notes.

Joseph A. Grassi, *Informing the Future: Social Justice in the New Testament*   Though *peace* is not cited in Grassi's Index, a few references (surprisingly few) occur. He cites Matt. 5:9 and links it to justice (p. 152). In discussing Luke, Grassi has a section on women, with Luke's teaching expressive of social justice (192ff.). He also mentions jubilee, and Jesus' power over demons (citing Luke 10; p. 191). But nowhere does he hint at Luke's emphasis on *peace.* For Paul, his only citation of *peace* is Gal. 5:22-23.

In summing up his contribution, he lists many important moral values related to justice, but not *peace* (p. 270). This failure to connect justice to *peace* is lamentable. This deficiency, however, is corrected *in part* by his more recent volume, *Peace on Earth: Roots and Practices from Luke's Gospel* (Collegeville: Liturgical, 2004). While this volume appeared late in my work, I refer to it briefly in Chapter 5.

David Bosch, *Transforming Mission: Paradigm Shifts in Theology of Mission*   Bosch's insightful treatment of the mission paradigm in the NT lacks any connection to the NT's teaching on *peace.* See my article on this topic, "Bosch and Beyond: Biblical Issues in Mission," *Mission Focus: Annual Review,* vol. 11 (2003 Supplement): 77-105.

Peter Stuhlmacher's Twelve Theses
on Peace in the New Testament[1]

THESIS 1: The manifold and multilevel way of speaking about *eirēnē* in the New Testament is rooted tradition-historically in the Old Testament/Jewish tradition of "peace."

THESIS 2: Whereas in the proclamation of Jesus and in the synoptic Gospels' traditional material *eirēnē* is spoken of entirely in connection to its usage in the Old Testament and Judaism, in Paul and his school, the Lucan redaction, and the Johannine tradition, there is a conscious New Testament theological reflection on the phenomenon of peace.

THESIS 3: The analysis of the Pauline way of speaking about peace within the New Testament confronts us in its most enduring depth with the christological content-problem of our topic. It is therefore advisable to make the Pauline statements the starting point for the theological concern for the New Testament problem of peace.

THESIS 4: In his genuine letters, Paul starts from the Old Testament/Jewish *shalom* tradition. But, nevertheless, he has a special interest in speaking of *eirēnē* as the salvation and gift of the end-time.

THESIS 5: For Paul, his unmistakable New Testament definition of *eirēnē* re-

---

1. These theses are from Peter Stuhlmacher, "Der Begriff des Friedens im Neuen Testament und seine Konsequenzen," in *Historische Beiträge zur Friedensforschung,* ed. Wolfgang Huber (Studien zur Friedensforschung, ed. Georg Picht and Heinz Eduard Tödt; Forschungsstätte der Evangelischen Studiengemeinschaft Heidelberg, vol. 4; Stuttgart: Klett-Cotta/Munich: Kösel, 1970), 21-69. Translated by David Stassen, edited by Willard M. Swartley. Used by permission.

ceives its eschatological salvation power from the Christ-event. Now, *eirēnē* indicates the reality and effect of reconciliation.

THESIS 6: Corresponding to the christological-anticipatory structure of Pauline theology, *eirēnē*, as defined by reconciliation, also marks an existence in eschatological movement (toward consummation).

THESIS 7: The Pauline *paraklēsis*, a means of proclaiming Christ that is an essential part of the Pauline Gospel, calls for witnessing to *eirēnē*, and making that witness faithfully in the world's everyday political life.

THESIS 8: According to Pauline thought, Christians are charged with the task of testifying to the world about *eirēnē* in a conciliatory manner. With this commission, they are thus entangled in the end-time confrontation between the world of the law and that of the Gospel, and are called to a testimony that allows the Gospel to remain the Gospel.

THESIS 9: Jesus' preaching and anticipatory practice of the reign of God have their most important, distinctive climax in the Passion-event. To the extent to which Jesus' Passion and its efficacy can be seen together, a wide-ranging agreement exists between Jesus' work and the Pauline message of reconciliation.

THESIS 10: The approximately simultaneous further development of the New Testament thought on *eirēnē* in the Gospel of John, the letters of the Pauline school, and the Lucan historical work allows us to recognize different accents, but all of them, nevertheless, uniformly define peace christologically.

THESIS 11: The New Testament tradition offers a historically differentiated picture of the Christian understanding of peace and, accordingly, knows of different means of the Christian hope for and realization of peace. Although within the New Testament, there is little need to compare these different interpretational models to one another and integrate them theologically, we can still establish certain essential characteristics of the New Testament thought of peace. The decisive traditional-historical background for all models of exposition is the Old Testament/Jewish tradition. What peace means, then (in the New Testament), will be unfolded by christology in view of this tradition. Thus, we have a wide-ranging identification of peace and salvation as the liberating community of God through Jesus Christ. The opposite concept of this peace is almost generally life lacking salvation outside the community of God in Christ, including the world; only occasionally is war a mysterious possibility, among others, of such life. The receiver of peace is, first, the believing community, and within it, the individual Christian. From the reception of peace, the commission grows, both in the Christian and with other people, to testify to and impart the received salvation to the world and to other people, although this commission is perceived with differing degrees of urgency and scope. The determining framework for the understanding of peace and salvation, nevertheless, remains eschatology in all levels of the tradition. But since, from Easter on, this eschatology is seen to an ever-stronger degree as the fulfillment of the mission of Jesus in his end-time appearance and reign, it follows that the Christian understanding of peace is always developed and lived out from Jesus, to his end-time appearance.

THESIS 12: A hermeneutically careful interpretation of the New Testament thought on peace will leave its historical independence as it is. It must keep in view the positive and aporetic results of the interpretation and the effectual history of this peace-thought, and it may not renege on the correlation of christology and eschatology that has been gained from the New Testament. Actually, in all sober-minded views of the limited possibilities of a final, ultimate realization of peace, it will flatly refuse war as a form of human confrontation, will recognize the inadequacy of any conception of peace that is only the opposite of war, and especially will point the church, as well as the individual believer, to their duty and freedom for founding and preserving peace.

Bibliography

Adams, Rebecca. "Loving Mimesis and Girard's 'Scapegoat of the Text': A Creative Re-assessment of Mimetic Desire." In *Violence Renounced,* ed. Swartley, 277-307.

———. "Violence, Difference, Sacrifice: A Conversation with René Girard." *Journal of Religion and Literature* 25 (1993): 22-26.

Alison, James. *Raising Abel: The Recovery of Eschatological Imagination.* New York: Crossroad, 1996.

Alison, James, and Sandor Goodhart. "Colloquium on Violence and Religion." Conference on Judaism and Christianity in the Ancient World. Purdue University, 2002.

Allison, Dale C. *The Sermon on the Mount: Inspiring the Moral Imagination.* New York: Crossroad, 1999.

Anderson, Bernhard W. "The Messiah as Son of God: Peter's Confession in Traditio-Historical Perspective." In *Christological Perspectives: Essays in Honor of Harvey K. McArthur,* ed. Robert F. Berkey and Sarah A. Edwards, 157-69. New York: Pilgrim, 1982.

Anderson, Paul N. *The Christology of the Fourth Gospel: Its Unity and Disunity in Light of the Fourth Gospel.* Valley Forge: Trinity, 1997.

Arnold, Clinton. *Ephesians, Power and Magic: The Concept of Power in Ephesians in Light of Its Historical Setting.* SNTSMS 63. Cambridge: University of Cambridge Press, 1989.

———. *Powers of Darkness: Principalities and Powers in Paul's Letters.* Downers Grove: InterVarsity, 1992.

———. *Three Crucial Questions about Spiritual Warfare.* Grand Rapids: Baker, 1997.

Augsburger, Myron. *The Peacemaker.* Nashville: Abingdon, 1987.

Avalos, Hector. *Fighting Words: The Origins of Religious Violence.* Amherst: Prometheus, 2005.

Bacchiocchi, Samuele. *From Sabbath to Sunday: A Historical Investigation.* Rome: Pontifical Gregorian University Press, 1977.

Balch, David. "Hellenization/Acculturation in 1 Peter." In *Perspectives on First Peter,* ed. Charles Talbert, 61-101. Macon: Mercer University Press, 1986.

―――. *Let Wives Be Submissive: The Domestic Code in 1 Peter.* SBLMS 26. Chico: Scholars, 1981.

Bammel, Ernst. "The Commands in I Peter II.17." *NTS* 11 (1965): 279-81.

Barcley, William B. *"Christ in You": A Study in Paul's Theology and Ethics.* Lanham: University Press of America, 1999.

Barr, David L. "Doing Violence: Moral Issues in Reading John's Apocalypse." In *Reading the Book of Revelation: A Resource for Students,* ed. David L. Barr, 97-108. Atlanta: Society of Biblical Literature, 2003.

Barrett, Charles Kingsley. *Paul: An Introduction to His Thought.* London: Chapman, 1994.

Barth, Heinz-Lothar. "Das Verhältnis des Frühen Christentums zum Militär." In *Alvarium (FS für Christian Gnilka),* 1-26. Jahrbuch für Antike und Christentum Ergängzungsband 33. Münster: Aschendorf, 2002.

Barth, Marcus. "The Faith of the Messiah." *HeyJ* 10 (1969): 363-70.

―――. "Jews and Gentiles: The Social Character of Justification in Paul." *Ecumenical Studies* 5 (1968): 241.

Bartlett, Anthony W. *Cross Purposes: The Violent Grammar of Christian Atonement.* Harrisburg: Trinity, 2001.

Bartlett, David. "The First Letter of Peter." *NIB* XII. Nashville: Abingdon, 1998.

Bass, Dorothy C., ed. *Practicing Our Faith: A Way of Life for a Searching People.* San Francisco: Jossey-Bass, 1997.

Bauckham, Richard. *The Climax of Prophecy: Studies on the Book of Revelation.* Edinburgh: Clark, 1993.

―――. *Gospel Women: Studies of the Named Women in the Gospels.* Grand Rapids: Eerdmans, 2002.

―――. *The Gospels for All Christians: Rethinking the Gospel Audiences.* Grand Rapids: Eerdmans, 1998.

―――. "The Parting of the Ways: What Happened and Why?" *ST* 47 (1993): 135-51.

―――. "Prayer in the Book of Revelation." In *Into God's Presence: Prayer in the New Testament,* ed. Richard N. Longenecker, 252-71. Grand Rapids: Eerdmans, 2001.

―――. *2 Peter, Jude.* WBC 50. Waco: Word, 1983.

―――. *The Theology of Jürgen Moltmann.* Edinburgh: Clark, 1995.

―――. *The Theology of the Book of Revelation.* Cambridge: Cambridge University Press, 1993.

Bauman, Clarence. *The Sermon on the Mount: The Modern Quest for Its Meaning.* Macon: Mercer University Press, 1985.

Bauman, Elizabeth. *Coals of Fire.* Scottdale: Herald, 1954.

Beale, G. K. *The Book of Revelation: A Commentary on the Greek Text.* Grand Rapids: Eerdmans, 1999.

―――. "Review Article." *TRINJ* 25 (2004): 93-101.

Beck, H., and C. Brown. "Peace." In *The New International Dictionary of New Testament Theology,* ed. Colin Brown. Vol. 2. Grand Rapids: Zondervan, 1976, 1986.

Beck, Robert. *Nonviolent Story: Narrative Conflict Resolution in the Gospel of Mark.* Maryknoll: Orbis, 1996.

Beker, Johan Christiaan. *Paul the Apostle: The Triumph of God in Life and Thought.* Philadelphia: Fortress, 1980.

Bender, Philip D. "The Holy War Trajectory in the Synoptic Gospels and the Pauline Writings." MA thesis, Associated Mennonite Biblical Seminary, 1987.

Berkhof, Hendrik. *Christ and the Powers.* Translated by J. H. Yoder. Scottdale: Herald, 1962.

Best, Ernest. *The Temptation and Passion: The Marcan Soteriology.* SNTSMS 2. Cambridge: Cambridge University Press, 1965.

Betz, Hans D. "The Sermon on the Mount: In Defense of a Hypothesis." *BR* 36 (1991): 74-80.

Bianchi, Ugo. "Dualism." In *Encyclopedia of Religion,* ed. Mircea Eliade. New York: Macmillan, 1987.

Bigg, Charles. *Epistles of St. Peter and St. Jude.* ICC. Edinburgh: Clark, 1901.

Birch, Bruce C., and Larry L. Rasmussen. *Bible and Ethics in the Christian Life.* Revised and expanded edition. Minneapolis: Augsburg Fortress, 1989.

Blank, Joseph. "Gewaltlosigkeit — Krieg — Militärdienst." *Orientierung* 46 (1982): 157-63.

———. *Im Dienst der Versöhnung: Friedenspraxis aus christlicher Sicht.* Munich: Kösel, 1984.

Boers, Arthur. *Lord, Teach Us to Pray.* Scottdale: Herald, 1992.

Boers, Hendrikus. *Neither on This Mountain nor in Jerusalem.* SBLMS 35. Atlanta: Scholars, 1988.

Boersma, Hans. *Violence, Hospitality, and the Cross: Appropriating the Atonement Tradition.* Grand Rapids: Baker, 2004.

Borg, Marcus. *Jesus, A New Vision: Spirit, Culture and the Life of Discipleship.* San Francisco: Harper and Row, 1988.

Bosch, David. *Transforming Mission: Paradigm Shifts in Theology of Mission.* ASMS 16. Maryknoll: Orbis, 1991.

Bovon, François. "Israel, die Kirche und die Völker im lukanischen Doppelwerk." *Theologische Literaturzeitung* 108 (1983): 403-14.

———. "Studies in Luke-Acts: Retrospect and Prospect." *HTR* 85 (1992): 175-96 = Bovon, *Studies in Early Christianity,* pp. 19-37. Grand Rapids: Baker, 2005.

Boyarin, Daniel. *Dying for God: Martyrdom and the Making of Christianity and Judaism.* Stanford: Stanford University Press, 1999.

———. *A Radical Jew: Paul and the Politics of Identity.* Berkeley: University of California Press, 1994.

Boyd, Gregory A. *God at War: The Bible and Spiritual Conflict.* Downers Grove: InterVarsity, 1997.

Brandenburger, Egon. *Frieden im Neuen Testament. Grundlinien urchristlichen Friedensverständnisse.* Gütersloh: Mohn, 1973.

———. "Grundlinien des Friedensverständnisses im Neuen Testament." *Wort und Dienst* 11 (1971): 21-72.

———. "Perspektiven des Friedens im Neuen Testament." *Bibel und Kirche* 37 (1982): 31-33.

Bredin, Mark. *Jesus, Revolutionary of Peace: A Nonviolent Christology in the Book of Revelation.* London: Paternoster, 2003.

———. "The Synagogue of Satan Accusation in Revelation 2:9." *BTB* 28 (1998): 160-64.

Brock, Peter. "Why Did St. Maximilian Refuse to Serve in the Roman Army?" *JEH* 45 (1994): 195-209.

Brodie, Thomas L. *The Gospel According to John: A Literary and Theological Commentary.* Oxford: Oxford University Press, 1993.

Brown, Dale W. *Biblical Pacifism.* Second edition. Nappanee: Evangel, 2003.

Brown, Raymond E. *The Gospel According to John I-XII.* Garden City: Doubleday, 1966.

Bruce, F. F. *The Spreading Flame.* Devon: Paternoster, 1958.

Brueggemann, Walter. *Peace.* St. Louis: Chalice Press, 2001. New edition of *Living toward a Vision: Biblical Reflections on Shalom.* Philadelphia: United Church, 1976.

Budde, Ludwig. *Ara Pacis Augustae. Der Friedensaltar des Augustus.* Hanover: Tauros, 1957.

Buell, Denise Kimber, and Carolyne Johnson Hodge. "The Politics of Interpretation: The Rhetoric of Race and Ethnicity in Paul." *JBL* 123 (2004): 235-51.

Bultmann, Rudolf. *Theology of the New Testament.* Volumes 1 and 2. New York: Scribner, 1951.

Burge, Gary. *The NIV Application Commentary: John.* Grand Rapids: Zondervan, 2000.

Burger, Christoph. *Jesus als Davidssohn. Eine traditionsgeschichtliche Untersuchung.* Göttingen: Vandenhoeck und Ruprecht, 1970.

Burton-Edwards, Taylor. "The Teaching of Peace in Early Christian Liturgies." M.A. Thesis, Associated Mennonite Biblical Seminary, 1997.

Caird, G. B. *New Testament Theology.* Completed and edited by L. D. Hurst. Oxford: Oxford University Press, 1994.

————. *Principalities and Powers: A Study in Pauline Theology.* Oxford: Clarendon, 1956.

————. *The Revelation of St John the Divine.* London: Black, 1966.

Campenhausen, H. von. "Zur Auslegung von Röm. 13. Die dämonische Deutung des ἐξουσία-Begriffs." In *Festschrift für S. A. Bertholet zum 80. Geburtstag,* ed. W. Baumgartner, 97-113. Tübingen: Mohr, 1950.

Carr, Wesley. *Angels and Principalities: The Background, Meaning and Development of the Pauline Phrase Hai Archai kai Hai Exousiai.* SNTMS 42. Cambridge: Cambridge University Press, 1981.

Carter, Warren. "Are There Imperial Texts in the Class? Intertextual Eagles and Matthean Eschatology as 'Lights Out' Time for Imperial Rome (Matthew 24:27-31)." *JBL* 122 (2003): 467-87.

————. *Matthew and Empire: Initial Explorations.* Harrisburg: Trinity, 2001.

————. *Matthew and the Margins: A Sociopolitical and Religious Reading.* Maryknoll: Orbis, 2000.

Cassidy, Richard J. *Jesus, Politics, and Society: A Study of Luke's Gospel.* Maryknoll: Orbis, 1978.

————. *John's Gospel in New Perspective: Christology and the Realities of Roman Power.* Maryknoll: Orbis, 1992.

————. *Society and Politics in the Acts of the Apostles.* Maryknoll: Orbis, 1987.

Castelli, Elizabeth A. *Imitating Paul: A Discourse of Power.* Louisville: Westminster John Knox, 1991.

Cerfaux, Lucien. *Christ in the Theology of St. Paul.* New York: Herder and Herder, 1959.

————. *The Christian in the Theology of St. Paul.* London: Chapman, 1967.

————.*The Church in the Theology of St Paul*. New York: Herder and Herder, 1959.

Charles, J. Daryl. "2 Peter, Jude." In *1-2 Peter, Jude*, by Erland Waltner and J. Daryl Charles, BCBC. Scottdale: Herald, 1999.

Charlesworth, James H. "Hillel and Jesus: Why Comparisons Are Important." In *Hillel and Jesus: Comparisons of Two Major Religious Leaders*, ed. J. H. Charlesworth and Loren L. Johns, 3-30. Minneapolis: Fortress, 1997.

————. *OTP* 1. New York: Doubleday, 1983.

Charlesworth, James H., ed. *The Messiah: Developments in Earliest Judaism and Christianity*. Minneapolis: Fortress, 1992.

Chilton, Bruce. *A Galilean Rabbi and His Bible: Jesus' Use of the Interpreted Scripture of His Time*. Wilmington: Glazier, 1984.

————. "Regnum Dei Deus Est." *Scottish Journal of Theology* 31 (1978): 261-70.

————. *The Temple of Jesus: His Sacrificial Program within a Cultural History of Sacrifice*. University Park: Pennsylvania State University Press, 1992.

Chow, John K. "Patronage in Roman Corinth." In *Paul and Empire*, ed. Horsley, 104-25.

Christensen, Torben. *Christus oder Jupiter. Der Kampf um die geistigen Grundlagen des römischen Reiches*. Göttingen: Vandenhoeck und Ruprecht, 1981.

Collins, Adela Yarbro. *Crisis and Catharsis: The Power of the Apocalypse*. Philadelphia: Fortress, 1984.

————. "Persecution and Vengeance in the Book of Revelation." In *Apocalypticism in the Mediterranean World and the Near East* (Uppsala Colloquium on Apocalyptic, 1979), ed. David Hellholm, 729-49. Tübingen: Mohr, 1983.

————. "The Political Perspective of the Book of Revelation." *JBL* 96 (1977): 241-56.

Collins, John J. *The Apocalyptic Imagination: An Introduction to the Jewish Matrix of Christianity*. New York: Crossroad, 1984.

————. *The Scepter and the Star: The Messiahs of the Dead Sea Scrolls and Other Ancient Literature*. New York: Doubleday, 1995.

Collins, Raymond F. "Speaking of the Jews: 'Jews' in the Discourse Material of the Fourth Gospel." In *Anti-Judaism and the Fourth Gospel*, ed. Reimund Bieringer, Didier Pollefeyt, and Frederique Vandecasteele-Vanneuville, 158-75. Louisville: Westminster John Knox, 2001.

Collins, Robin. "Girard and Atonement: An Incarnational Theory of Mimetic Participation." In *Violence Renounced*, ed. Swartley, 132-53.

Coloe, Mary L. "Welcome into the Household of God: The Foot Washing in John 13." *CBQ* 66 (2004): 400-15.

Comblin, Joseph. "La Paix dans la Théologie de saint Luc." *ETL* 32 (1956): 439-60.

Conrad, Edgar W. *Fear Not Warrior: A Study of 'al tîrā' Pericopes in the Hebrew Scriptures*. Brown Judaic Studies 75. Chico: Scholars, 1985.

Conzelmann, Hans. *An Outline of the Theology of the New Testament*. New York: Harper and Row, 1969.

Cook, Gerald. "The Israelite King as Son of God." *ZAW* 73 (1961): 202-25.

Corley, Kathleen E. *Private Women; Public Meals*. Peabody: Hendrickson, 1993.

Crosby, Michael. *Spirituality of the Beatitudes: Matthew's Challenge for First World Christians*. Maryknoll: Orbis, 1981.

Cross, Frank L. *1 Peter, A Paschal Liturgy*. London: Mobray, 1954.

Culbertson, Diana. "Response" to "Colloquium" draft of "Discipleship and Imitation of Jesus/Suffering Servant: The Mimesis of New Creation," by Willard M. Swartley. Unpublished, 1994.

Cullmann, Oscar. *The State in the New Testament*. New York: Scribner, 1956.

Culpepper, R. Alan. "Inclusivism and Exclusivism in the Fourth Gospel." In *Word, Theology, and Community in John*, ed. John R. Painter, Alan Culpepper, and Fernando F. Segovia, 85-108. St. Louis: Chalice, 2002.

————. "An Introduction to the Johannine Writings." In *The Johannine Literature*, ed. Barnabas Lindars, Ruth B. Edwards, and John M. Court, 4-27. Sheffield: Sheffield Academic, 2000.

Dalton, W. J. *Christ's Proclamation to the Spirits*. AnBib 23. Rome: Pontifical Biblical Institute, 1965.

Daly, Robert J. *Christian Biblical Ethics: From Biblical Revelation to Contemporary Christian Praxis: Method and Content*. New York: Paulist, 1984.

D'Angelo, Mary Rose. "Abba and 'Father': Imperial Theology and the Jesus Traditions." *JBL* 111 (1992): 611-30.

Davids, Peter. *The First Epistle of Peter*. NICNT. Grand Rapids: Eerdmans, 1990.

Davies, W. D. *Jewish and Pauline Studies*. Philadelphia: Fortress, 1984.

————. *The Setting of the Sermon on the Mount*. Brown Judaic Studies 186. Atlanta: Scholars, 1989.

Dawn, Marva J. "The Biblical Concept of 'the Principalities and Powers': John Yoder Points to Jacques Ellul." In *The Wisdom of the Cross: Essays in Honor of John Howard Yoder*, ed. Stanley Hauerwas, Chris K. Huebner, Harry J. Huebner, and Mark Thiessen Nation, 168-86. Grand Rapids: Eerdmans, 1999.

————. *Powers, Weakness, and the Tabernacling of God*. Grand Rapids: Eerdmans, 2001.

Dear, John. *The God of Peace: Toward a Theology of Nonviolence*. Maryknoll: Orbis, 1994.

de Boer, Martinus C. "The Depiction of 'the Jews' in John's Gospel: Matters of Behavior and Identity." In *Anti-Judaism and the Fourth Gospel*, ed. Reimund Bieringer, Didier Pollefeyt, and Frederique Vandecasteele-Vanneuville, 141-57. Louisville: Westminster John Knox, 2001.

Deissmann, Adolf. *Light from the Ancient East*. Tübingen: Mohr, 1908. Trans. Lionel R. M. Strachan. London, Hodder and Stoughton, 1910 (1927 edition). Reprint: Grand Rapids: Baker, 1965.

de Jonge, Hans Jan. "'The Jews' in the Gospel of John." In *Anti-Judaism and the Fourth Gospel*, ed. Reimund Bieringer, Didier Pollefeyt, and Frederique Vandecasteele-Vanneuville, 121-40. Louisville: Westminster John Knox, 2001.

Delling, Gerhard. "Die Bezeichnung 'Gott des Friedens' und ähnliche Wendungen in den Paulusbriefen." In *Jesus und Paulus*, ed. E. E. Ellis and E. Grässer, 76-84. Göttingen: Vandenhoeck und Ruprecht, 1975.

deSilva, David A. *Honor, Patronage, Kinship and Purity: Unlocking New Testament Culture*. Downers Grove: InterVarsity, 2000.

Desjardins, Michel. *Peace and Violence in the New Testament*. The Biblical Seminar 46. Sheffield: Sheffield Academic, 1997.

Dewey, Joanna. "Women in the Synoptic Gospels: Seen but Not Heard?" *BTB* 27 (1997): 53-60.

de Wit, Hans, Louis Jonker, Marleen Kool, and Daniel Schipani, eds. *Through the Eyes of Another: Intercultural Reading of the Bible.* Elkhart: Institute of Mennonite Studies/ Amsterdam: Vrije Universiteit, 2004.

Dibelius, Martin. *An die Kolosser, Epheser, an Philemon.* HNT 12. Third ed. Tübingen: Mohr, 1953.

———. *Die Geisterwelt im Glauben des Paulus.* Göttingen: Vandenhoeck und Ruprecht, 1909.

———. *James: A Commentary on the Epistle of James.* Revised by Heinrich Greeven, trans. M. A. Williams, ed. Helmut Koester. Hermeneia. Philadelphia: Fortress, 1976.

Dinkler, Erich. "*Eirēnē* — The Early Christian Concept of Peace." In *The Meaning of Peace,* ed. P. B. Yoder, 71-120 (1992 ed., pp. 164-212).

———. "Die Verkündigung als eschatologisch-sakramentales Geschehen." In *Die Zeit Jesu,* ed. G. Bornkamm and K. Rahner, 169-189. Freiburg: Herder, 1970.

Dodd, C. H. *According to the Scripture: The Sub-Structure of New Testament Theology.* London: Nisbet, 1952.

———. "The Theology of Pacifism." In *The Bases of Christian Pacifism,* ed. Charles Raven, 5-15. London: Council of Christian Pacifist Groups, 1938.

Donahue, John R. *Are You the Christ? The Trial Narrative in the Gospel of Mark.* SBLDS 10. Missoula: Society of Biblical Literature, 1973.

———. "Biblical Perspectives on Justice." In *The Faith That Does Justice: Examining the Christian Sources for Social Change,* ed. John C. Haughey, 68-112. New York: Paulist Press, 1977.

———. "The Good News of Peace." *The Way* 22 (April 1982): 88-89.

———. *The Gospel in Parable: Metaphor, Narrative, and Theology in the Synoptic Gospels.* Philadelphia: Fortress, 1988.

———. "Who Is My Enemy? The Parable of the Good Samaritan and Love of Enemies." In *Love of Enemy and Nonretaliation,* ed. Swartley, 137-56.

Driver, John. *Understanding the Atonement for the Mission of the Church.* Scottdale: Herald, 1986.

Duchrow, Ulrich, and Gerhard Liedke. *Shalom: Biblical Perspectives on Creation, Justice, and Peace.* Geneva: WCC, 1989.

Dunn, James D. G. "John VI — A Eucharistic Discourse?" *NTS* 17 (1971): 328-38.

———. "The New Perspective on Paul." In *Jesus, Paul, and the Law,* 183-214. Louisville: Westminster John Knox, 1990.

———. *The Partings of the Ways between Judaism and Christianity and Their Significance for the Character of Christianity.* London: SCM/Philadelphia: Trinity, 1991.

———. *The Theology of Paul the Apostle.* Grand Rapids: Eerdmans, 1998.

Dunn, James D. G., ed. *Jews and Christians: The Parting of the Ways, A.D. 70-135.* WUNT 66. Tübingen: Mohr, 1992/Grand Rapids: Eerdmans, 1993.

Eaton, John H. *Kingship and the Psalms.* SBT 2/32. Naperville: Allenson, n.d.

Edwards, George R. "Biblical and Contemporary Aspects of War Tax Resistance." In *The*

Peacemaking Struggle: Militarism and Resistance, ed. R. H. Stone and D. W. Wilbanks, 111-22. Lanham: University Press of America, 1985.

Egan, Eileen. *Peace Be with You: Justified Warfare or the Way of Nonviolence.* Maryknoll: Orbis, 1999.

Eisenbeis, Walter. "A Study of the Root Shalom in the Old Testament." Ph.D. Diss., University of Chicago, 1966. Published as *Die Würzel* שלם *im Alten Testament.* BZAW 113. Berlin: de Gruyter, 1969.

Elias, Jacob W. *1 and 2 Thessalonians.* BCBC. Scottdale: Herald, 1995.

———. "Jesus Who Delivers Us from the Wrath to Come." *SBL Seminar Papers,* 121-32. Atlanta: Scholars, 1992.

———. "The New Has Come: An Exegetical and Theological Discussion of 2 Corinthians 5:11–6:10." In *Beautiful upon the Mountains,* ed. Schertz, 197-214.

Eller, Vernard. *The Most Revealing Book of the Bible: Making Sense Out of Revelation.* Grand Rapids: Eerdmans, 1974.

Elliott, John H. "The Evil Eye and the Sermon on the Mount." *BibInt* 2 (1994): 51-84.

———. "I Peter, Its Situation and Strategy: A Discussion with David Balch." In *Perspectives on First Peter,* ed. Charles Talbert, 61-101. Macon: Mercer University Press, 1986.

———. *A Home for the Homeless: A Sociological Exegesis of 1 Peter, Its Situation and Strategy.* Philadelphia: Fortress, 1981.

———. "The Rehabilitation of an Exegetical Step-Child: 1 Peter in Recent Research." *JBL* 95 (1976): 243-54.

Elliott, Neil. "The Anti-Imperial Message of the Cross." In *Paul and Empire,* ed. Horsley, 167-83.

———. *Liberating Paul: The Justice of God and the Politics of the Apostle.* Maryknoll: Orbis, 1994.

Ellis, Peter F. *The Genius of John: A Composition-Critical Commentary on the Fourth Gospel.* Collegeville: Liturgical, 1984.

———. *Matthew: His Mind and His Message.* Collegeville: Liturgical, 1974.

Ellul, Jacques. *Apocalypse: The Book of Revelation.* Trans. G. W. Schreiner. New York: Seabury, 1977.

———. *The Ethics of Freedom.* Grand Rapids: Eerdmans, 1976.

Enns, Fernando, Scott Holland, and Ann K. Riggs, eds. *Seeking Cultures of Peace: A Peace Church Conversation.* Telford: Cascadia, 2004.

Erdmann, Martin. "Mission in John's Gospel and Letters." In *Mission in the New Testament: An Evangelical Approach,* ed. William F. Larkin, Jr., and Joel F. Carpenter, 207-26. Maryknoll: Orbis, 1998.

Evans, Craig A. *Mark 8:27–16:20.* WBC 34B. Nashville: Nelson, 2001.

———. "The New Testament and First-Century Judaism." In *Anti-Semitism and Early Christianity: Issues of Polemic and Faith,* ed. Craig A. Evans and Donald A. Hagner, 1-20. Minneapolis: Fortress, 1993.

Evans, Craig A., and James A. Sanders, eds. *Luke and Sacred Scripture: The Function of Sacred Scripture in Luke-Acts.* Minneapolis: Fortress, 1993.

Farley, Benjamin W. *In Praise of Virtue: An Exploration of the Biblical Virtues in a Christian Context.* Grand Rapids: Eerdmans, 1995.

Farmer, William R. *Jesus and the Gospel: Tradition, Scripture and Canon*. Philadelphia: Fortress, 1982.

————, ed. *Anti-Judaism and the Gospels*. Harrisburg: Trinity, 1999.

Farmer, William R., and Denis M. Farkasfalvy. *The Formation of the New Testament Canon: An Ecumenical Approach*. New York: Paulist, 1983.

Fawcett, Thomas. *Hebrew Myth and Christian Gospel*. London: SCM, 1973.

Ferguson, John. *The Politics of Love: The New Testament and Nonviolent Revolution*. Greenwood: Attic, n.d.

Finger, Reta Halteman. "'Reconciled to God through the Death of his Son': A Mission of Peacemaking in Romans 5:1-11." In *Beautiful upon the Mountains*, ed. Schertz, 183-96.

Finger, Thomas N. *Christian Theology: An Eschatological Approach*. Vol. 1. Scottdale: Herald, 1985.

Finger, Thomas N., and Willard M. Swartley. "Bondage and Deliverance: Biblical and Theological Perspectives," with response by Josephine M. Ford. In *Essays on Spiritual Bondage and Deliverance*, ed. Swartley, 10-45. OP 11. Elkhart: Institute of Mennonite Studies, 1988.

Fischer, Kathleen M., and Urban C. Von Wahlde. "The Miracles of Mark 4:35–5:43: Their Meaning and Function in the Gospel Framework." *BTB* 11 (1981): 13-16.

Fitzmyer, J. A. "'Now This Melchizedek. . . .'" *CBQ* 25 (1963): 305-21.

Fitzmyer, Joseph A. *Romans: A New Translation with Introduction and Commentary*. Anchor Bible 33. New York: Doubleday, 1993.

Flusser, David. "Blessed Are the Poor in Spirit." *Israel Exploration Journal* 10 (1960): 1-13.

————. *Jesus*. Jerusalem: Magnes, 1998.

Fodor, Jim. "Christian Discipleship as Participative Imitation: Theological Reflections on Girardian Themes." In *Violence Renounced*, ed. Swartley, 246-76.

————. "Imitation and Emulation: Training in Practical Christian Judgment." Manuscript for Stanley Hauerwas. The Divinity School of Duke University, n.d.

Foerster, W. Εἰρήνη. *TDNT* 2: 400-402. Grand Rapids: Eerdmans, 1964.

Ford, J. Massyngberde. *My Enemy Is My Guest: Jesus and Violence in Luke*. Maryknoll: Orbis, 1984.

————. "Reconciliation and Forgiveness in Luke's Gospel." In *Political Issues in Luke-Acts*, ed. R. J. Cassidy and P. J. Sharper, 80-98. Maryknoll: Orbis, 1983.

Forsyth, Neil. *The Old Enemy: Satan and the Combat Myth*. Princeton: Princeton University Press, 1987.

Fowl, Stephen E., and L. Gregory Jones. *Reading in Communion: Scripture and Ethics in Christian Life*. Grand Rapids: Eerdmans, 1991.

Franke, Peter Robert, and Max Hirmer. *Die griechische Münze*. Munich: Hirmer, 1964.

Frankemölle, Hubert. "Jesus als deuterojesajanische Freudenbote? Zur Rezeption von Jes 52,7 und 61,1 im Neuen Testament, durch Jesus und in den Targumim." In *Vom Christentum zu Jesus* (FS Joachim Gnilka), ed. Frankemölle, 34-67. Freiberg: Herder, 1989.

————. "Peace and the Sword in the New Testament," in *The Meaning of Peace*, ed. P. B. Yoder, 191-210 (1992 edition, pp. 213-33).

Franklin, E. *Christ the Lord: A Study in the Purpose and Theology of Luke-Acts*. Philadelphia: Fortress, 1975.

Frend, W. H. C. *Martyrdom and Persecution in the Early Church: A Study of Conflict from the Maccabees to Donatus*. Oxford: Blackwell, 1965.

Fretheim, Terence E. "Theological Reflections on the Wrath of God in the Old Testament." *HBT* 24 (2002): 1-26.

Friedrich, Johannes, Wolfgang Pöhlmann, and Peter Stuhlmacher. "Situation und Intention von Röm 13.1-7." *ZTK* 73 (1967): 131-66.

Friesen, Steven. *Imperial Cults and the Apocalypse of John*. Oxford: Oxford University Press, 2001.

———. "Myth and Symbolic Resistance in Revelation 13." *JBL* 123 (2004): 281-313.

Fuchs, Harald. *Augustin und der antike Friedensgedanke. Untersuchungen zum neunzehnten Buch der Civitas Dei*. Second edition. Berlin: Weidmann, 1965.

Furnish, Victor Paul. *The Love Command in the New Testament*. Nashville: Abingdon, 1972.

———. *Theology and Ethics in Paul*. Nashville: Abingdon, 1968.

———. "War and Peace in the New Testament." *Int* 38 (1984): 363-79.

Gager, John. *Kingdom and Community: The Social World of Early Christianity*. Englewood Cliffs: Prentice-Hall, 1976.

García, Ismael. "Reflections on Violence." *New Conversations* 16 (1994): 16-26.

Gardner, Richard B. *Matthew*. BCBC. Scottdale: Herald, 1991.

Garnsey, Peter, and Richard Saller. "Patronal Power Relations." In *Paul and Empire*, ed. Horsley, 96-103.

Garrett, Susan. *The Demise of the Devil: Magic and the Demonic in Luke's Writings*. Minneapolis: Fortress, 1989.

———. "Exodus from Bondage: Luke 9:31 and Acts 12:1-24," *CBQ* 52 (1990): 85-88.

Gaston, Lloyd. *No Stone on Another: Studies in the Significance of the Fall of Jerusalem in the Synoptic Gospels*. NovTSup 23. Leiden: Brill, 1970.

Gehman, Steven. "'Rejoice O Heaven! Babylon Is Fallen!'" Unpublished.

Georgi, Dieter. *Remembering the Poor: The History of Paul's Collection for the Poor*. Trans. John Bowden. Nashville: Abingdon, 1992.

———. *Theocracy in Paul's Praxis and Theology*. Trans. David E. Green. Minneapolis: Augsburg Fortress, 1991.

Gerbrandt, Gerald E. *Kingship according to the Deuteronomic History*. SBLDS 87. Atlanta: Scholars, 1986.

Gerleman, Gillis. "שׁלם." *THAT* 2:919-35.

Gibson, Jeffrey B. "Jesus' Wilderness Temptation according to Mark." *JSNT* 53 (1994): 3-34.

———. *The Temptations of Jesus in Early Christianity*. JSNTSS 112. Sheffield: Sheffield Academic, 1995.

Gilbertson, Michael. *God and History in the Book of Revelation: New Testament Studies in Dialogue with Pannenberg and Moltmann*. SNTSMS 124. Cambridge: Cambridge University Press, 2003.

Gingerich, Ray C. "Reimaging Power: Toward a Theology of Nonviolence." In *Peace and Justice Shall Embrace*, ed. Grimsrud, 192-216.

Girard, René. "How Can Satan Cast Out Satan?" In *Biblische Theologie und gesellschaft-*

licher Wandel für Norbert Lohfink SJ, ed. Georg Braulik, Walter Gross, and Sean McEvenue, 125-41. Freiburg: Herder, 1993.

———. *I See Satan Fall like Lightning.* New York: Orbis, 2001.

———. *The Scapegoat.* Translated by Yvonne Freccero. Baltimore: Johns Hopkins University Press, 1986.

———. *Things Hidden since the Foundation of the World.* Stanford: Stanford University Press, 1987.

———. *Violence and the Sacred.* Baltimore: Johns Hopkins, 1977.

Goetz, Ron. "The Primordial Violence of God." *New Conversations* 16 (1994): 27-37.

Goldsmith, Dale. *New Testament Ethics: An Introduction.* Elgin: Brethren, 1988.

Goldstein, H. "Die politischen Paränesen in 1 Petr 2 und Röm 13." *BibLeb* 14 (1973): 88-104.

Good, Deirdre J. *The Meek King.* Harrisburg: Trinity, 1999.

Goodhart, Sandor. "René Girard and the Innocent Victim." In *Violence Renounced,* ed. Swartley, 200-217.

———. "We Will Cling Fast to Your Torah. . . ." *COV & R Bulletin* 19 (2000): 15.

Gopin, Marc. "Judaism and Peacebuilding." In *Religion and Peacebuilding,* ed. Harold Coward and Gordon S. Smith, 111-27. Albany: SUNY Press, 2004.

Goppelt, Leonhard. *A Commentary on 1 Peter,* ed. Ferdinand Hahn, trans. and augmented by John E. Alsup. Grand Rapids: Eerdmans, 1993.

———. *A Theology of the New Testament.* Vols. 1 and 2. Trans. John E. Alsup. Grand Rapids: Eerdmans, 1981.

Gordon, Richard. "The Veil of Power." In *Paul and Empire,* ed. Horsley, 126-37.

Gorman, Michael J. *Cruciformity: Paul's Narrative Spirituality of the Cross.* Grand Rapids: Eerdmans, 2001.

Gornik, Mark R. *To Live in Peace: Biblical Faith and the Changing Inner City.* Grand Rapids: Eerdmans, 2002.

Grassi, Joseph A. *Informing the Future: Social Justice in the New Testament.* Mahwah: Paulist, 2003.

———. *Peace on Earth: Roots and Practices from Luke's Gospel.* Collegeville: Liturgical, 2004.

Green, Joel B., and Mark D. Baker. *Recovering the Scandal of the Cross: Atonement in New Testament and Contemporary Contexts.* Downers Grove: InterVarsity, 2000.

Griffiths, Michael. *The Example of Jesus.* Downers Grove: InterVarsity, 1985.

Grimsrud, Ted. "Peace Theology and the Justice of God in the Book of Revelation." In *Essays on Peace Theology and Witness,* ed. Willard M. Swartley, 135-53. OP 12. Elkhart: Institute of Mennonite Studies, 1988.

Grimsrud, Ted, and Loren L. Johns, eds. *Peace and Justice Shall Embrace: Power and Theopolitics in the Bible.* Telford: Pandora (now Cascadia)/Scottdale: Herald, 1999.

Guelich, Robert A. "What Is the Gospel?" *Theology, News, and Notes* (Fuller Theological Seminary) 51 (2004): 4-7.

Gundry, Robert H. *Jesus the Word According to John the Sectarian: A Paleofundamentalist Manifesto for Contemporary Evangelicalism, Especially Its Elites in North America.* Grand Rapids: Eerdmans, 2002.

———. *Mark: A Commentary on His Apology for the Cross.* Grand Rapids: Eerdmans, 1993.

―――. *Matthew: A Commentary on His Literary and Theological Art.* Grand Rapids: Eerdmans, 1982.

Gundry-Volf, Judith. "Spirit, Mercy and the Other." *Theology Today* 51 (1995): 508-23.

Haacker, Klaus. "Der Römerbrief als Friedensmemorandum." *NTS* 36 (1990): 25-41.

Haag, H. חָמַס. *Theological Dictionary of the Old Testament* IV, 485-86.

Habicht, Christian. "Die Augusteische Zeit und das erste Jahrhundert nach Christi Geburt." In *Le culte des souverains dans l'Empire Romain,* ed. E. J. Bickermann, et al., 41-69. Vandœuvres-Genève: Fondation Hardt, 1973.

Hamerton-Kelly, Robert. *The Gospel and the Sacred: Poetics of Violence in Mark.* Minneapolis: Fortress, 1994.

Hanson, A. T. *The Wrath of the Lamb.* New York: Seabury, 1957.

Hanson, Paul D. "Apocalypse, Genre," "Apocalypticism." In *IDBSupp,* 27-34. Nashville: Abingdon, 1976.

―――. "War and Peace in Hebrew Scripture." *Int* 38 (1984): 341-62.

Hanson, Paul D., ed. *Visionaries and Their Apocalypses.* Philadephia: Fortress, 1983.

Hardin, Michael. "Mimesis and Dominion: The Dynamics of Violence and the Imitation of Christ in Maximus Confessor." *St. Vladimir's Theological Quarterly* 36 (1992): 373-85.

Harnack, Adolf von. *Militia Christi: The Christian Religion and the Military in the First Three Centuries.* Trans. D. M. Gracie. Philadelphia: Fortress, 1981.

Harris, J. Douglas. *Shalom! The Biblical Concept of Peace.* Grand Rapids: Baker, 1970.

Harrisville, Roy A. *The Miracle of Mark.* Minneapolis: Augsburg, 1967.

Hasel, Gerhard. *New Testament Theology: Basic Issues in the Current Debate.* Rev. ed. Grand Rapids: Eerdmans, 1990.

Hastings, James. *The Christian Doctrine of Peace.* Edinburgh: Clark, 1922.

Hauerwas, Stanley. *Character and the Christian Life: A Study in Theological Ethics.* San Antonio: Trinity University Press, 1975.

―――. *A Community of Character: Toward a Constructive Christian Social Ethic.* Notre Dame: University of Notre Dame Press, 1981.

―――. "Explaining Christian Nonviolence: Notes for a Conversation with John Milbank." In *Must Christianity Be Violent? Reflections on History, Practice, and Theology,* ed. Kenneth R. Chase and Alan Jacobs, 172-82. Grand Rapids: Brazos, 2003.

―――. *The Peaceable Kingdom: A Primer in Christian Ethics.* Notre Dame: University of Notre Dame Press, 1983.

―――. *Unleashing the Scriptures: Freeing the Bible from the Captivity to America.* Nashville: Abingdon, 1993.

Hay, David M. *Glory at the Right Hand: Psalm 110 in Early Christianity.* SBLMS 18. Nashville: Abingdon, 1973.

Hays, Richard B. *The Faith of Jesus Christ: An Investigation into the Narrative Substructure of Galatians 3:1–4:11.* SBLDS 56. Chico: Society of Biblical Literature, 1983. Second edition: *The Faith of Jesus Christ: The Narrative Substructure of Galatians 3:1–4:11.* Grand Rapids: Eerdmans, 2002.

―――. *The Moral Vision of the New Testament.* San Francisco: HarperSanFrancisco, 1996.

―――. *New Testament Ethics: The Story Retold.* Winnipeg: CMBC, 1998.

Heil, J. P. "Ezekiel 34 and the Narrative Strategy of the Shepherd and Sheep Metaphor in Matthew." *CBQ* 55 (1993): 698-708.

Helgeland, John. "Roman Army Religion." *ANRW* 2.16.2, ed. Wolfgang Haase, 1470-1505. Berlin: de Gruyter, 1978.

Hengel, Martin. *Victory over Violence: Jesus and the Revolutionists.* Translated by David E. Green. Philadelphia: Fortress, 1973.

————. *The Zealots: Investigations into the Jewish Freedom Movement in the Period from Herod I until 70 A.D.* Trans. D. Smith. Edinburgh: Clark, 1989.

Herz, P. "Bibliographie zum römischen Kaiserkult." *ANRW* 2.16.2, ed. W. Haase, 834-910. Berlin and New York: de Gruyter, 1978.

Hesselink, I. J. "John 14:23-29." *Int* 43 (1989): 174-77.

Hinkle, Mary E. "The Lord's Prayer: Empowerment for Living the Sermon on the Mount." *World and World* 22 (2002): 9-17.

Hirmer, Max A. See Franke.

Holland, Scott. "The Gospel of Peace and the Violence of God." *Cross Currents* 51 (2002): 470-83.

————. "The Gospel of Peace and the Violence of God." In *Seeking Cultures of Peace,* ed. Enns, Holland, and Riggs, 132-46.

Holsopple, Mary Yoder, Ruth E. Krall, and Sharon Weaver Pittman. *Building Peace: Overcoming Violence in Communities.* Geneva: WCC, 2004.

Holtz, Traugott. *Die Christologie der Apokalypse des Johannes.* Berlin: Academie, 1962.

Hooker, Morna D. "ΠΙΣΤΙΣ ΧΡΙΣΤΟΥ." *NTS* 35 (1989): 321-42.

————. *The Son of Man in Mark.* Montreal: McGill University Press, 1967.

Horbury, William. "'Gospel' in Herodian Judaea." In *The Written Gospel,* ed. Markus Bockmuehl and Donald Hagner, 7-30. Cambridge: Cambridge University Press, 2005.

Horn, Clifford W. "Communicating the Gospel Cross-Culturally." *Missio Apostolica* 2 (1994): 41-46.

Horsley, Richard A. "'By the Finger of God': Jesus and Imperial Violence." In *Violence in the New Testament,* ed. Matthews, 51-80.

————. "Ethics and Exegesis: 'Love Your Enemies' and the Doctrine of Non-Violence." *JAAR* 54 (1986): 3-31. Repr. in *The Love of Enemy and Nonretaliation,* ed. Swartley, 72-101.

————. *Hearing the Whole Story: The Politics of Plot in Mark's Gospel.* Louisville: Westminster John Knox, 2001.

————. *Jesus and Empire: The Kingdom of God and the New World Disorder.* Minneapolis: Fortress, 2003.

————. *Jesus and the Spiral of Violence: Popular Jewish Resistance in Roman Palestine.* San Francisco: Harper and Row, 1987.

Horsley, Richard A., ed. *Paul and Empire: Religion and Power in Roman Imperial Society.* Harrisburg: Trinity, 1997.

————, ed. *Paul and Politics: Ekklesia, Israel, Imperium, Interpretation: Essays in Honor of Krister Stendahl.* Harrisburg: Trinity, 2000.

Horsley, Richard A., and Neil Asher Silberman. *The Message and the Kingdom: How Jesus and Paul Ignited a Revolution and Transformed the Ancient World.* Minneapolis: Fortress, 2002.

Horton, F. L. *The Melchizedek Tradition: A Critical Examination of the Sources to the Fifth Century A.D. and in the Epistle to the Hebrews.* Cambridge: Cambridge University Press, 1976.

Howard, George. "'On the Faith of Christ.'" *HTR* 60 (1967): 459 65.

Howard-Brook, Wes, and Anthony Gwyther. *Unveiling Empire: Revelation Then and Now.* Maryknoll: Orbis, 2003.

Huebner, Harry. "Christian Pacifism and the Character of God." In *The Church as Theological Community: Essays in Honour of David Schroeder,* ed. Harry Huebner, 247-72. Winnipeg: Canadian Mennonite Bible College, 1990.

Hunsinger, George. "The Politics of the Nonviolent God: Reflections on René Girard and Karl Barth." *Scottish Journal of Theology* 51 (1998): 61-85.

Hunter, A. M. *Introducing New Testament Theology.* London, SCM, 1957.

Hunter, David G. "A Decade of Research on Early Christians and Military Service." *RelStudRev* 18 (1992): 87-94.

Hurtado, Larry W. *Lord Jesus Christ: Devotion to Jesus in Earliest Christianity.* Grand Rapids: Eerdmans, 2003.

Jaeger, Werner. *Paideia: The Ideals of Greek Culture.* Second edition. New York: Oxford University Press, 1945.

Janzen, Anna. *Der Friede im lukanischen Doppelwerk vor dem Hintergrund der Pax Romana.* Frankfurt am Main: Lang, 2002.

Janzen, Waldemar. "'Ašrê in the Old Testament." *HTR* 58 (1965): 215-26.

———. *Old Testament Ethics: A Paradigmatic Approach.* Louisville: Westminster John Knox, 1994.

Jeremias, Joachim. *The Eucharistic Words of Jesus.* Revised edition based on third German edition. New York: Scribner, 1966.

———. *New Testament Theology: The Proclamation of Jesus.* New York: Scribner, 1971.

Jeske, Richard L. "Expository Article: John 14:27 and 16:33." *Int* 38 (1984): 403-11.

Jewett, Robert. "The God of Peace in Romans: Reflections on Crucial Lutheran Texts." *CurrTheolMiss* 25 (1998): 186-94.

Johns, Loren L. *The Lamb Christology of the Book of Revelation: An Investigation into Its Origins and Rhetorical Force.* WUNT[2] 167. Tübingen: Mohr, 2003.

———. "Leaning toward Consummation: Mission and Peace in the Rhetoric of Revelation." In *Beautiful upon the Mountains,* ed. Schertz, 249-68.

———. "The Violence of Revelation as a Theological Problem." Unpublished article.

Johns, Loren L., and James R. Krabill, eds. *Deliver Us from Evil: Stories of God's People Confronting the Spirit World.* Scottdale: Herald/Elkhart: Institute of Mennonite Studies, 2006.

Johnson, E. Elizabeth. "Romans 9–11: The Faithfulness and Impartiality of God." In *Pauline Theology* III: *Romans,* ed. David M. Hay and E. Elizabeth Johnson, 211-39. Minneapolis: Fortress, 1995.

Johnson, E. Elizabeth, and David M. Hay, eds. *Pauline Theology: Looking Back, Pressing On.* Vol. 4. Altanta: Scholars, 1997.

Johnson, Luke Timothy. "The Letter of James." In *NIB* vol. XII, 117-225. Nashville: Abingdon, 1998.

———. "Rom 3:21-26 and the Faith of Jesus." *CBQ* 44 (1982): 77-90.

Juel, Donald. *The Messiah and Temple.* Missoula: Scholars, 1977.

Kallas, James G. *Revelation: God and Satan in the Apocalypse.* Minneapolis: Augsburg, 1973.

———. *The Satanward View: A Study in Pauline Theology.* Philadelphia: Westminster, 1966.

———. *The Significance of the Synoptic Miracles.* Philadelphia: Westminster, 1961.

Kaminouchi, Albert de Mingo. *'But It Is Not So among You': Echoes of Power in Mark 10.32-45.* Edinburgh: Clark, 2003.

Kampling, Rainer. See Schreiner, Josef.

Karris, Robert J. *Jesus and the Marginalized in John's Gospel.* Collegeville: Liturgical, 1988.

Kee, Howard Clark. *Community of the New Age: Studies in Mark's Gospel.* Philadelphia: Westminster, 1977.

———. *Miracle in the Early Christian World.* New Haven: Yale University Press, 1983.

———. "The Terminology of Mark's Exorcism Stories." *NTS* 14 (1968-69): 232-46.

Keener, Craig S. *The Gospel of John: A Commentary,* vol. 1. Peabody: Hendrickson, 2003.

Keim, Paul. "Is God Nonviolent?" *CGR* 21 (2003): 25-32.

Kenneson, Philip D. *Life on the Vine: Cultivating the Fruit of the Spirit in Christian Community.* Downers Grove: InterVarsity, 1999.

Klassen, William. "The Ascetic Way: Reflections on Peace, Justice, and Vengeance in the Apocalypse of John." In *Asceticism and the New Testament,* ed. Leif E. Vaage and Vincent L. Wimbush, 393-410. New York: Routledge, 1999.

———. "The Authenticity of the Command: 'Love Your Enemies.'" In *Authenticating the Words of Jesus,* ed. Bruce Chilton and Craig A. Evans, 192-210. Leiden: Brill, 1999.

———. "'A Child of Peace' (Luke 10:6) in First Century Context." *NTS* 27 (1981): 484-506.

———. "Coals of Fire: Sign of Repentance or Revenge?" *NTS* 9 (1962): 337-50.

———. "The Eschatology of Jesus: Is Apocalyptic Really the Mother of Christian Theology?" In *Apocalypticism and Millennialism,* ed. Loren L. Johns, 75-90. Kitchener: Pandora, 2000.

———. "The God of Peace: New Testament Perspectives on God." In *Towards a Theology of Peace,* ed. S. Tunnicliffe, 121-31. London: European Nuclear Disarmament, 1989.

———. "Jesus and the Messianic War." In *Early Jewish and Christian Exegesis: Studies in Memory of William Hugh Brownlee,* ed. Craig A. Evans and William F. Stinespring, 155-175. Atlanta: Scholars, 1987.

———. "Jesus and the Zealot Option." In *The Wisdom of the Cross: Essays in Honor of John Howard Yoder,* ed. Stanley Hauerwas, Chris K. Huebner, Harry J. Huebner, and Mark Thiessen Nation, 131-49. Grand Rapids: Eerdmans, 1999.

———. *Love of Enemies: The Way to Peace.* Philadelphia: Fortress, 1984. Reprint Eugene: Cascade, 2005.

———. "'Love Your Enemies': Some Reflections on the Current Status of Research." In *The Love of Enemy and Nonretaliation,* ed. Swartley, 1-31.

———. "Love Your Enemy: A Study of New Testament Teaching on Coping with an Enemy." In *Biblical Realism Confronts the Nations: Ten Christian Scholars Summon the*

Church to the Discipleship of Peace, ed. Paul Peachey, 153-183. Scottdale: Fellowship, 1963.

—————. "The Novel Element in the Love Commandment of Jesus." In *The New Way of Jesus: Essays Presented to Howard Charles,* ed. William Klassen, 100-14. Newton: Faith and Life, 1980.

—————. "Peace." In *Anchor Dictionary of the Bible* 5 (1992): 207-12. See also "War (NT)" in vol. 6, 867-75.

—————. "Peace." In *A Dictionary of Jewish-Christian Relations,* ed. Edward Kessler and Neil Wenborn, 338. Cambridge: Cambridge University Press and Centre for the Study of Jewish-Christian Relations, 2005.

—————. "Peace." In *Illustrated Dictionary and Concordance of the Bible,* ed. G. Wigoder, 767-69. New York: Macmillan, 1986.

—————. "Pursue Peace: A Concrete Ethical Mandate (Romans 12:18-21)." In *Ja und Nein: Christliche Theologie im Angesicht Israels* (FS Wolfgang Schrage), ed. Klaus Wengst and Gerhard Saß, 195-207. Neukirchen-Vluyn: Neukirchner, 1998.

—————. *The Realism of Peace.* Sackville: Mount Allison University, 1986.

—————. "Religion and the Gift of Peace." *Tantur Yearbook, 1984-1985* (Jerusalem, 1986; also as *Tantur Occasional Paper* 1, 1986).

—————. Review of *The Meaning of Peace: Biblical Studies,* ed. Perry B. Yoder and Willard M. Swartley. *MQR* 67 (October 1993): 491-93.

—————. "The Sacred Kiss in the New Testament: An Example of Social Boundaries." *NTS* 39 (1993): 122-35.

—————. Summary of "Frieden, Altes Testament," by H. H. Schmid, W. Thiessen, and G. Delling. *TRE* 11 (1983): 605-18.

—————. "Vengeance in the Apocalypse of John." *CBQ* 28 (1966): 300-311.

Kobelski, P. J. *Melchizedek and Melchiresa.* CBQMS 10. Washington: Catholic Biblical Association of America, 1981.

Koenig, John. *The Feast of the World's Redemption: Eucharistic Origins and the World's Redemption.* Harrisburg: Trinity, 2000.

Koester, Craig. "The Savior of the World (John 4:42)." *JBL* 109 (1990): 665-80.

Koester, Helmut. "Jesus the Victim." *JBL* 111 (1992): 2-15.

Köstenberger, Andreas J. "The Challenge of a Systematized Biblical Theology of Mission: Missiological Insights from the Gospel of John." *Missiology: An International Review* 23 (1995): 449.

—————. *The Missions of Jesus and His Disciples according to the Fourth Gospel.* Grand Rapids: Eerdmans, 1998.

Kotva, Joseph J., Jr. *The Christian Case for Virtue Ethics.* Washington: Georgetown University Press, 1996.

Kraybill, Donald. *The Upside-Down Kingdom.* Scottdale: Herald, 1978. Revised third edition, 2003.

Kraybill, J. Nelson. *Imperial Cult and Commerce in John's Apocalypse.* JSNTSS 132. Sheffield: Sheffield Academic, 1996.

Kreider, Alan. *Journey toward Holiness: A Way of Living for God's Nation.* Scottdale: Herald, 1987.

————. "Light." *The Third Way* 11 (October 1988): 14-16.

————. "Military Service in the Church Orders." *JRE* 31 (2003): 415-42.

————. "Peacemaking in Worship in the Syrian Church Orders." *Studia Liturgica* 34 (2004): 177-90.

————. "Salt and Light." *The Third Way* 11 (September 1988): 14-16.

————. "Salty Discipleship." *The Other Side* 25 (March-April 1989): 34-37.

————. *Worship and Evangelism in Pre-Christendom.* Cambridge: Grove, 1995.

Kreider, Alan, Eleanor Kreider, and Paulus Widjaja. *A Culture of Peace: God's Vision for the Church.* Intercourse: Good, 2005.

Kreider, Eleanor. *Communion Shapes Character.* Scottdale: Herald, 1997.

————. "Let the Faithful Greet Each Other: The Kiss of Peace." *CGR* 5 (1987): 29-49.

Kremer, Jacob. "Peace — God's Gift: Biblical-Theological Considerations." In *The Meaning of Peace: Biblical Studies,* ed. P. B. Yoder, 21-35 (1992, 133-47). Original: "Der Frieden — Eine Gabe Gottes: Bibeltheologische Erwägungen." *Stimmen der Zeit* 200 (1982): 161-73.

Kümmel, Werner Georg. *The Theology of the New Testament: According to Its Major Witnesses Jesus — Paul — John.* Nashville: Abingdon, 1973.

Küng, Hans. *The Religious Situation of Our Time: Judaism.* Translated by John Bowden. London: SCM, 1992.

Ladd, George Eldon. *A Theology of the New Testament.* Grand Rapids: Eerdmans, 1974. Revised edition, 1993 (revised and edited by Donald A. Hagner).

Lampe, Peter. "The Eucharist: Identifying with Christ on the Cross." *Int* 48 (1994): 36-49.

Lapide, Pinchas. *The Sermon on the Mount: Utopia or Program for Action?* Maryknoll: Orbis, 1992.

Larsson, Edvin. *Christus als Vorbild. Eine Untersuchung zu den paulinischen Tauf- und Eikontexten.* Acta Seminarii Neotestamentici Upsaliensis 23; Lund: Gleerup, 1962.

Lasserre, Jean. "A Tenacious Misinterpretation: John 2:15." Translated by John H. Yoder. *Occasional Papers* 1, ed. Willard M. Swartley, 35-48. Elkhart: Institute of Mennonite Studies, 1981. Original in *Cahiers de la Reconciliation,* October 1967.

————. *War and the Gospel.* Translated by Oliver Coburn. Scottdale: Herald, 1962.

Lederach, John Paul. *The Journey toward Reconciliation.* Scottdale: Herald, 1999.

Lehman, Chester K. *Biblical Theology: New Testament.* Scottdale: Herald, 1974.

Lehn, Cornelia. *Peace Be with You.* Newton: Faith and Life, 1980.

Leivestad, Ragnar. *Christ the Conqueror: Ideas of Conflict and Victory in the New Testament.* London: SPCK, 1954.

Levine, Amy-Jill. *The Social and Ethnic Dimensions of Matthean Salvation History: "Go Nowhere among the Gentiles. . . ."* Studies in the Bible and the Church 14. Lewiston: Mellen, 1988.

Lieu, Judith M. "'Grace to You and Peace.'" *BJRL* 68 (1985): 161-78.

Lincoln, Andrew T. *Truth on Trial: The Lawsuit Motif in the Fourth Gospel.* Peabody: Hendrickson, 2000.

Lind, Millard C. *Ezekiel.* BCBC. Scottdale: Herald, 1996.

————. *The Sheer Sound of Silence and the Killing State: The Death Penalty and the Bible.* SPS 8. Telford: Cascadia/Scottdale: Herald, 2004.

————. "Transformation of Justice: From Moses to Jesus." In *Monotheism, Power, Justice: Collected Old Testament Essays,* by Millard C. Lind. Text Reader Series 3. Elkhart: Institute of Mennonite Studies, 1990.

————. *Yahweh Is a Warrior.* Scottdale: Herald, 1980.

Lischer, Richard. "The Sermon on the Mount as Radical Pastoral Care." *Int* 41 (1987): 152-63.

Lohfink, Gerhard. *Jesus and Community: The Social Dimension of the Christian Faith.* Translated by John P. Galvin. Philadelphia: Fortress/Ramsey: Paulist, 1984.

Lohmeyer, Ernst. *Lord of the Temple: A Study of the Relation between Cult and Gospel.* Translated by Stewart Todd. Edinburgh: Oliver and Boyd, 1962.

Lohse, Eduard. *Theologische Ethik des Neuen Testaments.* Stuttgart: Kohlhammer, 1988. English translation: *Theological Ethics of the New Testament.* Translated by M. Eugene Boring. Minneapolis: Augsburg Fortress, 1991.

Longenecker, Bruce W. "'Until Christ Is Formed in You': Suprahuman Forces and Moral Character in Galatians." *CBQ* 61 (1999): 92-108.

Love, Stuart L. "Jesus, Healer of the Canaanite Woman's Daughter in Matthew's Gospel: A Social-Scientific Inquiry." *BTB* 32 (2002): 11-20.

Lowery, Richard H. *Sabbath and Jubilee.* St. Louis: Chalice, 2000.

Luz, Ulrich. *Matthew 1–7.* Minneapolis: Augsburg, 1989.

Luz, Ulrich, et al. *Eschatologie und Friedenshandeln: Exegetische Beiträge zur Frage christlicher Friedensverantwortung.* Stuttgarter Bibelstudien 101; Stuttgart: Katholisches Bibelwerk, 1981.

————. "The Significance of the Biblical Witnesses for Church Peace Action." In *The Meaning of Peace,* ed. P. B. Yoder, 234-52 (1992, pp. 237-55).

Macgregor, G. H. C. "Does the New Testament Sanction War?" In *A Peace Reader,* ed. E. Morris Sider and Luke Keefer, Jr., 49-57. Nappanee: Evangel, 2002.

————. *The New Testament Basis of Pacifism.* Nyack: Fellowship of Reconciliation, 1954.

MacIntyre, Alasdair. *After Virtue: A Study in Moral Theology.* Second edition. Notre Dame: Notre Dame University Press, 1984.

Madsen, Catherine. "Notes on God's Violence." *Cross Currents* 51 (2001): 229-56.

Malbon, Elizabeth Struthers. "Galilee and Jerusalem: History and Literature in Marcan Interpretation." *CBQ* 44 (1982): 242-55.

————. "The Jesus of Mark and the Sea of Galilee." *JBL* 103 (1984): 363-77.

Malina, Bruce J. *On the Genre and Message of Revelation: Star Visions and Sky Journeys.* Peabody: Hendrickson, 1995.

Marcus, Joel. *The Way of the Lord: Christological Exegesis of the Old Testament in the Gospel of Mark.* Louisville: Westminster John Knox, 1992.

Marshall, Christopher D. *Beyond Retribution: A New Testament Vision for Justice, Crime, and Punishment.* Grand Rapids: Eerdmans, 2001.

————. *Crowned with Glory and Honor: Human Rights in the Biblical Tradition.* SPS 6. Telford: Pandora (now Cascadia), 2001.

————. *Faith as a Theme in Mark's Narrative.* SNTSMS 64. Cambridge: Cambridge University Press, 1989.

Marshall, I. Howard. *The Gospel of Luke: A Commentary on the Greek Text.* Grand Rapids: Eerdmans, 1978.

———. "New Testament Perspectives on War." *EvQ* 57 (1985): 115-32.

———. *New Testament Theology.* Downers Grove: InterVarsity, 2004.

Martin, Ernest D. *Colossians and Philemon.* BCBC. Scottdale: Herald, 1993.

Martin, Ralph P. *Mark: Evangelist and Theologian.* Grand Rapids: Zondervan, 1973.

———. *Reconciliation: A Study of Paul's Theology.* Atlanta: John Knox, 1981.

Matera, Frank J. *New Testament Ethics: The Legacies of Jesus and Paul.* Louisville: Westminster John Knox, 1996.

———. *Passion Narratives and Gospel Theologies: Interpreting the Synoptics through Their Passion Stories.* Mahwah: Paulist, 1986.

Matlock, R. Barry. "'Even the Demons Believe': Paul and the *pistis Christou.*" *CBQ* 64 (2002): 319-38.

Matthews, Shelly, and E. Leigh Gibson. *Violence in the New Testament.* Edinburgh: Clark, 2000.

Mauser, Ulrich. *The Gospel of Peace: A Scriptural Message for Today's World.* SPS 1. Louisville: Westminster John Knox, 1992.

McAlpine, Thomas. *Facing the Powers: What Are the Options?* Monrovia: MARC, 1991.

McClain, George. *Claiming All Things for God.* Nashville: Abingdon, 1998.

McCurley, Foster R. *Ancient Myths and Biblical Faith: Scriptural Transformations.* Philadelphia: Fortress, 1983.

McDonald, Patricia M. *God and Violence: Biblical Resources for Living in a Small World.* Scottdale: Herald, 2004.

McKay, Alastair J. M. "God's Covenant of Shalom-Peace: Some Porblems of and Arguments Supporting a Case for Christian Nonviolence and Peacemaking Based Primarily on a New Testament Biblical Theology." Unpublished, 1999.

McLean, Bradley H. "The Absence of an Atoning Sacrifice in Paul's Soteriology." *NTS* 38 (1992): 531-53.

McSorley, Richard. *New Testament Basis for Peacemaking.* Scottdale: Herald, 1985.

Meeks, Wayne A. "The Ethics of the Fourth Gospel." In *Exploring the Gospel of John* (FS D. Moody Smith), ed. R. Alan Culpepper and C. Clifton Black, 317-25. Louisville: Westminster John Knox, 1996.

———. "The Man from Heaven in Johannine Sectarianism." *JBL* 91 (1972): 44-72.

———. *The Origins of Christian Morality: The First Two Centuries.* New Haven: Yale University Press, 1993.

———. *The Prophet King: Moses Traditions and the Johannine Christology.* NovTSup 14. Leiden: Brill, 1967.

Meggitt, Justin J. *Paul, Poverty and Survival.* Edinburgh: Clark, 1998.

Mettinger, Tryggve N. D. "Fighting the Powers of Chaos and Hell — Towards a Biblical Portrait of God." *ST* 39 (1985): 21-38.

Michaelis, Wilhelm. Μιμέομαι, μιμητής. *TDNT* IV, 659-74.

Michaels, J. Ramsey. *1 Peter.* WBC 49. Waco: Word, 1988.

Milbank, John. *Being Reconciled: Ontology and Pardon.* New York: Routledge, 2003.

———. *Theology and Social Theory: Beyond Secular Reason.* Cambridge: Blackwell, 1991.

————. *The Word Made Strange: Theology, Language, Culture.* Cambridge: Blackwell, 1997.

Miller, Larry. "Christianisme et société dans la première lettre de Pierre. Histoire de l'interprétation, interprétation de l'histoire." Th.D. dissertation, Université de Strasbourg, 1995.

Miller, Marlin E. "Girardian Perspectives and Christian Atonement." In *Violence Renounced*, ed. Swartley, 19-48.

Minear, Paul S. *To Heal and to Reveal: The Prophetic Vocation According to Luke.* New York: Seabury, 1976.

Moessner, David P. *Lord of the Banquet: The Literary and Theological Significance of the Lukan Travel Narrative.* Minneapolis: Augsburg Fortress, 1989.

Moloney, Francis J. *The Gospel of John.* Sacra Pagina. Collegeville: Liturgical, 1998.

Moltmann, Jürgen. *The Crucified God: The Cross of Christ as the Foundation and Criticism of Christian Theology.* Translated by R. A. Wilson and John Bowden. New York: Harper and Row, 1974.

————. *Politics of Discipleship and Discipleship in Politics: Lectures and Dialogue with Mennonite Scholars*, ed. Willard M. Swartley. Eugene: Cascade, 2006.

————. *The Theology of Hope: On the Ground and the Implications of a Christian Eschatology.* New York: Harper and Row, 1967.

————. *The Way of Jesus Christ: Christology in Messianic Dimensions.* Translated by Margaret Kohl. Minneapolis: Fortress, 1993.

Montefiore, C. G., and H. Loewe, eds. *A Rabbinic Anthology: Selected and Arranged with Comments and Introductions.* New York: Schocken, 1974.

Moo, Douglas. "Response." "The Theology of Romans 9–11." In *Pauline Theology* III: *Romans*, ed. David M. Hay and E. Elizabeth Johnson, 240-58. Minneapolis: Fortress, 1995.

Mor, Menachem. "The Persian, Hellenistic, and Hasmonean Period." In *The Samaritans*, ed. Alan D. Crown, 1-31. Tübingen: Mohr, 1989.

Morris, Leon. *New Testament Theology.* Grand Rapids: Zondervan, 1986.

Morrison, Clinton D. *The Powers That Be: Earthly Rulers and Demonic Powers in Romans 13:1-7.* SBT 29. London: SCM, 1960.

Motyer, Stephen. *"Your Father the Devil"? A New Approach to John and "The Jews."* London: Paternoster, 1997.

Moulton, William Fiddian, and Alfred Shenington Geden. *A Concordance to the Greek Testament.* Third edition. Edinburgh: Clark, 1926. Reprinted 1957.

Mouw, Richard J. "Violence and the Atonement." In *Must Christianity Be Violent? Reflections on History, Practice, and Theology*, ed. Kenneth R. Chase and Alan Jacobs, 159-71. Grand Rapids: Brazos, 2003.

Mowery, Robert L. "God, Lord and Father: The Theology of the Gospel of Matthew." *BR* 33 (1988): 24-33.

————. "God the Father in the Gospel of Matthew." Society of Biblical Literature annual meeting, Boston, 1987.

————. "Son of God in Roman Imperial Titles and Matthew." *Biblica* 83 (2002): 100-110.

Muilenberg, James. *The Way of Israel: Biblical Faith and Ethics.* New York: Harper, 1961.

Munck, Johannes. *Christ and Israel: An Interpretation of Romans 9–11.* Translated by Ingeborg Nixon. Philadelphia: Fortress, 1967.

Murphy, Nancey. "John Howard Yoder's Systemic Defense of Christian Pacifism." In *The Wisdom of the Cross: Essays in Honor of John Howard Yoder,* ed. Stanley Hauerwas, Chris K. Huebner, Harry J. Huebner, Mark Thiessen Nation, 45-68. Grand Rapids: Eerdmans, 1999.

Myers, Ched. *Binding the Strong Man: A Political Reading of Mark's Story of Jesus.* Maryknoll: Orbis, 1988.

Nave, Guy D., Jr. "It's Time for a Change! Examining the Lukan Demand for Repentance within the Context of Roman Imperialism." *AAR/SBL Abstracts 2004,* 347-48.

Nickle, Keith F. *The Collection: A Study in Paul's Strategy.* SBT 48. London: SCM, 1966.

Nolan, Brian. *Royal Son of God: The Christology of Matthew 1–2 in the Setting of the Gospel.* OBO 23; Göttingen: Vandenhoeck und Ruprecht, 1979.

Nolt, Steven M. "Passion for the Prophets: Millard Lind Champions the Old Testament." *Christian Living* 47/7 (October–November 2000): 21-24.

North, Robert. "Violence and the Bible: The Girard Connection." *CBQ* 47 (1985): 1-27.

Oakman, D. E. "The Ancient Economy and St. John's Apocalypse." *Listening: Journal of Religion and Culture* 28 (1993): 200-214.

O'Brien, P. T. "Principalities and Powers: Opponents of the Church." In *Biblical Interpretation and the Church: The Problem of Contextualization,* ed. D. A. Carson, 110-50. Nashville: Nelson, 1984.

O'Day, Gail R. "Narrative Mode and Theological Claim: A Study in the Fourth Gospel." *JBL* 105 (1986): 657-68.

O'Donovan, Oliver. "The Political Thought of the Book of Revelation." *Tyndale Bulletin* 37 (1986): 61-94.

Oepke, A. *Nachfolge und Nachahmung Christi im NT.* AELKZ 71 (1938): 853-69.

Okure, Teresa. *The Johannine Approach to Mission: A Contextual Study of John 4:1-42.* WUNT 2/31. Tübingen: Mohr, 1988.

Ollenburger, Ben C. "Is God the Friend of Slaves and Wives?" In *Perspectives on Feminist Hermeneutics,* ed. G. G. Koontz and Willard M. Swartley, 97-112. OP 10. Elkhart: Institute of Mennonite Studies, 1987.

———. "Peace and God's Action against Chaos in the Old Testament." In *The Church's Peace Witness,* ed. Marlin E. Miller and Barbara Nelson Gingerich, 70-88. Grand Rapids: Eerdmans, 1994.

———. *Zion, City of the Great King: A Theological Symbol of the Jerusalem Cult.* Sheffield: JSOT, 1987.

Ollenburger, Ben C., and Amy L. Barker, "The Passion and God's Atonement." *Mennonite Life* 59/2 (June 2004), available at http://www.bethelks.edu/mennonitelife.

Ott, Bernhard. *God's Shalom Project.* Trans. Timothy Geddert. Intercourse: Good, 2004.

Overman, J. Andrew. *Matthew's Gospel and Formative Judaism: The Social World of the Matthean Community.* Minneapolis: Fortress, 1990.

Painter, John R., Alan Culpepper, and Fernando F. Segovia, eds. *Word, Theology, and Community in John.* St. Louis: Chalice, 2002.

Pancaro, Severino. *The Law in the Fourth Gospel: The Torah and the Gospel, Moses and Jesus, Judaism and Christianity according to John.* NovTSup 42. Leiden: Brill, 1975.

Pao, David W. *Acts and the Isaianic New Exodus.* WUNT 2/130. Tübingen: Mohr, 2000/ Grand Rapids: Baker, 2002.

Patte, Daniel. *The Gospel of Matthew: A Contextual Introduction for Group Study.* Nashville: Abingdon, 2003.

————. *Paul's Faith and the Power of the Gospel: A Structural Introduction to the Pauline Letters.* Philadelphia: Fortress, 1983.

Peck, M. Scott. *People of the Lie: The Hope for Healing Human Evil.* New York: Simon and Schuster, 1983.

Pennington, Jonathan. "The Kingdom of Heaven against All Earthly Kingdoms." *AAR/SBL Abstracts 2004,* 356.

Perkins, Pheme. "Apocalyptic Sectarianism and Love Commands: The Johannine Epistles and Revelation." In *Love of Enemy and Nonretaliation,* ed. Swartley, 287-96.

————. *Love Commands in the New Testament.* Ramsey: Paulist, 1982.

Phillips, Edward L. "The Ritual Kiss in Early Christian Worship." Ph.D. dissertation, University of Notre Dame, 1992.

Pilgrim, Walter E. *Uneasy Neighbors: Church and State in the New Testament.* Minneapolis: Fortress, 1999.

Piper, John. *The Justification of God: An Exegetical Study of Romans 9:1-23.* Revised edition. Grand Rapids: Baker, 1993.

————. *"Love Your Enemies": Jesus' Love Command in the Synoptic Gospels and in the Early Christian Paraenesis. A History of the Tradition and the Interpretation of Its Uses.* SNTSMS 38. Cambridge: Cambridge University Press, 1979.

Piper, Otto. "The Apocalypse of John and the Liturgy of the Ancient Church." *Church History* 20 (1951): 10-72.

Pippin, Tina. *Death and Desire: The Rhetoric of Gender in the Apocalypse of John.* Louisville: Westminster John Knox, 1992.

Pobee, John. *Persecution and Martyrdom in the Theology of Paul.* JSNTSS 6. Sheffield: JSOT, 1985.

Ravitsky, Aviezer. "Peace." In *Contemporary Jewish Religious Thought: Original Essays on Critical Concepts, Movements, and Beliefs,* ed. Arthur A. Cohen and Paul Mendes-Flohr, 685-89. New York: Macmillan, 1987.

Reid, David P. "Peace and Praise in Luke." In *Blessed Are the Peacemakers,* ed. Anthony J. Tambasco, 79. Mahwah: Paulist, 1989.

Reimer, James. "God Is Love but Not a Pacifist." In *Mennonites and Classical Theology: Dogmatic Foundations for Christian Ethics,* by James Reimer, 486-92. Kitchener: Pandora/Scottdale: Herald, 2001.

Reinhartz, Adele. *Befriending the Beloved Disciple: A Jewish Reading of the Gospel of John.* New York: Continuum, 2001.

————. "'Jews' and Jews in the Fourth Gospel." In *Anti-Judaism and the Fourth Gospel,* ed. Reimund Bieringer, Didier Pollefeyt, and Frederique Vandecasteele-Vanneuville, 213-27. Louisville: Westminster John Knox, 2001.

————. "The Johannine Community and Its Jewish Neighbors: A Reappraisal." In *What Is John?* ed. Fernando Segovia, 2:111-38. Atlanta: Scholars, 1998.

Reiser, Marius. "Love of Enemies in the Context of Antiquity." *NTS* 47 (2001): 411-27.

Rempel, John D. *The Lord's Supper in Anabaptism: A Study of the Christology of Balthasar Hubmaier, Pilgram Marpeck, and Dirk Philips.* Studies in Anabaptist and Mennonite History 33. Scottdale: Herald, 1993.

Rensberger, David. "Anti-Judaism and the Gospel of John," with responses by Mark Goodwin and Thomas D. Lea. In *Anti-Judaism and the Gospels,* ed. William R. Farmer, 120-75. Harrisburg: Trinity, 1999.

————. *Johannine Faith and Liberating Community.* Philadelphia: Westminster, 1988.

————. "Love for One Another and Love for Enemies." In *Love of Enemy and Nonretaliation,* ed. Swartley, 297-313.

Reploh, K. G. *Markus — Lehrer der Gemeinde. Eine redaktionsgeschichtliche Studie zu den Jüngerperikopen des Markusevangeliums.* SBM 9. Stuttgart: Katholisches Bibelwerk, 1969.

Repo, Eero. *Der "Weg" als Selbstbezeichnung des Urchristentums. Eine Traditionsgeschichtliche und Semasiologische Untersuchung.* Helsinki: Suomalainen Tudeakatemia, 1964.

Rhoads, David M. *Israel in Revolution, 6-74 C.E.: A Political History Based on the Writings of Josephus.* Philadelphia: Fortress, 1976.

Riches, John. "Intercultural Hermeneutics." In *Through the Eyes of Another: Intercultural Reading of the Bible,* ed. de Wit, 460-76.

Ridderbos, H. *Paul: An Outline of His Theology.* Grand Rapids: Eerdmans, 1975.

Ringgren, Helmar. *The Messiah in the Old Testament.* SBT. Chicago: Allenson, 1956.

Robinson, James M. *The Problem of History in Mark.* SBT 21. London: SCM, 1957.

Rossing, Barbara R. *The Rapture Exposed: The Message of Hope in the Book of Revelation.* Boulder: Westview, 2004.

Rowland, Christopher C. "The Book of Revelation." *NIB* 12:503-56. Nashville: Abingdon, 1998.

————. *The Open Heaven: A Study of Apocalyptic in Judaism and Early Christianity.* New York: Crossroad, 1982.

Ruiz, Jean-Pierre. "Betwixt and Between the Lord's Day." *SBLSP,* 654-72. Atlanta: Scholars, 1992.

————. "The Politics of Praise: A Reading of Revelation 19:1-10." *SBLSP,* 374-93. Atlanta: Scholars, 1997.

Ruppert, Lothar. *Jesus als der leidende Gerechte?* Stuttgart: KBW, 1972.

Sakenfeld, Kathryn D. *The Meaning of Hesed in the Hebrew Bible: A New Inquiry.* HSM 17. Missoula: Society of Biblical Literature, 1978.

Saldarini, Anthony J. *Matthew's Christian-Jewish Community.* Chicago: University of Chicago Press, 1994.

Sanders, E. P. *Paul and Palestinian Judaism: A Comparison of Patterns of Religion.* Philadelphia: Fortress, 1977.

Savage, Joseph M. "Shalom and Its Relationship to Health/Healing in the Hebrew Scriptures: A Contextual and Semantic Study of the Books of Psalms and Jeremiah." Ph.D. dissertation, Florida State University, 2001.

Scheibler, Ingeborg. "Götter des Friedens in Hellas und Rom." *Antike Welt* 15 (1984): 39-40, 45-46.

Schertz, Mary H. "'Likewise You Wives . . .': Another Look at 1 Peter 2:11–5:11." In *Perspectives on Feminist Hermeneutics,* ed. G. G. Koontz and Willard M. Swartley, 75-82. OP 10. Elkhart: Institute of Mennonite Studies, 1987.

———. "Nonretaliation and the Haustafeln in 1 Peter." In *Love of Enemy and Nonretaliation,* ed. Swartley, 268-69.

———. "Radical Trust in the Just Judge: The Easter Texts of 1 Peter." *Word and World* 24 (2004): 430-41.

———. "Swords and Prayer: Luke 22:31-62." Unpublished (see AAR/SBL *Abstracts 2005,* p. 230).

———. "Turn in the Road." *Christian Century* (April 14, 2004): 16.

Schertz, Mary H., and Ivan Friesen, eds. *Beautiful upon the Mountains: Biblical Essays on Mission, Peace, and the Reign of God.* Elkhart: Institute of Mennonite Studies/ Scottdale: Herald, 2004.

Schipani, Daniel. "Transformation in the Borderlands: A Study of Matthew 15:21-28." *Vision: A Journal for Church and Theology* 2 (2001): 13-24.

Schirch, Lisa. *The Little Book of Strategic Peacemaking.* Intercourse: Good, 2004.

Schlier, Heinrich. "Jesus und Pilatus nach dem Johannesevangelium." In *Die Zeit der Kirche: Exegetische Aufsätze und Vorträge,* 56-73. Third edition. Freiburg: Herder, 1962.

———. *Principalities and Powers in the New Testament.* QD 3. Freiburg: Herder/New York: Nelson, 1961.

Schmid, Hans Heinrich, W. Thiessen, and Gerhard Delling. "Frieden, Altes Testament," II-IV. *Theologische Realenzyklopädie* 11:605-18.

———. *Shalom. Frieden im Alten Orient und im Alten Testament.* SBS 51. Stuttgart: Katholisches Bibelwerk, 1971.

Schnackenburg, Rudolf. "Macht, Gewalt und Friede nach dem Neuen Testament." In *Maßstab des Glaubens. Fragen heutiger Christen in Licht des Neuen Testaments.* Freiburg: Herder, 1978.

———. *The Moral Teaching of the New Testament.* New York: Herder and Herder, 1965.

Schneider, Gerhard. *Lukas, Theologe der Heilsgeschichte. Aufsätze zum lukanischen Doppelwerk.* BBB 59. Bonn: Hanstein, 1985.

Schneiders, Sandra M. *The Revelatory Text: Interpreting the New Testament as Sacred Scripture.* San Francisco: HarperSanFrancisco, 1991.

———. *Written That You May Believe: Encountering Jesus in the Fourth Gospel.* New York: Crossroad, 1999.

Schottroff, Luise. "'Give to Caesar What Belongs to Caesar and to God What Belongs to God': A Theological Response of the Early Christian Church to Its Social and Political Environment." In *Love of Enemy and Nonretaliation,* ed. Swartley, 223-57.

———. "Non-Violence and the Love of One's Enemies." In *Essays on the Love Command,* by Schottroff, et al., 9-39.

————. "The Samaritan Woman and the Notion of Sexuality in the Fourth Gospel." In *"What Is John?"* II: *Literary and Social Readings of the Fourth Gospel,* ed. Gail R. O'Day and Fernando Segovia, pp. 157-81. Atlanta: Scholars, 1998.

Schottroff, Luise, Reginald H. Fuller, Christoph Burchard, and M. Jack Suggs. *Essays on the Love Commandment,* trans. Reginald H. and Ilse Fuller. Philadelphia: Fortress, 1978.

Schrage, Wolfgang. *The Ethics of the New Testament.* Minneapolis: Fortress, 1988.

Schreiner, Josef, and Rainer Kampling. *Der Nächste — der Fremde — der Feind. Perspektiven des Alten und Neuen Testaments.* Die Neue Echter Bibel: Themen 3. Würzburg: Echter, 2000.

Schrenk, G. "ὑπογραμμός." *TDNT* 1:772-73.

Schroeder, David. "Die Haustafeln des Neuen Testaments. Ihrer Herkunft und ihr theologischer Sinn." Th.D. dissertation, Hamburg Universität, 1959.

————. "The New Testament Haustafeln: Egalitarian or Status Quo?" In *Perspectives on Feminist Hermeneutics,* ed. Gayle Gerber Koontz and Willard M. Swartley, 56-65. OP 10. Elkhart: Institute of Mennonite Studies, 1987.

————. "'Once You Were No People. . . .'" In *The Church as Theological Community,* ed. Harry Huebner, 37-65. Winnipeg: Canadian Mennonite Publications, 1990.

Schur, Nathan. *History of the Samaritans.* Frankfurt am Main: Lang, 1989.

Schüssler Fiorenza, Elisabeth. *The Book of Revelation: Justice and Judgment.* Philadelphia: Fortress, 1985.

————. "The Ethics of Biblical Interpretation: Decentering Biblical Scholarship." *JBL* 107 (1988): 3-17.

————. *Invitation to the Book of Revelation: A Commentary on the Apocalypse with Complete Text from the Jerusalem Bible.* Garden City: Doubleday, 1981.

————. "Religion und Politik in der Offenbarung des Johannes." In *Biblische Randbemerkungen,* ed. H. Merklein and J. Lange, 269-70. Würzburg: Echter, 1974.

Schwager, Raymund. "Christ's Death and the Critique of Sacrifice." In *René Girard and Biblical Studies,* ed. Andrew J. McKenna. Semeia 33. Decatur: Scholars, 1985.

————. *Must There Be Scapegoats? Violence and Redemption in the Bible.* San Francisco: Harper and Row, 1987.

Schwank, P. Benedikt. "Wie Freie — aber als Sklaven Gottes (1 Petr 2,16). Das Verhältnis des Christen zur Staatsmacht nach dem Ersten Petrusbrief." *Erbe und Auftrag* 36 (1960): 5-12.

Schweitzer, Albert. *The Mysticism of St. Paul the Apostle.* New York: Seabury, 1968.

Schweizer, Eduard. *The Good News According to Mark.* Translated by D. H. Madwig. Richmond: John Knox, 1970.

Segal, Alan F. *Paul the Convert: The Apostolate and Apostasy of Saul the Pharisee.* New Haven: Yale University Press, 1990.

Senior, Donald. *Matthew.* Abingdon New Testament Commentaries. Nashville: Abingdon, 1998.

Sharp, Gene. *The Politics of Nonviolent Action.* Volume 3. Cambridge: Harvard University Press, 1973.

Sheffield, Julian. "The Father in the Gospel of Matthew." In *A Feminist Companion to Mat-*

thew, ed. Amy-Jill Levine with Marianne Blickenstaff. Sheffield: Sheffield Academic, 2001.

Shillington, George. "Salt of the Earth? (Mt 5:13/Lk 14:30f.)." *ExpT* 112 (2001): 120-21.

———. *2 Corinthians.* BCBC. Scottdale: Herald, 1999.

Shuck, Glenn W. *Marks of the Beast: The Left-Behind Novels and the Struggle for Evangelical Identity.* New York: New York University Press, 2004.

Sider, E. Morris, and Luke Keefer, Jr., eds. *A Peace Reader.* Nappanee: Evangel, 2002.

Sider, Ronald J. *Christ and Violence.* Scottdale: Herald, 1979.

Sleeper, C. F. "Political Responsibility according to 1 Peter." *NovT* 10 (1968): 270-86.

Smedes, Lewis. *Union with Christ.* Grand Rapids: Eerdmans, 1983.

Smith, D. Moody. "Ethics and Interpretation of the Fourth Gospel." In *Word, Theology, and Community,* ed. Painter, 109-22.

Smith, J. B. *Greek-English Concordance to the New Testament.* Scottdale: Herald, 1955.

Smith, Morton. "Zealots and Sicarii, Their Origins and Relations." *HTR* 64 (1971): 2-19.

Smith, Ralph F. "Eucharistic Faith and Practice." *Int* 48 (1994): 5-16.

Sordi, Marta. *The Christians and the Roman Empire.* Translated by A. Bedini. Norman: University of Oklahoma Press, 1986.

Stanton, Graham N. *A Gospel for a New People: Studies in Matthew.* Louisville: Westminster John Knox, 1993.

Stark, Rodney. *The Rise of Christianity: A Sociologist Reconsiders History.* Princeton: Princeton University Press, 1996.

Stassen, Glen H. "The Fourteen Triads of the Sermon on the Mount." *JBL* 122 (2003): 267-308.

———. "Jesus and Just Peacemaking Theory." In *Must Christianity Be Violent? Reflections on History, Practice, and Theology,* ed. Kenneth R. Chase and Alan Jacobs, 135-55. Grand Rapids: Brazos, 2003.

———. *The Journey into Peacemaking.* Second edition. Memphis: Brotherhood Commission, SBC, 1987.

———. *Just Peacemaking: Transforming Initiatives for Justice and Peace.* Louisville: Westminster John Knox, 1992.

Stassen, Glen H., ed. *Just Peacemaking: Ten Practices for Abolishing War.* Cleveland: Pilgrim, 1998.

Stassen, Glen H., and David P. Gushee. *Kingdom Ethics: Following Jesus in Contemporary Context.* Downers Grove: InterVarsity, 2003.

Stauffer, Ethelbert. *New Testament Theology.* London: SCM, 1955, 1963.

Steck, Odil Hannes.*Friedensvorstellungen im alten Jerusalem. Psalmen, Jesaja, Deuterojesaja.* Zurich: Theologischer Verlag, 1972.

———. "The Jerusalem Conceptions of Peace and Their Development in the Prophets of Ancient Israel." In *The Meaning of Peace,* ed. P. B. Yoder, 129-48 (1992, pp. 49-68). Original: "Jerusalemer Vorstellungen vom Frieden und ihre Abwandlungen in der Prophetie des Alten Israel." In *Frieden — Bibel — Kirche,* ed. Gerhard Liedke, 75-95. Stuttgart: Klett/Munich: Kösel, 1972.

Stendahl, Krister. *Paul among Jews and Gentiles.* Philadelphia: Fortress, 1976.

Stevens, Bruce A. "The Divine Warrior in the Gospel of Mark." *Biblische Zeitschrift* 31 (1987): 103-9.

Stopher, Wanda. "The Trial: John 18:28–19:16a, 19–22." Student paper, Associated Mennonite Biblical Seminary, 2004.

Stott, John R. W. *The Cross of Christ.* Downers Grove: InterVarsity, 1986.

———. *God's New Society: The Message of Ephesians.* Leicester: Intervarsity, 1979.

Stuhlmacher, Peter. "Der Begriff des Friedens im Neuen Testament und seine Konsequenzen." In *Historische Beiträge zur Friedensforschung,* ed. Wolfgang Huber, 21-69. Studien zur Friedensforschung 4. Stuttgart: Klett/Munich: Kösel, 1970.

———. *Reconciliation, Law and Righteousness: Essays in Biblical Theology.* Translated by Everett R. Kalin. Philadelphia: Fortress, 1986.

———. "The Theme: The Gospel and the Gospels." In *The Gospel and the Gospels,* ed. Peter Stuhlmacher, 1-25. Translated by John Vriend. Grand Rapids: Eerdmans, 1991. Original in *Das Evangelium und die Evangelien.* WUNT 28. Tübingen: Mohr, 1983.

Swartley, Willard M. "Bosch and Beyond: Biblical Issues in Mission." *Mission Focus: Annual Review* 11 (2003 Supplement): 77-105.

———. "Discipleship and Imitation of Jesus/Suffering Servant: The Mimesis of New Creation." In *Violence Renounced,* ed. Swartley, 218-45.

———. "God as Father: Patriarchy or Paternity?" *Daughters of Sarah* 16 (November-December 1990): 12-15.

———. "How to Interpret the Bible: A Case Study of Romans 13:1-7 and the Payment of Taxes Used for War." *Seeds* 3 (June 1984): 28-31.

———. "The Imitatio Christi in the Ignatian Letters." *Vigiliae Christianae* 27 (1973): 81-103.

———. "Introduction." In *Violence Renounced,* ed. Swartley, 19-28.

———. *Israel's Scripture Traditions and the Synoptic Gospels: Story Shaping Story.* Peabody: Hendrickson, 1994.

———. *Mark: The Way for All Nations.* Scottdale: Herald, 1981; Eugene: Wipf and Stock, 1999.

———. "Method and Understanding for Texts and Disciples." In *Perspectives on Feminist Hermeneutics,* ed. Gayle Gerber Koontz and Willard M. Swartley, 113-21. OP 10. Elkhart: Institute of Mennonite Studies, 1987.

———. "Mutual Aid Based in Jesus and Early Christianity." In *Building Communities of Compassion,* ed. Donald B. Kraybill and Willard M. Swartley, 21-39. Scottdale: Herald, 1998.

———. "Peace and Mission in John's Gospel: Jesus and the Samaritan Woman (John 4)." In *Beautiful upon the Mountains,* ed. Schertz, 161-82.

———. "Peace." In *The Westminster Theological Wordbook of the Bible,* ed. Donald E. Gowan, 354-60. Louisville: Westminster John Knox, 2003.

———. "Politics and Peace *(Eirēnē)* in Luke's Gospel." In *Political Issues in Luke-Acts,* ed. Richard J. Cassidy and Philip J. Scharper, 18-37. Maryknoll: Orbis, 1983.

———. Review of *Binding the Strong Man* by Ched Myers, *Critical Review of Books in Religion* (1990): 227-30.

———. Review of *Non-Retaliation in Early Jewish and New Testament Texts: Ethical*

Themes in Social Context, by Gordon Zerbe, *Critical Review* (1995): 328-30; adapted in *MQR* 69 (July 1995): 410-12.

―――. Review of *Peace, Violence and the New Testament*, by Michel Desjardins, in *CGR* 17 (1999): 122-24.

―――. "The Role of Women in Mark's Gospel: A Narrative Analysis." *BTB* 27 (1997): 16-22.

―――. *Slavery, Sabbath, War, and Women: Case Issues in Biblical Interpretation*. Scottdale: Herald, 1983.

―――. "Smelting for Gold: Jesus and Jubilee in John H. Yoder's *Politics of Jesus*." In *A Mind Patient and Untamed: Assessing John Howard Yoder's Contributions to Theology, Ethics, and Peacemaking*, ed. Gayle Gerber Koontz and Ben C. Ollenburger, 288-301. Telford: Cascadia/Scottdale: Herald, 2004.

―――. "The Structural Function of the Term 'Way' *(Hodos)* in Mark's Gospel." In *The New Way of Jesus* (FS Howard H. Charles), ed. William Klassen, 68-80. Newton: Faith and Life, 1980.

―――. "A Study in Markan Structure: The Influence of Israel's Holy History upon the Structure of the Gospel of Mark." Ph.D. dissertation, Princeton Theological Seminary, 1973.

―――. "Violence, Violent." In *The Westminster Theological Wordbook of the Bible*, ed. Donald E. Gowan, 520-22. Louisville: Westminster John Knox, 2003.

―――. "War." In *The Westminster Theological Wordbook of the Bible*, ed. Donald E. Gowan, 524-28. Louisville: Westminster John Knox, 2003.

―――. "War and Peace in the New Testament." In *ANRW* 2.26.3, ed. W. Haase and H. Temporini, 2298-2408. Berlin: de Gruyter, 1996.

Swartley, Willard M., ed. *The Love of Enemy and Nonretaliation in the New Testament*. Louisville: Westminster John Knox, 1992.

―――. *The Meaning of Peace*. See Yoder, Perry B.

―――. *Violence Renounced: René Girard, Biblical Studies and Peacemaking*. Telford: Pandora (now Cascadia), 2000.

Swartz, Herbert L. "Fear and Amazement Responses: A Key to the Concept of Faith in the Gospel of Mark." Th.D. dissertation, Toronto School of Theology, 1988.

Sylvan, Dennis D. "The Temple Curtain and Jesus' Death in Luke." *JBL* 105 (1986): 239-50.

Talbert, Charles. *Reading John: A Literary and Theological Commentary on the Fourth Gospel and the Johannine Epistles*. New York: Crossroad, 1992.

Talmon, Shemaryahu. "The Signification of שלם in the Hebrew Bible." In *The Quest for Context and Meaning: Studies in Biblical Intertextuality in Honor of James A. Sanders*, ed. Craig A. Evans and Shemaryahu Talmon. Leiden: Brill, 1997.

Tambasco, Anthony J. "Principalities, Powers and Peace." In *Blessed Are the Peacemakers: Biblical Perspectives on Peace and Its Social Foundations*, ed. Anthony J. Tambasco. New York: Paulist, 1989.

Tannehill, Robert C. "The 'Focal Instance' as a Form of New Testament Speech: A Study of Matthew 5:39b-42." *JR* 50 (1970): 372-85.

―――. "The Gospel of Mark as Narrative Christology." In *Semeia* 16:57-96. Missoula: Scholars, 1980.

————. *The Sword of His Mount: Forceful and Imaginative Language in the Synoptic Sayings.* Philadelphia: Fortress, 1975.

Tasker, R. V. G. "The Biblical Doctrine of the Wrath of God." *Themelios* 26/2 (2001): 4-17; 26/3 (2001): 5-21, reprinted from *ExpT* 63/44 (1951).

Taylor, Vincent. *The Atonement in New Testament Teaching.* London: Epworth, 1945.

Thissen, Werner. *Erzählung der Befreiung. Eine exegetische Untersuchung zu Mk 2, 1–3, 6.* Würzburg: Echter, 1976.

Thompson, J. W. "The Conceptual Background and Purpose of the Midrash in Hebrews VII." *NovT* 19 (1977): 209-39.

Thompson, Leonard. *The Book of Revelation: Apocalypse and Empire.* New York: Oxford University Press, 1990.

Thompson, Marianne Meye. *The God of the Gospel of John.* Grand Rapids: Eerdmans, 2002.

————. *The Promise of the Father: Jesus and God in the New Testament.* Louisville: Westminster John Knox, 2000.

Thurston, Bonnie. *Spiritual Life in the Early Church: The Witness of Acts and Ephesians.* Minneapolis: Fortress, 1993.

Tite, Philip L. *Conceiving Peace and Violence: A New Testament Legacy.* Dallas: University Press of America, 2004.

Toews, John E. *Romans.* BCBC; Scottdale: Herald, 2004.

Twelftree, Graham H. *Christ Triumphant: Exorcism Then and Now.* London: Hodder and Stoughton, 1985.

Ulrich, Daniel. "Did Jesus Love His Enemies?" In *Seeking Cultures of Peace: A Peace Church Conversation,* ed. Enns, 157-70.

Urbach, Ephraim E. *The Sages: The World and Wisdom of the Rabbis of the Talmud.* Translated by Israel Abrahams. Cambridge: Harvard University Press, 1975.

van der Ven, Johannes A. *Formation of the Moral Self.* Grand Rapids: Eerdmans, 1998.

Vanni, Ugo. "Liturgical Dialogue as a Literary Form in the Book of Revelation." *NTS* 31 (1991): 348-72.

Veltman, Fred. "The Defense Speeches of Paul in Acts." In *Perspectives on Luke-Acts,* ed. Charles H. Talbert, 243-56. Edinburgh: Clark, 1978.

Verhey, Allen. *The Great Reversal: Ethics and the New Testament.* Grand Rapids: Eerdmans, 1984.

————. *Remembering Jesus: Christian Community, Scripture, and the Moral Life.* Grand Rapids: Eerdmans, 2002.

Volf, Miroslav. *Exclusion and Embrace: A Theological Explanation of Identity, Otherness, and Reconciliation.* Nashville: Abingdon, 1996.

————. "Johannine Dualism and Contemporary Pluralism." *Modern Theology* 21 (2005): 189-217.

————. "Social Meaning of Reconciliation." *Int* 54 (April 2002): 158-72.

von Rad, Gerhard. "שלם in the Old Testament." *TDNT* 2: 402-6.

Walaskay, P. *"And So We Came to Rome": The Political Perspective of St Luke.* SNTSMS 49. Cambridge: Cambridge University Press, 1983.

Walsh, Brian, and Sylvia Keesmaat. *Colossians Remixed: Subverting the Empire.* Downers Grove: InterVarsity, 2004.

Walsh, William J., and John P. Langan. "Patristic Social Consciousness: The Church and the Poor." In *The Faith That Does Justice: Examining the Christian Sources for Social Change*, ed. John C. Haughey, 113-51. New York: Paulist, 1977.

Waltner, Erland. "1-2 Peter." In *1-2 Peter, Jude*. BCBC. Scottdale: Herald, 1999.

———. "Reign of God, Mission, and Peace in 1 Peter." In *Beautiful upon the Mountains*, ed. Schertz, 235-48.

Watson, Francis. *Paul, Judaism, and the Gentiles: A Sociological Approach*. SNTSMS 56. Cambridge: Cambridge University Press, 1986.

Watts, Rikki. *Isaiah's New Exodus and Mark*. Tübingen: Mohr, 1997. Reprint, Grand Rapids: Baker, 2000.

Watty, William W. "Jesus and the Temple — Cleansing or Cursing?" *ExpT* 93 (1982): 235-39.

Weaver, Dorothy Jean. "As Sheep in the Midst of Wolves: Mission and Peace in the Gospel of Matthew." In *Beautiful upon the Mountains*, ed. Schertz, 123-44.

———. *Matthew's Missionary Discourse: A Literary-Critical Analysis*. JSNTSS 38. Sheffield: JSOT, 1990.

———. "'Thus You Will Know Them by Their Fruits': The Roman Characters of the Gospel of Matthew." In *The Gospel of Matthew in Roman Imperial Context*, ed. John Riches and David C. Sim, 107-27. JSNTSS 276. Edinburgh: Clark, 2005.

———. "Transforming Nonresistance: From *Lex Talionis* to 'Do Not Resist the Evil One.'" In *Love of Enemy and Nonretaliation*, ed. Swartley, 32-71.

Weaver, J. Denny. "Atonement and the Gospel of Peace." In *Seeking Cultures of Peace*, ed. Enns, 109-23.

———. *The Nonviolent Atonement*. Grand Rapids: Eerdmans, 2001.

———. "Violence in Christian Theology." *Cross Currents* 51 (2001): 150-76.

Weinstock, Stefan. *Divus Iulius*. Oxford: Clarendon, 1971.

———. "Pax and the 'Ara Pacis.'" *JRS* 50 (1960): 44-58.

Wengst, Klaus K. *Humility: Solidarity of the Humiliated: The Transformation of an Attitude and Its Social Relevance in Graeco-Roman, Old Testament-Jewish and Early Christian Tradition*. Philadelphia: Fortress, 1988.

———. *Pax Romana and the Peace of Jesus Christ*. Translated by John Bowden. Philadelphia: Fortress, 1987.

Werblowsky, R. J. Zwi, and Geoffrey Wigoder, eds. *The Oxford Dictionary of Jewish Religion*. Oxford: Oxford University Press, 1997.

Westermann, C. "Der Frieden *(shalom)* im Alten Testament." In *Studien zur Friedensforschung* 1, ed. G. Picht and H. E. Tödt, 144-77. Stuttgart: Klett, 1969.

White, R. E. O. *Biblical Ethics*. Atlanta: John Knox, 1979.

Whiteley, D. E. H. *The Theology of St. Paul*. Oxford: Blackwell, 1964.

Wiebe, Ben. *Messianic Ethics: Jesus' Proclamation of the Kingdom of God and the Church in Response*. Scottdale: Herald, 1992.

Wiles, Virginia. *Making Sense of Paul: A Basic Introduction to Pauline Theology*. Peabody: Hendrickson, 2000.

Williams, James G. *The Bible, Violence, and the Sacred: Liberation from the Myth of Sanctioned Violence*. San Francisco: Harper, 1991.

———. *The Girard Reader*. New York: Crossroad, 1996.

————. "King as Servant, Sacrifice as Service: Gospel Transformations." In *Violence Renounced,* ed. Swartley, 178-99.

Williams, Margaret H. *The Jews among the Greeks and Romans: A Diaspora Sourcebook.* London: Duckworth, 1998.

Williams, Sam K. *Jesus' Death as Saving Event: The Background and Origin of a Concept.* HTR Dissertations 2. Chico: Scholars, 1975.

Windisch, Hans. *Der messianische Krieg and das Urchristentum.* Tübingen: Mohr, 1909.

Wink, Walter. "Counterresponse to Richard Horsley." In *Love of Enemy and Nonretaliation,* ed. Swartley, 133-36.

————. *Engaging the Powers: Discernment and Resistance in a World of Domination.* Minneapolis: Fortress, 1992.

————. *Naming the Powers.* Philadelphia: Fortress, 1984.

————. "Neither Passivity nor Violence: Jesus' Third Way." In *SBL Seminar Papers,* 210-24. Atlanta: Scholars, 1988. Slightly revised in *Love of Enemy and Nonretaliation,* ed. Swartley, 102-25.

————. *The Powers That Be: Theology for a New Millennium.* New York: Doubleday, 1998.

————. *Unmasking the Powers: The Invisible Forces That Determine Human Existence.* Philadelphia: Fortress, 1986.

————. *When the Powers Fall: Reconciliation in the Healing of the Nations.* Minneapolis: Fortress, 1998.

Winn, Albert Curry. *Ain't Gonna Study War No More: Biblical Ambiguity and the Abolition of War.* Louisville: Westminster John Knox, 1993.

Witherington, Ben, III. *John's Wisdom: A Commentary on the Fourth Gospel.* Louisville: Westminster John Knox, 1995.

Witherington, Ben, III, and Laura M. Ice. *The Shadow of the Almighty: Father, Son, and Spirit in Biblical Perspective.* Grand Rapids: Eerdmans, 2002.

Wolff, H. W. "Swords into Plowshares — Misuses of a Word of Prophecy?" *CurrTheolMission* 12 (1985): 133-47. Also in *The Meaning of Peace,* ed. P. B. Yoder, 211-28 (1992, pp. 110-26).

Wolterstorff, Nicholas. *Until Justice and Peace Embrace.* Grand Rapids: Eerdmans, 1983.

Wood, Charles. *The Formation of Christian Understanding: Theological Hermeneutics.* Valley Forge: Trinity, 1993.

Wood, John A. *Perspectives on War in the Bible.* Macon: Mercer University Press, 1998.

Wright, N. T. *Jesus and the Victory of God.* Minneapolis: Fortress, 1996.

————. *The Moral Vision of the New Testament: A Contemporary Introduction to New Testament Ethics.* San Francisco: HarperSanFrancisco, 1996.

————. "Paul's Gospel and Caesar's Empire." In *Paul and Politics,* ed. Horsley, 160-83.

Yamasaki, Gary. "Shalom for Shepherds: An Audience-Oriented Critical Analysis of Luke 2:8-14." In *Beautiful upon the Mountains,* ed. Schertz, 145-60.

Yeatts, John R. *Revelation.* BCBC. Scottdale: Herald, 2003.

Yoder, John Howard. *The Christian Witness to the State.* Newton: Faith and Life, 1964. Second edition Scottdale: Herald, 2002.

————. "'It Did Not Have to Be.'" In *The Jewish-Christian Schism Revisited,* ed. Michael C. Cartwright and Peter Ochs, 43-68. Grand Rapids: Eerdmans, 2003.

————. *The Original Revolution.* Scottdale: Herald, 1972.

————. *The Politics of Jesus: Vicit Agnus noster.* Grand Rapids: Eerdmans, 1972. Revised edition, 1994.

————. *The Priestly Kingdom: Social Ethics as Gospel.* Notre Dame: University of Notre Dame Press, 1984.

————. Review of *The Scapegoat* by René Girard. *Religion and Literature* 19 (1987): 89-92.

————. "Theological Critique of Violence." *New Conversations* 16 (1994): 3-6.

Yoder, Perry B. *Shalom: The Bible's Word for Salvation, Peace and Justice.* Newton: Faith and Life, 1988. Reprint, Nappanee: Evangel, 1997.

————. "Shalom Revisited." Unpublished, 1984.

Yoder, Perry B., and Willard M. Swartley, eds. *The Meaning of Peace: Biblical Studies.* SPS 2. Second edition, Elkhart: Institute of Mennonite Studies, 2001. First edition, Louisville: Westminster John Knox, 1992.

Yoder Neufeld, Thomas. *Ephesians.* BCBC. Scottdale: Herald, 2002.

————. "For He Is Our Peace: Ephesians 2:11-22." In *Beautiful upon the* Mountains, ed. Schertz, 215-34.

————. "Power, Love, and the New Creation: The Mercy of the Divine Warrior in the Wisdom of Solomon." In *Peace and Justice Shall Embrace,* ed. Grimsrud, 174-91.

————. *"Put On the Whole Armor of God": The Divine Warrior from Isaiah to Ephesians.* JSNTSS 141. Sheffield: Sheffield Academic, 1997.

————. "Resistance and Nonresistance: The Two Legs of a Biblical Peace Stance." *CGR* 21 (2003): 56-81.

Yokota, Paul. "Jesus the Messiah of Israel: A Study of Matthew's Narrative Christology with Reference to His Messianic Interpretation of Scripture." Ph.D. dissertation, St. Andrews University, 2004.

Young, Frances. *The Theology of the Pastoral Epistles.* Cambridge: Cambridge University Press, 1994.

Zanker, Paul. "The Power of Images." In *Paul and Empire,* ed. Horsley, 72-86.

Zehr, Howard. *Changing Lenses: A New Focus for Crime and Justice.* Scottdale: Herald, 1990.

Zerbe, Gordon. *Non-Retaliation in Early Jewish and New Testament Texts: Ethical Themes in Social Context.* Journal for the Study of the Pseudepigrapha Supplement Series 13. Sheffield: JSOT, 1993.

————. "Paul's Ethic of Nonretaliation and Peace." In *Love of Enemy and Nonretaliation,* ed. Swartley, 177-222.

————. "The Politics of Paul: His Supposed Social Conservatism and the Impact of Postcolonial Readings." *CGR* 21 (2003): 82-103.

Index of Authors

Index of Subjects

Index of Scripture and Other Ancient Writings